ACCA

STUDY TEXT

PAPER P4

ADVANCED FINANCIAL MANAGEMENT

In this edition approved by ACCA

- We **discuss** the **best strategies** for studying for ACCA exams
- We **highlight** the **most important elements** in the syllabus and the **key skills** you will need
- We **signpost** how each chapter links to the syllabus and the study guide
- We **provide** lots of **exam focus points** demonstrating what the examiner will want you to do
- We **emphasise key points** in regular **fast forward summaries**
- We **test your knowledge** of what you've studied in **quick quizzes**
- We **examine your understanding** in our **exam question bank**
- We **reference all the important topics** in our **full index**

BPP's **i-Learn** and **i-Pass** products also support this paper.

FOR EXAMS IN DECEMBER 2008 AND JUNE 2009

BPP LEARNING MEDIA

First edition 2007
Second edition July 2008

ISBN 9870 7517 4737 9
(Previous ISBN 9870 7517 3303 7)

British Library Cataloguing-in-Publication Data
A catalogue record for this book
is available from the British Library

Published by

BPP Learning Media Ltd
BPP House, Aldine Place
London W12 8AA

www.bpp.com/learningmedia

Printed in the United Kingdom

Your learning materials, published by BPP Learning Media Ltd, are printed on paper sourced from sustainable, managed forests.

We are grateful to the Association of Chartered Certified Accountants for permission to reproduce past examination questions. The suggested solutions in the exam answer bank have been prepared by BPP Learning Media Ltd, unless otherwise stated.

Contents

LEARNING MEDIA

How the BPP ACCA-approved Study Text can help you pass

Tackling studying

Studying can be a daunting prospect, particularly when you have lots of other commitments. The **different features** of the text, the **purposes** of which are explained fully on the **Chapter features** page, will help you whilst studying and improve your chances of **exam success**.

Developing exam awareness

Our Texts are completely **focused** on helping you pass your exam.

Our advice on **Studying P4** outlines the **content** of the paper, the **necessary skills** the examiner expects you to demonstrate and any **brought forward knowledge** you are expected to have.

Exam focus points are included within the chapters to highlight when and how specific topics were examined, or how they might be examined in the future.

Using the Syllabus and Study Guide

You can find the syllabus, Study Guide and other useful resources for P4 on the ACCA web site:

www.accaglobal.com/students/study_exams/qualifications/acca_choose/acca/professional/afm/

The Study Text covers **all aspects** of the syllabus to ensure you are as fully prepared for the exam as possible.

Testing what you can do

Testing yourself helps you develop the skills you need to pass the exam and also confirms that you can recall what you have learnt.

We include **Questions** – lots of them - both within chapters and in the **Exam Question Bank**, as well as **Quick Quizzes** at the end of each chapter to test your knowledge of the chapter content.

Chapter features

Each chapter contains a number of helpful features to guide you through each topic.

Topic list (Topic list / Syllabus reference)	Tells you what you will be studying in this chapter and the relevant section numbers, together the ACCA syllabus references.
Introduction	Puts the chapter content in the context of the syllabus as a whole.
Study Guide	Links the chapter content with ACCA guidance.
Exam Guide	Highlights how examinable the chapter content is likely to be and the ways in which it could be examined.
Knowledge brought forward from earlier studies	What you are assumed to know from previous studies/exams.
FAST FORWARD	Summarises the content of main chapter headings, allowing you to preview and review each section easily.
Examples	Demonstrate how to apply key knowledge and techniques.
Key terms	Definitions of important concepts that can often earn you easy marks in exams.
Exam focus points	Tell you when and how specific topics were examined, or how they may be examined in the future.
Formula to learn	Formulae that are not given in the exam but which have to be learnt.
 **Question**	Give you essential practice of techniques covered in the chapter.
Case Study	Provide real world examples of theories and techniques.
Chapter Roundup	A full list of the Fast Forwards included in the chapter, providing an easy source of review.
Quick Quiz	A quick test of your knowledge of the main topics in the chapter.
Exam Question Bank	Found at the back of the Study Text with more comprehensive chapter questions. Cross referenced for easy navigation.

Studying P4

As the name suggests, this paper examines advanced financial management topics and is particularly suited to those who are thinking about a career in treasury or are likely to be involved in strategic financial management decisions.

The examiner for this paper is **Bob Ryan** who is a new member of the ACCA examining panel. He expects you to demonstrate a highly **professional approach** to all questions – not just presenting information in a professional manner, but also **integrating knowledge and understanding** of topics from across the syllabus. The examiner is also very keen for students to demonstrate evidence of **wider reading** and the ability to incorporate **real life examples** into their answers where relevant and appropriate.

1 What P4 is about

The aim of the syllabus is to develop students' ability to **apply relevant knowledge and skills**, and exercise the **professional judgement** expected of a senior financial advisor, in taking or recommending financial management decisions that are likely to have an impact on the entire organisation.

This is an **advanced level** optional paper which builds on the topics covered in Paper F9 *Financial Management*. As an advanced paper it tests much more than just your ability to perform calculations. You must be able to **evaluate** data, **assess** the potential financial and strategic consequences of taking investment decisions and **advise** on alternative courses of action, amongst other things, in both a **domestic** and **international** context.

The syllabus is divided into **seven** main sections:

(a) **The role and responsibility towards stakeholders**

More than ever, company management's responsibility towards all stakeholders is under scrutiny. They must be aware of different stakeholder groups' **conflicting needs** and be able to develop suitable financial strategies that fulfil each group's interests as much as possible. The impact of **environmental factors** should also be uppermost in their minds given the increasing importance placed on such factors in the modern business world.

Ethical issues cannot be ignored – ethics are expected to be a consistent theme in the examination, with the examiner expecting students to be able to take a **practical approach** to identifying such issues in given scenarios.

(b) **Advanced investment appraisal**

This section revisits **investment** and **financing** decisions with the emphasis moving from straightforward technical knowledge towards the **strategic issues** associated with making investment decisions, both **domestic** and **international**.

(c) **Acquisitions and mergers**

You will be expected to distinguish between **different types** of acquisitions, **choose** and **apply** the most appropriate method of **valuation** and make **strategic decisions** regarding how the merger or acquisition should be **financed**. You will be required to act in an **advisory** as well as technical capacity.

(d) **Corporate reconstruction and re-organisation**

This section looks at the various models for **predicting corporate failure**, as well as how to put together a **restructuring package**. As above, you will be expected to act in both a **technical** and **advisory** capacity in questions on this section.

(e) **Treasury and advanced risk management techniques**

This section covers distinct areas of risk and how to measure and manage them. **Interest rate** and **currency risks** and the derivatives used to hedge against them are considered in detail. You will not only be required to know how the derivatives work but also to **advise** on the best methods of hedging in particular scenarios. This section also covers other risks such as **credit risk** and additional treasury functions such as **dividend policy**.

(f) **Economic environment for multinationals**

Multinational companies have their own unique set of challenges, including having operations in international locations. You will be expected to have detailed knowledge and understanding of how to manage international finances and strategic business and financial planning for companies with international operations.

(g) **Emerging issues in finance and financial management**

This is an area the examiner is very keen on and therefore cannot be ignored or treated lightly. Financial management is a continually developing area and finance executives have to keep **up to date** with the new **tools** and **techniques** that are emerging, as well as **developments** in the **international financial markets**.

2 What skills are required?

- Be able to **integrate** knowledge and understanding from across the syllabus
- Think in a **strategic** way – you are assumed to be a senior financial adviser for the purposes of this paper
- Be able to **criticise** financial techniques as well as apply them, and be able to make **reasoned judgements** and give **objective advice** based on calculated results
- Be able to **think internationally** as well as from the viewpoint of the domestic market
- If you read the main capabilities listed by ACCA that students are expected to have on completion of P4, you will find continued reference to the verbs '**evaluate**', '**assess**', '**advise**' and '**explain**' – make sure you can do **all of these** in relation to the different aspects of the syllabus

3 How to improve your chances of passing

- Study the **entire** syllabus – questions may span a number of syllabus areas and you must be prepared for anything!
- **Practise** as many questions as you can under **timed conditions** – this is the best way of developing good exam technique. Make use of the **Question Bank** at the back of this text. **BPP's Practice and Revision Kit** contains numerous exam standard questions (many of them taken from past exam papers) as well as three mock exams for you to try.
- Section A questions in particular will be based on scenarios – make sure you relate your answers to the scenario rather than being generic. Answers that are simply regurgitated from texts are unlikely to score highly.
- Present your answers in a **professional** manner – there are **up to five professional marks** available for setting answers out properly and for coherent, well structured arguments and recommendations. You should be aiming to achieve all of these marks.
- **Answer plans** will help you to focus on the requirements of the question and enable you to manage your time effectively.
- Answer the question that you are most comfortable with first – it will help to settle you down if you feel you have answered the first question well.

- **Answer all parts** of the question – leaving out a five mark discursive element for example may mean the difference between a pass and a fail.
- Read the financial press and relevant web sites for real life examples – the examiner is specifically looking for evidence of **wider reading**.
- Read **Student Accountant** (the ACCA's student magazine) regularly – it often contains technical articles written either by or on the recommendation of the examiner which can be invaluable for future exams.

4 Brought forward knowledge

As mentioned previously, this paper builds on knowledge brought forward from Paper F9 *Financial Management*. If you have not studied F9, you should be aware that the following topics are assumed knowledge and should be considered examinable.

- Management of working capital
- Business finance (including sources of finance and dividend policy)
- The capital structure decision
- Investment decisions
- Interest and discounting
- Investment appraisal
- Capital rationing
- Cost of capital (including CAPM and WACC)
- Business valuations
- Market efficiency
- Foreign currency and interest rate risk management

5 Change in terminology

In order to comply with IAS1, from the June 2008 exam setting onwards, **balance sheet** will be replaced with **statement of financial position** in all ACCA exams.

The exam paper

Format of the paper

		Number of marks
Section A:	Two compulsory case studies	60
Section B:	Choice of two from three questions, 20 marks each	40
		100

Time allowed: 3 hours

Guidance

Section A questions will usually require you to show a comprehensive understanding of issues from across the syllabus. The questions will be in the form of case studies or scenarios and will address significant issues likely to be faced by a senior financial manager or adviser. You will be expected to demonstrate your ability to evaluate the information thoroughly and relate it to the question requirements. The questions will be a mixture of computational and discursive elements, with marks being divided approximately evenly between these elements. The maximum marks that will be awarded to any single Section A question will not exceed 40 marks.

Section B questions are more likely to examine discrete subject areas. They may be based on short scenarios and requirements may include calculations, interpretation of results and discussions. There will always be one wholly discursive question in Section B.

Analysis of past papers – Professional and Fundamentals levels

The table below provides details of when each element of the syllabus has been examined and the question number and section in which each element appeared. Further details can be found in the Exam Focus Points in the relevant chapters.

Covered in Text chapter		Dec 2007	Pilot Paper
	ROLE AND RESPONSIBILITY TOWARDS STAKEHOLDERS		
1	Stakeholder interests		
2, 4	Role of senior financial adviser/financial strategy formulation	4a	
3, 5	Ethical/environmental issues	4b	5c
	ADVANCED INVESTMENT APPRAISAL		
6	Discounted cash flow techniques & use of free cash flows	1, 5b	3a
7	Impact of financing and adjusted present values	5c	4b
8	Application of option pricing theory to investment decisions	3	
9	International investment and financing decisions		
10	Impact of capital investment on financial reporting		
	ACQUISITIONS AND MERGERS		
11, 13, 14	Strategic/financial/regulatory issues	2b(iii)	1d
12	Valuation techniques	2a,b	1a,b,c
	CORPORATE RECONSTRUCTION & REORGANISATION		
15	Predicting corporate failure		
16	Financial reconstruction		
17	Business reorganisation		
	TREASURY & ADVANCED RISK MANAGEMENT TECHNIQUES		
18	Role of the treasury function		
19	Hedging foreign currency risk		2
20	Hedging interest rate risk		
21	Other forms of risk	5a,b	4a
22	Dividend policy & transfer pricing in multinationals		
	ECONOMIC ENVIRONMENT FOR MULTINATIONALS		
23	Management of international trade and finance		5a,b
24	Business and financial planning		
	EMERGING ISSUES		
25	Developments in markets, trade and finance		
26	Emerging derivative products		3b

Analysis of past papers – Professional and Fundamentals levels

PART A

Role and responsibilities toward stakeholders

1

Conflicting stakeholder interests

Topic list	Syllabus reference
1 Potential sources of stakeholder conflict	A (1) (a)
2 Strategies for the resolution of stakeholder conflict	A (1) (b)
3 Emerging governance structures	A (1) (c)

Introduction

The purpose of this chapter is to look at the ways in which a modern organisation is governed and more specifically at the possible conflicts between the various stakeholders of the organisation and the ways in which these conflicts can be resolved.

We first assess the possible sources of conflicts which may arise amongst stakeholders and review these in the light of alternative theories of managerial behaviour such as agency theory and transaction cost theory.

We then analyse alternative strategies for the resolution of conflict. Finally we compare the emerging governance structures of the European and UK/US models with respect to the role of the financial manager.

Study guide

		Intellectual level
A1	**Conflicting stakeholder interests**	
(a)	Assess the potential sources of the conflict within a given corporate governance/stakeholder framework informed by an understanding of the alternative theories of managerial behaviour. Relevant underpinning theory for this assessment would be: (i) The Separation of Ownership and Control (ii) Transaction cost economics and comparative governance structures (iii) Agency Theory	3
(b)	Recommend, within specified problem domains, appropriate strategies for the resolution of stakeholder conflict and advise on alternative approaches that may be adopted.	3
(c)	Compare the emerging governance structures and policies with respect to corporate governance (with particular emphasis upon the European stakeholder and the US/UK shareholder model) and with respect to the role of the financial manager.	3

Exam guide

You must be prepared to answer questions on key concepts such as agency theory or goal congruence, or developments in corporate governance and emerging governance structures. Questions are likely to be of a practical nature and are likely to require you to advise the board on the resolution of stakeholder conflict and alternative approaches that may be adopted.

1 Potential sources of shareholder conflict

FAST FORWARD

The central source of shareholder conflict is the difference between the interests of managers and those of owners.

1.1 Objectives of the organisation

The fundamental objective of any organisation should be the maximisation of shareholders' wealth. In its purest sense this means squeezing every last cent of profits out of the organisation's operations. This objective has its origins in the owner-manager set-up, where the owners actually managed their own businesses and paid little or no attention to other stakeholders such as the wider community and the government.

1.1.1 Separation of ownership from control

In most modern organisations the owners do not actually manage the company. Whilst the **equity shareholders** own the company, the day to day operations are managed on their behalf by the **board of directors**. The directors and managers within the organisation have their own personal goals that may **conflict** with those of the shareholders. The problem that shareholders have is that they are seen as being **passive** stakeholders – that is, they do not (and are not expected to) contribute to business decisions that affect the company. Whilst managers are privy to privileged information about the company, shareholders have to rely on publicly available details such as annual reports and press articles, a situation known as **information asymmetry**. As a result managers are very much left to their own devices when making business decisions

1.2 Examples of conflicts of interest between managers and shareholders

As mentioned in section 1.1.1 above, the fact that the managers of a company are not necessarily the owners of the company, leaves open the possibility that managers may not act in the interests of the owners. There are various ways in which this conflict can be demonstrated.

1.2.1 Short-termism

There is evidence that in many companies the primary driver of decision-making has been to **increase share prices** and hence **managerial rewards** in the short-term. The longer-term benefits of investment in **research and development** may be ignored in the short-term drive to cut costs and increase profits thus jeopardising the long term prospects of the company.

1.2.2 Sales maximisation

This strategy is often employed by managers to increase market share and therefore the importance of the company within its sector. An increase in importance for the company will mean greater status for management but will not necessarily be in the best interests of the shareholders.

1.2.3 Overpriced acquisitions

Takeovers is another manifestation of the non-alignment of the interests of shareholders and managers. In Chapter 12 we explore in more depth the issue of why so many takeovers or mergers fail to increase shareholder value. In brief, the explanation lies in the fact that managers have motives other than shareholder value maximisation.

1.2.4 Resistance to takeovers

The management of a company may tend to resist takeovers if they feel that their position is threatened even if in doing so shareholder value is also reduced.

1.2.5 Relationships

Many companies' pursuit of short-term cost reduction may lead to difficult relationships with their wider stakeholders. Relationships with **suppliers** may be disrupted by demands for major improvements in terms and in reduction of prices. **Employees** may be made redundant in a drive to reduce costs and **customers** may be able to buy fewer product lines and have to face less favourable terms. These policies may aid short-term profits, but in the long-term suppliers and employees are able to take full advantage of market conditions and move to other companies, and customers can shop elsewhere or over the internet.

1.3 Conflict between stakeholders

Although we discussed the **conflict** between **managers** and **owners**, there are other areas of potential conflict between managers, owners and **other stakeholders** who provide **capital**, namely the **debt holders**. The relationship between the long-term creditors of a company, the management and the shareholders of a company encompasses the following factors:

(a) Management may decide to raise finance for a company by taking out **long-term** or **medium-term loans**.

(b) Investors who provide debt finance will rely on the company's management to generate enough net cash inflows to make **interest payments** on time, and eventually to repay loans. Long-term creditors will often take **security** for their loan, perhaps in the form of a fixed charge over an asset (such as a mortgage on a building). Debentures are also often subject to certain **restrictive covenants**, which restrict the company's rights to borrow more money until the debentures have been repaid.

(c) The money that is provided by long-term creditors will be invested to **earn profits**, and the profits (in excess of what is needed to pay interest on the borrowing) will provide extra dividends or retained profits for the shareholders of the company. In other words, shareholders will expect to increase their wealth using creditors' money.

Sometimes the needs of shareholders and debtholders may conflict:

(a) Managers may be tempted to take **risky decisions** using debtholders' money to finance them, knowing that the benefits of these decisions will accrue to the shareholders. If the projects go badly and the company fails, the debtholders may suffer a greater loss than the equity shareholders.

(b) In many jurisdictions there are rules limiting the proportion of company assets that can be paid out as dividends. However, it may still be possible to pay out lawfully **considerable sums** as dividends, enough to jeopardise the company's future and hence the amounts that the debtholders have advanced, should trading results turn bad in the near future.

(c) Shareholders and managers may wish to **prolong the company's life** as long as possible, whereas debtholders may wish to safeguard the amount loaned and realise their security as soon as the company appears to be getting into difficulties.

(d) Managers may attempt to undermine the position of debtholders by seeking further loan capital, committing the company to an **increased interest burden** and hence greater risk of insolvency. The additional loan capital may also have superior claims on the company's assets to the original amounts borrowed.

Exam focus point

You may be asked about the differing interests of share and bond holders.

1.4 Conflict between headquarters and divisions

We have so far examined potential conflicts between managers and outside investors. However, there is another potential conflict between divisional managers and corporate headquarters. Example of this type of conflict usually arises over the allocation of capital to the various subdivisions by headquarters. If there are too many divisions competing for funds, then the allocation of capital may not be efficient. It is quite common for corporate headquarters to allocate capital in an equitable way which may not maximise the return on capital for the organisation as a whole.

1.5 Agency theory

FAST FORWARD

The **agency problem** arises when agents do not act in the best interests of their principals. **Agency theory** seeks to give insight in the relationship between the owners and the management of a firm.

The relationship between management and shareholders is sometimes referred to as an **agency relationship**, in which managers act as agents for the shareholders.

Key term

Agency theory proposes that, although individual members of the business team act in their own self-interest, the well-being of each individual depends on the well-being of other team members and on the performance of the team in competition with other teams.

1.5.1 The agency problem

Classical microeconomic theory views a firm as an homogenous entity which decides on profit maximisation and production levels according to market conditions. In this framework there is no distinction between ownership and management. However when such a distinction exists and managers are the agents of the shareholders, then the separation of ownership from management is sometimes characterised as the **'agency problem'**. For example, if managers hold none or very little of the equity shares of the company they work for, what is to stop them from working inefficiently, not bothering to look for profitable new investment opportunities, or giving themselves high salaries and perks?

We have already examined some manifestations of the **agency problem**. The costs of the agency problem include auditing systems to limit ill behaviour of the managers, various kinds of bonding assurances by the managers to ensure that such abuses will not be practised and changes in organisation systems that limit the ability of managers to engage in undesirable practices.

The goal of agency theory is to find **governance structures** and **control mechanisms** that minimise the problem caused by the separation of ownership and control. In that sense agency theory is the cornerstone of the theory of corporate governance. More specifically agency theory tries to find means for the owners to control the managers in such a way that the managers will operate in the interest of the owners. **Moral hazard problems** are related to the **agency problems** in that the managers, once appointed as representatives for the owner, do not always act in the interest of the owners although they should.

Whereas in the **classical microeconomic setting** a firm employs **labour** and **capital** to produce **output**, the starting point of the agency theory is that there are many more factors of production including management as well as the capital providers and that the firm is a nexus of contracts among these individual factor's of productions. The contracts between these individual factors of productions are constantly negotiated, each factor of production maximising in the process their own utility function.

In the **agency theory** set up, shareholders as the main providers of capital, enter into contractual agreements with managers so as the managers manage the assets of the company in a way that maximises the utility of shareholders. Thus the shareholders are the principals and the managers the agents. For the contracts that are negotiated between the principal and the agent to lead to the utility maximisation of both parties, it requires the existence of efficient markets for corporate control, managers and corporate information.

The **agency theory** suggests that the existence of the efficient markets for corporate control, managers and information ensures that management bears the cost of possible misconduct. It is in the interest of management to align its interest with the interest of the principals. One power that shareholders possess is the right to **remove the directors** from office. But shareholders have to take the initiative to do this, and in many companies the shareholders lack the energy and organisation to take such a step. Even so, directors will want the **company's report and accounts**, and the **proposed final dividend**, to meet with **shareholders' approval** at the AGM.

The agency theory implies heavy **monitoring costs** of the agents by the principals as well as high costs of enforcing the **negotiated contracts**. The resulting corporate structure is designed to monitor and control.

This view of the corporate world by the agency theory is, however, not universally accepted. The **stewardship theory** for example maintains that the interests of managers and shareholders are not always at variance, and management may have incentives such as **responsibility**, **altruism** or **recognition** that do not conflict with the interests of the shareholders. According to this theory, the managers of a company are the **stewards** of the company.

1.6 Transaction cost economics

FAST FORWARD

The **transaction cost economics** theory postulates that the **governance structure** of a corporation is determined by **transaction costs**.

The theory of **transaction cost economics** explains the organisational structure of a firm and its behaviour as a result of the costs that are incurred when the owners of the firm are making transactions. These transaction costs include **search** and **information costs**, **bargaining costs** and **policing** and **enforcement costs**. Bargaining costs arise from the process of agreeing (bargaining) on a contract, and the enforcement costs, are the costs of ensuring that every party complies with the contract.

Ronald Coase (1937) explained firm organisation as the result of the difference between markets and hierarchies. Markets are generally preferred when there is low uncertainty, low frequency of transactions and the assets being transacted have a low 'specificity'. Hierarchies are favoured when the reverse is the case.

Transaction costs imply limited liability for shareholders and limited liability enables investors to diversify. Diversification allows investors to ignore the idiosyncratic risks of individual companies. This implies that investors require relatively little direct monitoring of the operations of individual business firms.

Exam focus point

Although the detail of the theories is not examinable, you need to be aware of them in so far as they give insight into managerial behaviour and the development of corporate governance.

2 Strategies for the resolution of stakeholder conflict

FAST FORWARD

The **resolution** (of the **agency problem** arising when agents do not act in the best interests of their principals) is to bring about **goal congruence** between the objectives of the shareholders and those of management by devising **appropriate mechanisms**. Alternatively, the relevant authorities should enforce good **corporate governance** practice.

2.1 Agency theory resolution strategy

Agency theory analyses the problems that can arise when ownership and control are separated and how they might be mitigated by negotiating contracts that allow the principal to control the agent in such a way that the agent will operate in the interests of the principal. These contractual ways of resolving the problem include a variety of strategies some of which are discussed below.

2.2 Firm induced strategies

Agency theory sees employees of businesses, including managers, as individuals, each with his or her own objectives. Within a department of a business, there are departmental objectives. If achieving these various objectives leads also to the achievement of the objectives of the organisation as a whole, there is said to be **goal congruence**.

Key term

Goal congruence is accordance between the objectives of agents acting within an organisation and the objectives of the organisation as a whole.

Goal congruence may be better achieved and the 'agency problem' better dealt with by giving managers some profit-related pay, or by providing incentives which are related to profits or share price. Examples of such remuneration incentives are:

(a) **Profit-related/economic value-added pay**

Pay or bonuses related to the size of profits or economic value-added.

(b) **Rewarding managers with shares**

This might be done when a private company 'goes public' and managers are invited to subscribe for shares in the company at an attractive offer price. In a **management buy-out** or buy-in (the latter involving purchase of the business by new managers; the former by existing managers), managers become owner-managers.

(c) **Executive Share Options Plans (ESOPs)**

In a share option scheme, selected employees are given a number of share options, each of which gives the holder the right after a certain date to subscribe for shares in the company at a fixed price. The value of an option will increase if the company is successful and its share price goes up.

Exam focus point

Discussion of managerial priorities may be part of a longer question in the exam. The integrated approach to the syllabus may mean that a question on the effect on management motivation of the introduction of a share option scheme may be examined as part of a question on general option theory.

Such measures might merely encourage management to adopt **'creative accounting'** methods which will distort the reported performance of the company in the service of the managers' own ends.

2.3 Separation of roles

The agency theory suggests that not too much power should accrue to a single individual within an organisation. The role of the Chairman and the Chief executive for example should be split.

2.4 Accounting standards

The financial statements of a company are the main vehicle of corporate information to the shareholders. Agency theory suggests that **audited accounts** of limited companies are an important source of 'post-decision' information minimising investors' agency costs.

2.5 Corporate governance

An alternative approach to attempt to monitor managers' behaviour is through the adoption of a corporate framework of decision making that restricts the power of managers and increases the role of independent external parties in the monitoring of their duties. This can be achieved for example by establishing 'management audit' procedures, by introducing additional reporting requirements, or by seeking assurances from managers that shareholders' interests will be foremost in their priorities.

3 Emerging governance structures

3.1 Corporate governance in the UK

FAST FORWARD

Three UK reports – Cadbury, Greenbury and Hampel – recommend best practice in **corporate governance**, **financial reporting** and **accountability.** The Combined Code merges the recommendations of the three reports into best practice that should be followed by listed companies.

Key term

The Cadbury Report defines **corporate governance** as 'the system by which companies are directed and controlled'.

3.1.1 The Cadbury Report

The Cadbury Committee in the UK was set up because of the perceived lack of confidence in financial reporting and in the ability of auditors to provide the assurances required by the users of financial statements. The main difficulties were considered to be in the relationship between **auditors and boards of directors**. In particular, the commercial pressures on both directors and auditors caused pressure to be brought to bear on auditors by the board and the auditors often capitulated. Problems were also perceived in the ability of the board of directors to control their organisations.

3.1.2 Code of Best Practice

The **Code of Best Practice** included in the Cadbury Report and subsequently amended by later reports was aimed at the directors of all UK public companies, but the directors of all companies are encouraged to use the Code. Key points in the Code are summarised in the following paragraphs.

Directors should state in the annual report and accounts whether they comply with the Code and give reasons for any non-compliance.

3.1.3 The Greenbury Code

In 1995, the **Greenbury Committee** published a Code which established principles for the determination of directors' pay and detailing disclosures to be given in the annual reports and accounts. Most of the Greenbury Code principles have been adopted by The Stock Exchange in its Listing Rules.

3.1.4 The Hampel Report

The **Hampel Committee** followed up matters raised in the Cadbury and Greenbury reports, aiming to restrict the regulatory burden on companies and substituting principles for detail whenever possible.

3.1.5 Combined Code

The London Stock Exchange subsequently issued a combined corporate governance code, which was derived from the recommendations of the Cadbury, Greenbury and Hampel reports.

Provisions of the Combined Code	
Directors' responsibilities	
The Board	Should **meet regularly**, and have a **formal schedule of matters** reserved to it for its decision. There should be clear division of responsibilities between chairman and chief executive, preferably separation of the two roles. For FTSE 350 companies independent non-executive directors should make up at least half the board. Smaller companies should have two non-executive directors. Directors should submit themselves for re-election at regular intervals (at least every three years).
The AGM	Companies should propose **separate resolutions** at the AGM on each substantially different issue. The chairman should ensure that members of the audit, remuneration and nomination committees are available at the AGM to **answer questions**. Notice of AGMs should be sent out at least 20 working days before the meeting.
Accountability and audit	The directors should **explain** their **responsibility for preparing accounts**. They should **report that the business is a going concern**, with supporting assumptions and qualifications as necessary.
Remuneration	There should be a remuneration committee composed of independent non-executive directors to set directors' pay, which should provide pay which attracts, retains and motivates quality directors but avoids paying more than is necessary. The company's annual report should contain a statement of remuneration policy and details of the remuneration of each director.
Internal control	The directors should review the **effectiveness of internal control** systems, at least annually, and also **review the need for an internal audit function**.
Audit committee	The board **should establish an audit committee**.
Auditors' responsibilities	
Statement of responsibilities	The auditors **should include** in their report a statement of their reporting responsibilities.

3.2 Corporate governance internationally: comparisons with other countries

FAST FORWARD

The voluntary code-based UK approach can be contrasted with the American approach, very much founded in **regulation** and **legislation**.

Other examples of corporate governance models include Germany (**supervisory board**) and Japan (three boards, low level of regulation, **stakeholder collaboration** stressed).

The establishment of a voluntary code of practice on corporate governance in the Cadbury Report characterises a different approach to that adopted in many other countries.

(a) In continental Europe, **reporting requirements** tend to be more statutorily based in tax law, although all EU members are subject to EU company law directives.

(b) **Japanese** companies are characterised by what is sometimes called a flexible approach to corporate governance, with a low level of regulation. All stakeholders are supposed to collaborate in the company's best interests.

(c) In the USA, the system of corporate governance is rather more oriented to legal rules and **stock exchange regulation**, through the Securities and Exchange Commission (SEC), which imposes stringent quarterly reporting requirements on listed US companies and requires all such companies to maintain independent audit committees. This regime has been reinforced by the **Sarbanes-Oxley Act** (discussed further below).

3.2.1 Germany: institutional differences

A significant difference between companies in the UK and many German companies is the **distribution of power** between **workers and managers,** and **shareholders and managers.**

In the UK, ownership is something which can be easily traded on the Stock Exchange in the form of shares. Buyers of shares seek the best combination of risk and return. While managers have most power for practical purposes, in theory they are acting in the shareholders' interests. From the company's point of view, the **stock market** is the **principal source of** investment capital, especially for large companies. Banks generally provide credit, not capital.

In Germany the role of stock markets in company finance and management is not so important. **German banks** specialising in lending to industry and commercial enterprises have a relatively long-term interest in a company, and might even have an equity investment in it, as the sign of a long-term business relationship. It is argued that this makes them more sympathetic to a company's problems.

Institutional arrangements in German companies, typified by the **two-tiered board**, allow employees to have a formal say in the running of the company. A **supervisory board** has workers' representatives, and perhaps shareholders' representatives including banks' representatives, in equal numbers. The board has no executive function, although it does review the company's direction and strategy and is responsible for safeguarding **stakeholders**' interests. An **executive board**, composed entirely of managers, will be responsible for the **running** of the business.

3.2.2 Japan: cross shareholdings

The main emphasis of Japanese corporate governance is on **management** by **consensus** rather than directors following voluntary codes or statutory regulations.

In Japan, the stock market does have an important role to play, particularly in savings. However, the separation between investment and management is in practice drawn differently to the UK. The stock market is less 'open'. The corporate sector has close links with the banks, who are often represented on boards of directors.

There are three different types of board of director.

- **Policy boards** – concerned with long-term strategic issues
- **Functional boards** – made up of the main senior executives with a functional role
- **Monocratic boards** – with few responsibilities and having a more symbolic role

Japanese companies generally set up **long-term business relationships** with banks, suppliers and customers, even to the extent of buying each other's shares as a symbol of the relationship. When share prices fall, friendly companies do not sell shares in each other. If the web of interrelated companies is large enough, it may possibly include a bank which provides credit to participants in the group.

In Japan the long-term interests of the company are stressed rather than the short-term preferences of shareholders. These arrangements have enabled some companies to be protected from the rigours of profit-performance, so that long-term objectives such as market share have been traditionally favoured instead. There is evidence, however, that this system is gradually coming to an end.

3.2.3 USA: Sarbanes-Oxley

The Sarbanes-Oxley Act was introduced in America in 2002 in an attempt to prevent scandals such as the Enron affair. The Act has introduced a new **oversight board** and tighter regulations on certain accounting issues such as off-balance sheet finance, a particular problem in the Enron case.

Under the Act companies will not be able to obtain a listing unless they have an **audit committee**. **Disclosure requirements** are expanded.

The Act requires companies to produce a signed statement that their accounts are **accurate**; if their accounts have to be re-stated due to non-compliance with legislation or accounting standards, the chief executive and chief financial officer **forfeit their bonuses**.

Auditors are also subject to greater regulation, with **restrictions** on the **non-audit work** that they can perform for companies that they audit, and **compulsory rotation** of **audit partners**.

3.3 Recent developments in corporate governance in the UK

FAST FORWARD

The Higgs Report recommends that **independent non-executive directors** should comprise at least half the membership of the board, and that a **senior non-executive director** should be appointed as a contact for shareholder concerns.

The Smith report provides guidelines on the work of the **audit committee**, and its relations with external auditors.

3.4 Non-executive directors

Review of the Role and Effectiveness of Non-Executive Directors (The **Higgs Report**) was published in the UK in July 2003. This report contains a revised draft of the Combined Code.

The revised Code contains a principle that:

> 'The board should include a **balance of executive and non-executive directors** (and in particular independent non-executive directors) such that no individual or small group of individuals can dominate the board's decision taking.'

The provisions state that for larger companies **at least half the board**, excluding the Chairman, should be **non-executive directors** determined by the board to be **independent**. This is in addition to the fact that the Code requires that the **Chairman** and **Chief Executive** should be **clearly divided roles** and that they should not be exercised by the same individual. The Chairman should meet the **independence criteria** of a non-executive director. A chief executive should not normally later become chairman of the same company.

3.5 Audit committees

The **Smith Report** on the application of the Combined Code guidance to audit committees was published in the UK in early 2003. The guidance recommends that audit committees should:

- **Recommend** the **appointment** of the internal auditor and **approve** the **remuneration** and **terms of engagement**
- **Monitor** and **review** the external auditors' **independence**, **objectivity and effectiveness**
- **Develop and implement policy** on what, if any, **non-audit services** should be supplied by the external auditor
- **Monitor** and **review** internal audit, management systems and published financial information.

The audit committee should consist entirely of independent non-executive directors (excluding the chairman), and should include at least one member with significant and recent financial experience. A number of recommendations are similar to those in the Sarbanes-Oxley Act outlined previously.

Chapter Roundup

- The central source of shareholder conflict is the difference in the interest of managers and owners.
- The **agency problem** arises when agents do not act in the best interests of their principals. The **agency theory** tries to give insight in the relationship between the owners and the management of a firm.
- The **transaction cost economics** theory postulates that the governance structure of a corporation is determined by transaction costs.
- The **resolution** of the **agency problem** which arises when agents do not act in the best interests of their principals is to bring about **goal congruence** between the objectives of the shareholders and management by devising appropriate mechanisms. Alternatively, the relevant authorities should enforce good **corporate governance** practice.
- Three UK reports – Cadbury, Greenbury and Hampel – recommend best practice in **corporate governance**, **financial reporting** and **accountability.** The Combined Code merges the recommendations of the three reports into best practice that should be followed by listed companies.
- The voluntary code-based UK approach can be contrasted with the American approach, very much founded in **regulation** and **legislation**.
- Other examples of corporate governance models include Germany (**supervisory board**) and Japan (three boards, low level of regulation, **stakeholder collaboration** stressed).
- The Higgs report recommends that **independent non-executive directors** should comprise at least half the membership of the board, and that a **senior non-executive director** should be appointed as a contact for shareholder concerns.
- The Smith report provides guidelines on the work of the **audit committee**, and its relations with external auditors.

Quick Quiz

1 What is the key proposition of agency theory?

2 **Fill in the blank**

.... is accordance between the objectives of agents acting within an organisation.

3 To which code have the Cadbury, Greenbury and Hampel reports contributed?

4 **Fill in the blank**

The Cadbury report defines corporate governance as ....

5 What is the best way to achieve a division of responsibilities at the head of a company?

6 What target length of time for directors' service contracts was suggested by the Greenbury report?

7 Which two boards go to make up the German system of two-tiered boards?

Answers to Quick Quiz

1 Although individual members of the business team act in their own self-interest, the well-being of each individual depends on the well-being of other team members and on the performance of the team in competition with other teams.

2 Goal congruence

3 The combined corporate governance code

4 The system by which companies are directed and controlled

5 Separation of the posts of Chairman and Chief Executive

6 One year or less

7 A supervisory board (workers and shareholders)
An executive board (management)

Now try the question below from the Exam Question Bank

Number	Level	Marks	Time
1	Introductory	12	22 mins

The role and responsibility of the senior financial executive

Topic list	Syllabus reference
1 Financial goals and objectives	A (2) (a)
2 Financial management decisions	A (2) (a)
3 Strategies for achieving financial goals	A (2) (b) (c)
4 Ethical financial policy	A (2) (d) (e)

Introduction

In this chapter we discuss **the role and responsibility of the senior financial executive** in the context of setting strategic objectives, financial goals and financial policy development.

First we discuss the crucial decisions that financial executives have to make in an organisation with respect to investment decisions, and distribution and retention policy. Other aspects that are addressed in this context include communication with the stakeholders, financial planning and control and the management of risks.

Once the role of financial manager has been discussed, we deal with issues of strategy implementation and ethical considerations in the formulation of financial policy.

Study guide

		Intellectual level
A2	**The role and responsibility of senior financial executive/advisor**	
(a)	Advise the board of directors of the firm in setting the financial goals of the business and in its financial policy development with particular reference to: (i) Investment selection and capital resource allocation (ii) Minimising the firm's cost of capital (iii) Distribution and retention policy (iv) Communicating financial policy and corporate goals to internal and external stakeholders (v) Financial planning and control (vi) The management of risk	2
(b)	Develop strategies for the achievement of the firm's goals in line with its agreed policy framework.	3
(c)	Recommend strategies for the management of the financial resources of the firm such that they are utilised in an efficient, effective and transparent way.	3
(d)	Establish an ethical financial policy for the financial management of the firm which is grounded in good governance, the highest standards of probity and is fully aligned with the ethical principles of the Association.	3
(e)	Explore the areas within the ethical framework of the firm which may be undermined by agency effects and/or stakeholder conflicts and establish strategies for dealing with them.	3
(f)	Provide advice on personal finance to individual as well as groups of investors	3

1 Financial goals and objectives

FAST FORWARD

In financial management of businesses, the key objective is the **maximisation of shareholders' wealth**.

1.1 The prime financial objective of a company

The theory of company finance is based on the assumption that the objective of management is to **maximise the market value of the company's shares**, which is equivalent to maximising the **wealth** of its **ordinary shareholders**.

A company is financed by ordinary shareholders, preference shareholders, loan stock holders and other long-term and short-term creditors. All surplus funds, however, belong to the legal owners of the company, its ordinary shareholders. Any retained profits are undistributed wealth of these equity shareholders.

1.2 Measuring wealth and value

If the financial objective of a company is to maximise value, and in particular the value of its ordinary shares, we need to be able to put values on a company and its shares. How do we do it? Three possible methods of valuation might occur to us.

Methods of company valuation	
Going concern basis	Based on the company's balance sheet. Rising retained profits indication of potential dividends.
Break-up basis	Only of interest if company is threatened with insolvency, or if individual assets are being sold to raise cash.
Market values	Trading prices of stocks and shares, most relevant to financial objectives. Shareholders' return on investment comes from dividends received and increases in market value of shares (determined by expectations of future dividends).

The **wealth** of the shareholders in a company comes from **dividends** received and the **market value** of the shares. A shareholder's **return on investment** is obtained in the form of dividends received and capital gains from increases in the market value of his or her shares.

Dividends are generally paid by UK public companies just twice a year at most, whereas a current market value is always known from share prices. There is also a theory that market prices are influenced strongly by expectations of what future dividends will be. So we might conclude that the wealth of shareholders in quoted companies can be **measured** by the **market value** of the shares.

1.3 How is the value of a business increased?

If a company's shares are traded on a stock market, the wealth of shareholders is increased when the share price goes up. The price of a company's shares will go up when the company makes attractive profits, which it pays out as dividends or re-invests in the business to achieve future profit growth and dividend growth. However, to increase the share price the company should achieve its profits without taking business risks and financial risks which worry shareholders.

If there is an increase in earnings and dividends, management can hope for an increase in the share price too, so that shareholders benefit from both **higher revenue** (dividends) and also **capital gains** (higher share prices). Management should set **targets** for factors which they can influence directly, such as profits and dividend growth.

Earnings are the profits attributable to equity (that is, to ordinary shareholders) after tax. Earnings per share (EPS) are the earnings attributable to each equity share.

1.4 Financial targets

In addition to targets for earnings, EPS, and dividend per share, a company might set other financial targets:

Examples of other financial targets	
Restriction on gearing	Ratio of debt: equity shouldn't exceed 1:1 or finance costs shouldn't be higher than 25% of profit from operations for instance
Profit retentions	Dividend cover (Profit for the year/Dividends) should exceed 2.5 for instance
Profit from operations	Target profit from operations: revenue ratio or minimum return on capital employed
Cash generation	As well as generating profits, businesses need to generate enough cash to ensure they remain liquid
Value added	Creation of economic value for shareholders, to be discussed later in this text

In their annual report, Tate & Lyle identified the '**signposts to shareholder value'** as being:

- *Focus* – we focus on adding value to carbohydrates within a group that has clear objectives
- *Efficiency* – we initiate programmes to maximise efficiency, reduce costs and enhance the value on investment
- *Markets* – our extensive market knowledge and geographic reach enable us to serve global customers and maintain our leading market positions
- *Growth* – new products, innovative manufacturing processes and our strong brand portfolio deliver growth by adding value to consumer products
- *Investment* – selective investment, combined with volume manufacturing skills, enable us to grow our business and become a low-cost processor

These financial targets are not primary financial objectives, but they can act as subsidiary targets or constraints which should help a company to achieve its main financial objective without incurring excessive risks.

Case Study

Some recently privatised companies act within regulatory financial constraints imposed by 'consumer watchdog' bodies set up by government. For example, BT (British Telecom) is overseen by the telecommunications regulator OFTEL, which restricts price rises to protect consumers.

1.5 Short-term and long-term targets

Targets are usually measured over a year rather than over the long term, and it is the **maximisation of shareholder wealth** in the **long term** that ought to be the **corporate objective**. Short-term measures of return can encourage a company to pursue short-term objectives at the expense of long-term ones, for example by deferring new capital investments, or spending only small amounts on research and development and on training.

1.6 Multiple financial targets

A major problem with setting a number of **different financial targets**, either primary targets or supporting secondary targets, is that they might not all be consistent with each other, and so might not all be achievable at the same time. When this happens, some compromises will have to be accepted.

2 Financial management decisions

FAST FORWARD

In seeking to attain the financial objectives of the organisation or enterprise, a financial manager has to make the following types of decision:

- Investment
- Financing
- Dividends
- Financial planning and control
- Risk management

In the context of the overall objective of financial management, which is the maximisation of shareholder wealth, there are five main types of decisions facing financial managers: **investment decisions**, **financing**

decisions, dividend decisions, financial planning and control decisions and **risk management decisions.**

In practice, these areas are interconnected and should not be viewed in isolation. An equally important function of the financial manager is to **communicate the financial policy and corporate goals to internal and external stakeholders**.

2.1 Investment decisions

The financial manager will need to **identify** investment opportunities, **evaluate** them and decide on the **optimum allocation of scarce funds** available between investments.

Investment decisions may be on the undertaking of new **projects** within the existing business, the **takeover** of, or the **merger** with, another company or the **selling off** of a part of the business. Managers have to take decisions in the light of strategic considerations such as whether the business wants to **grow internally** (through investment in existing operations) or **externally** (through expansion).

2.1.1 Growth by acquisition

Companies may expand or diversify by developing their own internal resources, but they are also likely to consider growth through acquisitions or mergers. In both situations the result is a sudden spurt in company growth, which can clearly cause 'corporate indigestion' typified by problems of communication, blurring of policy decisions and decline in the staff's identity with company and products.

The aim of a merger or acquisition, however, should be to make **profits** in the long term as well as the short term. Acquisitions provide a **means of entering** a market, or building up a market share, more quickly and/or at a lower cost than would be incurred if the company tries to develop its own resources.

It will also be necessary to attempt an evaluation of the following.

- The **prospects** of **technological change** in the industry
- The size **and strength of competitors**
- The **reaction of competitors** to an acquisition
- The **likelihood of government intervention** and legislation
- The **state of the industry** and its long-term prospects
- The amount of **synergy** obtainable from the merger or acquisition

Whatever the reason for the merger or acquisition, it is unlikely to be successful unless it offers the **company opportunities** that cannot be found within the company itself and unless the new subsidiary fits closely into the strategic plan outlined for future growth.

2.1.2 Organic growth

A company which is planning to grow must decide on whether to pursue a policy of 'organic' internal growth or a policy of taking over other established businesses, or a mix of the two.

Organic growth requires funding in cash, whereas acquisitions can be made by means of share exchange transactions. A company pursuing a policy of organic growth would need to take account of the following.

(a) The company must make the **finance available**, possibly out of retained profits. However, the company should then know how much it can afford, and with careful management, should not over-extend itself by trying to achieve too much growth too quickly.

(b) The company can **use its existing staff and systems** to create the growth projects, and this will open up career opportunities for the staff. In contrast, when expansion is achieved by taking over other businesses, the company usually acquires and assimilates the staff of those businesses.

(c) **Overall expansion** can be **planned more efficiently**. For example, if a company wishes to open a new factory or depot, it can site the new development in a place that helps operational efficiency (eg close to other factories, to reduce transport costs). With acquisitions, the company must take on existing sites no matter where they happen to be.

(d) **Economies of scale** can be achieved from **more efficient use** of central head office functions such as finance, purchasing, personnel and management services. With acquisitions, a company buys the head office functions of other companies and there will either be fewer economies of scale, or more redundancies.

2.1.3 Organic growth versus acquisition

Acquisitions are probably only desirable if **organic growth alone cannot achieve the targets** for growth that a company has set for itself.

Organic growth takes time. With acquisitions, entire existing operations are assimilated into the company at one fell swoop. Acquisitions can be made without cash, if share exchange transactions are acceptable to both the buyers and sellers of any company which is to be taken over.

However, acquisitions do have their **strategic problems**.

(a) They might be **too expensive**. Some might be resisted by the directors of the target company. Others might be referred to the government under the terms of anti-monopoly legislation.

(b) **Customers** of the target company might **resent** a sudden takeover and consider going to other suppliers for their goods.

(c) In general, the problems of assimilating new products, customers, suppliers, markets, employees and different systems of operating might create **'indigestion'** and management overload in the acquiring company.

We shall discuss acquisitions in more detail in Chapter 12.

2.2 Financing decisions

Financing decisions include those for both the long term (**capital structure**) and the short term (**working capital management**).

The financial manager will need to determine the **source, cost** and effect on **risk** of the possible sources of long-term finance. A balance between **profitability** and **liquidity** (ready availability of funds if required) must be taken into account when deciding on the optimal level of short-term finance.

2.2.1 Sources of funds

Companies, whether public or private, obtain long-term funds from a variety of sources.

- New issues
  - Equity (ordinary) shares
  - Preference shares
  - Loan stock or bonds
- Retained profits
- Bank borrowing (medium-term)

Retained profits are the main source of long-term finance.

Shares

- Shares provide an ownership stake in the company. Income is in the form of **dividends or capital gains.**
- The main types of shares are **equity shares** with full voting rights and **preference shares**, with a prior right to be paid dividends.
- All types of company may use **rights issues**, offers to existing shareholders to buy more shares usually at a price below the current market price.
- Companies whose shares can be traded (are **listed**) on the stock exchange can use a variety of methods to issue shares, including an **offer for sale** (inviting the public to apply for shares) or a **placing** (an issue to small groups of investors or to institutions).

Loan stock and bonds

'Bonds' is a term used to describe various forms of long-term debt. Bonds or loans come in a variety of forms, for example as follows.

- **Floating rate debentures** are loans on which the coupon rate of interest can be varied at regular intervals, in line with changes in current market rates of interest.
- **Zero coupon bonds** are bonds issued at a large discount to their eventual redemption value, but on which no interest is paid. Investors obtain all their return from the capital gain on redemption.
- **Convertible loan stock**, loan stock that can ultimately be converted into shares.
- Loans might be **secured** or **unsecured**.
- **Mortgage loans** are loans secured on property.
- **Bank loans** might have a **fixed charge** over certain fixed assets (eg property) and a **floating charge** over current assets (eg stocks and debtors).

Leasing

There are two steps in arriving at a **lease or buy decision**.

- Establish whether it is worth having the equipment by discounting the project's cash flows at a suitable cost of capital.
- If the equipment is worth having, compare the cash flows of purchasing and leasing. The cash flows can be discounted at an after-tax cost of borrowing, and the financing method with the lowest PV of cost selected.

Other sources of long-term funds

- Private loans (fairly common with small private companies)
- Government grants
- Venture capital

2.2.2 Optimal financing mix

Key term

Capital structure refers to the way in which an organisation is financed, by a combination of long-term capital (ordinary shares and reserves, preference shares, loan notes, bank loans, convertible loan stock and so on) and short-term liabilities, such as a bank overdraft and trade creditors. The mix of finance can be measured by **gearing** ratios.

The assets of a business must be financed somehow. When a business is growing, the additional assets must be financed by additional capital.

However, using debt to finance the business creates financial risk. **Financial risk** can be seen from different points of view.

(a) **The company as a whole**

If a company builds up debts that it cannot pay when they fall due, it will be forced into liquidation.

(b) **Lenders**

If a company cannot pay its debts, the company will go into liquidation owing lenders money that they are unlikely to recover in full. Lenders will probably want a **higher interest yield** to compensate them for higher financial risk and gearing.

(c) **Ordinary shareholders**

A company will not make any distributable profits unless it is able to earn enough profit from operations to pay all its interest charges, and then tax. The lower the profits or the higher the interest-bearing debts, the less there will be, if there is anything at all, for shareholders.

Ordinary shareholders will probably want a **bigger expected return** from their shares to compensate them for a **higher financial risk**. The market value of shares will therefore depend on gearing, because of this premium for financial risk that shareholders will want to earn.

2.2.3 What determines the optimal financing mix

When we consider the capital structure decision, the question arises of whether there is an **optimal mix** of **capital and debt** that a company should try to achieve. Under one view (the traditional view) there is an optimal capital mix at which the **average cost of capital**, weighted according to the different forms of capital employed, is **minimised**.

However, the alternative view of **Modigliani and Miller** is that the firm's overall **weighted average cost of capital** is **not influenced** by changes in its **capital structure**. Their argument is that the issue of debt causes the cost of equity to rise in such a way that the benefits of debt on returns are exactly offset. Investors themselves adjust their level of personal gearing and thus the level of corporate gearing becomes irrelevant. We shall discuss this debate further in Chapter 7.

Taxes

The impact on the company's tax **overall tax position** will need to be considered, also how **tax efficient** the alternative sources of finance are.

Clientele effect

When considering whether to change gearing significantly, directors may take into account changes in the profile of shareholders. If gearing does change significantly, the company may adjust to a **new risk-return trade-off** that is unsuitable for many shareholders. These shareholders will look to sell their shares, whilst other investors, who are now attracted by the new gearing levels, will look to buy shares.

Bankruptcy risk

Increasing the level of debt may increase the probability of default as the company is much more exposed volatility in earnings. Higher levels of debt may also increase the cost of borrowing, making repayment of debt more difficult and triggering financial distress. The company may therefore choose a level of debt that balances the benefits of debt with the costs of bankruptcy.

Signalling

Some investors may see the issue of debt capital as a sign that the directors are confident enough of the future cash flows of the business to be prepared to commit the company to making **regular interest payments** to **lenders.**

2.2.4 Domestic and international borrowing

If the company is receiving income in a foreign currency or has a long-term investment overseas, it can try to limit the **risk of adverse exchange rate movements** by matching. It can take out a long-term loan and use the foreign currency receipts to repay the loan. Similarly it can try to **match its foreign assets** (property, plant etc) by a **long-term loan** in the foreign currency. However, if the asset ultimately generates home currency receipts, there will be a long-term currency risk.

In addition foreign loans may carry a lower **interest rate**, but the principle of **interest rate parity** (covered in Chapter 14) suggests that the **foreign currency** will ultimately strengthen, and hence loan repayments will become more expensive.

2.2.5 Risk attitudes

The choice of capital structure will not only depend on company circumstances, but also on the **attitudes** that directors and owners have towards the **principal risks**. This will include the risks that are specific to the business, more general economic risks, and also the risks of raising finance. It could for example adversely affect the company's reputation if it made a rights issue that was not fully subscribed. **Foreign exchange risk** will need to be considered if the company is considering using international sources of finance.

2.2.6 Loss of control

The directors and shareholders may be unwilling to accept the **conditions** and the **loss of control** that obtaining extra finance will mean. Control may be diminished whether equity or loan funding is sought:

(a) **Issuing shares** to outsiders may **dilute** the **control** of the existing shareholders and directors, and the company will be subject to greater regulatory control if it obtains a stock market listing.

(b) The price of additional debt finance may be **security** restricting disposal of the assets secured and **covenants** that limit the company's rights to **dispose of assets** in general or to pay dividends.

2.2.7 Costs

The directors may consider that the **extra interest costs** the company is committed to are too high; remember that companies are not legally obliged to pay dividends, although obviously if they don't do so, there may be an impact on the share price. On the other hand the effective **cost of debt** might be cheaper than the **cost of equity**, particularly if tax relief can be obtained.

The costs of **arranging new finance sources** may also be significant, particularly if the business is contemplating using a number of different sources over time.

2.2.8 Commitments

The interest and repayment schedules that the company is required to meet may be considered **too tight.** The collateral that loan providers require may also be too much, particularly if the directors are themselves required to provide **personal guarantees.**

2.2.9 Present sources of finance

Perhaps it's easy to find reasons why new sources of finance may not be desirable, but equally they may be considered more acceptable than drawing on current sources. For example shareholders may be **unwilling to contribute further funds** in a rights issue; the business may wish to improve its relations with its suppliers, and one condition may be lessening its reliance on trade credit.

2.3 Feasibility of capital structure

FAST FORWARD

The mix of finance chosen must be **feasible;** companies may face **restrictions** in the finance available, and may not be able to commit to repaying too much at any one time.

Even if directors and shareholders are happy with the implications of obtaining significant extra finance, the company may not be able to obtain that finance.

2.3.1 Lenders' attitudes

Whether lenders are prepared to lend the company any money will depend on the company's circumstances, particularly as they affect the company's ability to generate **cash** and **security** for the loan.

2.3.2 Availability and popularity of finance

If the **stock market** is **depressed**, it may be difficult to raise cash through share issues, so major amounts will have to be borrowed. On the other hand specific sources of finance may be particularly appealing to investors.

How quickly amounts are available may also be an issue.

2.3.3 Future trends

Likely **future trends** of **fund availability** will be significant if a business is likely to require a number of injections of funds over the next few years. The business needs to consider how much current decisions may affect its ability to raise funds in the future.

2.3.4 Restrictions in loan agreements

Restrictions written into agreements on current loans may prohibit a business from taking out **further loans**, or may require that its gearing does **not exceed specified limits**.

2.3.5 Maturity dates

If a business already has significant debt repayable in a few years' time, because of **cash flow restrictions** it may not be able to take out further debt repayable around the same time.

2.4 Dividend decisions

Dividend decisions refer to the amount of a company's distributable profits that can be distributed to the shareholders of a company. Most companies follow a target dividend policy whereby they distribute a constant proportion of their earnings as dividends.

Not all companies reward investors through dividends. Some companies prefer to return funds to investors by buying back their shares. The issue of how to transfer money from within the company to its shareholders depends very much on the tax treatment of the two types of payments. If dividends are taxed more heavily than capital gains then it make sense for the shareholders to prefer share repurchases rather than dividend payments.

There are of course other considerations that affect the decision between share repurchases and cash dividend and they discussed to a greater extent in Chapter 4.

2.5 Interaction of investment with financing and dividend decisions

Managers will need to consider whether **extra finance** will be required, and if it will be, what will be the consequences of obtaining it. They will have to consider the demands of **providers of finance**, particularly of equity shareholders who require **dividends**. Will equity shareholders be content with projects that maximise their long-term returns, or will they require a minimum return or dividend each year?

When taking financial decisions, managers will have to fulfil the **requirements of the providers of finance**, otherwise finance may not be made available. This may be particularly difficult in the case of equity shareholders, since dividends are paid at the company's discretion; however if equity shareholders do not receive the dividends they want, they will look to sell their shares, the share price will fall and the company will have more difficulty raising funds from share issues in future.

Although there may be risks in obtaining extra finance, the long-term risks to the business of **failing to invest** may be even greater and managers will have to balance these up. Investment may have direct consequences for decisions involving the **management of finance**; extra working capital may be required if investments are made and sales expand as a consequence. Managers must be sensitive to this and ensure that a balance is maintained between receivables and inventory, and cash.

A further issue managers will need to consider is the **matching** of the **characteristics** of investment and finance. **Time** is a critical aspect; an investment which earns returns in the long-term should be matched with finance which requires repayment in the long-term.

The amount of surplus cash paid out as **dividends** will have a direct impact on **finance** available for **investment**. Managers have a difficult decision here; how much do they pay out to shareholders each year to keep them happy, and what level of funds do they retain in the business to invest in projects that will yield long-term income? In addition funds available from retained profits may be needed if debt finance is likely to be unavailable, or if taking on more debt would expose the company to undesirable risks.

2.6 Financing planning and control

Financial planning is concerned with the monitoring of the firm's financial condition, the evaluation of a firm's productive capacity needs, and the finance it requires. These functions impact on the entire operations of the company and affect its performance. The main elements of financing planning and control are:

2.6.1 Strategic cash flow planning

In order to survive, any business must have an adequate inflow of cash. Cash flow planning at a strategic level is similar to normal cash budgeting, with the following exceptions.

(a) The **planning horizon** (the furthest time ahead plans can be quantified) is longer.

(b) The **uncertainties** about future cash inflows and cash outflows are much greater.

(c) The business should be able to respond, if necessary, to an **unexpected need** for cash. Where could extra cash be raised, and in what amounts?

(d) A company should have planned cash flows which are consistent with:

  (i) Its dividend payment policy, and
  (ii) Its policy for financial structuring, debt and gearing

Investments in new projects, such as new product developments, use up cash in the short term, and it will not be for some years perhaps that good profits and cash inflows are earned from them.

One aspect of strategic cash flow planning is to try to achieve a balance between the following.

(a) **Making and selling products** which are still in their **early stages of development**, and are still 'soaking up' cash

(b) **Making and selling products** which are **'cash cows'** – ie established products which are earning good profits and good cash inflows

A company should try to plan for adequate cash inflows, and be able to call on 'emergency' sources of cash in the event of an unforeseen need, but it might be unwise to hold too much cash.

When a company is **cash-rich**, it can invest the money, usually in short-term investments or deposits, such as the money market, to earn interest. However, for companies which are not in financial services or banking, the main function of money is to be spent. A cash-rich company could do one of the following.

(a) **Plan to use the cash**, for example for a project investment or a takeover bid for another company

(b) **Pay out the cash** to shareholders as **dividends**, and let the shareholders decide how best to use the cash for themselves

(c) **Re-purchase its own shares**

Strategic fund management is an extension of cash flow planning, which takes into consideration the ability of a business to overcome unforeseen problems with cash flows, recognising that the assets of a business can be divided into three categories.

(a) Assets which are needed to carry out the **'core' activities** of the business. A group of companies will often have **one or several main activities**, and in addition will carry on several peripheral activities. The group's strategy should be primarily to develop its main activities, and so there has to be enough cash to maintain those activities and to finance their growth.

(b) Assets which are **not essential for carrying out** the main activities of the business, and which could be **sold off** at **fairly short notice**. These assets will consist mainly of short-term marketable investments.

(c) Assets which are not essential for carrying out the main activities of the business, and which could be **sold off to raise cash**, although it would probably take time to arrange the sale, and the amount of cash obtainable from the sale might be uncertain. These assets would include: long-term investments (for example, substantial shareholdings in other companies); subsidiary companies engaged in 'peripheral' activities, which might be sold off to another company or in a management buyout; and land and buildings.

If an unexpected event takes place which threatens a company's cash position, the company could also meet the threat by:

(a) **Working capital management** to **improve cash flows** by reducing stocks and debtors, taking more credit, or negotiating a higher bank overdraft facility

(b) **Changes to dividend policy**

2.6.2 Financial controls

Strategic planning and control is 'the process of deciding on objectives of the organisation, on changes in these objectives, on the resources used to attain these objectives, and on the policies that are to govern the acquisition, use and disposition of these resources'.

Tactical or management control is 'the process by which managers assure that resources are obtained and used effectively and efficiently in the accomplishment of the organisation's objectives'.

Operational control is 'the process of assuring that specific tasks are carried out effectively and efficiently'.

Management control is sometimes called **tactics** or **tactical planning**. Operational control is sometimes called **operational planning**.

	Investment	Financing	Dividend
Strategic	Selection of products and markets Required levels of profitability Purchase of fixed assets fundamental to the business	Target debt/equity mix	Capital growth or high dividend payout
Tactical	Other fixed asset purchases Efficient use of resources Effective use of resources Pricing	Lease versus buy	Scrip or cash dividends
Operational	Working capital management	Working capital management	N/A

It is quite common for strategic plans to be in conflict with the shorter term objectives of management control. Examples are as follows.

(a) It might be in the long-term interests of a company to buy more expensive or technologically advanced machinery to make a product, in the expectation that when market demand for the product eventually declines, customers will buy from producers whose output is of a slightly better quality – ie made on better machinery. In the short run, however, new and expensive machinery will incur higher depreciation charges and therefore **higher unit costs** for the same volume of production.

(b) Similarly, it may be in the long-term interests of a company to invest in research and development, in spite of the costs and loss of profits in the short term.

2.7 Communicating policy to stakeholders

FAST FORWARD

For the financial strategy to be successful it needs to be communicated and supported by the **stakeholder groups.**

- **Internal** – managers, employees
- **Connected** – shareholders, banks, customers, suppliers
- **External** – government, pressure groups, local communities

Key term

Stakeholders are groups or individuals having a legitimate interest in the activities of an organisation, generally comprising customers, employees, the community, shareholders, suppliers and lenders.

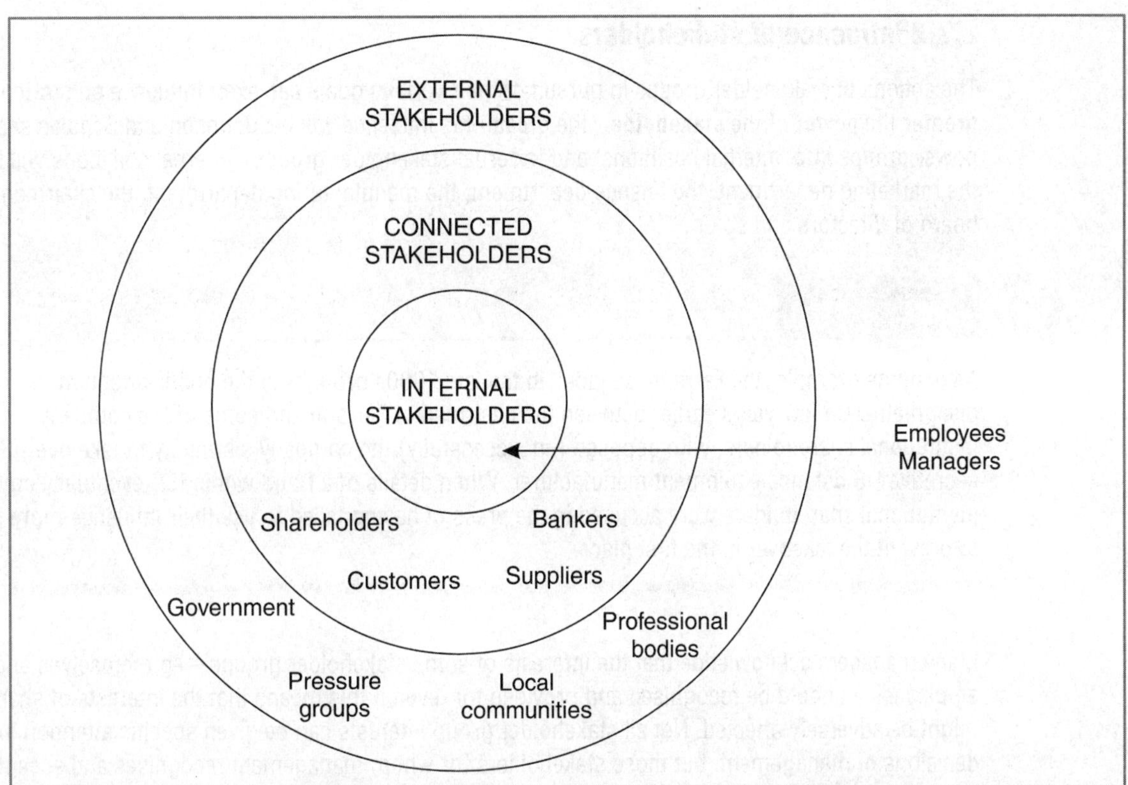

Exam focus point

You may be told in a question that a company aims to respect the interests of stakeholders, and determines its policies in the light of that aim. Even if you aren't, you will see at various times in this text circumstances when stakeholder interests become particularly important, for example in a merger and acquisition situation.

2.7.1 Objectives of stakeholder groups

The various groups of stakeholders in a firm will have different goals which will depend in part on the situation of the organisation.

STAKEHOLDER GOALS	
Shareholders	Providers of risk capital, aim to maximise wealth
Suppliers	Often other businesses, aim to be paid full amount by date agreed, but want to continue long-term trading relationship, and so may accept later payment
Long-term lenders	Wish to receive payments of interest and capital on loan by due date for repayment
Employees	Maximise rewards paid to them in salaries and benefits, also prefer continuity in employment
Government	Political objectives such as sustained economic growth and high employment.
Management	Maximising their own rewards

Exam focus point

You might be asked to comment on a situation where the interests of different stakeholders diverge.

2.7.2 Influence of stakeholders

The actions of stakeholder groups in pursuit of their various goals can exert influence on strategy. The **greater** the **power** of the **stakeholder**, the greater his influence will be. Johnson and Scholes separate power groups into 'internal coalitions' and 'external stakeholder groups'. Internal coalitions will include the marketing department, the finance department, the manufacturing department, the chairman and board of directors and so on.

Case Study

As just one example, the Ferranti 'scandal' in the late 1980s brought to the public attention the disagreement a few years earlier between the chairman of Ferranti and some of the company's major institutional shareholders, who opposed (unsuccessfully) the company's strategy to take over ISC, the secretive US defence equipment manufacturer. When details of a fraud within ISC eventually emerged, the institutional shareholders were accused in the press of having failed to use their influence more powerfully to prevent the takeover in the first place.

Many managers acknowledge that the interests of some stakeholder groups – eg themselves and employees – should be recognised and provided for, even if this means that the interests of shareholders might be adversely affected. Not all stakeholder group interests can be given specific attention in the decisions of management, but those stakeholders for whom management recognises and accepts a responsibility are referred to as **constituents** of the firm.

2.7.3 Stakeholders and objectives

The **stakeholder view** of company objectives is that many groups of people have a stake in what the company does. Shareholders own the business, but there are also suppliers, managers, workers and customers. Each of these groups has its own objectives so that a compromise or balance is required. Management must balance the profit objectives with the pressures from the non-shareholder groups in deciding the strategic targets of the business.

The **consensus theory** of company objectives was developed by Cyert and March. They argued that managers 'run' a business but do not own it and that 'organisations do not have objectives, only people have objectives'. Managers do not necessarily set objectives for the company but rather they look for objectives which suit their own inclinations. However, objectives emerge as a **consensus** of the differing views of shareholders, managers, employees, suppliers, customers and society at large, but (in contrast to the stakeholder view) they are not all selected nor controlled by management.

2.8 The management of risk

Any business activity that there is no uncertainty about the financial outcome is considered to be a risk-free investment. In a risk-free investment, the investor is compensated only for the fact that he or she postpones their consumption. The return on a risk-free investment is therefore the lowest investment return available in an economy. However if investors want to earn a return higher than that on the risk-free asset, they should be exposed to additional risk. This additional risk makes the realization of expected return from an investment uncertain, and risk averse investors as compensation for the uncertainty will require a premium over the risk-free rate in order to undertake this risky investment.

The relationship between risk and return is shown in the diagram below.

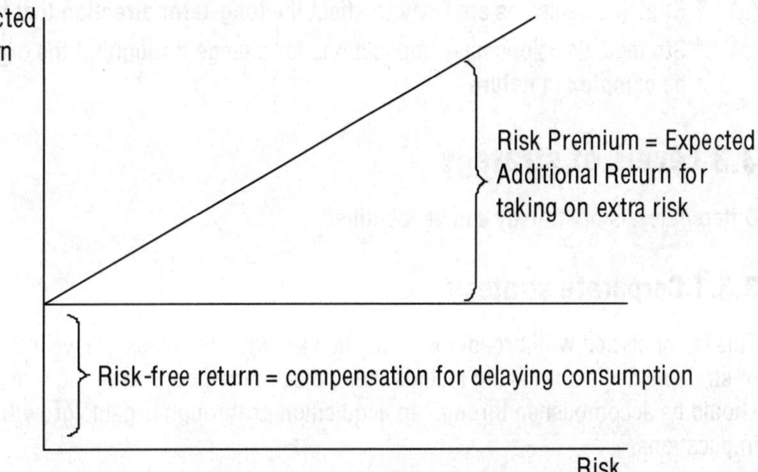

The diagram shows the risk-return trade-off that a company faces. This trade-off is established in the financial markets, and is given to the firm, in the sense that it cannot influence it. A firm's decision with regard to the risk exposure is to decide on the combination of risk and return that is consistent with the risk appetite of the firm. A firm can lower its exposure to risk by foregoing return.

3 Strategies for achieving financial goals

FAST FORWARD

Strategy is a course of action to achieve an objective. Strategies to accomplish the objective of maximising shareholder value are set at the corporate, business and operational levels.

3.1 Strategy

Key term

Strategy may be defined as a course of action, including the specification of resources required, to achieve a specific objective.

Strategy can be **short-term** or **long-term**, depending on the time horizon of the objective it is intended to achieve.

This definition also indicates that since strategy depends on objectives or targets, the obvious starting point for a study of corporate strategy and financial strategy is the **identification and formulation of objectives**.

3.2 Characteristics of strategic decisions

Johnson and Scholes (*Exploring Corporate Strategy*) have summarised the characteristics of strategic decisions for an organisation as follows.

(a) Strategic decisions will be concerned with the **scope** of the organisation's activities.

(b) Strategy involves the matching of an organisation's activities to the **environment** in which it operates.

(c) Strategy also involves the matching of an organisation's activities to its **resource capability**.

(d) Strategic decisions therefore involve major decisions about the **allocation** or **re-allocation of resources.**

(e) Strategic decisions will **affect operational decisions**, because they will set off a chain of 'lesser' decisions and operational activities, involving the use of resources.

(f) Strategic decisions will be affected by:
    (i) Environmental considerations
    (ii) Resources availability

(iii) The **values and expectations of the people in power** within the organisation

(g) Strategic decisions are likely to affect the **long-term direction** that the organisation takes.

(h) Strategic decisions have implications for change throughout the organisation, and so are likely to be **complex in nature**.

3.3 Levels of strategy

Different levels of strategy can be identified.

3.3.1 Corporate strategy

This is concerned with broader issues, such as 'what business are we in?' **Financial aspects** of this level of strategic decision-making include the choice of method in entering a market or business. Whether entry should be accomplished through an acquisition or through organic growth is a question with financial implications.

3.3.2 Business strategy or competitive strategy

This covers the question of how strategic business units compete in **individual markets**, and therefore of the resources which should be allocated to them.

Competitive strategy examines the threat on the performance of the company of factors such as

(a) The potential changes in the industry in which the firm operates, through entry of new competitors
(b) The competition between existing firms in terms of costs, pricing and product quality
(c) The development of substitute products that may affect the industry as a whole
(d) The monopolistic power of individual companies in the input markets
(e) The monopolistic power of companies in the various product markets.

Competitive strategy allows a company to forecast revenue and costs much more accurately. Operating profits together with financing and distribution decisions determine ultimately the value of a company.

3.3.3 Operational strategy

This is to do with how different functions within the business – including the finance function – contribute to corporate and business strategies.

3.4 The management of financial resources

Key term

The **management of financial resources** is part of the overall financial strategy and consists of the management of the balance sheet items to achieve the desired balance between risk and return.

Financial strategy determines the means for the attainment of stated **objectives** or **targets** An integral part of financial strategy is the **management of financial resources**.

The financial management process provides the framework for coordinating and controlling the firm's actions to achieve its financial objectives. It includes strategic financial plans which determines a company's actions and the resulting impact on shareholder value over a period of time, and which, in turn determine the short-term operating plans of the firm.

Long-term financial strategy is part of firm's overall strategy together with a company's marketing strategy, investment strategy and product development strategy. Financial strategy is expressed through a series of annual budget and profit plans.

The long-term financial strategy is supplemented by a **short-term financial strategy** which deals with the management of the financial resources of the company.

The goal of short-term financial management is to manage each of the firm's current assets and liabilities in order to achieve a balance between profitability and risk, which enhances shareholder value. Too much investment in current assets reduces profitability, whereas too little investment in current assets may

impair the ability of a company to meet debt payments. Either way, the effect on the value on the firm may be negative.

The efficient management of financial resources of a company is achieved through the construction of annual cash budgets which reflect the firm's planned inflows and outflows of cash. The cash budget presents a useful tool for the estimation of the short-term cash requirements or surpluses of a company. If a company is predicted to face a deficit, the most efficient method of financing should be considered. This will normally involve the issue of short-term money market instruments.

If a company is predicted to have a surplus, then an appropriate investment in short-term money market instruments should be considered.

Case Study

The following statements of objectives, both formally and informally presented, were taken from recent annual reports and accounts.

Tate & Lyle ('a global leader in carbohydrate processing')

The board of Tate & Lyle is totally committed to a strategy that will achieve a substantial improvement in profitability and return on capital and therefore in shareholder value. To that end we will:

- Continue to develop higher margin, higher-value-added and higher growth carbohydrate-based products, building on the Group's technology strengths in our world-wide starch business.
- Ensure that all retained assets produce acceptable returns.
- Divest businesses which do not contribute to value creation, and/or are no longer core to the Group's strategy.
- Conclude as rapidly as practicable our review of the strategic alternatives available to us in our US sugar operations.
- Continue to improve efficiency and reduce costs through our business improvement projects which include employee development and training programmes.

Kingfisher ('one of Europe's leading retailers concentrating on market serving the home and family')

Customers are our primary focus. We are determined to provide them with an unbeatable shopping experience built on great value, service and choice, whilst rapidly identifying and serving their ever-changing needs.

This goal is pursued through some of Europe's best known retail brands and increasingly through innovative e-commerce channels which harness our traditional retailing expertise.

By combining global scale and local marketing we aim to continue to grow our business, deliver superior returns to our shareholders and provide unique and satisfying opportunities for our people.

Hilton Group ('A global company operating in the hospitality and gaming markets with the leading brand names of Hilton and Ladbroke')

The group intends to enhance shareholder value by exploiting its prime position in these international markets both of which are expected to experience significant long-term growth.

4 Ethical financial policy

FAST FORWARD

Non-financial objectives such as **ethical considerations**, welfare, service provision and fulfilment of responsibilities are also important for businesses.

4.1 Ethical considerations

The subject of business ethics is discussed in greater detail in Chapter 5. We outline here how ethical problems may arise in the formulation and execution of a company's financial policy. Ethical problems arise when a company is able to exploit its stakeholders for the benefit of the management of the company.

Examples where the company can exploit its stakeholders are:

- Avoidance of minimum wage payments
- Discrimination on the basis of gender, race or age
- Abuse of market power, charging higher prices to their customers and paying lower prices to their suppliers
- Disregard of the environment and environmental damage
- Tax avoidance
- Marketing policy that targets weak groups
- Cultural impact on society

In any of the above examples the company could have avoided any restrictions that governments or other relevant authorities could have placed. An ethical financial policy adopted by a corporation should take these considerations into account. The actual incorporation of these guidelines should be formulated by the board of the company and its implementation should be closely monitored. It should become clear that financial objectives may have to be compromised in order to satisfy ethical objectives.

An ethical financial policy has become a requirement in most developed countries under the pressure of the various groups of stakeholders. Investors choose companies with explicit ethical policies in place, consumers prefer companies with an ethical attitude and employees are also more committed to companies which have a reputation for ethical policies.

4.2 Ethical framework and congruence with the institute's guidelines

Members are required to comply with the following fundamental principles

(a) **Integrity**. Members should be straightforward and honest in all professional and business relationships.

(b) **Objectivity**. Members should not allow bias, conflicts of interest or undue influence of others to override professional or business judgements.

(c) **Professional competence and due care**. Members have a continuing duty to maintain professional knowledge and skill at a level required to ensure that a client or employer receives competent professional service based on current developments in practice, legislation and techniques. Members should act diligently and in accordance with applicable technical and professional standards when providing professional services.

(d) **Confidentiality**. Members should respect the confidentiality of information acquired as a result of professional and business relationships and should not disclose any such information to third parties without proper and specific authority or unless there is a legal or professional right or duty to disclose. Confidential information acquired as a result of professional and business relationships should not be used for the personal advantage of members or third parties.

(e) **Professional behaviour**. Members should comply with relevant laws and regulations and should avoid any action that discredits the profession.

Chapter Roundup

- In financial management of businesses, the key objective is the **maximisation of shareholders' wealth**.
- In seeking to attain the financial objectives of the organisation or enterprise, a financial manager has to make the following decisions:
  - Investment
  - Financing
  - Dividends
  - Financial planning and control
  - Risk management
- The mix of finance chosen must be **feasible;** companies may face **restrictions** in the finance available, and may not be able to commit to repaying too much at any one time.
- For the financial strategy to be successful it needs to be communicated and supported by the **stakeholder groups.**
  - **Internal** – managers, employees
  - **Connected** – shareholders, banks, customers, suppliers
  - **External** – government, pressure groups, local communities
- **Strategy** is a course of action to achieve an objective. Strategies to accomplish the objective of maximising shareholder value are set at the corporate, business and operational levels.
- **Non-financial objectives** such as **ethical considerations**, welfare, service provision and fulfilment of responsibilities are also important for businesses.

Quick Quiz

1. Why is maximisation of the market value of shares the key objective in the theory of company finance?
2. State three ways of measuring the value of a company
3. What are the main financial management decisions?
4. What are the main ways of growth for a company?
5. What are the three groups of stakeholders?
6. What is the objective of risk management policy?
7. Why are ethical considerations important for a company?

Answers to Quick Quiz

1. Because it implies maximisation of the market value of shareholder wealth.

2. (1) Going concern basis (2) Break-up basis
   (3) Market values

3. (1) Investment decisions (2) Financing decisions
   (3) Dividend decisions (4) Planning and control decisions
   (5) Risk management decisions

4. Organic growth or through acquisitions

5. Internal, Connected and External.

6. To choose the combination of risk and return which is consistent with the risk attitude of the company.

7. Because of regulatory requirements and competitive pressures.

Now try the questions below from the Exam Question Bank

Number	Level	Marks	Time
2	Examination	20	36 mins

Impact of environmental issues on corporate objectives and governance

Topic list	Syllabus reference
1 Sustainability and environmental risk	A (3) (a)
2 The carbon trading economy and emissions	A (3) (a)
3 The role of the environment agency	A (3) (a)
4 Environmental audits	A (3) (a)
5 Triple bottom line (TBL) reporting	A (3) (a)
6 Wider reading	–

Introduction

In this chapter we discuss the impact of environmental issues on corporate objectives and governance.

Sustainability and environmental concerns are closely related to the ethical issues facing the financial manager.

Study guide

		Intellectual level
A3	**Impact of environmental issues on corporate objectives and on governance**	
(a)	Assess the issues which may impact upon corporate objectives and governance from (i) Sustainability and environmental risk (ii) The carbon-trading economy and emissions (iii) The role of the environment agency (iv) Environmental audits and the triple bottom line approach	3

Exam guide

You may be asked to discuss how the financial manager needs to take into account environmental issues when formulating corporate policy.

1 Sustainability and environmental risk

FAST FORWARD

Environmental and **social** factors contribute to **sustainable** business.

1.1 Sustainability

The extensive use of exhaustible resources and the adoption of production processes which are potentially harmful to the environment have jeopardised the welfare of future generations. There is a growing realisation and pressure from the wider stakeholders that companies need to take into account the long-term sustainability of their activities.

Although there is no single agreed or precise definition of sustainability a broad definition is given below based on the common understanding about its underlying principles.

Key term

Sustainability refers to the concept of balancing growth with environmental, social and economic concerns.

1.2 Environmental concerns

Business activities in general were formerly regarded as problems for the environmental movement, but the two are now increasingly complementary. There has been an increase in the use of the 'green' approach to market products. 'Dolphin friendly' tuna and paper products from 'managed forests' are examples.

1.3 The impact of green issues on business practice

Environmental impacts on business may be **direct**.

- Changes affecting costs or resource availability
- Impact on demand
- Effect on power balances between competitors in a market

They may also be **indirect,** as legislative change may affect the environment within which businesses operate. Finally, pressure may come from customers or staff as a consequence of concern over environmental problems.

1.4 Ecology and strategic planning

Physical environmental conditions are important.

(a) **Resource inputs**

Managing physical resources successfully (eg oil companies, mining companies) is a good source of profits.

The physical environment presents logistical problems or opportunities to organisations. Proximity to road and rail links can be a reason for siting a warehouse in a particular area.

(b) **Government**

The physical environment is under the control of other organisations.

(i) Local authority town planning departments can influence where a building and necessary infrastructure can be sited.

(ii) Governments can set regulations about some of the organisation's environmental interactions.

(c) **Disasters**

In some countries, the physical environment can pose a major 'threat' to organisations. The example of the earthquake in Kobe, Japan, springs to mind.

Issues relating to the effect of an organisation's activities on the physical environment (which, to avoid confusion, we shall refer to as 'ecology'), have come to the fore in recent years.

1.5 Environmental reporting

More companies are now producing an external report for external stakeholders, covering:

(a) What the **business does** and how it impacts on the environment
(b) An **environmental objective** (eg use of 100% recyclable materials within x years)
(c) The **company's approach** to achieving and monitoring these objectives
(d) An **assessment of its success** towards achieving the objectives
(e) An **independent verification** of **claims made**

1.6 Environmental policy

FAST FORWARD

Companies are acknowledging the advantages of having an **environmental policy**. These include **reduction/management of risk to the business, motivating staff** and enhancement of corporate reputation.

Many believe that development of a policy will mean a **long term improvement in profitability**. According to Shell plc 'we believe long-term competitive success depends on being trusted to meet society's expectations.'

Pressure is increasing on companies to widen their scope of corporate public accountability. This pressure stems from **increasing expectations of stakeholders** and knowledge about the consequences of ignoring such pressures. There is an increasing expectation on companies to follow **social policies** of their business in addition to **economic** and **environmental policies**.

The corporate world is responding to these pressures. Environmental and social factors are seen to **contribute** to a **sustainable business** that will enhance long-term shareholder value by addressing the needs of its stakeholders – employees, customers, suppliers, the community and the environment.

2 The carbon trading economy and emissions

Carbon trading allows companies which emit **less** than their **allowance** to **sell** the **right** to **emit** CO_2 to another company.

2.1 Background to emissions trading

The first world summit on the environment was convened in Stockholm in 1972, at which time world leaders declared the intention of having regular assessments of **global environmental issues**. In 1987, the Intergovernmental Panel on Climate Change was formed by the United Nations Environmental Programme (UNEP) together with the World Meteorological Organisation (WMO).

In 1992 the UN general assembly proposed a treaty now known as the United Nations Framework Convention on Climate Change (UNFCCC), which was subsequently accepted and signed by more than 150 nations represented at the second summit which was held in 1992 in Rio de Janeiro.

Countries ratifying the convention agreed:

(a) To develop programs to slow climate change
(b) To share technology and cooperate to reduce greenhouse gas emissions
(c) To develop a greenhouse gas inventory listing national sources and sinks

At the summit, it was also agreed that the responsibility falls upon the **developed nations** to lead the fight against **climate change**, as they are largely responsible for the current concentrations of **greenhouse gases** in the atmosphere. The original target for emission reductions that was generally accepted in 1992 was that the developed nations should, at a minimum, seek to return to 1990 levels of emissions by the year 2000. Additionally, developed nations should provide financial and technological aid and assistance to the developing nations to produce inventories and work toward more **efficient energy use**.

2.1.1 The Kyoto protocol

In December 1997 the countries which met in Rio in 1992 re-convened in Kyoto to develop a set of legally binding agreements on the reduction of greenhouse gas emissions.

The Kyoto Protocol to the UNFCCC could only come into force after two conditions had been fulfilled.

It had been ratified by at least 55 countries.

It had been ratified by nations accounting for at least 55% of emissions from what the Treaty calls 'Annex 1' countries – that is, 38 industrialised countries given targets for reducing emissions, plus Belarus, Turkey and Kazakhstan.

The Kyoto Protocol came into force on 16 February 2005 - 90 days after Russia ratified. As at March 2008, 176 countries had ratified the Treaty, the most recent being Australia whose ratification came into effect on 11 March 2008.

During the period 2008-2012 industrialised countries have to reduce their GHG emissions by on average 5% below their 1990 levels. For EU-15 the reduction target is 8%.

2.2 The European Union trading

Emissions trading is emerging as a key part of the strategy both within the EU and globally to reduce the emission of greenhouse gases.

2.2.1 The EU gas emissions allowance scheme

As part of their policy towards implementation of the Kyoto Protocol, the EU set the total amount of CO_2 emissions to be produced in the EU as a whole to no more than 2.2 billion tonnes per annum. This total amount was then allocated to member states based primarily on the historical emission of CO_2. Each

member state was therefore allocated a European Union Allowance to emit CO_2 for a specific compliance period.

The following table shows the allocation of the European Union Allowances to the biggest countries:

A general picture of the EU emissions trading scheme (ETS) in its first year.

	Allocation 2005 (tonnes of CO_2)	Emissions 2005 (tonnes of CO_2)	Difference (tonnes of CO_2)
TOTAL	**2,087.9**	**2,006.6**	**81.3**
Germany	495.0	474.0	20.9
Poland	235.6	205.4	30.1
Italy	215.8	225.3	–9.5
UK	206.0	242.5	–36.4
Spain	172.1	182.9	–10.8
France	150.4	131.3	19.1
Czech Republic	96.9	82.5	14.5
Netherlands	86.5	80.4	6.1
Greece	71.1	71.3	–0.1
Belgium	58.3	55.4	3.0
Finland	44.7	33.1	11.6
Denmark	37.3	26.5	10.8
Portugal	36.9	36.4	0.5
Austria	32.4	33.4	–1.0
Slovakia	30.5	25.2	5.2
Hungary	30.2	26.0	4.2
Sweden	22.3	19.3	3.0
Ireland	19.2	22.4	–3.2
Estonia	16.7	12.6	4.1
Lithuania	13.5	6.6	6.9
Slovenia	9.1	8.7	0.4
Latvia	4.1	2.9	1.2
Luxembourg	3.2	2.6	0.6

Source: CITL.

A National Allocation Plan was also established within each member state, which allocated the national total allowance to companies. A total of 12,000 CO_2 emitters were granted EU allowances in the whole of the EU. Each Member State establishes a national registry that links to the others and to the Community Independent Transaction Log (CITL).

2.2.2 The EU emissions trading scheme

FAST FORWARD

EU governments are addressing the challenge of reducing carbon emissions through a combination of increased regulation and market mechanisms.

The European Union Emissions Trading Scheme (ETS) commenced on 1 January 2005, creating the world's first multi-country emissions trading system and the largest scheme ever implemented. The EU ETS runs in two phases: 2005-2007 (Phase I) and 2008-2012 (Phase II, coinciding with the first commitment period of the Kyoto Protocol).

The EU allowance given to a company represents their target or 'cap' for a compliance period. If at the end of the period their total emissions during the period are below their cap then they have allowances to sell; if not, they must purchase allowances from companies which have exceeded their emissions reductions targets.

Thus the underlying commodity being traded are EU allowances (EUAs) as issued under the EU ETS. One EUA equals one tonne of CO_2 (right-to-emit). These allowances are traded on a special exchange, the ECX.

Emissions trading is using a **market-based mechanism** for **environment protection**. The rationale behind emission trading is to ensure that the required **overall emission** reductions take place where the cost of the reduction is lowest, thus lowering the overall costs of combating climate change. It does not impose a particular type of technology or set rigid limitations on how much can be emitted.

3 The role of the environment agency

FAST FORWARD

The role of an **environmental agency** is to protect the environment and promote sustainable development.

This section gives an example of good practice. Different countries have their own approaches to regulating the environment which are equally relevant to this syllabus.

3.1 The goal of the Environment Agency

The **Environment Agency** of England and Wales and the Scottish Environment Protection Agency were created in 1996.

The stated mission of the newly created agencies was *'to protect or enhance the environment, taken as a whole'* so as to promote *'the objective of achieving sustainable development'*.

3.2 The responsibilities of the environment agency

3.2.1 Flood risk management

The agency is the main body responsible for creating and maintaining flood defences and providing flood warning systems. Control of water levels is usually by systems of sluices, weirs and locks. The agency issues regular flood warnings and maintains maps of areas liable to flooding.

3.2.2 Waste regulation

The agency is the regulatory authority for all waste management activities including the licensing of sites such as landfill and incineration facilities. It also grants licenses for handling special waste such as radioactive, chemical or medical materials. The agency monitors waste management sites and any individuals or companies found to have caused pollution or have infringed their licence conditions can be prosecuted and potentially have waste handling licenses revoked by the Courts.

3.2.3 Pollution control

Under the provisions of a series of Acts of Parliament, the Agency is the main regulator of discharges to the aquatic environment, to air and to land. It does this through the issue of formal consents to discharge or, in the case of large, complex or potentially damaging industries, by means of a permit. Failure to comply with such a consent or permit or making a discharge without the benefit of a consent or permit can lead to criminal prosecution. Under recent legislation changes enforcement action regarding a pollution event can, through the Magistrates courts system, result in a fine of up to £50,000 or 5 years imprisonment, or unlimited fines and up to 5 years' imprisonment through the Crown courts.

3.2.4 Air quality management

The Agency regulates the release of air pollutants into the atmosphere from large, complex industrial processes. This will soon include emissions from some large-scale agricultural activities, but air pollutant releases from many agricultural activities will continue to be unregulated.

Emissions from major sources of pollution, such as transport, are subject to various measures at the European, national and local level. Local authorities control air pollution from smaller industrial processes.

The Agency works with local authorities, the Highways Agency and others to implement the UK government's air quality strategy in England and Wales as mandated in the Environment Act 1995.

4 Environmental audits

Environmental audits attempt to measure the economic, social and environmental impacts of a business.

4.1 A framework for social reporting

The provision of a framework for social reporting is being addressed in various ways. A green paper has been issued by the European Union to encourage companies to (voluntarily) 'contribute to a better society and a cleaner environment'. The current company law review in the UK sets out social and environmental reporting requirements. The Financial Times FTSE has launched a new index - **FTSE4good** - exclusively for companies who are deemed to be socially responsible. In the six months to March 2008 there were 41 new entrants to this index, including the Big Yellow Group (UK), Bank of Kyoto (Japan) and Google (USA).

The United Nations has backed a Global Reporting Initiative (GRI). This Initiative sets out a framework for reporting, including a **statement of vision and strategy** from the CEO together with **performance indicators** divided into economic, environmental and social performance indicators against which performance can be **measured** and **independently verified**.

The development of measurement and independent verification techniques are important, as in the past companies' own valuation of their contribution to the environment has sometimes been accepted uncritically. Enron was awarded six environmental awards in 2000, voted the best company to work for three years in a row and boasted its achievements in a report on its economic, environmental and social performance.

Exam focus point

Look out in investment appraisal questions for details of non-financial objectives. If a company is for example aiming to respect the interests of stakeholders and operate to the highest ethical standards, this could have an impact on the investments it undertakes.

4.2 Environmental accounting

In their capacity as information providers, accountants may be required to report on a firm's environmental impact and possible consequences. **Environmental management accounting** according to Frank Kirken in *Management Accounting*, (February 1996) is more advanced in Germany and Scandinavia than in the UK.

Examples of environmental management accounting objectives are as follows.

(a) **Eco-balance**

The firm identifies the raw materials it uses and outputs such as waste, noise etc, which it gives a notional value. The firm can identify these outputs as a social 'cost'.

(b) **Cleaner technology**

This can be used in the manufacturing process to avoid waste. Simple waste-minimisation measures can increase profit on purely economic grounds.

(c) **Corporate liabilities**

Firms are being sued for environmental damage, and this might need to be recorded as a liability, with a suitable risk assessment. This might have to be factored into the project appraisal and risk.

(d) **Performance appraisal**

This can include reducing pollution.

(e) **Life cycle assessments**

The total environmental impact of a product is measured, from the resources it consumes, the energy it requires in use, and how it is disposed of, if not recycled. It may be that a product's poor ecological impact (and consequent liability or poor publicity) can be traced back to one component or material, which can be replaced.

(f) **Budgetary planning and control system**

These can be used to develop variances analysing environmental issues.

4.3 Environmental audits and reporting

4.3.1 Environmental audits

Key term

An **environmental audit** is an audit that seeks to assess the environmental impact of a company's policies.

The starting point for assessing the impact of management decisions and company policies on the environment is for the auditor to obtain and review the company's environmental policy, where such a policy is formulated and documented.

The auditor will need to check whether the policy

- satisfies key stakeholder criteria
- meets legal requirements
- complies with British Standards or other local regulations

4.3.2 Impact of environmental issues on company reporting

Environmental issues are reflected in the financial accounts in the form of **contingent environmental liabilities**.

Potential environmental liabilities that are unrecorded in the financial statements can jeopardise the future profitability of the company.

As shown from asbestos claims, the number of environmental issues giving rise to liabilities is potentially quite large and increasing with enhanced environmental awareness and technological advances.

Examples of environmental exposures giving rise to liabilities include:

(a) soil contamination

(b) surface and ground water contamination

(c) site restructuring and rehabilitation

(d) removal of asbestos

(e) removal of controlled chemicals following new regulations eg recent international regulations on polychlorinated biphenyls (PCBs)

(f) air emissions

Certain industries, by the nature of their operations tend to be more exposed to environmental liabilities than others.

These industries include:

- chemical industries
- oil and gas industries
- pharmaceutical industries
- metallurgical and mining industries
- utility industries

4.3.3 The European eco-management and audit scheme (EMAS)

The main elements of the eco-management and audit scheme which was adopted in 1993 as a voluntary scheme are:

(a) Transparency of environmental statements
(b) Employee involvement in the implementation of the scheme
(c) Examination of the environmental effects of capital investments, planning decisions and procurement decisions.

Participating companies commit themselves to follow an environmental policy which will:

(a) Comply with environmental legislation
(b) Try to prevent pollution
(c) Strive to improve environmental improvements.

5 Triple bottom line (TBL) reporting

5.1 The main elements of TBL

Key term

Triple bottom line (TBL) reporting is external reporting that gives consideration to financial outcomes, environmental quality and social equity. *(Giekenson 1999)*

The term **triple bottom line** originated among investors seeking investments in enterprises that were socially just, economically profitable and environmentally sound.

The underlying principle is that in order to evaluate a company's true performance and assess the risk to the investor, one must look at a corporation's social, financial and environmental performance.

The triple bottom approach is often conceptualised as a pyramid or a triangle. An examples of how this approach has been represented diagrammatically are given below:

The triple bottom approach to decision making

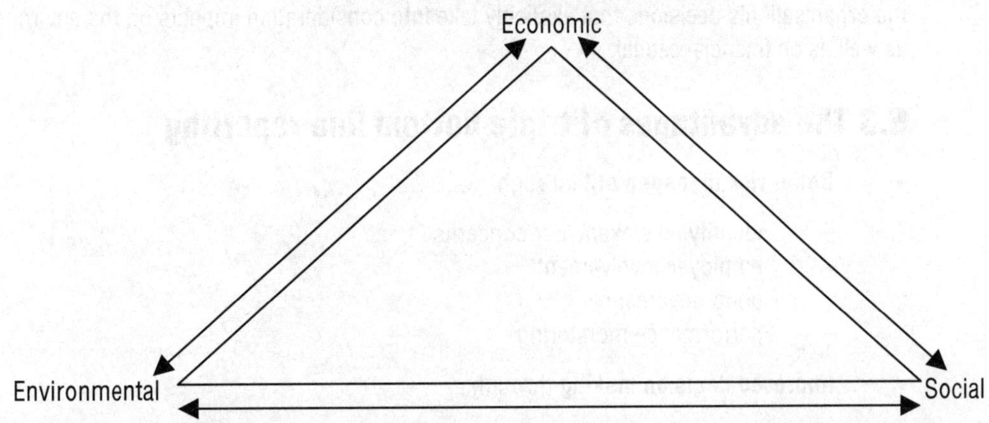

(Source: The Triple Bottom Line: A Viable Strategy for Rural Development? Cornelia Butler Flord)

Under the triple bottom approach decision making should ensure that each perspective is growing but not at the expense of the other. That is economic performance should not come at the expense of the environment or society.

The triple bottom line can be defined conceptually as **economic prosperity**, **environmental quality** and **social justice**. Triple bottom line reporting is the latest evolution of what is often reported as corporate sustainable development, or corporate social responsibility (sustainable development reporting). **Corporate sustainable development** tends to be very much **forward looking** and **qualitative**. By comparison, **triple bottom line reporting** is a more **quantitative summary** of a company's **economic**, **environmental** and **social performance** over the previous year.

However, more specific methods of measurement are still being defined, making management and reporting difficult. Many companies, thinking it is just a matter of **pollution control**, are missing the bigger picture that meeting the needs of the current generation will destroy the ability of future generations to meet theirs.

5.2 Reasons for triple bottom line

The concept of **triple bottom line** developed as a response to an increasing demand by community and business groups for reporting the environmental and social impacts as well as the economic impact of a company on the life of a community. Investors, taxpayers, consumers and other stakeholders are demanding that reporting extends beyond economic return or 'output' to cover issues of equity, justice and responsibility. Demands are being made to report on corporate performance in areas such as:

(a) assurances of food safety after highly public problems such as food recalls and food contamination.

(b) assurances of long-term sustainable production systems and environmental stewardship; eg. investments in renewable resources, recycling, waste reduction, or reducing green house gas emissions. Demands are on a global basis so that pollution problems are not exported offshore.

(c) looking after human rights, equity and equality; e.g. not using child labour, minimum working standards, no human rights violations, work/life balance, social equity for aboriginal communities.

(d) looking after the welfare of animals such as no testing on animals (Body Shop), humane transportation, feeding etc.

(e) ethical corporate conduct such as demonstrated due diligence and disclosure of conflicts of interest after the public spectacles of Enron, HIH, One Tel, Nippon Meat Packers and others.

(f) ethical business investments

The supporters of the TBL approach advocate that a corporation's (whether private or public) ultimate success is measured not just by the financial bottom line but by the corporation's social and ethical environmental performance.

Triple Bottom Line provides a framework for measuring and reporting **corporate performance** against **economic, social and environmental** benchmarks. Reporting on Triple Bottom Line makes transparent the organisation's decisions that explicitly take into consideration impacts on the environment and people, as well as on financial capital.

5.3 The advantages of triple bottom line reporting

- **Better risk management** through
  - identifying stakeholder concerns
  - employee involvement
  - good governance
  - performance monitoring
- **Improved decision making** through
  - stakeholder consultation
  - better information gathering
  - better reporting processes
- **Attracting and retaining higher calibre employees** through practising sustainability and ethical values

The critics of the triple bottom line argue that whereas the aspirations of the TBL movement are sound, on both practical and conceptual grounds, the TBL is an unhelpful addition to the corporate social responsibility debate and it promises more than it can deliver.

Some critics go so far as to argue that the rhetoric behind TBL can 'in fact provide a smokescreen behind which firms can avoid truly effecting social and environmental reporting and performance.'

(Getting to the Bottom of 'Triple Bottom Line' Wayne Normal and Chris MacDonald)

5.4 Triple bottom line indicators

Triple bottom line reporting requires proxies to indicate the economic, environmental and social impact of doing business. Examples of useful proxies are given below.

An indication of **economic impact** can be gained from such items as:

(a) gross operating surplus
(b) dependence on imports
(c) stimulus to the domestic economy by purchasing of locally produced goods and services.

An indication of **social impact** can be gained from, for example:

(a) the organisation's tax contribution
(b) employment.

An indication of **environmental impact** can be gained from such measures as:

(a) the ecological footprint
(b) emissions to soil, water and air
(c) water and energy use.

Such indicators can distil complex information into a form that is accessible to stakeholders. Organisations report on indicators that reflect their objectives and are relevant to stakeholders. One difficulty in identifying and using indicators is to ensure consistency within an organisation, over time, and between organisations. This is important for benchmarking and comparisons.

6 Wider reading

This is an extremely topical chapter and there are considerable amounts of information available in quality newspapers and websites. Make sure you keep up to date with latest developments by reading such materials and mention relevant real-life examples where appropriate in exam answers.

Chapter Roundup

- **Environmental** and **social** factors contribute to **sustainable** business.
- Companies are acknowledging the advantages of having an **environmental policy**. These include **reduction/management of risk to the business, motivating staff** and enhancement of corporate reputation.
- **Carbon trading** allows companies which emit **less** than their **allowance** to **sell** the **right** to **emit** CO_2 to another company.
- Emissions trading is emerging as a key part of the strategy both within the EU and globally to reduce the emission of greenhouse gases.
- EU governments are addressing the challenge of reducing carbon emissions through a combination of increased regulation and market mechanisms.
- The role of **environmental agency** is to protect the environment and promote sustainable development.
- **Environmental audits** and **triple bottom line accounting** attempt to measure the economic, social and environmental impacts of a business.

Quick Quiz

1 What does a company's external environmental report cover?

2 How can the triple bottom line be defined conceptually, and what are the differences between the triple bottom line accounting and corporate sustainable development?

3 Give two examples of triple bottom line indicators for each of the following impacts of doing business:

(i) economic
(ii) social
(iii) environmental

Answers to Quick Quiz

1
- What the business does and how it impacts on the environment
- The company's environmental objective(s)
- The company's approach to achieving and monitoring these objectives
- Assessment of success towards achieving objectives
- Independent verification of claims made

2 TBL can be defined conceptually as:

- Economic prosperity
- Environmental quality
- Social justice

Differences between TBL and Corporate Sustainable Development:

- CSD is forward looking and qualitative
- TBL is a quantitative summary of economic, environmental and social performance over the previous year, ie backward looking

3 Any two from:

(i) Gross operating surplus
Dependence on imports
Purchase of locally produced goods
Services

(ii) Tax contribution
Employment
'Giving back' to the community, eg Tesco's 'Computers for Schools' scheme

(iii) Water and energy use
Emissions to air, soil and water
Ecological footprint

Now try the questions below from the Exam Question Bank

Number	Level	Marks	Time
3	Introductory	15	27 mins

4

Financial strategy formulation

Topic list	Syllabus reference
1 Optimal capital structure	A (4) (a)
2 Dividend policy	A (4) (b)
3 Capital investment monitoring	A (4) (c)
4 Risk management	A (4) (d)

Introduction

This chapter looks in greater detail into four areas of financial strategy, namely the capital structure policy, the dividend distribution policy, the capital investment monitoring process and the risk management process. The Capital Asset Pricing Model (now part of the F9 syllabus) underpins a lot of what is covered in the following chapters. As this is assumed knowledge for students of P4, it is included in an appendix to this chapter.

Study guide

		Intellectual level
A4	**Financial strategy formulation**	
(a)	Recommend the optimum capital mix and structure within a specified business context and capital asset structure.	3
(b)	Recommend appropriate distribution and retention policy.	3
(c)	Establish capital investment monitoring and risk management systems.	3
(d)	Develop a framework for risk management comparing and contrasting risk mitigation, hedging and diversification strategies.	3

Exam guide

You may be asked about the contents of a strategic financial plan. Alternatively, as part of a longer question assessing a specific proposal, you may need to draw on your knowledge of the reasons for mergers and acquisitions, or the differences between vertical integration and diversification.

1 Optimal capital structure

FAST FORWARD

Decisions on how to finance the acquisition of assets are based on the cost of the various sources of finance.

Exam focus point

Part of a 20 mark optional question in December 2007 asked for a discussion of the advantages and disadvantages of debt as a mode of financing.

1.1 The capital structure decision

Suppose that a company has decided to expand its operations and has decided that the expansion will take place through organic growth rather than by acquiring another company. The company has therefore decided to expand its operation by increasing its productive capacity. This entails investment in plant and machinery. The increase in productive capacity need to generate cash flows that will increase the value of the firm. The question that the financial manger needs to address is how to finance the new investment.

1.2 Sources of finance

The main sources of finance for corporations are:

(a) Retained earnings
(b) Proceeds from the issue of new ordinary shares to existing or new shareholders
(c) Proceeds from a flotation of a company
(d) Preference shares
(e) Debt

1.3 The choice between debt and equity

1.3.1 Advantages of debt

(a) Debt is a **cheaper form of finance** than shares because, as debt interest is tax-deductible in most tax regimes.

(b) Debt should be **more attractive** to investors because it will be **secured** against the assets of the company.

(c) **Debt holders** rank above **shareholders** in the event of a liquidation.

(d) **Issue costs** are normally **lower** for debt than for shares.

(e) There is **no immediate change** in the existing structure of control, although this may change over time if the bonds are convertible to shares.

(f) There is **no immediate dilution** in earnings and dividends per share.

(g) Lenders do not participate in high profits compared with shares.

1.3.2 Disadvantages of debt

(a) **Interest** has to be paid on debt no matter what the company's profits in a year are. In particular the company may find itself locked into long-term debt at unfavourable rates of interest. The company is not legally obliged to pay dividends.

(b) Money has to be made available for **redemption** or **repayment** of debt. However, redemption values will fall in real terms during a time of inflation.

(c) Heavy borrowing **increases the financial risks** for ordinary shareholders. A company must be able to pay the interest charges and eventually repay the debt from its cash resources, and at the same time maintain a healthy balance sheet which does not deter would-be lenders. There might be insufficient security for a new loan.

(d) Shareholders may demand a **higher rate of return** because an increased interest burden increases the risks that dividends will not be paid.

(e) There might be restrictions on a company's power to borrow. The **company's constitution** may limit borrowing. These borrowing limits cannot be altered except with the approval of the shareholders at a general meeting of the company. **Trust deeds of existing loan stock** may **limit borrowing**. These limits can only be overcome by redeeming the loan stock.

1.4 Debt instruments

FAST FORWARD

Debt capital takes various forms such as **loan capital**, **debentures**, **zero coupon bonds** and the interest on debt is tax-deductible

1.4.1 Types of corporate debt

Corporate debt takes many forms which are differentiated in terms of maturity as **redeemable** or **irredeemable**, in terms of the coupon as fixed rate loan notes, **floating rate loan notes**, or **zero coupon bonds.** Finally there are callable bonds which can be redeemed before maturity and **convertible loan stock w**hich can be converted into equity.

(a) **Debentures** are **secure loan capital** secured either by a floating charge on all assets of the company, or by a fixed charge on specific assets of the company.

(b) **Unsecured loan stock** is debt which is not secured on any of the assets of the company and it carries a higher interest.

(c) **Deep Discount bonds** are bonds offered at a large discount on the face value of the debt so that a significant proportion of the return to the investor comes by way of a capital gain on redemption, rather than through interest payment. Deep discount bonds pay a low coupon and have **low servicing costs** but a high cost of redemption at maturity. The only tax advantage is that the gain gets taxed (as **income**) in one lump on maturity or sale, not as amounts of interest each year.

(d) **Zero coupon bonds** are bonds offering no interest payments, all investor return being gained through capital appreciation. They are issued at a discount to their redemption value, and the investor gains from the difference between the issue price and the redemption value. The advantage for borrowers is that zero coupon bonds can be used to raise cash immediately, and there is no cash repayment until redemption date. The cost of redemption is known at the time of issue, and so the borrower can plan to have funds available to redeem the bonds at maturity. The advantage for lenders is that that there is no exposure to interest rate risk and if held to maturity are free of market risk. The investor is of course exposed to credit risk.

(e) **Convertible unsecured debt** are debt instruments that give the option to the holder to convert them into equity at some time in the future at a predetermined price.

(f) **Mezzanine debt** is debt with conversion options. It is a subordinated debt because it ranks in terms of seniority of claims below straight debt like debentures and it requires a higher rate of return. Mezzanine debt is the preferred way of financing leveraged buyouts.

(g) **Leasing** is used for the financing of certain assets such as buildings, ship or aircraft.

(h) **Eurobonds** are bonds denominated in currency other than that of the issuer, usually dollar, yen or Euro, and trade in the international financial markets.

1.4.2 Trust deed

A **loan note (or debenture)** is a written acknowledgement of a debt by a company, usually given under its seal and normally containing provisions as to payment of interest and the terms of repayment of principal. A loan note may be secured on some or all of the assets of the company or its subsidiaries.

A **trust deed** would empower a trustee (such as an insurance company or a bank) to **intervene** on behalf of loan note holders if the conditions of borrowing under which the debentures were issued are not being fulfilled. This might involve:

- **Failure** to **pay interest** on the due dates
- An **attempt** by the company to **sell off important assets** contrary to the terms of the loan
- A company taking out **additional loans** and thereby exceeding previously agreed borrowing limits established either by its constitution or by the terms of the loan note trust deed. (A trust deed might place restrictions on the company's ability to borrow more from elsewhere until the loan notes have been redeemed.)

1.4.3 Issuing corporate bonds

A company that wants to issue corporate bonds will need to appoint an investment bank as the lead manager. The lead manager in turn sets up an underwriting syndicate which purchases the entire issue at an agreed price. The price reflects the coupon of the bond and the credit rating of the bond. The syndicate will then sell the issue to final buyers who are normally clients of the investment banks involved or other investment banks.

1.4.4 Cost of debt

The cost of debt capital is the after-tax cost of raising debt in the capital markets. It is the rate of return that investors require for investments with that specific risk. Other factors that influence the cost of debt capital include:

(a) The general level of interest rate

(b) The credit rating of the bond which is reflected in the spread over the risk-free rate .

(c) The maturity of the bond.

(d) The type of debt issue. For example callable bonds will be more expensive than non callable bonds.

(e) The cost of issuing a bond.

1.5 Preference shares

Preference shares have priority over ordinary shares in divided payments and capital repayment.

1.5.1 Characteristics of preference shares

Preference shares carry priority over ordinary shareholders with regard to dividend payments. They do not carry voting rights. They may be attractive to corporate investors, as (unlike interest receipts) dividends received are generally not subject to tax. However, for the issuing company, dividend payments (unlike interest payments) are generally not tax-deductible.

Preference shares are shares carrying a fixed rate of dividends, the holders of which, subject to the conditions of issue, have a prior claim to any company profits available for distribution. They are an example of prior charge capital.

Preferred shareholders may also have a prior claim to the repayment of capital in the event of winding up.

1.5.2 Types of preference shares

Cumulative preference shares are preference shares where any arrears of dividend are carried forward. When eventually the company decides to pay a dividend, the cumulative preference shareholders are entitled to all their arrears before ordinary shareholders are paid a dividend.

Participating preference shares are shares that have an additional entitlement to dividend over and above their specified rate. Participating preferred shareholders are entitled to participate along with ordinary shareholders in available profits, normally once the ordinary shareholders have themselves received a specified level of dividend.

Convertible preference shares are shares that can be converted into ordinary shares.

1.5.3 Advantages and disadvantages of preference shares

From the company's point of view, preference shares have some positive features.

- Dividends do **not have** to be **paid** in a year in which **profits are poor**, whilst this is not the case with interest payments on long-term debt.
- Since they do not normally carry voting rights, preferred shares **avoid diluting** the **control** of existing shareholders whilst an issue of equity shares would not.
- Unless they are redeemable, issuing preference shares will **lower** the company's **gearing**. Redeemable preference shares are normally treated as debt when gearing is calculated.
- The issue of preference shares does **not restrict** the company's **borrowing power**, at least in the sense that preferred share capital is not secured against assets of the business.
- The non-payment of dividend does **not give** the preferred shareholders the **right** to **appoint a receiver**, a right which is normally given to debenture holders.

From the point of view of the investor, preference shares are less attractive than loan stock because:

- They **cannot be secured** on the company's assets.
- The **dividend yield** traditionally offered on preferred dividends has been much **too low** to provide an attractive investment compared with the interest yields on loan stock in view of the additional risk involved.
- **Dividend payments on preference shares may not be tax deductible** in the way that interest payments on debt are. Furthermore, for preferred shares to be attractive to investors, the level of payment needs to be **higher than** for **interest on debt** to compensate for the additional risks.

1.5.4 Cost of preferred stock

The key feature of preferred stock is the **constant interest** that it pays to investors. The cost of preference shares should therefore be calculated in the same way as the cost of corporate bonds.

1.6 Retained earnings

FAST FORWARD

Retained earnings are the **cumulative undistributed earnings** of the company and can be used to finance the **capital expenditure** programme of the company.

For many businesses, the cash needed to finance investments will be available because the earnings the business has made have been retained within the business rather than paid out as dividends. This interaction of investment, financing and dividend policy is the most important issue facing many businesses.

Advantages of using retentions

Retentions are a **flexible source** of finance; companies are not tied to specific amounts or specific repayment patterns. Using retentions does **not involve** a **change in the pattern** of **shareholdings**.

Disadvantages of using retentions

Shareholders may be **sensitive** to the **loss of dividends** that will result from retention for re-investment, rather than paying dividends.

1.6.1 Cost of retained earnings

Retained profits is not a cost-free method of obtaining funds. There is an **opportunity cost** in that if dividends were paid, the cash received could be invested by shareholders to earn a return. The cost of retained earnings is the rate of return that stockholders require on equity capital that the company has obtained by retaining profits.

The shareholders could have received these earnings as dividends and invested them elsewhere, therefore, the company needs to earn at least as good a return as the investors could have got elsewhere for comparable risk. If the company cannot achieve this return they should return the funds to the shareholders and let them invest them elsewhere.

1.6.2 Alternative methods of estimating the cost of equity

There are three alternatives for calculating the cost of retained earnings.

- Firstly, by using theoretical Valuation Models such as the **Capital Asset Pricing Model (CAPM)** or the **Arbitrage Pricing Theory (APT)**.
- Secondly, the **bond yield-plus-premium approach**. This is a model used where analysts do not have confidence in the CAPM or the APT approach, they instead simply add a judgmental risk premium to the interest rate on the firm's own long-term debt.
- Thirdly, **market implied estimates** using variants of the discounted cash flow (DCF) approach. This model is however, based on particular assumption on the growth rate of earning of the company.

1.6.3 Valuation models – the CAPM

We have already discussed in Chapter 2 that companies and investors in general will earn a return above the yield of a risk-free asset only if they are prepared to undertake extra risk. The difference between the expected return from a risky investment and the risk-free return is called the **risk premium**. The capital asset pricing model (CAPM) and the other valuation models make the assumption that the risk premium is proportional to the risk premium of the market as a whole.

Risk premium on a portfolio = beta of portfolio x risk premium on the market

The formula for the CAPM is given below

$E(r_i) = r_f + \beta_i(E(r_m) - r_f)$

where

$E(r_i)$ = expected (target) return on a security by the investor (that is, K_e)

r_f = risk-free rate of return

$E(r_j) - r_f$ = risk premium for the security

$E(r_m)$ = expected return in the market

β_i = beta factor of the individual security, portfolio or project

$E(r_m) - r_f$ = market premium

Thus the risk premium of a portfolio depends on the beta of the portfolio. The higher the beta the riskier the portfolio and the higher the required return by the investor in order to invest in the portfolio. CAPM is assumed knowledge from Paper F9 – *Financial Management* thus details of this model are given in the appendix to this chapter.

1.6.4 Valuation models – beyond the CAPM

The CAPM specifies that the only risk factor that should be taken into account is the market risk premium. Subsequent empirical research has shown that there may be other factors in addition to market risk premium that explain differences in asset returns, such as **interest rates** and **industrial production**. The **Arbitrage Pricing Theory** (APT) generalises the CAPM and postulates the following model for the risk premium of a portfolio

$E(r_i) = r_f + (E(r_A) - r_f)\beta_A + (E(r_B) - r_f)\beta_B + \text{..........} +(E(r_m) - r_f)\beta_m + \text{.......}$

Where $(E(r_A) - r_f)\beta_A$ is the risk premium on factor A.

$E(r_B) - r_f)\beta_B$ is the risk premium on factor B and so on

The APT model calculates the risk premium by constructing a portfolio with a **beta of** 1 in relation to the factor under consideration (such as the interest rate) and a **beta of zero** in relation to all the other factors. The risk premium of that specific portfolio is then used as a proxy for the risk premium for the factor under consideration.

Fama and French identified **two factors** in addition to the **market portfolio** that explain company returns namely:

- **size** and
- **distress**

The **size factor** is measured as the difference in return between a portfolio of the smallest stocks and a portfolio of the largest stocks, whereas the **distress factor** is proxied by the difference in return between a portfolio of the highest book to market value stocks and portfolio of the lowest book to market value stocks.

The Fama and French three factor model is as follows

$E(r_j) = r_f + \beta_{i,m} (E(r_m) - r_f) + \beta_{i,S}\ SIZE + \beta_{i,D}\ DIST$

where $\beta_{i,m}$ is the stock's beta

$\beta_{i,S}$ is beta with respect to size

$\beta_{i,D}$ is the stock's beta with respect to distress

Unlike the CAPM, the APT leaves the factors to be determined empirically.

1.6.5 Bond-yield-plus premium approach

The bond yield-plus model is based on the empirical observation that the return on equity is higher than the yield on bonds. Since equities are riskier than bonds, the difference between the two is a reward the investor requires in order to invest in the riskier asset. Now if this equity market premium was constant, then the required rate of return for equity could simply be calculated by looking at the bond yields and then adding the fixed premium.

1.6.6 Market implied method

The market-implied method is based on a particular assumption about the growth rate or earnings or dividends of a company. For example, if we were to assume a constant rate of growth for dividends at the rate of g per annum, the shareholders' required rate of return is r_e per annum, and the next period's dividend payment is d_1 then the market value of the share will be

$$V_{ex\text{-}div} = \frac{d_0(1+g)}{r_e - g}$$

where $V_{ex\text{-}div}$ = the ex-div market value of the shares that may need to be calculated using

$V_{ex\text{-}div} = V_{cum\ div} - d_0$

where $V_{cum\ div}$ is the cum div market value of the shares

d_0 is the dividend about to be paid now if we are cum dividend

d_0 = the current dividend
r_e = the investors' required rate of return
g = the expected annual growth rate of the dividends

The formula can be rearranged as follows $k_e - g = \frac{d_0(1+g)}{V_{ex-div}}$

to produce the cost of equity

$$k_e = \frac{d_0(1+g)}{V_{ex-div}} + g$$

where d_0 = the current dividend
V_{ex-div} = the market value determined by the investor
g = the expected annual growth rate of the dividends

Growth Rates

The cost of capital we have derived is based on the current market price of shares but also on the growth rate assumptions we have made. If the constant growth assumption in the implied method is not appropriate, then the estimates we have derived will not be accurate.

Question

Cost of retained earnings

A company is about to pay a dividend of $1 on its common stock. The shares are currently quoted at $23.00. The dividend is expected to grow at the rate of 10% per annum. Calculate the cost of retained earnings for the company.

Answer

Since we are about to pay the dividend, we will assume that the share is currently cum div. Hence, since we need the ex-div value, we must use the expression

$$V_{ex\text{-}div} = V_{cum\text{-}div} - d_0$$

to calculate the ex-div price as

$$V_{ex\text{-}div} = \$23.00 - \$1.00 = \$22.00$$

Then using the above formula for the cost of equity, we get

$$k_e = \frac{d_0(1+g)}{E_{ex-div}} + g$$

$$k_e = \frac{\$1 \times 1.1}{\$22.00} + 0.1$$

$$k_e = \frac{1.10}{\$22.00} + 0.1$$

$k_e = 0.05 + 0.1 = 0.15$ or 15% per annum

Note that k_e is calculated as dividend yield plus growth rate here.

1.7 New share issues by quoted companies

FAST FORWARD

New shares can be issued either to existing shareholders or to new shareholders.

A new issue of shares might be made in a variety of different circumstances.

- The company might want to **raise more cash**, for example for expansion of its operations.
- The company might want to issue new shares partly to raise cash but more importantly to obtain a **stock market listing**. When a UK company is floated, for example on the main stock market, it is a requirement of the Stock Exchange that at least a minimum proportion of its shares should be made available to the general investing public if the shares are not already widely held.
- The company might issue new shares to the shareholders of another company, in order to **take it over**.

1.7.1 Practicalities for issuing new shares

A lot of the practicalities involved are specific to the type of issue. However, general factors apply to all types.

- **Costs.** There will be administrative costs, but how great these are will vary enormously.
- **Income to investors.** In Britain and other jurisdictions, companies are not obliged to pay dividends to shareholders in a particular year. However in the long-term shareholders will expect dividends and/or capital appreciation.
- **Tax.** Unlike loan finance interest or charges, dividends paid are **not normally tax-deductible**.
- **Effect on control.** Unless shares are issued to **existing shareholders** in proportion to their **current holdings**, the balance of voting power will change and there may ultimately be an impact on the **control** of the firm.

1.7.2 Timing of new share issue

New equity issues in general will be more common when share prices are high than when share prices are low.

- When **share price are high, investors' confidence** will probably be **high**, and investors will be more willing to put money into companies with the potential for growth.
- By issuing shares at a high price, a company will **reduce** the **number of shares** it must issue to raise the amount of capital it wants. This will reduce the dilution of earnings for existing shareholders.
- Following on from (b), the company's **total dividend commitment** on the new shares, to meet shareholders' expectations, will be **lower**.
- If **share prices are low**, business **confidence** is likely to be **low** too. Companies may not want to raise capital for new investments until expectations begin to improve.

1.7.3 A rights issue

A **rights issue** is an offer to existing shareholders for them to buy more shares, usually at lower than the current share price.

A rights issue is the raising of new capital by giving existing shareholders the right to subscribe to new shares in proportion to their current holdings. These shares are usually issued at a discount to market price. A shareholder not wishing to take up a rights issue may sell the rights.

A dilution is the reduction in the earnings and voting power per share caused by an increase or potential increase in the number of shares in issue.

Existing shareholders have **pre-emption rights** when new shares are issued. So that existing shareholders' rights are not diluted by the issue of new shares, legislation in many countries requires that before any equity shares are allotted for cash, they must first be offered to existing shareholders.

Rights issues are **cheaper** than offers for sale to the general public. This is partly because no **prospectus** is generally required (provided that the issue is for less than 10% of the class of shares concerned), partly because the **administration** is **simpler** and partly because the cost of underwriting will be less.

Rights issues are **more beneficial** to **existing shareholders** than issues to the general public. New shares are issued at a **discount** to the current market price, to make them attractive to investors. A rights issue secures the discount on the market price for existing shareholders, who may either keep the shares or sell them if they wish.

Relative voting rights are **unaffected** if shareholders all take up their rights.

The finance raised may be used to **reduce gearing** in book value terms by increasing share capital and/or to pay off long-term debt which will reduce gearing in market value terms.

A company making a rights issue must set a price which is low enough to **secure the acceptance** of shareholders, who are being asked to provide extra funds, but not so low that earnings per share are excessively diluted. Other possible problems include getting the issue **underwritten** and an excessive **fall** in the **share price.**

Example: rights issue (1)

Seagull can achieve a profit after tax of 20% on the capital employed. At present its capital structure is as follows.

	$
200,000 ordinary shares of $1 each	200,000
Retained earnings	100,000
	300,000

The directors propose to raise an additional $126,000 from a rights issue. The current market price is $1.80.

Required

(a) Calculate the number of shares that must be issued if the rights price is: $1.60; $1.50; $1.40; $1.20.

(b) Calculate the dilution in earnings per share in each case.

Solution

The earnings at present are 20% of $300,000 = $60,000. This gives earnings per share of 30c. The earnings after the rights issue will be 20% of $426,000 = $85,200.

Rights price	*No of new share ($126,000 ÷ rights price)*	*EPS ($85,200 ÷ total no of shares)*	*Dilution*
$		Cents	Cents
1.60	78,750	30.6	+ 0.6
1.50	84,000	30.0	–
1.40	90,000	29.4	– 0.6
1.20	105,000	27.9	– 2.1

Note that at a high rights price the earnings per share are increased, not diluted. The breakeven point (zero dilution) occurs when the rights price is equal to the capital employed per share: $300,000 ÷ 200,000 = $1.50.

A right issue is effectively a call option on the firm's equity and even if issued at the current price – that is, a zero intrinsic value – it may still have time value . The value of the call is effectively a deduction from the existing shareholder value. We will cover call options in more detail in Chapter 8.

1.7.4 Scrip dividends

Scrip dividends, **scrip issues** and **stock splits** are not methods of raising new equity funds, but they *are* methods of altering the share capital structure of a company, or in the case of scrip dividends and scrip issues, increasing the issued share capital of the company.

Scrip dividend is a dividend paid by the issue of additional company shares, rather than by cash.

A scrip dividend effectively converts profit and loss reserves into **issued share capital**. When the directors of a company would prefer to retain funds within the business but consider that they must pay at least a certain amount of dividend, they might offer equity shareholders the choice of a **cash dividend** or a **scrip dividend**. Each shareholder would decide separately which to take.

Recently **enhanced scrip dividends** have been offered by many companies. With enhanced scrip dividends, the value of the shares offered is much greater than the cash alternative, giving investors an incentive to choose the shares.

Advantages of scrip dividends

They can **preserve** a company's **cash position** if a substantial number of shareholders take up the share option.

Investors may be able to obtain **tax advantages** if dividends are in the form of shares.

Investors looking to **expand their holding** can do so **without incurring** the **transaction costs** of buying more shares.

A small scrip issue will **not dilute the share price significantly.** If however cash is not offered as an alternative, empirical evidence suggests that the share price will tend to fall.

A share issue will **decrease** the company's **gearing**, and may therefore **enhance** its **borrowing capacity.**

1.7.5 Bonus issues

A **bonus/scrip/capitalisation issue** is the capitalisation of the reserves of a company by the issue of additional shares to existing shareholders, in proportion to their holdings. Such shares are normally fully paid-up with no cash called for from the shareholders.

For example, if a company with issued share capital of 100,000 ordinary shares of $1 each made a one for five scrip issue, 20,000 new shares would be issued to existing shareholders, one new share for every five old shares held. Issued share capital would be increased by $20,000, and reserves (probably share premium account, if there is one) reduced by this amount.

By creating more shares in this way, a scrip issue does not raise new funds, but does have the advantage of making shares **cheaper** and therefore (perhaps) **more easily marketable** on the Stock Exchange. For example, if a company's shares are priced at $6 on the Stock Exchange, and the company makes a one for two scrip issue, we should expect the share price after the issue to fall to $4 each. Shares at $4 each might be more easily marketable than shares at $6 each.

1.7.6 Stock splits

The advantage of a scrip issue mentioned above is also the reason for a **stock split** which we discussed earlier.

1.8 Methods for obtaining a listing

An unquoted company can obtain a listing on the stock market by means of:

- Direct **offer by subscription** to the public
- **Offer for sale**
- **Placing**
- **Introduction**

Of these an offer for sale or a placing are the most common.

1.8.1 Direct offer by subscription to general public

Issues where the issuing firm sells shares directly to the general public tend to be quite rare on many stock exchanges, and the issues that are made tend to be quite large. These issues are sometimes known as **offers by prospectus**. This type of issue is very risky, because of the lack of guarantees that all shares will be taken up.

1.8.2 Offer for sale

Offer for sale is an invitation to apply for shares in a company based on information contained in a prospectus. It is a means of selling the shares of a company to the public at large. When companies 'go public' for the first time, a **large** issue will probably take the form of an offer for sale. Subsequent issues are likely to be **placings** or **rights issues**, described later.

An offer for sale entails the **acquisition by an issuing house** of a large block of shares of a company, with a view to offering them for sale to the public. An issuing house is usually a merchant bank (or sometimes a firm of stockbrokers). It may acquire the shares either as a direct allotment from the company or by purchase from existing members. In either case, the issuing house publishes an invitation to the public to apply for shares, either at a fixed price or on a tender basis.

The advantage of an offer for sale over a direct offer by the company to the public is that the issuing house **accepts responsibility** to the public, and gives to the issue the support of its own standing.

An issuing house has the job of trying to ensure a successful issue for the company's shares, by advising on an issue price for the shares, and trying to interest institutional investors in buying some of the shares.

The offer price must be **advertised a short time in advance**, so it is fixed without certain knowledge of the condition of the market at the time applications are invited. In order to ensure the success of an issue, share prices are often set **lower** than they might otherwise be. An issuing house normally tries to ensure that a share price rises to a **premium** above its issue price soon after trading begins. A target premium of 20% above the issue price would be fairly typical.

1.8.3 Offers for sale by tender

It is often very difficult to decide upon the price at which the shares should be offered to the general public. One way of trying to ensure that the issue price reflects the value of the shares as perceived by the market is to make an **offer for sale by tender.** A **minimum price** will be fixed and subscribers will be invited to tender for shares at prices equal to or above the minimum. The shares will be **allotted at the highest price** at which they will **all be taken up**. This is known as the **striking price**.

Example: offer for sale by tender

Byte Henderson is a new company that is making its first public issue of shares. It has decided to make the issue by means of an offer for sale by tender. The intention is to issue up to 4,000,000 shares (the full amount of authorised share capital) at a minimum price of 300 cents. The money raised, net of issue costs of $1,000,000, would be invested in projects which would earn benefits with a present value equal to 130% of the net amount invested.

The following tenders have been received. (Each applicant has made only one offer.)

Price tendered per share	*Number of shares applied for at this price*
$	
6.00	50,000
5.50	100,000
5.00	300,000
4.50	450,000
4.00	1,100,000
3.50	1,500,000
3.00	2,500,000

(a) How many shares would be issued, and how much in total would be raised, if Byte Henderson Inc chooses:

  (i) To maximise the total amount raised?
  (ii) To issue exactly 4,000,000 shares?

(b) Harvey Goldfinger, a private investor, has applied for 12,000 shares at a price of $5.50 and has sent a cheque for $66,000 to the issuing house that is handling the issue. In both cases (a)(i) and (ii), how many shares would be issued to Mr Goldfinger, assuming that any partial acceptance of

offers would mean allotting shares to each accepted applicant in proportion to the number of shares applied for? How much will Mr Goldfinger receive back out of the $66,000 he has paid?

(c) Estimate the likely market value of shares in the company after the issue, assuming that the market price fully reflects the investment information given above and that exactly 4,000,000 shares are issued.

Solution

(a) We begin by looking at the cumulative tenders.

Price	*Cumulative number of shares applied for*	*Amount raised if price is selected, before deducting issue costs*
$		$
6.00	50,000	300,000
5.50	150,000	825,000
5.00	450,000	2,250,000
4.50	900,000	4,050,000
4.00	2,000,000	8,000,000
3.50	3,500,000	12,250,000
3.00	6,000,000 (4,000,000 max)	12,000,000

(i) To maximise the total amount raised, the issue price should be $3.50. The total raised before deducting issue costs would be $12,250,000.

(ii) To issue exactly 4,000,000 shares, the issue price must be $3.00. The total raised would be $12,000,000, before deducting issue costs.

(b) (i) Harvey Goldfinger would be allotted 12,000 shares at $3.50 per share. He would receive a refund of 12,000 × $2 = $24,000 out of the $66,000 he has paid.

(ii) If 4,000,000 shares are issued, applicants would receive two thirds of the shares they tendered for. Harvey Goldfinger would be allotted 8,000 shares at $3 per share and would receive a refund of $42,000 out of the $66,000 he has paid.

(c) The net amount raised would be $12,000,000 minus issue costs of $1,000,000 which equals $11,000,000.

The present value of the benefits from investment would be 130% of $11,000,000 which equals $14,300,000. If the market price reflects this information, the price per share would rise to

$$\frac{£14,300,000}{4,000,000} = \$3.575 \text{ per share.}$$

1.8.4 A placing

A **placing** is an arrangement whereby the shares are not all offered to the public, but instead, the sponsoring market maker arranges for most of the issue to be bought by a **small number of investors**, usually institutional investors such as pension funds and insurance companies.

The choice between an offer for sale and a placing

When a company is planning a flotation, is it likely to prefer an offer for sale of its shares, or a placing?

- **Placings** are much **cheaper**. Approaching institutional investors privately is a much cheaper way of obtaining finance, and thus placings are often used for smaller issues.
- Placings are likely to be **quicker**.
- Placings are likely to involve **less disclosure** of **information.**
- However, most of the shares will be placed with a **relatively small number of (institutional) shareholders**, which means that most of the shares are unlikely to be available for trading after the flotation, and that institutional shareholders will have control of the company.

1.8.5 A Stock Exchange introduction

By this method of obtaining a quotation, no shares are made available to the market, neither existing nor newly created shares; nevertheless, the stock market grants a quotation. This will only happen where shares in a large company are already widely held, so that a market can be seen to exist. A company might want an **introduction** to obtain **greater marketability** for the shares, a known share valuation for inheritance tax purposes and easier access in the future to additional capital.

1.8.6 Underwriting

A company about to issue new securities in order to raise finance might decide to have the issue underwritten. **Underwriters** are financial institutions which agree (in exchange for a fixed fee, perhaps 2.25% of the finance to be raised) to buy at the issue price any securities which are **not subscribed** for by the investing public.

Underwriters **remove** the **risk** of a share issue's being under-subscribed, but at a cost to the company issuing the shares. It is not compulsory to have an issue underwritten. Ordinary offers for sale are most likely to be underwritten although rights issues may be as well.

Because of the costs of underwriting, there has been a trend in recent years for companies whose securities are marketable to adopt the practice known as the **'bought deal'**, whereby an investment bank buys the whole of a new issue at a small discount to the market.

1.8.7 Costs of share issue on the stock market

Companies may incur the following costs when issuing shares.

- Underwriting costs
- Stock market listing fee (the initial charge) for the new securities
- Fees of the issuing house, solicitors, auditors and public relations consultant
- Charges for printing and distributing the prospectus
- Advertising in national newspapers

1.8.8 Costs of equity for new share issue on the stock market

When we are dealing with newly issued equity, the company needs to take into account the flotation cost involved with the new stock. We need to adapt the formula used for retained earnings to allow for the additional cash outflow that the company suffers at time 0, being the **flotation costs**, f. Therefore the cost of equity for the company becomes

$$k_e = \frac{d_0(1+g)}{P_0(1-f)}$$

Example

Assume that there were flotation costs of 8% and d_0 = \$1.00, P_0 = \$22, g = 10%. What is the cost of new shares issued?

Solution

$$k_e = \frac{\$1.10}{\$22.00 - \$1.76} + 0.1 = 15.4\%$$

Note that the formula for new shares issued could be learned as a general formula for the cost of equity, with retained earnings being a special case where issue costs are zero (f = 0).

2 Dividend policy

Dividend decisions determine the amount of and the way that a company's profits are distributed to its shareholders.

2.1 Is dividend policy irrelevant?

Shareholders who hold the shares of a company are entitled to a portion of the income that the company generates and of the assets that it owns. The dividend policy of a company refers to the decision taken by the management of the company with regard to how much of a company's earnings will be distributed to shareholders and how much will be retained within the firm.

In reaching this decision, the management of the company should try, as in all financial management decisions, to maximise the wealth of the company's shareholders. However there is little agreement as to the impact of dividend policy on shareholder wealth, and the interaction between dividend payments, financing decision and the value of a company has been the subject of theoretical analysis and empirical investigation.

At one end of the debate Modigliani and Miller have maintained that the dividend policy of a corporation is irrelevant because the value of a company is not affected by its financial policy.

Suppose a company pays dividends without changing investment and financing policies. The money that the company will pay as dividends has to come from somewhere else. If the company maintains the amount of debt (does not borrow to pay the dividend), the company needs to issue new shares to finance the dividend. The new shareholders will pay only what the shares are worth, and the old shareholders will receive the money paid by the new shareholders as dividends. After the dividend is paid, the value per-share should be equal to the old price minus the dividend paid by the new shareholders. The value of the firm remains the same, but money changed hands from new to old shareholders. Dividend policies are therefore irrelevant.

2.2 Ways of paying dividend

Companies have many ways of returning money to the shareholders. The main ones are:

(a) **Cash dividends**. This the most common way of paying dividends by corporations. These dividends are paid in cash, usually quarterly. Companies can declare both regular and 'extra' dividends. Regular dividends usually remain unchanged in the future, but 'extraordinary' or 'special' dividends are unlikely to be repeated.

(b) **Stock dividends** are paid instead of cash dividends by allocating to existing shareholders shares of equivalent value. Shareholders receive new stock in the corporation as a form of a dividend. Like a 'stock split', the number of shares increases, but no cash changes hands

(c) **Share repurchases** is an alternative to distribute cash to its shareholders. The firm buys back its own shares. This can be done **on the open market, by tender offer or by buying stock from major shareholders.**

A **major difference** between dividends and share repurchases is their **tax treatment**. **Cash dividends** are **taxed as income** but **share repurchases** are subject to capital gains tax **only if a capital gain has been realised.**

Both cash and stock dividends reduce the value per share.

2.3 Dividend capacity

The **dividend capacity** of a corporation determines how much of a company's income can be paid out as dividend. The dividend capacity of the company is also known as the **free cash-flow** to equity (FCFE).

The estimation of dividend capacity of a firm is dealt with in Chapters 6 and 22. Here we simply give the definition of the free cash flow to equity.

Free Cash Flow to Equity = Net income (EBIT – Net Interest – Tax paid)

add Depreciation

less Total net investment
(change in capital investment + change in working capital)

add Net debt issued (new borrowings less any repayments)

add Net equity issued (new issues less any equity repurchases)

The FCFE represents the cash available to the company which could be paid out to shareholders as dividends.

The FCFE is usually not the same as actual dividends in a given year because normally the management of a company deliberately smoothes dividend payments across time. There are also rules which restrict the payment of distributable profits only as dividends.

2.4 Theories of dividend policy

The **Modigliani and Miller** argument that dividend policy is irrelevant should have led to a random pattern of dividend payments. In practice, dividend payments tend to be smoothed over time. In this section we review some of the reasons that have been put forward as explanation for the payment of dividends.

2.4.1 The residual theory of dividend payments

According to this theory, firms will only pay dividends if all the profitable investment opportunities have been funded. This theory assumes that internal funds are the cheapest source of financing, and the company will resort to external financing only if the available internal funds, current and retained earnings have been exhausted.

2.4.2 Target payout ratio

According to the target payout theory, companies pay out as dividends a fixed proportion of their earnings. Firms have long-run target dividend payout ratios.

(a) Mature companies with stable earnings usually have a higher dividend pay-out ratio than growth companies.
(b) Managers focus more on dividend changes than in absolute amounts.
(c) Transitory changes in earnings usually do not affect dividend pay-outs.
(d) Only long-term shifts in earnings can be followed by changes in dividends.
(e) Managers are reluctant to change dividend pay-out ratios due to the potential signals that such changes may send to the markets (see section 2.4.3 below).

2.4.3 Dividends as signals

Dividends can be used to convey good (or bad) information. A firm that increases its dividend payout ratio may be signalling that it expects future cash flows to increase as this ratio tends to remain steady over time. Bad firms can also increase dividends to try to convince the markets that they too are expecting increased future cash flows. However this increase may be unsustainable if the promised increases do not occur and the inevitable reduction in dividend payout ratio will mean heavy penalities from the markets.

2.4.4 Agency theory

Dividend payments can be an instrument to monitor managers. When firms pay dividends they often need to subsequently go to the capital markets to fund the projects. When firms go to the financial markets they will be scrutinised by different market participants. For instance, investors will require an analysis of the creditworthiness of the firm. Companies often announce dividend payments in conjunction with trying to raise new capital.

2.4.5 Dividends and taxes

A final theory explaining dividend payments is based on the presence of different corporate and personal taxes on one hand and of different income and capital gains taxes on the other. Modigliani and Miller assume that there are no personal taxes. Taxes on dividends (ordinary income) are higher than taxes on capital gains. Thus, under the presence of personal taxes, companies should not pay dividends because investors require a higher return to companies that pay dividends. If payments are to be made to shareholders, the company should opt for other alternatives, such as share repurchases. This is true if taxes on dividend income are higher than taxes on capital gains.

However, different investors have different tax rates. High tax rate individuals will prefer that the firm invest more, whereas low tax individuals may prefer that the firm does not invest and instead pay dividends. Investors try to select companies with dividend policies that approximate their requirements.

3 Capital investment monitoring

FAST FORWARD

Capital investment projects require appraisal, and implementation monitoring.

3.1 The need for investment monitoring

Capital investment projects require a large proportion of a company's monetary and human resources and its implementation is crucial for a company's performance. Implementation is one of the stages of the capital investment process which consist of the appraisal stage, the budgeting stage, the authorisation stage, the implementation stage and the post audit report.

The monitoring functions of the implementation stage seek to ensure

(a) That the project expenses are within the budgeted limits
(b) That any revenues budgeted are achieved.
(c) That the completion time schedule is adhered to..
(d) That the risk factors identified during the appraisal stage remain valid.

3.2 Aspects of the monitoring process

Monitoring is a multifaceted function which requires clearly delineated roles and planning as well as recommendations for responding to any violations of the planned targets. Monitoring sets milestones for the assessment of the implementation process and the assessment of the various risks associated with the project implementation. Such risks may stem from industrial action, from changes in raw material prices, from changes in interest and exchange rates or from changes in tastes which may affect the demand for the company's products and therefore its revenues. The monitoring process is therefore closely linked to periodic risk assessment of the project Below is a list of key activities in the monitoring process, which includes planning, execution and strategic reassessment.

3.2.1 Monitoring and risk management planning

1 Organisation of the monitoring function and roles and responsibilities assigned and communicated to individual members of the monitoring committee.

2 Milestones and risk tracking methods selected.

3 Determination of the critical path in the implementation phase. The critical path is a series of linked activities which make up the entire project.

3.2.2 Monitoring and risk management execution

4 Project risk factor database created and risk assessment against the deliverables at each time point to take place.

5 System of revenue and cost evaluation to be used along the critical path to verify compliance with budgets and time scheduling.

6 Project risks assigned impact and probability values eg risks could be classified as

	Probability	
Impact	Low probability High impact	High probability High impact
	Low probability Low Impact	High probability Low Impact

7 Risk mitigation actions decided and implemented.

3.2.3 Project reassessment

Produce final monitoring and risk management report on whether project requires revision of time schedules and financial assumptions and viability reassessed.

3.3 Post-completion auditing

Once a project has been completed, an audit should take place to compare the income, costs and timing with the corresponding budgeted items. A valuable aspect of the post-completion audit is the attribution to specific and identifiable factors of any deviations between budgeted items and actual outcomes. Such attribution will be valuable for a company that may undertake similar projects. However such attribution is not easy and it may be costly. It may not be easy to identify the causes of a delay for example in the execution of a project as there may several related and contingent factors. The usefulness of an audit may also be limited especially for projects that are unique..

4 Risk management

4.1 Risk management strategies

We have already discussed in Chapter 2 the principles of risk management in an organisation. Exposure to risk by corporations should be rewarded and **risk management** is the process through which the company determines the risk-return combination that is consistent with the company's risk appetite. Risk management requires the **identification**, **measurement** and **transfer** of risks. The decision whether to transfer any of the risks to which the company is exposed will depend on the cost of transfer and the risk aversion of the company.

The transfer of risk can take place through the financial or insurance markets, or through product markets. It should be clarified that risk management does not necessarily imply a reduction in risk. If the expected rewards for undertaking risks warrant it, a company may increase its exposure to risk. **Risk mitigation** on the other hand is the process through which a company reduces its exposure to risk.

4.2 Risk mitigation

Risk mitigation is attained through financial hedging, operational hedging, product differentiation and geographical diversification.

Risk mitigation is the process through which a corporation reduces its risk exposure. Risk mitigation is therefore closely linked with the process of risk transferring. The most common risk mitigation strategies are **hedging, insurance** and **diversification**.

4.3 Hedging

Hedging involves the creation of offsetting or counterbalancing flows so that the exposure of a company to risk is either eliminated or reduced. Depending of the instrument that is employed by the company, the hedging strategy can be classified as **financial** or **operational** hedging.

4.3.1 Financial hedging

Financial hedging involves the use of financial instruments, mainly derivatives to reduce or eliminate exposure to risks. A company that imports raw materials, for example, may worry about an increase in the price of raw materials due to a depreciation of the home currency, and may want to use forwards, futures or options to hedge such a risk.

4.3.2 Operational hedging

Operational hedging is the course of action that **hedges a firm's risk exposure** through operational activities using **non-financial instruments**, The main way of implementing an operational hedging strategy is through **real options**. Real options give the possibility of delaying, abandoning, enhancing or switching activities and are covered in more detail in Chapter 8.

Consider a manufacturing firm, for example, which decides to expand its scale of activity in an overseas subsidiary. The parent company is exposed to both demand and exchange rate risks. The exposure to foreign exchange risk can be hedged using financial instruments e.g. forward contracts. However financial tools cannot be used to alter the demand risk exposure. This risk can be managed by postponing the production decision until after more accurate information about the demand is acquired. This kind of operational hedging is achieved by exercising the real option to postpone the extra investment.

4.4 Diversification strategies

Diversification strategies seek to reduce the volatility of earnings of a company. This can be achieved through **product** or **geographical** diversification.

4.4.1 Product diversification

Diversification into new products is considered one of the main strategies of reducing the volatility of earnings and the main motivation of conglomerate mergers which are examined in Chapter 12. Examples of conglomerate mergers include the acquisition for example of hotels and holiday resorts by a car manufacturer. The main idea of diversification is that earnings in various industries are subject to different risk factors, which are offset against each other when companied, resulting in aggregate earnings with less volatility.

4.4.2 Geographical diversification

Geographical diversification is achieved when the costs and revenues of a firm are aligned in such a way that they are exposed to the same risks. For example domestic firms selling to overseas markets can ensure that their production costs and sales revenues are exposed to the same exchange rate risk by opening a production facility in the overseas markets.

Chapter Roundup

- Decisions on how to finance the acquisition of assets are based on the cost of the various sources of finance.
- Debt capital takes various forms such as **loan capital**, **debentures**, **zero coupon bonds** and the interest on debt is tax-deductible.
- Preference shares have priority over ordinary shares in divided payments and capital repayment.
- **Retained earnings** are the **cumulative undistributed earnings** of the company and can be used to finance the **capital expenditure** programme of the company.
- New shares can be issued either to existing shareholders or to new shareholders.
- Dividend decisions determine the amount of and the way that a company's profits are distributed to its shareholders.
- Capital investment projects require appraisal, and implementation monitoring.
- Risk mitigation is attained through financial hedging, operational hedging, product differentiation and geographical diversification.

Quick Quiz

1 Name three advantages and three disadvantages of debt as a source of finance

2 What is the main difference between operational and financial hedging?

3 What is the difference between a floating charge and a fixed charge?

Answers to Quick Quiz

1 Advantages:

Any three from:

- Debt holders rank above shareholders in the case of liquidation
- Debt is generally cheaper than equity, as interest is tax deductible in most tax regimes
- Debt is secured against assets ∴ should be more attractive to investors
- Issue costs are normally lower for debt than for equity
- No immediate change in control when debt is issued, but this may change over time if debt is converted into shares
- Lenders do not participate in high profits – payout is restricted to interest and principal
- No immediate dilution in earnings and dividends per share

Disadvantages:

Any three from:

- There is a legal obligation to pay interest, regardless of the size of annual profit, but there is no such obligation to pay dividends
- The increased burden of interest may cause shareholders to demand a higher return, as the greater burden increases the risk that dividends won't be paid
- The financial risks of ordinary shareholders is increased by heavy borrowing
- There may be restrictions on a company's power to borrow, either from a company's constitution or the trust deeds of existing stock
- Money has to be made available for redemption or repayment of debt

2 Financial hedging involves the use of financial instruments, usually derivatives, whereas operational hedging uses non-financial instruments usually real options

3 In a fixed charge, debt issued by the company is secured on specific assets of the company whereas in a floating charge the debt is secured on all assets of the company

Now try the questions below from the Exam Question Bank

Number	Level	Marks	Time
4	Introductory	15	27 mins

Appendix
The Capital Asset Pricing Model

1 Introduction

This appendix is primarily intended for those students who are attempting Paper P4 without having sat Paper F9 – *Financial Management*. Paper F9's old syllabus equivalent – Paper 2.4 – *Financial Management and Control* – did not cover CAPM and there may therefore be a 'gap' in knowledge.

If you are one of these students, you MUST read and understand this appendix, as the CAPM is a fundamental model in financial management.

You may also use this appendix to refresh your knowledge of CAPM if you are already familiar with the model.

2 The capital asset pricing model (CAPM)

FAST FORWARD

The **capital asset pricing model** can be used to calculate a cost of equity and incorporates **risk.**
The CAPM is based on a comparison of the **systematic risk** of **individual investments** with the **risks of all shares** in the **market**.

2.1 Systematic risk and unsystematic risk

FAST FORWARD

The **risk** involved in holding securities (shares) divides into **risk specific** to the company (unsystematic) and risk due to **variations** in **market activity** (systematic).

Unsystematic or business risk can be diversified away, while **systematic or market risk** cannot. Investors may mix a diversified market portfolio with risk-free assets to achieve a preferred mix of risk and return.

Whenever an investor invests in some shares, or a company invests in a new project, there will be some risk involved. The actual return on the investment might be better or worse than that hoped for. To some extent, risk is unavoidable (unless the investor settles for risk-free securities such as gilts).

Provided that the investor **diversifies** his investments in a suitably wide portfolio, the investments which perform well and those which perform badly should tend to cancel each other out, and much risk can be diversified away. In the same way, a company which invests in a number of projects will find that some do well and some do badly, but taking the whole portfolio of investments, average returns should turn out much as expected.

Risks that can be diversified away are referred to as **unsystematic risk**. But there is another sort of risk too. Some investments are by their very nature more risky than others. This has nothing to do with chance variations up or down in actual returns compared with what an investor should expect. This **inherent risk** – the **systematic risk** or **market risk** – cannot be diversified away.

Key terms

Market or **systematic risk** is risk that cannot be diversified away. **Non-systematic** or **unsystematic risk** applies to a single investment or class of investments, and can be reduced or eliminated by diversification.

In return for accepting systematic risk, a **risk-averse investor** will expect to **earn a return** which is **higher** than the return on a risk-free investment.

The amount of systematic risk in an investment varies between different types of investment.

Exam focus point

Common errors on this topic in exams include:

- Assuming risk-averse investors wish to eliminate risk. Risk-averse investors are prepared to accept risk, in exchange for higher returns
- Failing to link the risks of an investment with its returns
- Mixing up systematic and unsystematic risk

2.2 Systematic risk and unsystematic risk: implications for investments

The implications of systematic risk and unsystematic risk are as follows.

(a) If an investor wants to **avoid risk** altogether, he must **invest entirely** in **risk-free securities**.

(b) If an investor **holds shares in just a few companies**, there will be **some unsystematic risk** as well as systematic risk in his portfolio, because he will not have spread his risk enough to diversify away the unsystematic risk. To eliminate unsystematic risk, he must build up a well diversified portfolio of investments.

(c) If an investor holds a **balanced portfolio** of all the stocks and shares on the stock market, he will incur systematic risk which is exactly equal to the average systematic risk in the stock market as a whole.

(d) **Shares in individual companies** will have **different systematic risk characteristics** to this market average. Some shares will be less risky and some will be more risky than the stock market average. Similarly, some investments will be more risky and some will be less risky than a company's 'average' investments.

2.3 Systematic risk and the CAPM

FAST FORWARD

The **beta factor** measures a share's volatility in terms of market risk.

The capital asset pricing model is mainly concerned with how systematic risk is measured, and how systematic risk affects required returns and share prices. **Systematic risk** is measured using **beta factors**.

Key term

Beta factor is the measure of the systematic risk of a security relative to the market portfolio. If a share price were to rise or fall at double the market rate, it would have a beta factor of 2.0. Conversely, if the share price moved at half the market rate, the beta factor would be 0.5.

CAPM theory includes the following propositions.

(a) Investors in shares require a **return** in **excess of the risk-free rate**, to compensate them for systematic risk.

(b) Investors should **not require** a **premium** for **unsystematic risk**, because this can be diversified away by holding a wide portfolio of investments.

(c) Because systematic risk varies between companies, investors will require a **higher return** from shares in those companies where the systematic risk is bigger.

The same propositions can be applied to capital investments by companies.

(a) Companies will want a **return on a project** to **exceed** the **risk-free rate**, to compensate them for systematic risk.

(b) **Unsystematic risk** can be **diversified away**, and so a premium for unsystematic risk should not be required.

(c) Companies should want a **bigger return** on projects where **systematic risk is greater**.

2.4 Market risk and returns

Market risk (systematic risk) is the average risk of the market as a whole. Taking all the shares on a stock market together, the total expected returns from the market will vary because of systematic risk. The market as a whole might do well or it might do badly.

2.5 Risk and returns from an individual security

In the same way, an individual security may offer prospects of a return of x%, but with some risk (business risk and financial risk) attached. The return (the x%) that investors will require from the individual security will be higher or lower than the market return, depending on whether the security's systematic risk is greater or less than the market average. A major **assumption in CAPM** is that there is a

linear relationship between the return obtained from an individual security and the average return from all securities in the market.

2.5.1 Example: CAPM (1)

The following information is available about the performance of an individual company's shares and the stock market as a whole.

	Individual company	*Stock market as a whole*
Price at start of period	105.0	480.0
Price at end of period	110.0	490.0
Dividend during period	7.6	39.2

The expected return on the company's shares R_i and the expected return on the 'market portfolio' of shares $E(r_m)$ may be calculated as:

$$\frac{\text{Capital gain (or loss)} + \text{dividend}}{\text{Price at start of period}}$$

$$R_i = \frac{(110-105)+7.6}{105} = 0.12 \qquad E(r_m) = \frac{(490-480)+39.2}{480} = 0.1025$$

A statistical analysis of 'historic' returns from a security and from the 'average' market may suggest that a linear relationship can be assumed to exist between them. A series of comparative figures could be prepared (month by month) of the return from a company's shares and the average return of the market as a whole. The results could be drawn on a scattergraph and a 'line of best fit' drawn (using linear regression techniques) as shown in Figure 2.

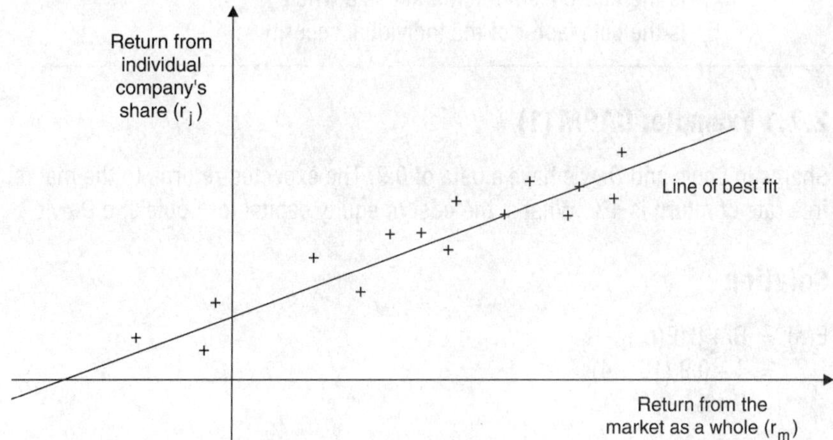

Figure 2

This analysis would show three things.

(a) The return from the security and the return from the market as a whole will tend to rise or fall together.

(b) The return from the security may be higher or lower than the market return. This is because the systematic risk of the individual security differs from that of the market as a whole.

(c) The scattergraph may not give a good line of best fit, unless a large number of data items are plotted, because actual returns are affected by unsystematic risk as well as by systematic risk.

Note that returns can be negative. A share price fall represents a capital loss, which is a negative return.

The conclusion from this analysis is that individual securities will be either more or less risky than the market average in a fairly **predictable** way. The measure of this relationship between market returns and an individual security's returns, reflecting differences in systematic risk characteristics, can be developed into a beta factor for the individual security.

2.6 The market risk premium

Key term

Market risk premium is the difference between the expected rate of return on a market portfolio and the risk-free rate of return over the same period.

The market risk premium ($E(r_m - R_f)$ represents the excess of market returns over those associated with investing in risk-free assets.

The CAPM makes use of the principle that **returns on shares** in the **market** as a whole are expected to be higher than the returns on risk-free investments. The difference between market returns and risk-free returns is called an **excess return**. For example, if the return on British Government stocks is 9% and market returns are 13%, the **excess** return on the market's shares as a whole is 4%.

The difference between the risk-free return and the expected return on an individual security can be measured as the **excess return for the market as a whole multiplied** by **the security's beta factor**.

2.7 The CAPM formula

The capital asset pricing model is a statement of the principles explained above. It can be stated as follows.

Exam Formula

$$E(r_i) = R_f + \beta_i(E(r_m) - R_f)$$

where $E(r_i)$ is the cost of equity capital
R_f is the risk-free rate of return
$E(r_m)$ is the return from the market as a whole
β_i is the beta factor of the individual security

2.7.1 Example: CAPM (1)

Shares in Louie and Dewie have a beta of 0.9. The expected returns to the market are 10% and the risk-free rate of return is 4%. What is the cost of equity capital for Louie and Dewie?

Solution

$$\begin{aligned} E(r_i) &= R_f + \beta_i(E(r_m) - R_f) \\ &= 4 + 0.9\,(10 - 4) \\ &= 9.4\% \end{aligned}$$

2.7.2 Example: CAPM (2)

Investors have an expected rate of return of 8% from ordinary shares in Algol, which have a beta of 1.2. The expected returns to the market are 7%.

What will be the expected rate of return from ordinary shares in Rigel, which have a beta of 1.8?

Solution

$$\begin{aligned} \text{Algol:}\quad E(r_i) &= R_f + \beta_i(E(r_m) - R_f) \\ 8 &= R_f + 1.2(7 - R_f) \\ 8 &= R_f + 8.4 - 1.2\,R_f \\ 0.2\,R_f &= 0.4 \\ R_f &= 2 \\ \text{Rigel:}\quad E(r_i) &= 2 + (7 - 2)\,1.8 \\ &= 11\% \end{aligned}$$

Question

The risk-free rate of return is 7%. The average market return is 11%.

(a) What will be the return expected from a share whose β factor is 0.9?

(b) What would be the share's expected value if it is expected to earn an annual dividend of 5.3c, with no capital growth?

Answer

(a) 7% + 0.9 (11% – 7%) = 10.6%

(b) $\frac{5.3c}{10.6\%}$ = 50c

2.8 Alpha values

FAST FORWARD

The **alpha value** is a measure of a share's **abnormal return.**

Key term

A share's **alpha value** is a measure of its abnormal return, which is the amount by which the share's returns are currently above or below the required return, given the level of systematic risk.

The alpha value can be seen as a measure of how wrong the CAPM is.

Alpha values:

(a) Reflect only temporary, abnormal returns, if CAPM is a realistic model
(b) Can be positive or negative
(c) Over time, will tend towards zero for any individual share, and for a well-diversified portfolio taken as a whole will be 0
(d) May exist due to the inaccuracies and limitations of the CAPM

Exam focus point

In the exam you may be asked to compare the required return (calculated by CAPM) with the expected current return of the portfolio, and hence calculate the alpha value.

If the **alpha value** is **positive**, investors who don't hold shares will be tempted to buy them (to take advantage of the abnormal return), and investors who do hold shares will want to hold on to them so share prices will rise. If the **alpha value** is **negative**, investors won't want to buy them, and current holders will want to sell them, so share prices will fall.

Exam focus point

In the exam you may need to identify which share has the largest alpha value and hence is the most attractive investment.

2.8.1 Example: Alpha values

ABC plc's shares have a beta value of 1.2 and an alpha value of +2%. The market return is 10% and the risk-free rate of return is 6%.

Required return 6% + (10% – 6%) × 1.2 = 10.8%

Current return = expected return ± alpha value = 10.8% + 2% = 12.8%

2.9 Problems with applying the CAPM in practice

FAST FORWARD

Problems of CAPM include **unrealistic assumptions** and the **required estimates being difficult to make.**

(a) The need to **determine** the **excess return** ($E(r_m) - R_f$). Expected, rather than historical, returns should be used, although historical returns are often used in practice.

(b) The need to **determine** the **risk-free rate**. A risk-free investment might be a government security. However, interest rates vary with the term of the lending.

(c) **Errors** in the **statistical analysis used** to calculate β values. Betas may also **change over** time.

(d) The CAPM is also **unable to forecast accurately returns** for companies with **low price/earnings** ratios and to take account of seasonal 'month-of-the-year' effects and 'day-of-the-week' effects that appear to influence returns on shares.

Question

Beta factor

(a) What does beta measure, and what do betas of 0.5, 1 and 1.5 mean?

(b) What factors determine the level of beta which a company may have?

Answer

(a) **Beta measures** the systematic risk of a risky investment such as a share in a company. The total risk of the share can be sub-divided into two parts, known as **systematic (or market) risk** and **unsystematic (or unique) risk**. The systematic risk depends on the sensitivity of the return of the share to general economic and market factors such as periods of boom and recession. The capital asset pricing model shows how the return which investors expect from shares should depend only on systematic risk, not on unsystematic risk, which can be eliminated by holding a well-diversified portfolio.

The average risk of stock market investments has a **beta of 1**. Thus shares with betas of 0.5 or 1.5 would have half or 1½ times the average sensitivity to market variations respectively.

This is reflected by higher volatility of share prices for shares with a beta of 1.5 than for those with a beta of 0.5. For example, a 10% increase in general stock market prices would be expected to be reflected as a 5% increase for a share with a beta of 0.5 and a 15% increase for a share with a beta of 1.5, with a similar effect for price reductions.

(b) The beta of a company will be the **weighted average** of the beta of its shares and the beta of its debt. The beta of debt is very low, but not zero, because corporate debt bears default risk, which in turn is dependent on the volatility of the company's cash flows.

Factors determining the beta of a company's equity shares include:

(i) **Sensitivity** of the company's **cash flows** to economic factors, as stated above. For example sales of new cars are more sensitive than sales of basic foods and necessities.

(ii) The company's **operating gearing**. A high level of fixed costs in the company's cost structure will cause high variations in operating profit compared with variations in sales.

(iii) The company's **financial gearing**. High borrowing and interest costs will cause high variations in equity earnings compared with variations in operating profit, increasing the equity beta as equity returns become more variable in relation to the market as a whole. This effect will be countered by the low beta of debt when computing the weighted average beta of the whole company.

3 Dividend growth model and CAPM

The two models will not necessarily give the same cost of equity and you may have to calculate the cost of equity using either, or both, models.

3.1 Example: Dividend growth model and CAPM

The following data relates to the ordinary shares of Stilton.

Current market price, 31 December 20X1	250c
Dividend per share, 20X1	3c
Expected growth rate in dividends and earnings	10% pa
Average market return	8%
Risk-free rate of return	5%
Beta factor of Stilton equity shares	1.40

(a) What is the estimated cost of equity using the dividend growth model?
(b) What is the estimated cost of equity using the capital asset pricing model?

Solution

(a) $k_e = \frac{d_0(1+g)}{P_0} + g$

$= \frac{3(1.10)}{250} + 0.10$

$= 0.1132$ or 11.32%

(b) $k_e = 5 + 1.40\ (8 - 5) = 9.2\%$

4 CAPM and portfolios

The **expected return** of a portfolio of shares can be calculated by calculating the weighted beta of the portfolio and using CAPM.

4.1 Beta factors of portfolios

Just as an individual security has a beta factor, so too does a portfolio of securities.

(a) A portfolio consisting of all the **securities** on the **stock market** (in the same proportions as the market as a whole), excluding risk-free securities, will have an expected return equal to the expected return for the market as a whole, and so will have a **beta factor of 1**.
(b) A portfolio consisting entirely of **risk-free securities** will have a beta factor of **0**.
(c) The beta factor of an investor's portfolio is the **weighted average** of the **beta factors** of the securities in the **portfolio**.

4.1.1 Example: Beta factors and portfolios

A portfolio consisting of five securities could have its beta factor computed as follows.

Security	*Percentage of portfolio*	*Beta factor of security*	*Weighted beta factor*
A Inc	20%	0.90	0.180
B Inc	10%	1.25	0.125
C Inc	15%	1.10	0.165
D Inc	20%	1.15	0.230
E Inc	35%	0.70	0.245
	100%	Portfolio beta =	0.945

If the risk-free rate of return is 12% and the average market return is 20%, the required return from the portfolio using the CAPM equation would be 12% + (20 – 12) × 0.945% = 19.56%

The calculation could have been made as follows.

Security	*Beta factor*	*Expected return* $E(r_j)$	*Weighting* %	*Weighted return* %
A Inc	0.90	19.2	20	3.84
B Inc	1.25	22.0	10	2.20
C Inc	1.10	20.8	15	3.12
D Inc	1.15	21.2	20	4.24
E Inc	0.70	17.6	35	6.16
			100	19.56

4.2 CAPM and portfolio management

Practical implications of CAPM theory for an investor are as follows.

(a) He should decide what **beta factor** he would **like to have** for his portfolio. He might prefer a portfolio beta factor of greater than 1, in order to expect above-average returns when market returns exceed the risk-free rate, but he would then expect to lose heavily if market returns fall. On the other hand, he might prefer a portfolio beta factor of 1 or even less.

(b) He should seek to invest in shares with **low beta factors** in a **bear market**, when average market returns are falling. He should then also sell shares with high beta factors.

(c) He should seek to invest in shares with **high beta factors** in a **bull market**, when average market returns are rising.

4.3 International CAPM

The possibility of international portfolio diversification increases the opportunities available to investors.

If we assume that the international capital market is a **fully integrated market** like an enlarged domestic market, then we have an international CAPM formula as follows.

$E(r_j) = r_f + [E(r_w) - r_f]\beta_w$

where $E(r_w)$ is the expected return from the world market portfolio and β_w is a measure of the world systematic risk.

This analysis implies that the risk premium is proportional to the world systematic risk, β_w, and that investors can benefit from maximum diversification by investing in the world market portfolio consisting of all securities in the world economy. New risk and return combinations may be available.

In practice, such complete diversification will of course not be practicable. However, significant international diversification can be achieved by the following methods:

- Direct investment in companies in different countries
- Investments in multinational enterprises
- Holdings in unit trusts or investment trusts which are diversified internationally

4.4 Segmentation and integration

The international picture may be complicated by market segmentation. Segmentation is usually caused by government-imposed restrictions on the movement of capital, leading to restricted capital availability within a country or other geographical segment. Therefore:

- Returns on the same security may differ in different markets
- Some investments may only be available in certain markets

In a segmented market the parent company of a international group would use its own country's risk-free rate and market return in CAPM calculations.

In practice the situation that a multinational company faces will often not be completely integrated nor completely segmented. In this situation a multinational can use CAPM to estimate a local cost of equity and a world cost of equity, and use a cost of equity that is somewhere in between the two.

4.5 Limitations of the CAPM for the selection of a portfolio

Under the CAPM, the return required from a security is related to its systematic risk rather than its total risk. If we relax some of the assumptions upon which the model is based, then the total risk may be important. In particular, the following points should be considered.

(a) The model assumes that the **costs of insolvency** are **zero**, or in other words, that all **assets** can be **sold** at **going concern prices** and that there are no selling, legal or other costs. In practice, the costs of insolvency cannot be ignored. Furthermore, the risk of insolvency is related to a firm's total risk rather than just its systematic risk.

(b) The model assumes that the **investment market** is **efficient**. If it is not, this will limit the extent to which investors are able to eliminate unsystematic risk from their portfolios.

(c) The model also assumes that **portfolios are well diversified** and so need only be concerned with systematic risk. However, this is not necessarily the case, and undiversified or partly-diversified shareholders should also be concerned with unsystematic risk and will seek a total return appropriate to the total risk that they face.

5 CAPM and investments

FAST FORWARD

CAPM can be used to produce a **cost of capital** for an **investment project**, based on the systematic risk of that investment.

5.1 The use of CAPM for capital investment decisions

CAPM can also be used to calculate a **project-specific cost of capital**.

The CAPM produces a required return based on the expected return of the market $E(r_m)$, the risk-free interest rate (R_f) and the variability of project returns relative to the market returns (β). Its main advantage when used for investment appraisal is that it produces a discount rate which is based on the **systematic** risk of the individual investment. It can be used to **compare projects of all different risk classes** and is therefore superior to an NPV approach which uses only one discount rate for all projects, regardless of their risk.

The model was developed with respect to securities; by applying it to an investment within the firm, the company is assuming that the shareholder wishes investments to be evaluated as if they were securities in the capital market and thus assumes that all shareholders will hold **diversified portfolios** and will not look to the company to achieve diversification for them.

5.2 Example: Required return

Panda Inc is all-equity financed. It wishes to invest in a project with an estimated beta of 1.5. The project has significantly different business risk characteristics from Panda's current operations. The project requires an outlay of $10,000 and will generate expected returns of $12,000.

The market rate of return is 12% and the risk-free rate of return is 6%.

Required

Estimate the minimum return that Panda will require from the project and assess whether the project is worthwhile, based on the figures you are given.

Solution

We do not need to know Panda's weighted average cost of capital, as the new project has different business characteristics from its current operations. Instead we use the capital asset pricing model so that:

Required return = 6 + 1.5(12 – 6)
= 15%

$$\text{Expected return} = \frac{12,000 - 10,000}{10,000}$$

= 20%

Thus the project is worthwhile, as expected return exceeds required return.

The CAPM produces a required return based on the expected return of the market, expected project returns, the risk-free interest rate and the variability of project returns relative to the market returns.

Its main advantage when used for investment appraisal is that it produces a **discount rate** which is based on the **systematic risk** of the individual investment. It can be used to compare projects of all different risk classes and is therefore superior to an NPV approach which uses only one discount rate for all projects, regardless of their risk.

The model was developed with respect to securities; by applying it to an investment within the firm, the company is assuming that the shareholder wishes **investments** to be evaluated as if they were securities in the capital market and thus assumes that all shareholders will hold diversified portfolios and will not look to the company to achieve diversification for them.

5.3 Limitations of using CAPM in investment decisions

5.3.1 Estimating market return

This is achieved by comparing movements in the stock market as a whole. It will be **volatile** and will overstate the returns achieved as it will not pick up the firms that have failed and have dropped out of the stock market.

5.3.2 Estimating the beta factor

Beta values are **historic** and will not give an accurate measure of risk if the firm has recently changed its gearing or its strategy.

5.3.3 Other risk factors

It has been argued that CAPM ignores the impact of **the size of the company** and the **ratio of book vlue of equity to market value of equity.**

Problems in using the model for investment appraisal in an **international** context arise from the fact that where the company is raising funds and operating in a number of countries, it may be difficult to establish exactly what the **risk-free** and **market rates of return are**. The problems of estimation increase when the economic situation in more than one country has to be taken into account. In practice, an international company will normally base its calculations on conditions in its **home country**.

6 CAPM and MM combined – geared betas

FAST FORWARD

When an investment has differing business and finance risks from the existing business, **geared betas** may be used to obtain an appropriate required return.

Geared betas are calculated by:

- Ungearing industry betas
- Converting ungeared betas back into a geared beta that reflects the company's own gearing ratio

6.1 Beta values and the effect of gearing

The gearing of a company will affect the risk of its equity. If a company is geared and its **financial risk is therefore higher** than the risk of an all-equity company, then the β value of the geared company's equity will be higher than the β value of a similar ungeared company's equity.

The CAPM is consistent with the propositions of Modigliani and Miller. MM argue that as gearing rises, the cost of equity rises to compensate shareholders for the extra financial risk of investing in a geared company. This financial risk is an aspect of systematic risk, and ought to be reflected in a company's beta factor.

6.2 Geared betas and ungeared betas

The connection between MM theory and the CAPM means that it is possible to establish a mathematical relationship between the β value of an ungeared *company* and the β value of a similar, but geared, company. The β value of a geared company will be higher than the β value of a company identical in every respect except that it is all-equity financed. This is because of the extra financial risk. The mathematical relationship between the 'ungeared' (or asset) and 'geared' betas is as follows.

Exam formula

$$\beta_a = \left[\frac{V_e}{(V_e + V_d(1-T))}\beta_e\right] + \left[\frac{V_d(1-T)}{(V_e + V_d(1-T))}\beta_d\right]$$

where β_a is the asset or ungeared beta
β_e is the equity or geared beta
β_d is the beta factor of debt in the geared company
V_D is the market value of the debt capital in the geared company
V_E is the market value of the equity capital in the geared company
T is the rate of corporate tax

Debt is often assumed to be risk-free and its beta (β_d) is then taken as zero, in which case the formula above reduces to the following form.

$\beta_a = \beta_g \times \frac{V_e}{V_e + V_d(1-T)}$ or, without tax, $\beta_a = \beta_g \times \frac{V_e}{V_e + V_d}$

However, just because beta is zero does not mean that the company is free from firm-specific risk. All that is assumed is that there is zero exposure to market risk. Default risk is an important driver of bond value, whereas market risk is much less significant.

6.2.1 Example: CAPM and geared betas

Two companies are identical in every respect except for their capital structure. Their market values are in equilibrium, as follows.

	Geared	*Ungeared*
	\$'000	\$'000
Annual profit before interest and tax	1,000	1,000
Less interest (4,000 × 8%)	320	0
	680	1,000
Less tax at 30%	204	300
Profit after tax = dividends	476	700
Market value of equity	3,900	6,600
Market value of debt	4,180	0
Total market value of company	8,080	6,600

The total value of Geared is higher than the total value of Ungeared, which is consistent with MM.

All profits after tax are paid out as dividends, and so there is no dividend growth. The beta value of Ungeared has been calculated as 1.0. The debt capital of Geared can be regarded as risk-free.

Calculate:

(a) The cost of equity in Geared
(b) The market return R_m
(c) The beta value of Geared

Solution

(a) Since its market value (MV) is in equilibrium, the cost of equity in Geared can be calculated as:

$$\frac{d}{MV} = \frac{476}{3,900} = 12.20\%$$

(b) The beta value of Ungeared is 1.0, which means that the expected returns from Ungeared are exactly the same as the market returns, and R_m = 700/6,600 = 10.6%.

(c) $$\beta_g = \beta_a \times \frac{V_e + V_d(1+T)}{V_e}$$

$$= 1.0 \times \frac{3,900 + (4,180 \times 0.70)}{3,900} = 1.75$$

The beta of Geared, as we should expect, is higher than the beta of Ungeared.

6.3 Using the geared and ungeared beta formula to estimate a beta factor

Another way of estimating a beta factor for a company's equity is to use data about the returns of other quoted companies which have similar operating characteristics: that is, to use the beta values of other companies' equity to estimate a beta value for the company under consideration. The beta values estimated for the firm under consideration must be **adjusted to allow for differences in gearing** from the firms whose equity beta values are known. The formula for geared and ungeared beta values can be applied.

If a company plans to invest in a project which involves diversification into a new business, the investment will involve a different level of systematic risk from that applying to the company's existing business. A discount rate should be calculated which is specific to the project, and which takes account of both the project's systematic risk and the company's gearing level. The discount rate can be found using the CAPM.

Step 1 Get an estimate of the systematic risk characteristics of the project's operating cash flows by obtaining published beta values for companies in the industry into which the company is planning to diversify.

Step 2 Adjust these beta values to allow for the company's capital gearing level. This adjustment is done in two stages.

(a) Convert the beta values of other companies in the industry to ungeared betas, using the formula:

$$\beta_a = \beta_e \left(\frac{V_e}{V_e + V_d(1-T)} \right)$$

(b) Having obtained an ungeared beta value β_a, convert it back to a geared beta β_e, which reflects the company's own gearing ratio, using the formula:

$$\beta_e = \beta_a \left(\frac{V_e + V_d(1-T)}{V_e} \right)$$

Step 3 Having estimated a project-specific geared beta, use the CAPM to estimate:

(a) A project-specific cost of equity, and

(b) A project-specific cost of capital, based on a weighting of this cost of equity and the cost of the company's debt capital

6.3.1 Example: Gearing and ungearing betas

A company's debt:equity ratio, by market values, is 2:5. The corporate debt, which is assumed to be risk-free, yields 11% before tax. The beta value of the company's equity is currently 1.1. The average returns on stock market equity are 16%.

The company is now proposing to invest in a project which would involve diversification into a new industry, and the following information is available about this industry.

(a) Average beta coefficient of equity capital = 1.59
(b) Average debt:equity ratio in the industry = 1:2 (by market value).

The rate of corporation tax is 30%. What would be a suitable cost of capital to apply to the project?

Solution

Step 1 The beta value for the industry is 1.59.

Step 2 (a) Convert the geared beta value for the industry to an ungeared beta for the industry.

$$\beta_a = 1.59 \left(\frac{2}{2+(1(1-0.30))} \right) = 1.18$$

(b) Convert this ungeared industry beta back into a geared beta, which reflects the company's own gearing level of 2:5.

$$\beta_e = 1.18 \left(\frac{5+(2(1-0.30))}{5} \right) = 1.51$$

Step 3 (a) This is a project-specific beta for the firm's equity capital, and so using the CAPM, we can estimate the project-specific cost of equity as:

$$k_{eg} = 11\% + (16\% - 11\%)\ 1.51 = 18.55\%$$

(b) The project will presumably be financed in a gearing ratio of 2:5 debt to equity, and so the project-specific cost of capital ought to be:

$$[5/7 \times 18.55\%\ ] + [2/7 \times 70\% \times 11\%\ ] = 15.45\%$$

Question

Ungeared and geared betas

Two companies are identical in every respect except for their capital structure. XY has a debt: equity ratio of 1:3, and its equity has a β value of 1.20. PQ has a debt: equity ratio of 2:3. Corporation tax is at 30%. Estimate a β value for PQ's equity.

Answer

Estimate an ungeared beta from XY data.

$$\beta_a = 1.20 \frac{3}{3+(1(1-0.30))} = 0.973$$

Estimate a geared beta for PQ using this ungeared beta.

$$\beta_e = 0.973 \ \frac{3+(2(1-0.30))}{3} = 1.427$$

6.4 Weaknesses in the formula

The problems with using the geared and ungeared beta formula for calculating a firm's equity beta from data about other firms are as follows.

(a) It is difficult to identify other firms with identical operating characteristics.

(b) Estimates of beta values from share price information are not wholly accurate. They are based on statistical analysis of historical data, and as the previous example shows, estimates using one firm's data will differ from estimates using another firm's data.

(c) There may be differences in beta values between firms caused by:

  (i) Different cost structures (eg, the ratio of fixed costs to variable costs)
  (ii) Size differences between firms
  (iii) Debt capital not being risk-free

(d) If the firm for which an equity beta is being estimated has **opportunities for growth** that are recognised by investors, and which will affect its equity beta, estimates of the equity beta based on other firms' data will be inaccurate, because the opportunities for growth will not be allowed for.

Perhaps the most significant simplifying assumption is that to link MM theory to the CAPM, it must be assumed that the **cost of debt** is a **risk-free rate of return**. This could obviously be unrealistic. Companies may default on interest payments or capital repayments on their loans. It has been estimated that corporate debt has a beta value of 0.2 or 0.3.

The consequence of making the assumption that debt is risk-free is that the formulae tend to **overstate** the financial risk in a geared company and to **understate** the business risk in geared and ungeared companies by a compensating amount.

Question

Gearing and ungearing betas

Backwoods is a major international company wanting to raise $150 million to establish a new production plant in the eastern region of Germany. Backwoods evaluates its investments using NPV, but is not sure what cost of capital to use in the discounting process for this project evaluation.

The company is also proposing to increase its equity finance in the near future for domestic expansion, resulting overall in little change in the company's market-weighted capital gearing.

The summarised financial data for the company before the expansion are shown below.

Income statement for the year ended 31 December 20X1

	$m
Revenue	1,984
Gross profit	432
Profit after tax	81
Dividends	37
Retained earnings	44

Balance sheet as at 31 December 20X1

	$m
Non-current assets	846
Working capital	350
	1,196
Medium term and long term loans (see note below)	210
	986
Shareholders' funds	
Issued ordinary shares of $0.50 each nominal value	225
Reserves	761
	986

Note on borrowings

These include $75m 14% fixed rate bonds due to mature in five years time and redeemable at par. The current market price of these bonds is £120.00 and they have an after-tax cost of debt of 9%. Other medium and long-term loans are floating rate UK bank loans at LIBOR plus 1%, with an after-tax cost of debt of 7%.

Company rate of tax may be assumed to be at the rate of 30%. The company's ordinary shares are currently trading at 376 cents.

The equity beta of Backwoods is estimated to be 1.18. The systematic risk of debt may be assumed to be zero. The risk free rate is 7.75% and market return 14.5%.

The estimated equity beta of the main German competitor in the same industry as the new proposed plant in the eastern region of Germany is 1.5, and the competitor's capital gearing is 35% equity and 65% debt by book values, and 60% equity and 40% debt by market values.

Required

Estimate the cost of capital that the company should use as the discount rate for its proposed investment in eastern Germany. State clearly any assumptions that you make.

Answer

The discount rate that should be used is the weighted average cost of capital (WACC), with weightings based on market values. The cost of capital should take into account the systematic risk of the new investment, and therefore it will not be appropriate to use the company's existing equity beta. Instead, the estimated equity beta of the main German competitor in the same industry as the new proposed plant will be ungeared, and then the capital structure of Backwoods applied to find the WACC to be used for the discount rate.

Since the systematic risk of debt can be assumed to be zero, the German equity beta can be 'ungeared' using the following expression.

$$\beta_a = \beta_g \frac{V_e}{V_e + V_d(1-T)}$$

where: β_a = asset beta
β_g = equity beta
V_e = proportion of equity in capital structure
V_d = proportion of debt in capital structure
T = tax rate

For the German company:

$$\beta_a = 1.5\left(\frac{60}{60+40(1-0.30)}\right) = 1.023$$

The next step is to calculate the debt and equity of Backwoods based on market values.

		$m
Equity	450m shares at 376c	1,692.0
Debt: bank loans	(210 – 75)	135.0
Debt: bonds	(75 million × 1.20)	90.0
Total debt		225.0
Total market value		1,917.0

The beta can now be re-geared

$$\beta_g = \frac{1.023(1{,}692 + 225\ (1-0.3))}{1{,}692} = 1.118$$

This can now be substituted into the capital asset pricing model (CAPM) to find the cost of equity.

$E(r_i) = R_f + \beta\ (E\ (r_m) - R_f)$

where: $E(r_i)$ = cost of equity

R_f = risk free rate of return

$E(r_m)$ = market rate of return

$E(r_i) = 7.75\% + (14.5\% - 7.75\%) \times 1.118 = 15.30\%$

The WACC can now be calculated:

$$\left[15.3\times\frac{1{,}692}{1{,}917}\right] + \left[7\times\frac{135}{1{,}917}\right] + \left[9\times\frac{90}{1{,}917}\right] = 14.4\%$$

Note. You have been given both costs of debt. In the exam you may well be asked to calculate the cost of debt.

7 The arbitrage pricing model

FAST FORWARD

The **arbitrage pricing model (APM)** assumes that the return on securities is based on a number of independent factors.

7.1 CAPM and APM

Exam focus point

You must be aware that there are other models apart from the CAPM, and know the benefits and limitations of the arbitrage pricing model relative to the CAPM.

The CAPM is seen as a useful analytical tool by financial managers as well as by financial analysts. However, critics suggest that the relationship between risk and return is more complex than the linear relationship assumed in the CAPM. One model which could replace the CAPM in the future is the **arbitrage pricing model** (APM).

7.2 Factors influencing APM

Unlike the CAPM, which analyses the returns on a share as a function of a single factor – the return on the market portfolio, the APM assumes that the return on each security is based on a number of **independent factors**. The actual return r on any security is shown as:

$r = E(r_j) + \beta_1 F_1 + \beta_2 F_2 \ldots + e$

where $E(r_j)$ is the expected return on the security

β_1 is the sensitivity to changes in factor 1

F_1 is the difference between actual and expected values of factor 1

β_2 is the sensitivity to changes in factor 2

F_2 is the difference between actual and expected values of factor 2

e is a random term

Factor analysis is used to ascertain the factors to which security returns are sensitive. Four key factors identified by researchers have been:

- Unanticipated inflation
- Changes in the expected level of industrial production
- Changes in the risk premium on bonds (debentures)
- Unanticipated changes in the term structure of interest rates

It has been demonstrated that when no further arbitrage opportunities exist, the expected return $E(r_j)$ can be shown as:

$E(r_j) = r_f + \beta_1(r_1 - r_f) + \beta_2(r_2 - r_f) \ldots$

where r_f is the risk-free rate of return

r_1 is the expected return on a portfolio with unit sensitivity to factor 1 and no sensitivity to any other factor

r_2 is the expected return on a portfolio with unit sensitivity to factor 2 and no sensitivity to any other factor

7.3 APM in practice

With the APM, the CAPM's problem of identifying the market portfolio is avoided, but this replaced with the problem of **identifying** the **macroeconomic factors** and their risk sensitivities. As is the case with the CAPM, what empirical evidence is available is inconclusive and neither proves nor disproves the theory of the APM. Both the CAPM and the APM do however provide a means of analysing how risk and return may be determined in conditions of competition and uncertainty.

8 Summary

This appendix is based on knowledge that is covered in Paper F9 – *Financial Management.* Now that you have covered the contents you should have sufficient understanding of CAPM to continue with your P4 studies.

7.2 Factors influencing [illegible]

7.3 APT in practice

8 Summary

Ethical issues in financial management

Topic list	Syllabus reference
1 The ethical dimension in business	A (5) (a)
2 Ethical aspects and functional areas of the firm	A (5) (b)
3 The elements of an ethical financial policy	A (5) (c)

Introduction

In this chapter we discuss the ethical dimension to the financial manager's role. The chapter provides a framework to enable the student to identify with reasons where ethical issues might arise in given scenarios in an examination.

Study guide

		Intellectual level
A5	**Ethical issues in financial management**	
(a)	Assess the ethical dimension within business issues and decisions and advise on best practice in the financial management of the firm.	3
(b)	Demonstrate an understanding of the interconnectedness of the ethics of good business practice between all of the functional areas of the firm.	2
(c)	Recommend an ethical framework for the development of a firm's financial policies and a system for the assessment of their ethical impact upon the financial management of the firm.	3

Exam guide

The ethical dimension to the financial manager's job is very important and will be a consistent issue in examinations. The concern with ethics is a practical one and the examiner will be concerned to see that candidates can identify with reasons where ethical issues might emerge in given scenarios. The student should be able to put forward soundly based arguments to support their views.

1 The ethical dimension in business

FAST FORWARD

In the **financial management** of businesses, the key objective is the **maximisation of shareholders' wealth**.

Ethical considerations are part of the **non-financial objectives** of a company and influence the decisions of management.

Exam focus point

There was a 20 mark optional discursive question in the December 2007 exam that dealt with the ethical issues of a company's financial strategy.

1.1 The prime financial objective of a company

The theory of company finance is based on the assumption that the objective of management is to **maximise the market value of the company's shares**. Specifically, the main objective of a company should be to maximise the wealth of its ordinary shareholders.

A company is financed by ordinary shareholders, preference shareholders, loan stock holders and other long-term and short-term creditors. All surplus funds, however, belong to the legal owners of the company, its ordinary shareholders. Any retained profits are undistributed wealth of these equity shareholders.

1.2 Non-financial objectives

The goal of **maximising shareholder wealth** implies that shareholders are the only stakeholders of a company. In fact the stakeholders of a company include employees, customers, suppliers and the wider community. The formulation of the financial policy of the firm takes into account the interests of the shareholders as a stakeholder group and the formulation of non-financial objectives addresses the concerns of other stakeholders. We have already discussed in Chapter 3, the measures that companies adopt in order to address issues related to **sustainability** and **environmental reporting**. Here we provide some further examples of non-financial objectives. Note that these **non-financial objectives**, could potentially limit the achievement of **financial objectives**.

Non-financial objectives	
Ethical considerations	**Actions and strategies**
Welfare of employees	Competitive wages and salaries, comfortable and safe working conditions, good training and career development
Welfare of management	High salaries, company cars, perks
Welfare of society	Concern for environment
Provision of service to minimum standard	For example regulations affecting utility (water, electricity providers)
Responsibilities to customers	Providing quality products or services, fair dealing
Responsibilities to suppliers	Not exploiting power as buyer unscrupulously
Leadership in research and development	Failure to innovate may have adverse long-term financial consequences

Most of these non-financial objectives reflect an **ethical dimension** of business activity.

1.3 Ethical dimensions in business

Businesses play an important role in the economic and social life of a nation. They provide **employment, tax revenues** and have been responsible through **research** and **development** for some of the greatest technological breakthroughs which have changed our everyday life. The **downside** of this **dominant role is abuse of power** in the market place, **disregard for the environment**, irresponsible use of **depletable resources**, adverse effect on local culture and customs. Companies like Coca Cola, Imperial Tobacco and Mc Donald's have had an impact on developing countries that transcended the economic sphere and affected dietary habits and ways of life.

Given the power that companies exercise how do we measure their impact on society? How do we assess their behaviour against some ethical norm as opposed to mere financial norms? The answer to this question is provided by the development of **business ethics**, as a branch of **applied morality** that deals specifically with the behaviour of firms and the norms they should follow so that their behaviour is judged as ethical.

It should be stressed that **business ethics** does not invoke a universally acceptable framework of principles that all companies should adhere to. Hence the requirement for a corporate governance framework that would ensure a minimum degree of **ethical commitment** by firms became apparent. These movements towards the adoption of **corporate governance norms** have been discussed in Chapter 1.

Ethical considerations are sometimes easy to be incorporated into the policy of a company. For example, during the apartheid years many companies were boycotting South Africa, without any governmental coercion. In this case the ethical aspect was clear and easily identifiable. However, for a multinational company in a developing country not to pay wages to its employees that would render a project uneconomical, may not be seen as unethical, as the employees of that country may have remained unemployed without the multinational company's presence.

2 Ethical aspects and functional areas of the firm

FAST FORWARD

Business ethics should govern the conduct of corporate policy in all functional areas of a company such as:

- Human resources management
- Marketing
- Market behaviour
- Product development

Maximising the wealth of shareholders generally implies maximising profits consistent with long-term stability. It is often found that short-term gains must be sacrificed in the interests of the company's long-term prospects. In the context of this overall objective of financial management, there are five main types of decisions facing financial managers:

- Investment decisions,
- Financing decisions,
- Dividend decisions,
- Financial planning and control decisions
- Risk management decisions.

In practice, these areas are interconnected and should not be viewed in isolation. An equally important function of the financial manager is to **communicate the financial policy and corporate goals to internal and external stakeholders**.

2.1 Human resources management

Employees in a modern corporation are not simply a factor of production which is used in a production process. Employees as human beings have feelings and are entitled to be treated by their employers with respect and dignity. In most advanced countries there are employment laws that determine the **rights** of employees and provide protection against the abuses of their employers.

Ethical problems arise when there is a conflict between the financial objectives of the firm and the rights of the employees. These ethical problems arise in relation to minimum wages, and discrimination.

2.1.1 Minimum wage

Companies are obliged to pay their employees at least the minimum wage. However when multinational companies operate in countries where there are no minimum wage requirements then the companies may try to take advantage of the lack of protection and offer low wages. Business ethics would require that companies should not exploit workers and pay lower than the warranted wages.

2.1.2 Discrimination

Discrimination on the basis of **race, gender, age, marital status, disability or nationality** is prohibited in most advanced economies, through **equal opportunity legislation**. However, companies may have the power in some instances to circumvent many of the provisions. Companies for example may be able to discriminate against black applicants for certain positions for which they may feel that they are appropriate.

Employers may also wish to discriminate against mothers in certain jobs for which overtime is required. In other circumstances a company may want to restrict applicants from a certain ethnic background when they deal with people of similar ethnic backgrounds. In all the cases of potential discrimination the company wishing to behave ethically should be aware of the risk of breaking the rules.

2.2 Marketing

Marketing decisions by the firm are also very important in terms of the impact on firm performance. Marketing is one of the main ways of communicating with its customers and this communication should be **truthful** and sensitive to the **social** and **cultural impact** on society. The marketing strategy should not target vulnerable groups, create artificial wants or reinforce consumerism. It should also avoid creating stereotypes or creating insecurity and dissatisfaction.

2.3 Market behaviour

FAST FORWARD

Companies should not take advantage of their **dominant position** in the market to **exploit suppliers** or **customers**.

Ethical behaviour in this context refers to the exercise of restraint in their pricing policies. Companies which are dominant in the product market and enjoy monopolistic power may charge a price which will result in abnormally high profits. For example a water company may charge high prices for water in order to increase its profits because the remuneration of managers may be linked to profitability. Similarly a company which in the input markets may be able to pay too low a price to their suppliers. For example in many developing countries multinational companies are the only buyers of raw materials and they determine the price they pay to their suppliers.

3 The elements of an ethical financial policy

FAST FORWARD

Ethical policy can be implemented through measures that ensure that the company takes into account the concerns of its stakeholders.

3.1 The ethical framework

The company should develop an ethical corporate philosophy and should make the enhancement of corporate governance as one of its most important management issues. The aim is to have customers and society, as well as shareholders and investors, place even greater trust in the company and to ensure that the company is one that society wants to exist. The ethical framework should be developed as part of the overall company's social responsibility which according to Carroll includes

(a) Economic responsibility
(b) Legal responsibility
(c) Ethical responsibility
(d) Philanthropic responsibility

The **four responsibilities** have been classified in terms of priority for the firm. **Economic responsibility** is the first and **philanthropic responsibility** the last. **Carroll's framework** is considered a useful way of integrating the various aspects of a company's activities and helpful as a means for management to set social responsibility targets within an organisation.

The only problem with the framework is the lack of an **explicit mechanism** for addressing **conflicting corporate responsibilities**, when for example **legal** and **regulatory** compliance may limit the **economic return** that a company can achieve.

3.2 Economic responsibility

The first responsibility of a company is to its shareholders. Shareholders have invested their money in the company and require a return. The company has therefore a responsibility to manage the funds of outside investors in such a way that the required return is generated. The main aspects of the economic responsibility were analysed in Chapter 2 and include the various decisions that the financial manager is responsible for, such as financing, investment, risk management and dividend.

3.3 Legal responsibility

Companies operate within a legal framework as defined by company law, the various accounting and environmental standards, labour law etc. It is a duty of the company to comply with all the legal and regulatory provisions, and to ensure that employees are aware of this policy.

As we have already said, ethical responsibilities arise in situations where there is no explicit legal or regulatory provision and the company needs to exercise its judgement as to what is right and fair.

3.4 Ethical responsibility

Ethical responsibilities arise not as a result of legal requirements but as a result of a moral imperative for companies to operate in an ethical and fair manner. We have already discussed examples where issues of business ethics arise. How does a company ensure that an ethical approach to the various aspects of a company's activities is adopted? The following are deemed to be the elements of a business ethics management in a European or US corporation:

(a) **Mission or value statement.** A corporation has a mission statement in which some social goal is included.

(b) **Codes of ethics** to be followed by the employees, and which specify their attitude and response to ethical dilemmas. The code of ethics should reflect **corporate values** but it should also incorporate **professional codes** of ethics, which individual employees as members of professional bodies need to observe.

(c) **Reporting/advice channels** for employees to notify unethical behaviour or to seek advice on specific situations.

(d) **Ethics managers**, officers and committees to coordinate or assume responsibility for the implementation of ethics in the corporation.

(e) **Ethics consultants** should be consulted by corporations on specific issues of business ethics on which the corporation needs advice as to the appropriate course of action or policy formulation.

(f) **Ethics education and training** should be provided to the managers and employees of a corporation to ensure that ethical problems are recognised and dealt with according to the ethics code of the corporation.

(g) **Auditing, accounting and reporting** are necessary aspects of a business ethics programme since the corporation needs to be able to measure and report its economic and social impact to its stakeholders.

3.5 Philanthropic responsibility

Philanthropy is the last of the responsibilities of a company and includes all those actions that the company needs to take in order improve the life of its employees, to contribute to the local community and to make a difference to society as a whole. Philanthropic activities include **charitable donations**, the provision of **recreation facilities** to **employees**, the support to **educational institutions**, the **sponsoring of athletic** and **cultural events** and so on.

Chapter Roundup

- In the **financial management** of businesses, the key objective is the **maximisation of shareholders' wealth**.
- **Ethical considerations** are part of the **non-financial objectives** of a company and influence the decisions of management.
- **Business ethics** should govern the conduct of corporate policy in all functional areas of a company such as:
  - Human resources management
  - Marketing
  - Market behaviour
  - Product development
- Companies should not take advantage of their **dominant position** in the market to **exploit suppliers** or **customers**.
- **Ethical policy** can be implemented through measures that ensure that the company takes into account the concerns of its stakeholders.

Quick Quiz

1. On what management objective is the theory of company finance primarily based?
2. To which areas might non-financial objectives of a company relate?
3. List two areas of a company's activity where ethical issues may arise.
4. What are the main corporate social responsibilities of a firm?
5. What are the main elements through which the ethical responsibility of a company is discharged?

Answers to Quick Quiz

1. The objective of management is to maximise the market value of the enterprise.

2. (1) Welfare of employees
   (2) Welfare of management
   (3) Welfare of society
   (4) Quality of service provision
   (5) Responsibilities to customers and suppliers
   (6) Leadership in research and development

3. Human resources management and marketing

4. Economic responsibility, legal responsibility, ethical responsibility, philanthropic responsibility

5. (a) Mission or value statement.
   (b) Codes of ethics.
   (c) Reporting/advice channels.
   (d) Ethics managers.
   (e) Ethics consultants.
   (f) Ethics education and training.
   (g) Auditing, accounting and reporting.

Now try the questions below from the Exam Question Bank

Number	Level	Marks	Time
5	Introductory	20	36 mins

PART B

Advanced investment appraisal

Discounted cash flow techniques and the use of free cash flows

Topic list	Syllabus reference
1 Net Present Value	B (1) (a)
2 Internal rate of return	B (1) (b)
3 Comparison of NPV and IRR	B (1) (b)
4 Modified internal rate of return (MIRR)	B (1) (b)
5 Forecasting a firm's free cash flow	B (1) (c)
6 Forecasting a firm's dividend capacity	B (1) (d)
7 Valuing a firm using free cash flow	B (1) (e)
8 Risk and uncertainty	B (1) (b)
9 Monte Carlo simulation and investment appraisal	B (2) (c)

Introduction

In this chapter we discuss two criteria for investment appraisal, the net present value (NPV) and the internal rate of return (IRR). A number of issues related to the two criteria are explored, such as inflation and taxation effects, free cash flow estimation and Monte Carlo simulation.

Study guide

		Intellectual level
B1	**Discounted cash flow techniques and the use of free cash flows**	
(a)	Evaluate the potential value added to a firm arising from a specified capital investment project or portfolio using the net present value model. Project modelling should include explicit treatment of:	3
(i)	Inflation and specific price variation	
(ii)	Taxation and the assessment of fiscal risk	
(iii)	Multi-period capital rationing to include the formulation of programming methods and the interpretation of their output.	
(b)	Establish the potential economic return (using internal rate of return and modified internal rate of return) and advise on a project's return margin and its vulnerability to competitive action.	3
(c)	Forecast a firm's free cash flow and its free cash flow to equity (pre and post capital reinvestment.)	2
(d)	Advise, in the context of a specified capital investment programme, on a firm's current and projected dividend capacity.	3
(e)	Advise on the value of a firm using its free cash flow and free cash flow to equity under alternative horizon and growth assumptions.	3
B2	**Impact of financing on investment decisions and adjusted present values**	
(c)	Outline the application of Monte Carlo simulation to investment appraisal. Candidates will not be expected to undertake simulations in an examination context but will be expected to demonstrate an understanding of:	2
(i)	Simple model design	
(ii)	The different types of distribution controlling the key variables within the simulation	
(iii)	The significance of the simulation output and the assessment of the likelihood of project success.	
(iv)	The measurement and interpretation of project value at risk	

Exam Guide

Discounted cash flow techniques may arise as a means of solving part of a larger problem in the exam. In the Pilot Paper, Question 3 required candidates to recommend procedures for the appraisal of capital investment projects from the point of view of a senior financial manager, including the provision of advice on a project and its likely impact on the company.

1 Net present value

This section covers material that should be familiar to you from previous studies. It is however important that you revise this section as net present value is a fundamental investment appraisal technique.

FAST FORWARD

Projects with a positive net present value should be undertaken.

Key term

The **net present value (NPV)** of a project is the sum of the discounted cash flows less the initial investment.

Question

Project X requires an immediate investment of $150,000 and will generate net cash inflows of $70,000 for the next three years. The project's discount rate is 8%. If net present value is used to appraise the project, should Project X be undertaken?

Answer

Time	*Cash Flow*	*Discount Factor*	*Present Value*
0	–150,000	1	–150,000
1	60,000	0.935	56,100
2	60,000	0.873	52,380
3	60,000	0.816	48,960
			7,440

The NPV of this project is $7,440

1.1 NPV and shareholder wealth maximisation

The main advantage of the NPV method is that it evaluates projects in the same way as shareholders would do – that is, it focuses on how individual projects would affect shareholders' wealth. Only those projects with a **positive** NPV are accepted, meaning that only those projects that will **increase** shareholders' wealth will be undertaken.

1.2 The effect of inflation

FAST FORWARD

Inflation is present in all economies and must be accounted for when evaluating projects.

Key terms

Real cash flows have been adjusted for inflation and should be discounted using the **real discount rate**. **Nominal cash flows** have not been adjusted for inflation and should be discounted using the **nominal discount rate**.

The above example (*NPV calculations*) assumes that net cash flows do not change from year to year. This is unrealistic, given the existence of inflation. It is important to take proper account of inflation when undertaking investment appraisal as it could change the NPV of the project and ultimately the decision as to whether the project should be accepted.

NPV calculations can be carried out using either **real** or **nominal** cash flows.

1.2.1 Real and nominal interest rates

The **real interest rate** incorporates inflation. When the nominal rate of interest **exceeds** the rate of inflation, the real interest rate will be **positive**. If the nominal rate of interest **is less than** the rate of inflation, the real interest rate will be **negative**.

Exam formula

$(1 + i) = (1 + r)(1 + h)$

Where i = nominal (money) rate
r = real rate
h = inflation rate

This is known as the **Fisher equation**.

Question — Nominal discount factor

If the real rate of interest is 5% and the expected inflation is 3% what is the nominal return?

Answer

(1 + i) = (1 + 0.05)(1 + 0.03) = 1.0815

The nominal rate is therefore 8.15%.

1.2.2 Real rate or nominal rate?

The rule is as follows.

(a) We use the **nominal** rate if cash flows are expressed in **actual numbers of dollars** that will be received or paid at various future dates.

(b) We use the real rate if cash flows are expressed in **constant price terms** (that is, in terms of their value at time 0).

1.2.3 Advantages and misuses of real values and a real rate of return

Although generally companies should discount money values at the nominal cost of capital, there are some advantages of using real values discounted at a real cost of capital.

(a) When all costs and benefits rise at the same rate of price inflation, **real values** are the **same as current day values**, so that **no further adjustments** need be made to cash flows before discounting. In contrast, when nominal values are discounted at the nominal cost of capital, the **prices** in **future years** must be **calculated** before discounting can begin.

(b) The government might prefer to set a real return as a target for investments, as being more suitable than a commercial money rate of return.

Question — Effect of inflation

Rice is considering a project which would cost $5,000 now. The annual benefits, for four years, would be a fixed income of $2,500 a year, plus other savings of $500 a year in year 1, rising by 5% each year because of inflation. Running costs will be $1,000 in the first year, but would increase at 10% each year because of inflating labour costs. The general rate of inflation is expected to be 7½% and the company's required money rate of return is 16%. Is the project worthwhile? (Ignore taxation.)

Answer

The cash flows at inflated values are as follows.

Year	*Fixed income*	*Other savings*	*Running costs*	*Net cash flow*
	$	$	$	$
1	2,500	500	1,000	2,000
2	2,500	525	1,100	1,925
3	2,500	551	1,210	1,841
4	2,500	579	1,331	1,748

The NPV of the project is as follows.

Year	Cash flow	Discount factor	PV
	$	16%	$
0	(5,000)	1.000	(5,000)
1	2,000	0.862	1,724
2	1,925	0.743	1,430
3	1,841	0.641	1,180
4	1,748	0.552	965
			+ 299

The NPV is positive and the project would appear to be worthwhile.

1.2.4 Expectations of inflation and the effects of inflation

When managers evaluate a particular project, or when shareholders evaluate their investments, they can only guess at what the rate of inflation is going to be. Their expectations will probably be wrong, at least to some extent, because it is extremely difficult to forecast the rate of inflation accurately. The only way in which uncertainty about inflation can be allowed for in project evaluation is by risk and uncertainty analysis.

Costs and benefits may rise at levels different from the general rate of inflation: inflation may be **general,** affecting prices of all kinds, or **specific** to particular prices. Generalised inflation has the following effects.

(a) Since **non-current assets, inventories** and **other working capital** will **increase in money value**, the same quantities of assets or working capital must be financed by **increasing amounts of capital**.

(b) Inflation means higher costs and higher selling prices. The effect of higher prices on demand is not necessarily easy to predict. A company that raises its prices by 10% because the general rate of inflation is running at 10% might suffer a serious fall in demand.

(c) Inflation, because it affects financing needs, is also likely to affect gearing, and so the cost of capital.

1.3 Allowing for taxation

FAST FORWARD

In investment appraisal, tax is often assumed to be payable **one year in arrears,** but you should read the question details carefully.

Tax allowable depreciation details should be checked in any question you attempt.

Typical assumptions which may be stated in questions are as follows.

(a) An assumption about the timing of payments will have to be made.

(i) Half the tax is **payable** in the **same year** in which the **profits are earned** and **half in the following year.** This reflects the fact that large companies have to pay tax **quarterly** in some regimes.

(ii) Tax is payable in the **year following** the one in which the taxable profits are made. Thus, if a project increases taxable profits by $10,000 in year 2, there will be a tax payment, assuming tax at (say) 30%, of $3,000 in year 3.

(iii) Tax is payable in the **same year** that the **profits arise.**

The question should make clear what assumptions you should use.

(b) Net cash flows from a project should be considered as the taxable profits arising from the project (unless an indication is given to the contrary).

1.3.1 Tax-allowable depreciation

Tax allowable depreciation is used to reduce taxable profits, and the consequent reduction in a tax payment should be treated as a cash saving arising from the acceptance of a project.

For example, suppose tax-allowable depreciation is allowed on the cost of **plant and machinery** at the rate of 25% on a **reducing balance** basis. Thus if a company purchases plant costing $80,000, the subsequent writing down allowances would be as follows.

Year		*Tax-allowable depreciation*	*Reducing balance*
		$	$
1	(25% of cost)	20,000	60,000
2	(25% of RB)	15,000	45,000
3	(25% of RB)	11,250	33,750
4	(25% of RB)	8,438	25,312

When the plant is eventually sold, the difference between the sale price and the reducing balance amount at the time of sale will be treated as:

(a) A taxable profit if the sale price exceeds the reducing balance, and
(b) A tax-allowable loss if the reducing balance exceeds the sale price

Exam focus point

Examination questions often assume that this loss will be available immediately, though in practice the balance less the sale price may continue to be written off at 25% a year as part of a pool balance.

The cash saving on the tax-allowable depreciation (or the cash payment for the charge) is calculated by multiplying the depreciation (or charge) by the tax rate.

Assumptions about tax-allowable depreciation could be simplified in an exam question. For example, you might be told that tax-allowable depreciation can be claimed at the rate of 25% of cost on a straight line basis (that is, over four years).

There are two possible assumptions about the time when tax-allowable depreciation start to be claimed.

(a) It can be assumed that the **first claim** occurs at the **start of the project** (at year 0).
(b) Alternatively it can be assumed that the **first claim** occurs **later in the first year**.

You should state clearly which assumption you have made. Assumption (b) is more prudent, but assumption (a) is also perfectly feasible. It is very likely, however that an examination question will indicate which of the two assumptions is required.

1.3.2 Example: taxation

A company is considering whether or not to purchase an item of machinery costing $40,000 in 20X5. It would have a life of four years, after which it would be sold for $5,000. The machinery would create annual cost savings of $14,000.

The machinery would attract tax-allowable depreciation of 25% on the reducing balance basis which could be claimed against taxable profits of the current year, which is soon to end. A balancing allowance or charge would arise on disposal. The tax rate is 30%. Tax is payable half in the current year, half one year in arrears. The after-tax cost of capital is 8%.

Should the machinery be purchased?

Solution

Tax-allowable depreciation is first claimed against year 0 profits.

Cost: $40,000

Year	*Tax-allowable depreciation*	*Reducing balance (RB)*	
	$	$	
(0) 20X5 (25% of cost)	10,000	30,000	(40,000 – 10,000)
(1) 20X6 (25% of RB)	7,500	22,500	(30,000 – 7,500)
(2) 20X7 (25% of RB)	5,625	16,875	(22,500 – 5,625)
(3) 20X8 (25% of RB)	4,219	12,656	(16,875 – 4,219)
(4) 20X9 (25% of RB)	3,164	9,492	(12,656 – 3,164)

	$
Sale proceeds, end of fourth year	5,000
Less reducing balance, end of fourth year	9,492
Balancing allowance	4,492

Having calculated the depreciation each year, the tax savings can be computed. The year of the cash flow is one year after the year for which the allowance is claimed.

Year of claim	*Tax-allowable depreciation*	*Tax saved*	*Year of tax payment/saving*
	$	$	(50% in each)
0	10,000	3,000	0/1
1	7,500	2,250	1/2
2	5,625	1,688	2/3
3	4,219	1,266	3/4
4	7,656	2,297	4/5
	35,000 *		

* Net cost $(40,000 – 5,000) = $35,000

These tax savings relate to tax-allowable depreciation. We must also calculate the extra tax payments on annual savings of $14,000.

The net cash flows and the NPV are now calculated as follows.

Year	*Equip-ment*	*Savings*	*Tax on savings*	*Tax saved on tax-allowable depreciation*	*Net cash flow*	*Discount factor*	*Present value of cash flow*
	$	$	$	$	$	8%	$
0	(40,000)			1,500	(38,500)	1.000	(38,500)
1		14,000	(2,100)	2,625	14,525	0.926	13,450
2		14,000	(4,200)	1,969	11,769	0.857	10,086
3		14,000	(4,200)	1,477	11,277	0.794	8,954
4	5,000	14,000	(4,200)	1,782	16,582	0.735	12,188
5			(2,100)	1,148	(952)	0.681	(648)
							5,530

The NPV is positive and so the purchase appears to be worthwhile.

1.3.3 An alternative and quicker method of calculating tax payments or savings

In the above example, the tax computations could have been combined, as follows.

Year	*0*	*1*	*2*	*3*	*4*
	$	$	$	$	$
Cost savings	0	14,000	14,000	14,000	14,000
Tax-allowable depreciation	10,000	7,500	5,625	4,219	7,656
Taxable profits	(10,000)	6,500	8,375	9,781	6,344
Tax at 30%	3,000	(1,950)	(2,512)	(2,934)	(1,903)

The net cash flows would then be as follows.

Year	*Equipment*	*Savings*	*Tax*	*Net cash flow*
	$	$	$	$
0	(40,000)		1,500	(38,500)
1		14,000	525	14,525
2		14,000	(2,231)	11,769
3		14,000	(2,723)	11,277
4	5,000	14,000	(2,418)	16,582
5			(952)	(952)

The net cash flows are exactly the same as calculated previously.

1.3.4 Taxation and DCF

The effect of taxation on capital budgeting is theoretically quite simple. Organisations must pay tax, and the effect of undertaking a project will be to increase or decrease tax payments each year. These incremental tax cash flows should be included in the cash flows of the project for discounting to arrive at the project's NPV.

When **taxation is ignored** in the DCF calculations, the discount rate will **reflect the pre-tax rate of return** required on capital investments. When taxation is included in the cash flows, a **post-tax required rate of return** should be used.

If there is inflation and tax in a question, remember that tax flows do not get inflated by an extra year even though they may be paid one year later.

Question — **Effect of taxation**

A project requires an initial investment in machinery of $300,000. Additional cash inflows of $120,000 at current price levels are expected for three years, at the end of which time the machinery will be scrapped. The machinery will attract tax-allowable depreciation of 25% on the reducing balance basis, which can be claimed against taxable profits of the current year, which is soon to end. A balancing charge or allowance will arise on disposal.

The tax rate is 50% and tax is payable 50% in the current year, 50% one year in arrears. The pre-tax cost of capital is 22% and the rate of inflation is 10%. Assume that the project is 100% debt financed.

Required

Assess whether the project should be undertaken.

Answer

Post-tax: Year	Purchase	Inflation factor	Cash flow after inflation	Tax on cash inflow	(W1-3) Tax saved on tax-allowable depreciation	Net cash flow	Discount factor	Present value
	$		$	$	$	$	11%	$
0	(300,000)	1.000	(300,000)		18,750	(281,250)	1.000	(281,250)
1		1.100	132,000	(33,000)	32,813	131,813	0.901	118,764
2		1.210	145,200	(69,300)	24,609	100,509	0.812	81,613
3		1.331	159,720	(76,230)	42,187	125,677	0.731	91,870
4				(39,930)	31,640	(8,290)	0.659	(5,463)
							NPV =	5,534

The project should be undertaken at least from the financial viewpoint.

Workings

1 *Tax-allowable depreciation* (Initial cost $300,000)

Year		*Tax-allowable depreciation*	*Reducing balance (RB)*
		$	$
0	(25% at cost)	75,000	225,000
1	(25% of RB)	56,250	168,750
2	(25% of RB)	42,188	126,562
3	(25% of RB)	31,641	94,921

2 *Balancing allowance*

	$
Sale proceeds, end of third year	–
RB, end of third year	94,921
Balancing allowance	94,921

3 *Tax saved on tax-allowable depreciation*

Year of claim	*Tax-allowable depreciation claimed*	*Tax saved*	*Year of tax saving*
	$	$	
0	75,000	37,500	0/1
1	56,250	28,125	1/2
2	42,188	21,094	2/3
3	126,562	63,281	3/4
	300,000		

Multi-period capital rationing

FAST FORWARD

Capital rationing problems exist when there are insufficient funds available to finance all available profitable projects.

Capital rationing may occur due to internal factors (**soft** capital rationing) or external factors (**hard** capital rationing).

When capital rationing is present across **multiple periods**, linear programming may be used to solve the problem of **which projects** to undertake.

Knowledge brought forward from earlier studies

Hard and soft capital rationing

Soft capital rationing may arise for such reasons as:

(a) Management may be **reluctant** to **issue additional share capital** because of concerns that this may lead to **outsiders** gaining control of the business.

(b) **Capital expenditure budgets** may restrict spending.

(c) Management may wish to **limit investment** to a level that can be financed solely from retained earnings.

Hard capital rationing may arise for one of the following reasons.

(a) There may be restrictions on bank lending due to government control.

(b) The costs associated with making small **issues** of capital may be too great.

(c) Lending institutions may consider an organisation to be **too risky** to be granted further loan facilities.

For **single period** capital rationing problems, projects are ranked according to the **profitability index**. This gives the shadow price of capital or the maximum rate a company should be prepared to pay to obtain short term funds to release the capital constraint.

1.3.5 Introduction

Companies do not have inexhaustible resources therefore it is likely that only limited funds will be available for capital investment in each period. The problem facing financial managers is how best to spend the money in order to meet their objective of maximising shareholders' wealth. This problem can be solved using **linear programming**.

1.3.6 An example

The board of Bazza Inc has approved the following investment expenditure over the next three years.

Year 1	*Year 2*	*Year 3*
$16,000	$14,000	$17,000

You have identified four investment opportunities which require different amounts of investment each year, details of which are given below.

		Required investment		*Project*
Project	*Year 1*	*Year 2*	*Year 3*	*NPV*
	7,000	10,000	4,000	8,000
Project 2	9,000	0	12,000	11,000
Project 3	0	6,000	8,000	6,000
Project 4	5,000	6,000	7,000	4,000

Which combination of projects will result in the highest overall NPV whilst remaining within the annual investment constraints?

The problem can be formulated as a linear programming problem as follows.

Let Y1 be investment in project 1
Y2 be investment in project 2
Y3 be investment in project 3
Y4 be investment in project 4

Objective function

Maximise $Y_1 \times 8{,}000 + Y_2 \times 11{,}000 + Y_3 \times 6{,}000 + Y_4 \times 4{,}000$

Subject to the three annual investment constraints:

$Y_1 \times 7{,}000 + Y_2 \times 9{,}000 + Y_3 \times 0 + Y_4 \times 5{,}000 \leq 16{,}000$ (Year 1 constraint)
$Y_1 \times 10{,}000 + Y_2 \times 0 + Y_3 \times 6{,}000 + Y_4 \times 6{,}000 \leq 14{,}000$ (Year 2 constraint)
$Y_1 \times 4{,}000 + Y_2 \times 12{,}000 + Y_3 \times 8{,}000 + Y_4 \times 7{,}000 \leq 17{,}000$ (Year 3 constraint)

When the objective function and constraints are fed into a computer programme, the results are:

$Y_1 = 1, Y_2 = 1, Y_3 = 0, Y_4 = 0$

This means that Project 1 and Project 2 will be selected and Project 3 and Project 4 will not. The NPV of the investment scheme will be equal to $19,000.

Note that the solution:

$Y_1 = 0, Y_2 = 0, Y_3 = 1, Y_4 = 1$

also satisfies the constraints. However this is not the optimal solution since the combined NPV of projects 3 and 4 is $10,000 which is lower than the value derived above.

2 Internal rate of return

FAST FORWARD

A project will only be selected if its internal rate of return **exceeds** the cost of capital or target rate of return.

Key term

The **internal rate of return** of any investment is the discount rate at which the NPV is equal to zero.

Knowledge brought forward from earlier studies

The IRR is used to calculate the exact discount rate at which NPV is equal to zero.

If calculating IRR manually we use the interpolation method as follows.

(a) Calculate a net present value using a discount rate that gives **a whole number** and gives an NPV **close to zero**.

(b) Calculate a second NPV using another discount rate. If the first NPV was **positive**, use a rate that is **higher** than the first rate; if it was **negative**, use a rate that is **lower** than the first rate.

(c) Use the two NPVs to calculate the IRR. The formula to apply is:

$$IRR = a + \left(\left(\frac{NPV_a}{NPV_a - NPV_b} \right) (b-a) \right) \%$$ This formula is not given in the exam.

where
- a = the lower of the two rates of return used
- b = the higher of the two rates of return used
- NPV_a = the NPV obtained using rate a
- NPV_b = the NPV obtained using rate b

The project should be accepted if the IRR is **greater** than the **cost of capital** or **target rate of return**.

2.1 Example of IRR calculation

A company is considering the purchase of a piece of equipment costing $120,000 that would save $30,000 each year for five years. The equipment could be sold at the end of its useful life for $15,000. The company requires every project to yield a return of 10% or more otherwise they will be rejected. Should this equipment be purchased?

Solution

Annual depreciation will be $\frac{\$(120{,}000 - 15{,}000)}{5}$ = \$21,000

Step 1 Calculate the first NPV, using a rate that is two thirds of the return on investment.

The return on investment would be:

$$\frac{30{,}000 - \text{depreciation of } 21{,}000}{0.5 \times (120{,}000 + 15{,}000)} = \frac{9{,}000}{67{,}500} = 13.3\%$$

Two thirds of this is 8.9% and so we can start by trying 9%.

The IRR is the rate for the cost of capital at which the NPV = 0.

Year	*Cash flow*	*PV factor 9%*	*PV of cash flow*
	\$		\$
0	(120,000)	1.000	(120,000)
1–5	30,000	3.890	116,700
5	15,000	0.650	9,750
		NPV =	6,450

This is fairly close to zero. It is also **positive**, which means that the actual **rate of return** is **more than 9%.** We can use 9% as one of our two NPVs close to zero.

Step 2 Calculate the second NPV, using a rate that is **greater** than the first rate, as the first rate gave a positive answer.

Suppose we try 12%.

Year	*Cash flow*	*PV factor12%*	*PV of cash flow*
	\$		\$
0	(120,000)	1.000	(120,000)
1–5	30,000	3.605	108,150
5	15,000	0.567	8,505
		NPV =	(3,345)

This is fairly close to zero and **negative**. The real rate of return is therefore greater than 9% (positive NPV of \$6,450) but less than 12% (negative NPV of \$3,345).

Step 3 Use the two NPV values to estimate the IRR.

The interpolation method assumes that the NPV rises in linear fashion between the two NPVs close to 0. The real rate of return is therefore assumed to be on a straight line between NPV = \$4,300 at 9% and NPV = –\$2,230 at 12%.

Using the formula

$$IRR \approx a + \left(\left(\frac{NPV_a}{NPV_a - NPV_b}\right)(b-a)\right)\%$$

$$IRR \approx 9 + \frac{6{,}450}{(6{,}450 + 3{,}345)} \times (12-9)\% = 10.98\%, \text{ say } 11\%$$

If it is company policy to undertake investments which are expected to yield 10% or more, this project would be undertaken.

2.2 The multiple IRR problem

FAST FORWARD

A project being accepted based on IRR may be misleading if the cash flows from the project are not positive.

The example employed to calculate the IRR indicates that the IRR and the NPV produce the same result, ie a positive NPV implies $IRR \geq k$ and a negative NPV implies $IRR < k$. However, this is true only when the project has normal cash flows, i.e. a negative initial cash flow followed by a series of positive cash flows. If the cash flows change signs then the IRR may not be unique. This is the multiple **IRR problem**.

Key term

The **multiple IRR** occurs when cash flows change sign and result in more than one value for the IRR.

2.2.1 Example

Consider the following example, where the cash flow for the second year is negative. Note that in this case the NPV is equated to zero for two values of IRR, when IRR = 5.1% and when IRR = 39.8%.

Time	*Cash Flow*	*Discount Factor*	*Present Value*
0	– 245,000	1	– 245,000
1	600,000	0.909	545,455
2	– 360,000	0.826	– 297,521
			2,934

If we plot the NPV for this project at various different discount rates, we find the following:

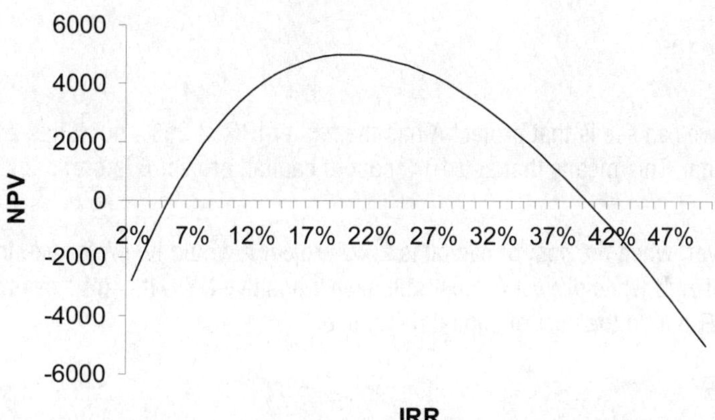

The NPV is initially negative, increases and becomes positive, reaches a maximum value and then declines and becomes negative again. According to the decision rule, we should accept projects for which IRR > k. However, the IRR takes two values.

3 Comparison of NPV and IRR

The rule for making investments under the NPV method is that where investments are mutually exclusive, the one with the higher NPV should be preferred. Where investments are independent, all investments should be accepted if they have positive NPVs. The reason for this is that they are generating sufficient cash flows to give an acceptable return to providers of debt and equity finance. This is known as the NPV rule.

The IRR rule states that, where an investment has cash outflows followed by cash inflows, it should be accepted if its IRR exceeds the cost of capital. This is because such investments will have positive NPVs.

3.1 Limitations of the IRR technique

Where we are dealing with independent investments, the IRR should usually come to the same decision as the NPV approach. However, it cannot be used to distinguish between mutually exclusive investments. This is because it merely indicates whether or not a project has a positive NPV. It does not tell us the magnitude of the NPV. Hence, it cannot decide which is the superior project.

3.2 Mutually exclusive projects

Question — **Mutually exclusive projects**

We have two projects that both require an initial investment of $10,000. Project A has an IRR of 25% per annum, project B has an IRR of 20% per annum. Which project should we select?

The answer may appear fairly clear cut, i.e. that we select the project with the higher IRR. However, we are also told that the company's cost of capital is 10% and are provided with the following data.

Time	*Project A*	*Project B*
0	(10,000)	(10,000)
1	12,000	1,000
2	625	13,200

Answer

It is incorrect to decide between these alternatives based on IRRs. If we were to work out the NPVs of these two projects, we could then summarize the findings as follows:

	Project A	*Project B*
NPV @ 10%	1,426	1,818
IRR	25%	20%

What we can see is that project A has the higher IRR of 25%, but it has a lower NPV at the company's cost of capital. This means that at a 10% cost of capital, project B is preferable, even though it has the lower IRR.

However, when the cost of capital is 20% project A would be preferred since project B would then have a NPV of zero while project A must still have a positive NPV. It can be seen that the decision depends not on the IRR but on the cost of capital being used.

Question — **NPV profile**

Considering this example more fully, if we calculate the NPVs at various costs of capital we find the following.

Rate %	*Project A NPV*	*Project B NPV*
	$	$
5.0	1,995	2,925
7.5	1,704	2,353
10.0	1,426	1,818
12.5	1,160	1,319
15.0	907	851
17.5	665	412
20.0	434	0
22.5	212	(387)
25.0	0	(752)
27.5	(204)	(1,096)
30.0	(399)	(1,420)

Answer

Plotting these on a graph we get the following.

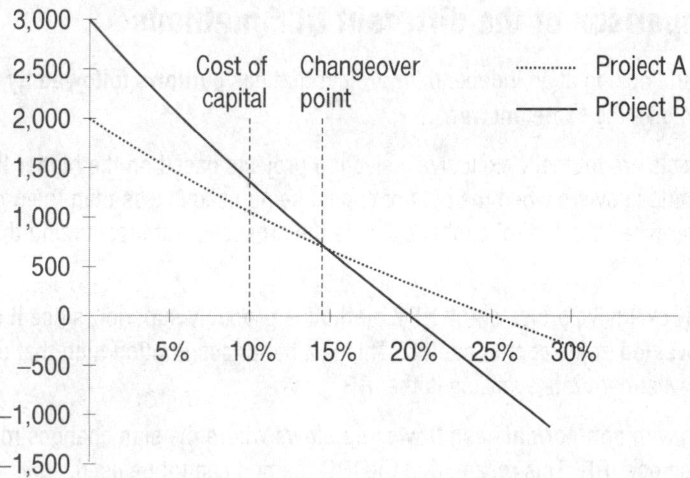

What we can see is that up to a cost of capital of just over 14%, project B has the highest NPV. Above that cost of capital, project A has the greater NPV and would, therefore, be preferable.
The assigned reading refers to the above graph as the NPV profile of the project. For both the above projects, the NPV profile is that the NPV falls as the discount rate increases.

3.3 Reasons why the NPV profiles differ

The NPV profiles cross over at a discount rate of 15%. There are two reasons why this may occur.

- Differences in the timing of the cash flows for each project
- Differences in the project sizes (or project scales)

In this case, there is no difference in project size, with both projects having an initial investment of $10,000. However, there are differences in the timing of the cash flows, with project B having high cash flows in Year 2 and project A having high cash flows in Year 1.

The NPV profile for project B shows a far steeper line. This is because it has higher cash inflows in the more distant year. Therefore, it is much more affected by an increasing discount rate. In contrast, project A has higher value cash flows in the earlier year. This means that it is less affected by the increase in discount rate.

3.4 Conflicting rankings using the NPV and IRR methods

Note that, where the discount rate is greater than 15% (the **changeover** or **crossover rate**), selecting an investment based on either the higher NPV or the higher IRR will give the same answer. In this case, for discount rates between 15% and 20%, project A has the higher NPV and it also has the higher IRR.

For discount rates of less than 15%, selecting an investment based on the higher IRR gives an answer which conflicts with the NPV method, since it will select project A, although project B has the higher NPV.

3.4.1 Re-investment rate

The problem with selecting investments based on the **higher IRR** is that it makes an assumption that **cash flows** can be **reinvested** at the **IRR** over the **life of the project**.

In contrast, the **NPV method** assumes that cash flows can be **reinvested** at the **cost of capital** over the life of the project.

If the assumption that the IRR as a reinvestment rate is valid, then the IRR technique will be superior. However, it is unlikely that this will be the case and therefore the NPV method is likely to be superior. The better reinvestment rate assumption will be the cost of capital used for the NPV method.

3.5 Comparison of the different DCF methods

Where we are looking at an independent project that has **outflows followed by inflows**, both the **NPV** and **IRR** method give the **same answer**.

Where projects are mutually exclusive, selecting projects based on the higher IRR or the higher NPV will give conflicting answers when the cost of capital being used is less than the crossover rate. It will give the same answer when the cost of capital exceeds the crossover rate (assuming that one project has a positive NPV).

For mutually exclusive projects, the **NPV method** is probably superior, since **it assumes** that **cash flows** can be **reinvested** at the **cost of capital**. This is a better assumption than that used in the IRR method, i.e. that the reinvestment rate available is the IRR.

For projects with **non-normal cash flows**, e.g. flows where the sign changes more than once, there may be more than one IRR. This means that the IRR method cannot be used.

The NPV method gives no indication as to the **sensitivity** of the project to changes in forecast figures or the amount of capital at risk, unlike the IRR method.

4 Modified internal rate of return (MIRR)

FAST FORWARD

The modified internal rate of return is the IRR that would result if it was **not assumed that project proceeds were reinvested at the IRR.**

The MIRR overcomes the problem of the **reinvestment assumption** and the fact that **changes in the cost of capital over the life of the project** cannot be incorporated in the IRR method.

4.1 Example of MIRR calculations

Consider a project requiring an initial investment of \$24,500, with cash inflows of \$15,000 in years 1 and 2 and cash inflows of \$3,000 in years 3 and 4. The cost of capital is 10%.

Solution

If we calculate the IRR:

Year	*Cash flow*	*Discount factor*	*Present value*	*Discount factor*	*Present value*
	\$	10%	\$	25%	\$
0	(24,500)	1.000	(24,500)	1.000	(24,500)
1	15,000	0.909	13,635	0.800	12,000
2	15,000	0.826	12,390	0.640	9,600
3	3,000	0.751	2,253	0.512	1,536
4	3,000	0.683	2,049	0.410	1,230
			5,827		(134)

$$\text{IRR} = 10\% + \left[\frac{5{,}827}{5{,}827+134} \times (25\% - 10\%)\right] = 24.7\%$$

The MIRR is calculated on the basis of **investing the inflows** at the **cost of capital**.

The table below shows the **values of the inflows if they were immediately reinvested at 10%**. For example the \$15,000 received at the end of year 1 could be reinvested for three years at 10% pa (multiply by $1.1 \times 1.1 \times 1.1 = 1.331$).

Year	Cash inflows	Interest rate multiplier	Amount when reinvested
	$		$
1	15,000	1.331	19,965
2	15,000	1.21	18,150
3	3,000	1.1	3,300
4	3,000	1.0	3,000
			44,415

The total cash outflow in year 0 ($24,500) is compared with the possible inflow at year 4, and the resulting figure of:

$$\frac{24{,}500}{44{,}415} = 0.552$$

is the discount factor in year 4. By looking along the year 4 row in present value tables you will see that this gives a return of 16%. This means that the $44,415 received in year 4 is equivalent to $24,500 in year 0 if the discount rate is 16%.

Alternatively, instead of using discount tables, we can calculate the MIRR as follows.

$$\text{Total return} = \frac{44{,}415}{24{,}500} = 1.813$$

$$\begin{aligned} \text{MIRR} &= \sqrt[4]{1.813} - 1 \\ &= 1.16 - 1 \\ &= 16\% \end{aligned}$$

In theory the MIRR of 16% will be a **better measure** than the IRR of 24.7%.

4.2 Alternative method

In the April 2008 issue of *Student Accountant*, an article by the Paper P4 examiner on MIRR suggested that, as the present value of a project is usually calculated as part of an investment appraisal exercise, it might be more efficient to use the following formula:

Formula to learn

$$\text{MIRR} = \sqrt[n]{\frac{\text{Present value of return phase}}{\text{present value of investment phase}}} \times (1 + i) - 1$$

Where
- the return phase is the phase of the project with cash inflows
- the investment phase is the phase of the project with cash outflows

i = the cost of capital

This approach removes the reinvestment problem and converts the return into the equivalent of receiving cash in one year's time.

Exam focus point

Make sure you read the examiner's article entitled 'A better measure?' in the April 2008 issue of *Student Accountant*..

4.3 Advantages of MIRR

MIRR has the advantage of IRR that it assumes the **reinvestment rate** is the **company's cost of capital**. IRR assumes that the reinvestment rate is the IRR itself, which is usually untrue.

In many cases where there is conflict between the NPV and IRR methods, the MIRR will give the same indication as NPV, which is the **correct theoretical method**. This helps when explaining the appraisal of a project to managers, who often find the concept of rate of return easier to understand than that of net present value.

4.4 Disadvantages of MIRR

However, MIRR, like all rate of return methods, suffers from the problem that it may lead an investor tor eject a project which has a **lower rate of return** but, because of its size, generates a **larger increase in wealth**.

In the same way, a **high-return** project with a **short life** may be preferred over a **lower-return** project with a longer life.

5 Forecasting a firm's free cash flow

FAST FORWARD

A firm's free cash flow is the actual amount of cash that a company has left from its operations that could be used to pursue opportunities that enhance shareholder value.

So far we have dealt with the two main decision rules for accepting investment projects. Both decision rules require estimates of the cash flows and the required rate of return. The issue of the required rate of return will be dealt extensively in Chapter 7. In this section we shall discuss the estimation of free cash flows.

5.1 Definition of free cash flow

Key term

The **free cash flow** is the cash flow derived from the operations of a company after subtracting working capital, investment and taxes and represents the funds available for distribution to the capital contributors, ie shareholders and debt holders.

The idea is to provide a measure of what is available to the owners of a firm, after providing for capital expenditures to maintain existing assets and to create new assets for future growth and is measured as follows:

Free Cash Flow = Earnings before Interest and Taxes (EBIT)
Less tax on EBIT
Plus non cash charges (eg depreciation)
Less capital expenditures
Less net working capital increases
Plus net working capital decreases
Plus salvage value received

Question — Free cash flow calculation

Albion Inc needs to invest $9,000 to increase productive capacity and also to increase its working capital by $1000. Earnings before taxes are $90,000 and it sets off against tax $6,000 of depreciation. Profits are taxed at 40 percent. What is the free cash flow?

Answer

The calculations for the free cash are given below:

	$
Earnings before interest and taxes (EBIT)	90,000
Less taxes	36,000
Operating Income After Taxes	54,000
Plus depreciation (non cash item)	6,000
Less capital Expenditures	9,000
Less changes to Working Capital	1,000
Free Cash Flow	50,000

5.2 Forecasting Free Cash Flows

Free cash flows can be forecast in similar ways to such other items as expenses, sales and capital expenditure. We must consider the likely behaviour of each of the elements that make up the free cash flow figure – such as movements in future tax rates, potential spending on capital projects and the associated working capital requirements.

5.2.1 Constant growth

One approach to forecasting free cash flows is to assume that they will grow at a constant rate. The calculation of free cash flows is therefore quite straightforward.

$FCF_t = FCF_{t-1}(1 + g)$

Where FCF_t = the free cash flow at time t
FCF_{t-1} = the free cash flow in the previous period
g = growth rate

If you wish to forecast the total free cash flow over a number of periods where the growth rate is assumed to be constant the following formula can be used.

$FCF = FCF_0(1 + g)^n$

Where FCF is the total forecast free cash flow
FCF_0 is the free cash flow at the beginning of the forecast period
n is the number of years for which the free cash flow is being forecast

Question — **Forecasting FCF**

The current value of the free cash flow is $6 million and it is estimated that the free cash flows will grow at a constant rate of 10 percent for the next seven years. What is the level of FCF predicted for year 7?

Answer

$FCF_7 = (1+0.1)^7 \times \$6 = \$11.7\text{ m}$

5.2.2 Differing growth rates

When the elements of free cash flow are expected to grow at different rates each element must be forecast separately using the appropriate rate. Free cash flow can then be estimated using the revised figures for each year.

Question — **Definite variables**

Pokey Inc is trying to forecast its free cash flow for the next three years. Current free cash flow is as follows.

	Expected annual increase	
	%	$
EBIT	4	500,000
Tax	30% of EBIT	150,000
Depreciation	5	85,000
Capital expenditure	2	150,000
Working capital requirements	3	60,000

By what percentage will free cash flow have increased between now and the end of year 3?

Answer

	Year 0	Year 3
	$	$
EBIT ($EBIT_0 \times (1 + 0.04)^3$)	500,000	562,432
Tax	(150,000)	(168,730)
Depreciation ($Depreciation_0 \times (1 + 0.05)^3$)	85,000	98,398
Capital expenditure ($Cap\ Ex_0 \times (1 + 0.02)^3$)	(150,000)	(159,181)
Working capital requirements ($WC_0 \times (1 + 0.03)^3$)	(60,000)	(65,564)
Free cash flow	225,000	267,355

$$\text{Percentage increase} = \frac{267{,}355 - 225{,}000}{225{,}000} = 18.8\%$$

6 Forecasting a firm's dividend capacity

FAST FORWARD

The dividend capacity of a firm is measured by its free cash flow to equity.

6.1 Free cash flow to equity

Exam focus point

Students were asked to produce a cash flow statement as part of a compulsory 30 mark question in the December 2007 exam. An appreciation of the free cash flow to equity concept was expected, although the examiner commented that only a small number of students made reasonable adjustments for net investment.

The free cash flow derived in the previous section is the amount of money that is available for distribution to the capital contributors. If the project is financed by equity only, then these funds could be potentially distributed to the shareholders of the company.

However, if the company is financing the project by issuing debt, then the shareholders are entitled to the residual cash flow left over after meeting interest and principal payments. This residual cash flow is called free cash flow to equity (FCFE).

6.1.1 Direct method of calculation

Free Cash Flow to Equity = Net income (EBIT – Net Interest – Tax paid)
Add depreciation
Less total net investment (change in capital investment + change in working capital)
Add net debt issued (new borrowings less any repayments)
Add net equity issued (new issues less any equity repurchases)

Question

Free cash flow to equity

The following information is available for ABC Co:

Capital expenditure $20 million
Corporate tax rate 35%
Debt repayment $23 million
Depreciation charges $10 million

	2008
	$m
Sales	650.00
Less: cost of goods sold	(438.00)
Gross profit	212.00
Operating expenses	(107.50)
EBIT	104.50
Less: interest expense	(8.00)
Earnings before tax	96.50
Less: taxes	(33.78)
Net Income	62.73

What is the FCFE?

Answer

The free cash flow to equity is calculated as follows:

	2008
	$m
Net Income	62.73
Plus: depreciation	10.00
Less: capital expenditures	(20.00)
Less: debt retirement	(23.00)
Free Cash Flow to Equity	29.73

6.1.2 Indirect method of calculation

Using the indirect method, FCFE is calculated as follows.

FCFE = Free Cash

Flow (calculated using the formula in section 5.1 above)
Less (net interest + net debt paid)
Add tax benefit from debt (net interest × tax rate)

Question

Free cash flow to equity – indirect method

Using the information in the question 'Free cash flow to equity' above, calculate the FCFE using the indirect method.

Answer

The free cash flow is given by:

EBIT(1 – Tax rate)	67.93
Plus: depreciation expense	10.00
Less: CAPEX	(20.00)
Free cash flow	57.93

FCFE = $57.93 – (8 + 23) + 0.35 × 8 = $29.73

6.2 How much can be paid as dividends?

In theory, the entire FCFE can be paid as dividends as this is the amount that is available for this purpose. In practice however only a portion of this figure will be given to the shareholders as dividends as the management team tends to prefer a smooth dividend pattern.

While the dividends can never be less than zero, the free cash flows to equity can be **negative**. This can occur even if earnings are positive, if the firm has **substantial working capital and capital expenditure needs**. Negative free cash flow to equity is not unusual in **small, high growth firms**, at least in the early years, as reinvestment needs will tend to be substantial. However, as growth rates and capital expenditure **slow down**, free cash flow to equity will eventually become **positive**.

7 Valuing a firm using free cash flow

In Section 6 above we saw that free cash flow could be calculated in two ways, either by calculating it directly or by calculating the free cash flow to equity and adding the **cash flows** to **debt holders**. Similarly we can value a firm using free cash flows by either using the predicted free cash flows or by adding together all the cash flows payable to the different claimants of the firm (equity and debt holders).

7.1 Firm valuation using free cash flows

The valuation of a firm using free cash flows is very similar to carrying out a net present value calculation. The value of the firm is simply the **sum of the discounted free cash flows** over the appropriate horizon.

If we assume that free cash flows remain **constant** (that is, with no growth) over the appropriate horizon, then the value of the firm is the **free cash flow divided by the cost of capital**.

Alternatively if the free cash flows are growing at a **constant rate** every year, the value of the firm can be calculated using the *Gordon Model* (also known as the *Constant Growth Model*).

$$PV_0 = \frac{FCF_0(1+g)}{k-g}$$

Where g is the growth rate
k is the cost of capital

7.1.1 Example

Rick Inc currently has free cash flows of $5 million per year and a cost of capital of 12%. Calculate the value of Rick Inc if

(a) The free cash flows are expected to remain constant
(b) The free cash flows are expected to grow at a constant rate of 4% per annum

Solution

(a) Value of Rick Inc = $\frac{\text{Free cash flow}}{\text{Cost of capital}} = \frac{\$5\text{ million}}{0.12\text{ million}}$ = $41.67 million

(b) Use the *Gordon Model*

Value of Rick Inc = $\frac{(\$5\text{ million}\times 1.04)}{(0.12-0.04)}$ = $65 million

7.2 Terminal values

Key term

> The **terminal value** of a project or a stream of cash flows is the value of all the cash flows occurring from period N + 1 onwards ie beyond the normal prediction horizon of periods 1 to N.

These flows are subject to a greater degree of uncertainty as they are beyond the horizon 1 to N where normal forecasts are acceptable. As such simplifying assumptions need to be made for any flows occurring after period N.

When we refer to a project, the terminal value is equivalent to the **salvage value** remaining at the end of the expected project horizon.

7.2.1 Terminal values and company valuation

Terminal values can be used in valuing a firm. The value of the firm will be calculated **as the sum of the discounted free cash flows plus the discounted terminal value.**

7.2.2 Calculating terminal values

Assume that free cash flows are constant

When calculating the terminal value, we can assume that the free cash flows after the 'normal' time horizon (period N) will be constant. Terminal value is determined by dividing the free cash flow at time (N + 1) by the cost of capital (required rate of return).

Question — **Terminal value**

Consider the following information on a project

Cash flow in period N+1 = $2 million
Required rate of return = 10%

Assuming that the free cash flow will remain at $2 million indefinitely and the initial investment is $18 million what is the terminal value?

Answer

The terminal value of the project is:

$$TV_N = \frac{2}{0.1} = \$20 \text{ million}$$

Assume that cash flows increase at a constant rate

An alternative assumption is to assume that cash flows increase from year to year at a constant rate g, ie:

$$FCF_{N+1} = (1 + g)\, FCF_N$$

and the terminal value will be:

$$TV_N = \frac{FCF_N(1+g)}{k-g}$$

Provided that $k > g$

Question

Terminal value

Assume the following values for the expected growth, current cash flows and required return:

$g = 0.05$
$FCF_N = \$2$ million
$k = 0.10$

What is the terminal value?

Answer

The terminal value according to the constant growth model will then be:

$$TV = \frac{2 \times (1+0.05)}{0.10-0.05} = \$24 \text{ million}$$

Question

Company value

You have completed the following forecast of free cash flows for an eight year period, capturing the normal business cycle of Marathon Inc:

Year	*FCF*
20X8	1,860.0
20X9	1,887.6
20Y0	1,917.6
20Y1	1,951.2
20Y2	1,987.2
20Y3	2,016.0
20Y4	2,043.6
20Y5	2,070.0

Free cash flows are expected to grow at 3% beyond 2015. The cost of capital is assumed to be 12%. What is Marathon's value?

Answer

Year	*FCF*	*Present value @ 12%*	*Present Value*
20X8	1,860.0	0.893	1,661
20X9	1,887.6	0.797	1,504
20Y0	1,917.6	0.712	1,365
20Y1	1,951.2	0.636	1,241
20Y2	1,987.2	0.567	1,127
20Y3	2,016.0	0.507	1,022
20Y4	2,043.6	0.452	924
20Y5	2,070.0	0.404	836

Total present value for forecast period = $9,680

$$\text{Terminal value} = \frac{(\$2{,}070 \times 1.03)}{(0.12-0.03)} = \$23{,}690$$

Total value of Marathon = $33,370

7.3 Firm valuation using FCFE

The techniques used for the valuation of a company using the FCFF can also be applied for the value of equity. The value of equity is simply the present value of the free cash flow to equity, discounted at the cost of equity (k_e), plus the terminal value discounted at the cost of equity.

Once the value of equity is calculated, the value of debt needs to be calculated next. The value of the firm is then simply the value of equity and the value of debt.

8 Risk and uncertainty

FAST FORWARD

Before deciding whether or not to undertake a project, financial managers will want to assess the project's **risk** (which can be predicted), and **uncertainty** (which is unpredictable).

Risk can be built into project appraisal using such tools as **expected values** and different **costs of capital**.

Project duration is a measure of how long it takes to recover approximately **half** of the value of the investment.

8.1 Risk

You should already be familiar with how financial managers incorporate risk into project appraisal. The **cost of capital** of a project gives an indication of its risk – the **higher** the cost of capital, the **greater** the risk. We will look at risk-adjusted discount rates in Chapter 7.

Risk can also be incorporated into project appraisal using **expected values**, whereby each possible outcome is given a probability. The expected value is obtained by multiplying each present value by its probability and adding the results together. The **lower** the expected value, the **higher** the risk.

Question — **Expected values**

A project has the following possible outcomes, each of which is assigned a probability of occurrence.

	Probability	*Present value*
		$
Low demand	0.3	20,000
Medium demand	0.6	30,000
High demand	0.1	50,000

What is the expected value of the project?

Answer

The expected value is the sum of each present value multiplied by its probability.

Expected value = (20,000 × 0.3) + (30,000 × 0.6) + (50,000 × 0.1) = $29,000

Question — **Expected values 2**

What would happen to the expected value of the project if the probability of medium demand fell to 0.4 and the probability of low demand increased to 0.5?

Answer

Expected value = (20,000 × 0.5) + (30,000 × 0.4) + (50,000 × 0.1) = $27,000

The project is more risky than before as there is a greater probability of demand being low, which results in a lower expected value.

8.2 Uncertainty

Uncertainty is more difficult to plan, for obvious reasons. There are several ways in which uncertainty can be dealt with in project appraisal. Three of them – **payback period, sensitivity analysis** and **discounted payback** will be familiar to you from earlier studies. Make sure you understand how each of them works.

8.2.1 Example – sensitivity analysis

Nevers Ure has a cost of capital of 8% and is considering a project with the following 'most-likely' cash flows.

Year	*Purchase of plant*	*Running costs*	*Savings*
	$	$	$
0	(7,000)		
1		2,000	6,000
2		2,500	7,000

Required

Measure the sensitivity (in percentages) of the project to changes in the levels of expected costs and savings.

Solution

The PVs of the cash flows are as follows.

Year	*Discount factor @ 8%*	*PV of plant cost*	*PV of` running costs*	*PV of savings*	*PV of net cash flow*
		$	$	$	$
0	1.000	(7,000)			(7,000)
1	0.926		(1,852)	5,556	3,704
2	0.857		(2,143)	5,999	3,856
		(7,000)	(3,995)	11,555	560

The project has a positive NPV and would appear to be worthwhile. The changes in cash flows which would need to occur for the project to break even (NPV = 0) are as follows.

(a) Plant costs would need to increase by a PV of $560, that is by:

$$\frac{560}{7,000} \times 100\% = 8\%$$

(b) Running costs would need to increase by a PV of $560, that is by:

$$\frac{560}{3,995} \times 100\% = 14\%$$

(c) Savings would need to fall by a PV of $560, that is by:

$$\frac{560}{11,555} \times 100\% = 4.8\%$$

8.2.2 Weaknesses of sensitivity analysis

These are as follows.

(a) The method requires that **changes** in each key variable are **isolated.** However management is more interested in the combination of the effects of changes in two or more key variables.

(b) Looking at factors in isolation is unrealistic since they are often **interdependent**.

(c) Sensitivity analysis does not examine the **probability** that any particular variation in costs or revenues might occur.

(d) **Critical factors** may be those over which managers have no control.

(e) In itself it does not provide a decision rule. Parameters defining **acceptability** must be laid down by managers.

8.2.3 Project duration

By calculating the project duration, the financial manager will be able to determine how long it will be before approximately 50% of the value of the investment is recovered.

Project duration is calculated by **weighting** each year of the project by the **percentage** of the present value of the cash flows **recovered** in that year.

Question

Project duration

Monty Inc is considering a project which requires an initial investment of $100,000. Projected cash flows discounted at Monty's cost of capital of 10% are as follows.

Year	*0*	*1*	*2*	*3*	*4*	*5*
Present value	(100,000)	45,455	36,364	26,296	13,660	6,209

Calculate the project duration.

Answer

The first thing we have to do is determine the total cash inflows over the life of the project, which is the sum of the present values of the cash inflows for years 1 to 5.

Total present value of cash inflows = $127,984

The second step is to calculate each present value as a percentage of $127,984.

Year	*1*	*2*	*3*	*4*	5
Present value	45,455	36,364	26,296	13,660	6,209
Percentage of total PV	36%	28%	21%	11%	4%

Project duration is the sum of the year number multiplied by the relevant percentage

$$= (1 \times 0.36) + (2 \times 0.28) + (3 \times 0.21) + (4 \times 0.11) + (5 \times 0.04)$$
$$= 2.19$$

This means that it takes **approximately** 2.19 years to recover half of the present value of the project. Unlike the payback period, this method looks at the cash flows earned in **every year** of the project, rather than just up to the point where the initial investment is paid back.

9 Monte Carlo simulation and investment appraisal

FAST FORWARD

The Monte Carlo method of estimating a project's NPV assumes that the key factors affecting NPV can be modelled as a probability distribution.

9.1 Monte Carlo method

This section provides a brief outline of the Monte Carlo method in investment appraisal. The method appeared in 1949 and is widely used in situations involving uncertainty. The method amounts to adopting a particular probability distribution for the uncertain (random) variables that affect the NPV and then using simulations to generate values of the random variables.

To deal with uncertainty the Monte Carlo method assumes that the uncertain parameters (such as the growth rate or the cost of capital k) or variables (such as the free cash flow) follow a specific probability distribution.

The basic idea is to generate through simulation thousands of values for the parameters or variables of interest and use those variables to derive the net present value for each possible simulated outcome.

From the resulting values we can derive the distribution of the NPV.

To illustrate the method, assume that a company has a project with an expected cash flow of \$2 million after the first year of operation. Cash flows will increase by 5% annually in perpetuity. The cost of capital is 10% and initial investment is \$18 million.

The present value of the project can be calculated using the constant growth model covered in section 7.1 above.

$$NPV = \frac{2 \times (1+g)}{(0.1-g)} - 18$$

In our simple example, since the only source of uncertainty is the growth rate, we can assume that the growth rate follows a particular probability distribution. For the sake of simplicity we shall assume that the growth rate follows a normal distribution with a mean of 5 percent and a standard deviation of 3 percent. Our model is thus $g \sim N(5, 3^2)$

The probability distribution of the growth rate is shown in the figure below. The Monte Carlo method works as follows. From the normal distribution we sample 1,000 random values of g. This can be done easily in EXCEL using the random number generator to generate 1,000 random numbers coming from a normal distribution with a mean of 5 and a standard deviation of 3. For each value of g we calculate the NPV from our model.

$$NPV = \frac{2 \times (1+g)}{(0.1-g)} - 18$$

Probability Distribution of Growth Rates

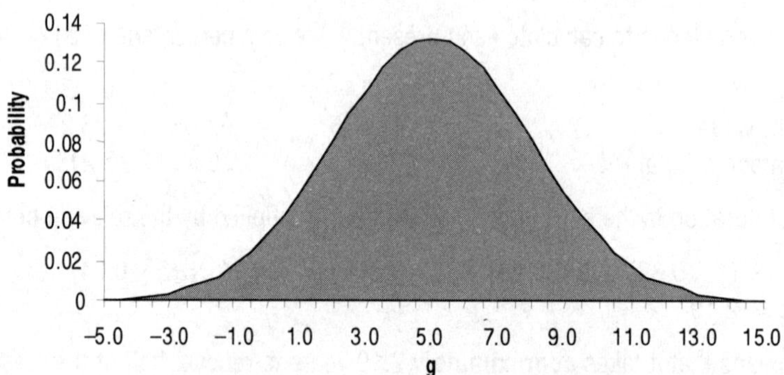

Calculating the NPV for all 1000 random values of g and plotting the resulting values for the NPV we obtain the following distribution of values for the NPV. Whilst the probability distribution of g is normal the distribution of the NPV is not normal. The empirical distribution can be constructed from the table below which shows the cumulative frequency distribution of the NPV

NPV	*Cumulative Frequency*
<–5.7	1
<–5.1	2
<–4.5	3
<–3.9	4
<–3.4	11
<–2.8	16
<–2.2	29
<–1.6	40
<–1.0	50
<–0.4	76
<0.0	100
<0.7	172
<1.3	217
<1.9	279
<2.5	351

NPV	Cumulative Frequency
<3.1	417
<3.6	480
<4.2	563
<4.8	628
<5.4	689
<6.0	756
<6.5	805
<7.1	846
<7.7	875
<8.3	899
<8.9	929
<9.5	951
<10.0	971
<10.6	981
<11.2	990
<11.8	996
<17.0	1,000
	1,000

The table provide a complete description of the distribution of the NPV of the model we have employed. For example the probability of getting a negative NPV is 10 percent since

$$\text{Probability (NPV < 0)} = \frac{100}{1{,}000} = 0.1.$$

Similarly the probability of getting a NPV of less than 3.6 is equal to:

$$\frac{480}{1{,}000} \text{ or } 48\%$$

The frequency distribution of the net present values resulting from the simulation are shown in the following diagram. The distribution shows that most of the values for the NPV are around 2 and 6 with a mean value of about 4. Statistical measures such as the standard deviation can be calculated to describe the dispersion of prices. The overwhelming conclusion from the analysis is that the NPV of the project under a wide range of assumptions for the growth rate is most likely to be positive.

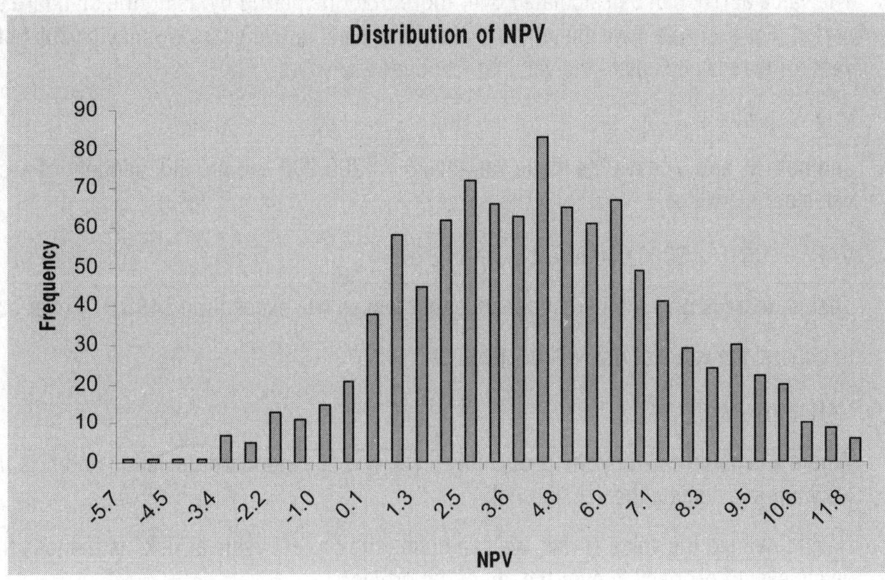

9.2 Project Value at Risk

FAST FORWARD

The project value at risk is the potential loss of a project with a given probability.

The empirical distribution of the NPV leads naturally to the concept of the project value at risk.

Value at Risk (VAR) is the minimum amount by which the value of an investment or portfolio will fall over a given period of time at a given level of probability. Alternatively it is defined as the maximum amount that it may lose at a given level of confidence. For example we may say that the Value at Risk is $100,000 at 5 percent probability, or that it is $100,000 at 95 percent confidence level. The first definition implies that there is a 5 percent chance that the loss will exceed $100,000, or that we are 95 percent sure that it will not exceed $100,000. VAR can be defined at any level of probability or confidence, but the most common probability levels are 1, 5 and 10 percent.

A formal definition of the VAR of a position where the value of the position is denoted by V is the value V* such that values of V less than V* have a chance of only p to appear. Formally this can be written as Probability (V < V*) =p and is shown below. The probability level is the area under the curve and it can be calculated as the value of the random variable that determines the desired area under the curve.

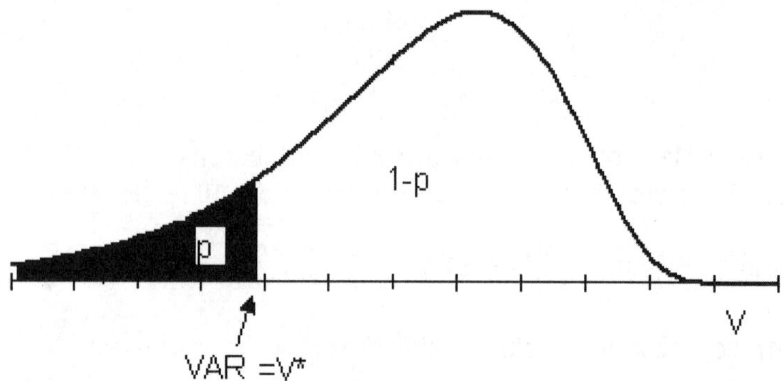

When the random variable follows the normal distribution, the value at risk at specific probability levels is easily calculated as a multiple of the standard deviation. For example the 5 percent VAR is simply 1.645σ, the 1 percent VAR is 2.33σ.

For example the annual standard deviation of a position is $200,000. The value at risk is 200,000 × 1.645) = $329,000. Only in 5 percent of the cases will the value fall by a larger amount within a year.

The value at risk can be calculated over more that one period by using the standard deviation for the entire period. For example if we assume the life of a project is two years we may calculate the value at risk for a year, or we may calculate the value at risk over two years.

$$V = V_1 + V_2$$

and both V_1 and V_2 have the same variance σ = $200,000 and are independent of each other, then the value at risk will be:

$$VAR = 1.645 \times \$200{,}000 \times \sqrt{2} = \$465{,}276$$

That is, there is only a 5 percent chance that losses will exceed the $465,276 over a two year period.

In general the value at risk will be given by:

$$VAR = k\sigma\sqrt{N}$$

Where k is determined by the probability level, σ is the standard deviation and N is the periods over which we want to calculate the value at risk.

Having defined the value at risk, we can define the project value at risk, as the loss that may occur at a given level of probability over the life of the project.

9.2.1 Example

The annual cash flows from a project are expected to follow the normal distribution with a mean of \$50,000 and standard deviation of \$10,000. The project has a 10 year life. What is the project value at risk?

The project value at risk for a year is:

PVAR = $1.645 \times \$10,000 = \$16,450$

The project value at risk that takes into account the entire project life is:

PVAR = $1.645 \times \$10,000 \times \sqrt{10} = \$52019$, this is the maximum amount by which the value of the project will fall at a confidence level of 95%.

So far we have used the normal distribution to calculate the value at risk. The assumption that project cash flows or values follow the normal distribution may not be plausible. An alternative way is to use the distribution from a Monte Carlo simulation. For example using the previous table we see that the probability of getting a net present value less or lower than –\$1 million is 5 percent. So the project value at risk at 5 percent probability is –\$1 million for the specific example. According to our notation $V^* = -1$ million. That means that the chance of losing more than \$1 million in the above project is only 5 percent.

The project value at risk can be calculated at different probability levels. The project value at risk at 1 percent probability level is –5.7 million. That means that the chance of losses exceeding \$5.7 million is only 1 percent.

Chapter Roundup

- Projects with a positive net present value should be undertaken
- Inflation is present in all economies and must be accounted for when evaluating projects.
- In investment appraisal, tax is often assumed to be payable **one year in arrears,** but you should read the question details carefully.

  Tax allowable depreciation details should be checked in any question you attempt.
- **Capital rationing** problems exist when there are insufficient funds available to finance all available profitable projects.
- **Capital rationing** may occur due to internal factors (**soft** capital rationing) or external factors (**hard** capital rationing).
- When capital rationing is present across **multiple periods**, linear programming may be used to solve the problem of **which projects** to undertake.
- A project will only be selected if its internal rate of return **exceeds** the cost of capital or target rate of return.
- A project being accepted based on IRR may be misleading if the cash flows from the project are not positive.
- The modified internal rate of return is the IRR that would result if it was **not assumed that project proceeds were reinvested at the IRR.**
- A firm's free cash flow is the actual amount of cash that a company has left from its operations that could be used to pursue opportunities that enhance shareholder value.
- The dividend capacity of a firm is measured by its free cash flow to equity.
- Before deciding whether or not to undertake a project, financial managers will want to assess the project's **risk** (which can be predicted), and **uncertainty** (which is unpredictable).
- Risk can be built into project appraisal using such tools as **expected values** and different **costs of capital**.
- **Project duration** is a measure of how long it takes to recover approximately **half** of the value of the investment.
- The Monte Carlo method of estimating a project's NPV assumes that the key factors affecting NPV can be modelled as a probability distribution.
- The project value at risk is the potential loss of a project with a given probability.

Quick quiz

1. Why is NPV preferable to IRR as a project selection criterion?
2. When does the multiple value IRR normally occur?
3. What is the appropriate criterion for ranking projects when there is a constraint of funds?
4. What is the main difference between modified IRR and IRR?
5. If Project A had a duration of 3.5 years and Project B had a duration of 2.6 years, which project would be preferable and why?
6. What is the advantage of the Monte Carlo calculation of the NPV?

Answers to quick quiz

1. The NPV criterion is consistent with the shareholder wealth maximisation whereas the IRR criterion is not
2. The multiple value of IRR occurs when there is a negative cash flow
3. The appropriate criterion is the profitability index
4. The IRR implies that the profits from a project are re-invested at the IRR whereas the modified IRR allows the re-investment rate to change
5. Project B would be preferable as it takes less time to recoup approximately half of the investment, which makes it appear less risky.
6. The Monte Carlo calculation of the NPV derives the NPV under a wide range of assumptions

Now try the questions below from the Exam Question Bank

Number	Level	Marks	Time
6	Examination	20	36 mins
7	Examination	20	36 mins

Impact of financing on investment decisions and adjusted present values

7

Topic list	Syllabus reference
1 Traditional theories of capital structure – Modigliani and Miller	B (2) (a)
2 Alternative theories of capital structure	B (2) (b)
3 The adjusted present value method	B (2) (b)

Introduction

The purpose of this chapter is to review some of the theories that seek to explain capital structure and the role of capital structure in investment appraisal. The traditional theories developed by Modigliani and Miller are briefly considered first, before moving onto some alternative theories of capital structure, including static trade-off theory and pecking order theory. We will then look at the adjusted present value approach to valuing a firm.

Study guide

		Intellectual level
B2	**Impact of financing on investment decisions and adjusted present values**	
(a)	Assess the impact of financing upon investment decisions of	3
	(i) Pecking order theory	
	(ii) Static trade-off theory	
	(iii) Agency effects and capital structure	
(b)	Apply the adjusted value technique to the appraisal of investment decisions that entail significant alterations in the financial structure of the firm, including their fiscal and transactions cost implications	3

Knowledge brought forward from earlier studies

1 **The relationship between risk and return**

Risk averse investors prefer less risk than more. In order to be persuaded to take on more risk, they must be 'compensated' in the form of higher returns.

2 **Diversifiable and non-diversifiable risk**

Diversifiable risk (also known as **unsystematic risk)** arises due to **random** and unpredicted factors. It can be diversified away by holding a portfolio of investments.

Non-diversifiable risk (also known as **systematic risk)** is caused by factors that **affect all firms** and therefore **cannot** be eliminated by diversification.

3 **The capital asset pricing model (CAPM)**

This model was covered in the appendix to Chapter 4 of this text. The following formula is given in the exam.

$E(r_i) = R_f + \beta(E(R_m - R_f))$

4 **Weighted average cost of capital (WACC)**

The formula for the WACC which is given in the exam is

$$WACC = \left[\frac{V_e}{V_e + V_d}\right]k_e + \left[\frac{V_d}{V_e + V_d}\right]k_d\,(1 - T)$$

This formula can be used to calculate the cost of capital at which potential investment projects should be discounted.

1 Traditional theories of capital structure – Modigliani and Miller

The issue of how to structure finance is one that has been raging on for many years and has never been fully resolved. **Traditional theory** suggests that using some debt will **lower** the WACC but if gearing rises above a certain level, WACC will start to rise, due to increased risk. This section looks at Modigliani and Miller's theories of capital structure.

1.1 Key principles

FAST FORWARD

The MM theory predicts that the financial structure has no impact on the cost of capital and therefore the way a project is financed has no impact on the value of the project.

Exam focus point

The examiner has stated that you will only need to know the key issues of the MM theory – you will not be asked to enter into any lengthy proofs.

The MM theory states that (**ignoring tax**) the use of debt simply transfers more risk to the shareholders, thus making equity more expensive. As a result, the use of **debt** does **not** reduce the WACC.

However **when tax was introduced** to the model, MM found that **debt actually saved tax** (due to tax relief on interest payments), thus finance costs (and **WACC**) would **fall** if debt was used. This finding suggested that firms should use debt **as much as possible**.

1.2 Formula for cost of equity

The principles of the MM theory with tax gave rise to the following formula for cost of equity.

Exam formula

$$k_e = k_e^i + (1-T)(k_e^i - k_d)\frac{V_d}{V_e}$$

Where k_e is the cost of equity in a geared company
k_e^i is the cost of equity in an ungeared company
V_d, V_e are the market values of debt and equity respectively
k_d is the cost of debt pre-tax

1.3 Example of MM cost of equity calculation

Shiny Inc is an ungeared company with a cost of equity of 10%. Shiny is considering introducing debt to its capital structure as it is tempted by a loan with a rate of 5%, which could be used to repurchase shares. Once the equity is repurchased, the ratio of debt to equity will be 1:4. Assume that corporation tax is 30%.

(a) What will be the revised cost of equity if Shiny takes out the loan?
(b) At what discount rate will Shiny now appraise its projects? Comment on your results.

Solution

(a) $k_e = 0.10 + (1 - 0.3)(0.10 - 0.05) \times 0.25 = 10.9\%$
(b) WACC $= (0.2 \times 0.7 \times 0.05) + (0.8 \times 0.109) = 9.42\%$

The new WACC figure is lower than that for the ungeared company. This means that future investments will be able to bring greater wealth to the shareholders. More projects will become acceptable to management, given that they are being discounted at a lower discount rate.

1.4 Limitations of the MM theory

In practice you will very rarely find firms with high levels of gearing, due to the risks involved. MM assumed that capital markets were perfect – that is, firms could always raise capital to fund profitable projects. In reality, this is not the case and firms have to face such problems as

(a) **Bankruptcy risks** – there is a legal obligation to pay interest when it is due. If firms take on too much debt, interest payments may become unsustainable, leading to the risk of bankruptcy.

(b) **Tax exhaustion** – one of the benefits of debt is the tax relief on interest. However there may come a time when tax relief is exhausted, meaning that there are no reductions in finance costs.

(c) **Agency costs** – the existence of restrictive covenants may prevent firms from investing.

(d) **Cost of borrowing** – as the level of gearing increases (and thus the perceived risk of the firm), finance providers will increase the interest rate on further debt, thus making debt a more expensive method of finance.

2 Alternative theories of capital structure

2.1 Static trade-off theory

FAST FORWARD

Static trade-off theory states that firms in a static position will seek to achieve a target level of gearing by adjusting their current gearing levels.

We know that a firm enjoys an increase in tax savings with an increase in debt financing due to the tax deductibility of interest. However, an increase in debt financing will also result in an increase in the chances of the firm going bankrupt because of its increased commitment in interest payments. This is the effect of financial leverage. It is important to remember that a firm can skip its dividend payments but not its interest payments. Failure to meet those interest payments because of inadequate cash on hand will cause the firm some financial distress, and the ultimate form of financial distress is bankruptcy.

What are some of the financial distress costs faced by a firm? We can classify them into two categories:

(a) Direct financial distress costs
(b) Indirect financial distress costs

2.1.1 Direct financial distress costs

The direct financial distress costs faced by a firm are the legal and administrative costs associated with the bankruptcy or reorganization of the firm. Studies have shown that such costs range from less than 1% to approximately 4-5% of the value of the firm.

2.1.2 Indirect financial distress costs

There are different types of cost (mostly implicit) that a firm faces when it is in a financially stressful situation (but not bankruptcy). The following are some of those costs:

- A higher cost of capital (either for debt or equity) due to its financial situation.
- Lost sales due to fear of impaired services and loss of trust.
- Managers and employees will try drastic actions to save the firm that might result in some long-term problems. Such actions include closing down plants, downsizing, drastic cost cuts, and selling off valuable assets. These actions will ultimately dilute the value of the firm.
- Firms might have trouble keeping highly skilled managers and employees, which is bad for the firms in the long run.

As a result of these costs the **leverage-adjusted** value of the firm should be decreased. The value of the company in this case will be:

Value of the unlevered firm + (tax rate × interest payments) – present value of the bankruptcy costs

This effect can be seen in the figure below. As the figure shows, when the present value of the bankruptcy costs increases with leverage, there is an optimal capital structure for the firm.

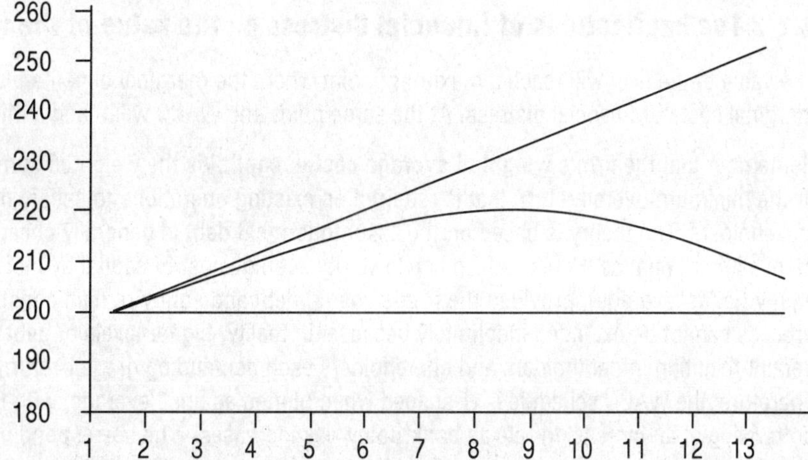

Starting from the empirical observation that firms do not have 100 percent leverage ratios, it is plausible to argue that a firm's WACC will start to increase and its value will start to decrease after a certain value of the leverage ratio, to reflect the increasing costs of leverage. Such as possible explanation is depicted in the graph below.

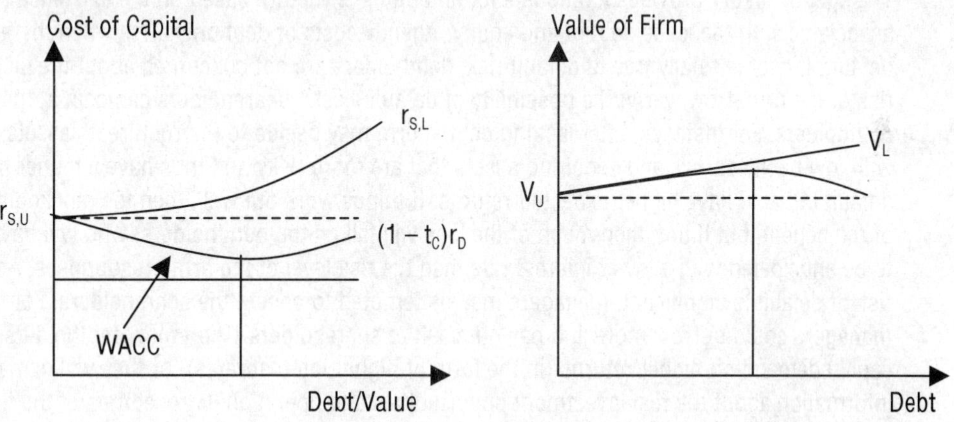

From the above graph, it is plausible that there exists a certain combination of **debt** and **equity financing** that will enable a firm to **minimize** its **cost of capital** and to **maximize** its **value**. The issue a financial manager is most concerned with is identifying the firm's **optimal capital structure** that will allow it to **minimize firm's WACC** and **maximize its value**.

In MM's propositions, debt was considered to be **risk free** and the company was considered not to have any risk of failing. In addition, it was assumed that EBIT will not be affected by capital structure. However, corporate failure is an unfortunate and expensive reality.

If a company actually becomes insolvent and has to be liquidated, there are many administrative and other costs to be borne (such as liquidators' fees) which would not otherwise have been suffered. As a result, the expected EBIT will fall.

Even if a company does not become insolvent, but merely has a rough ride for several years, there will be additional costs. These will arise because, among other factors, the management will need to spend extra time speaking to debt and equity investors and will be restricted in their actions due to loan covenants that prescribe various courses of action.

These additional costs of financial distress will reduce payouts to investors. As a company borrows more money, the probability that these cash outflows will occur increases, reducing the value of the company.

The conclusion is that a company should lever up to take advantage of any tax benefits available, but only to the extent that the **marginal benefits exceed** the **marginal costs** of **financial distress**. After this point, the market value of the firm will start to fall and its WACC will start to rise. This is known as the static trade-off theory of capital structure.

2.1.3 The implications of financial distress on the value of the firm and on WACC

The value of the firm will reach a maximum point where the marginal benefits of tax relief equal the marginal costs of financial distress. At the same point, the WACC will reach a minimum point.

Remember that the firm's **weighted average cost of capital** is the weighted sum of debt and equity costs or the minimum overall return that is required on existing operations to satisfy the demands of all stakeholders. The theory is based on the assumption that debt is generally cheaper than equity as a source of investment finance. Hence, a firm can lower its average cost of capital by increasing its debt relative to equity (ie. its leverage), provided the firm's cost of debt and equity remain constant. However, this process cannot be extended indefinitely because, in reality, higher levels of debt increase the likelihood of default resulting in debtholders and shareholders each demanding greater returns on their capital. Therefore, the WACC schedule is U-shaped when plotted against leverage, with the cost of debt and equity both rising at an increasing rate as bankruptcy risk increases. The corresponding company market value schedule is an inverted U-shape. **Optimal leverage** occurs where WACC is **minimised** and the value of the firm is **maximised**.

2.2 Agency theory

The agency theory provides a rationale for an optimal structure based on the existence of agency costs associated with the issue debt of and equity. Agency costs of debt only arise when there is a risk of default. If debt is totally free of default risk, debtholders are not concerned about the income, value or the risk of the firm. However, if the possibility of default exists, shareholders can gain at the expense of debtholders. For instance, after issuing debt, a firm may decide to restructure its assets, selling off those with low business risk and acquiring assets that are more risky and thus have a higher possibility of default but also have higher expected returns. If things work out well, then the stockholders will get most of the benefit, but if not, then much of the loss will fall on the bondholders, who will have already agreed to be anticipated with a lower interest rate than the risk level of the firm presupposes. Additionally, if the risk of default is significant, managers may be tempted to benefit the shareholders. For instance, managers could borrow more and pay out cash to shareholders. Therefore, debtholders will either provide capital demanding higher returns (in the form of higher interest rates), or they will demand more information about the real investment opportunities and operational procedures of the firm by setting monitoring mechanisms or they will set restrictive covenants. All these alternatives are costly and they result in agency costs. Moreover these costs will increase as the level of debt increases.

Agency costs also exist in relation to the **new share issues**. The cause of agency costs in this case is the potential conflict between **old shareholders** and **new shareholders**. New shareholders will want to monitor the management of the company to make sure that the original shareholders do not benefit at the expense of new shareholders. These monitoring mechanisms are expensive and the agency costs associated with the issue of new equity is increased with the amount of new equity issued.

The optimal capital structure of the firm will be formed at the particular level of debt and equity where the benefits of the debt that can be received by the shareholders balance with the costs of debt imposed by the debt holders.

2.3 Pecking order theory

Pecking order theory is based on the idea that shareholders have less information about the firm than directors do.

Shareholders and other investors will use directors' actions as signals to indicate what directors believe about the firm, given their superior information.

The pecking order hypothesis is based on the idea that investors have a lower level of information about the company than its directors do. This information asymmetry is in sharp contrast to the Modigliani

Miller model which assumes that investors and directors have the same information. As a result of information asymmetry, shareholders use directors' actions as a signal to indicate what directors believe about the company with their superior information.

2.3.1 The implication of information asymmetry

Assuming that directors want to maximize the wealth of the existing stockholders of the company, they will take decisions based on this criterion.

When a company is planning to invest in order to launch a successful new product, they will not want to finance this by the issue of shares. This is because any new shareholders will participate in the gains from the new investment, rather than just existing shareholders. Therefore, they would prefer to raise debt, even if this takes them beyond the target debt-to-equity ratio.

When the directors expect the value of the company to fall from its current level, they will prefer to issue new stock rather than debt, since any falls in value will affect the existing shareholders less. However, although this is what directors would like to do, their problem is that investors are aware of this information asymmetry. Hence they will not be prepared to buy new stock issues, since it merely suggests that the company is going to perform badly. The stock issue is an adverse signal to investors, depressing the stock price. Because of this the managers of a firm may be reluctant to issue new shares. The under-pricing of the equity may be so severe that new investors will capture more than the NPV of the new projects. This will result in a net loss to existing shareholders. Management and existing shareholders will therefore reject these projects even though the NPV may be positive.

2.3.2 The implications for capital structure

Firms can avoid this underinvestment by financing the investment with security that is not so heavily undervalued by the market. For this reason, internal funds and debt financing are preferred to the use of equity. In terms of the pecking order hypothesis, corporate debt decisions will be driven by the firm's desire to finance investment first internally, then with risky debt and finally with external equity. Thus the pecking order hypothesis postulates that directors will aim to keep reserve borrowing capacity available to enable them to borrow money at a reasonable cost to finance new investment when this is required, rather than having a new equity issue.

They will achieve this by using equity finance from retained earnings to finance new investments in normal years. Only when retained earnings are insufficient will they raise debt finance. Retained earnings may be insufficient due to the need to pay dividends or because the new investment required is exceptionally large. This suggests that in normal times, profitable firms will have lower debt levels than that suggested by Modigliani Miller model with taxes.

An additional factor to consider here is the impact of this on the marginal cost of finance. If the stock price falls, this may cause the cost of equity to rise, giving a higher marginal cost of finance and meaning that less projects can be accepted.

2.3.3 The main prediction of the pecking order hypothesis

If corporate managers operate in accordance with the pecking order model, highly profitable firms with limited investment opportunity would have a very low level of debt. Firms tend to use debt more conservatively than the trade-off theory predicts; this is especially true for large, profitable firms with stable cash flow. Conversely, firms that have more investment opportunities than their internally generated funds or firms that cannot generate sufficient funds internally for their operations tend to borrow more.

The main predictions of the **pecking order hypothesis**, are:

(a) To finance new investment, firms prefer internal finance to external finance. Asymmetric information creates the possibility that they may choose not to issue new securities and therefore miss a positive NPV investment; or may issue equity at a low price which disadvantages existing shareholders.

(b) If retained earnings are less than investment outlays, the firm first depletes its financial "slack" (its cash balances or marketable securities). If instead, retained earnings exceed investment, it first invests in cash or marketable securities, and then pays off debt. If the firm is persistently in surplus, it may increase its target payout rate.

(c) If financial slack is depleted and a sufficiently favourable investment opportunity is presented, the firm will resort to external finance. In this event, it starts with the safest security (plain debt); then hybrid securities such as convertible bonds. As it climbs up the pecking order, a firm faces increasing costs of financial distress inherent in the risk class of debt and equity securities. Only when it runs out of debt capacity, and the potential costs of financial distress become important, will it finally resort to a new equity issue.

Thus, internal finance is at the top, and equity is at the bottom, of the pecking order. A single "optimal" debt-equity ratio does not exist: a result which is similar to the Modigliani Miller model with no taxes. However, the rationale is different, for whereas the Modigliani Miller model suggests that firm financial policy is irrelevant this not an implication of the Pecking Order hypothesis.

3 The adjusted present value method

FAST FORWARD

The **APV** method suggests that it is possible to calculate an **adjusted** cost of capital for use in project appraisal, as well as indicating how the net present value of a project can be increased or decreased by project financing effects.

- Evaluate the project as if it was all equity financed
- Make adjustments to allow for the effects of the financing method

3.1 NPV and APV

We have seen that a company's gearing level has implications for both the value of its equity shares and its WACC. The viability of an investment project will depend partly on how the investment is financed, and how the method of finance affects gearing.

The net present value method of investment appraisal is to **discount** the **cash flows** of a project at a **cost of capital**. This cost of capital might be the WACC, but it could also be another cost of capital, perhaps one which allows for the risk characteristics of the individual project.

An alternative method of carrying out project appraisal is to use the **adjusted present value (APV) method**.

3.2 Carrying out an APV calculation

The APV method involves two stages.

Step 1 **Evaluate** the **project** first of all as if it was **all equity financed**, and so as if the company were an all equity company to find the 'base case NPV'

Step 2 **Make adjustments** to allow for the effects of the method of financing that has been used

3.3 Example: APV method

A company is considering a project that would cost $100,000 to be financed 50% by equity (cost 21.6%) and 50% by debt (pre-tax cost 12%). The financing method would maintain the company's WACC unchanged. The cash flows from the project would be $36,000 a year in perpetuity, before interest charges. Tax is at 30%.

Appraise the project using firstly the NPV method and secondly the APV method.

Solution

We can use the **NPV method** because the company's WACC will be unchanged.

	Cost	*Weighting*	*Product*
	%		%
Equity	21.6	0.5	10.8
Debt (70% of 12%)	8.4	0.5	4.2
		WACC	15.0

Annual cash flows in perpetuity from the project are as follows.

	$
Before tax	36,000
Less tax (30%)	10,800
After tax	25,200

NPV of project = –\$100,000 + (25,200 ÷ 0.15)
= –\$100,000 + £168,000
= +\$68,000

Note that the tax relief that will be obtained on debt interest is taken account of **in the WACC *not* in the project cash flows.**

Since £100,000 of new investment is being created, the value of the company will increase by £100,000 + \$68,000 = \$168,000, of which 50% must be debt capital.

The company must raise 50% × \$168,000 = \$84,000 of 12% debt capital, and (the balance) \$16,000 of equity. The NPV of the project will raise the value of this equity from \$16,000 to \$84,000 thus leaving the gearing ratio at 50:50.

The **APV approach** to this example is as follows.

(a) First, we need to know the cost of equity in an equivalent ungeared company. The MM formula we can use to establish this is as follows.

Exam formula

Cost of ordinary (equity) share capital in a geared firm (with tax):

$$k_e = k_e^i + (1+T)(k_e^i - k_d)\frac{V_d}{V_e}$$

Remember k_d = the **pre-tax** cost of debt. Using the information from the question:

$$21.6\% = k_e + \left[(k_e - 12\%) \times \frac{50 \times 0.7}{50}\right]$$

$$21.6\% = k_e + 0.70k_e - 8.4\%$$

$$1.70k_e = 30\%$$

$$k_e = 17.647\%$$

(b) Next, we calculate the **NPV of the project as if it were all equity financed.** The cost of equity would be 17.647%

$$NPV = \frac{\$25{,}200}{0.17647} - \$100{,}000 = +£42{,}800$$

(c) Next, we can use an MM formula for the relationship between the value of geared and ungeared companies, to establish **the effect of gearing on the value of the project**. £84,000 will be financed by debt.

V_g (APV) = V_u + (value of debt × corporate tax rate)
= + \$42,800 + (\$84,000 × 0.30)
= + \$42,800 + \$25,200
= \$68,000

The value of debt × corporate tax rate represents the **present value of the tax shield on debt interest,** that is the present value of the savings arising from tax relief on debt interest.

This can be proved as follows.

Annual interest charge = 12% of $84,000 = $10,080

Tax saving (30% × $10,080) = $3,024.00

Cost of debt (pre-tax) = 12%

PV of tax savings in perpetuity = $\frac{\$3,024}{0.12}$ (by coincidence only this equals the project net of tax cash flows)

= $25,200

Exam focus point

> Make sure you use the cost of debt to discount the tax relief on interest costs and not the cost of equity.

3.4 Example: APV method and limited cash flows

Suppose in the above example the cash flows only lasted for five years, and tax was payable one year in arrears. Calculate the present value of the tax shield.

Solution

The tax saving will now only last for years 2 to 6. (Remember interest will be paid in years 1 to 5, but the tax benefits will be felt a year in arrears).

PV of tax savings = 3,024 × Annuity factor years 2 to 6
= 3,024 × (Annuity factors years 1 to 6 – Annuity factor year 1)
= 3,024 × (4.111 – 0.893)
= $9,731

The APV and NPV approaches produce the same conclusion.

3.5 APV and changes in gearing

However, the APV method can also be adapted to allow for financing which **changes the gearing structure** and the WACC.

In this respect, it is superior to the NPV method. Suppose, for example, that in the previous example, the **entire project were to be financed by debt**. The APV of the project would be calculated as follows.

(a) The NPV of project if all equity financed is:

$$\frac{\$25,200}{0.17647} - \$100,000 = +\$42,800 \text{ (as before)}$$

(b) The adjustment to allow for the method of financing is the present value of the tax relief on debt interest in perpetuity.

$DT_c = \$100,000 \times 0.30 = \$30,000$

(c) APV = $42,800 + $30,000 = +$72,800

The project would increase the value of equity by $72,800.

Question **APV**

A project costing $100,000 is to be financed by $60,000 of irredeemable 12% loan stock and $40,000 of new equity. The project will yield an after-tax annual cash flow of $21,000 in perpetuity. If it were all equity financed, an appropriate cost of capital would be 15%. The tax rate is 30%. What is the project's APV?

Answer

	$
NPV if all equity financed: $21,000/0.15 – $100,000	40,000
PV of the tax shield: $60,000 × 12% × 30%/0.12	18,000
APV	58,000

3.6 Discounting tax relief at the risk-free rate

Often in exams you will be given the risk-free rate of return. As tax relief is allowed by the government and is almost certain, there is an argument for saying that **all tax relief** should be discounted at the **risk-free rate**. However there is the opposing argument that the **risk of the tax relief** is the same as the **risk of the debt** to which it relates, and therefore the tax relief should be discounted at the cost of debt. The risk-free rate would also not be used if the company was unlikely to be in a taxpaying position for some years.

In the exam we suggest that you make clear the reasons for choosing the discount rate that you have chosen to discount the tax relief, and add a comment that an alternative rate might be used.

3.7 Other elements in APV calculation

The tax shield may not be the only complication introduced into APV calculations.

3.7.1 Issue costs

The costs of issuing the finance needed for the project may also be brought into APV calculations.

3.7.2 Example: issue costs

Edted is about to start a project with an initial investment of $20 million, which will generate cash flow over four years. The project will be financed with a $10 million 10 year bank loan and a rights issue. Issue costs are 5% of the amount raised.

Calculate the issue costs that will be used in the APV calculation.

Solution

Issue costs will not equal 5% of $10 million ($20 million – $10 million). The $10 million will be the figure left after the issue costs have been paid. Therefore $10 million must be 95%, not 100% of the amount raised, and the

$$\text{Issue costs} = \frac{5}{95} \times \$10 \text{ million} = \$526{,}316$$

In the above example, the issue costs do not need to be discounted as they are assumed to be paid at time 0. The complication comes if issue costs are allowable for tax purposes.

3.7.3 Example: the tax implications of issue costs

Assume in the example above that issue costs are allowable for tax purposes, the tax is assumed to be 30% payable one year in arrears and the risk-free rate of return is assumed to be 8%.

Calculate the tax effect of the issuing costs to be included in the APV calculation.

Solution

$$\begin{aligned}\text{Tax effect} &= \text{Tax rate} \times \text{Issue costs} \times \text{Discount rate}\\ &= 0.3 \times 526{,}316 \times 0.926\\ &= \$146{,}211\end{aligned}$$

3.7.4 Spare debt capacity

Projects may yield other incremental benefits, for example increased borrowing or debt capacity. These benefits should be included in the APV calculations, even if the debt capacity is utilised elsewhere.

3.7.5 Example: spare debt capacity

Continuing with the Edted example, suppose the project increased the borrowing capacity of the company by $6 million, at the risk-free rate of return of 8%. Calculate the effect on the APV calculation.

Solution

Remember that we are concerned with the incremental benefit which is the **tax shield effect** of the increased debt finance.

$$\text{Present value of tax shield effect} = \text{Increased debt capacity} \times \text{Interest rate} \times \text{Tax rate} \times \text{Discount factor Years 2 to 5}$$

$$= \$6 \text{ million} \times 8\% \times 30\% \times 3.067$$

$$= \$441{,}648$$

3.7.6 Subsidy

You may face a situation where a company can obtain finance at a lower interest rate than its normal cost of borrowing. In this situation you have to include in the APV calculation the tax shield effect of the cheaper finance and the effect of the saving in interest.

3.7.7 Example: subsidy

Gordonbear is about to start a project requiring $6 million of initial investment. The company normally borrows at 12% but a government loan will be available to finance all of the project at 10%. The risk-free rate of interest is 6%.

Tax is payable at 30% one year in arrears. The project is scheduled to last for four years.

Calculate the effect on the APV calculation if Gordonbear finances the project by means of the government loan.

Solution

(a) The tax shield is as follows.

We assume that the loan is for the duration of the project (four years) only.

Annual interest = $6 million × 10%
= $600,000

Tax relief = $600,000 × 0.3
= $180,000

This needs to be discounted over years 2 to 5 (remember the one year time lag). We do not however use the 10% to discount the loan and the tax effect; instead we assume that the government loan is risk-free and the tax effect is also risk-free. Hence we use the 6% factor in discounting.

NPV tax relief = $180,000 × Discount factor Years 2 to 5
= $180,000 × 3.269
= $588,420

(b) We also need to take into account the benefits of **being able** to pay a **lower interest rate**.

Benefits = $6 million × (12% – 10%) × 6% Discount factor Years 1 to 4
= $6 million × 2% × 3.465
= $415,800

(c) Total effect = $588,420 + $415,800 = $1,004,220.

3.8 The advantages and disadvantages of the APV method

The main advantages of the APV are as follows.

(a) APV can be used to **evaluate** all the **effects of financing** a product including:

  (i) Tax shield
  (ii) Changing capital structure
  (iii) Any other relevant cost

(b) When using APV you do not have to adjust the WACC using assumptions of perpetual risk-free debt.

The main difficulties with the APV technique are:

(a) **Establishing** a **suitable cost of equity**, for the initial DCF computation as if the project were all-equity financed, and also establishing the all-equity β

(b) **Identifying all the costs** associated with the method of financing

(c) **Choosing the correct discount rates** used to discount the costs

Exam focus point

Always be prepared to discuss the limitations of a technique.

Chapter Roundup

- The MM theory predicts that the financial structure has no impact on the cost of capital and therefore the way a project is financed has no impact on the value of the project.
- Static trade-off theory states that firms in a static position will seek to achieve a target level of gearing by adjusting their current gearing levels.
- Pecking order theory is based on the idea that shareholders have less information about the firm than directors do.

  Shareholders and other investors will use directors' actions as signals to indicate what directors believe about the firm, given their superior information.
- The **APV** method suggests that it is possible to calculate an **adjusted** cost of capital for use in project appraisal, as well as indicating how the net present value of a project can be increased or decreased by project financing effects.
  - Evaluate the project as if it was all equity financed
  - Make adjustments to allow for the effects of the financing method

Quick Quiz

1 Using the beta values for the following companies calculate the cost of equity if the market risk premium is 4% and the return on a risk-free investment is 5 percent.

Company	*Beta*
Boeing	0.73
Hewlett-Packard	1.76
Intel	2.06

Answers to Quick Quiz

1 **Boeing**

r = 0.04 + 0.73 × 0.05 = 0.0765 or 7.65%

Hewlett-Packard

r = 0.04 + 1.76 × 0.05 = 0.128 or 12.8%

Intel

r = 0.04 + 2.06 × 0.05 = 0.143 or 14.3%

Now try the questions below from the Exam Question Bank

Number	Level	Marks	Time
8	Introductory	15	27 mins
9	Introductory	15	27 mins

Application of option pricing theory in investment decisions

Topic list	Syllabus reference
1 Overview	B (3)
2 Basic concepts	B (3) (a)
3 Determinants of option values	B (3) (a)
4 Real options	B (3) (b)
5 Valuation of real options	B (3) (c)

Introduction

In this chapter we look at how option valuation techniques can be applied to capital budgeting. First we review the basic theory underlying the pricing of financial options and then we examine a number of options embedded in projects, such as the option to delay, the option to abandon, the option to expand and the option to redeploy productive resources.

Study guide

		Intellectual level
B3	**Application of option pricing theory in investment decisions**	
(a)	Demonstrate an understanding of option pricing theory:	2
	(iii) Determine, using published data, the five principal drivers of option value (value of the underlying, exercise price, time to expiry, volatility and the risk free rate).	
	(iv) Discuss the underlying assumptions, structure, application and limitations of the Black-Scholes model	
(b)	Evaluate embedded real options within a project, classifying them into one of the real option archetypes	3
(c)	Assess and advise on the value of options to delay, expand, redeploy and withdraw using the Black-Scholes model	3

1 Overview

The topic of real options applies the option valuation techniques to capital budgeting exercises in which a project is coupled with a put or call option. For example, the firm may have the option to abandon a project during its life. This amounts to a put option on the remaining cash flows associated with the project. Ignoring the value of these real options (as in standard discounted cash flow techniques) can lead to incorrect investment evaluation decisions.

2 Basic concepts

FAST FORWARD

Options are contracts that give to one party the right to enter into a transaction but not the obligation to do so.

2.1 Types of options

2.1.1 Definition

An option is a contract that gives one party the option to enter into a transaction either at a specific time in the future or within a specific future period at a price that is agreed when the contract is issued.

2.1.2 Exercise price

The exercise or strike price is the price at which the future transaction will take place

2.1.3 Premium

Premium is the price paid by the option buyer to the seller, or writer, for the right to buy or sell the underlying shares.

2.1.4 Call and put options

The buyer of a call option acquires the right, but not the obligation, to buy the underlying at a fixed price. The buyer of a put option acquires the right, but not the obligation, to sell the underlying shares at a fixed price.

2.1.5 European, American and Bermudan options

A European option can only be exercised at expiration, whereas an American option can be exercised any time prior to expiration. A Bermudan option is an option where early exercise is restricted to certain dates during the life of the option. It derives its name from the fact that its exercise characteristics are somewhere between those of the American and the European style of options and the island of Bermuda lies between America and Europe.

2.1.6 Long and short positions

When an investor buys an option the investor is long, and when the investor sells an option the investor has a short position.

2.1.7 Price quotations

It should be noted that, for simplicity, only one price is quoted for each option in the national newspapers. In practice, there will always be two prices quoted for each option, ie a bid and an offer price. For example, the January option could be quoted as. This can be interpreted to mean that it would cost an investor to buy those options and that he would receive for selling it.

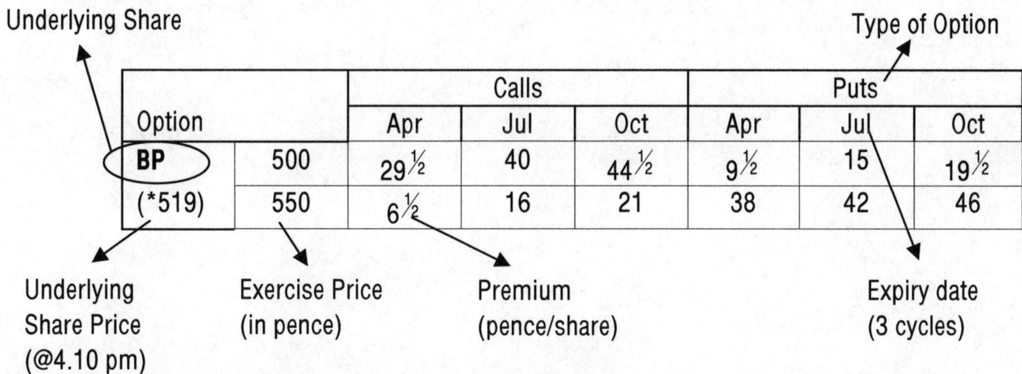

Option		Calls			Puts		
		Apr	Jul	Oct	Apr	Jul	Oct
BP	500	29½	40	44½	9½	15	19½
(*519)	550	6½	16	21	38	42	46

2.2 Profiles of call options at expiration

FAST FORWARD

A long call option position at expiration may lead to unlimited profits, and a short option position may lead to unlimited losses.

2.2.1 Long Call

A call option will be exercised at expiration only if the price of the underlying is higher than the exercise price. Otherwise the option will not be exercised. The value of a call option at expiration is the higher of

The difference between the value of the underlying security at expiration and the exercise price (if the value of the underlying security > exercise price)

Or

Zero, if value of the underlying security is equal to or less than the exercise price.

Since the buyer of a call option has paid a premium to buy the option, the profit from the purchase of the call option is the value of the option minus the premium paid. ie

Profit = value of call option – premium paid for the purchase of the option

Question — **Call option profile at expiration**

Suppose that you buy the October call option with an exercise price of 550. The premium is 21 cents. Calculate the potential profit/loss at expiration.

Answer

The profit loss/loss will be calculated for possible values of the underlying at expiration. Here we examine the profit/loss profile for prices ranging from 500 to 600.

Value of underlying at expiration	*Value of underlying – exercise price*	*Value of option*	*Profit/loss*
500	–50	0	–21
530	–20	0	–21
540	–10	0	–21
550	0	0	–21
560	10	10	–11
570	20	20	–1
600	50	50	29

The profit or loss at expiration is shown below:

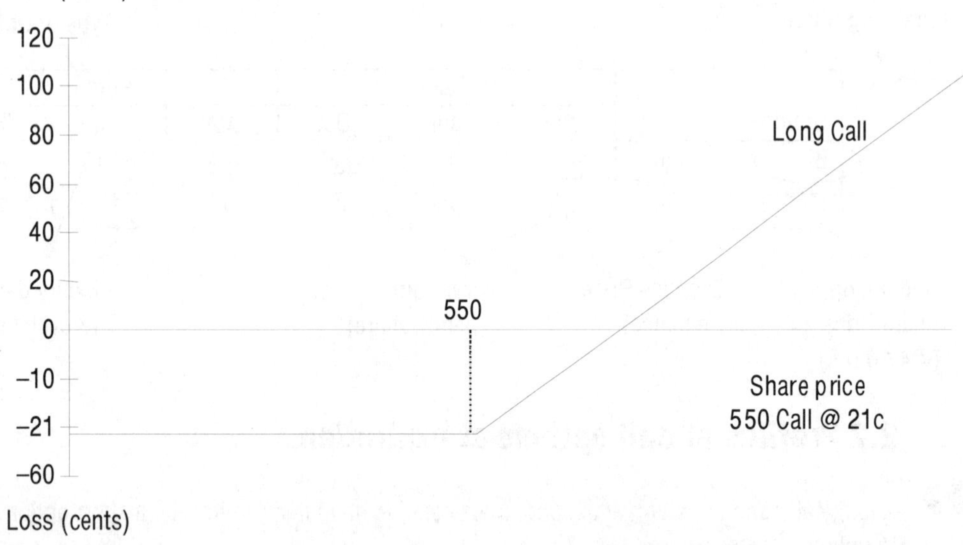

2.2.2 Short Call

The seller of a call loses money when the option is exercised and gains the premium if the option is not exercised. The value of the call option for a seller is exactly the opposite of the value of the call option for the buyer. The value of the short call at expiration is the negative of the long position. That is, the negative of

The greater of the difference between the value of the underlying and the exercise price

And

Zero.

The profit of the short position at expiration is:

Profit = premium received – value of call option

A short call option has a maximum profit, which is the premium, but unlimited losses.

Question

Call option profile at expiration

Suppose that you sell the October call option with an exercise price of 550. The premium is 21c. Calculate the potential profit/loss at expiration for the writer of the option

Answer

Column A *Value of the underlying at expiration*	*Column B* *Value of the underlying at expiration – exercise price*	*Column C* *– Maximum of zero and the difference between the value of the underlying and the exercise price*	*Negative Column C + premium*
500	–50	0	21
530	–20	0	21
540	–10	0	21
550	0	0	21
560	10	–10	11
570	20	–20	–1
600	50	–50	–29

The profit or loss at expiration is shown below:

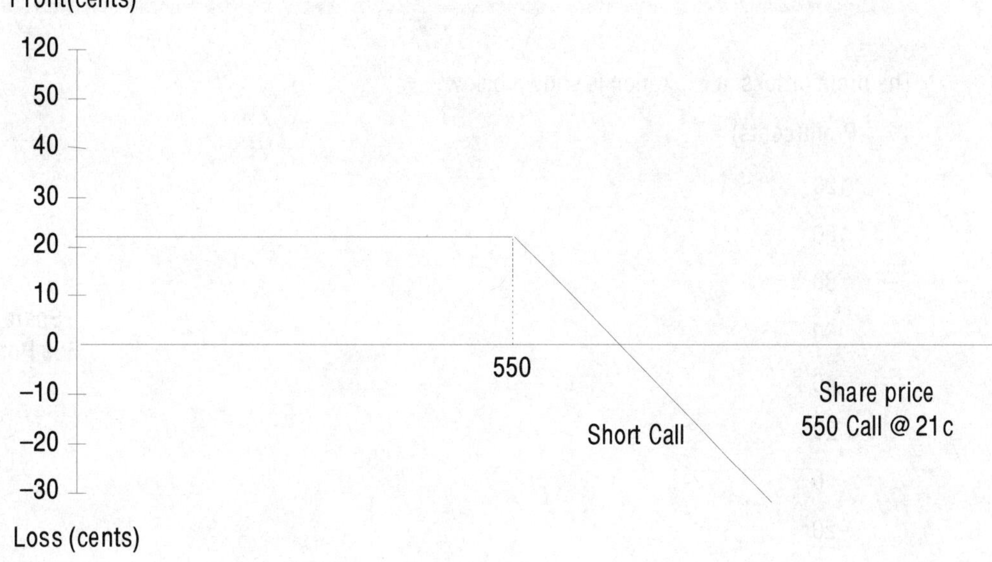

2.3 Profiles of put options at expiration

FAST FORWARD

The maximum profit from a long put position and the maximum loss from a short put position occurs when the price of the underlying becomes zero.

2.3.1 Long Put

A put will be exercised at expiration only if the price of the underlying asset is lower than the exercise price of the option. The **value** of the option when exercised is the **difference** between the **exercise price** and the **value of the underlying**.

The **profit** from a long position is the **difference** between the **value of the option** at expiration and the **premium paid**.

As in the case of the long call option, the buyer of the option has limited losses, that is the premium if the option is not exercised, but unlike the long call which has unlimited upside, the maximum value of the put option is X, which is attained when the price of the underlying is zero.

Question

Long put at expiration

Suppose that you buy the October put option with an exercise price of 550. The premium is 46c. Calculate the potential profit/loss at expiration.

Answer

Column A *Value of underlying at expiration*	*Column B* *Exercise price – value of underlying*	*Column C* *Maximum of Column B and zero*	*Column C – premium*
500	50	50	4
530	20	20	–26
540	–0	10	–36
550	0	0	–46
560	–10	0	–46
570	–20	0	–46
600	–50	0	–46

The profit or loss at expiration is shown below

Profit(cents)

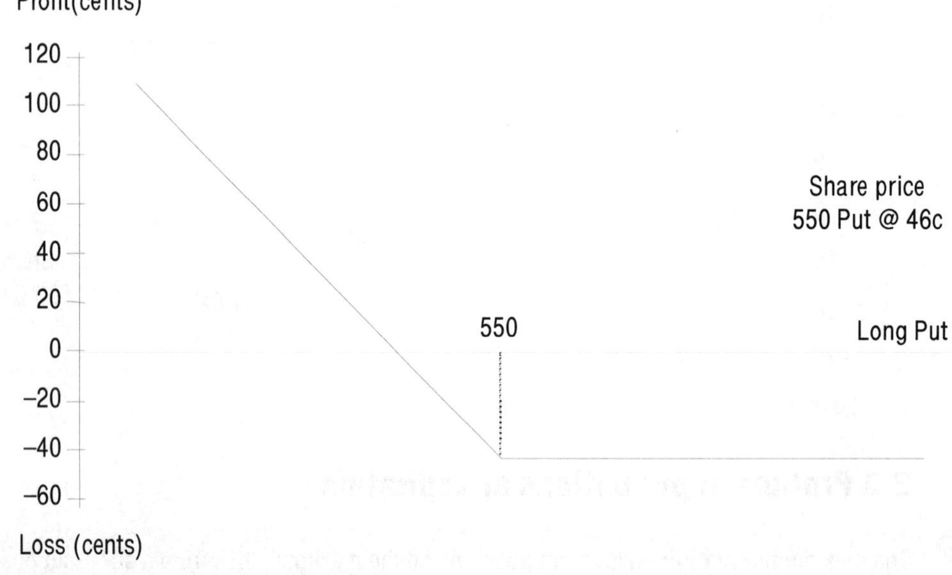

2.3.2 Short Put

Value of put option at expiration is the maximum of

The difference between the exercise price and the value of the underlying at expiration

And

Zero

Profit = Premium received – value of put option

The **maximum profit** for the writer of a put option is the **premium paid** which occurs when the put option is **not exercised** (that is, when the value at expiration = 0). This happens when the value of the underlying at expiration **is greater than** the exercise price.

The profit will be **zero** when the value of the underlying at expiration is **equal to** the sum of the exercise price and the premium paid.

The **highest loss** occurs when the value of the underlying = 0. The maximum loss will be equal to the **exercise price**.

Question — Short put at expiration

Suppose that you buy the October call option with an exercise price of 550. The premium is 46c. Calculate the potential profit/loss at expiration.

Answer

Column A *Value of underlying at expiration*	*Column B* *Exercise price – value of underlying*	*Column C* *(Maximum of column B and zero)*	*Column C + premium*
500	50	–50	–4
530	20	–20	26
540	–0	–10	36
550	0	0	46
560	–10	0	46
570	–20	0	46
600	–50	0	46

The profit or loss at expiration is shown below

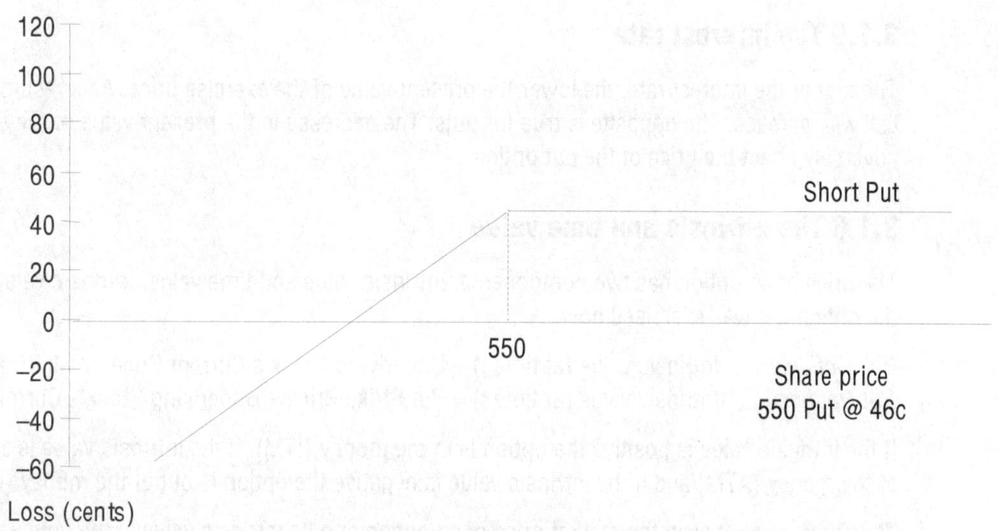

3 Determinants of option values

FAST FORWARD

> The value of an option is determined by the exercise price, the price of the underlying, the time to expiration, the volatility of the underlying and the interest rate.

3.1 Introduction

Options are financial instruments whose value changes all the time. The value of a call or a put option at expiration was derived earlier. In this section we shall identify the factors that affect the price of an option prior to expiration.

3.1.1 The exercise price

The higher the exercise price, the lower the probability that a call will be exercised. So call prices will decrease as the exercise prices increase. For the put, the effect runs in the opposite direction. A higher exercise price means that there is higher probability that the put will be exercised. So the put price increases as the exercise price increases.

3.1.2 The price of the underlying

As the current stock price goes up, the higher the probability that the call will be in the money. As a result, the call price will increase. The effect will be in the opposite direction for a put. As the stock price goes up, there is a lower probability that the put will be in the money. So the put price will decrease.

3.1.3 The volatility of the underlying

Both the call and put will increase in price as the underlying asset becomes more volatile. The buyer of the option receives full benefit of favourable outcomes but avoids the unfavourable ones (option price value has zero value).

3.1.4 The time to expiration

Both calls and puts will benefit from increased time to expiration. The reason is that there is more time for a big move in the stock price. But there are some effects that work in the opposite direction. As the time to expiration increase, the present value of the exercise price decreases. This will increase the value of the call and decrease the value of the put. Also, as the time to expiration increase, there is a greater amount of time for the stock price to be reduced by a cash dividend. This reduces the call value but increases the put value.

3.1.5 The interest rate

The higher the interest rate, the lower the present value of the exercise price. As a result, the value of the call will increase. The opposite is true for puts. The decrease in the present value of the exercise price will adversely affect the price of the put option.

3.1.6 The intrinsic and time value

The price of an option has two components; Intrinsic value and time value. Intrinsic value is the value of the option if it was exercised now.

Call Options: Intrinsic value (at time t) = Underlying Stock's Current Price – Call Strike Price
Put Options: Intrinsic value (at time t) = Put Strike Price – Underlying Stock's Current Price

If the intrinsic value is positive the option is in the money (ITM). If the intrinsic value is zero, the option is at the money (ATM) and if the intrinsic value is negative the option is out of the money (OTM)

The difference between the market price of an option and its intrinsic value is the time value of the option. Buyers of ATM or OTM options are simply buying time value, which decreases as an option approaches expiration. The more time an option has until expiration, the greater the option's chance of ending up in-the-money and the larger its time value. On the expiration day the time value of an option is zero and all an option is worth is its intrinsic value. It's either in-the-money, or it isn't.

3.2 The Black Scholes pricing model

FAST FORWARD The Black Scholes model predicts the value of an option for given values of its determinants.

The payoffs at expiration for a call option were derived earlier as

The difference between the value of the underlying at expiration and the exercise price (where value of underlying > exercise price)

Or

Zero (where value of underlying ≤ exercise price)

The expected value of the payoff will depend on the probability that the option will be on the money, which we do not know. The value of the call option today will be the present value of the expected payoff at expiration. Apart from the probability to be in the money we also need to specify a discount factor, which will reflect the risk of the option. The problem of option valuation concerned financial specialists for a long time until Black, Scholes and Merton resolved the problem.

3.2.1 Assumptions of the Black-Scholes Model

- There are perfect markets with no taxes, no transactions costs, perfect security divisibility, and no restrictions on short selling.
- Interest rates are constant over the option's life
- The stock pays no intervening dividends or interest over the option's life
- The distribution of possible asset prices at the end of any finite interval is lognormal, implying the percentage price changes over the interval are normally distributed with constant variance

3.2.2 The Black Scholes Formula

The Black Scholes formula for the value of a European call option is given by:

Exam formula

$$C = P_a N(d_1) - P_e N(d_2)e^{-rt}$$

where P_a is the current price of the underlying asset

P_e is the exercise price

r is the continuously compounded risk-free rate

t is the time to expiration measured as a fraction of one year , for example t =0.5 means that the time to expiration is six months.

e is the base of the natural logarithms

Exam formula

$$d_1 = \frac{\ln\left(\frac{P_a}{P_e}\right) + (r + 0.5s^2)t}{s\sqrt{t}}$$

$$d_2 = d_1 - s\sqrt{t}$$

where s is the standard deviation of S

$\ln\left(\frac{P_a}{P_e}\right)$ is the natural logarithm of the spot price over the exercise price

N(z) is the cumulative probability distribution function for a standardised normal variable (ie it is the probability that such a variable will be less than z).

3.2.3 Value of European put options

The value of a European put can be calculated in a similar way to a European call. The result is

$$C_0 = P_e N(-d_2)e^{-rt} - P_a N(-d_1)$$

3.2.4 Value of American call options

Although American options can be exercised any time during their lifetime it is never optimal to exercise an option earlier. The value of an American option will therefore be the same as the value of an equivalent European option and the Black-Scholes model can be used to calculate its price.

3.2.5 Value of American put options

Unfortunately, no exact analytic formula for the value of an American put option on a non-dividend-paying stock has been produced. Numerical procedures and analytic approximations for calculating American put values are used instead.

Question — **Black Scholes calculation**

Consider the situation where the stock price 6 months from the expiration of an option is \$42, the exercise price of the option is \$40, the risk-free interest rate is 10% p.a. and the volatility is 20% p.a. This means $P_a = 42$, $P_x = 40$, r = 0.1s = 0.2, t = 0.5.

Answer

$$d_1 = \frac{\ln(42/40) + (0.1 + \frac{0.2^2}{2})0.5}{0.2\sqrt{0.5}} = 0.7693 = 0.77$$

$$d_2 = 0.7693 - 0.2 \times \sqrt{0.5} = 0.6279 = 0.63$$

and

$$P_e^{-rT} = 40e^{-0.1 \times 0.5} = 40e^{-0.05} = 38.049$$

The values of the standard normal cumulative probability distribution can be found from the tables and are:

N(0.77) = 0.7794
N(–0.77) = 1 – N(0.77) = 1 – 0.7794 = 0.2206
N(0.63 = 0.7357
N(–0.63) = 1 – N(0.63) = 1 – 0.7357 = 0.2643

Hence if the option is a European call, its value, is given by:

c = 42N(0.7693) – 38.049N (0.6279) = 4.76

If the option is a European put, its value is given by:

P = 38.049N(–0.6279) – 42N(0.7693) = 0.81

The stock price has to rise by \$2.76 for the purchaser of the call to break even. Similarly, the stock price has to fall by \$2.81 for the purchaser of the put to break even.

4 Real options

FAST FORWARD Real options give the right to the management of a company to make decisions when it is profitable for the company.

In many project evaluation situations, the firm has one or more options to make strategic changes to the project during its life. For example, a natural resource company may decide to suspend extraction of copper at its mine if the price of copper falls below the extraction cost. Conversely, a company with the right to mine in a particular area may decide to begin operations if the price rises above the cost of extraction. These strategic options, which are known as real options, are typically ignored in standard discounted cash flow (DCF) analysis where a single expected present value is computed. These real options, however, can significantly increase the value of a project by eliminating unfavourable outcomes.

In this section we describe the various options embedded in projects and provide stylized examples. In the following section we illustrate how to estimate the value of real options using the Black Scholes method.

4.1 Option to delay

Exam focus point

> A 20 mark optional question in the December 2007 paper focused on the valuation of an option to delay.

When a firm has exclusive rights to a project or product for a specific period, it can delay taking this project or product until a later date. A traditional investment analysis just answers the question of whether the project is a "good" one if taken today. Thus, the fact that a project is not selected today either because its NPV is negative, or its IRR is less than its cost of capital, does not mean that the rights to this project are not valuable.

Consider a situation where a company considers paying an amount C to acquire a license to mine copper. The company needs to invest an extra amount I in order to start operations. The company has three years over which to develop the mine, otherwise it will lose the license. Suppose that today copper prices are low and the NPV from developing the mine is negative. The company may decide not to start the operation today, but it has the option to start any time over the next three years provided that the NPV is positive. Thus the company has paid a premium C to acquire an American option on the present value of the cash flows from operation, with an exercise price equal to the additional investment (I.) The value of the option to delay is therefore:

NPV = PV – I if PV >I
NPV = 0 otherwise

The payoff of the option to delay is shown below and it is the same as the payoff of a call option, the only difference being that the underlying is the present value (that is in this case S = PV) and the exercise price is the additional investment (X = I)

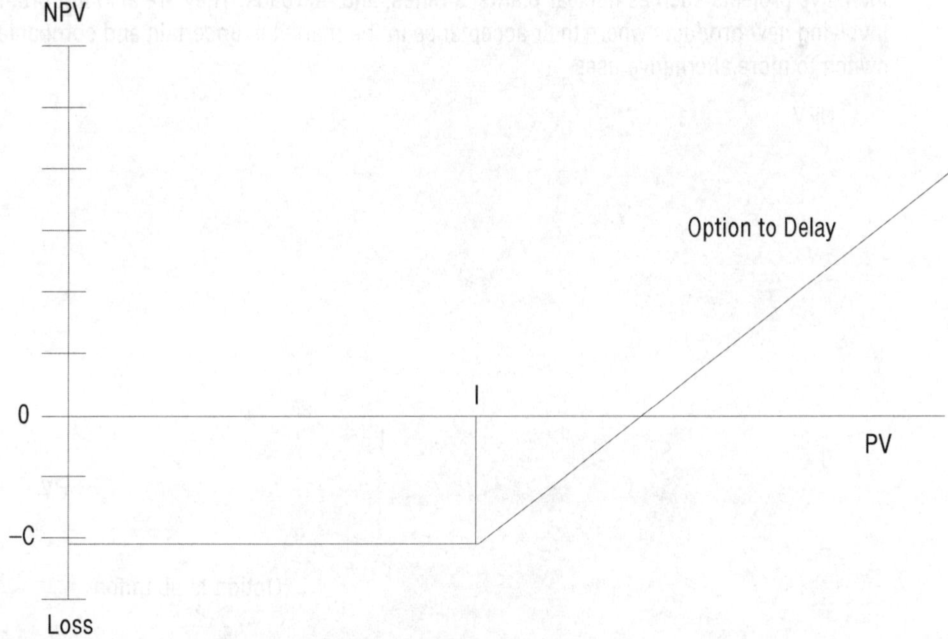

4.2 Option to expand

The option to expand exists when firms invest in projects which allow them to make further investments in the future or to enter new markets. The initial project may be found in terms of its NPV as not worth undertaking. However when the option to expand is taken into account, the NPV may become positive and the project worthwhile. The initial investment may be seen as the premium required to acquire the option to expand.

Expansion will normally require an additional investment, call it I. The extra investment will be undertaken only if the present value from the expansion will be higher than the additional investment, ie when PV > I. If PV ≤ I, the expansion will not take place. Thus the option to expand is again a call option of the present value of the firm with an exercise equal to the value of the additional investment.

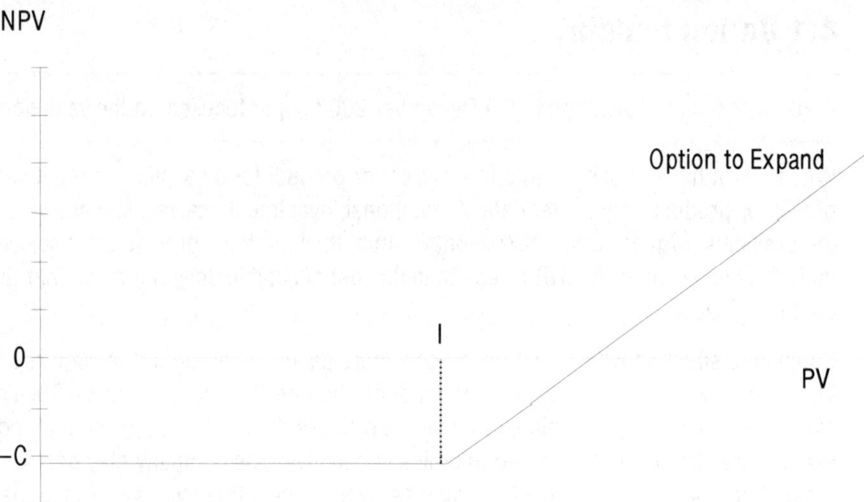

4.3 Option to abandon

Whereas traditional capital budgeting analysis assumes that a project will operate in each year of its lifetime, the firm may have the option to cease a project during its life. This option is known as an abandonment option. Abandonment options, which are the right to sell the cash flows over the remainder of the project's life for some salvage value, are like American put options. When the present value of the remaining cash flows (PV) falls below the liquidation value (L) , the asset may be sold. Abandonment is effectively the exercising of a put option. These options are particularly important for large capital intensive projects such as nuclear plants, airlines, and railroads. They are also important for projects involving new products where their acceptance in the market is uncertain and companies would like to switch to more alternative uses.

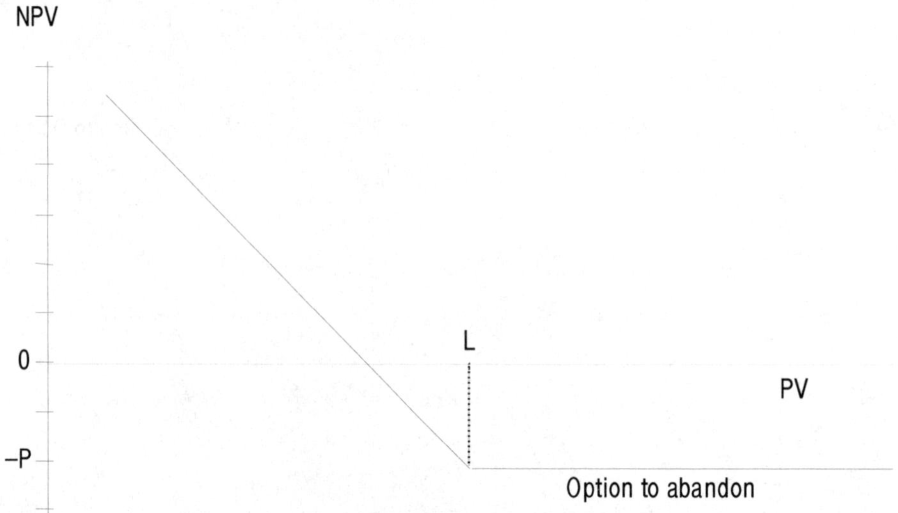

4.4 Option to redeploy

The option to redeploy exists when the company can use its productive assets for activities other than the original one. The switch from one activity to another will happen if the PV of cash flows from the new activity will exceed the costs of switching. The option to abandon is a special case of an option to redeploy.

These options are particularly important in agricultural settings. For example, a beef producer will value the option to switch between various feed sources, preferring to use the cheapest acceptable alternative.

These options are also valuable in the utility industry. An electric utility, for example, may have the option to switch between various fuel sources to produce electricity. In particular, consider an electric utility that has the choice of building a coal-fired plant or a plant that burns either coal or gas.

Naïve implementation of discounted cash flow analysis might suggest that the coal-fired plant be constructed since it is considerably cheaper. Whereas the dual plant costs more, it provides greater flexibility. Management has the ability to select which fuel to use and can switch back and forth depending on energy conditions and the relative prices of coal and gas. The value of this operating option should be taken into account.

5 Valuation of real options

FAST FORWARD

Real options can be valued using the Black-Scholes model, but certain adjustments need to be made since the underlying is not traded.

Exam focus point

Part of a 20 mark optional question in December 2007 asked students to discuss the limitations of the Black-Scholes model in valuing a real option.

5.1 Black-Scholes option analysis

Since American call options can be valued using the Black Scholes model, one could use in principle the Black Scholes model to estimate the value of the real options we have identified in the previous section. However there are certain differences between the application of the Black-Scholes model to financial options and real options. The main practical problem is the estimation of volatility. As the underlying asset is not traded, it is very difficult to established the volatility of the value. The main method to overcome this problem is to use simulation methods to estimate the volatility. Since the option to expand is a call option its value will be given by:

$c = P_a N(d_1) - P_e N(d_2)e^{-rt}$

In this case

P_a is the value of the project

P_e is the additional investment involved in expansion

$$d_1 = \frac{\ln(P_a/P_e) + (r + 0.5s^2)t}{s\sqrt{t}}$$

$d_2 = d_1 - s\sqrt{t}$

Similarly the option to abandon is a put option and its value is given by:

Put option = $P_e N(-d_2)\, e^{-rt} - P_a N(-d_1)$

Question — **Valuation of option to abandon**

Assume that Four Seasons International is considering taking a 20-year project which requires an initial investment of \$ 250 million in an real estate partnership to develop time share properties with a Spanish real estate developer, and where the present value of expected cash flows is \$ 254 million. While the net present value of \$ 4 million is small, assume that Four Seasons International has the option to abandon this project anytime by selling its share back to the developer in the next 5 years for \$ 150 million. A simulation of the cash flows on this time share investment yields a variance in the present value of the cash flows from being in the partnership of 0.09.

Answer

The value of the abandonment option can be estimated by determining the value of the put option using the Black-Scholes formula.

$C_0 = P_e\,N(-d_a)e^{-rt} - P_a\,N(-d_1)$

Where Value of the underlying asset (P_a) = PV of cash flows from Project = $ 254 million

Strike Price (P_e) = Salvage value from abandonment = $ 150 million

Variance in underlying asset's value = 0.09

Time to expiration = Life of the Project = 5 years

Assume that the five-year risk-free rate is 7%.

$$d_1 = \frac{\ln\left(\frac{P_a}{P_e}\right) + \left(r + 0.55^2\right)t}{s\sqrt{t}}$$

$d_2 = d_1 - s\sqrt{t}$

Furthermore we have:

$N(1.64) = 0.9495$, $N(-d_1) = 1 - N(d_1) = 0.050$

$N(-d_1) = 0.050$ and $N(-d_2) = 0.166$

The value of the put option can be estimated as follows:

$P = 150e^{-0.07 \times 5} \times 0.166 - 254 \times 0.050 = 4.743$

Put Value= $ 4.743 million

The value of this abandonment option has to be added on to the net present value of the project of $ 4 million, yielding a total net present value with the abandonment option of $ 8.743 million.

Chapter Roundup

- Options are contracts that give to one party the right to enter into a transaction but not the obligation to do so.
- A long call option position at expiration may lead to unlimited profits, and a short option position may lead to unlimited losses.
- The maximum profit from a long put position and the maximum loss from a short put position occurs when the price of the underlying becomes zero.
- The value of an option is determined by an exercise price, the price of the underlying, the time to expiration, the volatility of the underlying and the interest rate.
- The Black Scholes model predicts the value of an option for given values of its determinants.
- Real options give the right to the management of a company to make decisions when it is profitable for the company.
- Real options can be valued using the Black Scholes model, but certain adjustments need to be made since the underlying is not traded.

Quick Quiz

1. A call option with an exercise price of $60 is bought for $3. On expiry day the underlying is $61. Should the call option be exercised?
2. You have bought a put option, which expires in 3 months. The day after you bought the put option, the volatility of the underlying asset increased. What would happen to the value of the put options?
3. You have bought an out-of-the-money call option, with an exercise price of $40. The option cost $2 and it expires in 6 months. What would you expect the value of the call option to be in 5 months if the price and volatility of the underlying remain unchanged?

Answers to Quick Quiz

1 The option should be exercise since the price of the underlying is higher than the exercise price. The value of the option at expiration is \$61 – \$60 = \$1.

The overall result is a loss of \$2 since the option was bought for \$3.

2 The value of the put option will increase as the volatility increases, because it makes it more likely for the price of the underlying to fall below the exercise price.

3 As an option nears its expiration date its time value goes down. The value of the out-of-the-money option one month before expiration will be lower than the price 6 months before expiration since there is less time for the price of the underlying to exceed the exercise price.

Now try the questions below from the Exam Question Bank

Number	Level	Marks	Time
10	Examination	30	54 mins

International investment and financing decisions

9

Topic list	Syllabus reference
1 Overview	B (4)
2 Effects of exchange rate assumptions on project values	B (4) (a)
3 Forecasting cash flows from overseas projects	B (4) (b)
4 The impact of exchange controls	B (4) (c)
5 Translation, transaction and economic risks	B (4) (d)
6 Costs and benefits of alternative sources of finance for MNCs	B (4) (e)

Introduction

In this chapter we look at the international dimension of project appraisal.

Companies that undertake overseas projects are exposed to exchange rate risks as well as other risks such as exchange control, taxation and political risks.

In this chapter we look at capital budgeting techniques for multinational companies that incorporate these additional complexities in the decision-making process.

Study guide

		Intellectual level
B4	**International investment and financing decisions**	
(a)	Assess the impact upon the value of a project of alternative exchange rate assumptions	3
(b)	Forecast project or firm free cash flows in any specific currency and determine the project's net present value or firm value under differing exchange rate, fiscal and transaction cost assumptions	2
(c)	Evaluate the significance of exchange controls for a given investment decision and strategies for dealing with restricted remittance	3
(d)	Access the impact of a project upon a firm's exposure to translation, transaction and economic risk	3
(e)	Assess and advise upon the costs and benefits of alternative sources of finance available within the international financial markets	3

1 Overview

Many of the projects that companies are appraising may have an international dimension. For example, the assumption can be made that part of the production from a project may be exported. In appraising a tourist development, a company may be making assumptions about the number of tourists from abroad who may be visiting. Imported goods and materials could be a factor in the determination of cash flows. All these examples show that exchange rates will have an influence on the cash flows of the company.

Companies that undertake overseas projects are exposed, in addition to exchange rate risks, to other types of risk such as exchange control, taxation or political risks. The latter is particularly true in countries with undemocratic regimes that may be subject to changes in a rather disorderly fashion.

Capital budgeting techniques for multinational companies therefore need to incorporate these additional complexities in the decision making process. These can be based on similar concepts to those used in the purely domestic case which we have examined. Special considerations, examples of which were given above, may apply.

2 Effects of exchange rate assumptions on project values

FAST FORWARD

Changes in exchange rates are as important as the underlying profitability in selecting an overseas project.

In a domestic project the NPV is the sum of the discounted cash flows plus the terminal value (discounted at the WACC) less the initial investment.

When a project in a foreign country is assessed we must take into account some specific considerations such as local taxes, double taxation agreements, and political risk that affect the present value of the project. The main consideration of course in an international project is the exchange rate risk, that is the risk that arises from the fact that the cash flows are denominated in a foreign currency. An appraisal of an international project requires estimates of the exchange rate. In the rest of this section we discuss some fundamental relationships that help the financial manager form views about exchange rates.

2.1 Purchasing power parity

Purchasing power parity theory states that the exchange rate between two currencies is the same in equilibrium when the purchasing power of currency is the same in each country.

Purchasing power parity theory predicts that the exchange value of foreign currency depends on the relative purchasing power of each currency in its own country and that **spot exchange rates will vary over time according to relative price changes.**

Formally, purchasing power parity can be expressed in the following formula.

Exam formula

$$S_1 = S_0 \times \frac{(1+h_c)}{(1+h_b)}$$

Where S_1 = expected spot rate
S_0 = current spot rate
h_c = expected inflation rate in country c
h_b = expected inflation rate in country b

Note that the expected future spot rate will not necessarily coincide with the 'forward exchange rate' currently quoted.

2.1.1 Example: Purchasing power parity

The spot exchange rate between UK sterling and the Danish kroner is £1 = 8.00 kroners. Assuming that there is now purchasing parity, an amount of a commodity costing £110 in the UK will cost 880 kroners in Denmark. Over the next year, price inflation in Denmark is expected to be 5% while inflation in the UK is expected to be 8%. What is the 'expected spot exchange rate' at the end of the year?

Using the formula above:

Future (forward) rate, $S_1 = 8 \times \frac{1.05}{1.08}$

$= 7.78$

This is the same figure as we get if we compare the inflated prices for the commodity. At the end of the year:

UK price	=	£110 × 1.08 = £118.80
Denmark price	=	Kr880 × 1.05 = Kr924
S_t	=	924 ÷ 118.80 = 7.78

In the real world, exchange rates move towards purchasing power parity only over the **long term**. However, the theory is sometimes used to predict future exchange rates in **investment appraisal problems** where forecasts of relative inflation rates are available.

Case Study

An amusing example of purchasing power parity is the Economist's Big Mac index. Under PPP movements in countries' exchange rates should in the long-term mean that the prices of an identical basket of goods or services are equalised. The McDonalds Big Mac represents this basket.

The index compares local Big Mac prices with the price of Big Macs in America. This comparison is used to forecast what exchange rates should be, and this is then compared with the actual exchange rates to decide which currencies are over and under-valued.

2.2 International Fisher effect

FAST FORWARD

> The International Fisher effect states that currencies with high interest rates are expected to depreciate relative to currencies with low interest rates.

The term **Fisher effect** is sometimes used in looking at the relationship between **interest** rates and expected rates of **inflation** (see Chapter 6).

The rate of interest can be seen as made up of two parts: the real required rate of return (real interest rate) plus a premium for inflation. Then:

Exam formula

[1 + nominal (money) rate] = [1 + real interest rate] [1 + inflation rate]

$(1 + i) = (1 + r)(1 + h)$

Countries with relatively **high** rates of inflation will generally have high nominal rates of interest, partly because high interest rates are a mechanism for reducing inflation, and partly because of the Fisher effect: higher nominal interest rates serve to allow investors to obtain a high enough real rate of return where inflation is relatively high.

According to the **international Fisher effect**, interest rate differentials between countries provide an unbiased predictor of future changes in spot exchange rates. The currency of countries with relatively high interest rates is expected to depreciate against currencies with lower interest rates, because the higher interest rates are considered necessary to compensate for the anticipated currency depreciation. Given free movement of capital internationally, this idea suggests that the real rate of return in different countries will equalise as a result of adjustments to spot exchange rates.

The international Fisher effect can be expressed as:

Formula to learn

$$\frac{1+i_c}{1+i_b} = \frac{1+h_c}{1+h_b}$$

Where i_a is the nominal interest rate in country c
ib is the nominal interest rate in country b
ha is the inflation rate in country c
hb is the inflation rate in country b

Question

Forecasting exchange rates

Suppose that the nominal interest rate in the UK is 6 percent and the expected rate of inflation is 4 percent. If the expected rate of inflation in the US is 5 percent what is the nominal interest rate in the US? What is the real interest rate in each country?

Answer

The nominal interest rate in the US is:

$$\frac{1+i_c}{1+i_b} = \frac{1+h_c}{1+h_b}$$

$$1 + i_c = \left[\frac{1+h_c}{1+h_b}\right] \times (1+i_b)$$

$$= \left[\frac{1+0.05}{1+0.04}\right] \times (1+0.06)$$

$$= 1.070$$

The nominal interest rate in the US is therefore 7%

The real interest rate in both countries is approximately 2 percent (the difference between the nominal interest rate and the inflation rate for each country).

Question — Forecasting exchange rates

Suppose that the nominal interest rate in the UK is 6 percent and the nominal interest rate in the US is 7 percent. What is the expected change in the dollar/sterling exchange rate?

Answer

Since

$r_{\$} - r_{£} = 0.01$

It means that

$$\frac{e_1 - e_0}{e_0} = 1\%$$

And the implication is that the dollar will depreciate by 1 percent.

2.3 Expectations theory

Expectations theory looks at the relationship between differences in forward and spot rates and the expected changes in spot rates.

The formula for expectations theory is:

$$\frac{\text{Spot}}{\text{Forward}} = \frac{\text{Spot}}{\text{Expected future spot}}$$

2.4 Calculating NPV for international projects

FAST FORWARD

The NPV of an international project can be calculated either by converting the cash flows or the NPV.

There are **two alternative methods** for calculating the NPV from a overseas project. For a UK company investing overseas, we can:

(a) **Convert** the **project cash flows** into **sterling** and then **discount** at a **sterling discount rate** to calculate the NPV in sterling terms,

(b) **Discount the cash flows** in the **host country's currency** from the project at an **adjusted discount rate** for that currency and then **convert the resulting NPV** at the spot exchange rate.

Question — Overseas investment appraisal

Bromwich plc, a UK company, is considering undertaking a new project in Portugal. This will require initial capital expenditure of €1,250 million, with no scrap value envisaged at the end of the five year lifespan of the project. There will also be an initial working capital requirement of €500 million, which will be recovered at the end of the project. The initial capital will therefore be €1,750 million. Pre-tax net cash inflows of €800 million are expected to be generated each year from the project.

Company tax will be charged in Portugal at a rate of 40%, with depreciation on a straight-line basis being an allowable deduction for tax purposes. Portuguese tax is paid at the end of the year following that in which the taxable profits arise.

There is a double taxation agreement between the UK and Portugal, which means that no UK tax will be payable on the project profits.

The current €/£ spot rate is 1.6, and the Euro is expected to appreciate against the £ by 5% per year.

A project of similar risk recently undertaken by Bromwich plc in the UK had a required post-tax rate of return of 10%.

Calculate the present value of the project.

Answer

Method 1 – conversion of flows into sterling and discounting at the sterling discount rate

	0	*1*	*2*	*3*	*4*	*5*	*6*
Euro flows							
Capital	–1,750					500	
Net Cash flows		800	800	800	800	800	
Depreciation		250	250	250	250	250	
Tax			220	220	220	220	220
	–1,750	800	580	580	580	1080	–220
Exchange rate €/£	1.60	1.52	1.44	1.37	1.30	1.24	1.18
Cash flows in sterling	–1,093.75	526.32	401.66	422.80	445.05	872.34	–187.05
Discount factor	1	0.909	0.826	0.751	0.683	0.621	0.564
PV	–1,093.75	478.47	331.95	317.66	303.98	541.65	–105.59
NPV in sterling	774.38						

Method 2 – discounting foreign cash flows at an adjusted discount rate

When we use the second method we need to find the cost of capital for the project in the host country. If we are to keep the cash flows in Euros, and they need to be discounted at a rate that takes account of both the UK discount rate (10%) and the rate at which the exchange rate is expected to decrease (5%). This is in fact an application of the international Fisher effect.

$$\frac{\text{Future spot rate (€/£)}}{\text{Spot rate (€/£)}} = \frac{(1+\text{euro cost of capital})}{(1+\text{£ cost oc capital})}$$

We are trying to find the cost of capital for the euro.

$$\frac{\text{Future spot rate (€/£)}}{\text{Spot rate (€/£)}} \times (1 + \text{£ cost of capital}) = (1 + \text{euro cost of capital}) = \frac{(1.6\times 0.95)}{1.6} \times 1.10 = 1.045$$

The euro cost of capital is therefore 4.5%. Euro cash flows should be discounted at this rate.

	0	*1*	*2*	*3*	*4*	*5*	*6*
Euro flows							
Capital	–1,750					500	
Net Cash flows		800	800	800	800	800	
Depreciation		250	250	250	250	250	
Tax			220	220	220	220	220
Net Cash Flows	–1,750	800	580	580	580	1080	–220
Discount factor	1	0.961	0.925	0.889	0.855	0.822	0.790
PV	–1,750.00	769.23	536.24	515.62	495.79	887.68	–173.87
NPV in Euro	€1,280.69						

Translating this present value at the spot rate gives

$$\text{NPV} = \frac{€1{,}280.7}{1.6} = £800.43$$

2.5 The effect of exchange rates on NPV

Now that we have created a framework for the analysis of the effects of exchange rate changes on the net present value from an overseas project we can use the NPV equation to calculate the impact of exchange rate changes on the sterling denominated NPV of a project.

NPV = the sum of the discounted sterling cash flows

Add: discounted sterling terminal value
Less: initial sterling investment (converted at spot rate)

When there is a devaluation of sterling relative to a foreign currency, then the sterling value of the net cash flows increases and thus the NPV increases. The opposite happens when the domestic currency appreciates. In this case the sterling value of the cash flows decline and the NPV of the project in sterling declines. The relationship between NPV in sterling and the exchange rate is shown in the diagram below

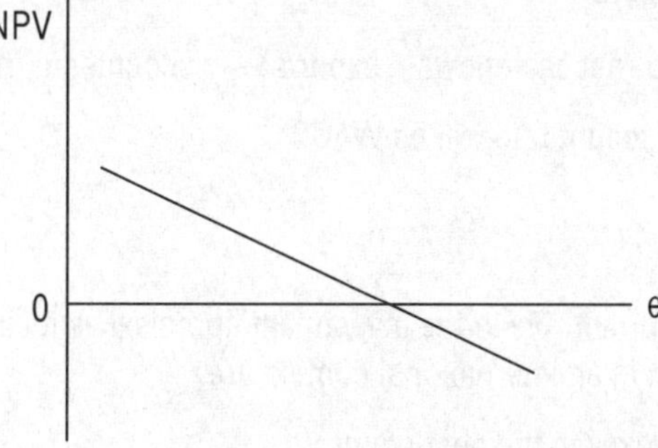

Question — **Effect of changes in the exchange rate**

Calculate the NPV for the Portugal project of Bromwich Inc under three different scenarios.

(a) The exchange rate remains constant at €1.63 for the duration of the project
(b) The dollar appreciates 5 percent every year
(c) The dollar depreciates 5 percent every year.

Answer

The NPV under the three scenarios is given in the table

			Cash flows in dollars	
Period	*Cash flows in Euros*	*Constant Exchange rate*	*Dollar Depreciates 5% per year*	*Dollar appreciates 5% per year*
0	–1,750	–1,093.75	–1,093.75	–1,093.75
1	800	500.00	526.32	476.19
2	580	362.50	401.66	328.80
3	580	362.50	422.80	313.14
4	580	362.50	445.05	298.23
5	1,080	675.00	872.34	528.88
6	–220	–137.50	–187.05	–102.60
Present Value in dollars		521.83	774.38	320.32

3 Forecasting cash flows from overseas projects

3.1 Forecasting project cash flows and APV

In Chapter 6 we computed the cash flows that are required for the valuation of a project. The calculation of cash flows for the appraisal of overseas projects requires a number of other factors to be taken into account.

3.2 Effect on exports

When a multinational company sets up a subsidiary in another country, in which it already exports, the relevant cash flows for the evaluation of the project should take into account the loss of export earnings in the particular country. The NPV of the project should take explicit account of this potential loss and it should be written as

Sum of discounted (net cash flows – exports) + discounted terminal value – initial investment

The appropriate discount rate will be WACC.

3.3 Taxes

Taxes play an important role in the investment appraisal as it can affect the viability of a project. The main aspects of taxation in an international context are:

- Corporate taxes in the host country.
- Investment allowances in the host country
- Withholding taxes in the host country
- Double taxation relief in the home country
- Foreign tax credits in the home country

The importance of taxation in corporate decision making is demonstrated by the use of **tax havens** by some multinationals as a means of deferring tax on funds prior to their repatriation or reinvestment. A tax haven is likely to have the following characteristics.

(a) Tax on foreign investment or sales income earned by resident companies, and withholding tax on dividends paid to the parent, should be low.

(b) There should be a stable government and a stable currency.

(c) There should be adequate financial services support facilities.

For example suppose that the tax rate on profits in the Federal West Asian Republic is 20% and the UK corporation tax is 30%, and there is a double taxation agreement between the two countries. A subsidiary of a UK firm operating in the Federal West Asian Republic earns the equivalent of £1 million in profit, and therefore pays £200,000 in tax on profits. When the profits are remitted to the UK, the UK parent can claim a credit of £200,000 against the full UK tax charge of £300,000, and hence will only pay £100,000.

Question

International investment I

Flagwaver Inc is considering whether to establish a subsidiary in Slovenia at a cost of €20,000, 000. The subsidiary will run for four years and the net cash flows from the project are shown below.

	Net Cash Flow
	€
Project 1	3,600,000
Project 2	4,560,000
Project 3	8,400,000
Project 4	8,480,000

There is a withholding tax of 10 percent on remitted profits and the exchange rate is expected to remain constant at €1.50/$. At the end of the four year period the Slovenian government will buy the plant for €12,000,000. The latter amount can be repatriated free of withholding taxes.

If the required rate of return is 15 percent what is the present value of the project?

Answer

Remittance net of withholding tax	*Remittance*	*Discounted*
€	$	$
3,240,000	2,160,000	1,878,261
4,104,000	2,736,000	2,068,809
7,560,000	5,040,000	3,313,882
19,632,000	13,088,000	7,483,106
		14,744,058

The NPV is $\frac{\$14{,}744{,}058 - €20{,}000{,}000}{1.50} = \$1{,}410{,}725$

Question

International Investment 2

Goody plc is considering whether to establish a subsidiary in the USA, at a cost of $2,400,000. This would be represented by fixed assets of $2,000,000 and working capital of $400,000. The subsidiary would produce a product which would achieve annual sales of $1,600,000 and incur cash expenditures of $1,000,000 a year.

The company has a planning horizon of four years, at the end of which it expects the realisable value of the subsidiary's fixed assets to be $800,000.

It is the company's policy to remit the maximum funds possible to the parent company at the end of each year.

Tax is payable at the rate of 35% in the USA and is payable one year in arrears. A double taxation treaty exists between the UK and the USA and so no UK taxation is expected to arise.

Tax allowable depreciation is at a rate of 25% on a straight line basis on all fixed assets.

Because of the fluctuations in the exchange rate between the US dollar and sterling, the company would protect itself against the risk by raising a eurodollar loan to finance the investment. The company's cost of capital for the project is 16%.

Calculate the NPV of the project.

Answer

The annual writing down allowance (WDA) is 25% of US$2,000,000 = $500,000, from which the annual tax saving would be (at 35%) $175,000.

Year	Investment	Contribution	Tax on contribution	Tax saving on WDA and tax on realisable value	Net cash flow	Discount factor @ 16%	Present value
	$m	$m	$m	$m	$m		$m
0	(2.4)				(2.400)	1.000	(2.400)
1		0.6		0.175	0.775	0.862	0.668
2		0.6	(0.21)	0.175	0.565	0.743	0.420
3		0.6	(0.21)	0.175	0.565	0.641	0.362
4	1.2*	0.6	(0.21)	0.175	1.765	0.552	0.974
5			(0.21)	(0.280)**	(0.490)	0.476	(0.233)
							(0.209)

* Fixed assets realisable value $800,000 plus working capital $400,000

** It is assumed that tax would be payable on the realisable value of the fixed assets, since the tax written down value of the assets would be zero. 35% of $800,000 is $280,000.

The NPV is negative and so the project would not be viable at a discount rate of 16%.

3.4 Subsidies

Many countries offer concessionary loans to multinational companies in order to entice them to invest in the country. The benefit from such concessionary loans should be included in the NPV calculation. The benefit of a concessionary loan is the difference between the repayment when borrowing under market conditions and the repayment under the concessionary loan.

For a UK company this benefit is calculated as

$$\text{Benefit} = \frac{L_0}{e_0} - \sum_{t=1}^{N} \frac{LP_t / e_t}{(1+i)^t}$$

Where L_0 is the amount of concessionary loan in foreign currency

LP is the periodic loan repayment in foreign currency

$i_£$ is the borrowing rate in the UK

e_0 is the foreign currency exchange rate

e_t is the foreign currency exchange rate at time t

3.5 Exchange restrictions

In calculating the NPV of an overseas project only the proportion of cash flows that are expected to be repatriated should be included in the calculation of the NPV.

3.6 Impact of transaction costs on NPV for international projects

Transaction costs are incurred when companies invest abroad due to currency conversion or other administrative expenses. These should also be taken into account.

3.7 A general model using adjusted present value

3.7.1 A recap of the APV approach

The APV method of investment appraisal was introduced in Chapter 7 in the context of domestic investments. Just to recap, there are essentially three steps.

Step 1 Estimate NPV assuming that the project is financed entirely by equity.

Step 2 Estimate the effects of the actual structure of finance (for example, tax effects of borrowing)

Step 3 Add the values from steps 1 and 2 to obtain the APV.

3.7.2 APV in the international context

You should follow the normal procedure of estimating the relevant cash flows and discounting them at an appropriate cost of capital. However you must also take account of the international dimension of the project, so that the steps become as follows.

Step 1 As the initial NPV assumes that the project is financed entirely by equity, the appropriate cost of capital is the cost of equity (allowing for project risk but excluding financial risk).

Step 2 Make adjustments for:

- Tax effects of debt and debt issue costs
- Any finance raised in the local markets
- Restrictions on remittances
- Subsidies from overseas governments

Step 3 Add the values from the first two steps to obtain the APV

The steps for calculating the APV of an international project are essentially the same as for domestic projects, although more care has to taken with the extra adjustments

4 The impact of exchange controls

4.1 The nature of exchange controls

Exchange controls restrict the flow of foreign exchange into and out of a country, usually to defend the local currency or to protect reserves of foreign currencies. Exchange controls are generally more restrictive in developing and less developed countries although some still exist in developed countries. These controls take the following forms:

Rationing the supply of foreign exchange. Anyone wishing to make payments abroad in a foreign currency will be restricted by the limited supply, which stops them from buying as much as they want from abroad.

Restricting the types of transaction for which payments abroad are allowed, for example by suspending or banning the payment of dividends to foreign shareholders, such as parent companies in multinationals, who will then have the problem of **blocked funds**.

4.2 Impact of exchange controls on investment decisions

In order to investigate the impact of exchange rate controls we can use the basic equation for the NPV.

Step 1 Convert net cash flows to home currency and discount at WACC

Step 2 Convert terminal value to home currency and discount at WACC

Step 3 Add the values from Steps 1 and 2 and deduct the initial investment (converted to home currency)

Assuming that **no repatriation** is possible until period N, when the life of the project will have been completed then the NPV will be calculated as follows.

Step 1 Add all net cash flows together and then add the terminal value

Step 2 Convert the value from Step 1 to home currency

Step 3 Discount the value from Step 2 at WACC

Step 4 Convert initial investment to home currency

Step 5 Deduct the value from Step 4 from the value in Step 3 to obtain NPV

The above formula assumes that non repatriated funds are not invested. If in fact we assume that the cash flow is invested each period and earns a return equal to i, then the NPV will be calculated as follows.

Step 1 Convert terminal value to home currency and discount at WACC

Step 2 Convert net cash flows to home currency, gross up for interest and add together, before discounting the total using WACC

Step 3 Convert initial investment to home currency and deduct from the sum of the values in Steps 1 and 2

The impact will depend on the interest rate earned and the cost of capital. An example will illustrate how this may be calculated.

Question — Exchange controls

Consider again the case of Flagwaver Inc, and its proposed subsidiary in Slovenia in question *International Investment 1*.

Now assume that no funds can be repatriated for the first three years, but all the funds are allowed to be remitted to the home market in year 4. The funds can be invested at a rate of 5 percent per year.

Answer

Year	*1st payment*	*2nd payment*	*3rd payment*	*4th payment*
1	€3,600,000			
2		€4,560,000		
3			€8,400,000	
4	4,167,450	5,027,400	8,820,000	€8,480,000

The total value payments are €26,494,850 which is subject to a 10 percent withholding tax. The net amount plus the salvage value is equal to €35,845,365, which is equal to $23,896,910. The present value of this is $13,663,136.

The net present value is:

$$\frac{\$20{,}000{,}000}{1.5 - £13{,}663{,}136} = £329{,}803$$

The exchange controls have reduced the NPV of the project from $1,410,725 to $329,803.

4.3 Strategies of dealing with exchange controls

Multinational companies have used many different strategies to overcome exchange controls the most common of which are

- **Transfer pricing** where the parent company sells goods or services to the subsidiary and obtain payment. The amount of this payment will depend on the volume of sales and also on the transfer price for the sales.
- **Royalty payments** when a parent company grants a subsidiary the right to make goods protected by patents. The size of any royalty can be adjusted to suit the wishes of the parent company's management.
- Loans by the parent company to the subsidiary. If the parent company makes a **loan** to a subsidiary, it can set the interest rate high or low, thereby affecting the profits of both companies. A high rate of interest on a loan, for example, would improve the parent company's profits to the detriment of the subsidiary's profits.
- **Management charges** may be levied by the parent company for costs incurred in the management of international operations.

5 Translation, transaction and economic risks

Exposure to foreign exchange risk can occur in a variety of ways. Most companies and certainly multinational corporations are affected by movements in exchange rates. Generally, exposure to foreign exchange risk can be categorized as transaction exposure, translation exposure, and economic exposure.

5.1 Transaction exposure

Transaction exposure occurs when a company has a future transaction that will be settled in a foreign currency. Such exposure could arise for example as the result of a UK company operating a foreign subsidiary. Operations in foreign countries encounter a variety of transactions for example, purchases or sales, financial transactions, and so on that are denominated in a foreign currency. Under these circumstances it is often necessary for the parent company to convert the home currency in order to provide the necessary currency to meet foreign obligations. This necessity gives rise to a foreign exchange exposure. The cost of foreign obligations could rise as a result of a weakening pound. Or the pound value of foreign revenues could depreciate as a result of a stronger pound. Even when foreign subsidiaries operate exclusively of the parent company, without relying on the parent company as a source of cash, they will ultimately remit dividends to the parent in the home currency. Once again, this will require a conversion from foreign to home currency.

The net impact of a project on the overall transaction exposure of the multinational company should be evaluated in a portfolio context.

Case Study

In 1971, Beecham Group a UK company borrowed SF100 million when the exchange rate for Swiss francs was close to 9.87 (SF/£). This implied that in 1976 when the loan came due, Beecham would need £10.13 million to repay the principal, assuming the SF—C exchange rate was unchanged. However, by 1976 the pound sterling had depreciated substantially against the Swiss franc. The exchange rate was then around 4.4 (SF/£)

To repay the SF100 million, Beecham Group needed £22.73 million, an additional cost of £12.6 million. Reportedly, the increase in the sterling value of the Swiss franc loan had actually exceeded Beecham Group's book value of net worth.

Case Study

During the late 1970s, Laker Airlines was expanding rapidly to accommodate a growing demand, primarily from British vacationers travelling to the United States. Laker purchased several DC-10s at that time, financing them in US dollars. By 1982, Laker Airlines was bankrupt. The problem was that Laker's revenues were primarily in pounds sterling and its debt was primarily in US dollars. When the dollar strengthened against the pound in 1981, two things happened. First, demand fell off because the higher cost of US dollars made travel to the US more expensive. At the same time, the £cost of Laker's US denominated debt went up.

5.2 Translation exposure

Translation exposure occurs in multinational corporations that have foreign subsidiaries with assets and liabilities denominated in foreign currency. Translation exposure occurs because the value of these accounts must eventually be stated in domestic currency for reporting purposes in the company's financial statements. In general, as exchange rates change, the home currency value of the foreign subsidiaries' assets and liabilities will change. Such changes can result in translation losses or gains, which will be recognized in financial statements. The nature and structure of the subsidiaries' assets and liabilities determine the extent of translation exposure to the parent company.

To some extent, the effects of exchange rate changes for translation purposes will be offsetting. For example, suppose a UK firm has a European subsidiary that has a European bank deposit of €1 million and payable of €1 million. Also, suppose the exchange rate between the € and sterling is €1.40 per £. The sterling value of the subsidiary's position in these two accounts is £714,285 in both cases. If the sterling were to suddenly appreciate against the €, say to €1.60/£ the asset and the liability accounts would lose sterling value in the same amount. Both would be revalued in sterling at £625,000. However, there would be no loss to the UK parent, since the sterling loss on the bank deposit is exactly offset by the sterling gain on the payable. In essence, these two accounts hedged each other from translation exposure to exchange rate changes.

5.3 Economic exposure

Economic exposure is the degree to which a firm's present value of future cash flows is affected by fluctuations in exchange rates.

Economic exposure differs from transaction exposure in that exchange rate changes may affect the value of the firm even though the firm is not involved in foreign currency transactions. Consider a UK manufacturer producing a product for the UK market only. The manufacturer does not use any imported materials and does not export to other countries. The manufacturer does not have any transactions exposure, but it has economic exposure because an appreciation of the pound in relation to other currencies may make imports cheaper and thus it may lead UK consumers to prefer the products of competitors resulting in lower revenues and profits.

For a company that is engaged in international trade changes in exchange rates affect both revenue and costs. A devaluation of the pound will increase the demand for exports and it will increase the price of competitive goods in the UK. Both effects will have a positive impact on a company's revenues. Costs will also increase because a devaluation will increase the price of imported raw materials. The net effect depends of the relative impact a devaluation has on revenues and costs.

An appreciation of the sterling will have the opposite effect on revenue and costs. That is revenues will be reduced as exports became more expensive and competitive goods in the domestic market cheaper, and costs will fall as the imported inputs become cheaper.

An exporting company faces economic exposure even if the exchange rate remains constant. Consider a UK manufacturer who exports in the US and its main competitor is a Japanese firm. A devaluation of the yen relative to the dollar will make Japanese imports cheaper in the US reducing the demand for UK

exports. Thus even though the dollar sterling exchange rate did not change, the company is still exposed to economic risk.

During the early 1980s, the appreciation of the US dollar against the Japanese yen caused similar problems for many US companies attempting to compete with Japanese competitors in the United States and abroad. One example is the difficulty experienced by Caterpillar. As the dollar strengthened against the yen, the price of Caterpillar equipment rose relative to that of a major Japanese competitor, Komatsu, giving Komatsu a competitive advantage. The result was a loss of market share for Caterpillar in both the US and international markets.

6 Costs and benefits of alternative sources of finance for MNCs

Multinational companies (MNCs) fund their investments from retained earnings from the issue of new equity or from the issue of new debt. Equity and debt funding can be secured by accessing both domestic and overseas capital markets. Thus multinational companies have to make decisions not only about their capital structure as measured by the debt/equity ratio and which was discussed extensively in Chapter 7, but also about the source of funding, that is whether the funds should be drawn from the domestic or the international markets.

6.1 Factors affecting capital structure of a MNC

The source of funding for a multinational company will be influenced by bankruptcy and agency costs as discussed in chapter 7, but also by a number of factors which are specific to multinational companies such as

(a) Global taxation
(b) Exchange risk
(c) Political risk
(d) Business risk

In Chapter 7 we discussed important role that interest tax deductibility plays in the determination of the optimal structure of the firm. **Global Taxation** is also an important factor in determining the capital structure of the multinational company. Tax deductibility in any specific country in which they operate is still the main aspect, but because multimodal companies operate in several tax jurisdictions, a multinational company will have to consider other issues, such as double taxation, withholding taxes investment tax allowances etc.

A multinational company may choose the level of debt and the type of debt in a way that minimises its global tax liabilities.

Exchange rate risk may also influence the capital structure of the multinational. When a UK company wishes to finance operations overseas, there may be a **currency** (foreign exchange) **risk** arising from the method of financing used. For example, if a UK company decides on an investment in the USA, to be financed with a sterling loan, the investment will provide returns in US dollars, while the investors (the lenders) will want returns paid in sterling. If the US dollar falls in value against sterling, the sterling value of the project's returns will also fall.

To reduce or to eliminate the currency risk of an overseas investment, a company might **finance** it with **funds** in the **same currency** as the investment. The advantages of borrowing in the same currency as an investment are as follows.

- Assets and liabilities in the same currency can be **matched**, thus avoiding exchange losses on conversion in the group's annual accounts.

- **Revenues** in the foreign currency can be used to **repay borrowings** in the same currency, thus eliminating losses due to fluctuating exchange rates.

Political risk to which companies may be exposed when investing overseas may also be reduced by the choice of an appropriate financing strategy. For example a multinational company may fund an international project by borrowing from banks in the country in which the project will be built. In this way the loss in the case of nationalisation will be borne by the local banks rather than by the parent company. In the absence of political risk, the company may prefer to finance the project by providing equity capital.

Business risk is also a determinant of the capital structure. As it was mentioned in chapter 7, business risk is normally proxied by the volatility of earnings and there is a negative relationship between business risk and leverage. As multinational companies are able to diversify and reduce the volatility of earnings, they should be able to take on more borrowing.

6.2 The advantages of borrowing internationally

There are three main advantages from borrowing for international capital markets, as opposed to domestic capital markets

(a) **Availability**. Domestic financial markets, with the exception of the large countries and the Euro zone, lack the depth and liquidity to accommodate either large debt issues or issues with long maturities.

(b) **Lower cost of borrowing.** In Eurobond markets interest rates are normally lower than borrowing rates in national markets

(c) **Lower issue costs**. The cost of debt issuance is normally lower than the cost of debt issue in domestic markets.

6.3 The risks of borrowing internationally

A multinational company has three options when financing an overseas project by borrowing. The first is to borrow in the same currency as the inflows from the project. The second option is borrowing in a currency other than the currency of the inflows but with a hedge in place and the third option is borrowing in a currency other than the currency of the inflows but without hedging the currency risk. The last case exposes the company to **exchange rate risk** which can substantially change the profitability of a project.

Question — Definite variables

Donegal plc is considering whether to establish a subsidiary in Ruritania, at a cost of Ruritanian $2,400,000. This would be represented by fixed assets of $2,000,000 and working capital of $400,000. The subsidiary would produce a product which would achieve annual sales of $1,600,000 and incur cash expenditures of $1,000,000 a year.

The company has a planning horizon of four years, at the end of which it expects the realisable value of the subsidiary's fixed assets to be $800,000. It expects also to be able to sell the rights to make the product for $500,000 at the end of four years.

It is the company's policy to remit the maximum funds possible to the parent company at the end of each year.

Tax is payable at the rate of 35% in Ruritania and is payable one year in arrears.

Tax allowable depreciation is at a rate of 25% on a straight line basis on all fixed assets.

Administration costs of £100,000 per annum will be incurred each year in the UK over the expected life of the project.

The UK taxation rate on taxable profits made in Ruritania and remitted to the UK, and on UK income and expenditure is 30%, payable one year in arrears.

The Ruritanian $:£ exchange rate is 5:1.

The company's cost of capital for the project is 10%.

Calculate the NPV of the project.

Answer

			Time			
$'000 cash flows	*0*	*1*	*2*	*3*	*4*	*5*
Sales receipts		1,600	1,600	1,600	1,600	
Costs		(1,000)	(1,000)	(1,000)	(1,000)	
Tax allowable depreciation		(500)	(500)	(500)	(500)	
$ taxable profit		100	100	100	100	
Taxation			(35)	(35)	(35)	(35)
Add back tax allowable depreciation		500	500	500	500	
Capital expenditure	(2,000)					
Scrap value					800	
Tax on scrap value (W1)						(280)
Terminal value					500	
Tax on terminal value						(175)
Working capital	(400)				400	
	(2,400)	600	565	565	2,265	(490)
Exchange rates	5:1	5:1	5:1	5:1	5:1	5:1
£'000 cash flows	*0*	*1*	*2*	*3*	*4*	*5*
From/(to) Ruritania	(480)	120	113	113	453	(98)
Additional UK tax (W2)			(6)	(6)	(6)	(84)
Additional UK expenses/income		(100)	(100)	(100)	(100)	
UK tax effect of UK expenses/income			30	30	30	30
Net sterling cash flows	(480)	20	37	37	377	(152)
UK discount factors	1	0.909	0.826	0.751	0.683	0.621
Present values	(480)	18	31	28	257	(94)

NPV = (£240,000), therefore the company should not proceed.

Workings

(1) Tax is payable on $800,000 as tax written down = $2,000,000 – (4 × $500,000) = 0

(2) *Years 1–3*

$ taxable profit = $100,000
At 5:1 exchange rate = £20,000
Tax at 30% = £6,000

Year 4

$ taxable profit = $100,000 + $800,000 + $500,000
= $1,400,000

At 5:1 exchange rate = £280,000

Tax at 30% = £84,000

Chapter Roundup

- Changes in exchange rates are as important as the underlying profitability in selecting an overseas project.
- **Purchasing power parity** theory states that the exchange rate between two currencies is the same in equilibrium when the purchasing power of currency is the same in each country.
- The International Fisher Effect states that currencies with high interest rates are expected to depreciate relative to currencies with low interest rates.
- The NPV of an international project can be calculated either by converting the cash flows or the NPV.

Quick Quiz

1 What does the absolute purchasing parity relationship state?

2 What are the two ways NPV can be calculated for an overseas project?

3 What is the impact of exchange controls on the decisions to invest in an international project?

4 What is the difference between transaction ad translation exposure?

5 How could economic exposure be measured?

Answers to Quick Quiz

1 The absolute purchasing parity relationship states that prices in different countries will be the same when expressed in the same currency.

2 The first way is to translate the overseas cash flows into domestic currency and use a domestic discount factor.

The second way is to use an appropriate overseas discount factor and calculate the NPV in foreign currency. The NPV can then be calculated into domestic currency.

3 Exchange controls will normally lower the NPV from an overseas investment unless they earn a sufficient return from reinvestment in the country of origin until repatriation is allowed.

4 Transaction exposure occurs when a company has a future transaction that will be settled as a foreign currency. Translation exposure occurs when a company has overseas subsidiaries whose assets are denominated in foreign currency.

5 Economic exposure can be measured by estimating the repressions coefficient of the rate of return of a company's stock on the exchange rate.

Now try the questions below from the Exam Question Bank

Number	Level	Marks	Time
11	Introductory	15	27 mins

10

Impact of capital investment on financial reporting

Topic list	Syllabus reference
1 Effect of alternative financing strategies on financial reporting	B (5) (a)
2 Effect of foreign exchange translation on financial reporting	B (5) (a)
3 Effect of taxation and double taxation on financial reporting	B (5) (a)
4 Effect of capital allowances and tax exhaustion on financial reporting	B (5) (a)

Introduction

In this chapter we look at how four aspects of a capital investment project can impact on the financial performance of a company. The four aspect we consider are: the **financing mix, foreign exchange translation, double taxation** and **capital allowances**.

Study guide

		Intellectual level
B5	**Impact of capital investment on financial decisions**	
(a)	Assess the impact of a significant capital investment project upon the reported financial position and performance of the firm taking into account: (i) Alternative financing strategies (ii) Foreign exchange translation (iii) Taxation and double taxation (iv) Capital allowances and the problem of exhaustion	3

Exam guide

You may be asked about the effect of leverage and taxation on the performance of a company.

1 Effect of alternative financing strategies on financial reporting

FAST FORWARD

Gearing affects the volatility of **earnings per share**. The higher the level of gearing the higher the **volatility of EPS**.

1.1 Financial gearing and debt

Fixed income securities issued by corporations to fund capital projects include **debt** and **preferred stock**.

Debt is **less risky** than **equity** for investors and therefore requires a **lower rate** of **return**. In addition, interest payments attract tax relief, hence the cost of debt will be lower than the cost of equity. The effect of this on the company's WACC is that as a company gears up, its WACC will be reduced due to the higher proportion of the cheaper debt financing in the company's overall financial structure.

The return on debt is not directly linked to the underlying performance of the business. The same predetermined amount is paid whether the profits are high or low and this in turn makes any residual claims that shareholders have on the income of a company more volatile.

1.2 Impact of gearing on earnings per share, EBIT and return on equity

To appreciate the impact of financial gearing we shall explain and calculate the effects of changes in earnings before interest and taxes (EBIT) on **earnings per share** for a company with differing amounts of **debt financing**.

Assume that a company has the following statement of financial position structure.

	Current	*Proposed*
Asset	500	500
Debt	–	300
Equity	500	200

The company currently has 100 shares in issue with a price of \$5. It is proposing to buy back 60 shares for a total cost of \$300, financing this by issuing debt at a cost of 10%. This will leave 40 shares in issue.

The earnings per share for the company when it has no debt is:

$$EPS(U) = \frac{EBIT}{100}$$

Whereas the earnings per share for the company under the proposed borrowing is:

$$EPS(G) = \frac{EBIT}{100}$$

The values of the ungeared earnings per share for different values of EBIT are shown in the table below:

	Scenario 1	*Scenario 2*	*Scenario 3*	*Scenario 4*	*Scenario 5*	*Scenario 6*	*Scenario 7*
EBIT	0	10	30	50	70	90	110
Interest payments	0	0	0	0	0	0	0
Net income	0	10	30	50	70	90	110
EPS(U)	0	0.1	0.3	0.5	0.7	0.9	1.1

Similarly, the values of the geared earnings per share for different values of EBIT are shown in the table below:

	Scenario 1	*Scenario 2*	*Scenario 3*	*Scenario 4*	*Scenario 5*	*Scenario 6*	*Scenario 7*
EBIT	0	10	30	50	70	90	110
Interest payments	30	30	30	30	30	30	30
Net income	–30	–20	0	20	40	60	80
EPS(L)	0.75	–0.5	0	0.5	1	1.5	2

As it can be seen from the two tables, the earnings for the geared company are more volatile. When the values of EPS are plotted against the values of EBIT, this is reflected in the gradient of the line showing the values of the geared earnings per share, which will be steeper than the line plotting showing the values of unleveraged earnings per share.

The breakeven level of EBIT where the two alternative financing schemes give the same earnings per share, ie when:

EPS(U) = EPS(G)

EBIT = \$50. This can be seen from the fact that:

$$\frac{EBIT - 30}{40} = \frac{EBIT}{100}$$

Implies EBIT = \$50

This breakeven point can be checked as follows.

Original all equity structure $\frac{50}{100} = \$0.50$

Revised structure $\frac{50 - 30}{40} = \$0.50$

Above an EBIT of \$50, the geared structure gives a higher earnings per share. In addition, the company's return on equity will exceed the interest cost of 10%. Below \$50, it gives a lower earnings per share and the return on equity is less than the cost of debt of 10%.

At the break-even point, the return on equity is equal to the interest rate on the debt, ie:

$$ROE = \frac{EBIT}{500} = \frac{50}{500} = 10\%.$$

At an EBIT of zero, the original ungeared earnings per share will also be zero. However, with debt, there will be a loss per share of $\frac{-30}{40} = -\$0.75$.

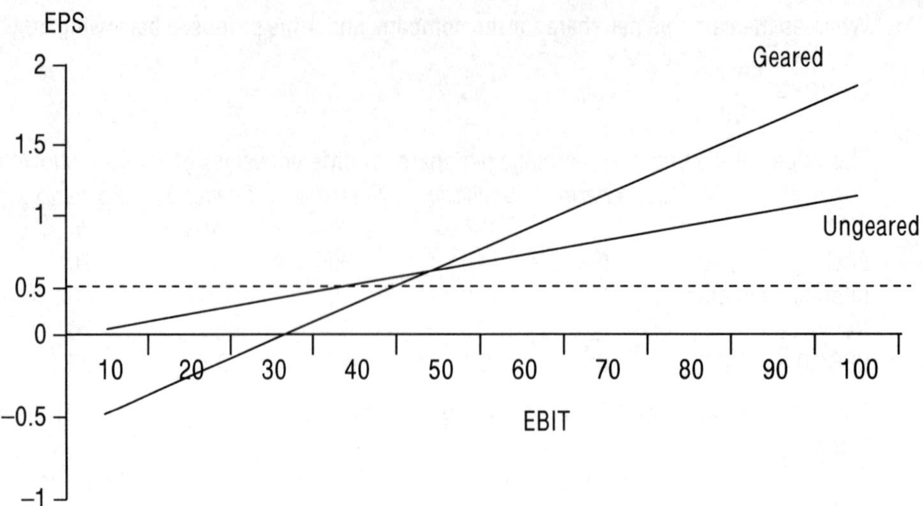

Note that, although the earnings per share and return on equity are more volatile for the geared company, the mean return is higher. This can be demonstrated by calculating the mean returns for the above two capital structures, assuming that each scenario has an equal likelihood of arising.

Ungeared Company

$$\text{Mean net income for ungeared company} = \frac{0+10+30+50+70+90+110}{7} = \$51.43$$

$$\text{Earnings per share} = \frac{51.43}{100} = \$0.5143$$

$$\text{Return on equity} = \frac{51.43}{500} = 10.286\%$$

Geared Company

$$\text{Mean net income for geared company} = \frac{-30-20+0+20+40+60+80}{7} = \$21.429$$

$$\text{Earnings per share} = \frac{21.429}{40} = \$0.5357$$

$$\text{Return on equity} = \frac{21.429}{200} = 10.714\%$$

1.3 Degree of financial gearing

The degree of financial gearing measures the sensitivity of EPS to changes in EBIT.

Key term

The **degree of financial gearing** is defined as the change in earnings per share (EPS) over the change in earnings before interest and tax (EBIT) or

$$\frac{\%\text{ Change in EPS}}{\%\text{ Change in EBIT}}$$

The degree of financial gearing can be calculated from the formula:

$$\frac{\text{EBIT}}{\text{EBIT} - \text{Interest}}$$

For the ungeared company in the example above, the degree of financial gearing can be calculated as follows, for a particular value of EBIT, say EBIT = $75. For the ungeared company we have:

$$\frac{75}{75-0} = 1$$

Whereas for the geared company, we have:

$$\frac{75}{75-30} = 1.67$$

The degree of gearing confirms our earlier finding that the geared EPS is more sensitive to changes in EBIT.

We have thus established that the relationship between the EPS and EBIT depends on the degree of **financial gearing**. The relationship can be expressed as follows:

$$\frac{\Delta \text{ EPS}}{\text{EPS}} = \text{degree of fdinancial gearing} \times \frac{\Delta \text{ EBIT}}{\text{EBIT}}$$

That is the relationship between earnings per share (EPS) and earnings before interest and tax in linear and is affected by the degree of financial gearing.

The higher the degree of financial gearing, the higher the impact of changes of EBIT on EPS.

When there is no debt DFL = 1 and EBIT changes are equal to EPS changes in percentage terms.

When there is debt DFL > 1 and EPS changes by more than the changes in EBIT due to the effect of DFL, the 'multiplier'.

Suppose for example that there is a 33% increase in EBIT from $75 to $100. There is a 55% increase in EPS from $45 to $70.The link between the two percentage increases is the degree of financial gearing – that is 1.67 × 33% = 55%.

2 Effect of foreign exchange translation on financial reporting

FAST FORWARD

Foreign exchange translation has an impact on both the **statement of financial position** and the **income statement** of a company.

2.1 Impact of exchange rate changes

Exchange rate changes affect the performance of an overseas subsidiary because they change the value of remittances to the parent company. A strong performance in the local currency can be enhanced by a depreciation of the parent company currency or it can be offset by an appreciation in the parent company currency. Thus it is important to disentangle changes in the exchange rate from the underlying performance. Consider a Portuguese subsidiary that is 100% owned by a US multinational company.

The impact of changes in local currency sales can be disentangled from changes in the exchange rate using the formula:

Parent Co. consolidated $ sales = Subsidiary Co. € sales × (1 + € Sales growth) × Exchange Rate ($/€).

Example

Assume Subsidiary Co. sales grow at 30% per year.

- Exchange Rate in Year 1 = €1 / $1.00
- Exchange Rate in Year 2 = €1 / $1.10

Year	*1*	*2*	*Cash Balance*
Subsidiary			*End Year 2 in €*
Revenues in LC	10,000	13,000	23,000
% change		**30%**	
Exchange Rate	€1 / $1.00	€ 1 / $1.10	€ 1 / $1.10
% change		**10%**	
Parent – Consolidated			*End Year 2 in $*
Revenues in HC	$10,000	$14,300	$25,300
% change		**43.0%**	

Note that the consolidated sales figure for the parent reflects the results of sales growth in local currency and movements in the value of the local currency.

Parent Consolidated Sales increase by 43.0% over the year as a result of:

- Subsidiary € Sales increase 30% over the year.
- Value of € increases 10% over the year.

The Year 2 column shows the 'flow effects' of an exchange rate change on the Parent's Consolidated Income Statement.

The effects of exchange rate changes on the balance sheet is shown on the last column of the table. The effects on the balance sheet are in general more difficult to be estimated because they reflect items that were collected over a period of time. The value of exchange rate that needs to be used in translating is considered below.

2.2 Exchange rate translation under IAS 21

Under IAS 21, all statement of financial position accounts are translated either at the closing or at the historic exchange rate and all income statement items are translated at the exchange rate at the dates the items are recognized. Since this is generally impractical, an appropriately weighted average exchange rate for the period may be used for the translation. A summary of the requirements of IAS 21 is given below

Statement of financial position item	**Exchange rate**
Monetary items	Closing rate, being the spot rate at the balance sheet date
Non-monetary items measured at historic cost	Rate of exchange at the date of original transaction
Non-monetary items measured at fair value	Exchange rate at the date when fair value was determined
Equity	The common stock account and any additional paid-in capital are carried at the exchange rates in effect on the respective dates of issuance. Year-end retained earnings equal the beginning balance of retained earnings plus any additions for the year.
Income statement	
Income/expenses	Actual rates or appropriate average for current period

A 'plug' equity account named **exchange differences** is used to make the statement of financial position balance since income and expense are translated using the exchange rate at the dates of the transaction and assets and liabilities are translated using the closing exchange rate.

2.3 Case study

An example of foreign currency translation is shown below by considering the statement of financial position and income statement of an overseas subsidiary, and looking at the effects of translation into sterling on earnings and the statement of financial position.

We assume that the subsidiary is at the end of its first year of operation. The first table presents the statement of financial position with the first column showing the statement of financial position in foreign

currency (FC). The historical exchange rate is assumed to be FC3.00/£1.00. The first table shows the translated statement of financial position after an assumed appreciation of the foreign currency to FC2.00/£1.00 and after an assumed depreciation of the foreign currency from FC3.00/£1.00 to FC4.00/£1.00.

The second table shows the translated income statements after the assumed appreciation of the foreign currency to FC2.00/£1.00 (the average exchange for the period is thus FC2.50/£1.00)

And the translated income statement after the depreciation of the foreign currency from FC3.00/£1.00 to FC4.00/£1.00 (the average exchange rate for the period is thus FC3.50/£1.00)

2.3.1 Impact on the statement of financial position

		Reporting Currency (£)	
	Local Currency (FC)	*Appreciation of local currency*	*Depreciation of local currency*
Cash	2,100	1,050	525
Inventory	1,500	750	375
Net Fixed assets	3,000	1,500	750
Total assets	6,600	3,300	1,650
Current liabilities	1,200	600	300
Long-term debt	1,800	900	450
Common Stock	2,700	900	900
Retained earnings	900	360	257
Exchange reserve		540	(257)
Total liabilities and equity	6,600	3,300	1,650

2.3.2 Impact on Income statement

		Reporting Currency (£)	
	Local Currency (FC)	*Appreciation of local currency*	*Depreciation of local currency*
Sales	10,000	4,000	2,857
Cost of sales	7,500	3,000	2,143
Depreciation	1,000	400	286
Profits before taxation	1,500	600	429
Taxation	600	240	171
Profit after taxation	900	360	257

Translating the income statement and the balance sheet of a subsidiary into the reporting currency of the parent company can make earnings and asset values more volatile. This translation exposure can be managed using the techniques discussed in Chapter 18.

3 Effect of taxation and double taxation on financial reporting

FAST FORWARD

Double taxation agreements reduce the tax liability of the parent company

3.1 Double taxation arrangements

Investments in overseas subsidiaries or projects are made for the prospect of profits from the overseas investment which need to be repatriated. However the amount that will eventually be received by the parent company will depend on the tax that will need to be paid to overseas and home tax authorities.

There are two main systems of cross-border double tax relief for dividends paid by subsidiaries to parent companies

- The credit method (used in the UK and the USA)
- The exemption method (used in most EU countries)

3.1.1 Credit method

Under the credit method, a UK firm that invests in an overseas subsidiary, say Ireland, pays corporation tax at the corporation tax rate of 12.5% in Ireland on profits of the Irish subsidiary

Any dividends paid from the Irish subsidiary to the UK parent are subject to UK corporation tax at the current corporation tax rate say 30%, with credit given for corporation tax paid by the Irish subsidiary to the Irish government on the underlying profits.

3.1.2 Exemption method

Under the exemption method a German firm that invests in Ireland pays corporation tax at say 12.5% in Ireland on profits of the Irish subsidiary.

Any dividends paid from the Irish subsidiary to the German parent are exempt from corporate income tax in Germany

As a result, a UK firm investing in Ireland may face a higher overall corporate tax charge than a German firm investing in Ireland and lower after tax earnings

3.2 Double taxation impact on earnings

Tax considerations can also be a factor that may affect the tax liability of the parent dividend policies inside the multinational firm. For example the parent company may reduce its overall tax liability by, for example, receiving larger amounts of dividends from subsidiaries in countries where undistributed earnings are taxed.

4 Effect of capital allowances and tax exhaustion on financial reporting

FAST FORWARD

Capital allowances in the form of **first-year allowances** or **writing down allowances** determine the tax liabilities and after tax earnings.

In most tax systems, capital expenditure is set off against tax liabilities so as to reduce the taxes a company pays and to encourage investment. These **capital allowances** take two forms; **first year allowances** which are set off against tax liabilities in the year the investment takes place and **writing down allowances** which are set off against tax liabilities in subsequent years.

The effect of capital allowances can be from the definition of after-tax – earnings

After tax earnings = Earnings before tax – Tax liability

Where tax liability = tax rate × (Earnings before tax – capital allowances)

There will be circumstances when the capital allowances in a particular year will equal or exceed before tax earnings. In such a case the company will pay no tax. In most tax systems unused capital allowances can be carried forward indefinitely, so that the capital allowance that is set off against the tax liability in any one year includes not only the writing down allowance for the particular year but also any unused allowances from previous years.

Question

Capital allowances

Suppose that a company has invested $10 million in a plant. The first year allowance is 40 percent, whereas the remaining amount is written down over a period of four years. The tax rate is 30 percent. Earnings before tax over a five year period are as follows:

Year 1	*Year 2*	*Year 3*	*Year 4*	*Year 5*
$m	$m	$m	$m	$m
3	2.5	3.5	3.8	4.2

(a) Calculate the tax liability every year and the after-tax earnings.
(b) Calculate the impact on earnings if the first year allowance is 60 percent

Answer

Capital allowances

(a) The first year allowance is 0.4 x $10 = $4m

Since the capital allowance exceeds the earnings before tax, the tax liability is 0 and the unused capital allowance of $1m will be added to the second year writing down allowance of 0.6 x$10/4 = $1.5 to yield a capital allowance for year 2 of $2.5m. The capital allowance is the same as the before tax earnings and the tax liability is again zero. However this time there is no unused capital allowance to be carried forward.

Capital allowance in each year are shown below

	Year 1	*Year 2*	*Year 3*	*Year 4*	*Year 5*
	$m	$m	$m	$m	$m
Earnings before tax	3	2.5	3.5	3.8	4.2
First Year allowance	4				
Unused capital allowance brought forward		1.0	0		
Writing Down Allowance		1.5	1.5	1.5	1.5
Total allowance	$4m	$2.5m	$1.5m	$1.5m	$1.5m

The tax liability for every year and the after tax earnings are shown in the table below

	Year 1	*Year 2*	*Year 3*	*Year 4*	*Year 5*
	$m	$m	$m	$m	$m
Tax liability	0	0.0	0.600	0.690	0.810
After-tax-Earnings	3	2.5	2.900	3.110	3.390

(b) When the first year allowance is 60 percent, the capital allowances are larger in the first three years but lower in the subsequent two years.

	Year 1	*Year 2*	*Year 3*	*Year 4*	*Year 5*
	$m	$m	$m	$m	$m
Earnings before tax	3	2.5	3.5	3.8	4.2
First Year allowance	6				
Unused capital allowance brought forward		3.0	1.5	0.0	0
Writing Down Allowance		1.0	1.0	1.0	1
Total allowance	6	4.0	2.5	1.0	1

The tax liability for every year and the after tax earnings are shown in the table below

	Year 1	*Year 2*	*Year 3*	*Year 4*	*Year 5*
	$m	$m	$m	$m	$m
Tax liability	0	0.0	0.300	0.840	0.960
After-tax-Earnings	3	2.5	3.200	2.960	3.240

After tax earnings are affected by the pattern of writing down allowances.

Chapter Roundup

- Gearing affects the volatility of **earnings per share**. The higher the level of gearing the higher the **volatility of EPS**.
- Foreign exchange translation has an impact on both the **statement of financial position** and the **income statement** of a company.
- Double taxation agreements reduce the tax liability of the parent company
- **Capital allowances** in the form of **first –year allowances** or **writing down allowances** determine the tax liabilities and after tax earnings.

Quick Quiz

1 **Choose the right answer**

The .... the degree of financial gearing the lower the volatility of EPS

Higher
Lower

2 What exchange rate is used to translate monetary assets?

3 The credit method of double taxation reduces earnings per share more than the exempt method.

True ☐

False ☐

Answers to Quick Quiz

1 Lower

2 Closing rate

3 True

Now try the questions below from the Exam Question Bank

Number	Level	Marks	Time
12	Examination	20	36 mins

P A R T C

Acquisition and mergers

11

Acquisitions and mergers versus other growth strategies

Topic list	Syllabus reference
1 Mergers and acquisitions as a method of corporate expansion	C(1) (a)
2 Evaluating the corporate and competitive nature of a given acquisition proposal	C(1) (b)
3 Developing an acquisition strategy	C(1) (b)
4 Criteria for choosing an appropriate target for acquisition	C(1) (c)
5 Creating synergies	C(1) (e)
6 Explaining high failure rate of acquisitions in enhancing shareholder value	C(1)(d)

Introduction

In this chapter we discuss the advantages and disadvantages of mergers and acquisitions as forms of expanding the scale of operations of a firm. We look at the types of mergers and their purpose illustrating these with real life examples. We evaluate the merits of a given acquisition proposal and set out the criteria for choosing an appropriate target. The evaluation of synergy in the context of two real life examples is also considered.

Study guide

		Intellectual level
C1	**Acquisitions and mergers versus other growth strategies**	
(a)	Discuss the arguments for and against the use of acquisitions and mergers as a method of corporate expansion	2
(b)	Evaluate the corporate and competitive nature of a given acquisition proposal	3
(c)	Advise upon the criteria for choosing an appropriate target for acquisition	3
(d)	Compare the various explanations for the high failure rate of acquisitions in enhancing shareholder value	3
(e)	Evaluate, from a given context, the potential for synergy separately classified as:	3
(i)	Revenue synergy	
(ii)	Cost synergy	
(iii)	Financial synergy	

1 Mergers and acquisitions as a method of corporate expansion

FAST FORWARD

Although **growth strategy through acquisition** requires high premiums, it is widely used by corporations as an alternative to **internal organic growth**.

Companies may decide to increase the scale of their operations through a strategy of **internal organic growth** by **investing money** to **purchase** or **create assets** and product lines **internally**.

Alternatively, companies may decide to grow by **buying** other **companies** in the market thus acquiring ready made tangible and intangible assets and product lines. Which is the right strategy? The decision is one of the most difficult the financial manager has to face.

The right answer is not easy to arrive at. **Organic growth** in areas where the company has been successful and has expertise may present **few risks** but it can be **slow**, **expensive** or sometimes **impossible**. On the other hand **acquisitions** require **high premiums** that make the **creation** of **value** difficult. Irrespective of the merits of a **growth strategy** by acquisition or not, the fact remains that this is used by corporations extensively.

The following chart shows the value of acquisitions globally from 1995 to 2006:

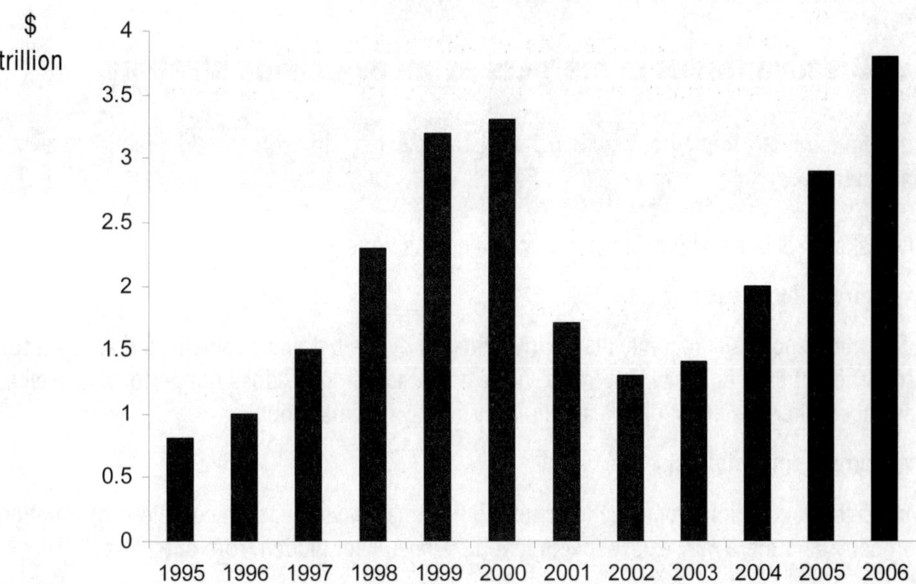

Source: McKinsey

When companies decide to expand their scale of operations by merging with or acquiring another company, there are many ways that this strategy can be implemented and many possible target companies.

In this section we will look at the each type of merger that companies have used for growth and present the arguments for and against each particular case. As a general rule, expansion either by building new plants or by acquisition should not be undertaken unless the expansion results in increased profitability for the company and enhances shareholder wealth.

1.1 Advantages of mergers as an expansion strategy

FAST FORWARD

As an **expansion strategy** mergers are thought to provide a quicker way of acquiring productive capacity and **intangible assets** and accessing **overseas markets**.

There are four main advantages that have been put forward in the literature and these are summarized below:

Speed

The acquisition of another company is a quicker way of implementing a business plan, as the company acquires another organization that is already in operation. An acquisition also allows a company to reach a certain optimal level of production much quicker than through organic growth. Acquisition as a strategy for expansion is particularly suitable for management with rather short time horizons.

Lower cost

An acquisition may be a cheaper way of acquiring productive capacity than through organic growth. An acquisition can take place for instance through an exchange of shares which does not have an impact on the financial resources of the firm.

Acquisition of intangible assets

A firm through an acquisition will acquire not only tangible assets but also intangible assets, such as brand recognition, reputation, customer loyalty and intellectual property which are more difficult to achieve with organic growth.

Access to overseas markets

When a company wants to expand its operations in an overseas market, acquiring a local firm may be the only option of breaking into the overseas market.

1.2 Disadvantages of mergers as an expansion strategy

FAST FORWARD

An **expansion strategy** through acquisition is associated with exposure to a higher level of **business and financial risk**.

The risks associated with expansion through acquisitions are:

Exposure to business risk

Acquisitions normally represent large investments by the bidding company and account for a large proportion of their financial resources. If the acquired company does not perform as well as it was envisaged, then the effect on the acquiring firm may be catastrophic.

Exposure to financial risk

During the acquisition process, the acquiring firm may have less than complete information on the target company, and there may exist aspects that have been kept hidden from outsiders.

Acquisition premium

When a company acquires another company, it normally pays a premium over its present market value. This premium is normally justified by the management of the bidding company as necessary for the benefits that will accrue from the acquisition. However, too large a premium may render the acquisition unprofitable.

Managerial competence

When a firm is acquired, which is large relative to the acquiring firm, the management of the acquiring firm may not have the experience or ability to deal with operations on the new larger scale, even if the acquired company retains its own management.

Integration problems

Most acquisitions are beset with problems of integration as each company has its own culture, history and ways of operation.

1.3 Types of mergers

FAST FORWARD

Mergers can be classified as **horizontal, vertical or conglomerate**, depending on the type of company that is acquired.

A merger generally involves two companies pooling their interests and having common ownership of the new company's assets.

An acquisition usually involves a stronger company (the 'predator') taking over the assets of a smaller company (the 'target') and assuming ownership of these assets.

Mergers and acquisitions can be classified in terms of the company that is acquired or merged with, as **horizontal**, **vertical** or **conglomerate**. Each type of merger represents a **different way** of **expansion** with **different benefits** and **risks**.

Horizontal mergers

A **horizontal merger** is one in which one company acquires another company in the **same line of business**. A horizontal merger happens between firms which were formerly competitors and who produce products that are considered **substitutes** by their buyers. The main impact of a horizontal merger is therefore to **reduce competition** in the market in which both firms operate. These firms are also likely to

purchase the same or substitute products in the input market. A **horizontal merger** is said to achieve **horizontal integration**.

Case Study

Examples of horizontal mergers include the acquisition of Safeway plc by WM Morrison Supermarkets plc, the merger of Daimler-Benz and Chrysler, the merger of Exxon and Mobil, the merger of Ford and Volvo.

In every one of the above examples, the company could have expanded its operation in the respective markets, but expansion through acquisition was considered a better option. WM Morrison was a supermarket chain with a strong presence in the North of England but with no presence in the populous and affluent south of the country. Instead of finding sites, waiting for planning permissions and delaying its expansion into the south of the country, it decided to acquire Safeway, a supermarket chain that was experiencing falling market share but which had a strong presence in the south of the country.

Vertical mergers

Vertical mergers are mergers between firms that operate at different stages of the same production chain, or between firms that produce complementary goods such as a newspaper acquiring a paper manufacturer. Vertical mergers are either backward when the firm merges with a supplier or forward when the firm merges with a customer.

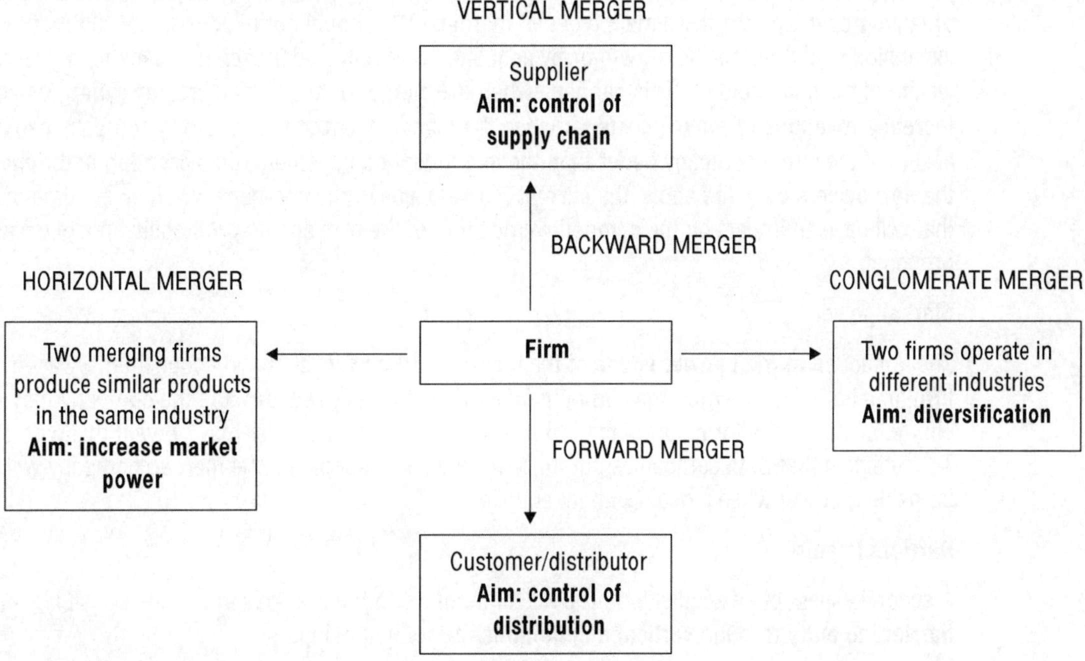

Case Study

An example of a vertical merger is the merger between Time Warner Incorporated, a major cable operation, and the Turner Corporation, which produces CNN, TBS, and other programmes. In this merger, the Federal Trade Commission (FTC) was alarmed by the fact that such a merger would allow Time Warner to monopolize much of the programming on television. Ultimately, the FTC voted to allow the merger but stipulated that the merger could not act in the interests of anti-competitiveness to the point that public good was harmed.

Conglomerate mergers

Conglomerate mergers are mergers which are neither vertical nor horizontal. In a conglomerate merger a company acquires another company in an unrelated line of business, for example a newspaper company acquiring an airline.

Case Study

Examples of conglomerate mergers include the expansion of Mercedes Benz into the aerospace industry, and the acquisition of Eagle Star an insurance company by BAT, the tobacco industry giant. Conglomerate mergers were the primary type of mergers in the 1960s.

2 Evaluating the corporate and competitive nature of a given acquisition proposal

FAST FORWARD

Expansion by **organic growth** or by acquisition should only be undertaken if it leads to an **increase** in the **wealth** of the **shareholders**.

We have discussed so far the reasons why a company may opt for growth by acquisition instead of organic growth and the three main types of mergers. We should not of course lose sight of the fact that expansion either by organic growth or by acquisitions is only undertaken if it leads to an increase in the wealth of the shareholders. This happens when the merger or acquisition creates **synergies** which either **increase revenues** or **reduce costs**, or when the management of the acquiring company can manage the assets of the target company better than the incumbent management, thus **creating additional** value for the new owners over and above the current market value of the company. We look at some of the aspects that will have an impact on the competitive position of the firm and its profitability in a given acquisition proposal.

Market power

The impact on **market power** is one of the most important aspects of an acquisition. By acquiring another firm, in a horizontal merger, the competition in the industry is reduced and the company may be able to charge higher prices for its products. Competition regulation however may prevent this type of acquisition. To the extent that both companies purchase for the same suppliers, the merged company will have greater bargaining power when it deals with its suppliers.

Barriers to entry

A second aspect of an acquisition proposal and related to the previous one is the possibility of creating **barriers to entry** through **vertical acquisitions** of production inputs.

FAST FORWARD

Aspects of a merger that will have an impact on the firm's **competitive position** include **increased market power**, the **creation of barriers to entry, supply chain security** and **economies of scope** and **scale**.

Case Study

A classic example of barriers to entry is the nearly exclusive ownership, before the Second World War, of all known bauxite deposits by ALCOA an aluminium refining company. If a firm wished to enter into aluminum refining in the USA it would have found it impossible.

Supply chain security

A third aspect that has an impact on the competitive position of a firm is the acquisition of a firm which has an important role in the **supply chain**. Companies acquire suppliers to ensure that there is no disruption in the supply of the inputs that will threaten the ability of the company to produce, sell and retain its competitive position. Although the risk of disruption can be eliminated by long-term contracts, acquisition is still considered an important option.

Case Study

The classic example of a company acquiring a supplier in spite of the presence of a long term supply contract is the acquisition of Fisher Body, the manufacturer of car bodies, by GM in 1926. This acquisition took place despite a 10 year contractual agreement between the companies that was signed in 1919.

Economies of scale

The merged company will be bigger in size than the individual companies and it will have a larger scale of operations. The larger scale of operations may give rise to what is called economies of scale from a reduction in the cost per unit resulting from increased production, realized through operational efficiencies. Economies of scale can be accomplished because as production increases, the cost of producing each additional unit falls.

Economies of scope

Scope economies or changes in product mix are another potential way in which mergers might help improve the performance of the acquiring company. Economies of scope occur when it is more economical to produce two or more products jointly in a single production unit than to produce the products in separate specializing firms. Scope economies can arise from two sources:

(a) the spreading of fixed costs over an expanded product mix; and
(b) cost complementarities in producing the different products.

Economies of scope have been invoked as the main reason driving mergers in the financial sector. The fixed capital of a bank branch for example, or its computer systems are more fully utilized when they issue not just banking products such as deposits and loans but also insurance products and investment services. These additional services allow the spreading of fixed costs over a larger number of activities reducing the unit cost of each activity.

2.1 Financial synergy: tax and debt benefits

The final aspect in an acquisition proposal has to do with the existence of financial synergies which take the form of diversification, tax and debt benefit synergies. This will be discussed in detail in **section five** of this chapter.

3 Developing an acquisition strategy

FAST FORWARD

The main reasons behind a strategy for acquiring a target firm includes the target being undervalued or to diversify operations in order to reduce risk.

Not all firms considering the acquisition of a target firm have acquisition strategies, and even if they do, they do not always stick to them. We are going to look at a number of different motives for acquisition in this section. A coherent acquisition strategy should be based on one of these motives.

3.1 Acquire undervalued firms

This is one of the main reasons for firms becoming targets for acquisition. If a predator recognises that a firm has been **undervalued** by the market it can take advantage of this discrepancy by purchasing the firm at a '**bargain**' price. The difference between the real value of the target firm and the price paid can then be seen as a '**surplus**'.

For this strategy to work, the predator firm must be able to fulfil three things.

3.1.1 Find firms that are undervalued

This might seem to be an obvious point but in practice it is not easy to have such **superior knowledge** ahead of other predators. The predator would either have to have access to **better information** than that available to other market players, or have **superior analytical tools** to those used by competitors.

3.1.2 Access to necessary funds

It is one thing being able to identify firms that are undervalued – it is quite another **obtaining** the funds to acquire them. Traditionally, **larger firms** tend to have **better access** to capital markets and internal funds than smaller firms. A history of success in **identifying** and **acquiring** undervalued firms will also make funds more accessible and future acquisitions easier.

3.1.3 Skills in executing the acquisition

There are **no gains** to be made from driving the share price up in the process of acquiring an undervalued firm. For example, suppose the estimated value of a target firm is $500 million and the current market price is $400 million. In acquiring this firm, the predator will have to pay a **premium**. If this premium exceeds 25% of the current market price (the difference between estimated value and current market price divided by current market price) then the price paid will actually **exceed** the estimated value. **No value** would thus be created by the predator.

3.2 Diversify to reduce risk

We mentioned in the appendix to Chapter 4 that firm-specific risk (**unsystematic risk**) can be reduced by holding a diversified portfolio. This is another potential acquisition strategy. Predator firms' managers believe that they may reduce earnings volatility and risk – and increase potential value – by acquiring firms in other industries.

3.2.1 Diversifying by acquisition versus diversifying across traded shares

Can diversification be achieved more efficiently at **company** level or at **individual investor** level? Obviously **individual investors** can diversify much more **cheaply** than companies can. All they have to do is buy shares in companies in different industries, whereas companies have to go through long, complicated and expensive processes in order to acquire other companies.

There are **two exceptions** to this.

(a) Owners of private firms with all or most of their wealth invested in the firm. The owner is exposed to all the risk therefore there is a greater case for diversification.

(b) Incumbent managers who have large amounts of their wealth invested in the firm. If these managers diversify through acquisition, they will reduce their exposure to total risk. This opens up other arguments as to whether these managers are acting in the best interests of the other shareholders, if the other shareholders do hold well diversified portfolios of other shares.

4 Criteria for choosing an appropriate target for acquisition

There are a number of different aspects to successful target identification. One important emerging need is to identify acquisitions in overseas markets. Acquirers must be able to assess the acquisition from the target's point of view, as well as from their own. But understanding the regulatory and competitive environment in another country can be complex and time-consuming.

Case Study

Microsoft uses the enormous resources of its extended enterprise to identify potential acquisitions. The business groups take the lead, looking within their own and related markets for opportunities. Ideas also come from venture capital relationships in both the United States and Europe, as well as through the company's alliance and partner community.

Acquirers must also be able to identify and capture new skills in the companies they buy.

Case Study

Cisco Systems, often known as the 'acquirer of choice' by target companies, is an outstanding example of success in this regard. The maker of Internet networking equipment emphasizes that it acquires people and ideas, not just technologies. The leadership and talent of the acquired company must be committed to seeing the acquisition and the integration of the company work. It is not the first version of a product that becomes a billion-dollar market, Cisco argues, but the subsequent versions. Cisco needs the acquired company's talent to stay and build those next versions.

The criteria that should be used to assess whether a target is appropriate will depend on the motive for the acquisition. The main criteria that are consistent with the underlying motive are:

Benefit for acquiring undervalued company

The target firm should trade at a price below the estimated value of the company when acquired. This is true of companies which have assets that are not exploited.

Diversification

The target firm should be in a business which is different from the acquiring firm's business and the correlation in earnings should be low.

Operating synergy

The target firm should have the characteristics that create the operating synergy. Thus the target firm should be in the same business in order to create cost savings through economies of scale. Or it should be able to create a higher growth rate through increased monopoly power.

Tax savings

The target company should have large claims to be set off against taxes and not sufficient profits. The acquisition of the target firm should provide a tax benefit to acquirer.

Increase the debt capacity

This happens when the target firm is unable to borrow money or is forced to pay high rates. The target firm should have capital structure such that its acquisition will reduce bankruptcy risk and will result in increasing its debt capacity.

Disposal of cash slack

This is where a cash rich company seeks a development target. The target company should have great projects but no funds. This happens when for example the target company has some exclusive right to product or use of asset but no funds to start activities.

Access to cash resources

A company with a number of cash intensive projects or products in their pipeline, or heavy investment in R&D might seek a company that has significant cash resources or highly cash generative product lines to support their own needs.

Control of the company

In this case the objective is to find a target firm which is badly managed and whose stock has underperformed the market. The management of an existing company is not able to fully utilize the potential of the assets of the company and the bidding company feels that it has greater expertise or better management methods. The bidding company therefore believes that the assets of the target company will generate for them a greater return than for their current owners. The criterion in this case is a market valuation of the company which is lower than for example the value of its assets.

Access to key technology

Some companies do not invest significantly in R&D but acquire their enabling technologies by acquisition. Pharmaceutical companies who take over smaller biotechs in order to get hold of the technology are a good example of this type of strategy.

5 Creating synergies

FAST FORWARD

The three main types of synergy to be gained from acquisitions or mergers are **revenue**, **cost** and **financial** synergies.

The existence of synergies has been presented as one of the two main explanations that may increase shareholder value in an acquisition. Indeed the identification, quantification and announcement of these synergies are an essential part of the process as shareholders of the companies need to be persuaded to back the merger.

The two examples below show how two takeover announcements presented their estimates of synergies.

Case Study

Euronext says the $10 billion takeover proposal by NYSE would generate cost and revenue synergies of $375 million of which $250 million will result from rationalising the combined group's IT's platforms.

The Exchange says these synergies should kick in over the first two or three years following the merger. As a result, Euronext says it is considering the 'progressive reduction' of trading fees on its equity markets by between 10 and 15% during that timeframe.

Case Study

Proposed Merger of Informa and Taylor & Francis

Released: 2 March 2004

Proposed Merger of Informa and Taylor & Francis to create a new force in specialist information

The boards of Informa and Taylor & Francis announce a proposed merger to create T&F Informa, a new international force in the provision of specialist information through its combined publishing and events businesses. T&F Informa will be a leading provider of high value specialist information to Informa and Taylor & Francis' overlapping academic, scientific, professional and commercial customer communities.

Its geographic, customer and product presence and enhanced financial strength will enable it to drive both organic and acquisition-led growth.

T&F Informa's future growth will benefit from:

- the existing strong momentum and prospects for both Informa and Taylor & Francis;
- enhanced revenue opportunities arising from new products and brand extensions across the Enlarged Group's markets;
- the cross-over demand for information in the academic, scientific, professional and commercial communities;
- a well balanced and robust portfolio of assets combining operationally geared professional and commercial operations with resilient and stable academic publishing;
- increased operational and financial scale and geographic reach; with approximately 2,500 subscription-based products and services, a book backlist of over 35,000 volumes, some 2,800 events per year and databases of approaching 10 million names; and
- annual pre-tax cost savings of at least £4.6 million by the beginning of 2005.

The one-off cost of achieving these savings is estimated at £1.3 million in 2004.

In this section we consider ways, through a series of examples, of identifying revenue, cost and financial synergies when a target company is evaluated for acquisition.

5.1 Revenue synergy

Revenue synergy exists when the acquisition of the target company will result in **higher revenues** for the acquiring company, **higher return on equity** or a **longer period of growth**. Revenue synergies arise from:

(a) Increased market power
(b) Marketing synergies
(c) Strategic synergies

Revenue synergies are more difficult to quantify relative to **financial** and **cost synergies**. When companies merge, cost synergies are relatively easy to assess pre-deal and to implement post-deal. But revenue synergies are more difficult. It is hard to be sure how customers will react to the new (in financial services mergers, massive customer defection is quite common),whether customers will actually buy the new, expanded 'total systems capabilities,' and how much of the company's declared cost savings they will demand in price concessions (this is common in automotive supplier M&A where the customers have huge purchasing power over the suppliers). Nevertheless, revenue synergies must be identified and delivered. The stock markets will be content with cost synergies for the first year after the deal, but thereafter they will want to see growth. Customer Relationship Management and Product Technology Management are the two core business processes that will enable the delivery of revenue.

5.2 Cost synergy

A **cost synergy** results primarily from the existence of **economies of scale**. As the level of operation increases, the marginal cost falls and this will be manifested in greater operating margins for the combined entity. The resulting **costs** from **economies of scale** are normally estimated to be substantial.

5.3 Sources of financial synergy

Diversification

Acquiring another firm as a way of reducing risk cannot create wealth for two publicly traded firms, with diversified stockholders, but it could create wealth for private firms or closely held publicly traded firms. A takeover, motivated only by diversification considerations, has no effect on the combined value of the two firms involved in the takeover. The value of the combined firms will always be the sum of the values of the independent firms. In the case of private firms or closely held firms, where the owners may not be diversified personally, there might be a potential value gain from diversification.

Cash slack

When a firm with significant excess cash acquires a firm, with great projects but insufficient capital, the combination can create value. Managers may reject profitable investment opportunities if they have to raise new capital to finance them. It may therefore make sense for a company with excess cash and no investment opportunities to take over a cash-poor firm with good investment opportunities, or vice versa. The additional value of combining these two firms lies in the present value of the projects that would not have been taken if they had stayed apart, but can now be taken because of the availability of cash.

Case Study

Assume that Softscape Inc, a hypothetical company, has a severe capital rationing problem, that results in approximately $500 million of investments, with a cumulative net present value of $100 million, being rejected. IBM has far more cash than promising projects, and has accumulated $4 billion in cash that it is trying to invest. It is under pressure to return the cash to the owners. If IBM takes over Softscape Inc, it can be argued that the value of the combined firm will increase by the synergy benefit of $100 million, which is the net present value of the projects possessed by the latter that can now be taken with the excess cash from the former.

Tax benefits

The tax paid by two firms combined together may be lower than the taxes paid by them as individual firms. If one of the firms has tax deductions that it cannot use because it is losing money, while the other firm has income on which it pays significant taxes, the combining of the two firms can lead to tax benefits that can be shared by the two firms. The value of this synergy is the present value of the tax savings that accrue because of this merger. The assets of the firm being taken over can be written up to reflect new market value, in some forms of mergers, leading to higher tax savings from depreciation in future years.

Debt capacity

By combining two firms, each of which has little or no capacity to carry debt, it is possible to create a firm that may have the capacity to borrow money and create value. Diversification will lead to an increase in debt capacity and an increase in the value of the firm. Has to be weighed against the immediate transfer of wealth that occurs to existing bondholders in both firms from the stockholders. When two firms in different businesses merge, the combined firm will have less variable earnings, and may be able to borrow more (have a higher debt ratio) than the individual firms.

6 Explaining high failure rate of acquisitions in enhancing shareholder value

FAST FORWARD

A number of theories have been put forward to explain the **high failure rate** of **acquisitions** in **enhancing shareholder value**. These include **agency theory**, **errors in valuing a target firm**, the **pre-emptive theory** and **market irrationality**.

The purpose of this section is to assess the various explanations put forward for the high failure rate of acquisitions in enhancing shareholder value.

One of the most common empirical findings is that in an acquisition the shareholders of the **acquiring company** seldom enjoy any benefits, whereas the shareholders of the **target company** do. What is the reason for the failure to enhance shareholder value? We said earlier that there must be some evidence of synergies or concrete proof of managerial superiority in the acquiring firm to produce an acquisition that would enhance shareholder value. A number of alternative theories explain the phenomenon of failure by

postulating that the main motive of the management of a company when they bid for another company is not maximization of the shareholder value but other motives which have been found to be consistent with empirical evidence.

6.1 Agency theory

The **agency theory** suggests that takeovers are primarily motivated by the **self-interest** of the acquirer's management. Reasons that have been advanced to explain the divergence in the interests of the management and the shareholder of a company include:

- Diversification of management's own portfolio
- Use of free cash flow to increase the size of the firm
- Acquiring assets that increase the firm's dependence on management

The common idea of these explanations is that acquisitions is a process that results in value being transferred from the shareholder of the acquiring firm to the managers of the acquiring firm.

The implication of the agency theory is that because the target firm knows that a bid is in the interest of the management rather than the shareholders of the acquiring firm, sees this bid opportunity to extract some of the value that would have gone to acquiring firm management. How much value the target firm can extract depends on the bargaining power they have.

6.2 Errors in valuing a target firm

Managers of the bidding firm may advise their company to bid too much as they do not know how to value an essentially recursive problem. A risk-changing acquisition cannot be valued without revaluing your own company on the presupposition that the acquisition has gone ahead. The value of an acquisition cannot be measured independently. As a result the merger fails as the subsequent performance cannot compensate for the high price paid.

6.3 Market irrationality

If a **rational manager** observes that his firm's stocks are overvalued in the short run, he has an incentive to exchange the overvalued stocks to real assets before the market corrects the overvaluation. A merger therefore occurs in order to take advantage of market irrationality and it is not related to either synergies or better management. The lack of the latter may in the end lead to a failing merger even though the acquired firm was bought cheaply through the exchange of over-valued shares.

6.4 Pre-emptive theory

This theory explains why acquiring firms pursue value-decreasing horizontal mergers even if managers are rational and are trying to maximize shareholders' value. If large cost savings can be achieved through the merger by several potential acquiring firms, these firms will compete for the opportunity to merge with the target. The winning firm who acquires the target could become a lower cost producer, improve its product market position and gain market share from the rivals. Intuitively, if a firm fears that one of its rivals will gain large cost savings or synergies from taking over some other firm, then it can be rational for the first firm to pre-empt this merger with a takeover attempt of its own.

6.5 Window dressing

Another reason for the high failure rate is that companies are not acquired because of the synergies that they may create, but in order to present a better financial picture in the short term.

Chapter Roundup

- Although **growth strategy through acquisition** requires high premiums, it is widely used by corporations as an alternative to **internal organic growth**.
- As an **expansion strategy** mergers are thought to provide a quicker way of acquiring productive capacity and **intangible assets** and accessing **overseas markets**.
- An **expansion strategy** through acquisition is associated with exposure to a higher level of **business and financial risk**.
- Mergers can be classified as **horizontal, vertical or conglomerate**, depending on the type of company that is acquired.

  A merger generally involves two companies pooling their interests and having common ownership of the new company's assets.

  An acquisition usually involves a stronger company (the 'predator') taking over the assets of a smaller company (the 'target') and assuming ownership of these assets.
- Expansion by **organic growth** or by acquisition should only be undertaken if it leads to an **increase** in the **wealth** of the **shareholders**.
- Aspects of a merger that will have an impact on the firm's **competitive position** include **increased market power**, the **creation of barriers to entry, supply chain security** and **economies of scope** and **scale**.
- The main reasons behind a strategy for acquiring a target firm includes the target being undervalued or to diversify operations in order to reduce risk.
- The three main types of synergy to be gained from acquisitions or mergers are **revenue**, **cost** and **financial** synergies.
- A number of theories have been put forward to explain the **high failure rate** of **acquisitions** in **enhancing shareholder value**. These include **agency theory**, **errors in valuing a target firm**, the **pre-emptive theory** and **market irrationality**.

Quick Quiz

1 State at least five criteria for choosing an appropriate target.

2 Provide three explanations for the failure of acquisitions to enhance shareholder value.

3 What are the sources of financial synergy?

4 What are the main advantages of mergers as an expansion strategy?

5 What are the main disadvantages of mergers as an expansion strategy?

Answers to Quick Quiz

1 Undervaluation of target
Diversification
Operating synergy
Tax Savings
Debt Capacity
Use of Cash slack
Control of company

2 Any three of the following

Hubris hypothesis
Market irrationality
Pre-emptive action
Window dressing

3 Diversification and reduction in volatility
Cash slack
Tax benefits
Debt capacity

4 Speed of growth
Lower cost
Acquisition of intangible assets
Access to overseas markets

5 Exposure to business risk
Exposure to financial risk
Acquisition premium
Managerial incompetence

Now try the questions below from the Exam Question Bank

Number	Level	Marks	Time
13	Introductory	8	15 mins
14	Examination	20	36 mins

12

Valuation of acquisitions and mergers

Topic list	Syllabus reference
1 The overvaluation problem	C (2) (a)
2 Estimation of the growth levels of a firm's earnings	C (2) (b)
3 The impact of an acquisition or merger upon the risk profile of the acquirer	C (2) (c)
4 Valuation of a type I acquisition of both quoted and unquoted entities	C (2) (d)
5 Valuation of type II acquisitions using the adjusted present value model	C (2) (e)
6 Valuation of type III acquisitions using iterative revaluation procedures	C (2) (f)
7 Valuation of high growth start-ups	C (2) (g)
8 Intangible assets	C (2) (d – f)
9 Firms with product options	C (2) (d – f)

Introduction

In this chapter we discuss ways of estimating the value of a target company. First we examine the various methods of predicting earnings growth for a company, using external and internal measures. We analyse the impact of an acquisition on the risk of the acquiring company and its cost of capital. We then examine the three possible types of impact of an acquisition on the risk of the acquiring company.

Study guide

		Intellectual level
C2	**Valuation for acquisitions and mergers**	
(a)	Outline the argument and the problem of overvaluation.	1
(b)	Estimate the potential near-term and continuing growth levels of a firm's earnings using both internal and external measures.	3
(c)	Assess the impact of an acquisition or merger upon the risk profile of the acquirer distinguishing:	3
(i)	Type I acquisitions that do not disturb the acquirer's exposure to financial or business risk	
(ii)	Type II acquisitions that impact upon the acquirer's exposure to financial risk	
(iii)	Type III acquisitions that impact upon the acquirer's exposure to both financial and business risk.	
(d)	Advise on the valuation of a type 1 acquisition of both quoted and unquoted entities using:	3
(i)	'Book value-plus' models	
(ii)	Market relative models	
(iii)	Cash flow models, including EVA™, MVA	
(e)	Advise on the valuation of type II acquisitions using the adjusted net present value model	3
(f)	Advise on the valuation of type III acquisitions using iterative revaluation procedures.	2
(g)	Demonstrate an understanding of the procedure for valuing high growth start-ups	2

1 The overvaluation problem

FAST FORWARD

When a company acquires another company, it always pays above its current market value. This is known as the overvaluation problem.

1.1 Examples of excessive payments for acquisitions

In Chapter 11, as part of the discussion on the causes of the failure of mergers, we have identified that excessive payments for target firms may make the acquisition uneconomical. Some examples of high prices are given below:

Case Study

Quaker Oats bought Snapple in 1994 for $1.7 billion. $500 million was lost on announcement and $100 million a year later. Snapple was spun off 2 years later at 20% of the acquisition price.

IBM bought Lotus for $3.2 billion which represented more than 100% premium probably never to be recouped.

1.2 What gives rise to the overvaluation problem?

We have already discussed the reasons why so many mergers fail to enhance shareholder value in Chapter 11.

Economic theory suggests that mergers only enhance shareholders' value if there are:

(a) **Synergies** which can be exploited or

(b) If there will be a **significant improvement** in the **management** of the **assets** of the **target** company that could be realised by an acquisition

In Chapter 11 we proposed a number of theories that could explain the **incidence** of **mergers** in the **absence** of the **two conditions** mentioned above.

Most of the theories were based on the existence of **agency problems** and the pursuit by management of takeovers that satisfied **management's goals** rather than those of the shareholders.

A reflection of these managerial motives is the control premium that management is prepared to pay in order to acquire the target company.

The larger the agency problem within the **acquiring** company, the larger the premium the **acquiring** company will be willing to pay.

Moreover, if the management/shareholders of the target company are aware that the merger will benefit the **management** of the **acquirer** rather than the **shareholders** of the **acquiring company**, then they will try to extract as much of the benefit as possible resulting in a high bid price.

Empirical studies have shown that during an acquisition, there is **normally** a **fall** in the **price** of the **bidder** and an **increase** in the **price** of the **target**.

The consensus of empirical studies is that the target company shareholders enjoy the benefit of the premium as they are paid more than the market value whereas the shareholders of the acquirer do not always benefit and sometimes even lose value as the result of the bidding.

In a sense there is a **transfer of value** from the **acquirer** to the **target**. This is reflected in the **premium** that is paid and is determined by the degree of the **agency problem** prevalent in the acquirer and the ability of the **target's shareholders** to **extract this premium**.

The overvaluation problem may of course arise as a miscalculation of the potential synergies or the overestimation of the ability of the acquiring firm's management to improve performance. Both errors will lead to a higher price being paid as compared to the current market price.

2 Estimation of the growth levels of a firm's earnings

FAST FORWARD

The growth rate of a company's earnings is the most important determinant of a company's value. The growth rate may be based on historical estimates, analyst's forecasts or company fundamentals.

The **growth rate** of a company's **earnings** is the most important factor in the **value** of the **company**. We have already considered this in the valuation formula derived from the Gordon constant growth model in section 7.1 of Chapter 6.

$$PV = \frac{FCF_0(1+g)}{k-g}$$

There are three ways to estimate the **growth rate** of earnings of a company. One is by extrapolating past values, the second is by relying on analysts' forecasts and a third is by looking at the fundamentals of the company.

2.1 Historical estimate

Historical estimates of the growth rate are estimated by observing the realised growth rates over a specific period.

The historical EPS for Megatera Inc is shown below

Year	EPS
20X6	0.53
20X5	0.43
20X4	0.37
20X3	0.26
20X2	0.25
20X1	0.18

The rate of growth is given by the formula

$$g = \left(\frac{53}{18}\right)^{1/5} - 1 = 24.1$$

There are several problems associated with historical estimates.

- First of all a decision needs to be made regarding the length of the estimation period. Too long a period may reflect conditions that are no longer relevant for the future.
- Secondly, even if the same conditions prevail, the average value estimated may not be relevant for the near term especially if growth rates are volatile. An average value may be close to the expected future growth rate over the medium term.

2.2 Analyst forecasts

The second way of estimating the growth in earnings is by using the forecasts of analysts. Analysts regularly produced forecasts on the growth of a company and these estimates can be the base for forming a view of the possible growth prospects for the company.

2.3 Company fundamentals

The determinants of the **rate of growth** of a company are the **return on equity** and the **retention rate of earnings** (that is, the proportion of earnings that are not distributed to shareholders as dividends).

The **retention rate** can be calculated by dividing the **retained earnings** by the **total earnings** during the period.

The **growth rate** can be found by multiplying **return on equity** by the **retention rate**.

Question **Implied retention rate**

On 21 December 20X6, the FT reported a dividend yield of 3.8% for BT and a price-earnings ratio (PE) of 15.3. What is the implied retention rate of BT?

Answer

The retention rate was defined above as: $\frac{\text{Retained earnings}}{\text{Total earnings}}$

Retained earnings are also defined as the difference between earnings and dividends.

Retained earnings can also be defined as:

Total earnings – dividends

Dividend yield = $\frac{\text{Diviednd per share}}{\text{Market price per share}}$

By substituting retained earnings = Total earnings – dividends into the retention rate equation, we can find that:

Retention rate = 1 – dividend yield × P/E ratio
Retention rate = 1 – 0.038 × 15.3 = 0.4186 or 41.86%

3 The impact of an acquisition or merger upon the risk profile of the acquirer

FAST FORWARD

An acquisition may have an impact on the financial and business risk exposure of the acquirer.

A Type I acquisition does not affect the acquiring firm's exposure to financial or business risk.

A Type II acquisition affects the acquiring firm's exposure to financial risk only – it does not affect exposure to business risk.

A Type III acquisition affects both the financial and business risk exposure of the acquiring firm.

We have already discussed in Chapter 7 that the total risk of the company can be divided into business risk and financial risk.

An acquisition may have an impact on both the financial and the business risk. There are three possibilities which also characterise the type of acquisitions.

(1) **Type I acquisition**

These are acquisitions that do not disturb the acquirer's exposure to financial or business risk.

(2) **Type II acquisition**

These are acquisitions that affect the acquirer's exposure to financial risk but it does not affect the exposure of the firm to business risk.

(3) **Type III acquisition**

These are acquisitions that affect the acquirer's exposure to both financial and business risk.

3.1 The business risk of the combined entity

FAST FORWARD

The business risk of the combined entity will be affected by the betas of the target and predator firs and the beta of the synergy that results from the acquisition.

3.1.1 The asset beta

The asset beta of the combined firm is the weighted average of the betas of the target firm, the predator firm and the synergy generated from the acquisition.

3.1.2 The equity beta

To obtain the equity beta for the combined entity you should follow these steps.

Step 1 Calculate the value of debt bet of tax and divide by the value of equity.

Step 2 Multiply the value from Step 1 by the difference between the beta of the combined entity an the beta of debt

Step 3 Add the value from Step 2 to the combined equity beta.

3.1.3 WACC

The WACC of the combined beta is the weighted average of the cost of equity and the cost of debt for the combined entity.

4 Valuation of a type I acquisition of both quoted and unquoted entities

FAST FORWARD

Type I acquisitions may be valued using one of the following valuation methods:

- Book value-plus models
- Market relative models
- Cash flow models, including EVA^{TM}, MVA

We defined earlier as **Type I acquisitions**, acquisitions that do not disturb the acquirer's exposure to financial or business risk.

4.1 Book value-plus models

FAST FORWARD

Book value or asset-based methods of company valuation are based on the balance sheet as the starting point in the valuation process.

Book value or asset-based methods of **company valuation** use the **balance sheet** as the starting point in the valuation process.

The balance sheet records the company's fixed assets (both tangible and intangible), current assets and liabilities to creditors, both short and long-term. After deducting long-term and short-term creditors from the total asset value, we arrive at the company's net asset value, (NAV). The book value of net assets is also referred to as 'equity shareholders' funds' as this represents the owners' stake in the company.

Question

Book value model

The summary statement of financial position of Cactus Co is as follows.

	$	$	$
Fixed assets			
Land and buildings			160,000
Plant and machinery			80,000
Motor vehicles			20,000
			260,000
Goodwill			20,000
Current assets			
Inventory		80,000	
Receivables		60,000	
Short-term investments		15,000	
Cash		5,000	
		160,000	
Current liabilities			
Payables	60,000		
Taxation	20,000		
Proposed ordinary dividend	20,000		
		(100,000)	
			60,000
			340,000
12% debentures			(60,000)
Deferred taxation			(10,000)
			270,000
			$
Ordinary shares of $1			80,000
Reserves			140,000
			220,000
4.9% preference shares of $1			50,000
			270,000

What is the value of an ordinary share using the net assets basis of valuation?

Answer

If the figures given for asset values are not questioned, the valuation would be as follows.

	$	$
Total value of net assets		340,000
Less: intangible asset (goodwill)		20,000
Total value of tangible assets (net)		320,000
Less: preference shares	50,000	
debentures	60,000	
deferred taxation	10,000	
		120,000
Net asset value of equity		200,000
Number of ordinary shares		80,000
Value per share		$2.50

4.2 Market relative models (P/E ratio)

FAST FORWARD

Market relative models may be based on the P/E ratio which produces an earnings based valuation of shares.

The P/E ratio is a very popular approach to share valuation. The P/E ratio compares a share's value to its latest earnings (profits).

Since P/E ratio = $\frac{\text{Market value}}{\text{EPS}}$, then market value per share = EPS × P/E ratio

The P/E ratio produce an **earnings-based** valuation of shares. This is done by deciding a suitable P/E ratio and multiplying this by the EPS for the shares which are being valued. The EPS could be a historical EPS or a prospective future EPS. For a given EPS figure, a higher P/E ratio will result in a higher price. **A high P/E ratio may indicate:**

Optimistic expectations

Expectations that the EPS will grow rapidly in the years to come, so that a **high price is being paid for future profit prospects.** Many small but successful and fast-growing companies are valued on the stock market on a high P/E ratio. Some stocks (for example those of some internet companies in the late 1990s) have reached high valuations before making any profits at all, on the strength of expected future earnings.

Security of earnings

A well-established low-risk company would be valued on a higher P/E ratio than a similar company whose earnings are subject to greater uncertainty.

Status

If a quoted company (the predator) made a share-for-share takeover bid for an unquoted company (the target), it would normally expect its own shares to be valued on a higher P/E ratio than the target company's shares. A quoted company ought to be a lower-risk company; but in addition, there is an advantage in having shares which are quoted on a stock market: the shares can be readily sold. **The P/E ratio of an unquoted company's shares might be around 50% to 60% of the P/E ratio of a similar public company with a full Stock Exchange listing** (and perhaps 70% of that of a company whose shares are traded on the AIM).

Case Study

Some sample P/E ratios taken from the *Financial Times* on 21 May 2004:

Market indices	
FTSE 100	16.56
FTSE all-share	17.16
FTSE all-small	>80.00
FTSE fledgling	Negative
FTSE AIM	Negative
Industry sector averages (main market)	
Chemicals	17.08
Construction	9.03
Food producers and processors	10.47
General retailers	14.61
Health	29.83
Telecommunications	23.30

Question

Offer price

Spider Inc is considering the takeover of an unquoted company, Fly Co. Spider's shares are quoted on the Stock Exchange at a price of $3.20 and since the most recent published EPS of the company is 20c, the company's P/E ratio is 16. Fly Co is a company with 100,000 shares and current earnings of $50,000, 50c per share. How might Spider Inc decide on an offer price?

Answer

The decision about the offer price is likely to be preceded by the estimation of a 'reasonable' P/E ratio in the light of the particular circumstances.

(a) If Fly Co is in the **same industry** as Spider plc, its P/E ratio ought to be lower, because of its lower status as an unquoted company.

(b) If Fly Co is in a **different industry**, a suitable P/E ratio might be based on the P/E ratio that is typical for quoted companies in that industry.

(c) If Fly Co is thought to be **growing fast**, so that its EPS will rise rapidly in the years to come, the P/E ratio that should be used for the share valuation will be higher than if only small EPS growth is expected.

(d) If the acquisition of Fly Co would **contribute substantially to Spider's own profitability and growth**, or to any other strategic objective that Spider has, then Spider should be willing to offer a higher P/E ratio valuation, in order to secure acceptance of the offer by Fly's shareholders.

Of course, the P/E ratio on which Spider bases its offer will probably be lower than the P/E ratio that Fly's shareholders think their shares ought to be valued on. Some haggling over the price might be necessary.

Spider might decide that Fly's shares ought to be valued on a P/E ratio of 60% × 16 = 9.6, that is, at 9.6 × 50p = $4.80 each.

Fly's shareholders might reject this offer, and suggest a valuation based on a P/E ratio of, say, 12.5, that is, 12.5 × 50c = $6.25.

Spider's management might then come back with a revised offer, say valuation on a P/E ratio of 10.5, that is, 10.5 × 50c = $5.25.

The haggling will go on until the negotiations either break down or succeed in arriving at an agreed price.

4.3 Market relative models – Q ratio

FAST FORWARD

Market relative models may be based on the Q ratio which is the market value of the assets divided by their replacement cost.

Key term

The **Q ratio** is defined as the market value of the assets (MV) of a company divided by the **replacement** cost of the assets (RC).

$$Q = \frac{MV}{RC}$$

Where MV = Market value of assets
RC = Replacement cost of assets

The equity version of Q is defined as:

$$Q_e = \frac{MV - \text{Market value of debt}}{RC - \text{total debt}}$$

The replacement cost of capital is difficult to estimate and in practice this is proxied by the book value of capital. The equity Q ie Q_e can therefore be approximated as:

$$Q_e = \frac{\text{Market value of equity}}{\text{Equity capital}}$$

The ratio simply shows how much the management of a company has increased the market value of the contributed capital. The Q ratio in this form is related to the **market to base ratio** and the **market value added measure** that will be discussed later.

If Q <1 then the management of the company has destroyed the value of contributed capital whereas if Q >1 then management has increased the value of the contributed capital.

As a guideline for valuing a potential target, a firm with a Q <1 is vulnerable since the assets of a company can be acquired at a cheaper price than they were bought on their own as assets. So, high-Q firms usually buy low Q-firms. In fact empirical studies have shown that in more than two thirds of all mergers the acquirer's Q exceeded the target's Q.

4.4 Free cash flow models

Exam focus point

There was a 30 mark compulsory question on acquisitions in the December 2007 exam. Part of the question focused on the validity of the use of the free cash flow model for valuing acquisitions so make sure you can critically evaluate the valuation methods in particular scenarios.

The free cash flow approach has been explained in detail in Chapter 6 in the context of project appraisal. The procedure for valuing a target company on the basis of its predicted cash flow is the same.

Step 1 Calculate the Free cash flow

The Free cash flow to the firm is defined as

FCF = EARNINGS BEFORE INTEREST AND TAXES (EBIT)
Less: TAX ON EBIT
Plus: NON CASH CHARGES
Less: CAPITAL EXPENDITURES
Less: NET WORKING CAPITAL INCREASES
Plus: SALVAGE VALUES RECEIVED
Plus: NET WORKING CAPITAL DECREASES

Example

	$
Earnings Before Interest and Taxes (EBIT)	80,000
Remove taxes (1 – Tax rate, τ)	× 70%
Operating Income After Taxes	56,000
Depreciation (non cash item)	14,000
Less Capital Expenditures	(9,000)
Less Changes to Working Capital	(1,000)
Free Cash Flow	60,000

Step 2 Forecast FCF and Terminal Value

For a time horizon of 6 years the following values need to be estimated:

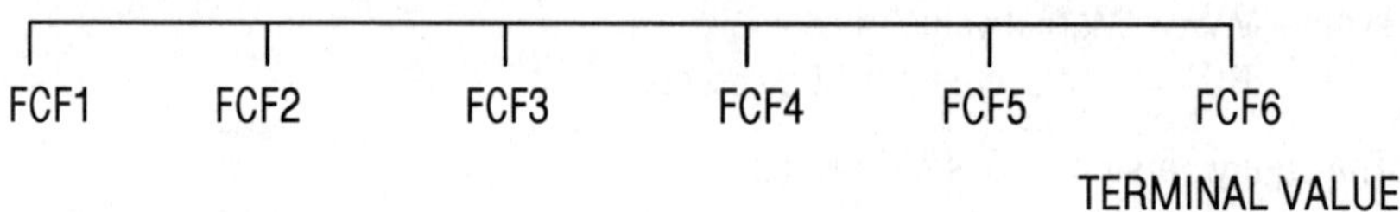

Step 3 Calculate the weighted average cost of capital (WACC)

$$WACC = K_e \times \frac{E}{D+E} + (1-T) \times K_d \times \frac{D}{D+E}$$

Where T is the tax rate
D is the value of the debt
E is the value of equity

Step 4 Discount **free cash flow** at **WACC** to obtain the value of the firm

Step 5 Calculate Equity values

Equity Value = Value of the firm – Value of Debt

Question

Aquisition

The management of Atrium Inc a company in the DIY industry considers making a bid for Tetrion Inc. a rival company. The current market price of Tetrion is $29 and a 20 percent premium will persuade Tetrion Shareholders to sell. In order to convince its shareholders, a valuation of Tetrion is undertaken. The following information is used:

Statement of financial position

	20X8	*20X7*	*Change*
	$	$	$
Cash	300	100	200
Receivables	2,500	1,500	1,000
Inventory	2,600	1,400	1,200
Property, plant and equipment	5,800	4,000	1,800
Accum depreciation	750	500	250
Net property, plant and equipment	5,050	3,500	1,550
Total assets	10,450	6,500	3,950
Accounts payables	3,600	2,560	1,040
Long-term debt	2,000	2,000	–
Common equity	5,130	2,040	3,090
Total liabilities and owners equity	10,730	6,600	4,130

Income Statement

	20X8
	$
Sales	12,000
cost of sales	3,500
Selling general administrative	3,000
Depreciation	250
Total expense	6,750
Interest	100
Income before tax	5,150
Taxes (40%)	2,060
Net income	3,090

Free Cash Flows

	20X8
	$
Cash Flows – Operations	
Revenue	12,000
Cash expenses	6,500
Taxes	2,100
Total	3,400
Cash Flows – Investments	
Working capital	1,360
Fixed assets	1,800
Total	3,160
Free Cash Flow	240

The following predictions are made by the management of Atrium for the next five years

	20X8	20X9	20Y0	20Y1	20Y2
	$	$	$	$	$
Free cash flows					
Sales	12,000	15,000	18,750	23,438	29,297
Operating costs excluding depreciation	6,500	8,125	10,156	12,695	15,869
EBDIT	5,500	6,875	8,594	10,742	13,428
Depreciation	250	300	360	432	518
EBIT	5,250	6,575	8,234	10,310	12,909
Less: tax on EBIT @ 40%	2,100	2,630	3,294	4,124	5,164
Plus depreciation	250	300	360	432	518
Less: capital expenditure	1,800	2,160	2,592	3,110	3,732
Less: additions to working capital	1,360	1,700	2,125	2,656	3,320
Free cash flow	240	385	583	851	1,211
Terminal value					10,093
Total free cash flow	240	385	583	851	11,305

If the WACC is 12 % and there are 100 shares outstanding what is the value of the shares of Tetrion Inc? If the market price of Tetrion is $29 should the shareholders of Atrium agree to the acquisition of Tetrion?

Answer

	$
PV @ 12%	7,892
Less debt	2,000
Equity value	5,892
Shares outstanding	100
Intrinsic value per share	$58.92
Market share price	$29
Discount of price from value	51%

The shareholders of Atrium should buy Tetrion at the offered price.

4.5 Economic Value Added (EVA) approach

Exam focus point

> EVA was examined as part of a 30 mark compulsory question in December 2007, in the context of analysing potential performance. The examiner commented that relatively few candidates were able to complete the EVA calculation and only a minority could explain the significance of the measure. Make sure you can do both.

Economic value added (EVA) gives the economic value or profit added per year. It can be used as a means of **measuring managerial performance**, by assessing the net present value of revenues (profits) less resources used (capital employed). We use EVA here to estimate the value of a company. EVA is calculated as follows:

EVA = Net operating profit after tax (NOPAT) – (WACC × book value of capital employed)

EVA can also be calculated as:

Book value of capital employed × (Return on invested capital – WACC)

Note that NOPAT cannot simply be lifted from the financial statements. There are numerous adjustments that may have to be made such as

(a) **Intangibles** (for example, advertising, research and development, training). These are viewed as investments and are added to the balance sheet.

(b) **Goodwill** written off and **accounting depreciation**. These are replaced by **economic depreciation**, which is a measure of the actual **decline** in the **market value** of the assets.

(c) **Net interest on debt capital** – debt is included in capital employed and the cost of debt is included in the WACC.

4.5.1 Example

	20X8	*20X7*
	$	$
Sales		2,000
Expenses other than interest		800
Depreciation		300
Earnings before interest and taxes (EBIT)		900
Taxes on EBIT @ 40%		360
Earnings before interest and after taxes (NOPAT)		540
Current assets less excess cash and securities	400	380
Non-interest bearing current liabilities	100	120
Adjusted net working capital	300	260
Gross property, plant and equipment	3,200	3,500
Accumulated depreciation	1,000	1,300
Net property, plant and equipment	2,200	2,200
Invested capital	2,500	2,460
Return on invested capital (EBIAT/invested capital) based on previous year's invested capital		21.6%

Solution

METHOD 1

Invested capital	2,500
Cost of capital	12%
Capital charge (12% of $2,500)	300
NOPAT	540
Less capital charge	(300)
EVA	240

METHOD 2

ROIC	21.6%
Less cost of capital	–12%
Excess return	9.6%
Invested capital	2,500
Times excess return	9.6%
EVA	240

4.5.2 Using EVA to calculate the value of a firm

The value of a firm can be calculated as

Value of invested capital + sum of discounted EVA

To arrive at the value of the **equity** as in the case of the free cash flow valuation, we need to **subtract** the **value of debt** from the value of the company. An example of how to calculate the value of a company using EVA is shown in the following example.

4.5.3 Example

Year	*0*	*1*	*2*	*3*	*4*	*5*
Invested capital	2,000	1,600	1,200	800	400	–
NOPAT	–	88	160	400	440	200
Less change in invested capital	(2,000)	400	400	400	400	400
Free cash flow	(2,000)	488	560	800	840	600
PV factor (WACC 10%)	1	0.91	0.83	0.75	0.68	0.62
PV of cash flow	(2,000)	444	463	601	574	373
Cumulative PV	(2,000)	(1,556)	(1,094)	(493)	81	454
NPV	454					
ROIC		4%	10%	33%	55%	50%
EVA = ROIC – WACC		(112)	–	280	360	160
PV factor	1	0.91	0.83	0.75	0.68	0.62
PV of EVA	–	(102)	–	210	246	99
Cumulative PV	–	(102)	(102)	109	354	454
Total PV of EVA	454					

4.6 Market value added approach

The Market Value Added (MVA) of a company is defined as:

MVA = Market Value of Debt + Market Value of Equity – Book Value of Equity

The MVA shows how much the management of a company has added to the value of the capital contributed by the capital providers.

The MVA is related to EVA because MVA is simply the present value of the future EVAs of the company.

In terms of the notation used in the previous section:

MVA = PV of EVA = 454

If the market value and the book value of debt is the same, then the MVA simply measures the difference between the market value of common stock and the equity capital of the firm.

A firm's equity MVA is sometimes expressed as a market to book ratio:

$$\frac{\text{MVA}}{\text{Book value}}$$

4.7 Dividend valuation basis

4.7.1 Using the dividend valuation model

The dividend valuation model is based on the theory that an equilibrium price for any share (or bond) on a stock market is:

- The **future expected stream of income** from the security
- **Discounted** at a suitable **cost of capital**

Equilibrium market price is thus a **present value** of a **future expected income stream**. The annual income stream for a share is the expected dividend every year in perpetuity.

The basic dividend-based formula for the market value of shares is expressed in the **dividend valuation model** as follows:

$$\text{MV (ex div)} = \frac{d}{1+k_e} + \frac{d}{(1+k_e)^2} + \frac{d}{(1+k_e)^3} + ... = \frac{d}{k_e}$$

Where MV = ex dividend market value of the shares
d = constant annual dividend
k_e = shareholders' required rate of return

4.7.2 The dividend growth model

Using the **dividend growth model** we have:

$$P_0 = \frac{d_0(1+g)}{(1+k_e)} + \frac{d_0(1+g)^2}{(1+k_e)^2} + ... = \frac{d_0(1+g)}{(k_e - g)}$$

where d_0 = Current year's dividend
g = Growth rate in earnings and dividends
$d_0(1+g)$ = Expected dividend in one year's time
P_0 = Market value excluding any dividend currently payable

4.7.3 Example: dividend growth

(a) If a company has a payout ratio of 40%, and retains the rest for investing in projects which yield 15%, the annual rate of growth in dividends could be estimated as 15% × 60% = 9%.

(b) If a company pays out 80% of its profits as dividends, and retains the rest for reinvestment at 15%, the current dividend would be twice as big as in (a), but annual dividend growth would be only 15% × 20% = 3%.

4.7.4 Example: dividend growth model

Tantrum has achieved earnings of $800,000 this year. The company intends to pursue a policy of financing all its investment opportunities out of retained earnings. There are considerable investment opportunities, which are expected to be available indefinitely. However, if Tantrum does not exploit any of the available opportunities, its annual earnings will remain at $800,000 in perpetuity. The following figures are available.

Proportion of earnings retained	*Growth rate in earnings*	*Required return on all investments by shareholders*
%	%	%
0	0	14
25	5	15
40	7	16

The rate of return required by shareholders would rise if earnings are retained, because of the risk associated with the new investments. What is the optimum retentions policy for Tantrum? The full dividend payment for this year will be paid in the near future in any case.

Solution

Since P_0 (MV ex div)= $\frac{D(1+g)}{(r-g)}$

$$\text{MV cum div} = \frac{D(1+g)}{(r-g)} + D$$

We are trying to maximise the value of shareholder wealth, which is currently represented by the cum div market value, since a dividend will soon be paid.

(a) If retentions are 0%:

$$\text{MV cum div} = \frac{800{,}000}{0.14} + 800{,}000 = \$6{,}514{,}286$$

(b) If retentions are 25%, the current dividend will be $600,000 and:

$$\text{MV cum div} = \frac{600{,}000(1.05)}{(0.15-0.05)} + 600{,}000 = \$6{,}900{,}000$$

(c) If retentions are 40%, the current dividend will be $480,000 and:

$$\text{MV cum div} = \frac{480{,}000(1.07)}{(0.16-0.07)} + 480{,}000 = \$6{,}186{,}667$$

The best policy (out of the three for which figures are provided) would be to retain 25% of earnings.

Question

Dividend valuation model

Target paid a dividend of $250,000 this year. The current return to shareholders of companies in the same industry as Target is 12%, although it is expected that an additional risk premium of 2% will be applicable to Target, being a smaller and unquoted company. Compute the expected valuation of Target, if:

(a) The current level of dividend is expected to continue into the foreseeable future, or
(b) The dividend is expected to grow at a rate of 4% pa into the foreseeable future

Answer

k_e = 12% + 2% = 14% (0.14) d_0 = $250,000 g (in (b)) = 4% or 0.04

(a) $P_0 = \frac{d_0}{k_e} = \frac{£250{,}000}{0.14} = \$1{,}785{,}714$

(b) $P_0 = \frac{d_0(1+g)}{k_e - g} = \frac{\$250{,}000(1.04)}{0.14-0.04} = \$2{,}600{,}000$

5 Valuation of type II acquisitions using the adjusted present value model

The theory behind the Adjusted Present Value (APV) has been explained in Chapter 6. An acquisition is valued by discounting the Free Cash Flows to the firm by the ungeared cost of equity and then adding the present value of the tax shield. The net present value is given by

APV = – Initial Investment + Value of acquired company if all – equity financed + Present Value of Debt Tax Shields

If the APV is positive then the acquisition should be undertaken

Steps for the Calculation of APV

Step 1 Calculation of FCF

FCFF = EARNINGS BEFORE INTEREST AND TAXES (EBIT)
Less: TAX ON EBIT
Plus NON CASH CHARGES
Less: CAPITAL EXPENDITURES
Less: NET WORKING CAPITAL INCREASES
Plus: SALVAGE VALUES RECEIVED
Plus: NET WORKING CAPITAL DECREASES

Step 2 Forecast FCFF and Terminal Value

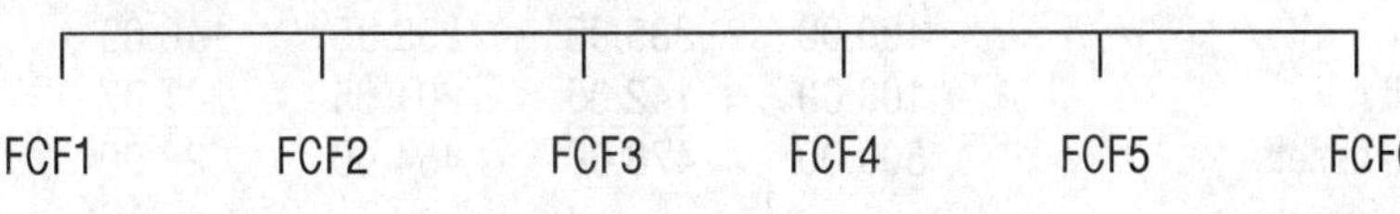

TERMINAL VALUE

Step 3 Calculation of ungeared cost of equity

The ungeared cost of equity requires the calculation of the unlevered beta of the firm, which can be calculated from the geared beta using the formula

$$\beta_U = \frac{\beta_G}{\left[1+(1-T)\frac{D}{E}\right]}$$

Step 4 Discount **free cash flow** at unlevered cost of equity to obtain

NPV of ungeared firm or project

Step 5 Calculation of ungeared cost of equity

Calculate interest tax shields

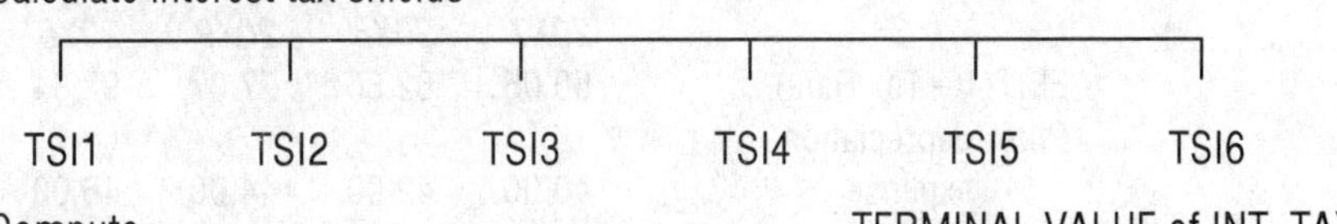

Compute

TERMINAL VALUE of INT. TAX SHIELDS

Step 6 Discount Interest tax shields

Discount at **pretax cost of debt** to obtain **PV of interest tax shields**

Step 7 Calculation of APV

APV = NPV OF UNGEARED FIRM OR PROJECT
Plus PV OF INTEREST TAX SHIELDS
Plus EXCESS CASH AND MARKETABLE SECURITIES
Less MARKET VALUE OF CONTINGENT LIABILITIES = MARKET VALUE OF FIRM
Less MARKET VALUE OF DEBT = MARKET VALUE OF EQUITY

Example

The use of the APV method will be illustrated using an example. Suppose that the management of XERON Inc is considering the acquisition of NERON Inc. an unquoted company. The owners of NERON want $500 million for the business. The analysis of the prospects of NERON by XERON is reflected in the following Income Statement and Statement of financial position.

Proforma income statements and statements of financial position

	Current Year	*Years*					
	20X7	*20X8*	*20X9*	*20Y0*	*20Y1*	*20Y2*	*20Y3*
Sales	620.00	682.00	750.20	825.22	907.74	998.52	998.52
Less: cost of goods sold	(410.00)	(441.00)	(475.10)	(512.61)	(553.87)	(599.26)	(599.26)
Gross profit	210.00	241.00	275.10	312.61	353.87	399.26	399.26
Operating expenses	(133.00)	(144.30)	(156.53)	(169.78)	(184.16)	(199.78)	(199.78)
EBIT	77.00	96.70	118.57	142.83	169.71	199.48	199.48
Less interest expense	–	(32.00)	(26.88)	(20.19)	(11.73)	(1.28)	–
Earnings before tax	77.00	64.70	91.69	122.64	157.98	198.21	199.48
Less taxes	(26.95)	(22.65)	(32.09)	(42.92)	(55.29)	(69.37)	(69.82)
Net Income	50.05	42.05	59.60	79.72	102.69	128.84	129.66
Current assets	100.00	100.00	100.00	100.00	100.00	242.90	404.55
Fixed assets	400.00	378.00	354.00	328.00	300.00	270.00	238.00
Total assets	500.00	478.00	454.00	428.00	400.00	512.90	642.55
Debt	400.00	335.95	252.35	146.63	15.94	–	–
Equity	100.00	142.05	201.65	281.37	384.06	512.90	642.55
Total assets	500.00	478.00	454.00	428.00	400.00	512.90	642.55

Assumptions

Growth rate for sales	10%
Depreciation expense (2007)	40
Interest rate on debt	8%
Tax rate	35%
All debt is interest bearing	
Capital expenditures/year	20.00
All available cash flow is applied to repaying debt until repaid in full	
Ungeared beta	1.1
Terminal value reflects level perpetuity equal to year five cash flow	
Risk free rate	6.0%
Market risk premium	7.5%

Step 1 **Calculation of Firm Free Cash Flow**

	20X7	*20X8*	*20X9*	*20Y0*	*20Y1*	*20Y2*	*20Y3*
EBIT(1 – Tax Rate)	50.05	62.86	77.07	92.84	110.31	129.66	129.66
Plus depreciation expense	40.00	42.00	44.00	46.00	48.00	50.00	52.00
Less CAPEX	(20.00)	(20.00)	(20.00)	(20.00)	(20.00)	(20.00)	(20.00)
Firm Free Cash Flow	70.05	84.86	101.07	118.84	138.31	159.66	161.66

Calculation of Capitalised Cash Flow

	2007	*2008*	*2009*	*2010*	*2011*	*2012*	*2013*
Firm Free Cash Flow	70.05	84.86	101.07	118.84	138.31	159.66	161.66
Plus interest Tax Savings	–	11.20	9.41	7.07	4.11	0.45	–
Total Cash Flow	70.05	96.06	110.48	125.91	142.42	160.11	161.66

Step 2 **Calculation of APV**

The Firm Free Cash Flow and the tax shield is discounted at the ungeared cost of equity capital which is:

$r_U = r_F + \beta_U [E(r_m) - r_F] = 6 + 1.1 \times 7.5 = 14.25$

Calculation of terminal value

The terminal value under the no-growth assumption is:

$$\frac{\$161.66}{0.1425} = \$1134.45$$

The present value of the terminal value is:

$$\frac{\$1134.45}{(1.1425)^5} = \$582.80$$

	2007	*2008*	*2009*	*2010*	*2011*	*2012*	*2013*
PV of total cash flows		84.07	84.64	84.42	83.59	82.25	582.80
Unlevered cost of equity	14.25%						
Firm value	1,001.76						
Less debt value	400.00						
Equity value	601.76						

The APV is therefore, APV = \$601.76 million – \$500 million = \$101.76 million

The managers of XERON Inc should proceed with the acquisition

Notice that the management of XERON would have arrived at the same recommendation if it had used the free cash flow to equity or to the firm approach. The calculations of both are given below.

Comparison to FCF valuation

		Years					
		2007	*2008*	*2009*	*2010*	*2011*	*2012*
WACC		11.66%	12.20%	12.99%	14.10%	14.25%	14.25%
PV of FCFs		76.00	80.67	83.95	85.63	86.52	614.79
Firm Value	1,027.57						
Less debt value	400.00						
Equity value	627.57						

Comparison to FCFE

		Years					
Direct equity valuation method		*2007*	*2008*	*2009*	*2010*	*2011*	*2012*
Geared beta		2.79	1.99	1.47	1.13	1.10	1.10
Cost of equity		26.93%	20.96%	17.04%	14.47%	14.25%	14.25%
PV of EFCFs		–	–	–	–	60.80	482.69
Equity value	543.49						

Each method gives a different answer because of the assumption we make regarding the capital structure.

6 Valuation of type III acquisitions using iterative revaluation procedures

6.1 Steps for valuing a type III acquisition

In a type III valuation both the **business** and the **financial risk** of the acquiring company change. The following steps are followed in order to value an acquisition.

Step 1 Estimate the value of the acquiring company before acquisition

Step 2 Estimate the value of the acquired company before acquisition

Step 3 Estimate the value of possible synergies resulting from the acquisition.

Step 4 Estimate the beta coefficients for the equity of the acquiring and the acquired company using the CAPM.

Step 5 Estimate the asset beta for each company

Step 6 Calculate the asset beta for the combined entity, which is the weighted average of the individual asset betas

Step 7 Calculate the geared beta of the combined firm

Step 8 Calculate the weighted average cost of capital for the combined entity

Step 9 Use the WACC derived in step 8 to discount the cash flows of the combined entity post acquisition.

The value of equity is the difference between the value of the firm and the value of the debt

6.2 Example

Omnivore Inc is considering the acquisition of Sweet Meals Co. The management of Omnivore have estimated that the cash flows of Sweet Meals will grow much faster than theirs over the next 10 years, and that considerable savings will be realised by integrating their distribution networks and marketing operations. The estimated cash flows for Omnivore, Sweet Meals and the synergies in the case of a merger are shown below. It is estimated that on acquisition Omnivore will be able to sell one of its storage sites realising an instant income of $5 million.

Year	*Sweet Meals*	*Synergies*	*Omnivore*	*Cash flows of combined entity*
20X5		5		5.00
20X6	12.00	6	42	60.00
20X7	14.40	6	45	65.40
20X8	17.28	6	48.01	71.29
20X9	20.74	6	50.97	77.70
20Y0	24.88	6	53.81	84.69
20Y1	29.86	6	56.46	92.32
20Y2	35.83	6	58.79	100.63
20Y3	39.41	6	64.27	109.68
20Y4	43.36	6	70.20	119.55
20Y5	45.52	6	78.79	130.31
Terminal value	682.86	50	1,663.97	2,396.84

The following information is available

	Omnivore	*Sweet Meals*
	$m	$m
Debt	100	20
Equity	900	280
Beta	0.9	2.4

Omnivore has decided to make a cash offer of $380 million to the shareholders of Sweet Meals for the purchase of 100 percent of their shares. The cash offer will be funded by additional borrowing.

The tax rate is 30%. Risk-free rate is 5% and the required rate of return for the combined company is 9%. Cost of debt for the combined company is expected to be 7%.

Calculate the change in equity for Omnivore's shareholders that would result from the acquisition.

Solution

The **asset beta of the combined company** is:

$$\frac{\text{Total value of Omnivore}}{\text{Total combined value}} \times \text{Beta (Omnivore)} + \frac{\text{Total value of Sweet Meals}}{\text{Total combined value}} \times \text{Beta (Sweet Meals)}$$

$$= \frac{1,000}{1,300} \times 0.9 + \frac{300}{1,300} \times 2.4 = 1.25$$

Geared beta of combined company

$$\text{Asset beta} \times \left(1+(1-T)\times\frac{\text{Total debt}}{\text{Total equity}}\right) = 1.25 \times \left(1+0.07\times\frac{500}{1,180}\right)$$ (Total debt includes $380m for 100% of Sweet Meals shares)

$$= 1.62$$

Cost of equity (using CAPM)

$K_e = 5 + 1.62 \times 4 = 11.48\%$

$$\text{WACC} = \frac{1,180}{1,680} \times 11.48 + \frac{500}{1,680} \times 7 \times 0.7 = 9.52\%$$

Discount cash flows at WACC to find the value of the combined firm = $1,422.76 million

Value of equity = Value of firm – value of debt
= $1,1,422.76 – 500
= $922.76 million

Omnivore's shareholders' value has increased by ($922.76 – 900) million = $22.76 million

6.3 A problem with the WACC

In the above example, however, we have introduced an inconsistency in the calculation of the WACC because we have assumed that equity represents 70 percent of the value of the firm (1180/1680) and debt represents 30 percent of the value of the firm (500/1680).

In the values we have derived the value of the equity represents 65 percent of the value of the firm (922.76/1422.76) and debt represents 35 percent of the value of the firm. That is, the WACC weights are not consistent with the values derived.

If the two sets of weights differ significantly, the valuation is internally inconsistent. In such circumstances, we need to adopt an iterative procedure that takes into account the interrelation between the market value of the firm and the WACC. In the iterative procedure we must go back and re-compute the beta using a revised set of weights that are closer to the weights derived from the valuation. This process is then repeated until the assumed weights and the weights calculated from the derived values are approximately equal. Because the value of the debt is assumed to be equal to its book values, the interrelation involves the WACC and the market value of the equity. A change in the WACC affects the market value of the equity, which alters the equity weight, and thereby affects the WACC.

The iteration proceeds as follows:

(a) First, the market value of FCF is initially set equal to its book value and the capital structure weights are computed.

(b) Second, given the capital structure weights the WACC is calculated and used to discount the forecast cash flows to present value.

(c) Third, the market value of the firm calculated from the discounting process is used to compute a revised value of the equity by subtracting the value of the debt. Based on this revised value, the initial assumption for the value of the equity is set equal to the original equity value plus one-half of the difference between the original value and the revised value and the program is rerun. This procedure is repeated until the change in the market value of the equity is less than a specified small value.

Fortunately this iterative procedure need not be done manually. It can be calculated in EXCELL using the Tools/Options/Calculation commands. The iteration box needs to be ticked and the maximum number of iterations to be set to a large number, 10,000 to ensure convergence. In practice since the iteration requires recalculation of the equity values, if the book values do not differ too much from the market values a few iterations will suffice for convergence.

The internally consistent results of the iterative procedure are presented below.

Value of the firm	$1,395.45 million
Value of equity	$1,395.45– 500 = $895.45 million
Geared beta	1.73
Cost of equity	11.93%
Weighted average cost of capital	9.41

The value of equity is reduced now to $895.45 million below pre-acquisition value of Omnivore. The increased debt has increased the leveraged beta and the cost of equity, but it has slightly reduced the WACC as a result of the larger proportion of debt.

The iterative procedure has shown that at this price, the acquisition of Sweet Meals is not in the interest of the Omnivore shareholders.

7 Valuation of high growth start-ups

7.1 Characteristics of high growth start-ups

FAST FORWARD

Due to their unique characteristics high growth Start-ups presents a number of challenges.

The valuation of **Start-ups** presents a number of challenges for the methods that we have considered so far due to their unique characteristics which are summarised below:

(1) Most start-ups typically have no track record
(2) Ongoing losses
(3) Few revenues, untested products
(4) Unknown market acceptance, unknown product demand
(5) Unknown competition
(6) Unknown cost structures, unknown implementation timing
(7) High development or infrastructure costs
(8) Inexperienced management

7.2 Projecting economic performance

All valuation methods require reasonable projections to be made with regard to the key drivers of the business. The following steps should be undertaken with respect to the valuation of a high-growth start up company.

Identifying the drivers

Any market-based approach or discounted cash flow analysis depends on the reasonableness of financial projections. Projections must be analyzed in light of the market potential, resources of the business, management team, financial characteristics of the guideline public companies, and other factors.

Period of projection

One characteristic of high growth start-ups is that in order to survive they need to grow very quickly. Start-ups that do grow quickly usually have operating expenses and investment needs in excess of their revenues in the first years and experience losses until the growth starts to slow down (and the resource needs begin to stabilize). This means that long-term projections, all the way out to the time when the business has sustainable positive operating margins and cash flows, need to be prepared. These projections will depend on the assumptions made about growth. However, rarely is the forecast period less than seven years.

Forecasting Growth

Forecasting growth in earnings can be accommodated in the framework we have already explained for the prediction of earnings. The growth in earnings will be:

$g = \text{retention rate} \times \text{ROIC}$

For most high growth start-ups retention rate = 1 as the company in order to achieve a high growth rate need to invest in research and development, expansion of distribution and manufacturing capacity, human resource development to attract new talent, and development of new markets, products, or techniques.

With a b =1, it means that the sole determinant of growth is the return on invested capital (ROIC). The ROIC can be estimated from industry projections from securities analysts or from an evaluation of the company's management, marketing strengths, and level of investment.

Estimation of the ROIC is possible by decomposing it further to get an insight:

$$\text{ROIC} = \frac{\text{EBIT}}{\text{IC}} = \frac{\text{EBIT}}{\text{Sales}} \times \frac{\text{Sales}}{\text{IC}} \qquad \text{(where IC = invested capital)}$$

That is the ROIC is determined by the profit margin and by revenue growth.

7.3 Valuation methods

Once growth rates have been estimated, the next step is to consider which is the most appropriate of the valuation approaches we have considered so far: net-assets, market or discounted cash flows.

Asset-based method

The asset based method is not appropriate because the value of capital in terms of tangible assets may not be high. Most of the investment of a start-up is in people, marketing and /or intellectual rights that are treated as expenses rather than as capital.

Market-based methods

The market approach to valuation also presents special problems for start-ups. This valuation process involves finding other companies, usually sold through private transactions, that are at a similar stage of development and that focus on existing or proposed products similar to those of the company being valued. Complicating factors include comparability problems, differences in fair market value from value paid by strategic acquirers, lack of disclosed information, and the fact that there usually are no earnings with which to calculate price-to-earnings ratios (in this case price-to-revenue ratios may be helpful).

Discounted cash flows

Using the DCF methodology, free cash flows are first projected and are then discounted to the present using a risk-adjusted cost of capital. For example, one could use the constant growth model which specifies that:

$$V = \frac{\text{FCF}}{r - g}$$

Our discussion of the high growth start-up indicates that the growth rates of revenues and costs may vary. Since FCF = Revenue – Costs = R – C, the value of company will be given by:

$$V = \frac{R - C}{r - g}$$

Now assuming that the growth rate of revenues g_R is different than the growth rate of costs g_C:

$$V = \frac{R}{r - g_R} - \frac{C}{r - g_C}$$

Question

Valuation of start-ups

QuickLeg is an internet legal services provider which next year expects revenue of $100 m and costs of $500 m. The revenues of the firm are expected to rise by 21 percent every year but costs will remain at the same level. The required rate of return is assumed to 22 percent. What is the value of QuickLeg?

Answer

$$V = \frac{\$100m}{0.22 - 0.21} - \frac{\$500m}{0.22 - 0} = \$7,727.27 \text{ million.}$$

The above model seems to capture the phenomenon observed in many start-ups of high losses in the first year of operations with high values of the company. The predicted profits for QuickLeg are shown in the diagram

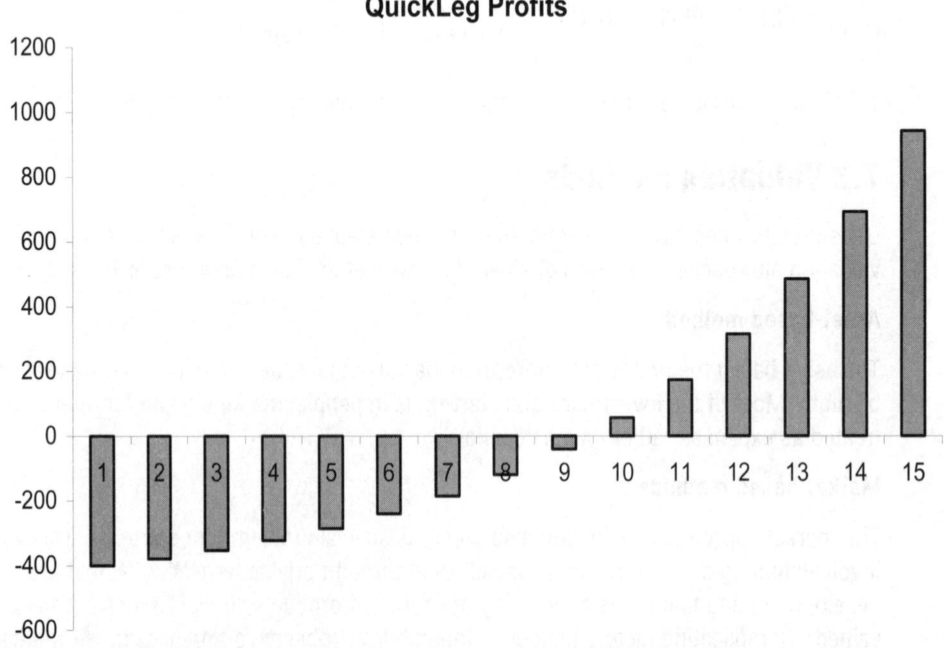

A very important problem with the discounted flow approach is the sensitivity of the valuation model to the underlying assumptions. Changes in the growth rate induced by changes in demand, technology, and management of other causes can have a dramatic effect on the value of the start-up. For example suppose that the growth rate of revenues falls from 21 percent to 20 percent. The value of the company now is:

$$V = \frac{\$100}{0.22 - 0.20} - \frac{\$500}{0.22 - 0} = \$2,727.27 \text{ million}$$

That is the company has lost $5 billion.

Another problem with the discounted cash flow is that it cannot reflect managerial flexibilities and the strategic options to expand, delay, abandon, or switch investments at various decision points. The best way of incorporating uncertainty into the discounted cash flow analysis for a new company, technology, or product is to assign probabilities of success to each of the various possibilities.

7.4 Probabilistic valuation methods

In a probabilistic cash flow model, we assume a number of scenarios for the drivers of value and derive a value under each scenario. The next step is to assign probabilities to each scenario and arrive at a weighted average value. The procedure to be followed is akin to the Monte Carlo methodology described in Chapter 6.

Example

Suppose you have calculated three valuations of QuickLeg over a 10 year forecast period. Based on your analysis of value drivers, strategies, competition, and other variables, you have assigned the following values to each scenario:

Scenario	Probability	Value Derived from Scenario	Expected value
Conservative	20	1,000	200
Normal	70	1,600	1,120
High Growth	10	2,200	220
	Overall value		1,540

Assigning the above values and respective probabilities to each scenario, the expected overall value of Quickleg is $1,540 million.

8 Intangible assets

FAST FORWARD

The valuation of **intangible assets** and **intellectual capital** presents special problems. Various methods can be used to value them including the relief from royalties, premium profits and capitalisation of earnings methods.

8.1 Valuation of intangibles

The book value-plus method discussed earlier specifically excluded most intangible assets from the computation. This rendered this method unsuitable for the valuation of most established businesses, particularly those in the service industry. Here we consider the various types of intangible assets that a business may benefit from and how they might be valued.

8.1.1 Intangible assets and goodwill

Key terms

Intangible assets are identifiable non-monetary assets without physical substance which must be controlled by the entity as the result of past events and from which the entity expects a flow of future economic benefits. *(IAS 38)*

Goodwill (acquired)is future economic benefits arising from assets that are not capable of being individually identified and separately recognised. *(IFRS 3)*

The above definition of intangible assets distinguishes:

(a) Intangible assets from tangible assets, by the phrase 'do not have physical substance'.

(b) Intangible assets from goodwill, by the word 'identifiable', an identifiable asset is legally defined as one that can be disposed of separately without disposing of a business of the entity.

The strict accounting distinctions do not need to concern us here. We are interested in any element of business that may have some value.

Certain intangible assets can be recorded at their **historical cost**. Examples include patents and trademarks being recorded at **registration value** and franchises being recorded at **contract cost**. However over time these historical values may become poor reflections of the assets' value in use or of their market value.

8.1.2 Intellectual capital

Key term

Intellectual capital is knowledge which can be used to create value. Intellectual capital includes:

(a) **Human resources**: the collective skills, experience and knowledge of employees

(b) **Intellectual assets**: knowledge which is defined and codified such as a drawing, computer program or collection of data

(c) **Intellectual property**: intellectual assets which can be legally protected, such as patents and copyrights *(OT 2005)*

As the demand for knowledge-based products grows with the changing structure of the global economy, knowledge plays an expanding role in achieving competitive advantage. Employees may thus be extremely valuable to a business, and they should be included in a full assets based valuation.

The principles of valuation discussed below should be taken as applying to all assets, resources or property that are defined as intangible assets or intellectual capital, which will include:

- Patents, trademarks and copyrights
- Franchises and licensing agreements
- Research and development
- Brands
- Technology, management and consulting processes
- Know-how, education, vocational qualification
- Customer loyalty
- Distribution channels
- Management philosophy

8.2 Measurement of intangible assets of an enterprise

The expanding intellectual capital of firms accentuates the need for methods of valuation for comparative purposes, for example when an acquisition or buy-out is being considered.

Ramona Dzinkowski (*The measurement and management of intellectual capital*, Management Accounting) identifies the following three indicators, which are derived from audited financial statements and are independent of the definitions of intellectual capital adopted by the firm.

- **Market-to-book values**
- **Tobin's 'q'**
- **Calculated intangible value**

8.2.1 Market-to-book values

This method represents the value of a firm's intellectual capital as **the difference between the book value of tangible assets and the market value of the firm**. Thus, if a company's market value is £8 million and its book value is £5 million, the £3 million difference is taken to represent the value of the firm's intangible (or intellectual) assets.

Although obviously **simple**, this method's simplicity merely serves to indicate that it fails to take account of **real world complexities.** There may be imperfections in the market valuation, and book values are subject to accounting standards which reflect historic cost and amortisation policies rather than true market values of tangible non-current assets.

In addition, the accounting valuation does not attempt to value a company as a whole, but rather as a sum of separate asset values computed under particular accounting conventions. The market, on the other hand, values the entire company as a going concern, following its defined strategy.

8.2.2 Tobin's 'q'

The Nobel prize-winning economist James Tobin developed the 'q' method initially as a way of predicting investment behaviour.

'q' is the ratio of the **market capitalisation of the firm** (share price × number of shares) to the **replacement cost** of its assets.

If the replacement cost of assets is **lower** than the market capitalisation, **q is greater than unity** and the company is enjoying higher than average returns on its investment ('monopoly rents'). Technology and so called 'human-capital' assets are likely to lead to high q values.

Tobin's 'q' is affected by the same variables influencing market capitalisation as the market-to-book method. In common with that method, it is used most appropriately to make comparisons of the value of intangible assets of companies within an industry which serve the same markets and have similar tangible non-current assets. As such, these methods could serve as performance benchmarks by which to appraise management or corporate strategy.

8.2.3 Calculated intangible values

NCI Research has developed the method of **calculated intangible value (CIV)** for calculating the fair market value of a firm's intangible assets. CIV calculates an 'excess return' on tangible assets. This figure is then used in determining the proportion of return attributable to intangible assets.

A step-by-step approach would be as follows.

Step 1 Calculate average pre-tax earnings over a time period.

Step 2 Calculate average year end tangible assets over the time period using balance sheet figures.

Step 3 Divide earnings by average assets to get the return on assets.

Step 4 Find the industry's return on assets.

Step 5 Multiply the industry's return on asset percentage by the entity's average tangible asset. Subtract this from the entity's pre-tax earnings to calculate the excess return.

Step 6 Calculate the average tax rate over the time period and multiply this by the excess return. Subtract this from the excess return to give the after-tax premium attributable to intangible assets.

Step 7 Calculate the NPV of the premium by dividing it by the entity's cost of capital.

8.2.4 Example of CIV method

Jools Inc is trying to value its intangible assets and has decided to use the CIV method. Details for Jools over the last three years are as follows.

	20X6	20X7	20X8
	$m	$m	$m
Pre-tax earnings	350.0	359.8	370.6
Tangible assets	1,507.5	1,528.9	1,555.9

The current return on assets ratio for the industry as a whole is 21%. Jools' WACC is 8%.

Calculate the fair value of Jools Inc's intangible assets, assuming an average tax rate of 30%.

Solution

Average pre-tax earnings = $\frac{350 + 359.8 + 370.6}{3}$ = \$360.13 million

Average tangible assets = $\frac{1{,}507.5 + 1{,}528.9 + 1{,}555.9}{3}$ = \$1,530.77 million

Return on assets = $\frac{360.13}{1{,}530.77}$ = 23.5%

Excess return = 360.13 – (0.21 × 1,530.77) = \$38.67 million

After-tax premium = 38.67 – (0.3 × 38.67) = \$27.07 million

NPV of premium = $\frac{27.07}{0.08}$ = \$338.38 million

8.2.5 Problems with the CIV approach

Whilst this seemingly straightforward approach, using readily available information, seems attractive, it does have two problems.

(a) It uses average industry ROA as a basis for computing excess returns, which may be distorted by extreme values.

(b) The choice of discount rate to apply to the excess returns to value the intangible asset needs to be made with care. To ensure comparability between companies and industries, some sort of average cost of capital should perhaps be applied. This again has the potential problems of distortion.

8.2.6 Lev's knowledge earnings method

FAST FORWARD

Lev's knowledge earnings method involves separating the earnings that are deemed to come from intangible assets and capitalise these earnings.

This method involves separating the earnings that are deemed to come from intangible assets and capitalise them. This model does produce results that are very close to the quoted share price, suggesting that it is a good method of valuation.

The main problem with this technique is that it can be very complicated and in the end unrealistic. In practice most valuations come from intense negotiations between the interested parties rather than complex calculations.

8.3 Valuation of individual intangible assets

8.3.1 Relief from royalties method

This method involves trying to determine:

(a) The value obtainable from licensing out the right to exploit the intangible asset to a third party, or

(b) The royalties that the owner of the intangible asset is relieved from paying through being the owner rather than the licensee

A **notional royalty rate** is estimated as a percentage of revenue expected to be generated by the intangible asset. The estimated royalty stream can then be **capitalised**, for example by discounting at a risk-free market rate, to find an estimated market value.

This relatively simple valuation method is easiest to apply if the intangible asset is already subject to licensing agreements. If they are not, the valuer might reach an appropriate figure from other comparable licensing arrangements.

8.3.2 Premium profits method

The premium profits method is often used for **brands**. It bases the valuation on capitalisation of the **extra profits generated** by the brand or other intangible asset in excess of profits made by businesses lacking the intangible asset or brand.

The premium profits specifically attributable to the brand or other intangible asset may be estimated (for example) by comparing the price of branded products and unbranded products. The estimated premium profits can then be capitalised by discounting at a risk-adjusted market rate.

8.3.3 Capitalisation of earnings method

With the capitalised earnings method, the **maintainable earnings accruing to the intangible asset** are estimated. An **earnings multiple** is then applied to the earnings, taking account of expected risks and rewards, including the prospects for future earnings growth and the risks involved. This method of valuation is often used to value **publishing titles**.

8.3.4 Comparison with market transactions method

This method looks at **actual market transactions** in similar intangible assets. A multiple of revenue or earnings from the intangible asset might then be derived from a similar market transaction. A problem with this method is that many **intangible assets are unique** and it may therefore be difficult to identify 'similar' market transactions, although this might be done by examining acquisitions and disposals of businesses that include similar intangible assets.

The method might be used alongside other valuation methods, to provide a comparison.

9 Firms with product options

FAST FORWARD

A product option is where a firm has the option to sell a product in the future but does not have the obligation to do so.

Traditional valuation techniques may not be suitable for valuing firms with product options – the option-based approach may be more suitable.

Examples of product options are patents and copyrights, and firms owning natural resources. Firms that have product options are often research and technology-based.

When a firm has a product option that is not currently generating cash flow, there is a risk that a discounted cash flow approach to valuation will not fully reflect that full value of the option. This is because a DCF approach may not incorporate all the possible future cash flows of the company.

9.1 Problems with traditional DCF techniques

The value of a firm usually comes from two different sources, as follows.

- The current assets of the business. Typically, the value of the current assets can be captured in the current cash flows of the firm.
- The present value of any future growth opportunities. Typically, the value of future growth opportunities is captured by the growth in cash flows in the future.

In the context of a product option, this approach is not fully appropriate, for the following reasons.

- The options represent a current asset of the business, but are not generating any cash flows.
- Any cash flows expected to be generated by the product could be outside of the detailed forecasting period.

9.2 Possible solutions to the valuation problem

There are three possible methods of valuing product options.

- **Value the option on the open market**. This is only possible if there is a traded market in such options. If there is no active market or if the option is difficult to separate from the other operations of the firm, this approach is probably not feasible.
- Use a traditional **DCF framework** and factor in a higher growth rate than would be justified given the existing assets of the firm. The problem with this is that any growth rate used will be subjective. In addition, it expresses contingent cash flows as expected cash flows.
- Use an **option-based approach** to valuation. This is considered below.

9.3 Use of option pricing models

Option pricing models for real options were covered in detail in chapter 8.

9.3.1 Benefits and problems of option pricing models

The benefit of using option pricing models is that the approach is based on **contingent claim valuation**, which reflects the situation more precisely than a DCF approach.

The problems of using option pricing models, such as Black-Scholes, are as follows.

(a) **They need the underlying asset to be traded**. This is because the model is based on the principle of arbitrage, which means that the underlying asset must be easy to buy and sell. This is not a problem when valuing options on quoted shares. However, the underlying asset in the context of product options will not be traded, meaning that arbitrage is not possible.

(b) **They assume that the price of the underlying asset follows a continuous pattern**. While this may be a reasonable approximation most of the time for quoted shares, it is clearly inappropriate in the context of product options. The impact of this is that the model will undervalue deeply out-of-the-money options, since it will underestimate the probability of a sudden large increase in the value of the underlying asset.

(c) **They assume that the standard deviation of price of the underlying asset is known** and does not vary over the life of the option. While this may be a reasonable assumption in the context of short-dated equity options, it is not appropriate for long-term product options.

(d) **They assume that exercise occurs at a precise point in time**. In the case of product options, exercise may occur over a long period of time. For example, if a firm has the right to mine natural resources, it will take time to extract the resources. This will reduce the present value of the asset.

9.4 Using option pricing models to value product patents

When valuing product patents as options, the key inputs for an option pricing will need to be identified, being the underlying asset price, the strike price, the expected volatility of the underlying asset price and the time to expiry. The following approach could be adopted.

Step 1 **Identify the value of the underlying asset**. This will be based on the expected cash flows that the asset can generate. Given the uncertain nature of the cash flows and the distant time periods in which they may arise, it clearly will be difficult to value the underlying asset precisely.

Step 2 **Identify the standard deviation of the cash flows above**. Again this will be difficult to identify, owing to changes in the potential market for the product, changes in technology and so on. It would, however, be possible to use techniques such as scenario analysis. The higher the standard deviation, the more valuable the asset.

Step 3 **Identify the** exercise price of the option. This is the cost of investing in the resources needed to produce the asset. It is typically assumed that this remains constant in present value terms, with any uncertainty being reflected in the cash flows of the asset.

Step 4 Identify the expiry date of the option. This is when the patent expires. Any cash flows after this date are expected to have an NPV of zero, since there will be generic competition after patent protection ends.

Step 5 **Identify the cost of delay.** If the product is not implemented immediately, this will reduce the value of the cash flows from the project as competing products will enter the market in future years.

A similar approach could be adopted to valuing other product options, such as **natural resources**. Where a company is investing in research and development, but has no patents developed, the same approach will apply, but the value of the option is clearly even more uncertain due to the greater uncertainty of the inputs.

Chapter Roundup

- When a company acquires another company, it always pays above its current market value. This is known as the overvaluation problem.
- The growth rate of a company's earnings is the most important determinant of a company's value. The growth rate may be based on historical estimates, analyst's forecasts or company fundamentals.
- An acquisition may have an impact on the financial and business risk exposure of the acquirer.

  A Type I acquisition does not affect the acquiring firm's exposure to financial or business risk.

  A Type II acquisition affects the acquiring firm's exposure to financial risk only – it does not affect exposure to business risk.

  A Type III acquisition affects both the financial and business risk exposure of the acquiring firm.
- The business risk of the combined entity will be affected by the betas of the target and predator firs and the beta of the synergy that results from the acquisition.
- Type I acquisitions may be valued using one of the following valuation methods:
  - Book value-plus models
  - Market relative models
  - Cash flow models, including EVA™, MVA
- Book value or asset-based methods of company valuation are based on the balance sheet as the starting point in the valuation process.
- Market relative models may be based on the P/E ratio which produces an earnings based valuation of shares.
- Market relative models may be based on the Q ratio which is the market value of the assets divided by their replacement cost.
- Due to their unique characteristics high growth Start-ups presents a number of challenges.
- The valuation of **intangible assets** and **intellectual capital** presents special problems. Various methods can be used to value them including the relief from royalties, premium profits and capitalisation of earnings methods.
- Lev's knowledge earnings method involves separating the earnings that are deemed to come from intangible assets and capitalise these earnings.
- A product option is where a firm has the option to sell a product in the future but does not have the obligation to do so.

  Traditional valuation techniques may not be suitable for valuing firms with product options – the option-based approach may be more suitable.

Quick Quiz

1. Give three ways in which the growth rate of a firm's earnings can be estimated.
2. What is the relationship between earnings growth and retained profits?
3. If the return on equity is 12 percent and the retention rate is 0.4 what is the growth rate of earnings?
4. What is a type I acquisition?
5. What is a type II acquisition?
6. What is a type III acquisition?
7. What is EVA™?
8. If the Q ratio is less than one, what does this tell you about the management of the company?
9. What is the most appropriate method for the valuation of type II acquisition?
10. What is the main problem with the WACC when valuing a type III acquisition?
11. If the profit margin is 30 percent and the revenue growth 20 percent what is the return on invested capital?

Answers to Quick Quiz

1. Historical estimates
   Analysts forecasts
   Company fundamentals
2. The higher the percentage of earnings retained the higher the earnings growth
3. Earnings growth = return on equity × retention rate = $0.12 \times 0.4 = 0.048$ or 4.8 percent
4. A type I acquisition is an acquisition that affects neither the business risk nor the financial risk of the acquiring company.
5. A type II acquisition is an acquisition that doesn't affect the business risk but does affect the financial risk of the acquiring company.
6. A type III acquisition is an acquisition that affects both the business risk and the financial risk of the acquiring company.
7. EVA™ is the difference between the dollar return on invested capital minus the capital charge the company needs to pay to the capital contributors.
8. A Q ratio of less than 1 means that management destroys value.
9. The Adjusted Present Value approach (APV).
10. The calculation of the WACC requires knowledge of the market value of debt and equity for which calculations we need knowledge of the WACC.
11. ROIC = Profit margin × revenue growth = $0.30 \times 0.20 = 0.06$ or 6 %

Now try the question below from the Exam Question Bank

Number	Level	Marks	Time
15	Introductory	15	27 mins
16	Examination	30	54 mins
17	Examination	40	72 mins
18	Examination	40	72 mins
19	Introductory	15	27 mins

13

Regulatory framework and processes

Topic list	Syllabus reference
1 The global regulatory framework	C(3) (a)
2 Key aspects of takeover regulation	C(3) (a)
3 Regulation in the UK	C(3) (b)
4 Defensive tactics in a hostile takeover	C(3) (b)

Introduction

In this chapter we discuss the main factors that have influenced the development of the regulatory framework for mergers and acquisitions globally and compare the two different models of regulation used in the UK and continental Europe respectively. We explain the convergence sought by the implementation of the EU Directive and discuss issues that are likely to arise in a given offer as well as defensive measures available to management in a hostile bid.

Study guide

		Intellectual level
C3	**Regulatory framework and processes**	
(a)	Demonstrate an understanding of the principal factors influencing the development of the regulatory framework for mergers and acquisitions globally and, in particular, be able to compare and contrast the shareholder versus the stakeholder models of regulation.	2
(b)	Identify the main regulatory issues which are likely to arise in the context of a given offer and (i) assess whether the offer is likely to be in the shareholders' best interests (ii) advise the directors of a target company on the most appropriate defence if a specific offer is to be treated as hostile.	3

1 The global regulatory framework

1.1 Introduction

FAST FORWARD

Takeover regulation is an important corporate governance device in protecting the interests of all stakeholders as the agency problem can have a significant potential impact on mergers and acquisitions.

The **agency problem** (discussed in Part A) and the issues arising from the separation of ownership and control have a significant potential impact on mergers and acquisitions.

In the 1980s there was both a merger boom and a succession of corporate scandals which made the need for adequate regulation both from the point of view of the shareholders and the wider group of stakeholders more pressing.

Takeover regulation is an important **corporate governance device** that seeks to protect the interests of **minority shareholders** and other types of **stakeholders** and ensure a **well-functioning market** for corporate control.

1.2 Potential conflicts of interest

Takeover regulation seeks to regulate the conflicts of interest between the management and shareholders of both the **target** and the **bidder**.

There are **two main agency problems** that emerge in the context of a takeover that regulation seeks to address.

(a) The first is the **protection of minority shareholders**. In addition to existing minority shareholders, transfers of control may turn existing majority shareholders of the target into minority shareholders.

(b) The second is the possibility that the management of the target company may implement **measures** to **prevent the takeover** even if these are **against stakeholder interests**.

1.3 Background and brief history of regulation in the UK and continental Europe

1.3.1 The City Code on Takeovers and Mergers and UK legislation

FAST FORWARD

The City Code on Takeovers and Mergers is a voluntary set of principles governing takeovers and mergers of UK companies. It is issued and administered by the Takeover Panel, an independent body of representatives from UK financial institutions with key members appointed by the Bank of England.

Takeover regulation in the UK goes back to 1968 when a **voluntary code**, the **City Code on Takeovers** and **Mergers** (known as the City Code) was introduced. Since then the Code, a set of general principles and rules governing takeovers and mergers of UK companies, has been frequently amended.

Mergers and acquisitions in the UK are also regulated by legislation through the **1985 Companies Act**, the **Financial Services and Markets Act 2000** (the FSMA) and the insider dealing provisions of the **Criminal Justice Act 1993**. The Companies Act 2006 (CA 2006) will repeat almost all of the provisions of CA 1985 and will re-state the law in plain English. Most of the provisions of CA 2006 will come into force in October 2008. However, provisions relating to public company takeovers and disclosure of major shareholding come into force in January 2007 under the new Financial Services Authority (FSA) Disclosure and Transparency rules, with FSA enforcement. See section 3.3.1.

In continental Europe, takeover regulation was put in place in the late 1980s based largely on voluntary codes following the UK City Code. However, these were soon replaced by legislation in the mid-1990s.

1.3.2 The Takeover Panel

The City Code is issued and administered by the Takeover Panel, an independent body made up of representatives from UK financial institutions and professional associations with key members currently appointed by the Bank of England.

1.3.3 Legal status of the City Code

Although the City Code (before the implementation of the EU Directive) was not legally binding, it was in practice mandatory for both UK and non-UK bidders. If a party to a takeover failed to comply with the Code they run the risk that facilities of the London Markets would be withdrawn.

In addition, the Panel could ask the Financial Services Authority under the FSMA to take action if a party's behaviour amounts to market abuse, with sanctions involving unlimited fines.

1.3.4 Scope and application of the City Code

The City Code applies to any offer where the target or offeree is a listed or unlisted public company resident in the UK, the Channel Islands or the Isle of Man.

The nature or country of residence of the company or entity making the offer, ie the bidder or offeror, does not affect the application of the City Code.

The main principles of the City Code are detailed in Section 3 below where the principal issues of which a bidder should be aware when making an offer are also discussed.

1.4 The two models of regulation

FAST FORWARD

Takeover regulation in the UK is centred around the City Code and is referred to as a 'market-based' model designed to protect a dispersed shareholder base.

Takeover regulation in the UK, centred around the City Code, is based upon what is often referred to as a **'market-based model'**[(1)] designed to protect a wide and dispersed shareholder base. This system which also prevails in the Commonwealth countries and the US is based on case law and the legal rules resulting from it. These seek to a great extent the protection of shareholder rights.

FAST FORWARD

> The system prevalent in continental Europe is referred to as the block-holder or stakeholder system and relies on codified civil law designed to protect a broader group of stakeholders.

The second system, prevalent in continental Europe, is referred to as the **'block-holder'**[1] or **stakeholder system** and relies on codified or civil law seeking to protect a broader group of stakeholders such as creditors, employees and the wider national interest.

The two systems differ not only in terms of their regulatory framework (civil versus common law) but also in terms of the underlying structure of ownership and control that they seek to address.

In the UK and the US the system is characterised by wider share ownership than in continental Europe where companies tend to be owned by majority or near-majority stakes held by a small number of investors.

In the Anglo-American model, the emphasis is on the agency problem and the protection of the widely distributed shareholder base.

The civil law countries rely via **legislation** on the monitoring by large shareholders, **creditors** and **employees**.

[1] *Georgen, Martynova and Renneboog (2005) Corporate governance convergence: evidence from takeover regulations reforms in Europe Oxford Review of Economic Policy*

1.5 Towards European harmonisation – the EU Takeovers Directive

FAST FORWARD

> The Takeovers Directive was introduced by the EU in 2002 and its principles became effective from May 2006 in order to achieve harmonisation and convergence of the market based and stakeholder systems.

The **Takeovers Directive** lays down for the first time minimum EU rules concerning the regulation of takeovers of companies whose shares are traded on regulated markets. It is one of the measures adopted under the EU Financial Services Action Plan and aims to strengthen the single market in financial services.

The **Takeover Directive** requires that certain of the activities of the **Takeover Panel** are placed within a legal framework bringing an end to the non-statutory approach to regulation in the UK. In terms of approach, the new regulatory model leads to the **convergence** of the **European system** to the **UK-US** one by adopting many of the elements of the **City Code**.

The **European Commission**, seeking to harmonise European takeover regulation presented a draft Takeover Directive in 2002. This draft introduced the following five main regulatory devices (the rationale of which is explained in Section 2 below).

(a) Mandatory-bid rule
(b) The principle of equal treatment of shareholders
(c) A squeeze-out rule and sell-out rights
(d) The principle of board neutrality
(e) A break-through rule

The break-through rule, described below, faced much resistance and the directive allowed individual countries to opt out of it.

2 Key aspects of takeover regulation

Goergen, Martynova and Renneboog [1] (2005) in their investigation of takeover reforms in Europe and the trend towards harmonisation, identify the following seven regulatory devices available to regulators and aimed at the protection of shareholders.

The mandatory-bid rule

The aim of this rule is to protect minority shareholders by providing them with the opportunity to exit the company at a fair price once the bidder has accumulated a certain percentage of the shares.

National thresholds vary between countries but the trend has been for these to decrease over the years.

In the UK, this threshold is specified by the City Code for Takeovers and Mergers and is at 30%.

The mandatory-bid rule is based on the grounds that once the bidder obtains control he may exploit his position at the expense of minority shareholders. This is why the mandatory-bid rule normally also specifies the price that is to be paid for the shares.

The bidder is normally required to offer to the remaining shareholders a price not lower than the highest price for the shares already acquired during a specified period prior to the bid.

The principle of equal treatment

The principle of treating all shareholders equally is fundamental in all western European countries.

In general terms, the principle of equal treatment requires the bidder to offer to minority shareholders the same terms as those offered to earlier shareholders from whom the controlling block was acquired.

Transparency of ownership and control

The disclosure of information about major shareholdings is an important element of investor protection and a well-functioning corporate market. The transparency enables the regulator to monitor large shareholders, minimise potential agency problems and investigate insider dealing. It also enables both minority shareholders and the market to monitor large shareholders who may be able to exercise undue influence or exact benefits at the expense of other shareholdings.

The squeeze-out and sell-out rights

Squeeze-out rights gives the bidder who has acquired a specific percentage of the equity (usually 90%) the right to force minority shareholders to sell their shares.

The threshold in the UK and in most European countries is 90%, although in Belgium, France, Germany and the Netherlands the threshold is 95% and in Ireland it is the lowest at 80%. The rule enables the bidder to acquire 100% of the equity once the threshold percentage has been reached and eliminates potential problems that could be caused by minority shareholders.

Sell-out rights enable minority shareholders to require the majority shareholder to purchase their shares.

[1] Georgen, Martynova and Renneboog (2005) Corporate governance convergence: evidence from takeover regulations reforms in Europe Oxford Review of Economic Policy

The one share-one vote principle

Where the one share-one vote principle is upheld, arrangements restricting voting rights are forbidden.

Differentiated voting rights, such as non-voting shares and dual-clan shares with multiple voting rights, enable some shareholders to accumulate control at the expense of other shareholders and could provide a significant barrier to potential takeovers.

The break-through rule

The effect of the break-through rule, where this is allowed by corporate law, is to enable a bidder with a specified proportion of the company's equity to break-through the company's multiple voting rights and exercise control as if one share-one vote existed.

Board neutrality and anti-takeover measures

Seeking to address the agency issue where management may be tempted to act in their own interests at the expense of the interests of the shareholders, several regulatory devices propose board neutrality. For instance the board would not be permitted to carry out post-bid aggressive defensive tactics (such as selling the company's main assets, known as crown jewels defence, or entering into special arrangements giving rights to existing shareholders to buy shares at a low price, known as poison pill defence), without the prior authority of the shareholders.

3 Regulation in the UK

3.1 The City Code: general principles

The City Code is divided into general principles and detailed rules which must be observed by persons involved in a merger or takeover transaction. The ten principles of the City Code are the following.

1 **All the shareholders of the target company must be treated similarly**

'All shareholders of the same class of an offeree company must be **treated similarly** by an offeror.' In other words, a company making a takeover bid cannot offer one set of purchase terms to some shareholders in the target company, and a different set of terms to other shareholders holding shares of the same class in that company.

2 **All information disclosed to one or more shareholders of the target company must be disclosed to all**

'During the course of a takeover, or when such is in contemplation, neither the offeror nor the offeree company ... may furnish information to some shareholders which is **not made available** to all shareholders.'

3 **An offer should only be made if it can be implemented in full**

Individuals or firms should not make an offer unless they have reason to believe that they will be able to implement this in full.

4 **Sufficient information, advice and time to be given for a properly informed decision**

'Shareholders must be given **sufficient information and advice** to enable them to reach a properly informed decision and must have sufficient time to do so. No relevant information should be withheld from them.'

5 **All documentation should be of the highest standards of accuracy**

All documentation produced by the bidding company or the directors of the target should be produced to the highest standards of accuracy.

6 **All parties must do everything to ensure that a false market is not created in the shares of the target company**

A false market is created when a deliberate attempt is made to distort the market in the offeror's or target's shares. An example would be where false information is either given or withheld in such a way as to prevent the free negotiation of prices.

7 **Shareholder approval**

'At no time after a *bona fide* offer has been communicated to the board of an offeree company ... may any action be taken by the board of the offeree company in relation to the affairs of the company, **without the approval of the shareholders** in general meeting, which could effectively result in any *bona fide* offer being frustrated or in the shareholders being denied an opportunity to decide on its merits.' In other words, directors of a target company are not permitted to frustrate a takeover bid, nor to prevent the shareholders from having a chance to decide for themselves.

8 **'Rights of control must be exercised in good faith and the oppression of a minority is wholly unacceptable'**

For example, a holding company cannot take decisions about a takeover bid for one of its subsidiaries in such a way that minority shareholders would be unfairly treated.

9 **The directors of both target and bidder must act in the interest of their respective companies**

The directors of both companies in the acquisition must act in the interest of their companies with no regard for their own holding or any of that of their family or any other special interest.

10 **'Where control of a company is acquired ... a general offer to all other shareholders is normally required'**

Control is defined as a 'holding, or aggregate holdings, of shares carrying 30% of the voting rights of a company, irrespective of whether that holding or holdings gives *de facto* control'.

3.2 Timetable for compliance with City Code

The City Code lays down time limits governing the overall period of an offer. The aim of the timetable is to minimise disruption of the normal activities of the target.

3.2.1 Outline timetable for a takeover offer

Day	Action Required	Note	Rule
–28	Announcement of intention to bid.	The offer document must be posted to the shareholders within 28 days of the notice of intention to make the offer.	30.1
0	Last day for posting offer document.		
+14	Last day for target's written response to offer.	The target company's board should advise its shareholders of its views on the offer. The target board's views may already be contained in the offer document if this is an offer which the board recommend.	30.2
+21	Earliest day for offer to close.	The offer cannot close before 21 days have passed from the day the intention to bid was announced.	31.1
+39	Last day for target to announce material new information including trading results, profit or dividend forecasts and any other relevant information.		
+42	Target shareholders may withdraw their acceptance if offer is not unconditional.		
+46	Last day for offeror to revise its offer.	Any subsequent revised offer must be kept open for at least 14 days after the revised offer document is posted. Therefore, because the acceptance condition (see 3.3.2 below) must be met within 50 days, no revised document may be posted after day 46.	32.1
+60	Last day for offer to be declared unconditional as to acceptances.	If the acceptance condition (see 3.3.2 below) is not satisfied by day 60 then the offer will lapse.	31.6
+81	Last day for offer to be made wholly unconditional.		
+95	Last day for paying the offer consideration to the target shareholders who accepted by day 81.		

3.2.2 The acceptance condition

Whether an offer is successful or not depends on whether the offeror has sufficient acceptances to give it the required degree of control over the target. Therefore the offeror makes the offer subject to the condition that a minimum level of acceptance is achieved. The minimum acceptance condition permitted is 50% of the target's voting rights. Normally, however, a 90% condition will be specified because this is the level that will enable the offeror to force the remaining minority shareholders to sell their shares under the compulsory acquisition per the Companies Act 1985.

If the specified level of acceptances is not reached within 60 days from posting the offer document, the offer will lapse.

3.3 Stake building and the relevant thresholds

Normally, a potential offeror will wish to build a stake prior to making an offer. The City Code places a number of restrictions to regulate the substantial acquisition of shares (SARs) where the resulting holding would represent between 15 and 30 percent of the voting rights. These rules were intended to make the market and the offeree board and shareholders aware of the potential offeror's interest and give them more time to decide how to proceed. However, these were abolished in May 2006. Following the abolition of SARS, any person can acquire a stake of up to 29.9 percent in a listed or AIM (Alternative Investment Market) company without being subject to any timing restrictions. Some of the important share stakes and their consequences are outlined below:

%	Consequence	Source of regulation
Any	Ability of the company to enquire as to the ultimate ownership under s212 CA 1985.	CA 1985
3%	Requirement to disclose interest in the company under ss198-199 CA 1985 (the material interests rules)	CA 1985
10%	Shareholders controlling not less than 10% of the voting rights may requisition the company to serve notices, under s212 CA 1985 to identify another shareholder. Notifiable interests rules of CA 1985 become operative for institutional investors and non-beneficial stakes.	CA 1985
30%	City Code definition of effective control. Mandatory bid triggered and takeover offer becomes compulsory. If the bidder holds between 30% and 50% (normally due to earlier attempts at a takeover) a mandatory offer is triggered with any additional purchase.	City Code rule 9 City Code rule 5
50%+	CA 1985 definition of control (since at this level the holder will have the ability to pass ordinary resolutions). First point at which a full offer could be declared unconditional with regard to acceptances. Minimum acceptance condition (see 3.2.2 above).	CA 1985 City Code
75%	Major control boundary since at this level the holder will be able to pass special resolutions.	
90%	Minorities may be able to force the majority to buy out their stake. Equally, the majority may, subject to the way in which the stake has been acquired, require the minority to sell out their position. Compulsory acquisition of remaining 10% is now possible.	CA 1985

3.3.1 Disclosure and Transparency Rules (DIR) – from 20 January 2007

The relevant sections of CA 1985 relating to disclosure have been repealed with effect from January 2007. These have been replaced by the new **Disclosure and Transparency Rules (DTR)** to be enforced by the FSA and introduced as part of the process of implementation of the **Transparency Directive**, which must be completed by 20 January 2007.

In the new rules, the FSA will retain the current notification threshold of a 3% holding, and every 1% thereafter.

Instead of disclosure of 'interests' in shares as under the Companies Act 1985, the Transparency Directive requires the disclosure of **holdings of shares to which voting rights are attached**.

3.4 The Competition Commission

A UK company might have to consider whether its proposed takeover would be drawn to the attention of the Competition Commission (formerly called the Monopolies and Mergers Commission). Under the terms of the Monopolies and Mergers Act, the Office of Fair Trading (OFT) is entitled to scrutinise and possibly reject all major mergers and takeovers. If the OFT thinks that a merger or takeover might be against the public interest, it can refer it to the **Competition Commission** (formerly called the Monopolies and Mergers Commission).

If a transaction is referred to the Competition Commission and the Commission finds that it results in a substantial lessening of competition in the defined market, it will specify action to remedy or prevent the adverse effects identified, or it may decide that the merger does not take place (or, in the case of a completed merger, is reversed).

Any person aggrieved by a decision of the OFT, the Secretary of State or the Competition Commission in connection with a reference or possible reference, may apply to the Competition Appeal Tribunal (CAT) for a review of that decision.

A number of tests may be used to decide whether there has been a **substantial lessening** of **competition** (SLC). These normally include:

The turnover test

No investigation will normally be conducted if the target's turnover is less than £70 million.

The share of supply test

An investigation will not normally be conducted unless, following the merger, the combined entity supplies 25 percent. The 25 percent share will be assessed by the commission.

The substantial lessening of competition test

Even if the thresholds in (a) and (b) above are met, the Competition Commission will only be involved if there has been a substantial lessening of competition (SLC) in the market.

3.5 The European Union

Mergers fall within the exclusive jurisdiction of the European Union where, following the merger, the following two tests are met

(a) **Worldwide turnover** of more than **€5 billion per annum**
(b) **European Union** turnover of more than **€250 million per annum**

The European Union will assess the merger in a similar way as the Competition Commission in the UK by considering the effect on competition in the market.

The merger will be blocked if the merged company results in a market oligopoly or results in such a dominant position in the market, that consumer choice and prices will be affected.

4 Defensive tactics in a hostile takeover

FAST FORWARD

There are a number of defensive measures that can be taken where the management of the takeover target perceives the bid to be hostile. Takeover defences can be categorised into **pre-offer** and **post-offer** defences.

Most takeovers may be referred to as **friendly** and take place when the management of the two firms negotiate an agreement that is **beneficial** to both sides.

However, not all takeovers are negotiated in this way and some are perceived as hostile and resisted by the directors.

There are a number of **defensive** measures that can be taken where the management of the takeover target perceives the bid as **hostile**.

Takeover defences can be categorised into **pre-offer defences** and **post-offer defences**. Both types of defence have developed over the years, mainly in the US during the wave of takeover bids of the 1980s.

The more **aggressive tactics** which often **risk shareholders' interests** in favour of those of management. The EU Takeover Directive seeks to override certain of the more aggressive tactics that may be taken by management to frustrate a bid and which may be at the expense of the shareholders.

Both **pre-offer** and **post-offer defences** are set out below, together with an explanation of what can be appropriately used in the UK following the implementation of the Takeover Directive.

(a) **Pre-bid defences** normally include provisions in the company's articles of association whereby **differential share structures** are set up under which **minority shareholders** exercise **disproportionate voting rights**, thus enabling the target to frustrate a takeover bid.

    The Takeover Directive, now being implemented in the UK, gives companies with voting shares traded on a regulated market to opt for the breakthrough provisions should they wish to do so, thereby breaking the restrictions on voting rights.

(b) **Post-bid defences** include actions such as selling the major assets of the company (crown jewels) in an attempt to make the target less attractive and setting up schemes where existing shareholders can but shares at very low prices (poison pill). The Takeover directive now incorporated into the **City Code** requires that the management of the company does not take any such defensive action unless this is authorised by the shareholders.

Summary of defensive tactics

Tactic	Explanation
Golden parachute	Large compensation payments made to the top management of the target firm if their positions are eliminated due to hostile takeover. This may include cash or bonus payments, stock options or a combination of these.
Poison pill	This is an attempt to make a company unattractive normally by giving the right to existing shareholders to buy shares at a very low price. Poison pills have many variants.
White knights and white squires	This would involve inviting a firm that would rescue the target from the unwanted bidder. The white knight would act as a friendly counter-bidder. A white squire is similar to a white knight but the former does not take control of the target firm.
Crown jewels	The firm's most valuable assets may be the main reason that the firm became a takeover target in the first place. By selling these or entering into arrangements such as sale and leaseback, the firm is making itself less attractive as a target.

Tactic	Explanation
Pacman defence	This defence is carried out by mounting a counter-bid for the attacker. The Pacman defence is an aggressive rather than defensive tactic and will only work where the original acquirer is a public company with diverse shareholdings. This tactic also appears to suggest that the company's management are in favour of the acquisition but they disagree about which company should be in control.
Litigation or regulatory defence	The target company can challenge the acquisition by inviting an investigation by the regulatory authorities or though the courts. The target may be able to sue for a temporary order to stop the predator from buying any more of its shares.

Chapter Roundup

- Takeover regulation is an important corporate governance device in protecting the interests of all stakeholders as the agency problem can have a significant potential impact on mergers and acquisitions.
- The City Code on Takeovers and Mergers is a voluntary set of principles governing takeovers and mergers of UK companies. It is issued and administered by the Takeover Panel, an independent body of representatives from UK financial institutions with key members appointed by the Bank of England.
- Takeover regulation in the UK is centred around the City Code and is referred to as a 'market-based' model designed to protect a dispersed shareholder base.
- The system prevalent in continental Europe is referred to as the block-holder or stakeholder system and relies on codified civil law designed to protect a broader group of stakeholders.
- The Takeovers Directive was introduced by the EU in 2002 and its principles became effective from May 2006 in order to achieve harmonisation and convergence of the market based and stakeholder systems.
- There are a number of defensive measures that can be taken where the management of the takeover target perceives the bid to be hostile. Takeover defences can be categorised into **pre-offer** and **post-offer** defences.

Quick Quiz

1 What are the two models of takeover regulation?

2 What are the key points of the takeover regulation?

3 What are the ten principles of the City Code?

4 Which mergers fall within the jurisdiction of the European Union?

5 What are the main defensive tactics in a takeover?

Answers to Quick Quiz

1 The market-based model
The stakeholder system

2 The mandatory-bid rule
The principle of equal treatment
Transparency of ownership and control
The squeeze-out and sell-out rights
The one share-one vote principle
The break through rule
Board neutrality and anti-takeover measures

3 All the shareholders of the target company must be treated similarly

All information disclosed to one or more shareholders of the target company must be disclosed

An offer should only be made if it can be implemented in full

Sufficient information, advice and time to be given for a properly informed decision

All documents should be of the highest standards of accuracy

All parties must do everything to ensure that false market is not created in the shares of the target company

Shareholder approval

Rights of control must be exercised in good faith and the oppression of a minority is wholly unacceptable

The directors of both target and bidder must act in the interest of their respective companies

Where control of a company is acquired a general offer to all other shareholders is normally required.

4 Mergers where the resulting combined company will have worldwide turnover of more than €5 billion per annum.

Mergers where the resulting combined company will have a European Union turnover in excess of €250 million per annum.

5 Golden parachute
Poison Pill
White knights and white squires
Crown jewels
Pacman Defence
Litigation or regulatory defence

Now try the question below from the Exam Question Bank

Number	Level	Marks	Time
20	Examination	20	36

Financing mergers and acquisitions

14

Topic list	Syllabus reference
1 Methods of financing mergers	C(4) (a)
2 Assessing a given offer	C(4) (b)
3 Effect of an offer on financial position and performance	C(4) (c)

Introduction

In this chapter we deal with three issues. First we discuss how a bidding firm can finance an acquisition, either by cash or by a share offer or a combination of the two, and discuss the funding of cash offers. Second we discuss ways to evaluate a financial offer in terms of the impact on the acquiring company and criteria for acceptance or rejection. Finally we discuss ways of estimating the possible impact of an offer on the performance and the financial position of the acquiring firm.

Study guide

		Intellectual level
C4	**Financing acquisitions and mergers**	
(a)	Compare the various sources of financing available for a proposed cash-based acquisition	3
(b)	Evaluate the advantages and disadvantages of a financial offer for a given acquisition proposal using pure or mixed mode financing and recommend the most appropriate offer to be made	3
(c)	Assess the impact of a given financial offer on the reported financial position and performance of the acquirer	3

Exam guide

Questions in this area are likely to involve some calculations so you will need to bring in your knowledge of company valuation. However, questions will not be purely numerical. Topics you might be asked to discuss include why companies might choose to make an offer in a particular form, takeover tactics, the effect on shareholder wealth, and what happens after the takeover including post-audits. Questions on the subjects discussed in this chapter will be **regularly** set in the compulsory section of this paper.

1 Methods of financing mergers

FAST FORWARD

Payment can be in the form of **cash**, a **share exchange** or **convertible loan stock**. The choice will depend on available cash, desired levels of gearing, shareholders' taxation position and changes in control.

1.1 Methods of payment

The terms of a takeover will involve a purchase of the shares of the target company for **cash** or for **'paper'** (shares, or possibly loan stock). A purchase of a target company's shares with shares of the predator company is referred to as a **share exchange**.

1.2 Cash purchases

If the purchase consideration is in **cash**, the shareholders of the target company will simply be bought out. For example, suppose that there are two companies.

	Big Co	*Small Co*
Net assets (book value)	$1,500,000	$200,000
Number of shares	100,000	10,000
Earnings	$2,000,000	$40,000

Big Co negotiates a takeover of Small Co for $400,000 in cash.

As a result, Big Co will end up with:

(a) Net assets (book value) of

$1,500,000 + $200,000 – $400,000 cash = $1,300,000

(b) 100,000 shares (no change)

(c) Expected earnings of $2,040,000, minus the loss of interest (net of tax) which would have been obtained from the investment of the $400,000 in cash which was given up to acquire Small Co

1.3 Funding cash offers

A cash offer can be financed from:

(a) **The company's retained earnings.** This is a common way when the firm to be acquired is small compared to the acquiring firm, but not very common if the target firm is large relative to the acquiring firm. A company occasionally may divest of some of its own assets to accumulate cash prior to bidding for another company.

(b) **The proceeds of a debt issue.** That is the company may raise money by issuing bonds. This is not an approach that is normally taken, because the act of issuing bonds will alert the markets to the intentions of the company to bid for another company and it may lead investors to buy the shares of potential targets, raising their prices.

(c) **A loan facility from a bank.** This can be done as a short term funding strategy, until the bid is accepted and then the company is free to make a bond issue.

(d) **Mezzanine finance**. This may be the only route for companies that do not have access to the bond markets in order to issue bonds.

1.4 Purchases by share exchange

One company can acquire another company by **issuing shares** to pay for the acquisition. The new shares might be issued:

(a) **In exchange** for shares in the target company. Thus, if A Inc acquires B Co, A Inc might issue shares which it gives to B Co's shareholders in exchange for their shares. The B Co shareholders therefore become new shareholders of A Inc. This is a takeover for a 'paper' consideration. Paper offers will often be accompanied by a **cash alternative.**

(b) **To raise cash** on the stock market, which will then be used to buy the target company's shares. To the target company shareholders, this is a cash bid.

Sometimes, a company might acquire another in a share exchange, but the shares are then **sold immediately** on a stock market to raise cash for the seller.

Whatever the detailed arrangements of a takeover with paper, the end result will be an **increase in the issued share capital of the predator company**.

1.5 Use of convertible loan stock

Alternative forms of paper consideration, including debentures, loan stock and preference shares, are not so commonly used, due to

- **Difficulties** in **establishing a rate of return** that will be attractive to target shareholders
- The **effects** on the **gearing levels** of the acquiring company
- The **change** in the **structure** of the target shareholders' portfolios
- The **securities** being potentially **less marketable**, and possibly lacking voting rights

Issuing **convertible loan stock** will overcome some of these drawbacks, by offering the target shareholders the option of partaking in the future profits of the company if they wish.

Key term

Convertible loan stock is a loan which gives the holder the right to convert to other securities, normally ordinary shares, at a predetermined price/rate and time.

1.6 The choice between a cash offer and a paper offer

The choice between cash and paper offers (or a combination of both) will depend on how the different methods are viewed by the company and its existing shareholders, and on the attitudes of the shareholders of the target company. Generally speaking, firms which believe that their stock is under valued will not use stock to do acquisitions. Conversely, firms which believe that their stock is over or correctly valued will use stock to do acquisitions. Not surprisingly, the premium paid is larger when an acquisition is financed with stock rather than cash. There might be an accounting rationale for using stock as opposed to cash. You are allowed to use pooling instead of purchase. There might also be a tax rationale for using stock. Cash acquisitions create tax liabilities to the selling firm's stockholders.

The use of stock to finance a merger may be a sign of an agency problem – that is, trying to exploit the information advantage the acquirer has over the target firm's shareholders. There is also the possibility that mergers may reflect agency problems between the acquiring firm's managers and its shareholders. There is evidence that mergers increase the private benefits of managers even when they do not benefit a firm's shareholders. A declining stock price may indicate that management is pursuing its own goals rather than solely attempting to maximize shareholder value.

The factors that the directors of the bidding company must consider include the following.

COMPANY AND ITS EXISTING SHAREHOLDERS	
Dilution of EPS	Fall in EPS attributable to existing shareholders may occur if purchase consideration is in equity shares
Cost to the company	Use of loan stock to back cash offer will attract tax relief on interest and have lower cost than equity. Convertible loan stock can have lower coupon rate than ordinary stock
Gearing	Highly geared company may not be able to issue further loan stock to obtain cash for cash offer
Control	Control could change considerably if large number of new shares issued
Authorised share capital increase	May be required if consideration is in form of shares. This will involve calling a general meeting to pass the necessary resolution
Borrowing limits increase	General meeting resolution also required if borrowing limits have to change

SHAREHOLDERS IN TARGET COMPANY	
Taxation	If consideration is cash, many investors may suffer immediate liability to tax on capital gain
Income	If consideration is not cash, arrangement must mean existing income is maintained, or be compensated by suitable capital gain or reasonable growth expectations
Future investments	Shareholders who want to retain stake in target business may prefer shares
Share price	If consideration is shares, recipients will want to be sure that the shares retain their values

1.7 Mezzanine finance and takeover bids

When the purchase consideration in a takeover bid is cash, the cash must be obtained somehow by the bidding company, in order to pay for the shares that it buys. Occasionally, the company will have sufficient cash in hand to pay for the target company's shares. More frequently, the cash will have to be raised, possibly from existing shareholders, by means of **a rights issue** or, more probably, by **borrowing from banks** or other financial institutions.

When cash for a takeover is raised by borrowing, the loans would normally be **medium-term** and **secured**.

However, there have been many takeover bids, with a cash purchase option for the target company's shareholders, where the bidding company has arranged loans that:

(a) Are **short-to-medium term**

(b) Are **unsecured** (that is, 'junior' debt, low in the priority list for repayment in the event of liquidation of the borrower)

(c) Because they are unsecured, attract a **much higher rate of interest** than secured debt (typically 4% or 5% above LIBOR)

(d) Often, give the lender the **option to exchange** the loan for shares after the takeover

This type of borrowing is called **mezzanine finance** (because it lies between equity and debt financing) – a form of finance which is also often used in **management buyouts** (which are discussed later in this chapter).

1.8 Earn-out arrangements

The purchase consideration may not all be paid at the time of acquisition. Part of it may be deferred, payable upon the target company reaching certain performance targets. You should refer back to Chapter 6.

2 Assessing a given offer

FAST FORWARD

Shareholders of both the companies involved in a merger will be sensitive to the effect of the merger on **share prices** and **earnings per share**.

2.1 The market values of the companies' shares during a takeover bid

Market share prices can be very important during a takeover bid. Suppose that Velvet Inc decides to make a takeover bid for the shares of Noggin Inc. Noggin Inc shares are currently quoted on the market at \$2 each. Velvet shares are quoted at \$4.50 and Velvet offers one of its shares for every two shares in Noggin, thus making an offer at current market values worth \$2.25 per share in Noggin. This is only the value of the bid so long as Velvet's shares remain valued at \$4.50. If their value falls, the bid will become less attractive.

This is why companies that make takeover bids with a share exchange offer are always concerned that the market value of their shares should not fall during the takeover negotiations, before the target company's shareholders have decided whether to accept the bid.

Case Study

In November 2000, **PricewaterhouseCoopers (PwC)**, the accountancy group, were about three days away from signing a \$18bn deal with computer group Hewlett-Packard (HP) to sell HP PwC's consultancy division. Then HP announced that it had missed its Wall Street earnings estimate by a wide margin, its share price dropped by nearly 13%, to \$34.13, taking the share price down to a level 45% below that at which the talks had started. The bid, unsurprisingly, failed. With HP trading at well below its year-high price of \$78, the acquisition would have been a pricey one.

If the market price of the target company's shares rises above the offer price during the course of a takeover bid, the bid price will seem too low, and the takeover is then likely to fail, with shareholders in the target company refusing to sell their shares to the bidder.

2.2 EPS before and after a takeover

If one company acquires another by issuing shares, its EPS will **go up or down** according to the P/E ratio at which the target company has been bought.

(a) If the **target company's shares** are **bought** at a **higher P/E** ratio than the predator company's shares, the predator company's shareholders will suffer a **fall in EPS**.

(b) If the target company's shares are valued at a lower **P/E ratio**, the **predator company's shareholders** will benefit from a **rise in EPS**.

2.3 Example: Mergers and takeovers (1)

Giant Inc takes over Tiddler Co by offering two shares in Giant for one share in Tiddler. Details about each company are as follows.

	Giant Inc	*Tiddler Co*
Number of shares	2,800,000	100,000
Market value per share	$4	–
Annual earnings	$560,000	$50,000
EPS	20p	50p
P/E ratio	20	

By offering two shares in Giant worth $4 each for one share in Tiddler, the valuation placed on each Tiddler share is $8, and with Tiddler's EPS of 50p, this implies that Tiddler would be acquired on a P/E ratio of 16. This is lower than the P/E ratio of Giant, which is 20.

If the acquisition produces no synergy, and there is no growth in the earnings of either Giant or its new subsidiary Tiddler, then the EPS of Giant would still be higher than before, because Tiddler was bought on a lower P/E ratio. The combined group's results would be as follows.

	Giant group
Number of shares (2,800,000 + 200,000)	3,000,000
Annual earnings (560,000 + 50,000)	610,000
EPS	20.33p

If the P/E ratio is still 20, the market value per share would be $4.07 ($20.33 \times 20$), which is 7c more than the pre-takeover price.

The process of buying a company with a higher EPS in order to boost your own EPS is known as **bootstrapping**. Whether the stock market is fooled by this process is debatable. The P/E ratio is likely to fall after the takeover in the absence of synergistic or other gains.

2.4 Example: Mergers and takeovers (2)

Redwood Inc agrees to acquire the shares of Hawthorn Co in a share exchange arrangement. The agreed P/E ratio for Hawthorn's shares is 15.

	Redwood Inc	*Hawthorn Co*
Number of shares	3,000,000	100,000
Market price per share	$2	–
Earnings	$600,000	$120,000
P/E ratio	10	

The EPS of Hawthorn Co is $1.20, and so the agreed price per share will be $1.20 × 15 = $18. In a share exchange agreement, Redwood would have to issue nine new shares (valued at $2 each) to acquire each share in Hawthorn, and so a total of 900,000 new shares must be issued to complete the takeover.

After the takeover, the enlarged company would have 3,900,000 shares in issue and, assuming no earnings growth, total earnings of $720,000. This would give an EPS of:

$$\frac{\$720{,}000}{3{,}900{,}000} = 18.5\text{p}$$

The pre-takeover EPS of Redwood was 20p, and so the EPS would fall. This is because Hawthorne has been bought on a higher P/E ratio (15 compared with Redwood's 10).

2.5 Buying companies on a higher P/E ratio, but with profit growth

Buying companies with a higher P/E ratio will result in a fall in EPS unless there is profit growth to offset this fall. For example, suppose that Starving Inc acquires Bigmeal Inc, by offering two shares in Starving for three shares in Bigmeal. Details of each company are as follows:

	Starving Inc	*Bigmeal Inc*
Number of shares	5,000,000	3,000,000
Value per share	\$6	\$4
Annual earnings		
Current	\$2,000,000	\$600,000
Next year	\$2,200,000	\$950,000
EPS	40p	20p
P/E ratio	15	20

Starving Inc is acquiring Bigmeal Inc on a higher P/E ratio, and it is only the profit growth in the acquired subsidiary that gives the enlarged Starving group its growth in EPS.

	Starving group
Number of shares (5,000,000 + 3,000,000 × 2/3)	7,000,000

Earnings

If no profit growth (2,000,000 + 600,000) \$2,600,000	EPS would have been 37.14p
With profit growth (2,200,000 + 950,000) \$3,150,000	EPS will be 45p

If an acquisition strategy involves buying companies on a higher P/E ratio, it is therefore essential for continuing EPS growth that the acquired companies offer prospects of strong profit growth.

2.6 Further points to consider: net assets per share and the quality of earnings

FAST FORWARD

There are circumstances where a dilution of earnings is acceptable if any of the following benefits arise as a result:

- Earnings growth
- Quality of earnings acquired is superior
- Dilution of earnings compensated by an increase in net asset backing

You might think that **dilution of earnings** must be avoided at all costs. However, there are **three** cases where a dilution of earnings might be accepted on an acquisition if there were other advantages to be gained.

(a) **Earnings growth** may hide the dilution in EPS as above

(b) A company might be willing to accept earnings dilution if the **quality of the acquired company's earnings** is superior to that of the acquiring company

(c) A trading company with high earnings, but with few assets, may want to increase its assets base by acquiring a company which is strong in assets but weak in earnings so that assets and earnings get more into line with each other. In this case, **dilution in earnings is compensated for by an increase in net asset backing.**

Question — Effect of acquisition

Intangible Inc has an issued capital of 2,000,000 \$1 ordinary shares. Net assets (excluding goodwill) are \$2,500,000 and annual earnings average \$1,500,000. The company is valued by the stock market on a P/E ratio of 8. Tangible Co has an issued capital of 1,000,000 ordinary shares. Net assets (excluding goodwill) are \$3,500,000 and annual earnings average \$400,000. The shareholders of Tangible Co accept an all-equity offer from Intangible Inc valuing each share in Tangible Co at \$4. Calculate Intangible Inc's earnings and assets per share before and after the acquisition of Tangible Co.

Answer

(a) Before the acquisition of Tangible Co, the position is as follows.

$$\text{Earnings per share (EPS)} = \frac{\$1,500,000}{2,000,000} = 75c$$

$$\text{Assets per share (APS)} = \frac{\$2,500,000}{2,000,000} = \$1.25$$

(b) Tangible Co's EPS figure is 40c ($400,000 ÷ 1,000,000), and the company is being bought on a multiple of 10 at $4 per share. As the takeover consideration is being satisfied by shares, Intangible Inc's earnings will be diluted because Intangible Inc is valuing Tangible Co on a higher multiple of earnings than itself. Intangible Inc will have to issue 666,667 (4,000,000/6) shares valued at $6 each (earnings of 75c per share at a multiple of 8) to satisfy the $4,000,000 consideration. The results for Intangible Inc will be as follows.

$$\text{EPS} = \frac{\$1,900,000}{2,666,667} = 71.25c \text{ (3.75c lower than the previous 75c)}$$

$$\text{APS} = \frac{\$6,000,000}{2,666,667} = \$2.25 \text{ (\$1 higher than the previous \$1.25)}$$

If Intangible Inc is still valued on the stock market on a P/E ratio of 8, the share price should fall by approximately 30c (8 × 3.75c, the fall in EPS) but because the asset backing $\left(\frac{\text{Net assets exc goodwill}}{\text{Shares}}\right)$ has been increased substantially the company will probably now be valued on a higher P/E ratio than 8.

The shareholders in Tangible Co would receive 666,667 shares in Intangible Inc in exchange for their current 1,000,000 shares, that is, two shares in Intangible for every three shares currently held.

(a) **Earnings**

	$
Three shares in Tangible earn (3 × 40c)	1.200
Two shares in Intangible will earn (2 × 71.25c)	1.425
Increase in earnings, per three shares held in Tangible	0.225

(b) **Assets**

	$
Three shares in Tangible have an asset backing of (3 × $3.5)	10.50
Two shares in Intangible will have an asset backing of (2 × $2.25)	4.50
Loss in asset backing, per three shares held in Tangible	6.00

The shareholders in Tangible Co would be trading asset backing for an increase in earnings.

Question — Effect of acquisition

Roytel Inc is a ready- meal preparing company for schools in Gooland. The market for school meals is satiated and there are few profitable investment opportunities for the company in its current line of business. The board has decided to look outside the ready-meal sector into other sectors for possible candidates for acquisition. They have narrowed down the potential candidates to two. Quinnon Co which owns a number of hotels in the south east of Gooland, and Geranium Co which owns a number of leisure centres for children in the area of Katycille, which is the capital of Goodland.

The current return on assets and the expected growth rates for the three companies are shown below.

	Roytel	*Quinnon*	*Geranium*
Return on Assets	0.04	0.12	0.15
Growth Rate	0.04	0.18	0.14

The profit and loss account and the balance sheet of the three companies are:

INCOME STATEMENT

	Roytel	*Quinnon*	*Geranium*
Net Operating Income	3.71	8.91	18.4
Interest On Debt	1.50	1.20	1.20
Profit before taxation	2.21	7.71	17.2
Taxes	0.66	2.31	5.16
Net Income	1.55	5.40	12.04
Number of Shares (millions)	5	1	2
Earnings per share	0.31	5.40	6.02

STATEMENT OF FINANCIAL POSITION

	Roytel	*Quinnon*	*Geranium*
Debt	15	12	12
Equity	50	40	80
Total Assets	65	52	92

Find which of the two firms should be acquired based on the impact on the EPS of Roytel.

Answer

The analysis shows that an acquisition of Quinnon by Roytel will result in a decline in the earnings per share for the Roytel shareholders. On the other hand an acquisition of Geranium will nearly double EPS.

	Roytel Acquiring Quinnon	*Roytel Acquiring Geranium*
Number of new shares in the combined company	25	23
Total earnings of the combined company	6.95	13.59
EPS in the combined company	0.28	0.59
Change in EPS of Roytel Shareholders	–0.03	0.28

3 Effect of offer on financial position and performance

FAST FORWARD

Often takeovers fail to achieve their full potential because of lack of attention paid to **post-acquisition integration**. A clear programme should be in place, designed to re-define objectives and strategy, and take appropriate care of the human element.

3.1 Effects on earnings

Failures of takeovers often result from **inadequate integration** of the companies after the takeover has taken place. There is a tendency for senior management to devote their energies to the next acquisition rather than to the newly-acquired firm. The particular approach adopted will depend upon the **culture** of the organisation as well as the **nature** of the company acquired and **how it fits** into the amalgamated organisation (eg horizontally, vertically, or as part of a diversified conglomerate).

One obvious place to start is to assess how the merger will affect earnings. P/E ratios (price to earnings per share) can be used as a rough indicator for assessing the impact on earnings. The higher the P/E Ratio of the acquiring firm compared to the target company, the greater the increase in Earnings per Share (EPS) to the acquiring firm. Dilution of EPS occurs when the P/E ratio paid for the target exceeds the P/E ratio of the acquiring company. The size of the target's earnings is also important; the larger the target's earnings are relative to the acquirer, the greater the increase to EPS for the combined company. The following examples will illustrate these points.

Question

Effect of acquisition I

Greer Company has plans to acquire Holt Company by exchanging stock. Greer will issue 1.5 shares of its stock for each share of Holt. Financial information for the two companies is as follows:

	Greer	*Holt*
Net income	$400,000	$100,000
Shares outstanding	200,000	25,000
Earnings per share	$2.00	$4.00
Market price of stock	$40.00	$48.00

Greer expects the P/E Ratio for the combined company to be 15. What is the expected share price after the acquisition?

Answer

Combined earnings = $400,000 + $100,000 = $500,000

Combined shares = 200,000 shares + (25,000 x 1.5) = 237,500

Combined EPS = $500,000/237,500 = $2.11

Expected price of stock = expected P/E ratio × combined EPS = 15 × $2.11 = $31.65

Question

Effect of acquisition II

Romer Company will acquire all of the outstanding stock of Dayton Company through an exchange of stock. Romer is offering $65.00 per share for Dayton. Financial information for the two companies is as follows.

	Romer	*Dayton*
Net income	$50,000	$10,000
Shares outstanding	5,000	2,000
Earnings per share	$10.00	$5.00
Market price of stock	$150.00	
P/E ratio	15	

Required

(a) Calculate shares to be issued by Romer

(b) Calculate combined EPS

(c) Calculate P/E ratio paid: price offered/EPS of target

(d) Compare P/E ratio paid to current P/E ratio

(e) Calculate maximum price before dilution of EPS

Answer

(a) Shares to be issued by Romer: $65/$150 × 2,000 shares = 867 shares to be issued.

(b) Combined EPS: ($50,000 + $10,000)/(5,000 + 867) = $10.23

(c) Calculate P/E ratio paid: price offered/EPS of target or $65.00/$5.00 = 13

(d) P/E ratio paid to current P/E ratio: since 13 is less than the current ratio of 15, there should be no dilution of EPS for the combined company.

(e) Maximum price before dilution of EPS: 15 = price/$5.00 or $75.00 per share. $75.00 is the maximum price that Romer should pay before EPS are diluted.

3.2 Effects on the statement of financial position

In this example we investigate the effects of a takeover of the financial position of a company by looking at the statement of financial position sheet of the company. ABC Co is planning to bid for DEZ Co. The acquisition will be funded by cash which ABC will borrow.

STATEMENT OF FINANCIAL POSITION OF ABC

ASSETS	$m	LIABILITIES	$m
Fixed assets	600	Short-term liabilities	30
Equity investments	20	Long-term liabilities	100
Receivables	15	Equity capital	15
Cash	45	Share premium	35
		Profit and loss reserve	500
	680		680

STATEMENT OF FINANCIAL POSITION OF DEZ CO

ASSETS	$m	LIABILITIES	$m
Fixed assets	80	Short-term liabilities	10
Equity investments	5	Long-term liabilities	10
Receivables	25	Equity capital	20
Cash	10	Share premium	30
		Profit and loss reserve	50
	120		120

This is a cash offer funded entirely by the issue of debt. The company makes an offer of $120m which is raised by issuing corporate bonds worth $120m.

STATEMENT OF FINANCIAL POSITION OF ABC AFTER THE OFFER

ASSETS	$m	LIABILITIES	$m
Fixed assets	600	Short-term liabilities	30
Equity Investments	20	Long-term liabilities	220
Receivables	15	Equity capital	15
Cash	45	Share premium	35
Investment	120	Profit and loss reserve	500
	800		800

CONSOLIDATED STATEMENT OF FINANCIAL POSITION

ASSETS	$m	LIABILITIES	$m
Fixed Assets	680	Short –term liabilities	40
Equity Investments	25	Long – term liabilities	230
Receivables	40	Equity Capital	15
Cash	55	Share premium	35
Goodwill	20	Profit and loss reserve	500
	820		820

Chapter Roundup

- Payment can be in the form of **cash**, a **share exchange** or **convertible loan stock**. The choice will depend on available cash, desired levels of gearing, shareholders' taxation position and changes in control.
- Shareholders of both the companies involved in a merger will be sensitive to the effect of the merger on **share prices** and **earnings per share**.
- There are circumstances where a dilution of earnings is acceptable if any of the following benefits arise as a result:
  - Earnings growth
  - Quality of earnings acquired is superior
  - Dilution of earnings compensated by an increase in net asset backing
- Often takeovers fail to achieve their full potential because of lack of attention paid to **post-acquisition integration**. A clear programme should be in place, designed to re-define objectives and strategy, and take appropriate care of the human element.

Quick Quiz

1 What are the main factors a bidding company needs to consider in order to decide between a paper and a cash offer?

2 What are the main factors the shareholders of a target company need to consider in order to decide between a cash or a paper offer?

3 Yellow Company has plans to acquire Brown Company by exchanging stock. Yellow will issue 2 shares of its stock for each share of Brown. Financial information for the two companies is as follows:

	Yellow	*Brown*
Net income	500	200
Shares outstanding	300	50
Earnings per share $	2.5	3.8
Market price of stock	38	50

Yellow expects the P/E Ratio for the combined company to be 12. Produce an estimate of the value of the shares of the combined company.

Answers to Quick Quiz

1. Dilution of EPS
   Cost of the company
   Gearing
   Control
   Authorised share capital increase
   Borrowing limits increase

2. Taxation
   Income
   Future investments
   Share price

3. Combined earnings = $500,000 + $200,000 = $700,000
   Combined shares = 300,000 shares + (50,000 x 2) = 400,000
   Combined EPS = $700,000/400,000 = $1.75

   Expected price of stock = expected P/E ratio × combined EPS
   = 12 × $1.75 = $21.00

Now try the question below from the Exam Question Bank

Number	Level	Marks	Time
21	Introductory	15	27 mins

PART D

Corporate reconstruction and reorganisation

15

Predicting corporate failure

Topic list	Syllabus reference
1 Overview	D 1(a)
2 Financial and non-financial characteristics of companies	D 1(a)
3 Financial ratios	D 1(a)
4 Issues in the use of financial ratios	D 1(a)
5 Other information from companies' accounts	D 1(a)
6 Use of financial ratios, Z-scores and Zeta scores	D 1(a)
7 Financial distress models in emerging markets	D 1(b)

Introduction

In this chapter, we discuss the main methodology for predicting corporate failure based on the financial characteristics of companies. The chapter reviews industry accepted models such as the Z and Zeta models.

The application of these models to emerging markets and the problems of implementation are also discussed.

Study guide

		Intellectual level
D1	**Predicting corporate failure**	3
(a)	Assess the risk of corporate failure within the short to medium term using a range of appropriate financial evaluation methods (this will require an ability to use multivariate techniques such as the Z and Zeta score models)	3
(b)	Advise on the application of financial distress models to firms in emerging markets given local regulatory and financial market conditions.	3

1 Overview

The financial stability of a company is of great concern to its many stakeholders (employees, investors, lenders, government). Financial stability of a company is particularly important to its lenders and this and this importance is reflected both in the vast literature on measuring credit risk and in a series of proposals on the assessment of credit risks by the Bank of International Settlements.

Key term

The **credit risk** of a borrower is defined as the potential that a borrower will fail to meet its obligations in accordance with agreed terms.

In this chapter we concentrate on a review of the most common techniques used to predict business failure.

There are two major approaches to predicting corporate failure.

(a) The first approach is based on **option pricing theory**, and views equity as an option on the assets of a firm. The exercise price of the option is the level of the debt of the company. Thus a company will be bankrupt when the value of the assets is less than the outstanding debt. That is, bankruptcy occurs when the option at expiration is not in the money. Estimating the **probability** of **default** of a company is then equivalent to estimating the **probability** that a **call option** will **not be exercised**.

The option pricing model is explained fully in Chapter 21. Factors that affect the **probability of default** according to the **option pricing model** are the **leverage ratio**, the **volatility of assets** and the **maturity of debt**. Thus the model could be used to derive the probability of default for every company and thus predict business failure. However, the model is considered too simple to accommodate other factors that may impact on the behaviour of companies, such as liquidity and quality of management. This approach is discussed in Chapter 21.

(b) The second approach discussed in this chapter generalises the option pricing methodology to include a variety of **other financial ratios**. Indeed the published credit scoring models of rating companies are based on sets of financial ratios.

2 Financial and non-financial characteristics of companies

FAST FORWARD

Company characteristics are the means of discriminating between firms that may fail and firms that may survive.

Business failure can be predicted by models such as **Argenti's model**, which emphasises defects, mistakes and symptoms.

In describing the state of a company, analysts normally rely on **financial characteristics**, as well as on characteristics such as **size**, **quality of management** and **industry structure**. It is possible of course that good management and monopolistic power in an industry would ultimately be reflected in financial performance. However, timing issues may also be important and therefore the effect of management

change which is measured today may not be fully reflected within the time frame of our analysis. Thus one may want to investigate differences in companies in terms of **non-financial characteristics**.

The fundamental factors that may cause corporate failure have been identified by Argenti and are classified as **internal factors** and **external factors**.

(a) The main **internal factor** is **bad management** manifested through **lack of responsiveness to change in technology**, **bad communication**, **misfeasance** and **fraud**, **insufficient consideration for cost factors**, **poor knowledge** of **financial matters** and **high leverage position**.

(b) The main **external factors** are effect of **labour unions** where **too high a wage settlement** causing the firm to pay its employees in excess of their marginal product, **government regulations** which impede, in some instances, the functioning of the market system distorting in the process its signals to the corporate decision makers, and natural causes such as natural disasters, demographic changes, etc. All the above causes may or may not be reflected on the balance sheet in a timely or accurate fashion for use by the analyst.

So in addition to the analysis of the information contained in the financial statements, **non-financial factors** exist that may modify the evaluation of the company. Some of these **non-financial** factors are discussed below:

- Foreign exposure
- Quality of management
- Ownership structure

Foreign exposure is important for exporting or importing companies, as part of the revenue or expenses may be influenced by events outside the country of operation. Foreign currency exposure is an important possible source of risk, especially if the publication of information on hedging currency risk is not obligatory.

The **quality of management** and the depth of administrative structure in a company are more difficult to evaluate. **Positive aspects** of management will be reflected in a **steady growth pattern**. **Negative aspects** would include a firm founded and headed by one person who is approaching retirement and has made **no plan for succession.** Equally **negative** is the firm that has had **numerous changes of management** and philosophy. On the other hand excessive stability is not always desirable. Characteristics of a good management team include **depth**, a clear line of **succession** if the chief officers are nearing retirement, and a **diversity of age** within the management team.

Ownership of the firm should also be considered as a factor. If one family or group of investors owns a controlling interest in a firm, they may be too conservative in reacting to changes in the market. Owners should also be judged in terms of whether they are strategic or financial. Often financial buyers invest for the short to intermediate term, hoping to sell their positions (or the entire company) at a profit. In such a case a company may not plan for **longer-term growth** and it may be in its interest to boost **short-term growth** at the expense of **long term prospects**.

From historical data on a wide range of actual cases, **Argenti** mapped company characteristics into **measurable financial symptoms** which were used to predict the likelihood of company failure. A summary of Argenti's method is shown below:

FACTORS IN ARGENTI'S MODEL	
Defects	Autocratic Chief Executive (Robert Maxwell is an example here) Passive board Lack of budgetary control
Mistakes	Over-trading (expanding faster than cash funding) Gearing – high bank overdrafts/loans Failure of large project jeopardises the company
Symptoms	Deteriorating ratios Creative accounting – signs of window-dressing Declining morale and declining quality

A second issue that faces the investigator is to determine when a financial characteristic of a company deviates from the norm. In other words we need a norm in order to compare these characteristics to other companies or to the industry. For example, a financial characteristic of a company such as sales growth may appear attractive on its own for a company, but for an industry it may not be. There are many industry considerations that should be taken account of such as:

- Economic cyclicality
- Growth prospects
- Research and development expenses
- Competitors
- Sources of supply
- Degree of regulation
- Labour relationships
- Accounting policies

An additional degree of complexity is added because these factors should be considered in a global context since the elimination of trade barriers seems to have increased the competitive pressures on all sectors of an economy. The economic crisis in the Far East, the Russian bond crisis, oil price volatility, all constitute factors that make the economic analysis of a company from the view point of domestic market seriously deficient.

3 Financial ratios

FAST FORWARD

Financial ratios provide a means of summarising financial information about a company. They can be grouped under the headings **profitability**, **liquidity**, **gearing** and **shareholders' investment**. It is important to calculate **relevant ratios** and to take into account the **limitations** of **ratio analysis.**

Ratios can be grouped into the following four categories:

- Profitability and return
- Debt and gearing
- Liquidity: control of cash and other working capital items
- Shareholders' investment ratios (or 'stock market ratios')

The Du Pont system of ratio analysis involves constructing a pyramid of interrelated ratios like that below:

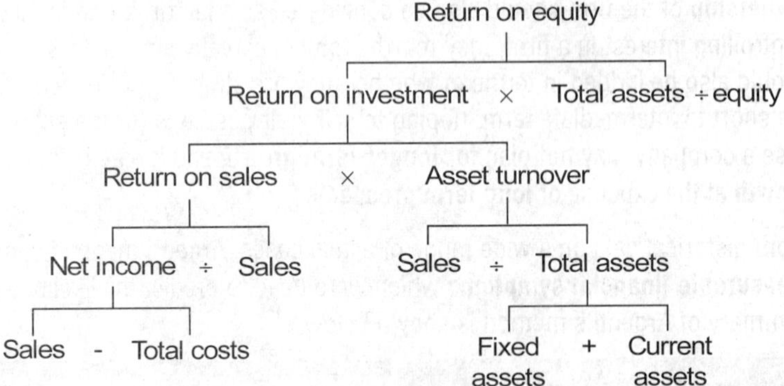

Such **ratio pyramids** help in providing for an overall management plan to achieve profitability, and allow the interrelationships between ratios to be checked.

Exam focus point

Although you will have encountered most or all of the ratios that we are about to define before, make sure you know how to calculate them in the exam. Performance measures were examined in December 2007, not just the calculations, but also interpretation.

A useful classification of financial ratios has been suggested by Bob Ryan in his book *Finance and Accounting for Business*. The PERL framework developed by Bob Ryan classifies ratios into four categories:

- **Performance**
- **Efficiency**
- **Risk**
- **Liquidity**

The complete PERL framework of financial ratios is shown below:

PERFORMANCE	**EFFICIENCY**
ROCE ROE RFCE (Return on fixed capital employed) ROTA (Return on total assets) Margins (gross, operating, net)	CER (Cash exhaustion ratio) FAT (Fixed asset turnover ratio) Labour asset turnover (LAT) Labour productivity ratio (LPR) Debtor age Creditor age Stock turnover (days)
RISK	**LIQUIDITY**
Gearing Interest cover Interest gearing Cost (operational gearing) Beaver failure ratio	CAR (current asset ratio) Acid test Cash exhaustion ratio Operating cash flow to maturing obligations

Source: Bob Ryan: Financial and Accounting for Business. Published by Thomson

3.1 Profitability and return: the return on capital employed (ROCE)

A company ought of course to be profitable, and obvious checks on **profitability** are:

- Whether the company has made a profit or a loss on its ordinary activities
- By how much this year's profit or loss is bigger or smaller than last year's profit or loss

It is impossible to assess profits or profit growth properly without relating them to the amount of funds (the capital) employed in making the profits. An important profitability ratio is therefore **return on capital employed (ROCE)**, which states the profit as a percentage of the amount of capital employed. **Profit** is usually taken as PBIT, and **capital employed** is shareholders' capital plus long-term liabilities and debt capital. This is the same as total assets less current liabilities.

The underlying principle is that we must compare like with like, and so if capital means share capital and reserves plus long-term liabilities and debt capital, profit must mean the profit earned by all this capital together. This is PBIT, since interest is the return for loan capital.

$$\text{Thus ROCE} = \frac{\text{Profit on ordinary activities before interest and taxation (PBIT)}}{\text{Capital employed}}$$

Capital employed = Shareholders' funds plus 'creditors: amounts falling due after more than one year' plus any long-term provisions for liabilities and charges.

3.1.1 Evaluating the ROCE

What does a company's ROCE tell us? What should we be looking for? There are three comparisons that can be made.

(a) The **change** in ROCE from one year to the next
(b) The **ROCE** being **earned** by other companies, if this information is available
(c) A comparison of the ROCE with **current market borrowing rates**
   (i) What would be the cost of extra borrowing to the company if it needed more loans, and is it earning an ROCE that suggests it could make high enough profits to make such borrowing worthwhile?
   (ii) Is the company making an ROCE which suggests that it is making profitable use of its current borrowing?

3.1.2 Profit margin

A company might make a high or a low profit margin on its sales. For example, a company that makes a profit of 25c per $1 of sales is making a bigger return on its turnover than another company in the same industry making a profit of only 10c per $1 of sales.

3.2 Asset turnover

Asset turnover is a measure of how well the assets of a business are being used to generate sales. For example, if two companies each have capital employed of $100,000, and company A makes sales of $400,000 a year whereas company B makes sales of only $200,000 a year, company A is making a higher turnover from the same amount of assets. This will help company A to make a higher return on capital employed than company B.

Profit margin and asset turnover together explain the ROCE, and if the ROCE is the primary profitability ratio, these other two are the secondary ratios. The relationship between the three ratios is as follows.

Profit margin $\times$ Asset turnover = ROCE

$$\frac{\text{PBIT}}{\text{Sales}} \times \frac{\text{Sales}}{\text{Capital employed}} = \frac{\text{PBIT}}{\text{Capital employed}}$$

It is also worth commenting on the **change in turnover** from one year to the next. Strong sales growth will usually indicate volume growth as well as turnover increases due to price rises, and **volume growth** is one sign of a prosperous company.

3.3 Debt and gearing ratios

Debt ratios are concerned with how much the company **owes in relation to its size** and whether it is getting into heavier debt or improving its situation.

(a) When a company is heavily in debt, and seems to be getting even more heavily into debt, banks and other would-be lenders are very soon likely to refuse further borrowing and the company might well find itself in trouble.
(b) When a company is earning only a **modest profit** before interest and tax, and has a **heavy debt burden**, there will be very little profit left over for shareholders after the interest charges have been paid.

3.4 The debt ratio

The **debt ratio** is the **ratio** of a **company's total debts** to its **total assets**.

(a) **Assets** consist of fixed assets at their balance sheet value, plus current assets.
(b) **Debts** consist of all creditors, whether amounts falling due within one year or after more than one year.

You can ignore long-term provisions and liabilities, such as deferred taxation.

There is no absolute rule on the **maximum safe debt ratio**, but as a very general guide, you might regard 50% as a safe limit to debt. In addition, if the debt ratio is over 50% and getting worse, the company's debt position will be worth looking at more carefully.

3.5 Capital gearing

Capital gearing is concerned with the amount of debt in a company's **long-term** capital structure. **Gearing ratios** provide a long-term measure of liquidity.

$$\text{Gearing ratio} = \frac{\text{Prior charge capital (long-term debt)}}{\text{Prior charge capital + equity (shareholders' funds)}}$$

Prior charge capital is long-term loans and preference shares (if any). It does not include loans repayable within one year and bank overdraft, unless overdraft finance is a permanent part of the business's capital.

3.6 Operating gearing

Operating gearing is concerned with the relationship in a company between its **variable/fixed cost operating structure** and its profitability. It can be calculated as the ratio of **contribution** (sales minus variable costs of sales) **to PBIT**. The possibility of rises or falls in sales revenue and volumes means that operating gearing has possible implications for a company's business risk.

3.7 Interest cover

The **interest cover** ratio shows whether a company is earning enough profits before interest and tax to pay its interest costs comfortably, or whether its interest costs are high in relation to the size of its profits, so that a fall in profit before interest and tax (PBIT) would then have a significant effect on profits available for ordinary shareholders.

$$\text{Interest cover} = \frac{\text{PBIT}}{\text{Interest charges}}$$

An interest cover of 2 times or less would be low, and it should really exceed 3 times before the company's interest costs can be considered to be within acceptable limits. Note it is usual to exclude preference dividends from 'interest' charges.

3.8 Cash flow ratio

The **cash flow ratio** is the ratio of a company's net annual cash inflow to its total debts:

$$\frac{\text{Net annual cash inflow}}{\text{Total debts}}$$

(a) **Net annual cash inflow** is the amount of cash which the company has coming into the business each year from its operations. This will be shown in a company's cash flow statement for the year.

(b) **Total debts** are short-term and long-term creditors, together with provisions for liabilities and charges.

Obviously, a company needs to earn enough cash from operations to be able to meet its foreseeable debts and future commitments, and the cash flow ratio, and changes in the cash flow ratio from one year to the next, provides a useful indicator of a company's cash position.

3.9 Liquidity ratios: cash and working capital

Profitability is of course an important aspect of a company's performance, and debt or gearing is another. Neither, however, addresses directly the key issue of liquidity. **A company needs liquid assets so that it can meet its debts when they fall due.**

Liquidity is the amount of cash a company can obtain quickly to settle its debts (and possibly to meet other unforeseen demands for cash payments too). **Liquid funds** consist of:

(a) **Cash**

(b) **Short-term investments for which there is a ready market,** such as investments in shares of other companies. (Short-term investments are distinct from investments in shares in subsidiaries or associated companies.)

(c) **Fixed term deposits** with a bank or building society, for example six month deposits with a bank

(d) **Trade debtors.** (These are not cash, but ought to be expected to pay what they owe within a reasonably short time.)

(e) **Bills of exchange receivable.** (Like ordinary trade debtors, these represent amounts of cash due to be received soon.)

If an analysis of a company's published accounts is to give us some idea of the company's liquidity, profitability ratios are not going to be appropriate for doing this. Instead, we look at **liquidity ratios** and **working capital turnover ratios.**

Knowledge brought forward from earlier studies

Liquidity ratios

- The **current ratio** is defined as:

$$\frac{\text{Current assets}}{\text{Current liabilities}}$$

- In practice, a current ratio comfortably in excess of 1 should be expected, but what is 'comfortable' varies between different types of businesses.
- The **quick ratio**, or **acid test ratio**, is:

$$\frac{\text{Current assets less stocks}}{\text{Current liabilities}}$$

- This ratio should ideally be at least 1 for companies with a slow stock turnover. For companies with a fast stock turnover, a quick ratio can be less than 1 without suggesting that the company is in cash flow difficulties.
- An excessively large current/quick ratio may indicate a company that is **over-investing in working capital**, suggesting poor management of debtors or stocks by the company.
- We can calculate **turnover periods** for stock, debtors and creditors (debtor and creditor days). If we add together the stock days and the debtor days, this should give us an indication of how soon stock is convertible into cash. Both debtor days and stock days therefore give us a further indication of the company's liquidity.

Question

Ratios

Calculate liquidity and working capital ratios from the accounts of a manufacturer of products for the construction industry, and comment on the ratios.

	20X8	*20X7*
	$m	$m
Turnover	2,065.0	1,788.7
Cost of sales	1,478.6	1,304.0
Gross profit	586.4	484.7

	20X8	20X7
	$m	$m
Current assets		
Inventory	119.0	109.0
Receivables (note 1)	400.9	347.4
Short-term investments	4.2	18.8
Cash at bank and in hand	48.2	48.0
	572.3	523.2
Payables: amounts falling due within one year		
Loans and overdrafts	49.1	35.3
Corporation taxes	62.0	46.7
Dividend	19.2	14.3
Payables (note 2)	370.7	324.0
	501.0	420.3
Net current assets	71.3	102.9

Notes

		20X8	20X7
		$m	$m
1	Trade receivables	329.8	285.4
2	Trade payables	236.2	210.8

Answer

	20X8	20X7
Current ratio	$\frac{572.3}{501.0} = 1.14$	$\frac{523.2}{420.3} = 1.24$
Quick ratio	$\frac{453.3}{501.0} = 0.90$	$\frac{414.2}{420.3} = 0.99$
Receivables' payment period	$\frac{329.8}{2{,}065.0} \times 365 = 58$ days	$\frac{285.4}{1{,}788.7} \times 365 = 58$ days
Inventory turnover period	$\frac{119.0}{1{,}478.6} \times 365 = 29$ days	$\frac{109.0}{1{,}304.0} \times 365 = 31$ days
Payables' turnover period	$\frac{236.2}{1{,}478.6} \times 365 = 58$ days	$\frac{210.8}{1{,}304.0} \times 365 = 59$ days

As a manufacturing group serving the construction industry, the company would be expected to have a comparatively lengthy receivables' turnover period, because of the relatively poor cash flow in the construction industry. It is clear that the company compensates for this by ensuring that they do not pay for raw materials and other costs before they have sold their stocks of finished goods (hence the similarity of receivables' and payables' turnover periods).

The company's current ratio is a little lower than average but its quick ratio is better than average and very little less than the current ratio. This suggests that inventory levels are strictly controlled, which is reinforced by the low inventory turnover period. It would seem that working capital is tightly managed, to avoid the poor liquidity which could be caused by a high receivables' turnover period and comparatively high payables.

Payables' turnover is ideally calculated by the formula:

$$\frac{\text{Average payables}}{\text{Purchases}} \times 365$$

However, it is rare to find purchases disclosed in published accounts and so cost of sales serves as an approximation. The payables' turnover ratio often helps to assess a company's liquidity; an increase in payables days is often a sign of lack of long-term finance or poor management of current assets, resulting in the use of extended credit from suppliers, increased bank overdraft and so on.

Exam focus point

The emphasis in the exam questions is likely to require you to

- Comment on the financial health of a company or
- Highlight financial problems

3.10 Stock market ratios

The final set of ratios to consider are the ratios which help equity shareholders and other investors to assess the value and quality of an investment in the ordinary shares of a company.

You have covered the computations of stock market ratios in your previous studies, and the formulae for the main ones are summarised below. We shall then consider their significance in the analysis of performance.

Knowledge brought forward from earlier studies

Stock market ratios

- **Dividend yield** = $\frac{\text{Dividend per share}}{\text{Market price per share}}$
- **Interest yield** = $\frac{\text{Interest payable}}{\text{Market value of loan stock}}$
- **Earnings per shares** = $\frac{\text{Pr ofit after tax, extraordinary items and preference dividends}}{\text{Number of equity shares in issue and ranking for dividend}}$
- **Price/Earnings ratio** = $\frac{\text{Market value per share}}{\text{Earnings per share}}$
- **Dividend cover** = $\frac{\text{Earnings available for distribution to ordinary shareholders}}{\text{Actual dividend for ordinary shareholders}}$

Exam focus point

Ratio analysis is an important technique in your toolkit for analysing companies even though you may not always be specifically required to calculate particular ratios.

Investors are interested in:

- The value (market price) of the securities that they hold
- The return that the security has obtained in the past
- Expected future returns
- Whether their investment is reasonably secure

3.10.1 Dividend and interest yields

In practice, we usually find with quoted companies that the **dividend yield** on shares is less than the interest yield on debentures and loan stock (and also less than the yield paid on gilt-edged securities). The share price generally rises in most years, giving shareholders **capital gains**. In the long run, **shareholders** will want the **return on their shares**, in terms of **dividends received** plus **capital gains**, to exceed the return that investors get from fixed interest securities.

Exam focus point

Note that the interest yield, which is the **investor's** rate of return, is different from the **coupon** rate payable by the company as the nominal value of the loan stock. (Many students confuse these.)

3.10.2 Earnings per share (EPS)

EPS is widely used as a measure of a company's performance and is of particular importance in comparing results over a period of several years. A company must be able to sustain its earnings in order to pay dividends and re-invest in the business so as to achieve future growth. Investors also look for **growth** in the EPS from one year to the next.

Question — Earnings per share

Walter Wall Carpets Inc made profits before tax in 20X8 of $9,320,000. Tax amounted to $2,800,000.

The company's share capital is as follows.

	$
Ordinary shares (10,000,000 shares of $1)	10,000,000
8% preference shares	2,000,000
	12,000,000

Required

Calculate the EPS for 20X8.

Answer

	$
Profits before tax	9,320,000
Less tax	2,880,000
Profits after tax	6,520,000
Less preference dividend (8% of $2,000,000)	160,000
Earnings	6,360,000
Number of ordinary shares	10,000,000

EPS = 63.6c

EPS must be seen in the context of several other matters.

(a) EPS is used for **comparing the results** of a company over time. Is its EPS growing? What is the rate of growth? Is the rate of growth increasing or decreasing?

(b) Is there likely to be a significant **dilution** of EPS in the future, perhaps due to the exercise of share options or warrants, or the conversion of convertible loan stock into equity?

(c) EPS should not be **used blindly** to compare the earnings of one company with another. For example, if A plc has an EPS of 12c for its 10,000,000 10c shares and B plc has an EPS of 24c for its 50,000,000 25c shares, we must take account of the numbers of shares. When earnings are used to compare one company's shares with another, this is done using the P/E ratio or perhaps the earnings yield.

(d) If EPS is to be a reliable basis for comparing results, it must be **calculated consistently**. The EPS of one company must be directly comparable with the EPS of others, and the EPS of a company in one year must be directly comparable with its published EPS figures for previous years. Changes in the share capital of a company during the course of a year cause problems of comparability.

Note that EPS is a figure based on **past data**, and it is easily manipulated by changes in accounting policies and by mergers or acquisitions.

3.10.3 Price/earnings ratio

The P/E ratio is, simply, a measure of the relationship between the **market value** of a company's shares and the **earnings** from those shares.

The value of the P/E ratio reflects the market's appraisal of the shares' future prospects. In other words, if one company has a higher P/E ratio than another it is because investors either expect its earnings to **increase faster** than the others or consider that it is a **less risky** company or in a more 'secure' industry.

As we shall see later in the text, one approach to assessing what share prices ought to be, which is often used in practice, is a P/E ratio approach:

(a) The relationship between the EPS and the share price is **measured** by the **P/E ratio**.

(b) There is no reason to suppose, in normal circumstances, that the P/E ratio will vary much over time.

(c) So if the EPS goes up or down, the share price should be expected to move up or down too, and the new share price will be the new EPS multiplied by the constant P/E ratio.

For example, if a company had an EPS last year of 30c and a share price of $3.60, its P/E ratio would have been 12. If the current year's EPS is 33c, we might expect that the P/E ratio would remain the same, 12, and so the share price ought to go up to 12 × 33c = $3.96.

Changes in the P/E ratios of companies over time will depend on several factors.

(a) If **interest rates go up**, investors will be attracted away from shares and into debt capital. Share prices will fall, and so P/E ratios will fall.

(b) If **prospects** for **company profits improve**, share prices will go up, and P/E ratios will rise. Share prices depend on expectations of future earnings, not historical earnings, and so a change in prospects, perhaps caused by a substantial rise in international trade, or an economic recession, will affect prices and P/E ratios.

(c) **Investors' confidence** might be changed by a variety of circumstances, such as:

  (i) The prospect of a change in government

  (ii) The prospects for greater exchange rate stability between currencies

3.10.4 The dividend cover

The dividend cover is the number of times the actual dividend could be paid out of current profits and indicates:

(a) The **proportion** of distributable profits for the year that is being **retained** by the company

(b) The level of **risk** that the company will **not be able to maintain the same dividend** payments in future years, should earnings fall

A high dividend cover means that a high proportion of profits are being retained, which might indicate that the company is investing to achieve earnings growth in the future.

3.10.5 The Beaver failure ratio

This ratio is named after William Beaver whose studies on business failure provided the basis of further work in the field. (See Section 6.1 in this chapter.)

The Beaver failure ration is derived from the cash flow statement and is defined as:

$$\text{Beaver failure ratio} = \frac{\text{Operating cash flow}}{\text{Short and long} - \text{term borrowings}}$$

It is an excellent signal of impending failure and studies show that an estimated 70 percent of firms with values of less than 0.3 fail within five years.

3.11 Limitations of ratio analysis

Although ratio analysis can be a very useful technique, it is important to realise its limitations.

Availability of comparable information

When making comparisons with other companies in the industry, industry averages may hide **wide variations** in figures. Figures for 'similar' companies may provide a better guide, but then there are problems identifying which companies are similar, and obtaining enough detailed information about them.

Use of historical/out-of-date information

Comparisons with the previous history of a business may be of limited use, if the business has recently undergone, or is about to undergo, **substantial changes**. In addition, ratios based on published accounts suffer from the disadvantage that these accounts are filed some months after the end of the accounting period. Comparisons over time may also be distorted by **inflation**, leading to assets being stated at values that do not reflect replacement costs, and revenue increasing for reasons other than more sales being made.

Ratios are not definitive

'Ideal levels' vary from industry to industry, and even they are not definitive. Companies may be able to exist without any difficulty with ratios that are rather worse than the industry average.

Need for careful interpretation

For example, if comparing two businesses' liquidity ratios, one business may have higher levels. This might appear to be 'good', but further investigation might reveal that the higher ratios are a result of higher inventory and receivable levels which are a result of poor working capital management by the business with the 'better' ratios.

Manipulation

Any ratio including profit may be distorted by **choice of accounting policies**. For smaller companies, working capital ratios may be distorted depending on whether a big customer pays, or a large supplier is paid, before or after the year-end.

Ratios lack standard form

For example, when calculating **gearing** some companies will include bank overdrafts, others exclude them.

Other information

Ratio analysis on its own is not sufficient for interpreting company accounts, and there are other items of information that should be looked at. We shall consider this further below.

Exam focus point

Bear these limitations in mind when using ratios and be aware of over-simplification.

4 Issues in the use of financial ratios

FAST FORWARD

Ratio analysis often forms the basis of comparisons with performance over time or with other companies. Comments on a company based on such ratios are far more likely to be right than comments based on a casual read through a set of accounts.

4.1 Results of the same company over successive accounting periods

Useful comparisons over **time** include:

- **Percentage growth** in **profit** (before and after tax) and percentage growth in turnover
- **Increases or decreases** in the **debt ratio** and the gearing ratio
- **Changes** in the **current ratio**, the stock turnover period and the debtors' payment period
- **Increases** in the **EPS**, the dividend per share, and the market price

The principal advantage of making comparisons over time is that they give some indication of progress: are things getting better or worse? However, there are some weaknesses in such comparisons.

(a) The effect of **inflation** should not be forgotten.

(b) The progress a company has made needs to be set in the context of **what other companies have done**, and whether there have been any **special environmental or economic influences** on the company's performance.

4.1.1 Allowing for inflation

Ratio analysis is not usually affected by **price inflation**, except as follows.

(a) **Return on capital employed** (ROCE) can be misleading if fixed assets, especially property, are valued at **historical cost net of depreciation** rather than at current value. As time goes by and if property prices go up, the fixed assets would be seriously undervalued if they were still recorded at their historical cost.

(b) Some growth trends can be misleading, in particular the **growth in sales turnover**, and the **growth in profits or earnings**.

4.2 Comparisons between different companies in the same industry

Making comparisons between the results of different companies in the same industry is a way of assessing which companies are outperforming others.

(a) Even if two companies are in the **same broad industry** (for example, retailing) they might not be direct competitors. For example, in the UK, the Kingfisher group does not compete directly with the Burton/Debenhams group. Even so, they might still be expected to show **broadly similar performance**, in terms of growth.

(b) If two companies are **direct competitors**, a comparison between them would be particularly interesting.

Comparisons between companies in the same industry can help investors to rank them in order of desirability as investments, and to judge relative share prices or future prospects. It is important, however, to make comparisons with caution: **a large company and a small company in the same industry might be expected to show different results**, not just in terms of size, but in terms of:

(a) **Percentage rates of growth** in sales and profits

(b) **Percentages of profits re-invested** (Dividend cover will be higher in a company that needs to retain profits to finance investment and growth.)

(c) **Fixed assets** (Large companies are more likely to have freehold property in their balance sheet than small companies.)

4.3 Comparisons between companies in different industries

Useful information can also be obtained by comparing the financial and accounting ratios of companies in different industries. An investor ought to be aware of how companies in one industrial sector are performing in comparisons with companies in other sectors. For example, it is important to know:

(a) Whether sales growth and profit growth is higher in **some industries** than in others (for example, how does growth in the financial services industry compare with growth in heavy engineering, electronics or leisure?)

(b) How the **return on capital employed** and **return on shareholder capital compare** between different industries

(c) How the **P/E ratios and dividend** yields vary between industries

Exam focus point

You may be asked to compare the return from two companies based on a variety of measures, and then to go on to consider the risk profiles of the two companies.

5 Other information from companies' accounts

As well as ratios, **other information** can be used to analyse a company's performance and identify possible problem areas. This will include information relating to **non-current assets** and **financial obligations, contingencies** and **post balance sheet events.**

5.1 The revaluation of fixed assets

Fixed assets may be stated in the balance sheet at cost less accumulated depreciation. They may also be revalued from time to time to a current market value to avoid understatement of current value. When this happens:

(a) The increase in the balance sheet value of the fixed asset is matched by an increase in the **revaluation reserve**

(b) **Depreciation** in subsequent years is based on the revalued amount of the asset, its estimated residual value and its estimated remaining useful life

5.2 Share capital and share issues

The **capital and reserves** section of a company's accounts contains information which appears to be mainly the concern of the various classes of shareholder. However, because the shareholders' interest in the business acts as a **buffer for the creditors** in the event of any financial problems, this section is also of some importance to creditors.

For example, if a company has increased its total share capital and reserves in the year:

(a) Did it do so by **issuing new shares** resulting in a higher allotted share capital and share premium account?

(b) Did it do so by **revaluing some fixed assets**, resulting in a higher revaluation reserve?

(c) Did it make a substantial profit and **retain a good proportion of this profit** in the business resulting in a higher profit and loss account balance?

A **scrip issue** might also be of some interest. It will result in a **fall** in the **market price** per share. If it has been funded from a company's profit and loss account reserves, a scrip issue would indicate that the company recognised and formalised its long-term capital needs by now making some previously distributable reserves non-distributable.

If a company has **issued shares in the form of a dividend**, are there obvious reasons why this should be so? For example, does the company need to retain capital within the business because of poor trading in the previous year, making the directors reluctant to pay out more cash dividend than necessary?

5.3 Financial obligations

Financial obligations of a company may also be significant, and the timescale over which these become or could become repayable should be considered.

Examples are:

(a) Levels of **redeemable debt**

(b) **Earn out arrangements**

(c) **Potential or contingent liabilities,** such as liabilities under unresolved legal cases or insurance claims

(d) **Long-term commitments** (eg the Private Finance Initiative in the UK)

5.4 Debentures, loans and other liabilities

Two points of interest about debentures, loans and other liabilities are:

- Whether or not loans are **secured**
- The **redemption dates** of loans

For debentures and loan stock which are **secured**, the details of the security are usually included in the terms of a trust deed. Details of any **fixed or floating charges against assets** must be disclosed in a note to the accounts.

In analysing a set of accounts, particular attention should be paid to some significant features concerning **debenture or loan stock redemption**. These are:

(a) The **closeness of the redemption date**, which would indicate how much finance the company has to find in the immediate future to repay its loans. It is not unusual, however, to repay one loan by taking out another, and so a company does not necessarily have to find the money to repay a loan from its own resources.

(b) The **percentage interest rate** on the loans being redeemed, compared with the **current market rate of interest**. This would give some idea, if a company decides to replace loans by taking out new loans, of the likely increase (or reduction) in interest costs that it might face, and how easily it might accommodate any interest cost increase.

5.5 Contingencies

Contingencies are conditions which exist at the balance sheet date where the outcome will be confirmed only on the occurrence or non-occurrence of one or more uncertain future events.

Contingencies can result in contingent gains or contingent losses. The fact that the condition **exists at the balance sheet date** distinguishes a contingency from a post balance sheet event.

Some of the **typical types of contingencies** disclosed by companies are as follows.

- Guarantees given by the company
- Discounted bills of exchange
- Uncalled liabilities on shares or loan stock
- Lawsuits or claims pending
- Tax on profits where the basis on which the tax should be computed is unclear

Again, knowledge of such contingencies will enhance the quality of the information used in analysis.

5.6 Post balance sheet events

Key term

Post balance sheet events are those events both favourable and unfavourable which occur between the balance sheet date and the date on which the financial statements are approved by the board of directors.

The following are examples of post balance sheet events which should normally be disclosed.

- Mergers and acquisitions
- The issue of new shares and debentures
- The purchase and sale of major fixed assets and investments
- Losses of fixed assets or stocks as a result of a catastrophe such as fire or flood
- The opening of new trading activities
- The closure of a significant part of the trading activities
- A decline in the value of property and investments held as fixed assets
- Changes in exchange rates (if there are significant overseas interests)
- Government action, such as nationalisation
- Strikes and other labour disputes
- The augmentation of pension benefits to employees

Knowledge of such events allows the analyst to 'update' the latest published figures by taking account of their potential impact.

Exam focus point

> You should try to develop a mental checklist of areas where accounts can be distorted, whether intentionally or unintentionally. These may include:
>
> - Asset values
> - Off balance sheet items
> - Equity restructuring
> - Loan terms
> - Post balance sheet events

6 Use of financial ratios, Z-scores and Zeta scores

FAST FORWARD

The **univariate analysis** to predicting business failure is based on a **single financial ratio** to discriminate between **failed** and **non-failed companies**, whereas the **multivariate approach** combines individual financial ratios into an **index** where the **weight** of each ratio in the index is estimated **empirically**.

We have so far reviewed the various characteristics of a company, and placed emphasis on financial characteristics as measured by the various ratios. In this section we explain how these ratios can be used in predicting financially distressed companies. The main idea underlying the use of financial ratios is based on the fact that companies that are going to experience financial distress exhibit, sometime before the financial distress is manifested, characteristics that are different from those that are not going to exhibit financial distress.

There are two main approaches to using financial ratios:

(a) The univariate approach that looks at the discriminating power of individual ratios, an introduction to which was given earlier in this chapter and

(b) The multivariate analysis that looks at the discriminating power of a number of financial ratios combined into an index.

6.1 Univariate approach

In the univariate approach we use individual ratios to discriminate between companies that are going to experience financial distress and those which are not. For example, companies with high **retained earnings** relative to **total assets** are less likely to experience financial difficulties. Thus one could classify companies into **two groups**. One group will contain companies that have a **high retained earnings** ratio whereas the second group will contain the companies with the **low retained earnings ratio**. The approach is based on the assumption that the companies in the second group are more likely to go bankrupt.

The following table shows the basic idea of the univariate approach. The table shows the average values of the financial ratios of two groups of companies. One group are the companies that failed one year later. The second group are the companies that did not fail. The table shows that a year before they failed, bankrupt companies had on average **negative profitability** (EBIT/TA), **lower market value** over **total capital, smaller sales** over **total assets** and so on.

	Values of sample means	
	Failed	*Non-failed*
EBIT/TA	–0.0055	0.1117
Sales/TA	1.3120	1.6200
EBIT/Sales	0.0020	0.0070
interest coverage	–0.5995	5.3410
Earnings/Debt	–0.0792	0.1806
WC/LTD	0.3532	2.4433
Retained earnings /TA	–0.0006	0.2935
Current ratio	1.5757	2.6040
WC/total assets	0.1498	0.3086
MN equity/total liabilities	0.6113	1.8449
Sales/fixed assets	3.1723	4.1790
MV equity/TC	0.3423	0.6022

Source: Edward I. Altman :'Predicting financial distress of companies:

Revisiting the z-score and zeta® models' New York University, July 2000

Where EBIT = earnings before interest and taxes
TA = total tangible assets
LTD = long term debt
MV = market value of equity
TC = total capital
TD = total debt
WC = working capital

The first study that employed univariate analysis to predict corporate failure was by **Beaver** in 1966 who used more than 30 financial ratios. In most cases he found that the **individual ratios** were able to differentiate between potentially **bankrupt** and **non-bankrupt** firms providing the first empirical evidence that financial ratios can predict the financial health or credit risk of a company.

Beaver's study can be summarised as follows:

- The **worst predictor** of failure is the current ratio (current assets/current liabilities).
- The **best predictor** of failure is cash flow borrowings.

Beaver's study was criticized for its dependence on **single ratios** rather than looking at **combinations of factors** that may affect the financial state of a company and its probability of default. However, despite the statistical shortcomings, as Beaver's results indicate, a univariate analysis allows the analyst to understand the nature of the data and provides valuable insights for the **multivariate analysis**.

6.2 The multivariate approach

The multivariate approach to predicting business failure, rather than relying on a single characteristic, which may give rise to conflicting results, relies on a combination of ratios. The relative importance or weighting of these ratios in the combination is calculated using a statistical technique called discriminant analysis.

6.2.1 Altman's Z score

FAST FORWARD

Altman researched the multivariate approach to predicting business future by analysing a number of variables for failed and non-failed companies. Five key indicators emerged which are used to derive Altman's Z score model.

Altman researched into the simultaneous analysis of several financial ratios as a **combined predictor of business failure**. Altman analysed 22 **accounting** and **non-accounting variables** for a selection of **failed** and **non-failed** firms in the USA and from these, five **key indicators** emerged.

These five indicators were then used to derive a **Z score**. Firms with a Z score above a certain level would be predicted to be financially sound, and firms with a Z score below a certain level would be categorised as probable failures. Altman also identified a range of Z scores in between the **non-failure** and **failure categories** in which eventual failure or non-failure was uncertain.

Altman's Z score model emerged as:

$$Z = 1.2X_1 + 1.4X_2 + 3.3X_3 + 0.6X_4 + 1.0X_5$$

Where X_1 = working capital/total assets
X_2 = retained earnings/total assets
X_3 = earnings before interest and tax/total assets
X_4 = market value of equity/book value of total debt (a form of gearing ratio)
X_5 = sales/total assets

Exam focus point

It is not necessary for you to memorise this formula, which would be given in the exam if needed.

In Altman's model, a Z score of **2.7 or more** indicated **non-failure**, and a Z score of **1.8 or less** indicated **failure**. Values of the Z variable **between 1.8 and 2.7** were **inconclusive**.

6.2.2 The value of Z scores

A current view of the link between **financial ratios** and **business failure** would appear to be as follows:

(a) The financial ratios of firms which fail can be seen in retrospect to have **deteriorated significantly** prior to failure, and to be worse than the ratios of non-failed firms. In retrospect, financial ratios can be used to suggest why a firm has failed.

(b) No fully accepted **model for predicting** future business failures has yet been established, although some form of Z score analysis would appear to be the most promising avenue for progress. In the UK, several Z score-type failure prediction models exist.

(c) Because of the use of X_4: market value of equity/book value of debt, Z score models cannot be used for unquoted companies which lack a market value of equity.

(d) Some Z score models have been developed specifically for **individual industries** or **sizes of organisation**.

Z score models are used widely in the banking sector, in risk assessment, loan grading and corporate finance activities. They are also used by accountancy firms, fund management houses, stockbrokers and credit insurers (such as Trade Indemnity).

Question — **z-score use**

The following values were observed for a company

X_1 = 0.16
X_2 = 0.10
X_3 = 0.05
X_4 = 1.10
X_5 = 1.40

Calculate the z-score for this company and assess whether the company is likely to experience financial distress on the basis of the result.

Answer

Plugging the values into the Z-score formula yields

$Z = 1.2 \times 0.16 + 1.4 \times 10 + 3.3 \times 0.05 + 0.6 \times 1.10 + 1.0 \times 1.40 = 2.557$

The value of the z-score is in the inconclusive range and we cannot therefore conclude whether the company will experience financial distress. The fact however that the value of the z-score is close to the upper end of the inconclusive range, means that the company should be considered as risky.

6.2.3 The Zeta model

FAST FORWARD

A new version of the Z score model referred to as the Zeta model was later developed by Altman and his associates based on seven variables which is reported to predict more accurately than the original.

In 1977 Altman and his associates developed a new version of the initial Z-score, referred to as the Zeta model. The new model used some of the original model's ratios but introduced some new ones as well. The ratios used in the Zeta model were:

1 Return on assets defined as earnings before interest and tax over total assets
2 Stability of earnings
3 Debt service
4 Cumulative profitability
5 Liquidity
6 Capitalisation
7 Size

Unfortunately, the authors have not published the actual function and the weights used, because of commercial confidentiality, but they report results of the empirical application that indicates that the Zeta model predicts better that the original model.

6.3 Ratios used by credit rating companies

The two main credit rating agencies – Moody's and Standard and Poor's – employ a variety of financial ratios as well as methodologies which are consistent with the option pricing model. The ratios employed by the two agencies are:

Moody's Risk Factors (2000)*

Moody's use the following set of seven factors in a model that combines discriminant analysis and logistic regression.

- Assets/Consumer Price Index
- Inventories/Cost of goods sold
- Liabilities/Assets
- Net Income Growth
- Net Income/Assets
- Quick Ratio
- Retained Earnings/Assets
- Sales Growth
- Cash/Assets
- Debt Service Coverage Ratio

Standard and Poor (2000)**

Standard and Poor report the following eight factors as important in terms of classifying issuers of corporate bonds.

- EBIT interest coverage
- EBITDA interest coverage
- Funds flow/total debt
- Free open cash flow/total debt
- Return on capital
- Operating income/sales
- Long-term debt/capital
- Total debt/capital

* Moody's Investor Service, Rating Methodology for Private Companies May 2000

** 'Adjusted Key US Industrial Financial Ratios' Standard and Poor's Credit Week, 20 September 2000

6.3.1 The Kaplan-Urwitz model

The Kaplan-Urwitz model is used to classify a company into a credit rating category. The model is discussed in full in Chapter 21 section 3.4.

6.4 Weaknesses of prediction methods

Using the available **financial information** to predict business failure presents the following problems:

(a) **Significant events** can take place between the end of the financial year and the publication of the accounts. An extreme example of this would be the collapse of the Barings merchant bank. A further feature of the Barings case that is worthy of comment is the fact that the factors that led up to the collapse were essentially internal to the business and would never have become apparent in the published accounts.

(b) The information is essentially **backward looking** and takes no account of current and future situations. An extreme example would be the Central American banana producers. There would be nothing in their published accounts to predict the effect on their businesses of Hurricane Mitch.

(c) The **underlying financial information** may not be reliable.

The use of **creative, or even fraudulent, accounting** can be significant in situations of corporate failure. Similarly, the **pressure to deliver earnings growth** may result in companies making poor decisions that eventually lead to their downfall. It is arguable that a deterioration in the performance of BTR (now Invensys) is attributable to its policy of aggressive acquisition followed by **price increases** and **stringent cost reduction**. Although this delivered growth in earnings for a while and made it a highly regarded company in which to invest, the effects of this policy are now being felt in a shrinking customer base and the consequences of a lack of investment in the underlying businesses.

Exam focus point

Although you don't need to learn the formula for Z-scores, or any other corporate failure model, by heart, you do need to know how they operate, how they can be used in practice and their weaknesses.

6.5 Other indicators of financial difficulties

You should not think that **ratio analysis of published accounts** and **Z score analysis** are the only ways of spotting that a company might be running into financial difficulties. There are other possible indicators too.

6.5.1 Other information in the published accounts

Some information in the published accounts might not lend itself readily to ratio analysis, but still be an indicator of financial difficulties, for example:

- Very **large increases** in **intangible fixed assets**
- A **worsening net liquid funds** position, as shown by the funds flow statement
- Very large **potential or contingent liabilities**

- Important **post balance sheet events**
- **Excess** of **current liabilities** over **current assets**
- Imminent **debt repayment** and **limited cash resources**

6.5.2 Information in the chairman's report, the directors' report and the audit report

The **report of the chairman** or chief executive that accompanies the published accounts might be very revealing. Although this report is not audited, and will no doubt try to paint a rosy picture of the company's affairs, any difficulties the company has had and not yet overcome will probably be discussed in it. There might also be warnings of problems to come in the future. The **audit report** itself may indicate difficulties.

6.5.3 Information in the press

Newspapers and financial journals are a source of information about companies, and the difficulties or successes they are having and the **markets** in which they operate. There may be reports of strikes, redundancies and closures.

6.5.4 Credit ratings

Ratings from specialist agencies or banks may be useful.

6.5.5 Published information about environmental or external matters

There will also be published information about matters that will have a direct influence on a company's future, although the connection may not be obvious. Examples of external matters that may affect a company adversely are:

- **New legislation**, for example on product safety standards or pollution controls, which affect a company's main products
- **International events**, for example political disagreements with a foreign country, leading to a restriction on trade between the countries
- **New and better products** being launched on to the market by a competitor
- A big **rise in interest rates**, which might affect a highly-geared company seriously
- A big **change in foreign exchange rates**, which might affect a major importer or exporter seriously.

7 Financial distress models in emerging markets

FAST FORWARD

Application of financial distress models in emerging markets is problematic because the information required for prediction may not be accurate.

The growth of emerging markets as an important sector of the global financial market, has necessitated the evaluation of companies but also countries in emerging markets in terms of business failure. Credit rating agencies have developed models for the assignment of credit ratings to both companies and countries. However, unlike their performance in developed economies, credit ratings failed to predict the Mexican and Asian crises as well as the ensuing domestic bankruptcies.

The failure of the credit rating companies has been attributed primarily to the lack of consistency in the data that have been used in the construction of the credit rating models. It has been well established in particular how financial ratios are affected by the operation of the financial markets and the apparent lack of a strict regulatory framework.

7.1 Financial market conditions

The main problems with the market conditions include :

- Lack of liquid markets for shares or debt needed to validate the real worth of a company as opposed to its accounting value

- Excess volatility due to exposure to international capital flows.
- Quickly changing market conditions as the result of privatisations and foreign investment
- Inflation may be endemic in some countries resulting in distortion of information

The above problems make the application of credit scoring models difficult.

7.2 Regulatory deficiencies

Regulatory deficiencies in emerging economies can be identified in a number of areas.

(a) Absence of **rigorous disclosure regulation**s contributes to the lack of transparency in financial data of emerging economies.

(b) Lack of sufficient data to statistically estimate relationships using multivariate analysis.

(c) Financial reporting does not follow internationally accepted standards making interpretation of the financial statements and the resulting ratios difficult.

(d) The definition of bankruptcy may differ from country to country making the application of models difficult. For example, a company in an emerging market may be technically insolvent, but the government may keep it in operation in order to protect employment.

Increasing globalisation and standardisation of accounting reporting requirements means that the application of business failure models to emerging markets is increasingly more credible.

7.3 Non-financial characteristics

Some of the non-financial characteristics of a firm discussed in section 2.1 are particularly relevant to emerging markets and may render their influence on the performance or survival of a company more important that that of the financial ratios.

Chapter Roundup

- **Company characteristics** are the means of discriminating between firms that may fail and firms that may survive.

  Business failure can be predicted by models such as **Argenti's model**, which emphasises defects, mistakes and symptoms
- **Financial Ratios** provide a means of summarising financial information about a company. They can be grouped under the headings **profitability**, **liquidity**, **gearing** and **shareholders' investment**. It is important to calculate **relevant ratios** and to take into account the **limitations** of **ratio analysis.**
- **Ratio analysis** often forms the basis of comparisons with performance over time or with other companies. Comments on a company based on such ratios are far more likely to be right than comments based on a casual read through of a set of accounts.
- As well as ratios, **other information** can be used to analyse a company's performance and identify possible problem areas. This will include information relating to **non-current assets** and **financial obligations, contingencies** and **post balance sheet events.**
- The **univariate analysis** to predicting business failure is based on a **single financial ratio** to discriminate between **failed** and **non-failed companies**, whereas the **multivariate approach** combines individual financial ratios into an **index** where the **weight** of each ratio in the index is estimated **empirically**.
- Altman researched the **multivariate approach** to predicting business future by analysing a number of variables for **failed** and **non-failed** companies. **Five key indicators** emerged which are used to derive Altman's **Z score model**.
- A **new version** of the **Z score model** referred to as the **Zeta model** was later developed by Altman and his associates based on **seven variables** which is reported to predict more accurately than the original.
- Application of financial distress models in emerging markets is problematic because the information required for prediction may not be accurate.

Quick Quiz

1 Identify terms (A) to (F) to complete the equation.

Profit margin × Asset turnover = ROCE

$$\frac{(A)}{(B)} \times \frac{(C)}{(D)} = \frac{(E)}{(F)}$$

2 Complete the following in respect of capital gearing.

$$\text{Gearing ratio} = \frac{(A)}{(B)+(C)}$$

3 Complete the following.

$$\text{Interest cover} = \frac{(A)}{(B)}$$

4 $$\frac{\text{Current assets less stock}}{\text{Current liabilities}} = ?$$

5 **Fill in the blanks**, using the terms in the box

$$\text{Dividend yield} = \frac{(1)}{(2)} \times 100\%$$

$$\text{Interest yield} = \frac{(3)}{(4)} \times 100\%$$

$$\text{EPS} = \frac{(5)}{(6)}$$

$$\text{P/E ratio} = \frac{(7)}{(8)}$$

$$\text{Dividend cover} = \frac{(9)}{(10)}$$

6 Identify three weaknesses of corporate failure models.

7 Give three methods of funding a deficiency of cash.

8 Give three methods of measuring uncertainty in forecasts.

Answers to Quick Quiz

1 (A) PBIT
(B) Sales
(C) Sales
(D) Capital employed
(E) PBIT
(F) Capital employed

2 (A) Prior-charge capital
(B) Prior-charge capital
(C) Equity

3 (A) PBIT
(B) Interest charges

4 Quick or acid test ratio

5 (1) Gross dividend per share
(2) Share price
(3) Gross interest
(4) Loan stock market value
(5) Profit after tax
(6) Number of shares
(7) Share price
(8) Earnings attributable to one share
(9) Earnings available for distribution
(10) Actual dividend

6 Any three of the following

(a) They relate to the past
(b) They share the limitations of accounting
(c) Accounting figures are published after a delay
(d) Measures are subject to manipulation
(e) The definition of corporate failure is unclear

7 (a) Borrowing
(b) Selling short-term financial investments
(c) Leading and lagging creditors and debtors

8 (a) Ask what if questions
(b) Prepare a probability distribution of possible outcomes
(c) Prepare pessimistic, optimistic and most likely forecasts

Now try the questions below from the Exam Question Bank

Number	Level	Marks	Time
22	Examination	20	36

16

Financial reconstruction

Topic list	Syllabus reference
1 Reconstruction schemes	D 2(a)
2 Financial reconstructions	D 2(a)
3 Financial reconstruction and firm value	D 2(b), 2(c)
4 Leveraged buy-outs (LBOs)	D 2(a), (b), (c)
5 Market response to financial reconstruction	D 2 (b)
6 Case study in financial reconstruction	D 2 (c)

Introduction

In this chapter we discuss financial restructuring in companies. Financial restructuring and other means of corporate re-shaping can take place when companies are in difficulties or seeking to change their focus.

Study guide

		Intellectual level
D2	**Financial reconstruction**	
(a)	Assess a company situation and determine whether a financial reconstruction is the most appropriate strategy for dealing with the problem as presented.	3
(b)	Assess the likely response of the capital market and/or individual suppliers of capital to any reconstruction scheme and the impact their response is likely to have upon the value of the firm.	3
(c)	Recommend a reconstruction scheme from a given business situation, justifying the proposal in terms of its impact upon the reported, performance and financial position of the firm.	3

Exam guide

As with mergers and acquisitions, most questions in this area are likely to be a mixture of calculations (for example assessing the financing mix for a management buy-out) and narrative (discussing the implications of a scheme of reconstruction on various interested parties). You may be asked to consider a reconstruction scheme and various alternatives (liquidation, selling off part or all of the company).

1 Reconstruction schemes

FAST FORWARD

Reconstruction schemes are undertaken when companies have got into difficulties or as part of a strategy to enhance the value of the firm for its owners.

1.1 Reconstruction schemes to prevent business failure

Not all businesses are profitable. Some incur losses in one or more years, but eventually achieve profitability. Others remain unprofitable, or earn only very small and unsatisfactory profits. Other companies are profitable, but run out of cash. (We looked at **indicators of business failure** in Chapter 15.)

(a) A poorly performing company which is unprofitable, but has enough cash to keep going, might eventually decide to **go into liquidation**, because it is not worth carrying on in business. Alternatively, it might become the target of a successful takeover bid.

(b) A company which runs out of cash, even if it is profitable, might be forced into liquidation by **unpaid creditors**, who want payment and think that applying to the court to wind up the company is the best way of getting some or all of their money.

However, a company might be on the brink of going into liquidation, but hold out good promise of profits in the future. In such a situation, the company might be able to attract fresh capital and to persuade its creditors to accept some securities in the company as 'payment', and achieve a **capital reconstruction** which allows the company to carry on in business.

1.2 Reconstruction schemes for value creation

Reconstruction schemes may also be undertaken by companies which are not in difficulties as part of a strategy to create value for the owners of the company. The management of a company can improve operations and increase the value of the company by

(a) Reducing costs through the sale of a poorly performing division or subsidiary

(b) increasing revenue or reducing costs through the acquisition of a company to exploit revenue or cost economies

(c) improving the financial structure of the company.

1.3 Types of reconstruction

Depending on the actions that a company needs to take as part of its reconstruction plans, these schemes are usually classified in three categories

(a) **Financial reconstruction** which involves changing the capital structure of the firm

(b) **Portfolio reconstruction**, which involves making additions to or disposals from companies' businesses eg through acquisitions or spin-offs.

(c) **Organisational restructuring**, which involves changing the organisational structure of the firm.

1.4 Step-by-step approach to designing reconstructions

You can use the following approach to designing reconstructions.

Step 1 **Estimate** the **position** of each party if **liquidation** is to go ahead. This will represent the minimum acceptable payment for each group.

Step 2 **Assess additional sources of finance**, for example selling assets, issuing shares, raising loans. The company will most likely need more finance to keep going.

Step 3 **Design the reconstruction**. Often the question will give you details of how to do it.

Step 4 **Calculate** and **assess** the new position, and also how each group has fared, and compare with Step 1 position.

Step 5 Check that the company is **financially viable** after the reconstruction.

In addition you should remember the following points when designing the reconstruction.

(a) Anyone providing extra finance for an ailing company must be persuaded that the expected return from the extra finance is attractive. A **profit forecast** and a **cash forecast** or a **funds flow forecast** will be needed to provide reassurance about the company's future, to creditors and to any financial institution that is asked to put new capital into the company. The reconstruction must indicate that the company has a **good chance** of being **financially viable**.

(b) The actual reconstruction might involve the **creation of new share capital** of a **different nominal value** than existing share capital, or the cancellation of existing share capital.

It can also involve the conversion of equity to debt, debt to equity, and debt of one type to debt of another.

(c) For a scheme of reconstruction to be acceptable it needs to **treat all parties fairly** (for example, preference shareholders must not be treated with disproportionate favour in comparison with equity shareholders), and it needs to offer creditors a better deal than if the company went into liquidation. If it did not, the creditors would press for a winding up of the company. A reconstruction might therefore include an arrangement to pay off the company's existing debts in full.

Exam focus point

Although assumptions may sometimes need to be made (and should be stated), you would not be expected to 'invent' basic financial data.

2 Financial reconstructions

Key term

A **financial reconstruction scheme** is a scheme whereby a company reorganises its capital structure, including leveraged buyouts, leveraged recapitalisations and debt for equity swaps.

There are many possible reasons why management would wish to restructure a company's finances. A reconstruction scheme might be agreed when a company is in danger of being put into liquidation, owing debts that it cannot repay, and so the creditors of the company agree to accept securities in the company,

perhaps including equity shares, in settlement of their debts. On the other hand a company may be willing to undergo some financial restructuring to better position itself for long term success.

2.1 Leveraged recapitalisations

In leveraged recapitalisation a firm replaces the majority of its equity with a package of debt securities consisting of both senior and subordinated debt. Leveraged capitalisations are employed by firms as defence mechanisms to protect them from takeovers. The high level of debt in the company discourages corporate raiders who will not be able to borrow against the assets of the target firm in order to finance the acquisition.

In order to avoid the possible financial distress arising from the high level of debt, companies that engage in leveraged recapitalisation should be relatively debt free, they should have stable cash flows and they should not require substantial ongoing capital expenditure in order to retain their competitive position.

2.2 Debt-equity swaps

A second way of changing its capital is to issue a debt/equity or an equity/debt swap. In the case of an equity/debt swap, all specified shareholders are given the right to exchange their stock for a predetermined amount of debt (ie bonds) in the same company. A debt/equity swap works the opposite way: debt is exchanged for a predetermined amount of equity (or stock). The value of the swap is determined usually at current market rates, but management may offer higher exchange values to entice share and debt holders to participate in the swap. After the swap takes place, the preceding asset class is cancelled for the newly acquired asset class.

One possible reason that the company may engage in debt-equity swaps is because the company must meet certain contractual obligations, such as a maintaining a debt/equity ratio below a certain number. Also a company may issue equity to avoid making coupon and face value payments because they feel they will be unable to do so in the future. The contractual obligations mentioned can be a result of financing requirements imposed by a lending institution, such as a bank, or may be self-imposed by the company, as detailed in the company's prospectus. A company may self-impose certain valuation requirements to entice investors to purchase its stock. Debt/equity swaps may also be carried out to rebalance a firm's WACC.

Question — **Financing policy**

For illustration, assume there is an investor who owns a total of $2,000 in ABC Inc stock. ABC has offered all shareholders the option to swap their stock for debt at a rate of 1:5. What is the amount worth of debt that the investor will receive?

Answer

The investor would receive, if he or she elected to take the swap, $3,000 (1.5 * $2,000) worth of debt, gaining $1000 for switching asset classes. However, the investor would lose all rights as a shareholder, such as voting rights, if he swapped his equity for debt.

2.3 Leveraged buy-outs

A leveraged buy out is a transaction in which a group of private investors uses debt financing to purchase a company or part of a company. In a leveraged buy out, like a leveraged capitalisation, the company increases its level of leverage, but unlike the case of leveraged capitalisations, the company does not have access to equity markets any more. This is covered in more detail in section 4 of this chapter.

2.4 Dividend policy

A company may change its dividend policy as part of financial restructuring and increase retained earnings and therefore its equity base.

3 Financial reconstruction and firm value

FAST FORWARD

The impact of a financial reconstruction scheme on the **value** of the firm can be assessed in terms of its impact on the **growth rate** of the company, its **risk**, and its **required rate of return**.

3.1 Effect on growth rate

The impact of changes in financial policy on the value of the firm can be assessed through one of the valuation models that we have considered in previous chapters. For example the growth rate following a financial restructuring can be calculated from the formula

Formula to learn

$$g = b\left(ROA + \frac{D}{E}(ROA - i(1-T)\right)$$

Where ROA is the return on the net assets of the company
b is the retention rate
D is the book value of debt
E is the book value of equity
i is the cost of debt
t is the corporate tax rate

Changes in the level of debt will be reflected in the growth rate through its impact on the debt ratio D/E. Similarly, changes in dividend policy can be reflected in the earnings growth rate. Changes in the dividend policy will change the value of b. Decreasing dividends (a higher b) will increase the growth rate, and increasing dividends will decrease the growth rate.

Question **Financing policy**

A firm currently has a debt-equity ratio of 0.12 and a return on assets (ROA) equal to 15 percent. The optimal debt ratio is however much lower than the optimal level, since it can raise the debt-equity ratio up to 0.30 without increasing the risk of bankruptcy. The firm plans to borrow and repurchase stock to get to this optimal ratio. The interest rate is expected to increase from 7 percent to 8 percent. The tax rate is 25 percent and the retention rate is 50 percent. Find the impact of the increase in debt on the growth rate.

Answer

Before the increase in the debt ratio we have:

ROA = 0.15
b = 0.50
D/E = 0.12
i = 0.07
t = 0.25

$$g = b\left(ROA + \frac{D}{E}(ROA - i(1-t)\right) = 0.5(0.15 + 0.12(0.15 - 0.07(1-0.25)) = 0.08085$$

After the increase in the debt ratio we have:

ROA = 0.15
b = 0.50
D/E = 0.30
i = 0.08
t = 0.25

$$g = b\left(ROA + \frac{D}{E}(ROA - i(1-T)\right) = 0.5(0.15 + 0.30(0.15 - 0.08(1-0.25)) = 0.0896$$

The increase in the debt-equity ratio will raise the growth rate from 8.085 percent to 8.96 percent, that is by nearly one percentage point.

Question

Dividend policy

Continuing the previous example suppose that the firm plans to reduce its dividend payout to 30 percent after the restructuring. What is the impact on the growth rate?

Answer

The growth rate before the reduction in the dividend payout ratio is 0.08085. The growth rate after the decrease in the payout rate (ie increase in b) is:

$$g = b\left(ROA + \frac{D}{E}(ROA - i(1-T)\right) = 0.7(0.15 + 0.12(0.15 - 0.07(1-0.25)) = 0.1132$$

The increase in the retention rate will raise the growth rate from 8.085 percent to 11.2 percent, that is by nearly three percentage points.

3.2 Effect on systematic risk

The impact of changes in financial policy on the value of the firm can be assessed through one of the valuation models that we have considered in previous chapters. For example the growth rate following a financial restructuring can be calculated from the formula

$$\beta_e = \beta_a\left(1 + \frac{D}{E}(1-t)\right)$$

Where β_a = is the asset beta and
β_e = is the geared beta

A higher level of debt relative will increase the geared beta of the company, and a lower level of debt will reduce it.

Question

Effect on risk

A firm currently has a debt equity ratio of 0.12 and a beta of 0.9. The optimal debt ratio is however much lower than the optimal level, since it can raise the debt equity ratio up to 0.30 without increasing the risk of bankruptcy. The firm plans to borrow and repurchase stock to get to this optimal ratio. The interest rate is expected to increase from 7 percent to 8 percent. The tax rate is 25 percent. Find the impact of the increase in debt on the geared beta.

Answer

Before the increase in the debt ratio we have:

D/E = 0.12
t = 0.25
β_a = 0.9

$$\beta_e = \beta_a\left(1+\frac{D}{E}(1-T)\right) = 0.9(1+0.12(1-0.25)) = 0.981$$

After the increase in the debt ratio we have:

D/E = 0.30
T = 0.25
β_a = 0.9

The new beta following the change in the level of debt will be

$$\beta_e = \beta_a\left(1+\frac{D}{E}(1-T)\right) = 0.9(1+0.30(1-0.25)) = 1.1025$$

Question

Dividend policy

If the current EPS for a firm is $2, the asset beta 0.9, the retention rate 0.5, the tax rate 0.25, the debt-equity ratio 0.12, the risk free rate is 5 percent and the equity market risk premium is 6 percent, what is the impact on the price of the share if the debt equity ratio increases to 0.30?

Answer

To calculate the price of the share we shall use the constant growth model, which was introduced in Chapter 6.

$$PV = \frac{FCF_0(1+g)}{k-g}$$

Where k is the cost of equity calculated using the Capital Asset Pricing Model

k = risk-free rate + β_e(equity market risk premium)

FCF can be calculated as EPS × retention rate

Before the financial reconstruction we have:

EPS = $2
b = 0.5
g = 0.08085
β_e = 0.981
k = 5% + 0.981 × 6 % = 10.886 %

and the price of the share is

$$P = \frac{\$2 \times 0.5 \times (1+0.08085)}{0.10886-0.08085} = \$38.588$$

After the financial reconstruction we have:

EPS = $2
b = 0.5
g = 0.0896
β_e = 1.1025
k = 5% + 1.1025 × 6 % = 11.615 %

$$P = \frac{\$2 \times 0.5 \times (1+0.0896)}{0.11615 - 0.0896} = \$41.040$$

As a result of the financial restructuring the price of the share increased by 6.4 percent

4 Leveraged buy-outs (LBOs)

FAST FORWARD

In an LBO a publicly quoted company is **acquired** by a specialist established **private company.** The private company funds the acquisition by substantial borrowing.

4.1 Procedures for going private

A public company **'goes private'** when a **small group of individuals**, possibly including existing shareholders and/or managers and with or without support from a financial institution, **buys all of the company's shares.** This form of restructuring is relatively common in the USA and may involve the shares in the company ceasing to be listed on a stock exchange.

4.2 Advantages of leveraged buy-outs

(a) The **costs of meeting listing requirements** can be saved.

(b) The **company is protected** from **volatility** in share prices which financial problems may create.

(c) The company will be **less vulnerable** to hostile takeover bids.

(d) Management can **concentrate** on the **long-term needs** of the business rather than the short-term expectations of shareholders.

(e) Shareholders are likely to be **closer to management** in a private company, reducing costs arising from the separation of ownership and control (the 'agency problem').

4.3 Disadvantages of leveraged buy-outs

The main disadvantage with leveraged buy outs is that the company loses its ability to have its shares publicly traded. If a share cannot be **traded** it may **lose some of its value**. However, one reason for seeking private company status is that the company has had difficulties as a quoted company, and the prices of its shares may be low anyway.

Case Study

One example of going private was Richard Branson's repurchase of shares in the **Virgin Company** from the public and from financial institutions. Another example was **SAGA** the tour operator which changed status from public to private in 1990. While public, 63% of the company was owned by one family. The family raised finance to buy all of the shares, to avoid the possibility of hostile takeover bids and to avoid conflicts between the long-term needs of the business and the short-term expectations which institutional shareholders in particular are often claimed to have.

More recently, the Matthews family have been considering an MBO (see later) to buy back the publicly held shares in their family turkey business, Bernard Matthews. It was held that the company was being undervalued by the stock market and, after 29 years as a listed company, the Matthews family wanted it back. At the time of writing, there was a possibility of a counter bid being made by Sara Lee, another food producer.

5 Market response to financial reconstruction

FAST FORWARD

> The **market response** to financial reconstruction has been estimated from **empirical studies** of the **behaviour** of **share prices**.

The empirical evidence shows that the market responds positively to financial restructuring. The available empirical evidence shows that the market reacts positively to firms raising their level of debt up to a certain level, since the constraint that debt imposes on future cash flows makes companies choosier when selecting investment opportunities.

A number of studies have dealt with the performance of **leveraged buyouts**. Since the company becomes private as a result of the leveraged buyout we cannot assess the impact of the market. However most studies show that a company does significantly better after the leveraged buyout. More specifically leveraged buy-outs result in increases in free cash flow, improved operational efficiency and a greater focus on the company's core business. The causes of the improvement following financial restructuring are reportedly benign and cannot be attributed to lay-offs of employees – rather the increased efficiency of operations coupled with improved control of capital expenditure seem to account for much of the difference.

The empirical evidence also shows that leveraged buy-outs which involve divisions of companies seem to display larger improvement gains than corporate leveraged buy-outs. On the other hand, the authors do enter a caveat, as the risk of bankruptcy and financial disaster with leveraged buy-outs seems to be greater. Moreover, leveraged buy-outs would appear to under-invest in long-term assets where the risk is greater.

The market reaction to dividend changes has been studied extensively. Most studies show abnormally high returns for dividend increases and abnormally low returns for dividend decreases around the announcement days.

6 Case study in financial reconstruction

FAST FORWARD

> A company **goes private** when a small group of individuals buys all the company's shares. Going private may **decrease costs** and make the company **less vulnerable** to hostile takeover bids.

6.1 Example: Financial reconstruction schemes

Crosby and Dawson Co is a private company that has for many years been making mechanical timing mechanisms for washing machines. The management was slow to appreciate the impact that new technology would have and the company is now faced with rapidly falling sales.

In July 20X1, the directors decided that the best way to exploit their company's expertise in the future was to diversify into the high precision field of control linkages for aircraft, rockets, satellites and space probes. By January 20X2, some sales had been made to European companies and sufficient progress had been made to arouse considerable interest from the major aircraft manufacturers and from NASA in the USA. The cost, however, had been heavy. The company had borrowed $2,500,000 from the Vencap Merchant Bank plc and a further $500,000 from other sources. Its bank overdraft was at its limit of $750,000 and the dividend on its cumulative preference shares, which was due in December, had been unpaid for the fourth year in succession. On 1 February 20X2, the company has just lost another two major customers for its washing machine timers. The financial director presents the following information.

If the company remains in operation, the expected cash flows for the next five periods are as follows.

	9 months to 31.12.X2	*Years ending 31 December 20X3*	*20X4*	*20X5*	*20X6*
	$'000	$'000	$'000	$'000	$'000
Receipts from sales	8,000	12,000	15,000	20,000	30,000
Payments to suppliers	6,000	6,700	7,500	10,800	18,000
Purchase of equipment	1,000	800	1,600	2,700	2,500
Other expenses	1,800	4,100	4,200	4,600	6,400
Interest charges	800	900	700	400	100
	9,600	12,500	14,000	18,500	27,000
Net cash flow	(1,600)	(500)	1,000	1,500	3,000

The above figures are based on the assumption that the present capital structure is maintained by further borrowings as necessary.

STATEMENTS OF FINANCIAL POSITION

	31.12.X0	*31.12.X1*	*31.3.X2 Projected*
	$'000	$'000	$'000
Assets employed			
Fixed assets			
Freehold property	2,780	2,770	2,760
Plant and machinery	3,070	1,810	1,920
Motor vehicles	250	205	200
Deferred development expenditure	–	700	790
Current assets			
Inventory	890	970	1,015
Receivables	780	795	725
	1,670	1,765	1,740
Current liabilities			
Trade payables	1,220	1,100	1,960
Bank overdraft (unsecured)	650	750	750
	1,870	1,850	2,710
	(200)	(85)	(970)
	5,900	5,400	4,700
Long-term liabilities			
10% debentures 20X8 (secured on Freehold property)	(1,000)	(1,000)	(1,000)
Other loans (floating charges)	–	(3,000)	(3,000)
	4,900	1,400	700
	$'000	$'000	$'000
Ordinary shares of $1	3,500	3,500	3,500
8% Cumulative preference shares	1,000	1,000	1,000
Accumulated reserves/(accumulated deficit)	400	(3,100)	(3,800)
	4,900	1,400	700

Other information

1 The freehold property was revalued on 31 December 20X0. It is believed that its net disposal value at 31 March 20X2 will be about $3,000,000.

2 A substantial quantity of old plant was sold during the second six months of 20X1 to help pay for the new machinery needed. It is estimated that the break up value of the plant at 31 March 20X2 will be about $1,400,000.

3 The motor vehicles owned at 31 March 20X2 could be sold for $120,000.

4 Much of the work done on the new control linkages has been patented. It is believed that these patents could be sold for about $800,000, which can be considered as the break-up value of development expenditure incurred to 31 March 20X2.

5 On liquidation, it is expected that the current assets at 31 March 20X2 would realise $1,050,000. Liquidation costs would be approximately $300,000.

Suggest a scheme of reconstruction that is likely to be acceptable to all the parties involved. The ordinary shareholders would be prepared to invest a further $1,200,000 if the scheme were considered by them to be reasonable.

A full solution follows. Complete the first step yourself as a short question.

Question

Liquidation

Ascertain the likely result of Crosby & Dawson Co (see above) going into liquidation as at 31 March 20X2.

Answer

Break-up values of assets at 31 March 20X2	$'000
Freehold	3,000
Plant and machinery	1,400
Motor vehicles	120
Patents	800
Current assets	1,050
	6,370

Total liabilities at 31 March 20X2	$'000
Debentures	1,000
Other loans	3,000
Bank overdraft	750
Trade payables	1,960
	6,710

Solution to remainder of the example

If the company was forced into liquidation, the debentures and other loans would be met in full but that after allowing for the expenses of liquidation ($300,000) the bank and trade creditors would receive a total of $2,070,000 or 76c per dollar. The ordinary and preference shareholders would receive nothing.

If the company remains in operation, the cash position will at first deteriorate but will improve from 20X4 onwards. By the end of 20X6 net assets will have increased by $11,800,000 before depreciation (plant $8,600,000 and cash $3,400,000). If the figures can be relied on and the trend of results continues after 20X6 the company will become reasonably profitable.

In the immediate future, after taking into account the additional amounts raised from the existing ordinary shareholders, the company will require finance of $400,000 in 20X2 and $500,000 in 20X3.

Vencap might be persuaded to subscribe **cash for ordinary shares**. It is unlikely that the company's clearing bank would be prepared to accept any shares, but as they would only receive 76c per dollar on a liquidation they may be prepared to transfer part of the overdraft into a (say) five year loan whilst maintaining the current overdraft limit. It is unlikely that a suitable arrangement can be reached with the trade payables as many would be prepared to accept 76c per dollar, rather than agree to a moratorium on the debts or take an equity interest in the company.

A possible scheme might be as follows.

1 The **existing ordinary shares** to be **cancelled** and **ordinary shareholders** to be **issued** with **$1,200,000 new $1 ordinary shares** for cash.

2 The **existing preference shares** to be **cancelled** and the holders to be issued with **$320,000 new $1 ordinary shares** at par.

3 The **existing debentures** to be **cancelled** and replaced by **$800,000 15% secured debentures** with a 15 year term and the holders to be issued with $400,000 of new $1 ordinary shares at par.

4 The **loan** 'from other sources' to be **repaid**.

5 The **Vencap Bank to receive $2,000,000 15% secured debentures** with a **15 year term** in part settlement of the existing loan, to be issued **$680,000 new ordinary shares** in settlement of the balance and to **subscribe cash for $800,000** of new ordinary shares.

6 The clearing bank to **transfer the existing overdraft** to a **loan account repayable over five years** and to keep the overdraft limit at $750,000. Both the loan and overdraft to be secured by a floating charge.

Comments

1 **Debenture holders**

The debentures currently have **more than adequate asset backing**, and their current nominal yield is 10%. If the reconstruction is to be acceptable to them, they must have either **the same asset backing** or **some compensation** in terms of increased nominal value and higher nominal yield. Under the scheme they will receive securities with a total nominal value of $1,200,000 (an increase of $200,000) and an increase in total yield before any ordinary dividends of $20,000. The new debentures issued to Vencap can be secured on the freehold property (see below).

2 **Loans from other sources**

It has been suggested that the 'loans from other sources' should be **repaid as**, in general, it is easier to arrange a successful reconstruction that involves fewer parties.

3 **Vencap**

Vencap's existing loan of $2,500,000 will, under the proposed scheme, be changed into $2,000,000 of 15% debentures secured on the property and $680,000 of ordinary shares. This gives total loans of $2,800,000 secured on property with a net disposal value of $3,000,000. This is **low asset cover** which might increase if property values were to rise. The scheme will **increase the nominal value of Vencap's interest** by $180,000 with an improvement in security on the first $2,000,000 to compensate for the risk involved in holding ordinary shares. It has also been suggested that Vencap should be asked to subscribe $800,000 for new ordinary shares. The money is required to repay the 'loans from other sources' and to provide additional working capital. The issue of share capital would give the bank a total of 1,480,000 ordinary shares or 43.5% of the equity. From the company's point of view issuing new equity is to be preferred to loan stock as it will improve the gearing position.

4 **The clearing bank**

In a liquidation now, the clearing bank would **receive approximately $573,000**. In return for the possibility of receiving the full amount owed to them they are being asked under the scheme to **advance a further $750,000**. By way of compensation, they are receiving the **security of a floating charge**.

5 **Preference shares**

In a liquidation at the present time, the preference shareholders would receive nothing. The issue of 320,000 $1 ordinary shares should be acceptable as it is **equivalent to their current arrears of dividend**. If the preference shares were left unaffected by the scheme, the full arrears of dividend

would become payable on the company's return to profitability, giving preference shareholders an undue advantage.

6 **Ordinary shareholders**

In a liquidation, the ordinary shareholders would also receive nothing. Under the scheme, they will **lose control of the company** but, in exchange for their additional investment, will still hold about 35.3% of the equity in a company which will have sufficient funds to finance the expected future capital requirements.

7 **Cash flow forecast, on reconstruction**

	$'000
Cash for new shares from equity shareholders	1,200
Cash for new shares from Vencap	800
	2,000
Repayment of loan from other sources	(500)
Cash available	1,500

The overdraft of $750,000 is converted into a long-term loan, leaving the company with a further $750,000 of overdraft facility to use.

8 **Adequacy of funds**

The statement of financial position below shows the company's position after the implementation of the scheme but before any repayments of short-term debt.

	$'000	$'000
Fixed assets		
Freehold property		2,760
Plant and machinery		1,920
Motor vehicles		200
Deferred development expenditure		790
		5,670
Current assets		
Inventory	1,015	
Receivables	725	
Cash	1,500	
	3,240	
Less current liabilities: Trade payables	1,960	
		1,280
		6,950
Less long-term liabilities		
15% debentures		(2,800)
Loan from clearing bank		(750)
		3,400
Ordinary shares of $1		3,400

It would seem likely that the company will have to make a bigger investment in working capital (ignoring cash) for the following reasons.

(a) Presumably a substantial proportion of the sales will be exports which generally have a longer collection period than domestic sales.

(b) It is unlikely that the trade creditors will accept the current payment position (average credit takes over two months) in the long term.

9 **Will the reconstructed company be financially viable?**

Assuming that net current assets excluding cash and any overdraft will, by the end of 20X2, rise from the projected figure of –$220,000 (1,015,000 + 725,000 – 1,960,000) to $500,000 and increase in proportion to sales receipts thereafter, that the equipment required in 20X2 and 20X3 will be leased on five year terms and that the interest charges (including the finance elements in the

lease rentals) will be approximately the same as those given in the question, then the expected cash flows on implementation could be as shown below.

	9 months to 31.12.X2	*20X3*	*20X4*	*20X5*	*20X6*
	$'000	$'000	$'000	$'000	$'000
Receipts from sales	8,000	12,000	15,000	20,000	30,000
Purchase of equipment			1,600	2,700	2,500
Payments to suppliers	6,000	6,700	7,500	10,800	18,000
Other expenses	1,800	4,100	4,200	4,600	6,400
Interest charges	800	900	700	400	100
Lease rentals (excluding finance element) (say)	200	360	360	360	360
Bank loan repayment (say)	150	150	150	150	150
Invt. in working capital	720	250	190	310	630
	9,670	12,460	14,700	19,320	28,140
Net movement	(1,670)	(460)	300	680	1,860
Cash balance b/f	1,500	(170)	(630)	(330)	350
Cash balance c/f	(170)	(630)	(330)	350	2,210

These figures suggest that with an agreed overdraft limit of $750,000 the company will have **sufficient funds** to carry it through the next five years, assuming that the figures are reliable and that no dividends are paid until perhaps 20X4 at the earliest.

This scheme of reconstruction might not be acceptable to all parties, if the **future profits of the company** seem **unattractive**. In particular, Vencap and the clearing bank might be reluctant to agree to the scheme. In such an event, an alternative scheme of reconstruction must be designed, perhaps involving another provider of funds (such as another venture capitalist). Otherwise, the company will be forced into liquidation.

Exam focus point

In a reconstruction question you may be asked to set out the attributes of a successful reconstruction and discuss alternative strategies.

Chapter Roundup

- **Reconstruction schemes** are undertaken when companies have got into difficulties or as part of a strategy to enhance the value of the firm for its owners.
- The impact of a financial reconstruction scheme on the **value** of the firm can be assessed in terms of its impact on the **growth rate** of the company, its **risk**, and its **required rate of return**.
- In an LBO a publicly quoted company is **acquired** by a specialist established **private company.** The private company funds the acquisition by substantial borrowing.
- The **market response** to financial reconstruction has been estimated form **empirical studies** of the **behaviour** of **share prices**.
- A company **goes private** when a small group of individuals buys all the company's shares. Going private may **decrease costs** and make the company **less vulnerable** to hostile takeover bids.

Quick Quiz

1 Describe the procedures that should be followed when designing a financial reconstruction scheme.

2 Give five advantages of a public company going private.

Answers to Quick Quiz

1 (a) Calculate what each party's position would be in a liquidation
(b) Assess possible sources of finance
(c) Design the reconstruction
(d) Assess each party's position as a result of the reconstruction
(e) Check that the company is financially viable

2 (a) Saving of costs of legal formalities
(b) Protection from volatility in share prices
(c) Less vulnerability to hostile takeover
(d) More concentration on long-term needs of business
(e) Closer relationships with shareholders

Now try the question below from the Exam Question Bank

Number	Level	Marks	Time
23	Examination	30	54 mins

17

Business reorganisation

Topic list	Syllabus reference
1 Business reorganisation	D 3(a)
2 Unbundling	D 3(a), (b)
3 Management buy-outs (MBOs) and buy-ins	D 3(c)
4 Unbundling and firm value	D 3(a), (b)

Introduction

In this chapter we discuss methods of business reorganisations concentrating primarily on methods of unbundling companies. Methods discussed include sell-offs, spin-offs, carve-outs, and management buy-outs.

Study guide

		Intellectual level
D3	**Business re-organisation**	
(a)	Recommend, with reasons, strategies for unbundling parts of a quoted company	3
(b)	Evaluate the likely financial and other benefits of unbundling	3
(c)	Advise on the financial issues relating to a management buy-out and buy-in	3

Exam guide

As with mergers and acquisitions, most questions in this area are likely to be a mixture of calculations (for example assessing the financing mix for a management buy-out) and narrative analysis (discussing the implications of a scheme of reconstruction on various interested parties). You may be asked to consider a reconstruction scheme and advise the board on the various alternatives (liquidation, selling off part or all of the company).

1 Business reorganisation

FAST FORWARD

Business reorganisations consist of portfolio restructuring and organisational restructuring.

Reorganisations of the operations and the structures of business is a constant feature of business life. Companies are restructuring in the pursuit of long term strategy in order to achieve a higher level of performance or in order to survive when existing structures and activities are problematic. Corporate restructuring is usually the result of extreme changes in corporate governance such as takeovers and bankruptcy, but it can also be initiated as a response to product market pressures and internal corporate controls. Companies which experience negative earnings due to competition, overexpansion, high costs and excessive debt respond in many ways such as cutting research and development expenditure, reducing debt levels, reducing employment levels and introducing changes in the internal organisation.

In Chapter 16 we classified business restructuring as financial, portfolio and organisational. The last two types of restructuring are collectively known as business reorganisations. However, all three types of restructuring are linked and it may be necessary for all types to be undertaken for a restructuring to be successful. In this chapter we concentrate primarily on portfolio restructuring.

1.1 Portfolio restructuring

FAST FORWARD

Portfolio restructuring consists of changes in the mix of assets owned by the firm or the lines of business in which the firm operates in order to increase the performance of the firm.

Key term

Portfolio restructuring is the acquisition or disposal of assets or business units by a company in the form of divestments, demergers, spin-offs or management buy-outs.

Portfolio restructuring involves a number of one-off diverse transactions such as the sale of underperforming assets, spin-offs and acquisitions which have permanent effects on the financial performance of the company. Thus portfolio restructuring can be seen as part of a strategy to increase the performance of the company which involves not only the buying and selling of a business but also the establishment of performance monitoring and evaluation systems.

According to Copeland, Koller and Murrin (Valuation of Companies), constant portfolio restructuring is necessary in order to improve value, otherwise external raiders will get an opportunity to take-over the company. It is therefore in the best interest of both management and shareholders to keep the gap between

the potential and actual value as close as possible. This can be achieved by improving the operations of the company leading to increasing revenue or declining costs, by acquiring or disposing of assets and by improving the financial structure of the company as we have already discussed in Chapter 16.

1.2 Organisational restructuring

FAST FORWARD

Organisational restructuring consists of changes in the organisational structure of the firm, such as divisional changes and hierarchical structures.

Organisational restructuring involves significant changes in the way a company is organised. As part of such a restructuring a company may redraw divisional boundaries, it may flatten the hierarchical structure, it may streamline processes, it may adopt a different system of corporate governance and it may reduce employment.

Organisational restructuring on its own does not seem to have a significant effect on the performance of the company. However when in conjunction with other forms of restructuring it seems to be a more potent means of increasing performance.

2 Unbundling

FAST FORWARD

Unbundling is a portfolio restructuring strategy which involves the disposal and sale of assets, facilities, production lines, subsidiaries, divisions or product units.

Unbundling can be either voluntary or it can be forced on a company. A company may voluntarily decide to divest part of its business for strategic, financial or organisational reasons. An involuntary unbundling on the other hand may take place for regulatory or financial reasons. The main forms of unbundling are:

(a) Divestments
(b) Demergers.
(c) Sell-offs.
(d) Spin-offs
(e) Carve-outs
(f) Management buy-outs .

2.1 Divestments

FAST FORWARD

Divestment is the partial or complete sale or disposal of physical and organisational assets, the shut-down of facilities and reduction in workforce in order to free funds for investment in other areas of strategic interest.

In a divestment the company ceases the operation of a particular activity in order to concentrate on other activities. The rationale for divestment is normally to reduce costs or to increase return on assets. Divestments differ from the other forms of unbundling because they do not require the formation of a new company.

Key term

A **Divestment** is the disposal of a company's assets.

Divestments are undertaken for a variety of reasons. They may take place as a corrective action in order to reverse unsuccessful previous acquisitions, especially when the acquisition has taken place for diversification purposes. Divestments may also be take place as a response to a cyclical downturn in the activities of a particular unit or line of business. However, divestments may be proactive in the sense that a company may want to exit lines of business which have become obsolete and redeploy resources to activities with a higher return on invested capital.

Where divestments are part of a strategic response for business realignment, the issue of which assets to divest is as important as the decision of which assets to acquire. A company has to decide what constitutes core activities and where the next growth opportunities exist. The growth opportunities may be realized by concentrating on the core business, organic growth and development of the right product lines, or by acquisitions and investment in the right markets.

This refocus of the company priorities may imply that the company may decide to disengage from certain business activities. ING, the financial services conglomerate, is a good example. In 2004 it divested 16 business units or subsidiaries freeing capital to use for the acquisition of 8 new businesses.

2.2 Demergers

FAST FORWARD

A **demerger** is the splitting up of corporate bodies into two or more separate bodies, to ensure share prices reflect the true value of underlying operations.

Key term

A **demerger** is the opposite of a merger. It is the **splitting up of a corporate body into two or more separate and independent bodies.**

For example, the ABC Group plc might demerge by splitting into two independently operating companies AB plc and C plc. Existing shareholders are given a stake in each of the new separate companies.

Demerging, in its strictest sense, stops short of selling out, but is an attempt to ensure that share prices reflect the true value of the underlying operations.

Case Study

British Gas demerged into BG plc and Centrica plc in 1996, allowing Centrica to develop fully its retail business and BG to build up a strong investment portfolio. In March 2000, it was announced that BG itself was to demerge, separating its international business (BG International) from the UK part (Lattice). These two businesses are unrelated, the international part being focused on oil and gas exploration and Lattice owning and operating the gas pipeline system in the UK, and this was an attempt to realise a fuller value for them.

The market looked upon the news of the demerger favourably, and BG's share price hit a five-year high shortly afterwards. BG International was widely seen as a takeover target, having important strategic assets in its field, but lacking in the critical mass thought necessary.

Just prior to the demerger date, BG's share price was 443p, as compared to analysts' estimates of break-up share values of 211p for BG International and 216p for Lattice. Takeover potential, however meant that shareholders were advised to hold on.

2.2.1 Advantages of demergers

The main advantage of a demerger is its greater operational efficiency and the greater opportunity to realise value. A two-division company with one loss making division and one profit making, fast growing division may be better off by splitting the two divisions. The profitable division may acquire a valuation well in excess of its contribution to the merged company.

2.2.2 Disadvantages of demergers

(a) **Economies of scale** may be **lost**, where the demerged parts of the business had operations in common to which economies of scale applied.

(b) The **smaller companies** which result from the demerger will have **lower turnover**, profits and status than the group before the demerger.

(c) There may be **higher overhead** costs as a percentage of turnover, resulting from (b).

(d) The **ability** to raise **extra finance**, especially debt finance, to support new investments and expansion may be reduced.

(e) **Vulnerability to takeover** may be **increased**. The impact on a firm's risk maybe significant when a substantial part of the company is spun off. The result maybe a loss in shareholder value if a relatively low beta element is unbundled.

2.3 Sell-offs

FAST FORWARD

A **sell-off** is the sale of part of a company to a third party, generally for cash.

Key term

A **sell-off** is a form of **divestment** involving the sale of part of a company to a third party, usually another company. Generally, cash will be received in exchange.

2.3.1 Reasons for sell-offs

As part of its strategic planning, it has decided to **restructure**, concentrating management effort on particular parts of the business. Control problems may be reduced if peripheral activities are sold off.

It wishes to sell off a part of its business which **makes losses**, and so to improve the company's future reported consolidated profit performance. This may be in the form of a management buy-out (MBO) – see below.

In order to **protect the rest of the business from takeover**, it may choose to sell a part of the business which is particularly attractive to a buyer.

The company may be **short of cash**.

A **subsidiary** with **high risk** in its operating cash flows could be sold, so as to reduce the business risk of the group as a whole. However as in point(e) in section 2.2.2 above, the reverse may actually be the case.

A **subsidiary** could be sold at a **profit**. Some companies have specialised in taking over large groups of companies, and then selling off parts of the newly-acquired groups, so that the proceeds of sales more than pay for the original takeovers.

Case Study

The *Financial Times* 26 April 2002 reported that the parent company of Burger King restaurants, Diageo, had put the chain up for sale. In the late 1990s Burger King had not grown as fast as its principal rival, McDonalds, and suffered management and investment problems. It has also suffered problems in relationships with franchisees.

Diageo decided to concentrate on becoming a pure premium drinks business and separate off the Burger King chain. A new chief executive, John Dasburg, was appointed to Burger King and money spent on developing new products and installing drive-through technology. The results were a small increase in turnover but an initial decrease in operating profits because of the heavy level of investment. However if the investments paid off, payments could rise rapidly.

The investment required meant that bidders would need to team up to provide a reasonable offer. The main distinguishing feature of bids was likely to be finance structure, particularly the possible securitisation of royalty and rental revenues. The successful bidder also required the support of the current franchisees.

2.3.2 Liquidations

The extreme form of a sell-off is where the entire business is sold off in a **liquidation**. In a voluntary dissolution, the shareholders might decide to close the whole business, sell off all the assets and distribute net funds raised to shareholders.

2.4 Spin-offs

FAST FORWARD

A **spin-off** is the creation of a new company, where the shareholders of the original company own the shares.

Key term

In a **spin-off**, a new company is created whose shares are owned by the shareholders of the original company which is making the distribution of assets.

In a spin-off:

(a) There is **no change** in the **ownership of assets**, as the shareholders own the same proportion of shares in the new company as they did in the old company.

(b) Assets of the part of the business to be separated off are transferred into the new company, which will usually have different management from the old company.

(c) In more complex cases, a spin-off may involve the original company being split into a number of separate companies.

For a number of possible reasons such as those set out below, a spin-off appears generally to meet with favour from stock market investors.

(a) The change may make a **merger** or takeover of some part of the business **easier** in the future, or may protect parts of the business from predators.

(b) There may be **improved efficiency** and more streamlined management within the new structure.

(c) It may be easier to see the value of the **separated parts** of the business now that they are no longer hidden within a conglomerate.

(d) The **requirements** of **regulatory agencies** might be met more easily within the new structure, for example if the agency is able to exercise price control over a particular part of the business which was previously hidden within the conglomerate structure.

(e) After the spin-off, shareholders have the opportunity to **adjust** the **proportions** of their **holdings** between the different companies created.

Case Study

In November 2000, **Invensys**, the UK automations and controls group, announced it was to spin-off its power systems business in an attempt to improve the group's prospects by clearer recognition of the value of the division. The new company was to be listed on the London Stock Exchange, and up to 25% of Invensys's interest in the spun-off unit would be offered to investors. The market reacted positively to the news, with a rapid increase in Invensys's share price, though some reservations were expressed about the 'partial' nature of the flotation, with suggestions that it was a means of raising cash quickly or to fend off a takeover bid.

2.5 Carve-outs

FAST FORWARD

A **carve-out** is the creation of a new company, by detaching parts of the company and selling the shares of the new company to the public.

Key term

In a **carve-out**, a new company is created whose shares are owned by the public with the parent company retaining a substantial fraction of the shares.

Parent companies undertake carve-outs in order to raise funds in the capital markets. These funds can be used for the repayment of debt or creditors or it can be retained within the firm to fund expansion. Carved out units tend to be highly valued.

3 Management buy-outs (MBOs) and buy-ins

FAST FORWARD

A **management buy-out** is the purchase of all or part of the business by its managers. Management buy-outs can be the best way of maintaining links with a subsidiary, and can ensure the co-operation of management if a disposal is inevitable.

The main complication with **management buy-outs** is obtaining the consent of all parties involved. Venture capital may be an important source of financial backing.

Key term

A **management buy-out** is the purchase of all or part of a business from its owners by its managers.

For example, the directors of a subsidiary company in a group might buy the company from the holding company, with the intention of running it as proprietors of a separate business entity.

(a) **To the managers,** the buy-out would be a method of setting up in business for themselves.

(b) **To the group**, the buy-out would be a method of **divestment**, selling off the subsidiary as a going concern.

3.1 The parties to a buy-out

There are usually three parties to a management buy-out.

(a) A **management team** wanting to make a buy-out. This team ought to have the skills and ability to convince financial backers that it is worth supporting.

(b) **Directors** of a group of companies, who make the divestment decision.

(c) **Financial backers** of the buy-out team, who will usually want an equity stake in the bought-out business, because of the **venture capital risk** they are taking. Often, several financial backers provide the venture capital for a single buy-out.

The management team making the buy-out would probably have the aims of setting up in business themselves, being owners rather than mere employees; or avoiding redundancy, when the subsidiary is threatened with closure.

3.2 Reasons for a management buy-out

A large organisation's board of directors may agree to a management buy-out of a subsidiary for any of a number of different reasons.

(a) The **subsidiary** may be **peripheral** to the group's mainstream activities, and no longer fit in with the group's overall strategy.

(b) The **group may** wish to **sell off a loss-making subsidiary**, and a management team may think that it can restore the subsidiary's fortunes.

(c) The parent company may need to **raise cash quickly**.

(d) The subsidiary may be part of a **group** that has just been **taken over** and the new parent company may wish to sell off parts of the group it has just acquired.

(e) The **best offer price** might come from a **small management group** wanting to arrange a buy-out.

(f) When a group has taken the decision to sell a subsidiary, it will probably get better co-operation from the management and employees of the subsidiary if the sale is a management buy-out.

(g) The sale can be arranged more quickly than a **sale** to an **external party**.

(h) The selling organisation is more likely to be able to maintain beneficial links with a segment sold to management rather than to an **external party**.

A private company's shareholders might agree to sell out to a management team because they need cash, they want to retire, or the business is not profitable enough for them.

To help convince a bank or other institution that it can run the business successfully, the management team should prepare a **business plan** and estimates of sales, costs, profits and cash flows, in reasonable detail.

3.3 The role of the venture capitalist

Knowledge brought forward from earlier studies

Venture capital

- **Venture capital** is risk capital, normally provided in return for an equity stake.
- Examples of **venture capital organisations** in the UK are 3i, Equity Capital for industry and the various venture capital subsidiaries of the clearing banks.
- Venture capital **may be provided to fund** business start-ups, business development, MBOs and the purchase of shares from one of the owners of the business.
- Venture capital can also be provided through **venture capital funds**, which is a pool of finance provided by a variety of investors, which will then be applied to MBOs or expansion projects.
- Venture capitalists will normally require an **equity stake** in the company and may wish to have a **representative on the board** to look after its interests.
- A number of clearly defined **exit routes** will be sought by the venture capitalists in order to ensure the easy realisation of their investment when required.

Venture capitalists are far more inclined to fund MBOs, management buy-ins (MBI) and corporate expansion projects than the more risky and relatively costly early stage investments such as start-ups. The minimum investment considered will normally be around £100,000, with average investment of £1m-£2m.

Whilst the return required on venture capital for the high-risk, early stage investments may be as high as 80%, where the funding is for a well established business with sound management, it is more commonly around the 25-30% mark. Whilst this may be achieved by the successful investments, of course there will be many more that fail, and the overall returns on venture capital funds averages out at around 10-15%.

For MBOs and MBIs the venture capitalist will not necessarily provide the majority of the finance – a £50m buy-out may be funded by, say, £15m venture capital, £20m debt finance and £15m mezzanine debt, discussed earlier.

Venture capital funds may require:

- A 20–30% shareholding
- Special rights to appoint a number of directors
- The company to seek their prior approval for new issues or acquisitions

3.3.1 Exit strategies

Venture capitalists generally like to have a predetermined **target exit date,** the point at which they can recoup some or all of their investment in an MBO. At the outset, they will wish to establish various **exit routes**, the possibilities including:

(a) The sale of shares to the public or to institutional investors following a **flotation** of the company's shares on a recognised stock exchange, or on the equivalent of the UK's Alternative Investment Market (AIM)

(b) The **sale** of the company to another firm

(c) The **repurchase** of the venture capitalist's shares by the company or its owners

(d) The sales of the venture capitalist's shares to an **institution** such as an investment trust

3.4 The appraisal of proposed buy-outs

3.4.1 How likely is a management buy-out to succeed?

Management-owned companies seem to achieve better performance probably because of:

- A **favourable buy-out price** having been achieved
- **Personal motivation and determination**
- **Quicker decision making** and so **more flexibility**
- **Keener decisions** and action on pricing and debt collection
- **Savings in overheads**, eg in contributions to a large head office

However, many management buy-outs, once they occur, begin with some redundancies to cut running costs.

3.4.2 How should an institutional investor evaluate a buy-out?

An institutional investor (such as a venture capitalist) should evaluate a buy-out before deciding whether or not to finance. Aspects of any buy-out that ought to be checked are as follows.

(a) Does the management team have the **full range of management skills** that are needed (for example a technical expert and a finance director)? Does it have the right blend of experience? Does it have the commitment?

(b) **Why** is the **company for sale**? The possible reasons for buy-outs have already been listed. If the reason is that the parent company wants to get rid of a loss-making subsidiary, what evidence is there to suggest that the company can be made profitable after a buy-out?

(c) What are the **projected profits and cash flows** of the business? The prospective returns must justify the risks involved.

(d) What is **being bought**? The buy-out team might be buying the shares of the company, or only selected assets of the company. Are the assets that are being acquired sufficient for the task? Will more assets have to be bought? When will the existing assets need replacing? How much extra finance would be needed for these asset purchases? Can the company be operated profitably?

(e) What is the **price**? Is the price right or is it too high?

(f) What **financial contribution** can be made by members of the management team themselves?

(g) What are the **exit routes** and when might they be taken?

3.5 The financial arrangements in a typical buy-out

Typically, the **buy-out team** will have a **minority** of the equity in the bought-out company, with the **various financial backers** holding a **majority** of the shares between them. A buy-out might have several financial backers, each providing finance in exchange for some equity.

Investors of venture capital usually want the **managers to be financially committed**. Individual managers could borrow personally from a bank, say £20,000 to £50,000.

The suppliers of equity finance might insist on investing part of their capital in the form of **redeemable convertible preference shares**. These often have voting rights should the preference dividend fall in arrears, giving increased influence over the company's affairs. They are issued in a redeemable form to give some hope of taking out part of the investment if it does not develop satisfactorily, and in convertible form for the opposite reason: to allow an increased stake in the equity of a successful company.

3.6 Problems with buy-outs

A common problem with management buy-outs is that the managers have little or no experience in **financial management** or **financial accounting**.

Other problems are:

(a) Tax and legal complications

(b) Difficulties in deciding on a fair price to be paid

(c) Convincing employees of the need to change working practices

(d) Inadequate cash flow to finance the maintenance and replacement of tangible fixed assets

(e) The maintenance of previous employees' pension rights

(f) Accepting the board representation requirement that many sources of funds will insist upon

(g) The loss of key employees if the company moves geographically, or wage rates are decreased too far, or employment conditions are unacceptable in other ways

(h) Maintaining continuity of relationships with suppliers and customers

3.7 Buy-ins

Key term

'Buy-in' is when a team of **outside managers**, as opposed to managers who are already running the business, mount a takeover bid and then run the business themselves.

A management buy-in might occur when a business venture is running into trouble, and a group of outside managers see an opportunity to take over the business and restore its profitability.

Alternatively, research suggests that buy-ins often occur when the major shareholder of a small family company wishes to retire.

Many features are common to management buy-outs and buy-ins, including **financing**.

Buy-ins work best for companies where the existing managers are being replaced by managers of **much better quality**. However, managers who come in from outside may take **time** to get used to the company, and may encounter **opposition** from employees if they seek to introduce significant changes.

4 Unbundling and firm value

FAST FORWARD

The main effect of **unbundling** on the **value** of the **firm** comes through changes in the **return on assets** and the **asset beta**.

4.1 Effect on growth rate

The impact of unbundling on the value of the firm can be assessed through one of the valuation models that we have considered in previous chapters. For example the growth rate following a restructuring can be calculated from the formula:

$$g = b\left(ROA + \frac{D}{E}(ROA - i(1-T)\right)$$

Where ROA is the return on the net assets of the company
b is the retention rate
D is the market value of debt
E is the market value of equity
i is the cost of debt
T is the corporate tax rate

When firms divest themselves of existing investments, they affect their expected return on assets, as good projects increase the return on assets, (ROA) and bad projects reduce the return –and any investment decision taken by firms affects their riskiness and therefore the asset beta β_a.

Question

Divestment policy

A firm is expected to divest itself of unrelated divisions, which have historically had lower returns on assets. As a result of the divestment the return on equity is expected to increase from 10 percent to 15 percent. Calculate the effect on the earnings growth rate if the debt to equity ratio is 0.30, the tax rate is 0.25, the retention rate is 0.50 and the interest rate on debt is 8 percent.

Answer

Before the restructuring the growth rate is equal to:

$$g = b\left(ROA + \frac{D}{E}(ROA - i(1-T))\right) = 0.5(0.10 + 0.3(0.10 - 0.08(1-0.25))) = 0.056$$

After the restructuring the growth rate is equal to:

$$g = b\left(ROA + \frac{D}{E}(ROA - i(1-T))\right) = 0.5(0.15 + 0.3(0.15 - 0.08(1-0.25))) = 0.0885$$

The restructuring has increased the growth rate from 5.6 percent to 8.85 percent.

Question

Divestment policy and business risk

The business risk of an oil company which has diversified into a number of other activities such as leisure and tourism is 1.3. If the oil company divested itself of all other activities and concentrated on its core business, its beta, based on the observed beta of oil companies with similar financial structure is expected to be 1.4 (β_L =1.4). If the tax rate is 0.25 and the debt to equity ratio is 0.30, calculate the business risk following the divestment of business.

Answer

The beta of the company is related to its business beta through the relationship:

$$\beta_e = \beta_a\left(1 + \frac{D}{E}(1-T)\right)$$

The business risk is calculated from:

$$\beta_a = \frac{\beta_e}{\left(1 + \frac{D}{E}(1-T)\right)} = \frac{1.4}{(1 + 0.3(1-0.25))} = 1.143$$

After the restructuring the business risk of the company is reduced from 1.3 to 1.143 implying a lower cost of equity and consequently a higher value of equity.

Chapter Roundup

- **Business reorganisations** consist of portfolio restructuring and organisational restructuring.
- **Portfolio restructuring** consists of changes in the mix of assets owned by the firm or the lines of business in which the firm operates in order to increase the performance of the firm.
- **Organisational restructuring** consists of changes in the organisational structure of the firm, such as divisional changes and hierarchical structures.
- **Unbundling** is a portfolio restructuring strategy which involves the disposal and sale of assets, facilities, production lines, subsidiaries, divisions or product units.
- **Divestment** is the partial or complete sale or disposal of physical and organisational assets, the shut-down of facilities and reduction in workforce in order to free funds for investment in other areas of strategic interest.
- A **demerger** is the splitting up of corporate bodies into two or more separate bodies, to ensure share prices reflect the true value of underlying operations.
- A **sell-off** is the sale of part of a company to a third party, generally for cash.
- A **spin-off** is the creation of a new company, where the shareholders of the original company own the shares
- A **carve-out** is the creation of a new company, by detaching parts of the company and selling the shares of the new company to the public.
- A **management buy-out** is the purchase of all or part of the business by its managers. Management buy-outs can be the best way of maintaining links with a subsidiary, and can ensure the co-operation of management if a disposal is inevitable
- The main complication with **management buy-outs** is obtaining the consent of all parties involved. Venture capital may be an important source of financial backing.
- The main effect of **unbundling** on the **value** of the **firm** comes through changes in the **return on assets** and the **asset beta**.

Quick Quiz

1 **Fill in the blank**

A .... is a splitting up of a corporate body into two independent bodies

2 **Fill in the blank**

A .... involves the sale of part of a company to a third party.

3 **Fill in the blank**

In a .... , a new company is created whose shares are owned by the shareholders of the old company.

4 Name three factors that an institutional investor will consider when deciding whether to invest in a management buy-out.

5 Give four examples of possible exit strategies for a venture capitalist.

6 What is a management buy-in?

Answers to Quick Quiz

1 Demerger

2 Sell-off

3 Spin-off

4 Any three of:

(a) Management skills
(b) Reason why company is for sale
(c) Projected profits and cash flows of the business
(d) What is being bought
(e) Price
(f) Financial contribution made by the management team
(g) Exit routes

5 (a) Sale of shares to public or institutional investors following a flotation
(b) Sale of shares to another company
(c) Sale to company itself or its owners
(d) Sale to institution management

6 A buy-in is when a team of outside managers mount a takeover bid and run the business.

Now try the question below from the Exam Question Bank

Number	Level	Marks	Time
24	Introductory	12	22 mins

PART E

Treasury and advanced risk management techniques

LEARNING MEDIA

18 The role of the treasury function in multinationals

Topic list	Syllabus reference
1 The role of financial and money markets	E1 (a)
2 Banks and other financial institutions in the money markets	E 1(b)
3 Money market instruments	E1 (c)
4 Money market derivatives	E2 (a)
5 The treasury management function	E1 (d)

Introduction

The purpose of this chapter is to discuss the role of the **treasury function** within a **multinational company**. The treasury function deals primarily with **short-term** decisions but in a way which is consistent with the **long-term** management objective of **maximising shareholder value**.

The chapter starts with a discussion of the role of the **money markets**, and how these provide **short-term finance** to companies. The chapter then discusses the role of banks and **financial institutions** in **financial intermediation** and the various instruments that are traded on this market. Having completed a description of the money market, its instruments and players, the chapter ends with a discussion of how the **treasury function** deals with the management of **short-term assets** of a company, its risk exposure and how it promotes the achievement of long-term company objectives.

Study guide

		Intellectual level
E1	**The role of the treasury function in multinationals**	
(a)	Describe the role of the money markets in: (i) Providing short-term liquidity to industry and the public sector (ii) Providing short-term trade finance (iii) Allowing a multinational firm to manage its exposure to FOREX and interest rate risk.	1
(b)	Explain the role of the banks and other financial institutions in the operation of the money markets.	1
(c)	Describe the characteristics and role of the principal money market instruments: (i) Coupon bearing (ii) Discount instruments (iii) Derivatives	1
(d)	Outline the role of the treasury management function within: (i) The short term management of the firm's financial resources (ii) The longer term maximisation of shareholder value (iii) The management of risk exposure	2

1 The role of financial and money markets

1.1 Financial markets

FAST FORWARD

Financial markets are the markets where economic units with surplus funds, such as individuals, corporations, the government, or overseas investors lend funds to other economic units that want to borrow.

This function is shown diagrammatically in Figure 1.

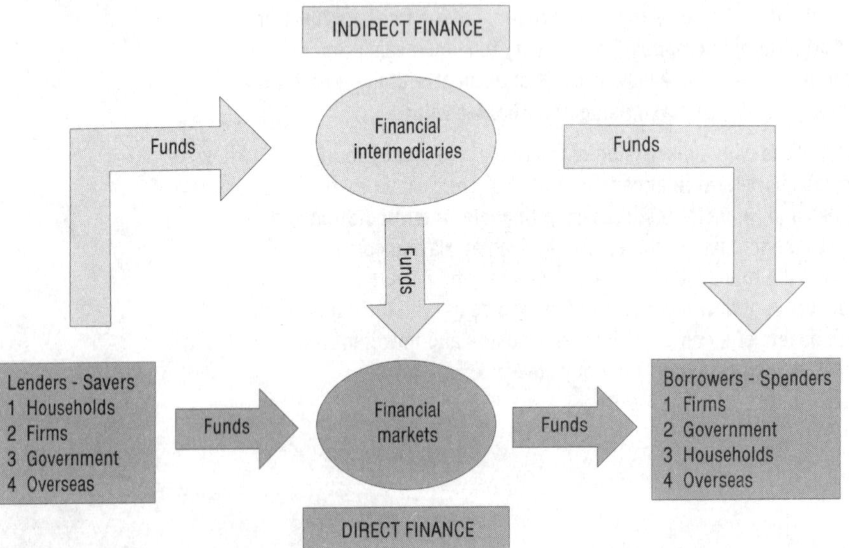

Those who have saved and are lending funds, the lender savers, are on the left, and those who must borrow funds to finance their spending, the borrower spenders, are on the right. The principal lender-

savers are **households**, as well as **overseas institutions** and their **governments**, who sometimes also find themselves with excess funds and so lend them out. The most important borrower-spenders are corporations and governments, although individuals also borrow to finance the acquisition of durable goods or houses. The arrows show that funds flow from **lender-savers** to **borrower-spenders** via two routes.

The first route is the direct finance route at the bottom of the diagram, when borrowers borrow funds directly from lenders in financial markets by selling them **securities** (called financial instruments), which are **claims** on the **borrowers' future income** or **assets**.

Securities are **assets** for the **buyer** but **liabilities** for the seller. For example, if British Airways needs to borrow funds to pay for a new aircraft, it might borrow the funds from a saver by **selling** the saver a **bond**, a **debt security** that promises to make payments periodically for a specified period of time.

The channelling of funds from **savers** to **spenders** is a crucial function for the economy because the people who save are frequently not the same people who have profitable investment opportunities available to them, ie the entrepreneurs. Without financial markets, it is hard to transfer funds from a person with surplus funds and no investment opportunities to one who has investment opportunities but no funds. They would be unable to transact and both would be worse off as result. Financial markets are thus essential to promoting **economic efficiency**.

Financial markets not only allow funds to move from people who lack **productive investment opportunities** to people who have such opportunities but they also directly improve the well-being of consumers by allowing them to time their purchases better. They provide funds to young people to buy what they need and can eventually afford without forcing them to wait until they have saved up the entire purchase price. Financial markets that are operating efficiently improve the economic welfare of everyone in the society.

Financial markets can be classified in a variety of ways depending on the criterion selected. The most common groupings are primary and secondary markets, over the counter and exchange -based markets and money and capital markets. A brief description follows.

1.2 Primary and secondary markets

FAST FORWARD

Markets where a security is first issued are known as primary, and markets where a security is subsequently traded are known as secondary.

Key term

A **primary market** is a financial market in which new issues of a security are sold by the issuer to initial buyers. A **secondary market** is a market in which securities that have already been issued can be bought and sold.

1.3 Exchange and over the counter markets

FAST FORWARD

Secondary markets can be organised as exchanges or over the counter (OTC).

Secondary markets for financial securities can be organised as **exchanges**, where buyers and sellers of securities buy and sell securities in one location, the exchange. Examples of exchanges include the **London Stock Exchange** and the **New York Stock Exchange** for the trading of shares, the **Chicago Board of Trade** for the trading of commodities, and the **London International Financial Futures and Options Exchange (LIFFE)** for the trading of derivatives.

Alternatively, secondary markets can operate as **over-the-counter (OTC)** markets, where buyers and sellers transact with each other not through an exchange but through individual negotiation. The prices at which securities are bought over the counter do not differ from the corresponding transactions in an exchange because participants are in constant contact through computers with other market participants and can therefore transact at the most competitive price.

Securities that are issued in an **over the counter market** and can be **resold** are called **negotiable**, and securities that are **not allowed** to be **resold** after they are issued are called **non-negotiable**.

1.4 Money and capital markets

Capital markets are markets in which the securities that are traded have **long maturities**, ie represent **long-term obligations** for the **issuer**. Securities that trade in capital markets include shares and bonds. **Money markets,** on the other hand, are markets in which the securities that are traded have short maturities, less than a year, and the repayment of funds borrowed is required within a short period of time.

2 Banks and other financial institutions in the money markets

Financial intermediaries borrow money from the **lenders-savers** and then in turn make loans to the borrowers-spenders. The most common financial intermediaries are banks, insurance companies, pension funds, mutual funds, and finance companies. The process of **borrowing** and **lending** through **intermediaries** is called **financial intermediation or indirect finance**. As a source of funds for businesses, **indirect finance** is far more common than **direct finance**.

2.1 The importance of financial intermediation

Financial intermediation is important for two main reasons, namely the presence of **transaction costs** and the presence of **credit risk**.

The presence of transaction costs

Transactions costs (time and money spent carrying out financial transactions) are often prohibitively high for individual borrowers and lenders. Financial intermediaries, by handling a large volume of such transactions, develop an expertise that allows them to make additional transactions much more cheaply than any individual could. Financial intermediaries exploit **economies of scale**. By conducting a very **high volume of business,** they reach a point where the unit cost of transactions becomes smaller and smaller.

The presence of credit risk

The second reason for the importance of financial intermediaries is **asymmetric information**. The borrower has much better information about his ability and intention to repay than the lender does. This exposes the lender to **credit risk**. An individual lender will not normally have the ability to ascertain the **credit risk** of another individual. A bank on the other hand employs a number of specialists who are in a better position to evaluate the **credit quality** of an individual and it may have access to information on an individual that would be too costly for an individual lender to acquire.

2.2 Securitisation

FAST FORWARD

Securitisation is the process of converting **illiquid assets** into **marketable asset-backed securities**. The development of **securitisation** has led to **disintermediation** and a reduction in the role of financial intermediaries as borrowers can reach lenders directly.

Securitisation is the process of converting **illiquid assets** into **marketable securities**. These securities are backed by specific assets and are normally called **asset-backed securities** (ABS). Securitisation started with banks converting their long term loans such as mortgages into securities and selling them to institutional investors. One of the problems of banks as financial intermediaries, is the fundamental mismatch between the maturities of assets and liabilities. Securitisation of loans and sale to investors with more long-term liabilities reduces the mismatch problem and a bank's overall risk profile.

The oldest and most common type of asset securitization is the **mortgage-backed bond** or **security (MBS)**, although today one can expect virtually anything that has a cash flow to be a candidate for securitization.

In a typical ABS transaction, the first step is to identify the underlying **asset pool** that will serve as **collateral** for the **securities**. The assets in this pool should be relatively homogeneous with respect to credit, maturity, and interest rate risks; common examples of ABS include credit card receivables, trade receivables, and car loans. Once a suitably large and homogenous asset pool is identified, the pooled assets are sold to a grantor trust or other bankruptcy-remote, special purpose financing vehicle (SPV).

The development of securitisation has led to **disintermediation** and a reduction in the role of financial intermediaries as borrowers can reach lenders directly.

Key term

> **Disintermediation** describes a decline in the traditional deposit and lending relationship between banks and their customers and an increase in direct relationships between the **ultimate suppliers** and **users** of financing.

Cash flows before securitisation

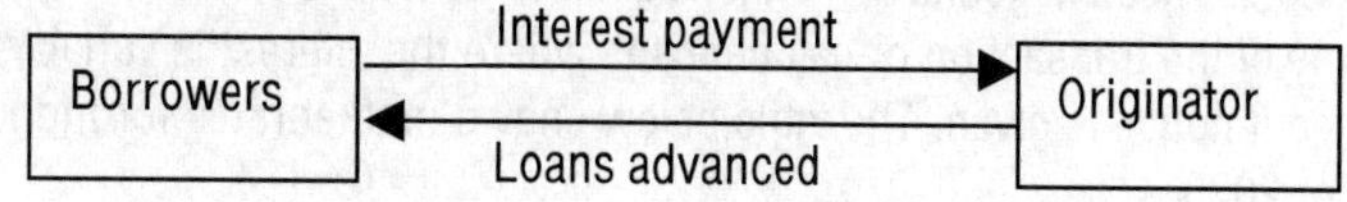

Cash flows after securitisation

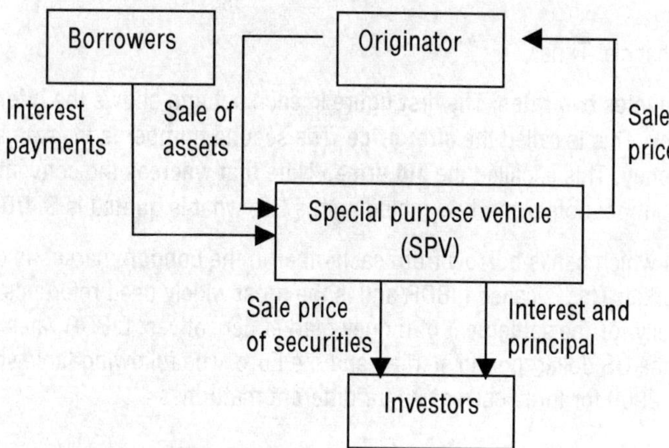

3 Money market instruments

FAST FORWARD

> **Money markets** are the markets where **short-term instruments** are traded.

Money markets are the markets where **short-term instruments** are traded. Money markets are over the counter markets and the transactions take place between **institutions** rather than individual investors. The main characteristic of money market instruments apart from their short maturities (up to 12 months) is that they normally have only one cash flow. Money market instruments can be either **negotiable** or **non-negotiable**. They can also be **coupon bearing** or **discount instruments**.

Discount instruments do not pay interest. They are issued and traded at a **discount to the face value**. The discount is equivalent to the interest paid to the investor and is the difference between the purchase price of the instrument and the price at maturity.

> Purchase Price = Face value – discount

The table below shows some of the **money market instruments** in the UK.

Coupon Bearing	Discount	Derivatives
Money Market Deposits	Treasury Bill (T-bill)	Forwards and Futures
Certificate of Deposit (CD)	Banker's Acceptance (BA)	Swaps
Repurchase Agreement (Repo)	Commercial Paper (CP)	Options

3.1 Money market deposits

Key term

LIBOR (London Interbank Offered Rate) is the rate of interest at which banks borrow from each other in the London interbank market

Money market deposits are very short-term loans between banks or other institutions including governments. These deposits can either be fixed, where the rate of interest and maturity dates are agreed at the time of the transaction or call deposits where the interest is variable and the deposit can be terminated if notice is given. The table below shows market rates for money market instruments on 21 December 2006.

	Over-night	*7 days notice*	*One month*	*Three months*	*Six months*	*One year*
Interbank Sterling	$5\frac{3}{32} - 5$	$6 - 5\frac{3}{4}$	$6\frac{1}{16} - \frac{15}{16}$	$6\frac{3}{16} - 6\frac{1}{16}$	$6\frac{5}{16} - \frac{3}{16}$	$6\frac{3}{8} - 6\frac{1}{4}$

Source: Financial Times

The table quotes **two rates**. The first figure in each column shows the **interest rate** at which a bank will **lend money**. This is called the **offer price**. The second number is the **rate** at which the bank will pay to **borrow money**. This is called the **bid price**. Note that whereas the convention in London is to quote **Offer/Bid,** in most other markets including the US, what is quoted is **Bid/Offer**.

The rate at which banks borrow from each other in the London market is of particular importance for money market. This is called LIBOR and is the most widely used reference rate for short-term interest rates globally for the settlement of money market derivatives. LIBOR rates are calculated for 10 currencies including the US dollar, pound sterling and the Euro. The following table shows the LIBOR rates on 12 December 2006 for three currencies for different maturities.

	EUR	*USD*	*GBP*
Overnight	3.413	5.289	5.141
1 week	3.592	5.305	5.150
1 month	3.653	5.350	5.241
3 months	3.672	5.360	5.279
9 months	3.851	5.313	5.420
12 months	3.898	5.250	5.459

Source: British Bankers Association

The LIBOR rates at **different maturities** define the **short-term yield curve** which is shown below.

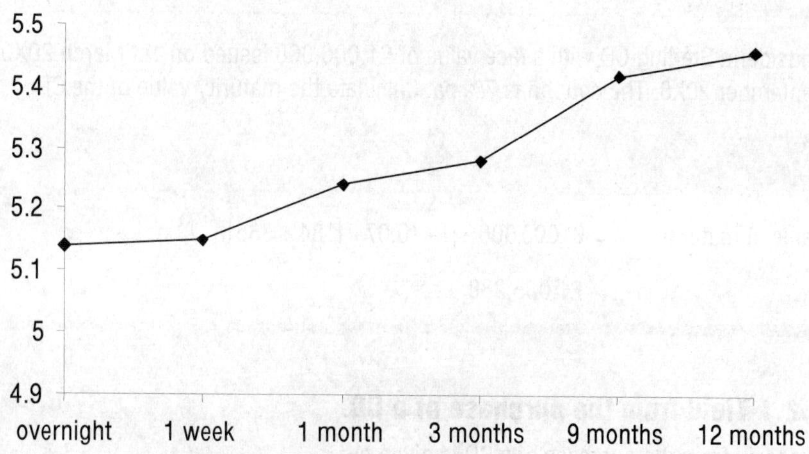

Note that whereas the yield curve is given for specific maturities, the yield curve can be constructed by interpolation.

The LIBOR yield curve can also be used to estimate the forward yield curve which gives the interest rate between two future periods. The forward yield curve is used to price many money market derivatives. The principle underpinning the derivation of the forward yield curve, is that the 1 period spot rate, the two-period spot rate and the forward rate are linked by the relationship

$$(1+r_2)^2 = (1+r_1)(1+r_{12})$$

Where r_1 s the one-period spot rate

r_2 is the two period spot rate

r_{12} is the forward rate between periods 1 and 2

The forward rate can be calculated from the above as:

$$r_{12} = \frac{(1+r_2)^2}{(1+r_1)} - 1$$

3.2 Certificates of deposit

Key term

> A **Certificate of Deposit (CD)** is a certificate of receipt for funds deposited at a bank or other financial institution for a specified term and paying interest at a specified rate.

Certificates of deposit can be either **negotiable** or **non-negotiable**. The holder of a **negotiable CD** has two options: to hold it until maturity, receiving the interest and the principal or to sell it before maturity at the market price. A typical range of dollar certificates of deposit in terms of coupon and maturity is shown below, together with the corresponding yield.

Term	*Coupon*	*Annual percentage yield*
3 Months	5.950	6.080
3 Months	6.150	6.290
3 Months	6.200	6.350
6 Months	6.200	6.300
6 Months	6.300	6.400
9 Months	6.400	6.450

The coupon is expressed as an annual percentage rate and needs to be adjusted to reflect the fact that its maturity is less than a year. Sterling CDs assume there are 365 days in the year, whilst US CDs assume 360 days.

The value of the CD on maturity = face value × $[1+(\text{coupon rate} \times \text{days to maturity} \div \text{days in the year})]$

Question

Maturity value

Consider a Sterling CD with a face value of £1,000,000 issued on 1st March 20X0 maturing on 1st September 20X0. The coupon is 7% pa. Calculate the maturity value of the CD.

Answer

Value at maturity $= £1{,}000{,}000 \times [1+(0.07 \times [184 \div 365])]$

$= £1{,}035{,}288$

3.2.1 Yield from the purchase of a CD

The yield from the purchase of a CD is given by

$$\frac{\text{Sale price} - \text{Purchase price}}{\text{Purchase price}} \times \frac{\text{Days in year}}{\text{Days to maturity}}$$

Question

Yield of CD

You have bought a sterling certificate of deposit for £1,012,000 and sold it 28 days later for £1,018,290. What is the yield ?

Answer

$$\frac{1{,}018{,}290 - 1{,}012{,}000}{1{,}012{,}000} \times \frac{365}{28} = 0.0810 \text{ or } 8.10\%$$

3.2.2 Fair price of a CD

Step 1 Divide days to maturity by number of days in the year (360 or 365) and multiply results by the yield (calculated in section 3.2.1 above)

Step 2 Add 1 to the result of Step 1

Step 3 Divide the selling price of the CD by the result of Step 2.

Question

Value of CD after rate increase

What will be the maturity value of a 90-day US CD yielding 10% if the investor pays $1,000,000 for it at the time of issue? If yields rise to 12% and the security is sold after 5 days, how much will it be worth?

Answer

Selling price (adapting the steps for calculating purchase price above)

$$\left[1+\left[\frac{\text{Days to maturity}}{\text{Days in a year}} \times \text{yield}\right]\right] \times \text{Purchase price}$$

$$= \left[1+\frac{90}{360} \times 0.10\right] \times 1{,}000{,}000$$

= $1,025,000

If yield increases to 12% with 85 days remaining, the selling price will be

$$\left[1+\left(\frac{85}{360}\times 0.12\right)\right]\times 1{,}000{,}000 = \$1{,}028{,}333$$

Note: remember that US CDs assume that there are 360 days in a year.

3.3 Repos

Key term

A **repurchase agreement** is an agreement between two counterparties under which one counterparty agrees to sell an instrument to the other on an agreed date for an agreed price, and simultaneously agrees to buy back the instrument from the counterparty at a later date for an agreed price.

A repurchase agreement is a loan secured by a marketable instrument, usually a treasury bill or a bond. The typical term is 1-180 days and is an attractive instrument because it can accommodate a wide spectrum of maturities. A repo involves two sets of transactions. First on the start date, the dealer sells the security for cash. On maturity, the dealer will repay the cash with interest and take back the security. The flows in a repo are shown in the following diagram.

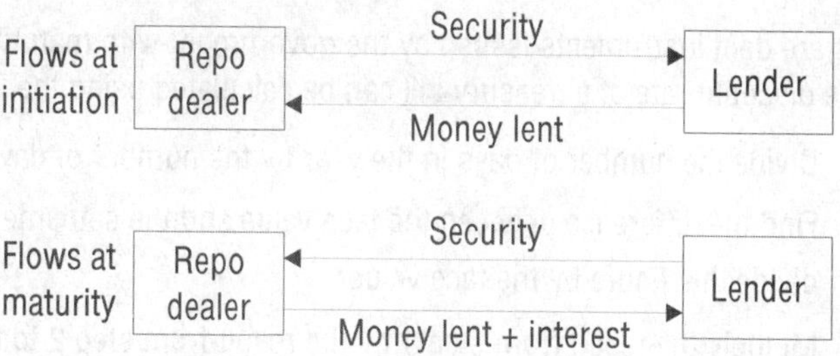

Question

Repo cash flows

A company enters into a repo agreement with a bank and it sells $10,000,000 of government bonds with an obligation to repurchase the security in 60 days. If the repo rate is 8.2% what is the repurchase price of the bond?

Answer

The repurchase price of the bond is the sale price plus the interest on the cash received.

$$\text{Interest} = \$10{,}000{,}000 \times 0.082 \times \frac{60}{365} = \$134{,}794.52$$

Repurchase price = $10,000,000 + $134,794.52 = $10,134,794.52

3.3.1 Yield

You should follow the following steps when calculating the yield on a repo.

Step 1 Divide days to maturity by the number of days in the year

Step 2 Find the difference between the selling price and the purchase price and divide the result by the purchase price

Step 3 Multiply the result from step 1 by the result from step 2 to find the yield on the repo

Question

Repo yield

A company enters into a repo agreement with a bank and it sells $10,000,000 of government bonds with a repurchase price in 60 days of $10,002,993. What is the yield?

Answer

$$y = \frac{10{,}002{,}993 - 10{,}000{,}000}{10{,}000{,}000} \times \frac{365}{60} = 0.182\%$$

Key term

A **reverse repurchase** agreement (reverse repo) is an agreement for the purchase of an instrument with the simultaneous agreement to resell the instrument at an agreed future date and agreed price.

In a **reverse repo**, the dealer purchases the security initially and then sells it on maturity. Because the two parties in a **repo** agreement act as a buyer and a seller of the security, a **repo** to one party is a **reverse repo** to the other.

3.4 Treasury bills

Treasury bills are debt instruments issued by the government with maturities ranging from one month to one year. The discount rate of a treasury bill can be calculated using the following steps.

Step 1 Divide the number of days in the year by the number of days to maturity

Step 2 Find the difference between the face value and the settlement price of the treasury bill and divide this figure by the face value

Step 3 Multiply the result from step 1 by the result from step 2 to find the discount rate

Question

Treasury bill discount

A 91-day Treasury bill with a face value of $10,000,000 is issued for $9,870,000. What is the discount rate?

Answer

$$\text{Discount rate} = \frac{365}{91} \times \frac{10{,}000{,}000 - 9{,}870{,}000}{10{,}000{,}000} = 5.2\%$$

3.4.1 Settlement price

You can calculate the settlement price of a treasury bill by following these steps.

Step 1 Divide the days to maturity by the days in the year and multiply the result by the discount rate (calculated in section 3.4 above)

Step 2 Deduct the result in Step one from 1

Step 3 Multiply the result from Step 2 by the face value of the treasury bill

3.4.2 Yield when held to maturity

Calculate the yield on a treasury bill by following these steps.

Step 1 Divide the number of days in the year by the number of days to maturity

Step 2 Find the difference between the face value and settlement price of the bill and divide the result by the face value

Step 3 Multiply the result from Step 1 by the result from Step 2 to obtain the yield when held to maturity

3.4.3 Yield when sold before maturity

By following these steps you can calculate the yield on a treasury bill if it is sold before maturity.

Step 1 Divide the days in the year by the days to maturity

Step 2 Find the difference between the selling price and the purchase price of the treasury bill and divide the result by the purchase price

Step 3 Multiply the result from step 1 by the result from Step 2 to find the yield on the treasury bill when it is sold before maturity

Alternatively the yield can be calculated using the discount rate as follows.

Step 1 Divide the days to maturity by the days in the year and multiply the result by the discount rate

Step 2 Deduct the result from Step 1 from 1

Step 3 Divide the discount rate by the result from Step 2 to find the yield on the treasury bill when it is sold before maturity

3.4.4 Bond Equivalent Yield

The Bond Equivalent Yield is required to allow comparisons between US and UK treasury bills (remember that the assumption about the length of a year is different for each of these bills). The Bond Equivalent Yield of a US treasury bill (where the length of a year is assumed to be 360 days) can be calculated as follows.

Step 1 Divide the days to maturity by 360 (US treasury bill assumption about days in the year) and multiply the result by the discount rate

Step 2 Deduct the result from step 1 from 1

Step 3 Divide the discount rate by the result from step 2

Step 4 Divide 365 by 360 (UK v US days in the year) and multiply the result by the result from step 3 to find the bond equivalent yield for a US treasury bill

Question — **Treasury bill yield**

An investor buys a US Treasury Bill for $98 expiring in 91-days with a face value of $100. What is the yield?

Answer

$$y = \frac{100-98}{98} \times \frac{360}{91} = 8.073\%$$

3.5 Commercial paper

Commercial paper is short-term unsecured corporate debt with maturity up to 270 days. The typical term of this debt is about 30 days. Commercial paper is unsecured debt so can only be issued by large organisations with good credit ratings, normally to fund short-term expenditure. The debt is issued at a discount that reflects the prevailing interest rates. The yield on commercial paper can be calculated using the following steps.

Step 1 Divide the days in the year by the days to maturity

Step 2 Deduct the purchase price of the paper from the selling price and divide the result by the purchase price

Step 3 Multiply the result from Step 1 by the result from Step 2

Question

Treasury bill yield

Wobbly Inc purchased commercial paper when it was issued on 30 April with a maturity date of 30 August. The paper has a face value of $5 million and a yield to maturity of 10%.

How much will Wobbly Inc have to pay for the commercial paper?

Answer

Rather than calculating the yield using the steps above we have to adapt these steps to calculate the purchase price.

Purchase price can be calculated as follows.

Step 1 Divide the days in the year by the days to maturity and multiply the result by the yield

$(122 \div 360) \times 0.10 = 0.034$

Step 2 Add 1 to the result from Step 1

$= 1.034$

Step 3 Divide the face value by the result from step 2 to obtain the purchase price

$5 million ÷ 1.034 = $4,835,590

3.6 Banker's acceptance

Key term

> **Banker's acceptances** are negotiable bills issued by companies and guaranteed by a bank.

Banker's acceptances are issued by firms to finance commercial transactions such as imports or the purchase of goods. The name derives from the fact that the bank has guaranteed the payment to the holder of the banker's acceptance, that is the bank has accepted responsibility for the payment. Banks guaranteed the payment by the company for a fee.

Banker's acceptances are sold on a discounted basis like T-bills and commercial paper. Because banker's acceptances are negotiable instruments, they can be bought and sold until they mature. The rates on banker's acceptances are low because, as they are guaranteed by a bank, the credit risk is low. The yield on a banker's acceptance can be calculated in exactly the same way as the yield on commercial paper given in section 3.5 above.

UK Banker's Acceptance are calculated on a Actual/365 days basis while in US they are calculated on an Actual/360 days basis.

The typical term is between 30 to 180 days and are issued by firms which do not have a sufficiently high credit rating to issue commercial paper.

4 Money market derivatives

Key term

> **Derivatives** are contracts that derive their value from movements in the value of an **underlying asset price**, **interest rate**, or **commodity price**.

Exam focus point

The fundamental properties of the various types of derivatives will be assumed to be known in examination questions that involve the use of derivatives.

Derivative contracts trade either in organised exchanges or over the counter (OTC). These contracts can utilize significant leverage since an underlying may represent a large notional amount. We have already looked at a class of derivative instruments, options, in Chapter 8. This section introduces the markets for the main interest rate derivative instruments such as forward, futures, swaps and options, all of which are based on money market instruments.

Certain options contracts and futures contracts are exchange-traded derivatives, whereas forward and swaps and some options contracts are privately negotiated in the so-called over-the-counter (OTC) market. OTC derivatives, are essentially bilateral contracts, privately negotiated transactions between counterparties. Nevertheless, many OTC derivatives are traded using standardized agreements, resulting in low transaction costs. Interest rate swaps, which have an extremely active, liquid market, are an example of such derivatives. The main benefit of OTC derivatives is that they can be tailored to the needs of the two parties; their major drawback is that they pose a higher risk of default than do exchange-traded derivatives. Some very specialized agreements may also be illiquid.

To be 'exchange-traded', derivative contracts must be standardized with regard to the amount of the underlying, the settlement or expiration date, and so forth. They are then listed and traded on the exchange, and accounts are settled through a clearinghouse. Legally, the clearinghouse is the counterparty for exchange-traded derivatives – that is, the agent responsible for upholding the derivative contract. A benefit of that system is that transactions can occur in an active, liquid market and there is no risk.

Certain derivative products require the delivery of some underlying asset or commodity. A derivative instrument is **physically settled** if the underlying is to be **physically delivered** in exchange for the specified payment in the contract.

When derivative contracts do not require the physical delivery of an asset or commodity they are said to be cash settled. With **cash settlement**, the underlying is not physically delivered. Instead, the derivative settles for an amount of money equal to what the derivative's market value would be at maturity/expiration if it were a physically settled derivative. In the case of a forward, this equals the notional amount multiplied by the difference between the market price of the underlying at maturity and the forward's delivery. In the case of an option, it is the intrinsic value.

Certain types of derivatives are cash settled because physical delivery would be inconvenient or impossible. For example, an option on an index such as the S&P 500, will generally be cash settled because it would be inconvenient and entail considerable transaction costs to deliver all five hundred stocks that comprise that index. An interest rate cap has to be cash settled because the underlying is an interest rate, which cannot be physically delivered.

In commodity and energy markets, people informally distinguish between the **physical market** and **paper market**. The physical market encompasses all transactions in which there is physical delivery ie cash, spot and physically-settled forward transactions. Paper markets encompass all derivatives transactions that have cash settlement.

4.1 Forward rates

4.1.1 Description of a forward contract

Key term

A **forward contract** is an agreement between two parties, now (ie period t) to buy or sell a particular asset or commodity at some set time (T) in the future for a set price.

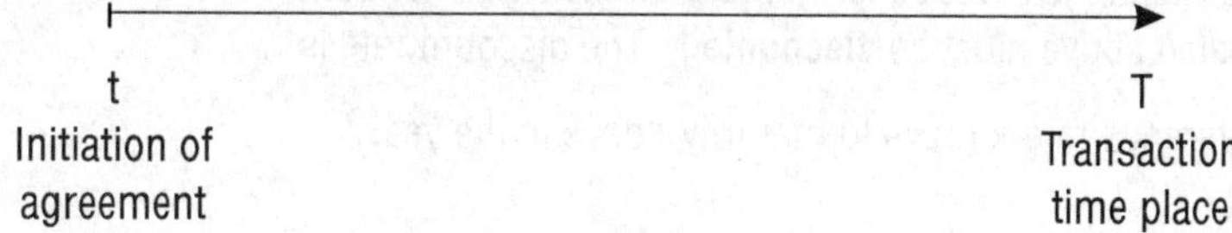

4.1.2 Profits/loss from a forward contract

Suppose that the price at which the two parties have agreed to transact in the future is denoted by F(t, T). The buyer of a forward contract has agreed to buy the underlying at time T, say in three months, at a price F(t, T). The seller of the forward contract has agreed to sell the underlying at time T at a price F(t, T). Denoting the price of the asset at time T as S(T), the buyer of a futures contract will profit if S(T) > F(t, T), since the purchase price is lower than the market price and will lose money if S(T) < F(t, T), ie when the current market price of the underlying is lower than the agreed price. The payoff for a seller of a forward contract is a mirror mage of the payoff of the buyer.

4.1.3 Price of a forward contract

At time t, the agreed forward price at which the transaction will take place in the future is higher than the current price of the underlying S(t), to reflect the cost of money, or more generally the 'cost of carry'. The forward price will be given by

$$F(t, T) = S(t)(1 + r)^{T-t}$$

where r is the relevant interest rate for the period T – t.

Forward contracts exist for a variety of commodities and underlying assets including metals, energy products, interest rates and currency exchange rates. Because forward contracts are not formally regulated by or traded on an organised exchange, each party to the contract is subject to potential default risk of the other party. This is known as settlement risk.

4.1.4 Forward rate agreements

Key term

A **forward rate agreement** (FRA) is a cash-settled forward contract on a short-term loan.

FRAs are over-the-counter (OTC) instruments which are typically issued by investment banks to end users and are not traded on exchanges. Thus the terms for the FRA can be set according to the end user's requirements but they tend to be illiquid as they can only be sold back to the issuing investment bank. For example, a 2 × 5 FRA is a 2-month forward on a 3-month loan. The interest rate on the loan, called the **FRA rate**, is set when the contract is first entered into.

The date on which the FRA is dealt is called the **trade date.** The **spot date** is usually two business days after the traded date. This is the date on which the value of the reference rate is determined.

Because FRAs are cash settled, no loan is ever actually extended. Instead, contracts settle with a single cash payment made on the first day of the underlying loan, which is called the **settlement date.** The period referred in the FRA terms is the period between the spot date and the settlement date. For example a **2 × 5 FRA** will have a settlement date **two calendar months after the spot rate**. The reference rate used for the settlement is determined on the **fixing date.**

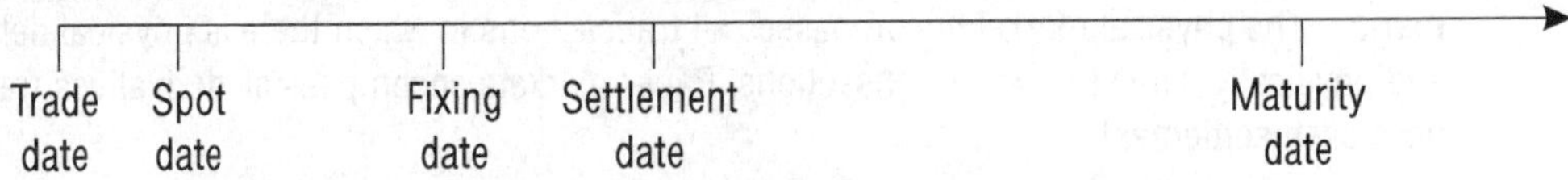

The exchange of cash flows on the maturity date will be calculated as follows.

Step 1 Divide days to maturity by days in the year

Step 2 Calculate the difference between the reference rate (usually LIBOR or EURIBOR rate) and multiply this figure by the result from step 1

Step 3 Multiply the result from step 2 by the notional amount of the loan

As the exchange of funds takes place on the settlement date (rather than the maturity date), the value calculated above must be **discounted**. The discount rate is

1 + reference rate × (days to maturity / days in the year)

The settlement value is therefore the **cash flows on the maturity date divided by the discount rate** (similar to an NPV calculation).

Question

FRA settlement value

Suppose a 4×10 $10 million FRA is transacted with an FRA rate of 3.5%. The four month forward period starts on the spot date and extends to the settlement date. For this FRA, the reference rate is 6-month USD LIBOR. Suppose 6-month LIBOR is 3.8% on the fixing date. The USD money market uses a 360 day basis. What is the settlement amount?

Answer

On the settlement date, the borrower (the party that is long the FRA) receives from the lender (the party that is short the FRA) the amount

$$S = 10m \times \frac{(0.038 - 0.035) \times \frac{180}{360}}{\left(1 + 0.038 \times \frac{180}{360}\right)} = \$14{,}720.31$$

4.2 Futures contracts

4.2.1 Description of futures contracts

Key term

A **futures contract** is a standardised agreement between two parties to buy or sell a particular asset or commodity at a set date in the future for a set price.

The terms of the contract specify the amount and precise type of the asset to be delivered, the delivery date or dates, the place of delivery, and certain options that the contract seller may have with respect to the delivery process. Futures' contracts exist for currencies, interest rates, commodities stock indices, individual stock and bonds.

The profit/loss profile of a buyer of a futures contract is the same as that of a forward contract and the price of a futures contract is determined in the same way. However, there are some important differences between the two types of contracts. The main differences are:

- Futures are standardized contracts that are traded on an **organized exchange**, whereas forwards are not. Futures contracts are highly uniform contracts that specify the quantity and quality of the good that can be delivered, the delivery date(s), the method for closing the contract, and the permissible minimum and maximum price fluctuations permitted in a trading day.
- Futures are generally more liquid and have less credit risk than forwards because organized exchanges have clearinghouses that guarantee that all of the traders in the futures market will honour their obligations
- Futures contracts are marked-to-market and require initial and maintenance margin deposits. As a result, futures contracts require daily cash settlements for the change in the contract's value. In contrast, cash payments on forward contracts generally do not occur until the contract's maturity date.

4.2.2 Interest rate futures contracts

Key term

An **interest rate futures** contract is a contract which either has a debt security as an underlying or is based on an interbank deposit.

An interest rate futures contract is a contract which either has a debt security as an underlying or is based on an interbank deposit. For example, the three-month sterling interest rate futures contract traded on LIFFE has as underlying a notional fixed-term deposit of £500,000 for a three-month period starting at a specified time in the future. Similarly the three-month Euro interest rate futures contract has as underlying a notional deposit of €1,000,000.

Three Month Sterling (Short Sterling) Interest Rate Futures	
Unit of trading	£500,000
Delivery months	March, June, September, December, and two serial months, such that 23 delivery months are available for trading, with the nearest three delivery months being consecutive calendar months.
Quotation	100.00 minus the rate of interest
Minimum price movement (tick size and value)	0.01 (£12.50)
Last trading day	11:00 – Third Wednesday of the delivery month.
Delivery day	First business day after the Last Trading Day.
Trading hours	07:30 – 18:00

Source: Euronex

4.2.3 Price quotation

The price of futures contract is quoted as 100 minus the interest rate for the contract period. The interest rate used is the LIBOR

Futures price = 100 – LIBOR

This convention makes sure that as interest rates rise, the value of the notional deposit falls and the price of the futures contract falls in order to reflects this.

4.2.4 Tick points

The price of a futures contract moves in 'ticks'. The minimum price change (**tick size**) and the value of the tick sizes varies according to the contract. The tick size for interest rate futures is usually **one basis point** or 0.01% interest rate movement in the underlying market. Therefore a futures contract which currently trades at 96 can move at least up to 96.01 or down to 95.99. (That is the interest rate can move from 4% either to 3.99% or to 4.01%)

Since the maturity of the contract is for **three months**, the tick size needs to be converted into a quarterly size by dividing by 4. Thus:

$$\text{Tick size} = \frac{0.01}{100} \times \frac{1}{4}$$

A futures contract's tick value is the **cash value** of one tick (one minimum price change) and is the **product of the tick size and the size of the contract**.

Tick value = tick size × contract size = \$0.0001/€× €125,000 = \$12.50

This tick value means that the for every 0.0001 that the price moves up or down, the profit or loss of a trade would increase or decrease by \$12.50.

4.2.5 Margin

Futures contracts and short positions in exchange-traded options require both an initial margin deposit and subsequent maintenance margin deposits. As a result, exchange traded contracts have a lower credit risk than OTC derivative contracts.

4.2.6 Basis risk

FAST FORWARD

Basis risk is the risk that the price of a future will vary from the price of the **underlying assets**.

In futures markets, the spread between a futures price and the underlying spot price is known as the futures **basis** (b) and is defined as **the difference between the spot price and the futures price**.

As expiry approaches the price of futures contract **moves toward** the price of the underlying instrument and on expiry date, they should be **the same**. If the asset to be hedged is the same as the one underlying the futures, then the basis on expiration is equal to zero.

Basis risk is the risk that the price of a future will vary from the price of the **underlying cash instrument** as expiry approaches, creating an imperfect hedge. This can occur when futures contracts are used for hedging and the futures contract is not written on the underlying that is being hedged – for example using a futures contract written on a 10y T-note to hedge a 30y T-bill.

A bond trader might hedge a long position in corporate bonds by shorting Treasury bonds. The hedge eliminates exposure to changes in Treasury yields, but the trader remains exposed to changes in the spread between corporate and Treasury yields. He too is still exposed to basis risk.

The second reason for the existence of basis risk is the use of a futures contract whose maturity is **not the same** as the time horizon of the hedger. For example if you expect a payment in three months and you want to look into a specific interest rate now, the appropriate futures contract would be a three month contract. A six month contract will expose the investor to basis risk since after 3 months the futures price and the spot price will not be the same.

To understand the nature of basis risk we shall first make use of the pricing equation for forward given by:

$$F(t, T) = S(t)(1 + r)^{T-t}$$

where r is the relevant risk interest rate for the period T – t. The above equation is also valid for the pricing of futures. We also need to understand what we mean by a perfect hedge. A perfect hedge is one which eliminates the risk of a position. Since the position has no risk the return on the position should be the same as the return on the risk-free asset.

Consider the profit for an investor who has bought the underlying asset and has sold futures contracts. In a sense this investor has created a portfolio with a long position on the underlying and a short position on the futures contract. The profit of the portfolio is:

$$\text{profit} = (S_T - S_t) - (F(T,T) - F(t,T))$$

Using the pricing relationship we can write the profit equation as:

$$\text{profit} = (S_T - S_t) - (F(T,T) - S_t(1+r)^{T-t})$$

If there is no basis risk, then $S_T = F(T,T)$ and the profit equation is simply $\text{profit} = S_t(1+r)^{T-t} - S_t$ whereas the rate of return is:

$\text{rate of return} = \frac{\text{profit}}{S_t} = (1+r)^{T-t} - 1 = r$ That is in the absence of basis risk, the hedged position will earn only the risk-free return.

In the situation when $S_T \neq F(T, T)$ then the rate of return will be:

$$\text{rate of return} = \frac{\text{profit}}{S_t} = (1+r)^{T-t} - 1 + \frac{S_T - S_t}{S_t} = r + \frac{\text{Basis}}{S_t}$$

When the basis is different from zero, then the return on hedged portfolio will not be the return on the risk-free asset. It means that the portfolio is still risky.

Question

Profit from futures trading

A 3-month sterling interest rate futures contract is quoted on a recognised investment exchange. Its delivery day is 20 December 20X6.

On November 22, the future is trading at 94.63, implying that the market believes 3-month LIBOR will be 5.37% (100 – 94.63) on 20 December.

On 24 November 20X6 future is quoted at 94.53. If you sell the future on 22 November at 94.63 and buy on 24 November at 94.53,how much profit would you make?

Answer

The asset underlying the future is a notional 3-month deposit of £500,000. For every 0.01% change in interest rates, the interest earned on such a deposit would change by:

£500,000 × 0.01% × 3/12 = £12.50

This is the tick value of the contract. In the example, the price of the future alters by 0.10 (94.63 – 94.53), or 10 ticks. So the profit on each contract would be:

£12.50 × 10 ticks = £62.50

4.3 Interest rate options

FAST FORWARD

An interest rate option gives the option holder the right, but not the obligation (before a specified expiry date) to:

- borrow a notional quantity of funds for a specified term at a specified (ie fixed)rate of interest
- lend or deposit a notional quantity of funds for a specified term at a specified interest yield;
- purchase or sell one interest rate future at a specified price.

The specified rate of interest for borrowing or lending is the **strike price** of the option. (With options on futures, the strike price is the specified purchase or sale price for the underlying future.) Options on interest rate are exchange-traded instruments, bought and sold on the same exchange, where the futures themselves are traded. All other interest rate options are purchased over-the-counter from a bank, on terms negotiated between the bank (the option writer) and the customer.

Over-the-counter options consist of:

- borrowers' options
- lenders' options
- caps
- floors
- collars

4.3.1 Characteristics of interest rate options

A **call option** gives its holder the right to **buy** an underlying instrument at the **strike price**, and obliges the option writer to **sell** the instrument at that price when and if the option is exercised. A borrower's option and an interest rate cap are types of OTC call option, giving their holder the right to obtain ('buy') a notional quantity of funds for the cost of the strike price, which is a specific interest rate.

A **put** option gives its holder the right to **sell** an underlying instrument at the **strike price**, and obliges the option writer to **buy** the instrument at that price if and when the option is exercised. A lender's option and an interest rate floor are types of OTC put option, giving their holder the right to 'sell' (lend or deposit) a notional quantity of funds at the strike price.

An option is written for a **specified term** and has an **expiry date**. An **American** option can be exercised **at any time** up to and including its expiry date. A **European** option can be exercised **on its expiry date only**, and not before. If an option is not exercised by its expiry date, it lapses.

The strike price of an OTC option is for a **benchmark or reference interest rate**, such as three-month LIBOR or six-month LIBOR. The option gives its holder the right to borrow or lend the notional funds with the reference rate of interest fixed at the strike price. For example, if the strike price of a borrower's option is 10% for six-month LIBOR, the option holder has the right to borrow the notional funds on or before the expiry date.

The strike price of an option can be more favourable (to the option holder), less favourable, or the same as the current market rate of interest for the reference rate. An option is in-the-money if its strike price is more favourable than the current market rate, out-of-the-money if it is less favourable and at-the-money if the strike price and the current market rate are the same. For example, if a borrower's option has a strike price of 11% for three-month LIBOR, and the current market rate for three-month LIBOR is 12.5%, the option is in-the-money because it is cheaper to borrow with LIBOR at 11% than with LIBOR at 12.5%.

4.3.2 Exercising an option

When an OTC option is **exercised**, the option holder takes up the right to **borrow or lend** the notional quantity of funds for a specified term with the reference interest rate at the strike price. There is no actual loan however, and an option is settled by a cash payment from the option writer to the option holder. For example, suppose that a lender's option has a strike price of 11% for three-month LIBOR, and a notional principal amount of $10 million. On expiry, if the market rate for three-month LIBOR is 9%, the option will be exercised, because it is more profitable to lend $10 million at the strike price of 11% than at the market of 9%.

On exercise of the option, there is no transaction of a $10 million loan at 11% interest. Instead, a compensatory payment will be made, based on the difference of 2% (11% - 9%) between the strike price and the LIBOR. The difference is applied to the notional principal of $10 million for the term of the notional loan as specified in the option agreement (in this example, probably for a three-month period since the reference rate is three-month LIBOR).

In the case of borrowers' and lenders' options, the compensatory payment is made **immediately**, when the option is exercised. With caps, floors and collars, however, the compensatory payment does not take place until the end of the interest rate period to which it relates.

4.3.3 Borrower's option

A **borrower's option** is an OTC derivative that protects the holder from rises in short-term interest rates by making a payment to the buyer when an underlying interest rate (the 'index' or 'reference' interest rate) exceeds a specified strike rate (the 'cap rate'). Such options are purchased for a premium but the holder has **no obligation** or liability to make any payments if interest rates fall below the cap rate.

Each period, the payment is determined by comparing the current level of the index interest rate with the cap rate. If the reference rate (such as three month LIBOR) **exceeds** the cap rate, the payment will be:

Notional amount of the loan, multiplied by
The difference between the reference rate and the cap rate, multiplied by
Days to maturity divided by days in the year

If the reference rate is **less than or equal to** the cap rate, then the payment will be **zero**.

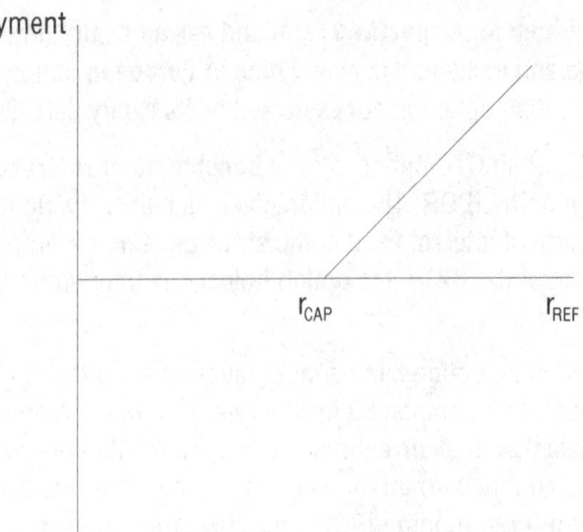

Such options are used by issuers of floating rate debt who wish to protect themselves from the increased financing costs that would result from a rise in interest rates. To reduce the up-front cost of such protection, a long cap may be combined with a short floor to form a collar.

4.3.4 Lender's option

Lender's options are OTC derivatives that protect the holder from declines in short-term interest rates by making a payment to the holder when an underlying interest rate (the 'index' or 'reference' interest rate) falls below a specified strike rate (the '**floor rate**'). They are purchased for a premium and typically have maturities between 1 and 7 years. They may make payments to the holder on a monthly, quarterly or semi-annual basis, with the period generally set equal to the maturity of the index interest rate.

The payment to the option holder is determined by comparing the current level of the reference interest rate with the floor rate. If the reference rate **exceeds** the floor rate, the payment to the option holder will be calculated as:

Notional amount of the loan, multiplied by

The difference between the reference rate and the floor rate, multiplied by

Days to maturity divided by days in the year

If the reference rate is **less than or equal to** the floor rate, the payment to the option holder will be **zero**.

4.3.5 Interest rate collar

A **colla**r is a combination of a cap and a floor carrying on the same period and amount. A **lending collar** is constructed by buying a floor and selling a cap. The premium received through the sale of the cap allows to finance, partly or completely, the premium paid for the purchase of the floor. The level of the floor is lower than that of the cap. By entering into a lending collar, the contract holder is hedged against a decrease of interest rates below the floor rate and simultaneously foregoing the benefit from an increase in interest rates above the cap rate.

A **borrowing collar** is constructed by buying a cap and selling a floor. The borrower reduces the cost of this hedge by selling a floor with the lower strike rate than that of the cap. The borrower foregoes the benefit from a decrease of interest rates below a certain rate.

4.4 Interest rate swaps

An interest rate **swap** is a contract between two parties, a swaps bank and a customer. The two parties agree to exchange a stream of payments at one interest rate for a stream of payments at a different rate, normally at regular intervals for a period of several years. The interest rates are applied to an agreed notional amount of principal, and payments are normally exchanged.

The most popular interest rate swaps are **fixed-for-floating** swaps under which cash flows of a fixed rate loan are exchanged for those of a floating rate loan. Among these, the most common use a 3-month or 6-month LIBOR rate (or EURIBOR, if the currency is the Euro) as their floating rate. These are called **vanilla**

interest rate swaps. There is also a liquid market for floating-floating interest rate swaps, which are known as **basis swaps**. An example of a basis swap is a swap of 1-month USD LIBOR for 6-month USD LIBOR. This might be used to customize exposures to specific points on the yield curve. More common are basis swaps between two floating indices from different segments of the money market. A bank that lends at prime but finances itself at LIBOR, would be a natural user of a prime-LIBOR basis swap.

In order to minimize settlement risk, that is the risk that one party may perform on its obligation but the other might not, concurrent cash flows are netted. In a typical arrangement, both loans have an initial payment (loan) of principal but those net to zero. Both loans have a final return of the same principal, but those also net to 0. Also, the periodic interest payments are generally scheduled to occur on concurrent dates, so they too can be netted. The principal amount is called the notional amount of the swap.

4.4.1 Features of swaps

The exchanges of payments under a swap agreement are based on a **notional amount of principal**, which in sterling will be at least £5 million. A swaps bank will usually agree to the amount of notional principal that the customer asks for (subject to an acceptable minimum). The term of a swap is typically between two and ten years. The timing of payments between the swap counterparties can be tailored to the requirements of the customer, but it is usual for payments to occur at regular intervals, typically every six months or one year.

The amount payable by each party to the other is usually decided at the start of a notional interest rate period, but paid at the end of the period. For example, if Alpha and Beta Bank arrange a swap with a six-monthly exchange of payments, the amount payable by each party would be calculated at the start of each six-month period, and paid at the end of six months. In practice, only a net payment is made (if both payments are in the same currency). For example, if Alpha must pay Beta Bank $A and Beta Bank must pay $B in return, there will be a net payment of $(A - B) from Alpha to Beta or of $(B - A) from Beta to Alpha, depending on which party must pay the larger amount. Although it is convenient to refer to them as such, swap payments are technically not interest payments, since there is no actual loan between the parties to the swap. Swap payments are payments calculated by applying an interest rate to a notional amount of principal.

In a **coupon swap**, the parties agree to exchange a stream of payments at a fixed rate of interest for a stream of payments at a floating rate of interest. The floating rate of interest is a reference market rate, such as three-month LIBOR or six-month LIBOR, which is specified in the swap agreement.

Coupon swap

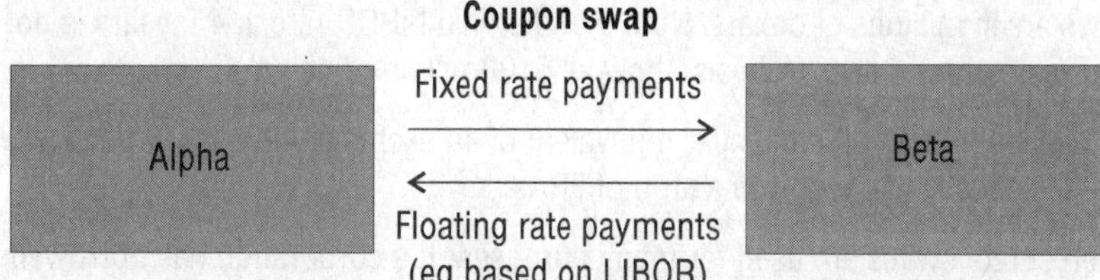

One party therefore pays a fixed rate of interest on the notional principal and receives a variable rate; the other receives a variable rate and pays a fixed rate. A bank that specialises in swaps transactions will quote a fixed rate that it is prepared to receive and a fixed rate that it is prepared to pay in exchange for floating rate interest at a reference market rate, such as six-month LIBOR. Its quoted receive-rate will be higher than its pay-rate, and the difference between the two rates represents the profit margin that the bank would expect to make in a two-legged swap transaction.

Swaps bank as market-maker

Swap 1 | Swap 2

Gamma — Pay floating rate at LIBOR → Swaps bank — Pay floating rate at LIBOR → Delta

Gamma ← Receive 10% fixed — Swaps bank ← Receive 10.20% fixed — Delta

If the swaps bank can arrange matching but opposite swaps with two customers, Gamma and Delta, for the same notional principal amount, it will make a net profit of 0.20% of the notional principal (10.20% – 10.00%) on the combined 'legs' of the arrangements with its two customers.

4.4.2 Example

Two banks enter into a vanilla interest rate swap. The term is four years. They agree to swap fixed rate USD payments at 4.8% in exchange for 6-month USD LIBOR payments. At the outset, the fixed rate payments are known. The first floating rate payment is also known, but the rest will depend on future values of LIBOR. Table 1 calculates the swap payments under a hypothetical scenario for LIBOR rates over the life of the swap.

Fixed 4.80%
Notional 100

Time	6-month LIBOR	Fixed Rate Cash Flows	Floating Rate Cash Flows	Swap Net Cash Flows
0.0	3.40%	–100.0	–100.0	0.0
0.5	3.60%	2.4	1.7	0.7
1.0	4.20%	2.4	1.8	0.6
1.5	4.40%	2.4	2.1	0.3
2.0	4.80%	2.4	2.2	0.2
2.5	5.20%	2.4	2.4	0.0
3.0	5.00%	2.4	2.6	–0.2
3.5	4.60%	2.4	2.5	–0.1
4.0	4.00%	102.4	102.3	0.1

The fixed payments in the four-year vanilla swap are based on a 4.8% semi-annual rate. Floating payments are based on 6-month LIBOR. The initial LIBOR rate is known to be 3.4% at the outset, so the swap's first payment is certain. Subsequent LIBOR rates are not known at the outset. The last column indicates cash flows to the receive-fixed party. Cash flows to the receive-floating party are the negatives of these. All cash flows are in millions of dollars. Note that the final LIBOR rate at 4.0 years is not used to calculate any of the swap's cash flows. Note also how all $100million principal payments net to zero.

In addition to being the financial equivalent of an exchange of loans, a vanilla fixed income swap is also mathematically equivalent to a strip of FRAs.

Interest rate swaps are used for many purposes. If a corporation has borrowed money at a floating rate of interest but would prefer to lock in a fixed rate, it can swap its floating rate payments into fixed rate payments. This is illustrated below.

Swapping Floating Debt into Fixed

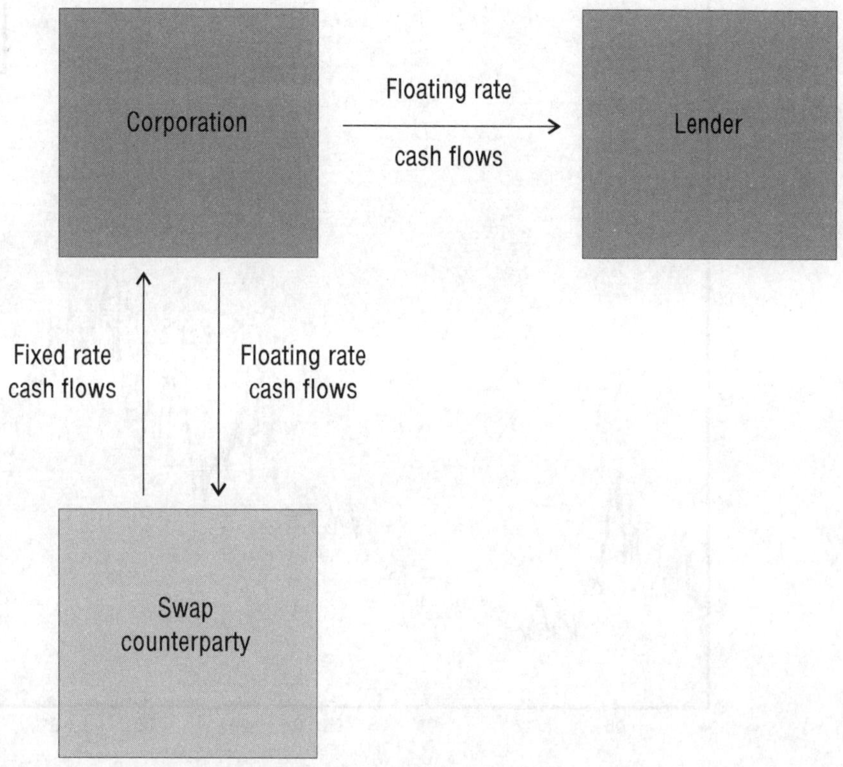

By entering into a swap with a third party, a corporation can convert floating rate payments into fixed rate payments.

Interest rate swaps can also be used to speculate on interest rates. A trader who believes that interest rates will rise could incur the expenses of borrowing and then shorting bonds. A simpler and less expensive solution would be to put on a pay-fixed swap.

Vanilla interest rate swaps are quoted in terms of the fixed rate to be paid against the floating index. The fixed rate is usually quoted as an absolute rate, so a quote of 4.3% against 3-month LIBOR would indicate that the fixed rate would be 4.3% paid quarterly. The floating rate is always 'flat', that is, any spreads are added or subtracted from the fixed rate only. In USD markets, vanilla swaps are often quoted, not as an absolute rate, but as the fixed rate's spread over the corresponding Treasury yield. In the interdealer market, **bid-ask spreads** on vanilla interest rate swaps are typically one or two basis points.

The fixed rates on vanilla swaps are called **swap rates**. The **swap curve** is a yield curve comprising swap rates for different maturities of swap. Due to high liquidity in the USD swap market, the swap curve has emerged as an alternative to Treasuries as a benchmark for USD interest rates at maturities exceeding a year.

4.4.3 Credit risk of swaps

Swaps are agreements between two parties to exchange payments. One of the parties may not be able to fulfil its obligation exposing the other party to risk. This risk is reflected in the spread of swap rates over the Treasury bills. The greater the spread the greater the risk associated with the swap. Spreads of rates on interest rate swaps over comparable U.S. Treasury yields widened dramatically during the severe financial market turmoil that followed the Russian default crisis of 1998 .

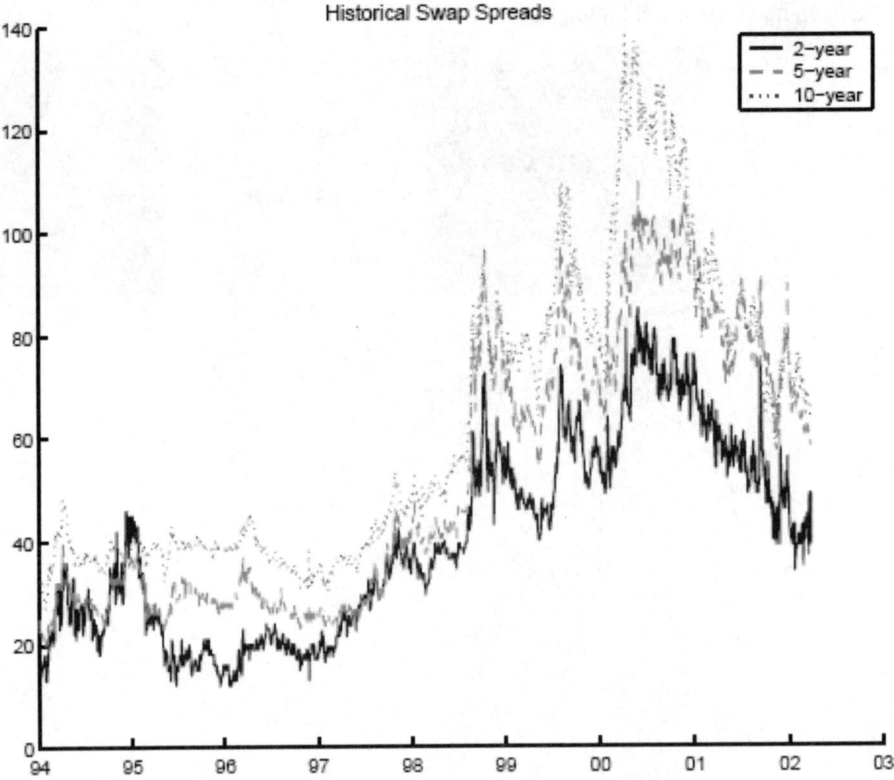

4.5 Interest rate swaptions

A **swaption** is an OTC option on a swap. Usually, the underlying swap is a vanilla interest rate swap. However, the term 'swaption' might be used to refer to an option on any type of swap. Swaptions can be for American, European, or Bermudan exercise. They can be physically settled, in which case an option is actually entered into upon exercise. They can also be cash settled, in which case the market value of the underlying swap changes hands upon exercise

Consider a corporation that has issued debt in the form of callable bonds paying a fixed semi-annual interest rate. The corporation would like to swap the debt into floating rate debt. The corporation enters into a fixed-for-floating swap with a derivatives dealer. To liquidate the call feature of the debt, it also sells the dealer a swaption. For derivatives dealers, clients often want to sell them swaptions while other clients want to buy caps from them. The dealers then face the challenge of hedging the short caps with the long swaptions.

The purchaser of the swaption pays an up front premium which depends on the expiration date of the option, the fixed rate on the underlying swap and the time to maturity at exercise of the swap. If the purchaser exercises, there is no strike price to pay. The two parties simply put on the prescribed swap. Note, however, the fixed rate specified for the swaption plays a role very similar to that of a strike price. The holder of the swaption will decide whether or not to exercise based on whether swap rates rise above or fall below that fixed rate. For this reason, the fixed rate is often called the strike rate.

By symmetry, a call on a pay-fixed swap is the same thing as a put on a receive-fixed swap. Similarly, a call on a receive-fixed swap is the same as a put on a pay-fixed swap. For this reason, it is often more convenient to speak in terms of two basic forms of swaption:

Key terms

A **payer swaption** is a call on a pay-fixed swap – the swaption holder has the option to pay fixed on a swap.

A **receiver swaption** is a call on a receive fixed swap – the swaption holder has the option to receive fixed on a swap.

4.5.1 Example

Suppose a party purchases a 1 x 5 payer swaption struck at 5%. A year later, if the four-year swap rate is 6%, the buyer will exercise the swaption and pay 5% fixed for LIBOR flat on a four-year swap. If instead, the four-year swap rate is 4%, the buyer will not exercise the swaption.

5 The treasury management function

FAST FORWARD

The treasury management function within an organisation is responsible for the management of the cash flows of the company, which is the most important measure of the financial health of a company.

The management of cash flows has three fundamental aspects.

(a) First the treasury management should determine the best ways of financing the short term operations of a company, in a way that minimises funding costs, and matches the cash flow needs of the company.

(b) The second fundamental aspect is the management of short-term assets of the company.

(c) The third aspect is the management of financial risks to which the cash flows of the company are exposed.

5.1 The short term management of the firm's financial resources

FAST FORWARD

The management of short term assets and liabilities of a company, known as the management of working capital is extremely important to any company as holding too much working capital is inefficient, holding too little is dangerous to the company's survival.

The management of short term assets and liabilities of a company, known as the management of working capital is extremely important to any company. Holding too much working capital is inefficient, holding too little is dangerous to the company's survival. The main current assets are stock, debtors and cash. The current liabilities are creditors and accrued expenses. The key characteristic of current assets and current liabilities is that they are expected to turn into cash, or be paid from cash, within twelve months.

As a general rule the company wants as little money tied up in working capital as possible. However, there are always trade-offs. The most obvious problem is running out of cash so a company cannot pay the wages, or is unable to provide a service because it has run out of a vital resource: for example, a manufacturing company being unable to produce the required quantity of products because it does not have enough raw materials in stock.

If on the other hand a company has too much liquidity in the long term, it may well be invested in fairly low return areas, such as bank deposit accounts instead of being invested in projects that would make the company grow.

Companies of course may hold cash in order to take advantage of special opportunities such as purchasing extra inventory at a discount that is greater than the carrying costs of holding the inventory. This is known as the speculative motive for holding cash.

Holding cash as a precaution serves as an emergency fund for a firm. If expected cash inflows are not received as expected, cash held on a precautionary basis could be used to satisfy short-term obligations that the cash inflow may have been bench marked for.

5.2 The management of risk exposure

FAST FORWARD

Cash flows generated by business operations are subject to a wide variety of fluctuations and risks and are particularly vulnerable to unexpected fluctuations in financial markets.

Cash flows generated by business operations are subject to a wide variety of fluctuations and risks. They are particularly vulnerable to unexpected fluctuations in financial markets. Changes in exchange rates may affect future selling prices, purchase prices and volumes, and thus influence a company's market position and hence its value. Similarly changes in interest rates may influence the cost of funding if interest rates go up or it may reduce the yield earned on short-term assets if interest rates go down. The value of the firm in either case will be affected. The value of the treasury function is therefore to manage the risks that affect the cash flows of the firm and in so doing to enhance the value of the company. This can be attained by using the derivative contracts that have been discussed in this chapter.

5.3 The longer term maximisation of shareholder value

FAST FORWARD

Maximisation of shareholder value has emerged as the dominant goal of corporate governance.

Maximisation of shareholder value has emerged as the dominant goal of corporate governance. Shareholder value refers to the total benefit to shareholders from investing in a company and includes dividends and capital appreciation of the shareholders' investments. Both components of shareholder value are related to the capacity of the company to generate cash flows and on the risks associated with these cash flows.

Companies earn profits from their operations and from continued investment in profitable ventures. Shareholder value is created when the returns from investments exceed the company's weighted average cost of capital and conversely it is destroyed if the returns were to be lower than the WACC.

Shareholder value should not be confined to stock market valuations. It is a long term concept which is driven by the strategic success of the company and also its operational performance. It is driven by the company's competitive landscape, the fit of its products to what its customers require, and its positioning vis-à-vis new technology. In other words, it is the traditional drivers of value that drive shareholder value.

Chapter Roundup

- Financial markets are the markets where economic units with surplus funds, such as individuals, corporations, the government, or overseas investors lend funds to other economic units that want to borrow.
- Markets where a security is first issued are known as primary, and markets where a security is subsequently traded are known as secondary.
- Secondary markets can be organised as exchanges or over the counter (OTC).
- **Securitisation** is the process of converting **illiquid assets** into **marketable securities**. The development of securitisation has led to disintermediation and a reduction in the role of financial intermediaries as borrowers can reach lenders directly.
- **Money markets** are the markets where **short-term instruments** are traded.
- **Basic risk** is the risk that the price of a future will vary from the price of the **underlying asset**.
- An interest rate option gives the option holder the right, but not the obligation, (before a specified expiry date) to
  - borrow a notional quantity of funds for a specified term at a specified term at a specified (ie fixed) rate of interest;
  - or deposit a notional quantity of funds for a specified term at a specified interest yield;
  - purchase or sell one interest rate future at a specified price.
- The treasury management function within an organisation is responsible for the management of the cash flows of the company, which is the most important measure of the financial health of a company.
- The management of short term assets and liabilities of a company, known as the management of working capital is extremely important to any company as holding too much working capital is inefficient, holding too little is dangerous to the company's survival.
- Cash flows generated by business operations are subject to a wide variety of fluctuations and risks and are particularly vulnerable to unexpected fluctuations in financial markets.
- Maximisation of shareholder value has emerged as the dominant goal of corporate governance.

Quick Quiz

1. You have bought a certificate of deposit for £1,012,000 and sold it 28 days later for £1,035,290. What is the yield?
2. A 91-day Treasury bill with a face value of $10,000,000 is issued for $9,830,000. What is the discount rate?
3. Why do you need to calculate the Bond Equivalent Yield for a treasury bill?
4. What happens to the price of interest rate futures contract if interest rates are increased?
5. What is the difference between a physically settled and a cash settled derivatives instrument?
6. What is basis risk?
7. When a treasury department is trying to decide which financial instrument to use, what are the key areas that should be considered?

Answers to Quick Quiz

1 $y = \frac{1,035,290 - 1,028,000}{1,028,000} \times \frac{365}{45} = 0.057519 \text{ or } 5.75\%$

2 $d = \frac{10,000,000 - 9,830,000}{10,000,000} \times \frac{365}{91}$

$= 6.82\%$

3 Because for the US market, the length of a year is different for Treasury bills and bonds.

4 Interest rate futures are quoted as

Futures price = 100 – reference interest rate. As interest rates go up the price of futures contract goes down.

5 Physical settlement means that the underlying is delivered, whereas cash settlement means that what is delivered is the cash equivalent of the underlying.

6 It is the risk that at expiration the price of the futures contract is not the same as the price of the underlying asset. Basis risk creates an imperfect hedge.

7 The key areas that should be considered by the treasury department are:

- The risk involved
- The effective interest rate (which is linked to default risk)
- The availability of the instruments
- The amount of cash involved
- The cost of each instrument (options can be expensive for example)
- The timescale involved
- How marketable are the instruments? Those that cannot be sold on may prove to be expensive if they are not ultimately required

Now try the question below from the Exam Question Bank

Number	Level	Marks	Time
25	Introductory	15	27 mins

19

The use of financial derivatives to hedge against foreign exchange risk

Topic list	Syllabus reference
1 Exchange rates	E (2) (a)
2 The foreign exchange derivatives market	E (2) (a)
3 Hedging strategies with forward contracts	E (2) (b)
4 Money market hedges	E (2) (b)
5 Exchange-traded currency futures contracts	E (2) (b)
6 Currency swaps	E (2) (b)
7 FX swaps	E (2) (b)
8 Currency options	E (2) (b)
9 Netting and matching in forex markets	E (2) (c)
10 Devising a foreign currency hedging strategy	E(2)(b)

Introduction

Future payments or distributions payable in a foreign currency carry the risk that the foreign currency will depreciate in value before the foreign currency payment is received and is exchanged into the **home currency**. While there is a chance of profit from the currency exchange in the event the price of the foreign currency increases, most investors and lenders would give up the possibility of **currency exchange profit** if they could avoid the risk of **currency exchange loss.**

The **foreign exchange market** comprises the **spot market** and the **forward or future market**. The spot market is for foreign exchange delivered in two days or less. Transactions in the spot market quote rates of exchange prevalent at the time of the transactions. A bank will typically quote a bid and offer rate for the particular currency. The forward market is for foreign exchange to be delivered in three days or more. In quoting the forward rate of currency, a bank will use a rate at which it is willing to buy the currency (bid) and a rate at which it will sell a currency (offer) for delivery, typically one, two, three or six months after the transaction date.

For the company that wants to eliminate short-term transaction exposure (exposure of less than one year), a variety of hedging instruments are available at varying costs to the company.

Study guide

		Intellectual level
E2	**The use of financial derivatives to hedge against forex risk**	
(a)	Demonstrate an understanding of the operations of the derivatives market, including: (i) The relative advantages and disadvantages of exchange traded versus OTC agreements. (ii) Key features, such as standard contracts, tick sizes, margin requirements and margin trading. (iii) The source of basis risk and how it can be minimised.	3
(b)	Evaluate, for a given hedging requirement, which of the following is the most appropriate strategy, given the nature of the underlying position and the risk exposure: (i) The use of the forward exchange market and the creation of a money market hedge (ii) Synthetic foreign exchange agreements (SAFE's) (iii) Exchange-traded currency futures contracts (iv) Currency swaps (v) FOREX swaps (vi) Currency options	3
(c)	Advise on the use of bilateral and multilateral netting and matching as tools for minimizing FOREX transactions costs and the management of market barriers to the free movement of capital and other remittances.	3

1 Exchange rates

FAST FORWARD

Currencies are quoted at Counter currency X units: Base currency 1 unit.

The **spot rate** is the rate at which currencies can be exchanged now. The **forward rate** is the rate at which currencies will be exchanged on a set future date.

1.1 Exchange rates

Key terms

An **exchange rate** is the rate at which a currency can be traded in exchange for another currency.

The **spot exchange rate** is the rate at which currencies can be bought or sold for **immediate delivery.**

The **forward rate** is an exchange rate set for currencies to be exchanged at a future date.

Every traded currency in fact has many exchange rates. There is an exchange rate with every other traded currency on the foreign exchange markets. Foreign exchange dealers make their profit by buying currency for less than they sell it, and so there are really two exchange rates, a selling rate and a buying rate.

1.2 Foreign exchange demand

If an importer has to pay a foreign supplier in a foreign currency, he might ask his bank to sell him the required amount of the currency. For example, suppose that a bank's customer, a trading company, has imported goods for which it must now pay US$10,000.

(a) The company will ask the bank to sell it US$10,000. If the company is buying currency, the bank is selling it.

(b) When the bank agrees to sell US$10,000 to the company, it will tell the company what the spot rate of exchange will be for the transaction. If the bank's selling rate (known as the **'offer'**, or **'ask'** price) is, say $1.7935 for the currency, the bank will charge the company:

$$\frac{\$10,000}{\$1.7935 \text{ per } £1} = £5,575.69$$

Similarly, if an exporter is paid, say, US$10,000 by a customer in the USA, he may wish to exchange the dollars to obtain sterling. He will therefore ask his bank to buy the dollars from him. Since the exporter is selling currency to the bank, the bank is buying the currency.

If the bank quotes a buying rate (known as the **bid** price) of, say $1.8075, for the currency the bank will pay the exporter:

$$\frac{\$10,000}{\$1.8075 \text{ per } £1} = £5,532.50$$

A bank expects to make a profit from selling and buying currency, and it does so by offering a rate for selling a currency which is different from the rate for buying the currency.

If a bank were to buy a quantity of foreign currency from a customer, and then were to re-sell it to another customer, it would charge the second customer more (in sterling) for the currency than it would pay the first customer. The difference would be profit. For example, the figures used for illustration in the previous paragraphs show a bank selling some US dollars for £5,575.69 and buying the same quantity of dollars for £5,532.50, at selling and buying rates that might be in use at the same time. The bank would make a profit of £43.19.

Question — **Sterling receipts**

Calculate how much sterling exporters would receive or how much sterling importers would pay, ignoring the bank's commission, in each of the following situations, if they were to exchange currency and sterling at the spot rate.

(a) A US exporter receives a payment from a Danish customer of 150,000 kroners.
(b) A US importer buys goods from a Japanese supplier and pays 1 million yen.

Spot rates are as follows.

	Bank sells (offer)		*Bank buys (bid)*
Danish Kr/$	9.4340	–	9.5380
Japan Y/$	203.650	–	205.781

Answer

(a) The bank is being asked to buy the Danish kroners and will give the exporter:

$$\frac{150,000}{9.5380} = \$15,726.57 \text{ in exchange}$$

(b) The bank is being asked to sell the yen to the importer and will charge for the currency:

$$\frac{1,000,000}{203.650} = \$4,910.39$$

1.3 The foreign exchange (FX) markets

Banks buy currency from customers and sell currency to customers – typically, **exporting and importing firms**. Banks may buy currency from the **government** or sell currency to the government – this is how a government builds up its official reserves. Banks also buy and sell currency **between themselves**. Consider what is actually happening when currencies are bought and sold: essentially, bank deposits denominated in one currency are being exchanged for bank deposits denominated in another currency.

International trade involves foreign currency, for either the buyer, the seller, or both (for example, a Saudi Arabian firm might sell goods to a UK buyer and invoice for the goods in US dollars). As a consequence, it is quite likely that exporters might want to sell foreign currency earnings to a bank in exchange for domestic currency, and that importers might want to buy foreign currency from a bank in order to pay a foreign supplier.

Since most foreign exchange rates are not fixed but are allowed to vary, rates are continually changing and each bank will offer new rates for new customer enquiries according to how its dealers judge the market situation.

Although exchange rates in the market are influenced by the forces as exercised through the actions of the central bank of supply and demand, a **government's policy on the exchange rate** for its currency can have an important effect on how the exchange rate is determined. In the case of the common European currency, the **euro**, the actions of the **European central bank** influence its exchange rate.

1.4 Direct and indirect currency quotes

Key terms

A **direct quote** is the amount of domestic currency which is equal to one foreign currency unit.

An **indirect quote** is the amount of foreign currency which is equal to one domestic currency unit.

In the UK indirect quotes are invariably used but, in most countries, direct quotes are more common.

Currencies may be quoted in either direction. For example, the US dollar and Euro might be quoted as □/$ = 0.7745 or $/□= 1.2912. In other words 0.7745□ = $1 and 1.2912$ = □1. One rate is simply the reciprocal of the other.

Key term

If a currency is quoted at $1.8500:£, the $ is the **counter currency** (the **reference or term currency**), the £ is the **base currency**.

1.4.1 Buying low and selling high

When considering the prices banks are using, remember that the bank will **sell the counter currency low**, and **buy the counter currency high**. For example if a UK bank is buying and selling dollars, the selling (offer) price may be $1.8500, the buying (bid) price may be $1.8700.

The examination will not be confined to the activities of UK companies. Exchange rates given in the examination could be as quoted in foreign countries. Because of these complications you should always double-check which rate you are using when choosing between the bid or offer rate. One sure method is to recognise that the bank **makes money** out of the transaction and will therefore offer you the worse of the two possible rates!

A simple example may help. If you come back to the United Kingdom from a holiday in America with spare dollars, and you are told the spread of $/£ rates is 1.8500 – 1.8700, will you have to pay the bank $1.85 or $1.87 to obtain £1? Answer: you will have to pay the higher price, $1.87.

1.5 Spread

FAST FORWARD

The difference between the bid price and the offer price is known as the **spread.**

One of the easiest ways to find the closing (end of day) exchange rates is to use the *Financial Times*.

The difference between the bid price and the offer price, covering dealers' costs and profit, is called the **spread**. The spread can be quoted in different ways.

\$/£1.9505 +/- 0.0005 or \$/£1.9500 – 1.9510

1.5.1 Exporters and importers

Exporters and importers will not be offered the same rate by the bank. Banks will charge different rates to **make a profit** on the spread. Remember that the company will always be offered the **worst** rate.

Exporters buying their home currency will pay a **high** rate; **importers** selling their home currency to pay invoices in a foreign currency will receive a **low** rate.

Question — **Exchange rate spreads**

Pratt Inc, a US based company, is engaged in both import and export activities. During a particular month, Pratt sells goods to Posh plc, a UK company, and receives £5 million. In the same month, Pratt imports goods from a UK supplier, which cost £5 million.

If the exchange rates were £/\$0.5075 +/- 0.0003, calculate the dollar values of the sterling receipt and payment.

Answer

(i) As an exporter, Pratt will pay a high rate to buy dollars (sell pounds) – that is, they will be quoted a rate of 0.5075 + 0.0003 = 0.5078. Pratt will therefore receive

£5 million / 0.5078 = \$9,846,396

(ii) As an importer, Pratt will receive a low rate to sell dollars (buy pounds) – that is, a rate of 0.5075 – 0.0003 = 0.5072. Pratt will therefore pay

£5 million / 0.5072 = \$9,858,044

2 The foreign exchange derivatives market

FAST FORWARD

If the forward rate is higher than the spot rate, the currency is quoted at a discount; if forward rate Is lower than the spot rate, the currency is quoted at a premium.

2.1 Forward exchange rates

As you will already appreciate, a forward exchange rate might be higher or lower than the spot rate. If it is higher, the quoted currency will be cheaper forward than spot. For example, if in the case of Swiss francs against sterling (i) the spot rate is 2.1560 – 2.1660 and (ii) the three months forward rate is 2.2070 – 2.2220:

(a) A bank would sell 2,000 Swiss francs:

(i) At the spot rate, now, for £927.64 $\left(\frac{2,000}{2.1560}\right)$

(ii) In three months time, under a forward contract, for £906.21 $\left(\frac{2,000}{2.2070}\right)$

(b) A bank would buy 2,000 Swiss francs

(i) At the spot rate, now, for £923.36 $\left(\frac{2,000}{2.1660}\right)$

(ii) In three months time, under a forward contract, for £900.09 $\left(\frac{2,000}{2.2220}\right)$

In both cases, the quoted currency (Swiss franc) would be worth less against sterling in a forward contract than at the current spot rate. This is because it is quoted forward 'at a discount', against sterling.

If the forward rate is thus higher than the spot rate, then it is 'at a discount' to the spot rate.

The forward rate can be calculated today without making any estimates of future exchange rates. **Future exchange rates** depend largely on future events and will often turn out to be very different from the forward rate. However, the forward rate is probably an **unbiased predictor of the expected value of the future exchange rate**, based on the information available today. It is also likely that the spot rate will move in the direction indicated by the forward rate.

2.1.1 The rule for adding or subtracting discounts and premiums

Forward rates as adjustments to spot rates	
Forward rate cheaper	Quoted at discount
Forward rate more expensive	Quoted at premium

A **discount** is therefore **added** to the spot rate, and a **premium** is therefore **subtracted** from the spot rate. (The mnemonic **ADDIS** may help you to remember that we ADD Discounts and so subtract premiums.) The longer the duration of a forward contract, the larger will be the quoted premium or discount.

2.2 Interest rate parity

FAST FORWARD

The principle of **interest rate parity** links the currency and money markets and explains differences between the **forward and spot rates**.

The difference between **spot and forward rates reflects differences in interest rates**. If this were not so, then investors holding the currency with the lower interest rates would switch to the other currency for (say) three months, ensuring that they would not lose on returning to the original currency by fixing the exchange rate in advance at the forward rate. If enough investors acted in this way (known as **arbitrage**), forces of supply and demand would lead to a change in the forward rate to prevent such risk-free profit making.

The principle of **interest rate parity** (not to be confused with purchasing power parity) links the foreign exchange markets and the international money markets. The principle can be stated as follows.

Exam formula

$$f_0 = s_0 \frac{(1+i_c)}{(1+i_b)}$$

where f_0 is the forward rate

s_0 is the spot rate

i_c is the interest rate in the country overseas

i_b is the interest rate in the base country

This equation links the spot and forward rates to the difference between the interest rates.

2.3 Example: Interest rate parity

Exchange rates between two currencies, the £ and the Southland dollar (S$) are listed in the financial press as follows.

Spot rates	4.7250	£/$S
	0.21164	$S/£
90 day rates	4.7506	£/$S
	0.21050	$S/£

The money market interest rate for 90 day deposits in £s is 7.5% annualised. What is implied about interest rates in Southland?

Assume a 365 day year. (*Note.* In practice, foreign currency interest rates are often calculated on an alternative **360-day basis**, one month being treated as 30 days.)

Solution

Today, $S1.000 buys £4.7250.

£4.7250 could be placed on deposit for 90 days to earn interest of £(4.7250 × 0.075 × 90/365) = £0.0874, thus growing to £(4.7250 + 0.0874) = £4.8124.

This is then worth $S1.0130 at the 90 day exchange rate.

This tells us that the annualised expected interest rate on 90-day deposits in Southland is:

0.013 × 365/90 = 5.3%.

Alternatively, we can reach the same answer as follows.

UK interest rate on 90 day deposit = i_b = 7.5% × 90/365 = 1.85%

Southland interest rate on 90 day deposit = i_b

90-day forward exchange rate = 0.21050

Spot exchange rate = 0.21164

$$\frac{i_C - 0.0185}{1+0.0185} = \frac{0.21050}{0.21164} - 1$$

$$i_c = 0.013, \text{ or } 1.3\%$$

Annualised, this is 0.013 × 365/90 = 5.3%

2.4 Use of interest rate parity to forecast future exchange rates

As seen above, the **interest rate parity** formula links the forward exchange rate with interest rates in a fairly exact relationship, because risk-free gains are possible if the rates are out of alignment. We have previously noted that the forward rate tends to be an unbiased predictor of the future exchange rate. So does this mean that future exchange rates can be predicted using interest rate parity, in the same way as **purchasing power parity** can be used?

The simple answer is 'yes', but of course the prediction is subject to very large inaccuracies, because events which arise in the future can cause large currency swings in the opposite direction to that predicted by interest rate parity. In general, interest rate parity is regarded as less accurate than purchasing power parity for predicting future exchange rates.

2.4.1 Example: Interest rate parity

A US company is expecting to receive Kuwaiti dinars in one year's time. The spot rate is US dollar/dinar 5.4670. The company could borrow in dinars at 9% or in dollars at 14%. There is no forward rate for one year's time. Predict what the exchange rate is likely to be in one year.

Solution

Using interest rate parity, dollar is the numerator and dinar is the denominator. So the expected future exchange rate dollar/dinar is given by:

$$\text{Forward rate} = \text{spot rate} \times \frac{1+i_{US}}{1+i_{KUW}}$$

or

$$5.4670 \times \frac{1.14}{1.09} = 5.7178$$

This prediction is subject to great inaccuracy, but note that the company could 'lock into' this exchange rate, working a money market hedge by borrowing today in dinars at 9%, converting the cash to dollars at spot and repaying some of its 14% dollar overdraft. When the dinar cash is received from the customer, the dinar loan is repaid.

2.4.2 Example

Assume the following interest rates for 90-day Treasury instruments in the US and Japan:

	US	*Japan*
Annual rate	4.93%	0.48%
Quarterly rate	1.21%	0.12%
Spot rate	140.22 J¥ / US$	

Given these assumptions, the forward foreign exchange rate of Japanese Yen for US dollars at the end of the first quarter must be:

$$\text{Forward rate} = 140.22 \times \frac{(1+0.0012)}{(1+0.0121)} = 138.71 \text{ J¥/US\$}$$

2.5 Use of interest rate parity to compute the effective cost of foreign currency loans

As we have seen, loans in some currencies are cheaper than in others. However, when the likely strengthening of the exchange rate is taken into consideration, the cost of apparently cheap foreign loans becomes a lot more expensive. This is illustrated in the following example.

2.5.1 Example: Effective cost of foreign currency loans

Cato, a Polish company, needs a one year loan of about 50 million zlotys. It can borrow in zlotys at 10.80% pa but is considering taking out a sterling loan which would cost only 6.56% pa. The current spot exchange rate is zloty/£ 5.1503. The company decides to borrow £10 million at 6.56% per annum. Converting at the spot rate, this will provide zloty51.503 million. Interest will be paid at the end of one year along with the repayment of the loan principal.

Assuming the exchange rate moves in line with interest rate parity, you are required to show the zloty values of the interest paid and the repayment of the loan principal. Compute the effective interest rate paid on the loan.

Solution

By interest rate parity, the zloty will have weakened in one year to:

$$5.1503 \times \frac{1.1080}{1.0656} = 5.3552$$

Time		£'000	*Exchange rate*	Zloty '000
Now	Borrows	10,000	5.1503	51,503
In 1 year	6.56% interest	(656)		
	Repayment	(10,000)	5.3552	(57,065)
		(10,656)		

The effective interest rate paid is $\frac{57,065}{51,503} - 1 = 10.80\%$, the same as it would have paid in £.

2.5.2 The Fisher effect revisited

We first looked at the relationship between interest rates and expected rates of inflation in Chapter 6 section 1.2, when we considered the effect of inflation on NPV calculations. As a reminder, the **Fisher equation** is as follows.

Exam formula

$$(1 + i) = (1 + r)(1 + h)$$

Countries with relatively high rates of inflation will generally have high nominal rates of interest, partly because interest rates are a mechanism for dealing with inflation and partly because of the Fisher effect.

2.5.3 The International Fisher effect revisited

We covered the International Fisher effect in Chapter 9 section 2.2. Interest rate differentials between two countries can be used as an unbiased predictor of the future spot exchange rates. You should refer back to Chapter 9 to remind yourself of the workings of the International Fisher effect but we have reproduced the formula here.

Formula to learn

$$\frac{1+i_a}{1+i_b} = \frac{1+h_a}{1+h_b}$$

2.6 Forward exchange contracts

Forward exchange contracts hedge against transaction exposure by allowing the importer or exporter to arrange for a bank to sell or buy a quantity of foreign currency at a future date, at a **rate of exchange determined** when the **forward contract is made**. The trader will know in advance either how much local currency he will receive (if he is selling foreign currency to the bank) or how much local currency he must pay (if he is buying foreign currency from the bank).

Forward contracts are very popular with small companies. The current spot price is irrelevant to the outcome of a forward contract.

Key term

A **forward exchange contract** is:

(a) An immediately firm and binding contract, eg between a bank and its customer
(b) For the purchase or sale of a specified quantity of a stated foreign currency
(c) At a rate of exchange fixed at the time the contract is made
(d) For performance (delivery of the currency and payment for it) at a future time which is agreed when making the contract (This future time will be either a specified date, or any time between two specified dates.)

2.7 Example: Forward exchange contracts (1)

A US importer knows on 1 April that he must pay a foreign seller 26,500 Swiss francs in one month's time, on 1 May. He can arrange a forward exchange contract with his bank on 1 April, whereby the bank undertakes to sell the importer 26,500 Swiss francs on 1 May, at a fixed rate of say 2.6400 to the $.

The US importer can be certain that whatever the spot rate is between Swiss francs and US dollars on 1 May, he will have to pay on that date, at this forward rate:

$$\frac{26,500}{2.6400} = \$10,037.88$$

(a) If the spot rate is **lower than 2.6400**, the importer would have successfully protected himself against a weakening of the dollar, and would have avoided paying more dollars to obtain the Swiss francs.

(b) If the spot rate is **higher than 2.6400**, the dollar's value against the Swiss franc would mean that the importer would pay more under the forward exchange contract than he would have had to pay if he had obtained the francs at the spot rate on 1 May. He cannot avoid this extra cost, because a forward contract is binding.

2.8 What happens if a customer cannot satisfy a forward contract?

A customer might be unable to satisfy a forward contract for any one of a number of reasons.

(a) An **importer** might find that:
   (i) His supplier **fails to deliver the goods** as specified, so the importer will not accept the goods delivered and will not agree to pay for them
   (ii) The **supplier sends fewer goods** than expected, perhaps because of supply shortages, and so the importer has less to pay for
   (iii) The supplier is **late with the delivery**, and so the importer does not have to pay for the goods until later than expected

(b) An **exporter** might find the same types of situation, but in reverse, so that he does not receive any payment at all, or he receives more or less than originally expected, or he receives the expected amount, but only after some delay.

2.9 Close-out of forward contracts

If a customer cannot satisfy a forward exchange contract, the bank will make the customer fulfil the contract.

(a) If the customer has arranged for the bank to buy currency but then cannot deliver the currency for the bank to buy, the bank will:
   (i) **Sell currency** to the **customer** at the **spot rate** (when the contract falls due for performance)
   (ii) **Buy** the **currency back**, under the terms of the **forward exchange contract**

(b) If the customer has contracted for the bank to sell him currency, the bank will:
   (i) Sell the customer the specified amount of currency at the forward exchange rate
   (ii) Buy back the unwanted currency at the spot rate

Thus, the bank arranges for the customer to perform his part of the forward exchange contract by either selling or buying the 'missing' currency at the spot rate. These arrangements are known as **closing out** a forward exchange contract.

3 Hedging strategies with forward contracts

Key term

> A **foreign currency forward contract** is a contract that specifies the **exchange rate** at which purchase or sale of a currency will take place at some time in the future.

3.1 Example 1

Suppose that on November 2, 20X4, a US company sold goods to a German company for €100,000, with remittance due in 90 days. The spot rate on November 2 20X4, was €1 = $1.160. On that same day, the US company entered into a forward contract to sell €100,000 in 90 days at €1 = $1.162.

A useful starting point for analysing how these contracts can reduce risk is to first describe the exposure of the firm conceptually as a gain/loss profile.

No matter what happens to the exchange rate over the three months, the company is assured of being able to convert the €100,000 into $116,200 on January 30 20X5.

Scenario 1

On January 30 20X5 the spot rate is €1 = $1.20. The euro has appreciated and the US will receive on translation of the €100,000 the amount of $120,000. However since it sells €100,000 for $116,200 (€1 = $1.162) it suffers a loss of $3,800 on the forward position so that the amount received from the cash transaction is reduced to $116,200.

Scenario 2

On January 30 20X5 the spot rate is €1 = $1.12. The euro has depreciated and the US will receive on translation of the €100,000 the amount of $112,000. However since it sells €100,000 for $116,200 (€1 = $1.162) it has a profit of $4,200 on the forward position so that the amount received from the cash transaction is increased to $116,200.

That is irrespective of the depreciation or appreciation of the dollar, the US company will receive an amount equal to $116,200.

If the US Company faced an account payable instead of a receivable, it could eliminate its transaction exposure by buying the Euros at the forward rate.
However, the transaction exposure is eliminated only if the German buyer pays its €100,000 obligation. A default by the German buyer would not relieve the US producer of its obligation to deliver €100,000 to the bank in return for $116,200. The US exporter would have to buy the €100,000 at the spot rate three months later.

Forward rate contracts are often inaccessible for many small businesses. Banks often tend to quote unfavourable rates for smaller companies.

3.2 Synthetic foreign exchange agreements (SAFEs)

A SAFE is a type of forward currency exchange rate agreement designed to provide a currency hedge over a specific forward period. It differs from a usual currency forward in that no cash or physical delivery takes place. Instead, the underlying is a notional principal like an FRA, and the agreement calls for settlement of the net amount in local currency. A SAFE is equivalent to a forward period currency swap without a principal exchange.

4 Money market hedges

4.1 Money market hedges

Because of the close relationship between forward exchange rates and the interest rates in the two currencies, it is possible to 'manufacture' a forward rate by using the spot exchange rate and money market lending or borrowing. This technique is known as a **money market hedge** or **synthetic forward**.

4.2 Setting up a money market hedge for a foreign currency payment

Suppose a British company needs to **pay** a Swiss creditor in Swiss francs in three months' time. It does not have enough cash to pay now, but will have sufficient in three months' time. Instead of negotiating a forward contract, the company could:

Step 1 Borrow the appropriate amount in pounds now

Step 2 Convert the pounds to francs immediately

Step 3 Put the francs on deposit in a Swiss franc bank account

Step 4 When the time comes to pay the company:

(a) Pays the creditor out of the franc bank account
(b) Repays the pound loan account

The effect is exactly the same as using a forward contract, and will usually cost almost exactly the same amount. If the results from a money market hedge were very different from a forward hedge, speculators could make money without taking a risk. Therefore market forces ensure that the two hedges produce very similar results.

4.3 Example: Money market hedge (1)

A UK company owes a Danish creditor Kr3,500,000 in three months' time. The spot exchange rate is Kr/£ 7.5509 – 7.5548. The company can borrow in Sterling for 3 months at 8.60% per annum and can deposit kroners for 3 months at 10% per annum. What is the cost in pounds with a money market hedge and what effective forward rate would this represent?

Solution

The interest rates for 3 months are 2.15% to borrow in pounds and 2.5% to deposit in kroners. The company needs to deposit enough kroners now so that the total including interest will be Kr3,500,000 in three months' time. This means depositing:

Kr3,500,000/(1 + 0.025) = Kr3,414,634.

These kroners will cost £452,215 (spot rate 7.5509). The company must borrow this amount and, with three months interest of 2.15%, will have to repay:

£452,215 × (1 + 0.0215) = £461,938.

Thus, in three months, the Danish creditor will be paid out of the Danish bank account and the company will effectively be paying £461,938 to satisfy this debt. The effective forward rate which the company has 'manufactured' is 3,500,000/461,938 = 7.5768. This effective forward rate shows the kroner at a discount to the pound because the kroner interest rate is higher than the sterling rate.

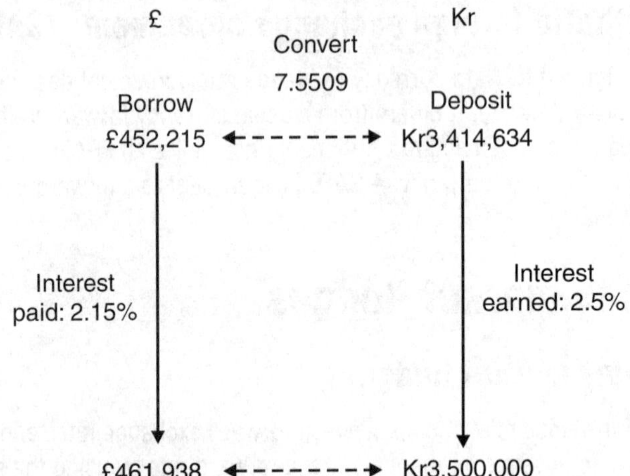

4.4 Setting up a money market hedge for a foreign currency receipt

A similar technique can be used to cover a foreign currency **receipt** from a debtor. To manufacture a forward exchange rate, follow the steps below.

Step 1 Borrow an appropriate amount in the foreign currency today

Step 2 Convert it immediately to home currency

Step 3 Place it on deposit in the home currency

Step 4 When the debtor's cash is received:

(a) Repay the foreign currency loan

(b) Take the cash from the home currency deposit account

Exam focus point

Variations on these money market hedges are possible in an examination.

4.5 Example: money market hedge (2)

A UK company is owed SFr 2,500,000 in three months' time by a Swiss company. The spot exchange rate is SFr/£ 2.2498 – 2.2510. The company can deposit in Sterling for 3 months at 8.00% per annum and can borrow Swiss Francs for 3 months at 7.00% per annum. What is the receipt in pounds with a money market hedge and what effective forward rate would this represent?

Solution

The interest rates for 3 months are 2.00% to deposit in pounds and 1.75% to borrow in Swiss francs. The company needs to borrow SFr2,500,000/1.0175 = SFr 2,457,003 today. These Swiss francs will be converted to £ at 2,457,003/2.2510 = £1,091,516. The company must deposit this amount and, with three months interest of 2.00%, will have earned

£1,091,516 × (1 + 0.02) = £1,113,346

Thus, in three months, the loan will be paid out of the proceeds from the debtor and the company will receive £1,113,346. The effective forward rate which the company has 'manufactured' is 2,500,000/1,113,346 = 2.2455. This effective forward rate shows the Swiss franc at a premium to the pound because the Swiss franc interest rate is lower than the sterling rate.

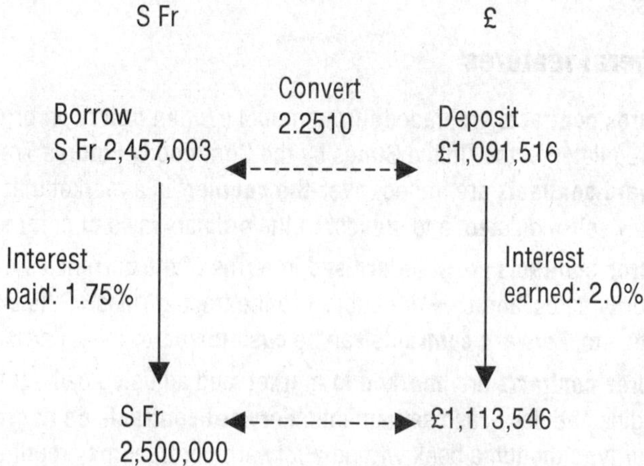

5 Exchange-traded currency futures contracts

Key term

A **foreign exchange futures contract** is an agreement between two parties to buy/sell a particular currency at a particular rate on a particular future date

When entering into a foreign exchange futures contract, no one is actually buying or selling anything – the participants are **agreeing** to buy or sell currencies on pre-agreed terms at a specified future date if the contract is allowed to reach maturity, which it rarely does.

The table below shows the most important foreign currency futures trading on the Chicago Mercantile Exchange. Contracts for each currency are of a standard size – eg for the pound sterling the face amount is £62,500; for the Euro it is €125,000. There are trading rules – for example, there is a minimum allowable price move between trades, and a maximum allowable price movement in a day.

The delivery dates fall on the third Wednesday of the months of March, June, September, and December. The longest maturity is for one year. Note that the futures exchange rates of all of the contracts are quoted in terms of the value of the foreign currency as measured in US dollars, and premiums are quoted in US cents per euro or pound – that is, in 'direct' or 'American' terms. But it differs from conventions in other parts of the exchange market – a Swiss franc forward would be priced at, say, '1.6000' (in CHF per dollar) while a Swiss franc future would be priced at the reciprocal, or '0.6250' (in dollars per CHF).

Denomination of Foreign Currency Futures Contracts

Currency	Underlying Amounts	Minimum Fluctuation
British Pound	62,500 L	$0.002 = $12,50
Canadian Dollar	100,000 C$	$0,0001 = $10
Euro	125,000 Euros	0.0001 = $12.50
Japanese Yen	12,500,000 Y	$0.000001 = $12.50
Swiss Franc	125,000 SF	$0.000025 = $5
Australian Dollar	125,000 A$	$0.0001 = $12.5

5.1 Comparison between futures and forward contracts

FAST FORWARD

Although a foreign exchange *futures* contract is conceptually similar to a *forward* foreign exchange contract, there are important structural and institutional differences between the two instruments:

A foreign exchange *futures* contract is conceptually similar to a *forward* foreign exchange contract, in that both are agreements to buy or sell a certain amount of a certain currency for another at a certain price on a certain date. However, there are important structural and institutional differences between the two instruments:

5.1.1 General features

(a) **Futures contracts** are traded through public **'open outcry'** in organised, centralised exchanges that are regulated in the United States by the Commodity Futures Trading Commission. In contrast, **forward contracts** are traded **'over-the counter'** in a market that is geographically dispersed, largely self-regulated, and subject to the ordinary laws of commercial contracts and taxation.

(b) **Futures contracts** are **standardised** in terms of the currencies that can be traded, the amounts, and maturity dates, and they are subject to the trading rules of the exchange with respect to daily price limits, etc. **Forward contracts** can be **customised** to meet particular customer needs.

(c) **Futures contracts** are **'marked to market'** and adjusted daily; there are initial and maintenance margins and daily cash settlements. **Forward contracts** do **not** require any cash payment until maturity (although a bank writing a forward contract may require collateral). Thus, a futures contract can be viewed as a portfolio or series of forwards, each covering a day or a longer period between cash settlements.

(d) **Futures contracts** are **netted** through the clearinghouse of the exchange, which receives the margin payments and guarantees the performance of both the buyer and the seller in every contract. **Forward contracts** are made **directly** between the two parties, with no clearinghouse between them.

5.1.2 Credit risk

The differences between the two instruments are very important. The fact that **futures contracts** are channeled through a clearinghouse and 'marked to market' daily means that **credit risk is reduced**. The fact that the clearinghouse is guaranteeing the performance of both sides also means that a contract can be cancelled (or 'killed') simply by buying a second contract that reverses the first and nets out the position. Thus, there is a good 'secondary market.' In a **forward contract**, if a holder wanted to close or reverse a position, there would have to be a second contract, and if the second contract is arranged with a

different counterparty from the first, there would be two contracts and two counterparties, with **credit risk** on both.

5.1.3 Uses

Because of the differences in the two markets, it is not hard to understand why the two markets are used differently. **Futures contracts seldom** go to maturity – less than two percent result in delivery – and are widely used for purposes of **financial hedging** and **speculation**. The ease of liquidating positions in the futures market makes a futures contract attractive for those purposes. The high degree of standardisation in the futures market means that traders need only discuss the number of contracts and the price, and transactions can be arranged quickly and efficiently.

Forward contracts are generally intended for **delivery**, and many market participants may need more flexibility in setting delivery dates than is provided by the foreign exchange futures market, with its standard quarterly delivery dates and its one-year maximum maturity. Transactions are typically for much larger amounts in the forward market while most standardised futures contracts are each set at about $100,000 or less, though a single market participant can buy or sell multiple contracts, up to a limit imposed by the exchange. Also, forward contracts are **not limited** to the relatively small number of currencies traded on the futures exchanges.

The foreign currency futures market provides, to some extent, an **alternative** to the OTC forward market, but it also **complements** that market. Like the forward market, the currency futures market provides a mechanism whereby users can **alter portfolio positions** other than through the alternative of the cash or spot market. It can accommodate both short and long positions, and it can be used on a highly geared basis for both hedging and speculation. It thus facilitates the **transfer of risk** – from hedgers to speculators, or from speculators to other speculators.

5.2 Hedging with currency futures

In principle, no differences exist between a futures market hedge and a forward market hedge. For example, a US business has an account payable for $50,000 Canadian, due on the third Wednesday in September. The company could buy one September Canadian Dollar futures contract. If the value of the Canadian dollar increased, the US dollar value of the company's account payable would increase, resulting in a reduction in the company's value. However, the value of the futures contract would increase by an equal amount, leaving the net value of the company unchanged. If the value of the Canadian Dollar decreased, the US dollar value of the payable account would increase, but the value of the futures contract would decrease by an equal amount.

A US business with an account receivable for Canadian Dollars would hedge its position by selling short the Canadian Dollar futures contract. A short sale of a future contract puts the business in a position opposed to that of a business owning the futures contract. When the futures contract increases in value, the company loses that amount. When the futures contract decreases in value, it gains that amount.

Despite their advantages, futures contracts also contain some disadvantages. Because futures contracts are marked to market on a daily basis, any losses must be made up in cash on a daily basis, while the offsetting gain on the currency transaction will be deferred until the transaction actually occurs. This imbalance can result in a severe liquidity crisis for small companies and for individuals.

Another disadvantage of using futures contracts for hedging is that they trade only in standardized amounts and maturities. Companies may not have the choice of timing their receivables and payables to coincide with standardized futures contracts. Consequently, the hedges are not perfect.

5.2.1 Example

A US company expects to receive a payment of £1,000,000 on October 29. The spot rate on September 12 is S_{SEP12} = 1.60 $/£. The operation of a futures hedge is similar to that of a forward contract. We can construct the same kind of graphical perspective to visualize how the futures position hedges the firm's risk.

The December futures contract trades on September 12 at $F_{SEP12,DEC}$ = 1.55 $/£.

In order to hedge its exposure, the firm could use futures contracts on the British Pound. The standard denomination on this contract, traded in Chicago Mercantile Exchange, is £62,500. The firm should sell (go short) 16 December contracts.

$$16 = \frac{1,000,000}{62,500}$$

On October 29 the spot exchange rate and the price of the December contract are:

$S_{OCT29} = 1.50$ \$/£

$F_{OCT29,DEC} = 1.45$ \$/£

The company will receive less in USD because of the appreciation of the dollar relative to the pound. Whereas on September 12 the company would have received \$1,600,000, on October 29, the company receives \$1,500,000, a loss of \$100,000.

The loss on the cash position will be offset by the gain on the futures position. The gain on the futures short position is:

$$(F_{SEP12,DEC} - F_{OCT29,DEC}) \times 1,000,000 = (1.55 - 1.45) \times 1,000,000 = \$100,000$$

The gain in the futures position has completely offset the loss in the cash position. The end result is equivalent to the company receiving the £1,000,000 at the spot rate of September 12, ie $S_{SEP12} = 1.60$ \$/£. The use of futures has eliminated the exchange rate risk completely.

The reason that the hedge was perfect was because there was no basis risk. Basis risk was defined as the difference at expiration between the value of the underlying and the value of the futures contract. It also encompasses the case when the basis change between the opening of a futures position and the closing of the futures position prior to expiration. In our example we have

$$B_{SEP12} = F_{SEP12,DEC} - S_{SEP12} = 1.60 - 1.55 = 0.05$$

$$B_{OCT29} = F_{OCT29,DEC} - S_{OCT29} = 1.55 - 1.50 = 0.05$$

ie $B_{SEP12} = B_{OCT29}$

The perfect hedge is due to the fact that the basis between the two dates has not changed. Had the basis changed the hedge would not have been perfect. For example is the basis contracted ie $B_{SEP12} > B_{OCT29}$ the profit on the futures position will more than offset the loss on the cash position.

The source of movements in the basis can be analysed looking at the covered interest rate relationship between the spot and the futures price

$$F(t,T) = S(t)\frac{(1+i_F)}{(1+i_H)}$$

This can be rearranged to be written as

$$F(t,T) - S(t) = S(t)\frac{i_F - i_H}{1+i_H}$$

That is the basis is proportional to the interest rate differential. As interest rates change the basis changes too, affecting the effectiveness of the hedge.

6 Currency swaps

Key term

A **currency swap** (or cross currency swap) is an interest rate swap with cash flows in different currencies.

Essentially, a currency swap is an **agreement** to make a loan in one currency and to receive a loan in another currency. With the currency swap, there are **three sets** of cash flows. Initially, the underlying principals are exchanged when the swap starts. Then, interest payments are made over the life of the swap. Finally, the underlying principal amounts are re-exchanged.

A currency swap could also be interpreted as issuing a bond in one currency (and paying interest on this bond), while investing in a bond in another currency (and receiving interest on this bond). In our example, the swap could be viewed as issuing a sterling bond and investing in a dollar bond.

The **lack of credit risk** arises from the nature of a currency swap. **Default** on a currency swap means that the currencies are **not exchanged** in the future, while default on a parallel loan means that the loan is not repaid. Unlike a parallel loan, default on a currency swap entails no loss of investment or earnings. The only risk in a currency swap is that the companies must exchange the foreign currency in the foreign exchange market at the new exchange rate.

Frequently, multinational banks act as brokers to match partners in parallel loans and currency swaps. However, finding companies whose needs mutually offset one another is difficult, imperfect and only partially reduces currency exposure risk. If a company cannot find a match, a **credit swap** may be used. Credit swaps involve a deposit in one currency and a loan in another. The deposit is returned after the loan is repaid. For example, a US business could deposit dollars in the New York branch of a British bank, which would, in turn, lend the depositor British pounds for an investment in the UK. After the British bank loan is repaid in British pounds, the dollar deposit would be returned.

6.1 Example of a currency swap

Company B borrows $l0m with a maturity of four years from third party investors, paying a fixed cost of 7.5%. It swaps this into UK pounds sterling for four years, receiving £6.5m in exchange for the $l0 m (based on an exchange rate of 1.538). The interest rates for the swap are 7% on the dollars and 8% on the sterling. Over the four years, Company B receives 7% x $l0m ($0.7m) and pays 8% x £6.5m (£0.52) in interest each year.

In four years' time, the swap is reversed. Company B repays the swap dealer £6.5m and receives $1m back. It then uses this $10m to repay the third-party investors.

Effectively, in net terms, Company B has borrowed sterling funds for four years, paying a fixed rate of interest of 8% in sterling + 0.5% in dollars (due to the fixed rate receipt under the swap only being 7% compared to the rate on the bond of 7.5%). The transaction can be viewed diagrammatically as follows.

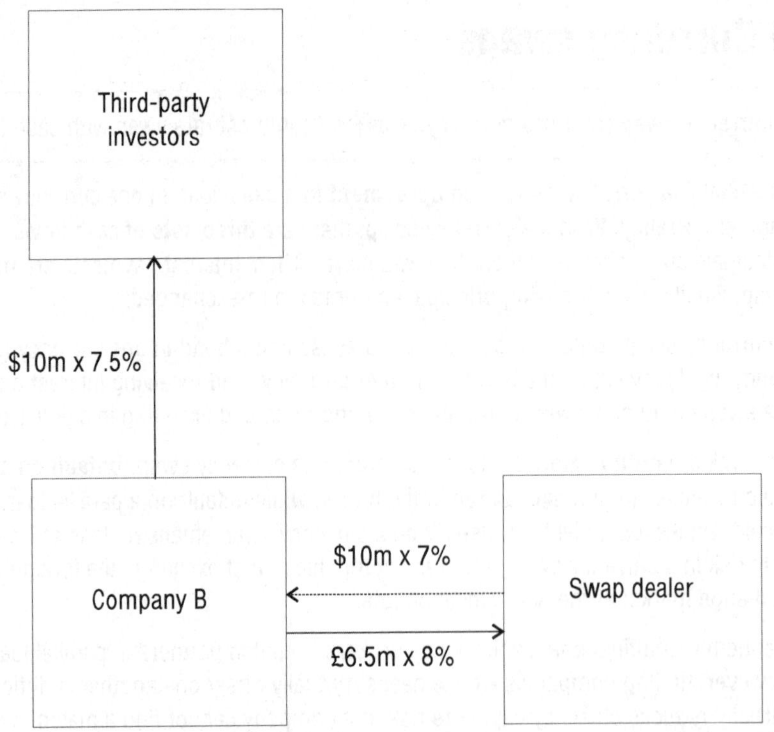

It can be seen that the dollar cash flows cancel out except for the 0.5% margin on the loan, leaving a net annual cost of $50,000 (being 0.5% x $l0m). This leaves the company with an exposure to UK pounds.

The swap rate for dollars is 7% compared to Company B's borrowing rate of 7.5% because the swap rate is based on LIBOR. Company B is unable to borrow at LIBOR in the loan market (see below for more detail on this point).

6.1.1 Fixed or floating interest rates

In the previous example, all interest payments were fixed rate flows (a fixed-for-fixed currency swap). It is also possible to have floating/fixed or floating/floating currency swaps.

A company would prefer to pay a fixed rate under the swap if it believes that the relevant interest rate is going to rise. It would prefer to receive a fixed rate if it believes that the rate will fall.

A company would prefer to pay a floating rate under the swap if it believes that the relevant interest rate is going to fall. it would prefer to receive a floating rate if it believes that the rate will rise.

For example, Company B might believe that UK interest rates are going to rise. This is why it has entered into a fixed rate for the sterling leg of the swap. The reason that Company B selected the fixed rate for dollars was because the underlying bond was fixed rate and it wanted to eliminate the exposure to dollar interest rates. Of course, if Company B subsequently believes that US interest rates will fall, it could use a receive fixed interest rate swap to swap out of fixed rate dollars and into floating rate dollars.

6.1.2 Interest periods and day counts

As with interest rate swaps, interest payments may be made semi-annually. Calculation of interest payments will be according to a specified day count convention.

6.1.3 Credit risk of the company

The swap rates are based on the credit risk of a high quality bank. LIBOR has within it a margin over the short-term risk free rate (ie T-bill rates) and the fixed rate will be at a margin over the relevant government bond rate.

Company B cannot borrow a fixed rate at a rate of 7% in the fixed rate bond market, because it is of lower credit quality than a high quality bank. This is why it has to pay 7.5% on its borrowing and end up with the extra cost of $50,000 a year. This cost will exist regardless of how it finances the borrowing.

6.1.4 Using a currency swap to reduce financing costs

In the above example, company B found it easier and possibly cheaper to borrow in dollars and swap into sterling than to borrowing in sterling directly. Suppose that Company B could only borrow directly in sterling at a rate of 9%. The swap has reduced its financing costs, since its net cost under the swap is 8% in sterling + 0.5% in dollars.

Reasons for this might be as follows.

- Company B is better known in the US than the UK, making it easier to borrow in dollars at competitive interest rates than in sterling.
- The swap dealer will be a large bank with whom Company B already has an established relationship.
- The bank will have access to global financial markets and can finance/hedge this transaction cheaply. Some of the benefit of this will be passed on to company B.
- Company B will be assuming some additional credit risk. There is a risk that the swap dealer will default on its obligations. If Company B had borrowed directly in sterling, this credit risk would not exist.

6.1.5 Currency swaps without exchange of the notional principal

A currency swap may involve the exchange of interest payments on each currency, but no exchange of notional principal. This has various uses, for example, to hedge a series of known cash flows in a foreign currency, or to create/hedge a dual currency bond (see the next section for this). We will demonstrate here the use of such a swap to hedge a series of known cash flows in a foreign currency.

6.1.6 Example

A US company has entered into a contract where it will receive from an Australian customer a sum of A$100,000 a year for three years, payable at the end of each year. The company wishes to hedge this into US dollars. The company enters into a three-year currency swap based on a notional principal of A$2m and US $1.3m. The A$ interest rate is 5% and the US $ interest rate is 4%. There is no exchange of notional principal under the swap. The company agrees to pay A$ interest and receive US $ interest under the swap.

For each of the next three years, the company will be paying A$100,000 (5% x A$2m) and receiving US $52,000 (4% x US$1.3m), under the swap. The company will also be receiving A$100,000 a year under the contract with its customer. The A$ flows cancel out, leaving a net receipt of US $52,000.

An alternative to this would have been to enter into three currency forwards, selling A$100,000 one year, two years, and three years forward. The approaches are equivalent, but the forward rates will be different from each other whereas the swap rates are the same for all three payments.

The risks faced by the company are the credit risk of the swap dealer since the dealer may default on its payments, which in this example is the risk that the company will not receive A$100,000 from its customer on the specified dates.

7 FX swaps

Key term

An **FX swap** is a spot currency transaction coupled with an agreement that it will be reversed at a pre-specified date by an offsetting forward transaction.

Although the FX swap is arranged as a single transaction, it consist of two distinct separate legs. The counterparties agree to exchange two currencies at a particular rate on one date and to reverse payments normally at a different rate on a specified future date. The two legs can therefore be seen as one spot **transaction** and **one forward transaction** going the **opposite direction**.

An FX swap is called a *buy/sell* swap when the base currency eg the dollar is bought on the near date and sold on the far date, and is called a *sell/buy* swap when the base currency is sold on the near date and bought on the far date.

An FX swap is useful for hedging because it allows companies to shift temporarily into or out of one currency in exchange for a second currency without incurring the exchange rate risk of holding an open position in the currency they temporarily hold. This avoids a change in currency exposure which is the role of the forward contract.

An example of an FX swap is where Bank ABC enters into an FX swap with Bank 123 to:

- Sell USD1,000,000 worth of Japanese Yen (JPY) today
- Buy USD1,000,000 worth of JPY in one week's time.

This FX swap (known as a spot to forward date swap) would look something like this:

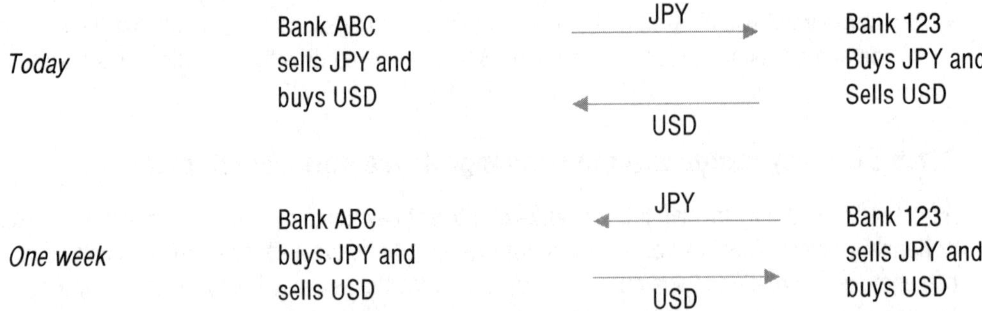

In the above example the FX swap is made up of a spot FX transaction and a one-week forward transaction. Other types of FX swaps include transactions where both the first and second halves (legs) occur in the future. These are known as forward against forward swaps, and are, in effect, two forward transactions operating in parallel.

8 Currency options

FAST FORWARD

Currency options protect against adverse exchange rate movements while allowing the investor to take advantage of favourable exchange rate movements. They are particularly useful in situations where the cash flow is not certain to occur (eg when tendering for overseas contracts).

8.1 Currency options as hedging mechanism

Forward exchange contracts and currency futures contracts are contracts to buy or sell a given quantity of foreign exchange, which must be carried out because they are binding contracts. Some exporters might be uncertain about the amount of currency they will earn in several months' time, and so would be unable to enter forward exchange contracts or futures contracts without the risk of contracting to sell more or less currency to their bank than they will actually earn when the time comes. An alternative method of obtaining foreign exchange cover which overcomes much of the problem is the **foreign currency option**.

Key term

A **currency option** is an agreement involving a right, but not an obligation, to buy or to sell a certain amount of currency at a stated rate of exchange (the **exercise price**) at some time in the future.

As with other types of option, **buying** a currency option involves **paying a premium**, which is the most the buyer of the option can lose. **Selling** (or 'writing') options, unless covered by other transactions, is risky because the seller ('writer') bears the whole of the cost of the variation and can face potentially unlimited losses. Such risks received much publicity with the Barings Bank failure in 1995.

8.2 Currency option quotations

A company wishing to purchase an option to buy or sell sterling might use currency options traded on the important Philadelphia Stock Exchange. The schedule of prices for £/$ options is set out in tables such as the one shown below.

Philadelphia SE £/$ options £31,250 (cents per pound)

Strike		*Calls*			*Puts*	
price	*Aug*	*Sep*	*Oct*	*Aug*	*Sep*	*Oct*
1.5750	2.58	3.13	–	–	0.67	–
1.5800	2.14	2.77	3.24	–	0.81	1.32
1.5900	1.23	2.17	2.64	0.05	1.06	1.71
1.6000	0.50	1.61	2.16	0.32	1.50	2.18
1.6100	0.15	1.16	1.71	0.93	2.05	2.69
1.6200	–	0.81	1.33	1.79	2.65	3.30

Note the following points

(a) The contract size is £31,250

(b) If a firm wished to have the **option to buy pounds** (selling dollars) in September, it can buy a **call option on sterling**. To have the option to buy pounds at an exchange rate of $1.5800/£, it would need to pay a premium of 2.77 cents per pound (check for yourself in the table). For a higher exchange rate, the premium is lower, since the higher exchange rate is less favourable to the buyer of the option: more dollars are needed to buy the same number of pounds

(c) A **put option** here is the **option to sell sterling** in exchange for dollars. Note that a put option with a strike price of 1.6000 $/£ exercisable in September is, at 1.50 cents per pound, cheaper than a September put option exercisable at 1.6100 $/£, which is available at a premium of 2.05 cents per pound. The premium on put options is higher for the higher exchange rate since the purchaser will receive more dollars for each pound sold than with the lower exchange rate

(d) Note that a call option with a strike price of 1.6000 $/£ exercisable in September will **cost more** than an option with the same strike price which is exercisable in August. This difference reflects the fact that for the September option there is a **longer period** until the exercise date and consequently the likelihood of it being beneficial to exercise the option is increased (ie it is more likely to be 'in the money' at the exercise date). The difference also reflects the market's view of the direction in which the exchange rate is likely to move between the two dates

8.3 Using currency options

The main purpose of currency options is to **reduce exposure** to **adverse currency movements**, while allowing the holder to profit from favourable currency movements. They are particularly useful for companies in the following situations:

(a) Where there is **uncertainty** about **foreign currency receipts** or **payments**, either in timing or amount. Should the foreign exchange transaction not materialise, the option can be sold on the market (if it has any value) or exercised if this would make a profit.

(b) To **support the tender** for an **overseas contract**, priced in a foreign currency (see example below).

(c) To **allow the publication of price lists** for its goods in a foreign currency.

(d) To **protect the import or export** of price-sensitive goods. If there is a favourable movement in exchange rates, options allow the importer/exporter to profit from the favourable change (unlike forward exchange contracts, when the importer/exporter is **tied** to a **fixed rate of exchange** by the binding contract). This means that the gains can be passed on in the prices to the importer's or exporter's customers.

In both situations (b) and (c), the company would not know whether it had won any export sales or would have any foreign currency income at the time that it announces its selling prices. It cannot make a forward exchange contract to sell foreign currency without becoming exposed in the currency.

8.4 Pricing of currency options

Currency options are priced using a variation of the Black-Scholes formula for stock prices. The main revision comes from the fact that the opportunity cost to invest in a foreign currency is not the domestic risk-free rate, as for an ordinary asset, but rather the interest rate differential (domestic minus foreign). The intuition behind this modification is very simple: an investment in a foreign currency costs the domestic interest rate (to finance the purchase of currency) but earns the foreign interest rate.

8.4.1 The Black-Scholes model revisited

The Black-Scholes formula for European currency call options was covered in Chapter 8 section 3.2. A reminder of the formulae is given below.

Exam formulae

$$C = P_aN(d_1) - P_eN(d_2)e^{-rt}$$

$$\text{Where } d_1 = \frac{\ln\left(\frac{P_a}{P_e}\right) + \left(r + 0.5s^2\right)t}{s\sqrt{t}}$$

$$d_2 = d_1 - s\sqrt{t}$$

The put-call parity relationship implies that the price of a European currency put option, P, is given by:

$$c = P_eN(-d_2)e^{-rt} - P_aN(-d_1)$$

8.4.2 The Grabbe model of the Black-Scholes formula

The Grabbe variation of the Black-Scholes model is used to price currency options. As mentioned above, the revision is necessary due to interest rate differentials. If a firm invests in a foreign currency, the money used to purchase the currency is subject to interest at domestic rates, whereas the foreign currency invested abroad earns interest at the foreign interest rate.

When pricing currency options, you should use the following formulae.

Exam formula

$$c = e^{-rt}\left[F_0N(d_1) - XN(d_2)\right]$$

$$d_1 = \frac{\ln(F_0 \div X) + s^2T \div 2}{s\sqrt{T}}$$

$$d_2 = d_1 - s\sqrt{T}$$

Where F_0 = forward rate; X = exercise price

r = risk free rate; T = time to expiry of option in years

s = annual standard deviation

8.5 Pricing currency options

Question — Pricing currency options

ShoreSchmidt is hoping to build a new manufacturing plant in France in three months' time, and will need euros at that time to finance the project. Exchange rates and interest rates are as follows.

£/€ = 0.6762

Three month LIBOR is 4.53067%

Three month Euro LIBOR is 2.71032%

The annual volatility (standard deviation) of the £/€ is 24%.

The forward exchange rate can be calculated using interest rate parity.

$$f_0 = s_0 \times \frac{(1+i_c)}{(1+i_b)}$$

Exchange rate risk will be hedged using 'at the money' options – contract size is 100,000 euros.

Required

Calculate the likely option price of a three month call option.

Answer

Step 1 Calculate the three month forward rate

Euro three month interest rate = 2.71032 / 4 quarters = 0.67758%
UK three month interest rate = 4.53067 / 4 quarters = 1.13267%

$$\text{Three month forward rate} = \frac{1+0.0113267 \times 0.672}{1+0.0067758} \text{ (using interest rate parity)}$$

Step 2 Calculate d_1 and d_2 using the Grabbe variation formulae

$$d_1 \frac{\ln(0.6793/0.6762)+0.24^2 \times 0.25 \div 2}{0.24 \times \sqrt{0.25}} = 0.0981$$

$d_2 = 0.0981 - 0.24 \times \sqrt{0.25} = -0.0219$

Step 3 Find $N(d_1)$ and $N(d_2)$ using normal distribution tables

$N(d_1) = 0.5 + 0.0398 = 0.5398$

$N(d_2) = 0.5 - 0.008 = 0.4920$

Step 4 Calculate the option price using the Grabbe variation of Black-Scholes

$c = e^{-rt}[F_0\, N(d_1) - X\, N(d_2)]$

$c = e^{-0.0453067 \times 0.25} \times [0.6793 \times 0.5398 - 0.6762 \times 0.4920]$

$c = 0.9887 \times (0.3667 - 0.3327)$

$c = 0.0336$

This means that the price of the option will be 3.36p per euro.

8.6 Example: Using currency options

Tartan Inc has been invited to tender for a contract in Blueland with the bid priced in Blues (the local currency). Tartan thinks that the contract would cost $1,850,000. Because of the fierce competition for the bid, Tartan is prepared to price the contract at $2,000,000, and since the exchange rate is currently B2.8 = $1, it puts in a bid of B5,600,000. The contract will not be awarded until after six months.

What can happen to Tartan with the contract? There are two 'worst possible' outcomes.

(a) Tartan Inc decides to **hedge against the currency risk**, and on the assumption that it will be awarded the contract in six months' time, it enters into a **forward exchange contract** to sell B5,600,000 in six months' time at a rate of B2.8 = $1.

As it turns out, the company fails to win the contract and so it must buy B5,600,000 spot to meet its obligation under the forward contract. The exchange rate has changed, say, to B2.5 = $1.

	$
At the outset:	
Tartan sells B5,600,000 forward at B2.8 to $1	2,000,000
Six months later:	
Tartan buys B5,600,000 spot to cover the hedge, at B2.5 to $1	(2,240,000)
Loss	(240,000)

(b) Alternatively, Tartan Inc might decide not to make a forward exchange contract at all, but to wait and see what happens. As it turns out, Tartan is awarded the contract six months later, but by this time, the value of the Blue has fallen, say, to B3.2 = $1.

	$
Tartan wins the contract for B5,600,000, which has a dollar value of (B3.2 = $1)	1,750,000
Cost of the contract	(1,850,000)
Loss	(100,000)

(c) A **currency option** would, for a fixed cost, **eliminate these risks** for Tartan Inc. When it makes its tender for the contract, Tartan might purchase an over-the-counter currency option to sell B5,600,000 in six months' time at B2.8 to $1, at a cost of $40,000.

The worst possible outcome for Tartan plc is now a loss of $40,000.

(i) If the company **fails to win the contract**, Tartan will abandon the option (unless the exchange rate has moved in Tartan's favour and the Blue has weakened against sterling so that the company can make a profit by buying B5,600,000 at the spot rate and selling it at B2.8 = $1).

(ii) If the company **wins the contract** and the exchange rate of the Blue has weakened against sterling, Tartan will **exercise the option** and sell the Blues at 2.80.

	$	$
Proceeds from selling B5,600,000		2,000,000
Cost of contract	1,850,000	
Cost of currency option	40,000	
		1,890,000
Net profit		110,000

(d) If the Blue has **strengthened against the dollar**, Tartan will **abandon the option**. For example, if Tartan wins the contract and the exchange rate has moved to B2.5 = $1, Tartan will sell the B5,600,000 at this rate to earn $2,240,000, and will incur costs, including the abandoned currency option, of $1,890,000.

	$	$
Proceeds from selling B5,600,000		2,240,000
Cost of contract	1,850,000	
Cost of currency option	40,000	
		1,890,000
Net profit		350,000

8.7 Comparison of currency options with forward contracts and futures contracts

In the last chapter, we saw that a hedge using a currency future will produce approximately the same result as a currency forward contract, subject to hedge inefficiencies. When comparing currency options with forward or futures contracts we usually find the following.

(a) If the currency movement is adverse, the option will be exercised, but the hedge will not normally be quite as good as that of the forward or futures contract; this is because of the **premium cost of the option**.

(b) If the currency movement is favourable, the option will not be exercised, and the result will normally be better than that of the forward or futures contract; this is because the option allows the holder to **profit from the improved exchange rate**.

These points are illustrated by the next series of examples.

8.8 Example: Currency options (1)

Crabtree Inc is expecting to receive 20 million South African rands (R) in one month's time. The current spot rate is R/£ 19.3383 – 19.3582. Compare the results of the following actions.

(a) The receipt is hedged using a forward contract at the rate 19.3048.

(b) The receipt is hedged by buying an over-the-counter (OTC) option from the bank, exercise price R/$ 19.3000, premium cost 12 cents per 100 schillings.

(c) The receipt is not hedged.

In each case compute the results if, in one month, the exchange rate moves to:

(a) 21.0000
(b) 17.6000

Solution

The target receipt at today's spot rate is 20,000,000/19.3582 = $1,033,154.

(a) The receipt using a forward contract is fixed with certainty at 20,000,000/19.3048 = $1,036,012. This applies to both exchange rate scenarios.

(b) The cost of the option is 20,000,000/100 × 12/100 = $24,000. This must be paid at the start of the contract.

The results under the two scenarios are as follows.

Scenario	*(a)*	*(b)*
Exchange rate	21.0000	17.6000
Exercise price	19.3000	19.3000
Exercise option?	YES	NO
Exchange rate used	19.3000	17.6000
	$	$
Pounds received	1,036,269	1,136,364
Less option premium	24,000	24,000
Net receipt	1,012,269	1,112,364

(c) The results of not hedging under the two scenarios are as follows.

Scenario	*(a)*	*(b)*
Exchange rate	21.0000	17.6000
Dollars received	$952,381	$1,136,364

Summary. The option gives a result between that of the forward contract and no hedge.

- If the South African rand weakens to 21.0000, the best result would have been obtained using the forward market ($1,036,012).
- If it strengthens to 17.6000, the best course of action would have been to take no hedge ($1,136,364).
- In both cases the option gives the second best result, being $24,000 below the best because of its premium cost.

8.9 Example: Currency options (2)

In **Example: currency options (1)**, by how much would the exchange rate have moved if the forward and option contracts gave the same result? Comment on your answer.

Solution

The forward contract gives a receipt of $1,036,012 whatever the movement in exchange rate. If the option is to give a net receipt of $1,036,012, it must give a gross amount (before deducting the premium) of $1,036,012 + $24,000 = $1,060,012. This implies that the exchange rate has moved to 20,000,000/1,060,012 = 18.8700 rands to the dollar.

The option will not be exercised at this exchange rate. It is allowed to lapse, giving an exchange gain which just covers the premium cost. The option becomes advantageous over a forward contract if the exchange rate strengthens beyond 18.8700 rands to the dollar.

8.10 Example: Currency options (3)

Prices (premiums) on 1 June for Sterling traded currency options on the Philadelphia Stock Exchange are shown in the following table:

Sterling £31,250 contracts (cents per £)

Exercise price	*Calls*		*Puts*	
$/£	*September*	*December*	*September*	*December*
1.5000	5.55	7.95	0.42	1.95
1.5500	2.75	3.85	4.15	6.30
1.6000	0.25	1.00	9.40	11.20

Prices are quoted in cents per £. On the same date, the September sterling futures contract (contract size £62,500) is trading at $/£ 1.5390 and the current spot exchange rate is $1.5404 – $1.5425. Stark Inc, a US company, is due to receive sterling £3.75 million from a debtor in four months' time at the end of September. The treasurer decides to hedge this receipt using either September £ traded options or September £ futures.

Required

Compute the results of using

(a) Futures
(b) Options hedges

(illustrating the results with all three possible option exercise prices) if by the end of September the spot exchange rate moves to (i) 1.4800; (ii) 1.5700; (iii) 1.6200. Assume that the futures price moves by the same amount as the spot rate and that by the end of September the options contracts are on the last day before expiry.

Solution

The target receipt is 3,750,000 × 1.5404* = $5,776,500.

*The American company gets the lower number of dollars for selling sterling.

A receipt of £3.75 million will represent 3,750,000/62,500 = 60 futures contracts or 3,750,000/31,250 = 120 option contracts. The value of a one-tick movement will be $6.25 on the futures contract (and $3.125 on the options contract, although this figure will not be needed in the calculation).

(a) If we make the assumption that the futures price moves by the same amount as the spot rate, there will be no basis risk and the future will give a perfect hedge.

On 1 June, 60 sterling futures contracts are sold for $1.5390 (a price which is $0.0014 below the spot rate). The results of this hedge are as follows.

Scenario	*(i)*	*(ii)*	*(iii)*
Spot rate, 30 Sept	1.4800	1.5700	1.6200
Sell 60 at	1.5390	1.5390	1.5390
Buy 60 at (spot – 0.0014)	1.4786	1.5686	1.6186
Gain/(loss) in ticks	604	(296)	(796)

	$	$	$
Value of gain/(loss)	226,500	(111,000)	(298,500)
£3.75 million sold at spot for	5,550,000	5,887,500	6,075,000
Total net receipt	5,776,500	5,776,500	5,776,500

(b) Using options, the treasurer will purchase 120 September *put* options. The premium cost will vary with the exercise price as follows.

Exercise price	*Cost $*
1.5000	$120 \times 0.42/100 \times 31{,}250 = \$15{,}750$
1.5500	$120 \times 4.15/100 \times 31{,}250 = \$155{,}625$
1.6000	$120 \times 9.40/100 \times 31{,}250 = \$352{,}500$

Scenario 1

Spot rate moves to 1.4800.

In all cases, exercise the option and sell £3.75 million at the exercise price.

Exercise price	*Cash received*	*Premium cost*	*Net*	
$/£	$	$	$	
1.5000	5,625,000	(15,750)	5,609,250	
1.5500	5,812,500	(155,625)	5,656,875	← Best result
1.6000	6,000,000	(352,500)	5,647,500	

Scenario 2

Spot rate moves to 1.5700.

Exercise price	*Exercise option?*	*Exchange rate used*	*Cash received*	*Premium cost*	*Net*	
			$	$	$	
1.5000	No	1.57	5,887,500	(15,750)	5,871,750	←Best
1.5500	No	1.57	5,887,500	(155,625)	5,731,875	
1.6000	Yes	1.60	6,000,000	(352,500)	5,647,500	

Scenario 3

Spot rate moves to 1.6200.

In all cases, abandon the option.

Cash received = $6,075,000

Exercise price	*Cash received*	*Premium cost*	*Net*	
$/£	$	$	$	
1.5000	6,075,000	(15,750)	6,059,250	←*Best*
1.5500	6,075,000	(155,625)	5,919,375	
1.6000	6,075,000	(352,500)	5,722,500	

Summary. The futures hedge achieves the target exactly. The options give a range of possible results around the target. As in the previous example when the option is exercised, it does not give as good a result as the future. However, when the option is allowed to lapse because of a favourable movement in the exchange rate, it allows the company to make a gain over target.

Exam focus point

Make sure you appreciate the differences between how futures and options work.

8.11 Best exercise price

It is possible to do a **simple computation** to predict the best exercise price under each scenario. If the pound strengthens, as in scenarios (ii) and (iii), the options are not needed, so, with the benefit of hindsight, the best option is the one with the cheapest premium (just as the best car insurance is the cheapest, provided you don't need to use it!) In this case it is the 1.50 exercise price.

However, if the pound weakens the **options** will be **exercised**. The best exercise price will be the one which gives the highest net $ per £ when the premium is deducted. For this purpose, the premium must be expressed as $ per £ (ie divide the quoted premium by 100).

Best option if exercised

Exercise price	*Premium*	*Net*	
$/£	$/£	$/£	
1.5000	(0.0042)	1.4958	
1.5500	(0.0415)	1.5085	← *Best*
1.6000	(0.0940)	1.5060	

Thus, in scenario (i), the best option is the 1.5500 exercise price.

9 Netting and matching in forex markets

FAST FORWARD

Netting inter company transfers is a common international cash management strategy to manage foreign currency risk.

Netting inter company transfers is another common international cash management strategy to manage foreign currency risk. The basis of netting is that, within a closed group of related companies, total payables will always equal total receivables. The advantages of netting are reduction in foreign exchange conversion fees and funds transfer fees and a quicker settlement of obligations reducing the group's overall exposure.

Multilateral netting systems net the amounts owed among a group of counterparties through a clearinghouse arrangement, resulting in one payment each day in a given currency to or from the clearing house by each counter party.

One of the primary difficulties faced by multilateral netting systems has been making netted contracts legally enforceable. Compared with other types of clearinghouses, a foreign exchange netting system cannot operate effectively without resolving the legal status of contracts in many different jurisdictions. The clearinghouse itself needs to be able to guarantee that the contracts it enters into are legally binding, and institutions from different legal jurisdictions need to guarantee their ability to net and enter into contracts with the clearinghouse. In addition, in situations of insolvency, the counterparties and clearinghouse need to assure themselves of access to collateral that may be held outside any of their legal jurisdictions.

To attract members and satisfy regulators, netting systems need to ensure that the clearinghouse does not take on settlement exposures that cannot be covered in the unlikely event of a failed payment or the bankruptcy of a user. As a general rule, netting systems are required to meet the minimum standards established by the Group of Ten's central banks, which require that the multilateral netting system 'be capable of ensuring timely completion of daily settlements in the event of an inability to settle by the participant with the largest single net debit position.' To meet this requirement, the multilateral netting system relies on a combination of real time exposure limits, the collection of collateral or margin, and precise operating procedures for limiting the duration of settlement risks and for dealing with a defaulting member.

To avoid transferring a failure to its other members, a multilateral netting system needs to be able to acquire funding if payments are withheld and to continue payments to other members. Multilateral netting systems have broached the funding issue either by holding collateral or by assuring themselves of outside sources of liquidity – for example, lines of credit and foreign exchange swap facilities, mostly with member banks. However, it is unclear whether the systems can rely on lines of credit with member banks, because these may also be affected by a liquidity problem during a period of stress. Ultimately, then, central banks would serve as the backstop in a liquidity crisis, just as they do without private multilateral netting systems.

It is worth emphasizing that netting systems are not stand-alone methods for eliminating settlement risk. After payments are netted, banks must still use a payment system that guarantees finality of payments. Thus, once the netting has been accomplished, the system's operating procedures are critical in

determining the amount of time between the settlement of the two legs of the transactions. Both netting systems have the ability to collect payments from participants a few hours before releasing their payments to the recipient participants for currencies in which it is feasible to access large-value RTGS systems simultaneously, shortening the exposure period.

But, unless there is simultaneous finality of received payments, there remains some degree of risk. Two multilateral netting systems may not be sustainable. The degree of risk reduction is a function of the number of linked counterparties and is therefore greatest when all the largest participants join the same system. It may not be cost-effective for a single bank to become a member unless the other banks with which it does business join the same netting system.

10 Devising a foreign currency hedging strategy

Given the wide range of financial instruments (both internal and external) available to companies that are exposed to foreign currency risk, how can an appropriate strategy be devised that will achieve the objective of reduced exposure whilst at the same time keeping costs at an acceptable level and not damaging the company's relationship with its customers and suppliers?

There is no individual best way of devising a suitable hedging strategy – each situation must be approached on its own merits. Unless you are told otherwise, it should be assumed that the company will be wanting to minimise its risk exposure – it is up to you to come up with the most appropriate way of doing so.
You should be prepared to justify your choice of strategy.

The following example will give you an idea of how to put together a suitable strategy while justifying your choice of doing so.

10.1 Example – foreign currency hedging strategy

IOU Inc is a large company based in the USA that trades mainly within the USA and with the UK. It has a significant amount of borrowing in sterling. Debt interest of £725,000 is due to be paid on 31 October and a further £530,000 on 31 December. IOU Inc's policy is to hedge the risks involved in all foreign currency transactions.

Assume it is now 30 September. The company's bank quotes the following rates of exchange, US$ per £:

Spot	*1 month forward (mid rate)*	*3 months forward (mid rate)*
1.5584 – 1.5590	1.5601	1.5655

Prices for a £/US$ option on a US stock exchange (cents per £, payable on purchase of the option, contract size £31,250) are:

Strike price	*Calls*		*Puts*	
(US$/£)	*October*	*December*	*October*	*December*
1.56	2.02	3.00	1.00	2.16
1.57	1.32	n/a	n/a	n/a
1.58	0.84	2.12	2.18	3.14

The treasurer is considering two methods of hedging the risk, forward or option contracts. Market expectations, based on current published economic forecasts, are that sterling will appreciate against the US$ over the next three months. The treasurer thinks the £ might weaken or at least remain stable against the $. He suggests that if options are to be used, one-month options should be bought at a strike price of 1.57 and three-month options at a strike price of 1.58.

Ignore transaction costs.

Required

(a) Recommend, with reasons, the most appropriate method for IOU Inc to hedge its foreign exchange risk on the two interest payments due in one and three months' time. Your answer should include appropriate calculations, using the figures in the question, to support your recommendation and a discussion of the factors to consider when choosing between the two hedging mechanisms.

Assume you are a financial manager with the nationally-owned postal and telecommunications company in Zorro, a country in Asia. In organisations such as this, periodic settlements are made between local and foreign operators. Net receipts or payments are in US$.

(b) Explain the main types of foreign exchange risk exposure that are likely to affect the organisation and advise the company on policies it could consider to reduce exposure to these risks.

Solution

(a) **Spot market position**

The company expects to pay £1,255,000. At today's spot rate this would be converted to $ at $1.5590, giving 1,255,000 × 1.5590 = $1,956,545.

Forward contracts

Forward contracts remove the **risk** from **future short-term currency fluctuations** by fixing an exchange rate in advance. If forward contracts are used, the following dollar costs will be incurred:

One month:	£725,000 × 1.5601 = $1,131,073
Three months:	£530,000 × 1.5655 = $829,715
Total payment:	1,131,073 + 829,715 = $1,960,788

A forward contract will mean that the interest payment is of a **predictable amount** and the possibility of exchange losses is **eliminated**. However, IOU will not be able to participate in **exchange gains** if the pound weakens.

Options

Options can be used to put a '**ceiling**' (or 'cap') on the amount payable while allowing the user to take advantage of **favourable exchange rate movements**.

Option set-up October payment

(i) Contract date – October

(ii) Option type – Call option; buy £ with $

(iii) Strike price – Choose $1.57 as recommended by the treasurer

(iv) Number of contracts

$$\frac{725,000}{31,250} = 23.2 \text{ contracts. Say 23 contracts hedging } 31,250 \times 23$$

= £718,750, leaving £6,250 to be hedged on forward market.

(v) Premium = 23 × 31,250 × $0.0132 = $9,488

Outcome

Option will be exercised if dollar weakens to more than $1.57 in £.

Exercise 23 contracts @ $1.57

	$
Option outcome 1.57 × 23 × £31,250	1,128,438
Option premium	9,488
Unhedged amount covered by forward contract £6,250 × 1.5601	9,751
	1,147,677

Option set-up December payment

(i) Contract date – December contract

(ii) Option type – Call option

(iii) Strike price – Choose $1.58

(iv) Number of contracts

$$\frac{530,000}{31,250} = 16.96 \text{ contracts, say 17 contracts hedging £31,250} \times 17$$

= £531,250, with difference taken to forward market (531,250 – 530,000 = £1,250)

(v) Premium = 17 × 31,250 × $0.0212 = $11,263

Outcome

Option will be exercised if dollar weakens to more than $1.58 in £.

	$
Option outcome 1.58 × 17 × 31,250	839,375
Option premium	11,263
Forward contract receipt £1,250 × 1.5655	(1,957)
Net payment	848,681

Breakeven rate

The disadvantage of options is that they can be expensive to buy because of the premium. The breakeven rate, the rate below which options will give a more favourable outcome than a forward contract, can be calculated as follows, ignoring the issue of whole contracts.

(Breakeven rate × Amount hedged) + Premium = Forward contract payment

$$\text{For October breakeven rate} = \frac{1,131,073 - 9,488}{725,000} = \$1.5470$$

$$\text{For December breakeven rate} = \frac{829,715 - 11,263}{530,000} = \$1.5442$$

Recommendation

Options should only be used if it is thought to be a good chance that the pound will weaken (but protection is still required against its strengthening). If, as the market believes, the pound is likely to strengthen, forward contracts will offer better value.

(b) **Exchange risks in Zorro**

Transactions exposure

This is the risk that the exchange rate **moves unfavourably** between the **date of agreement** of a contract price and the **date of cash settlement**.

Economic exposure

This is the risk of an **adverse change in the present value** of the organisation's future cash flows as a result of longer-term exchange rate movements.

Netting off

The Zorro postal and telecommunications company will receive **domestic income** in its local currency but will make **settlements** (net receipts or payments) with foreign operators in US dollars. It may appear that most of the **currency risk** is **hedged** because **dollar payments** are balanced against **dollar receipts** before settlement. However, although this is a good way of reducing currency transaction costs, it does not remove currency risk.

Residual risk

Although the foreign transactions are denominated in dollars, the exchange risk involves all the **currencies of the countries** with which the company deals. For example, if money is owed to Germany and the euro has strengthened against the dollar, then the dollar cost of the transaction has increased. Also, although all of these transactions are short term, their combined effect is to expose the company to **continuous exchange risk** on many currencies. The company needs a strategy to manage this form of **economic exposure**.

Management of currency risk

One way to manage currency risk in this situation is to attempt to **match assets and liabilities** in each currency as follows.

(i) The company needs to examine each country with which it deals and, having selected those with which it has a material volume of transactions, **determine in each case** whether there is a **net receipt** or **net payment** with that country and the average amount of this net receipt/payment.

(ii) If for a given country there is normally a net receipt, currency risk can be hedged by **borrowing an amount** in that currency equal to the **expected net receipt** for the period for which hedging is required, and **converting this amount** to the home currency.

(iii) For countries where there is **normally a net payment**, a **deposit account** in this currency should be maintained.

Recommendation

This strategy will go some way towards hedging currency risk in the various countries involved, but will involve **increased currency transaction costs** and possibly **increased interest costs**. It is therefore probably only feasible for major currencies (eg dollar, euro, yen) and for currencies of Asian countries with which there are major transaction volumes.

Chapter Roundup

- Currencies are quoted at Counter currency X units: Base currency 1 unit.

  The **spot rate** is the rate at which currencies can be exchanged now. The **forward rate** is the rate at which currencies will be exchanged on a set future date.
- The difference between the bid price and the offer price is known as the **spread**.
- If the forward rate is higher that the spot rate, the currency is quoted at a discount; if the forward rate is lower than the spot rate, the currency is quoted at a premium.
- The principle of **interest rate parity** links the currency and money markets and explains differences between the **forward and spot rates**.
- Although a foreign exchange *futures* contract is conceptually similar to a *forward* foreign exchange contract, there are important structural and institutional differences between the two instruments.
- **Currency options** protect against adverse exchange rate movements while allowing the investor to take advantage of favourable exchange rate movements. They are particularly useful in situations where the cash flow is not certain to occur (eg when tendering for overseas contracts).
- Netting inter company transfers is a common international cash management strategy to manage foreign currency risk.

Quick Quiz

1 Suppose that the annual interest rate is 5 percent in the United states and 6 percent in the United Kingdom, and that the spot exchange rate is \$1.756/£ and the forward exchange rate, with one-year maturity, is \$1.749/£. Does interest rate parity hold?

2 Using the data in question 1 how can you profit?

3 Suppose a company wants to hedge receivables. Should the company buy or sell futures contracts?

4 Suppose a company wants to hedge payables. Should the company buy or sell futures contracts?

5 What are the factors that affect the value of currency options?

6 Trebzon Ltd a UK company plans to use a money market hedge to hedge its payment of €4,000,000 for Spanish goods in one year. The UK interest rate is 6 percent and the Euro interest rate is 4 percent. The spot exchange rate is €1.46/£, while the one year forward rate is €1.46/£. Determine the amount of GBP needed if a money market hedge is used.

7 Thalmes Inc is a multinational company that has a bid on a project funded by the Slovenian government. If the company succeeds in its bid it will have to invest €2,000,000. The decision will be announced in three months from now. The management of Thalmes is afraid that dollar devaluation will increase the cost of investment and would like to hedge against the risk of devaluation. Which of the following three strategies (buy forward, buy futures, buy call option) is in your view the most appropriate?

Answers to Quick Quiz

1 Interest rate parity means that

$$\frac{1+i_{US}}{1+i_{uk}} = \frac{\text{Forward rate}}{\text{Spot rate}}$$

However

$$\frac{1+0.05}{1+0.06} < \frac{1.756}{1.749}$$

so interest rate parity does not hold.

2 Borrow $1,000,000 at 5 percent – amount to be repaid $1,050,000

Buy £569,476 spot using $1,000,000

Invest £569,476 in the UK for a year. The value of the investment in a year's time will be £603,645

Sell £603,645 forward in exchange for $1,055,775 (= £603,645 x $1.749/£)

Resulting profit = $1,055,774 – $1,050,000 = $5,774

3 It should sell futures contracts

4 It should buy futures contracts

5 The current exchange rate
The strike price
The time to expiration
The volatility of the exchange rate
The domestic interest rate
The foreign interest rate

6 Deposit amount to hedge in Euro = $\frac{4,000,000}{1+0.04} = 3,846,154$

The amount of GBP needed is €3,846,154/1.46 = £2,634,352

7 The most appropriate strategy is to buy a call option which will expire in three months. If the bid is successful Thalmes can use the option to purchase the euros needed. Even if the bid is not accepted it will still exercise the option if the euro spot rate exceeds the exercise price and sell the euros in the open market.

Now try the question below from the Exam Question Bank

Number	Level	Marks	Time
26	Introductory	15	27 mins
27	Introductory	15	27 mins
28	Introductory	15	27 mins
29	Introductory	15	27 mins
30	Examination	30	54 mins

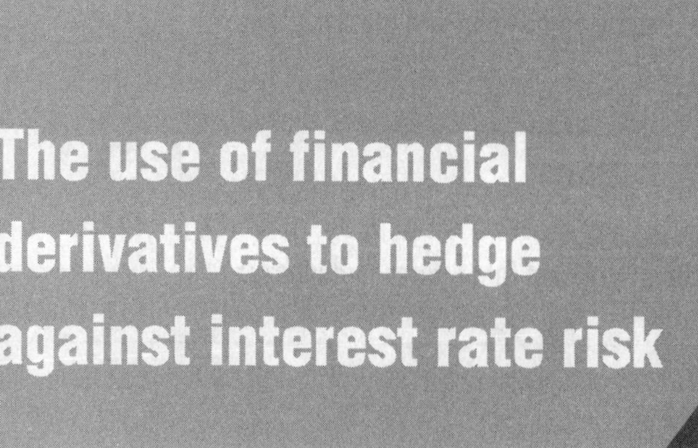

20 The use of financial derivatives to hedge against interest rate risk

Topic list	Syllabus reference
1 Hedging with FRAs	E (3) (a)
2 Hedging with interest rate futures	E (3) (a)
3 Hedging with interest rate swaps	E (3) (a)
4 Hedging with interest rate options	E (3) (a)
5 Interest rate hedging strategies	E (3) (a)

Introduction

A typical corporation will have **assets, liabilities** and **cashflows** whose values are affected by **changes** in **interest rates**. The range of **derivative instruments** available for the **elimination** of **interest rate risk** includes **forward rate agreements**, **interest rate futures contracts**, **interest rate swaps** and **options**.

The characteristics of these instruments have been discussed in Chapter 18. This chapter deals with the application of these derivative contracts for hedging. In Section 1, the simplest contract, the **forward rate agreement**, is studied. In Section 2 the use of **futures contracts** for hedging purposes is discussed, and their advantages and disadvantages are evaluated. Section 3 presents the features of an **interest rate swap** and explains through examples their use in **risk management**. In the final section, Section 4, we present the various types of **options** used by corporations to manage **interest rate risk**. The options discussed include **borrowers' options**, **lenders' options**, **caps**, **floors** and **collars**.

Study guide

		Intellectual level
E3	**The use of financial derivatives to hedge against interest rate risk**	
(a)	Evaluate for a given hedging requirement which of the following is the most appropriate given the nature of the underlying position and the risk exposure: (i) Forward Rate Agreements (ii) Interest Rate Futures (iii) Interest rate swaps (iv) Options on FRA's (caps and collars), Interest rate futures and interest rate swaps.	3

1 Hedging with FRAs

The range of **derivative instruments** available for the **elimination of interest rate risk** includes **forward rate agreements, interest rate futures contracts**, **interest rate swaps** and **options**.

Key term

A **forward rate agreement** is a contract in which two parties agree on the **interest rate** to be paid on a notional amount at a specified future time. Principal or notional amounts are agreed upon but never exchanged, and the contracts are settled in cash.

The **'buyer'** of a FRA is the party wishing to protect itself against a **rise in rates**, while the **'seller'** is a party protecting itself against an **interest rate decline**.

FRAs have symmetrical risk profiles identical to swaps. In fact, swaps are comprised of a series of FRAs.

At the settlement date, the difference between the agreed-upon interest rate on the FRA and the reference rate specified in the contract, usually LIBOR is calculated. That rate difference is multiplied by the agreed principal amount to determine the amount due. If LIBOR on the settlement date is higher than the agreed rate, the buyer on the FRA receives payment of the difference from the seller; if LIBOR is lower than the agreed rate, the seller receives payment.

FRAs can be used to hedge transactions of any size or maturity and offer an alternative to interest rate futures for hedging purposes. FRAs are not traded on exchanges and therefore do not offer the liquidity or protection provided by those exchanges. Credit risk is a primary concern because the entity usually deals directly with the counterparty and is directly at risk in the event of default by that counterparty.

1.1 Example of hedging with an FRA

A company knows that it will need to borrow $10 million in three months for a twelve-month period. It can borrow funds at LIBOR+50 basis points. LIBOR rates today are at 5% but the company's treasurer expects rates to go up to about 6% over the next few weeks. So the treasurer is concerned that the company will be forced to borrow at higher rates unless some sort of hedge is transacted to protect the borrowing requirement.

The treasurer decides to buy a 3-v-15 ('three-fifteens') FRA to cover the twelve-month period beginning three months from now. A bank quotes 5½% for the FRA which the company buys for a notional £10 million. Three months from now rates have indeed gone up to 6%, so the treasurer must borrow funds at 6½% (the LIBOR rate plus spread). However, the company will receive a settlement amount which will be the difference between the rate at which the FRA was bought and today's twelve-month LIBOR rate (6%) as a percentage of £10 million, which will compensate for some of the increased borrowing costs.

The interest paid on the loan will be:

6½% × 10,000,000 = $650,000

The payment the company will receive from the FRA is:

(6% – 5½%) × 10,000,000 = $50,000

The net cost to the company is therefore $600,000 which is equates the cost of borrowing to 6% instead of the actual 6½%.

Note that if the company were able to borrow at the LIBOR rate of 6%, the cost of borrowing would have been £600,000. The forward rate would have been 5% and the payment from the FRA would have been £100,000. In this case there would be complete protection from an increase in the interest rates. The borrower cannot achieve full protection due to the risk premium he has to pay over and above LIBOR.

The FRA therefore, does not protect the **borrower** from the **risk premium** that he has to pay due to his **credit rating**.

2 Hedging with interest rate futures

FAST FORWARD

Futures can be used to hedge an exposure to a rise or fall in short term interest rates over a period of up to approximately two years.

Futures can be used to hedge an exposure to a rise or fall in short term interest rates over a period of up to approximately two years. In practice most futures trading is in contracts with near-delivery dates, and hedging with futures is principally against the risk of adverse movements in a short-term interest rates over the ensuing six months.

- A company expecting to **borrow** can lock in an interest rate by **selling** futures.
- A company expecting to **lend** or invest can lock in an interest yield by **buying** futures.

The underlying item for a short-term interest rate future is a notional deposit, not an actual deposit. An interest rate can be fixed, however, in a similar way to hedging with FRAs. The company borrows or invests/lends at the current market rate, but there is a compensating profit or loss on the futures position. The net borrowing cost or net investment yield is the same as if the borrowing or investment had been at the fixed rate.

Several contracts will normally have to be bought or sold to hedge an exposure in full. For example, to hedge an exposure of $20 million to the risk of an increase in interest rates, it would be necessary to sell 40 short sterling futures contracts.

A hedge is obtained in a similar way to FRAs. The underlying item in short-term interest rate futures is a notional deposit, and buyers and sellers are trading in the price of short-term deposits (ie in interest rates) independently from the loan or investment itself.

If a company at the beginning of January expects to borrow $500,000 for three months from mid-February, and wishes to hedge against the risk of an increase in interest rates, it can sell one March three-month sterling future, and close its position in mid-February when the loan is obtained. The loan will be arranged at the current market rate. There will be a profit or a loss however, on closing the futures position. Taking this profit or loss together with the actual cost of the loan, the net cost to the company will be the interest rate fixed by the original sale of the future. The profit or loss on the future is therefore comparable to the compensatory payment with an FRA.

2.1 Example 1: fixing the cost of borrowing

Echo expects to borrow \$5 million for three months, starting in two months' time in early June, and expects to pay interest at three-month dollar LIBOR plus 0.50%. It wishes to use LIFFE Short sterling futures to hedge the exposure to rising interest rates. It therefore sells 10 June Short Sterling contracts (\$5 million ÷ \$500,000 per contract) at a price of 93.40. Echo subsequently closes the position in early June at a price of 92.70, when it also borrows \$5 million at 7.80%, which is the current three-month LIBOR rate of 7.30% plus 0.50%.

2.1.1 Analysis

By selling five short sterling futures at 93.40, Echo has locked in a rate of 6.60% (100 – 93.40) for LIBOR for its \$5 million loan. Borrowing at LIBOR plus 0.50%, this will lock in a total rate of 7.10%.

A three-month loan of \$5 million at 7.10% would have an interest cost of \$88,750 (\$5 million × 7.10% × 3/12).

In practice, Echo borrows at 7.80% and will pay interest of \$97,500 on its loan (\$5 million × 7.80% × 3/12). However, there is a profit on its futures position.

	\$
Original sale price per contract	93.40
Purchase price on closing position	92.70
Profit per contract	0.70

= 70 ticks

Total profit for 5 contracts = 5 × 70 ticks × \$12.5 per tick = \$8,750

The profit, taken with the actual cost of loan interest, produces a net cost equal to borrowing \$5 million for three months at 7.10%, the rate locked in by the original futures transaction.

	\$
Actual loan cost (7.80%)	97,500
Profit on futures	(8,750)
Net loan cost (7.10%)	88,750

2.2 Example 2: fixing the interest to be received

Foxtrot expects to invest \$3 million for three months at LIBOR minus 0.5%, starting next month in early November, and wishes to use futures to hedge against a fall in interest rates before then. It therefore buys six December three-month sterling futures at a price of 89.40 (six contracts × \$500,000 per contract = \$3 million). In early November when it makes the investment, Foxtrot closes the futures position by selling six December contracts at 89.35, and invests \$3 million at 10.15%, which is the three-month LIBOR rate of 10.65% minus 0.50%.

2.2.1 Analysis

By purchasing futures at 89.40, Foxtrot has locked in an interest rate of 10.60% for three-month LIBOR (100 – 89.40) and so has locked in an interest yield on its investment of 10.10%, which is LIBOR minus 0.50%.

The yield from a three-month investment of \$3 million at 10.10% should be \$75,750 (million × 10.10% × 3/12).

The investment is made at an interest rate of 10.15%, yielding \$76,125 (3 million × 10.15% × 3/12) over the three months. However, Foxtrot has made a loss on its futures position.

	\$
Original purchase price per contract	89.40
Sale price on closing position	89.35
Loss per contract	0.05

= 5 ticks

Total loss on six contracts 6×5 ticks $\times$ \$12.50 per tick = \$375

This loss taken with the actual yield on the investment, produces a net yield equal to investing \$3 million for three months at 10.10%, the rate locked in by the original futures transaction.

	\$
Actual interest yield on investment (10.15%)	76,125
Loss on futures	(375)
Net yield (10.10%)	75,750

2.3 Advantages and disadvantages of futures

2.3.1 Advantages of futures

Futures are just one method of hedging interest rate exposures by fixing an interest rate for anticipated short-term borrowing, lending or investing, or by fixing in advance a price or value for bonds. An important advantage of futures as a hedging instrument is the flexibility of closing a position at any time before delivery date, so that the hedge can be timed to match exactly the underlying borrowing, lending or investment transaction. In contrast, the settlement date or exercise date for FRAs and European-style interest rate options is set for an exact date when the transaction is arranged; giving the user no timing flexibility should the loan or investment date be slightly delayed or brought forward.

The user of futures also has the opportunity to benefit from current market prices, should these seem particularly favourable, by closing a position before the loan or investment takes place.

2.3.2 Example

In April, a company sells September Eurodollar futures at 93.00 to fix the interest rate on anticipated borrowings (in mid-September) at 7%. The dollar interest rate subsequently increases to 9%, and in mid-August the futures price is 91.00. The company at this time believes that the interest rate has peaked and might fall during the next few weeks.

2.3.3 Analysis

The company can close its position in mid-August, securing a profit on its futures trading of 200 ticks per contract (93.00 – 91.00). If, as the company expects, the dollar interest rate subsequently falls before the company has to borrow in mid-September, say to 7.5%, the futures price will rise to 93.50. If the company had delayed closing the position its profit would have been less (just 50 ticks per contract in this example). By closing its position early, the effect of the subsequent fall in interest rates would be to reduce the net cost of borrowing below the 7% that the company was originally trying to fix.

2.3.4 Disadvantages of futures

There are also some disadvantages in using futures. **Initial margins** and **variation margins** tie up cash in deposits for the sale or purchase transaction until the futures position is closed.

There can be a considerable amount of administrative work to manage futures positions efficiently. Direct debit arrangements can be established for the payment of margins, but positions in each contract must be monitored continually, and regular decisions taken about opening or closing positions to ensure that the intended interest rate hedges work effectively.

Futures are a short-term hedging method, and most contracts traded on an exchange are for the next one or two delivery dates. The range of available interest rate contracts is fairly limited and restricted to the major currencies; most short-term interest rate futures are for notional three-month deposits or instruments.

2.3.5 Summary

A significant proportion of futures transactions are carried out for **speculation** and **arbitrage**, with a lesser proportion of transactions intended as a **hedge**. Even so, futures are used extensively for hedging by both banks and non-bank companies.

Banks are the biggest users of futures for hedging. With very large quantities of financial assets and liabilities in different currencies, the interest rate and currency exposures which arise from their transactions in other markets (lending and borrowing markets, options markets, FRAs, etc.) can be significant. They can hedge their over-the-counter transactions with customers by executing matching trades in futures. For example, if a customer buys an FRA on notional principal of £5 million for a three-month interest period, the bank can hedge its exposure to rising interest rates (which selling the FRA has created) by selling ten short sterling futures. The customer gets a fixed borrowing rate with the FRA, and the bank fixes a borrowing rate with futures.

3 Hedging with interest rate swaps

FAST FORWARD

Swaps can be used for the management of interest rate risk.

There are two broad types of interest rate swap: a coupon swap and a basis swap.

The main features of interest rate swaps were reviewed in Chapter 18. Here we shall examine how swaps can be used for the management of interest rate risk. There are two broad types of interest rate swap: a coupon swap and a basis swap.

- In a **coupon swap**, one party makes payments at a fixed rate of interest in exchange for receiving payments at a floating rate (which is reset for each payment). The other party pays the floating rate and receives the fixed rate.
- In a **basis swap**, the parties exchange payments on one floating rate basis (eg at three-month LIBOR or at a six-month CD rate) for payments on another floating rate basis (eg at six-month LIBOR).

Most interest rate swaps are **coupon swaps**. There are also **cross-currency coupon swaps** in which the parties exchange interest payments at a **fixed rate** in **one currency** for payments at a **variable rate** in a **second currency**.

3.1 Hedging with coupon swaps

Coupon swaps can be used to hedge a long-term exposure to the risk of rising or falling interest rates, by allowing the user to manage the mix of fixed rate and floating rate obligations in its debt portfolio, or the mix of fixed rate and floating rate income in its investment portfolio. (Swaps that change payments from fixed rate to floating rate, or vice versa, for paying fixed rate interest an underlying debt are called liability swaps. Those that change an income stream on investments from fixed to floating rate, or vice versa, versa, are called asset swaps. Both liability swaps and asset swaps operate in the same way.)

- If a company believes that it has an exposure to an increase in interest rates because too much of its borrowing is at floating rate, it can arrange a swap to change some (or all) of its floating rate interest obligations into fixed rate obligations, without altering its underlying loans.
- Similarly, if a company believes that it has an exposure to falling interest rates, and that it has too much fixed rate borrowing (at a high markets at a fixed rate can fixed rate) it can arrange a swap to change some (or all) of its fixed rate interest rate obligations into variable rate obligations.

There is an active swaps market and companies should be able to switch from fixed to variable rate obligations, or vice versa, without difficulty so as to achieve a suitable floating rate/fixed rate mix. The mix can be adjusted whenever required by means of further swap arrangements, without having to redeem actual loans or obtain new loans, since swaps do not affect existing loans or investments in any way.

Companies might be unable to borrow long term at a fixed rate directly from a bank or the bond market, but can obtain a loan at a floating rate. If they want to pay interest at a fixed rate, they can borrow at a variable rate and arrange a swap to exchange the floating rate obligation for a fixed rate.

3.1.1 Example 1

Gamma wants to borrow £20 million for five years, with interest payable at six-monthly intervals. It can borrow this money from a bank at a floating rate for LIBOR plus 1%, but wants to obtain a fixed rate for the full five-year period. A swaps bank indicates that it will be willing to receive a fixed rate of 9.7% in exchange for payments of six-month LIBOR.

3.1.2 Analysis

5-year swap: notional principal £20 million

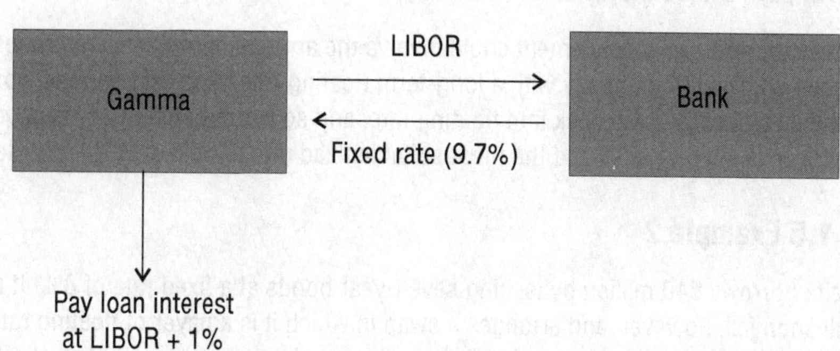

Gamma borrows $20 million with interest at six-month LIBOR plus 1%. In the swap, it receives six-month LIBOR and pays fixed interest at 9.7%. The net effect is to acquire a fixed rate obligation at 10.7% for the full term of the swap.

	%
Borrow at LIBOR plus 1%	–(LIBOR + 1%)
Swap: receive floating rate	+LIBOR
Pay fixed rate	–9.7%
Net payment (fixed rate)	–10.7%

Gamma will therefore fix its payments at $1,070,000 ($20 million × 10.7% × 6/12) every six months for the five-year term of the swap.

At each six-monthly fixing date for the swap, the payment due from Gamma to the swaps bank or from the bank to Gamma will depend on the market rate for six-month LIBOR at that date.

3.1.3 Outcome 1

Suppose that on the first fixing date for the swap, at the end of month six in the first year, six-month LIBOR is 11%. The payments due by each party to the swap will be as follows:

	$
Gamma pays fixed rate of 9.7% ($20 million × 9.7% × 6/12)	970,000
Swaps bank pays LIBOR rate of 11% ($20 million × 11% × 6/12)	1,100,000
Net payment from bank to Gamma	130,000

This payment will be made six months later at the end of the notional interest rate period. Gamma will pay interest on its loan at LIBOR + 1% which for this six-month period is 12% (11% + 1%). Taken with the payment received under the swap agreement, the net cost to Gamma is equivalent to interest payable at 10.7%.

	$
Loan payment at 12% ($20 million × 12% × 6/12)	1,200,000
Payment received from the swaps bank	(130,000)
Net payment (equivalent to 10.7% interest)	1,070,000

3.1.4 Outcome 2

Suppose that at the next six-monthly fixing date, six-month LIBOR is 8.8%. The swap payments will be as follows:

	$
Gamma to swaps bank (fixed at 9.7%)	970,000
Swaps bank to Gamma (at 8.8%)	(880,000)
Net payment by Gamma to swaps bank	90,000

Under its loan arrangement, Gamma will pay 9.8% (LIBOR + 1%) for the six-month period. Adding the net swap payment gives a total cost for the six-month period of $1,070,000, equivalent to an interest rate of 10.7% for the period.

	$
Loan payment at 9.8%	
($20 million × 9.8% × 6/12)	980,000
Swap payment	90,000
Total payment (equivalent to 10.7% interest)	1,070,000

Active interest rate management could involve the arrangement of several swaps over time for the same underlying loan. A company with a long-term floating rate debt, for example, could swap into fixed rate, and subsequently swap back into floating rate, and so on, depending on management's view of future changes in interest rates and the most suitable fixed rate and floating rate mix for its debts.

3.1.5 Example 2

Delta borrows $40 million by issuing seven-year bonds at a fixed rate of 8%. It believes that interest rates will soon fall, however, and arranges a swap in which it is a payer of floating rate at LIBOR and a receiver of 7.7% fixed. The net effect is that Delta will pay a floating rate on its loan at LIBOR plus 0.3%.

	%
Bond interest payment	(8)
Swap: receive	+7.7
pay	(LIBOR)
Net payable	(LIBOR + 0.3)

Interest rates do fall, but a year or so later, Delta believes that they might rise again. It therefore decides to arrange another swap, in which it receives floating rate (LIBOR) and pays a fixed rate. The fixed rate payment for the swap is 7% (reflecting lower market interest rates at the time).

With the second swap, Delta will become a fixed rate payer again, but at a lower interest rate than the amount payable on the bonds.

	%
Bond interest payment	(8)
Swap 1: receive	7.7
pay	(LIBOR)
Swap 2: receive	LIBOR
pay	(7)
Net payment (fixed rate)	7.3

3.2 Basis swaps

In a basis swap, the parties agree to exchange a stream of floating rate payments on one basis for a stream of floating rate payments on a different basis. Floating rate basis might be three-month LIBOR, six-month LIBOR, a Treasury bill rate, certificate of deposit rate, or a commercial paper rate. Basis swaps are much less common than coupon swaps, but can be used by banks as a hedge against basis risk and gap

3.2.1 Example

West Bank is partly funded by customer deposits for which it pays interest at six-month LIBOR minus 0.5%. It has used the funds to lend at three-month LIBOR, but is concerned about its exposure to a shift in the yield curve and that six-month LIBOR could rise relative to three-month LIBOR. It arranges a basis swap with another bank in which it receives six-month LIBOR minus 0.20% and pays three-month LIBOR.

3.2.2 Analysis

By arranging the swap, West Bank matches its income at three-month LIBOR with the amount payable for the swap, and matches the basis for its payments to depositors with the rate receivable from the swap. The net effect is to lock in a profit of 0.30% on its funding.

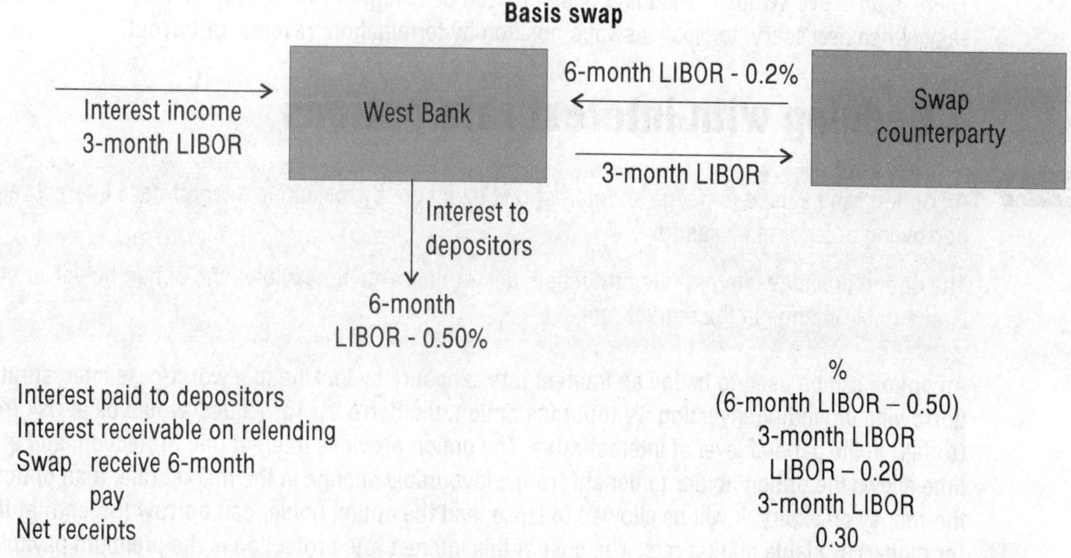

		%
Interest paid to depositors		(6-month LIBOR – 0.50)
Interest receivable on relending		3-month LIBOR
Swap	receive 6-month	LIBOR – 0.20
	pay	3-month LIBOR
Net receipts		0.30

3.3 Reaching hedging decisions

To determine whether to use swaps to hedge interest rate exposures, a company should first identify all those exposures arising from its long corporate funding or investment activity (for maturities of two or more years). It should establish whether the exposures are on a fixed or floating rate basis and the duration of each. For all but the largest companies this should be a straightforward exercise.

Previous hedging activity should not be overlooked, and the precise interest rate status of each exposure should be checked and confirmed. The company could have in place several interest rate hedges for an exposure; for example, it could have a swap to change interest rate payments from a floating rate to a fixed rate.

The company should then decide on the optimal blend of fixed and floating rate debt, and the required duration of this optimal blend. The most common split of fixed and floating rate debt is 50:50, simply because a change in interest rates will have both beneficial and adverse effects, which ought to be largely self-cancelling.

The required duration of the hedge will depend upon the term of both existing debt and new debt, and also on management's view of whether a hedge is required for the full term of each loan. The most common duration for fixing the cost of debt tends to be five years since this is the standard term for floating rate bank loan facilities.

As a result of their analysis, management should establish the company's interest-rate swap requirements in terms of specific amounts and duration, and the terms of each swap (fixed into floating or vice versa, etc.) The necessary swaps should then be executed if suitable prices are available.

3.4 Advantages of swaps

Swaps are flexible instruments for managing interest rates for longer- term funding (and investments), as a separate measure from managing the debt (or investment portfolio) itself. As a hedging instrument, swaps give management the opportunity to:

- manage the fixed/floating rate balance of debts or investments, and
- take action in anticipation of future interest rate changes, without having to repay existing loans, take out new loans or alter an investment portfolio.

Fixing the cost of debt for an extended period can improve the credit perception of a company, particularly in an environment of rising interest rates, as it reduces a company's financial risk exposures.

There is an active swaps market and positions can be changed over time as required. It is also relatively easy, when necessary, to close a swaps position by termination, reversal or buyout.

4 Hedging with interest rate options

FAST FORWARD

An option can be used to hedge an interest rate exposure by locking in a worst-case interest rate for borrowing or lending/investing.

The option provides interest rate protection, and at the same time allows the option holder to benefit from a favourable change in the market rate.

An option can be used to hedge an interest rate exposure by locking in a worst-case interest rate for borrowing or lending/investing. Without the option, the borrower (or lender) would be at risk from a rise (or fall) in the general level of interest rates. The option provides interest rate protection, and at the same time allows the option holder to benefit from a favourable change in the market rate. If an option is out-of-the-money on expiry, it will be allowed to lapse, and the option holder can borrow (or lend) at the lower (or higher) available market rate. The cost of this interest rate protection is the premium payable for the option.

Since an option will only be used in circumstances where it benefits the option holder, it can be described as a conditional hedging instrument. This is distinct from binding contracts such as FRAs and futures, which can be described as outright hedging instruments.

4.1 Hedging with a borrower's option

A borrower's option can be used to secure a maximum effective interest rate for future short-term borrowing, whilst allowing the option holder the option to benefit from lower market rates of interest if these are available when the loan is eventually transacted.

4.1.1 Example

Alpha will need to borrow $10 million for six months in two months' time. It expects to be offered an interest rate of six-month LIBOR + 1.5% by its bank. Six-month LIBOR is currently 10%, and Alpha does not want to pay more than 12.5% in interest.

Alpha therefore decides to buy a European borrower's option from the bank at a strike price of 10.5% for six-month LIBOR for a notional principal amount of $10 million, and with an expiry date in two months' time scheduled to coincide with the start of the loan period. The premium costs 0.5% of the notional principal amount.

4.1.2 Analysis

Alpha expects to borrow at LIBOR plus 1.5%, but does not want to pay an effective rate in excess of 12.5%. The effective interest rate includes the cost of the premium, which for a borrower's option at a strike price of 10.5% is 0.5%.

A strike price of 10.5% would therefore secure a maximum borrowing cost of 12.5%, as follows:

Premium for, option	0.5
Strike price	10.5
Excess borrowing rate over LIBOR	1.5
Maximum effective borrowing rate	12.5

4.1.3 Outcome 1

On the expiry date, if six-month LIBOR is 12% (higher than the strike price) the borrower's option will be exercised. Alpha will borrow $10 million for six months at 13.5%, which is LIBOR plus 1.5%. However, the bank (option writer) will make a compensatory payment equivalent to the difference between the strike price (10.5%) and the current market rate (12%). The effective cost of borrowing will be as follows:

	%
Loan at LIBOR plus	13.5
Less compensatory payment (12 – 10.5)	(1.5)
Premium for option	0.5
Effective borrowing rate	12.5

4.1.4 Outcome 2

On the expiry date, if six-month LIBOR is 10% (below the strike price) the borrower's option will be allowed to lapse. Alpha will borrow $10 million at 11.5%, which is LIBOR plus 1.5%. The effective borrowing cost, including the premium for the option, will be 12%.

	%
Loan at LIBOR plus	11.5
Premium for option	0.5
Effective borrowing rate	12.0

Whatever the market rate for LIBOR on expiry of the option, the effective borrowing cost for Alpha will not exceed 12.5%. If interest rates are below the strike price for the option, and the option is not exercised, the effective borrowing cost will be less than 12.5%, and Alpha will have paid a premium for an unused option. The premium might therefore be described as the cost of an interest rate 'insurance policy'.

4.2 Hedging with a lender's option

A lender's option can be used to secure a minimum effective interest yield on future short-term lending or investment whilst allowing the option holder to benefit from higher market rates of interest, if these are available when the loan or investment is eventually made.

4.2.1 Example

Beta expects to invest $15 million in one month's time for a period of three months, but is anxious about the possibility that interest rates will soon fall. It expects to deposit the funds at three-month LIBOR minus 0.75%. Three-month LIBOR is currently 11%, and Beta would like to ensure that its minimum yield is 9%. A lender's option on a notional three-month deposit of £15 million at a strike price of 10% would have a premium cost of 0.25% of the notional principal amount.

4.2.2 Analysis

Beta expects to invest at LIBOR minus 0.75%, but wants to secure a minimum yield of 9%. The effective interest yield for Beta is calculated after deducting the premium cost, which would be 0.25% for an option with a strike price of 10%. A strike price of 10% would give Beta the following minimum yield:

	%
Strike price	10.00
Rate below LIBOR for investing	-0.75
Premium for option	-0.25
Minimum effective investment rate	9.00

On the expiry date, if three-month LIBOR is lower than 10%, say 9.5%, the option will be exercised and Beta will secure the minimum yield of 9%. Beta would invest at 8.75% (LIBOR minus 0.75%) but would receive a compensatory payment from the bank (option writer) for the difference between three-month LIBOR and the strike price.

	%
Investment rate (9.5 – 0.75)	8.75
Compensatory payment (10 – 9.5)	0.50
Less premium for option	-0.25
Effective net yield	9.00

The effective net yield for Beta will be a minimum of 9%, and higher if the option is not exercised when the market rate for investing or lending exceeds the strike price. As with a borrower's option, the premium for a lender's option can be described as the cost of an 'insurance policy' (which the option holder would prefer not to use)

4.3 Interest rate caps

FAST FORWARD

Under a cap agreement, the seller (writer) agrees to compensate the buyer (holder) if interest rates rise above the strike price at each reset date (rollover date) for the loan.

The cap buyer pays the seller a premium, normally in advance of the transaction being made.

Key term

An **interest rate cap** is a series of borrowers' options, setting a maximum interest rate on a variable-rate borrowing.

A cap can be arranged for just one reset date (in which case it would be a borrower's option) or for a whole series of rollover dates. The term of a cap can therefore range from three months up to 12 years, but most are between two and five years.

The terms of a cap can be structured to the customer's requirements, for strike price, maturity and rollover dates, and can match the maturity and rollover dates for the underlying floating rate loan.

4.3.1 The purpose of a cap

The purpose of a cap is to provide its holder with protection from adverse movements in interest rates, by setting a maximum borrowing cost for any rollover date on a variable rate loan. At the same time, the holder has the flexibility to take advantage of lower market rates of interest when they occur.

Although a cap is used to provide a hedge against an increase in interest rates on an underlying loan, it is (like a borrower's option) a completely separate transaction from the loan itself. The cap is for a notional principal amount, which until fairly recently was unlikely to be less than $5 million, or an equivalent amount in another currency. Some banks, however, will now sell caps for notional amounts for as little as £100,000.

The reference interest rate for the strike price is normally three-month or six-month LIBOR (although another reference rate such as one-month LIBOR, a US Treasury bill rate or a commercial rate, could be used).

With a borrower's option, the option holder has to notify the option from the cap writer, writer of his intention to exercise the option, and there is a compensatory payment on exercise, at the beginning of the interest rate period, to which the option relates. In contrast, with a cap each option is automatically exercised on a rollover date when the market rate of interest is higher than the strike price, but the compensatory payment by the cap writer to the cap holder does not occur until the end of the interest rate period to which the option relates (typically three or six months later).

4.3.2 Example

Gamma is arranging a three-year floating rate loan of $20 million with six-monthly rollover dates. Interest is payable at six-month LIBOR plus 1%. Six-month LIBOR is currently 10%, and Gamma wishes to buy a cap to ensure that interest payable does not exceed 12% at any rollover date (ignoring the cost of the cap premium). The premium for a three-year cap at a strike price of 11% for six-month LIBOR would be 1.5% of the notional principal.

During the term of the loan and the cap, six-month LIBOR was as follows:

	6-month LIBOR
	%
Start of loan/cap period	10.0
After: 6 months	11.5
1 year	9.5
18 months	11.0
2 years	11.5
2½ years	12.0

4.3.3 Analysis

The strike price of 11% for six-month LIBOR ensures that Gamma, paying interest at LIBOR plus 1%, will not pay more than 12% for any rollover period on the loan (ignoring the cap premium cost). The cap writer will make a compensatory payment whenever six-month LIBOR exceeds 11% on a rollover date.

Reset date	*Interest rate for next 6 months**	*Amount of compensation*	*Net loan cost*
	%	%	%
Start of loan	11.0	None	11.0
End of 6 months	12.5	0.5	12.0
End of 1 year	10.5	None	10.5
End of 18 months	12.0	None	12.0
End of 2 years	12.5	0.5	12.0
End of 2½ years	13.0	1.0	12.0

*LIBOR + 1%

Compensation receivable (in arrears) would be $50,000 (0.5% of $20 million x 6/12) at the end of the first year and after two-and-a-half years, and $100,000 (1% of $20 million x 6/12) for the final rollover period, payable at the end of the loan term.

In this example, since the cap premium was $300,000 (1.5% of $20 million), Gamma has paid in premium more than the compensatory payments received, and so can be said to have made a 'loss' on the hedge.

However, Gamma not only had the security for three years of knowing that the interest rates payable would not exceed 12% net, but also the flexibility to take advantage of lower interest rates; in this example at the rollover date after one year when LIBOR was down to 9.5%.

4.4 Interest rate floors

FAST FORWARD

An interest rate floor is comparable to a cap in the same way that a lender's option can be compared to a borrower's option.

It is a series of lenders' options which sets a minimum interest yield on a variable rate investment or loan to a customer. The floor buyer pays a premium to the writer (seller). In return, the writer agrees to compensate the buyer if interest rates fall below the strike price at each reset date for the investment or loan. As with a cap, the terms of a floor agreement can be tailored to the requirements of the customer for strike price, interest reference rate, rollover dates and maturity.

A floor can provide a hedge against falling interest rates, and fix a minimum interest yield for a lender or investor, whilst at the same time giving the holder the flexibility to benefit from higher market rates of interest when these occur.

4.4.1 Example

Delta is arranging a two-year investment of $20 million, on which interest receivable will be 0.75% below three-month US dollar LIBOR. Rollover dates will be every three months. Three-month dollar LIBOR is currently 6.5%, and Delta does not want its interest yield to be less than 5% at any rollover date on the investment.

For a premium of $280,000, Delta could buy a floor with a notional principal of $20 million and a strike price of 6% (with caps and floors, available strike prices are quoted as whole percentage figures).

4.4.2 Analysis

A strike price of 6% will fix the minimum interest yield for any rollover period on the investment at 5.25% (6% – 0.75%). Suppose, for example, that three-month LIBOR is 6.5% at the start of the investment and then 6%, 5%, 4.75%, 4%, 4.25%, 7% and 8% at the subsequent three-monthly rollover dates on the investment.

Delta's net income would be as follows:

Reset date	*Interest yield for next 3 months**	*Amount of compensation*	*Net yield*
	%	%	%
Start of investment	5.75	None	5.75
After 3 months	5.25	None	5.25
After 6 months	4.25	1.00	5.25
After 9 months	4.00	1.25	5.25
After 12 months	3.25	2.00	5.25
After 15 months	3.50	1.75	5.25
After 18 months	6.25	None	6.25
After 21 months	7.25	None	7.25

*LIBOR – 0.75%

Delta would receive the following compensation (three months in arrears):

End of month	*Compensation*	
		$
9	($20 million × 1% × 3/12)	50,000
12	($20 million × 1.25% × 3/12)	62,500
15	($20 million × 2% × 3/12)	100,000
18	($20 million × 1.75% × 3/12)	87,500

In this example, since the floor premium was $280,000, Delta could be said to have made a 'profit' on the hedge. More significantly, however, Delta has also had the risk protection of a guaranteed minimum yield over the two-year period. It has also been able to benefit from higher interest rates, at the end of months 18 and 21.

4.5 Interest rate collars

FAST FORWARD

Collars are a lower cost alternative to caps and floors.

A major disadvantage of caps and floors as a hedge for interest rate exposures is their high cost. Premiums typically range from 1-5% of the notional principal, and are payable up front. Collars were devised as a lower-cost alternative to caps and floors. A collar is a combination of buying a cap and selling a floor, or buying a floor and selling a cap.

A company wishing to fix a maximum interest rate cost for a variable rate loan and at the same time wanting some flexibility to benefit from more favourable interest rates when they occur, could transact a collar with a bank in which it buys a cap with a strike price at the required maximum limit, and simultaneously sells a floor to the bank at a lower strike price, for the same maturity and notional principal.

The net premium is the cost of the premium payable for the cap minus the premium receivable for selling the floor.

The effect of a collar is to set both a maximum and a minimum interest rate on the borrowing. If interest rates rise above the cap strike price, the collar holder will receive compensation, but if interest rates fall below the floor strike price, the collar holder must pay compensation to the bank. This limits the flexibility to benefit from lower interest rates, but in return the net premium is lower.

Similarly, a company wishing to fix a minimum interest yield for a floating rate investment whilst retaining some flexibility to benefit from higher market rates of interest, should they occur, could transact a collar in which it buys a floor with a strike price at the required minimum level, and simultaneously sells a cap to the bank at a higher strike price.

The net premium is the premium payable for the floor minus the premium receivable for selling the cap. The effect of the collar would be to fix a minimum interest yield with the floor's strike price, but limit the maximum yield obtainable (in the event that market interest rates rise) to the cap strike price level.

Exam focus point

In an exam you may be asked to choose the most suitable hedging instrument.

4.6 Summary

Options provide a form of conditional hedge. They provide protection against adverse movements in interest rates by fixing a maximum cost on floating rate borrowing or a minimum yield on floating rate lending or investing, but are not exercised if market interest rates are more beneficial. They can be used to hedge exposures over a short-to-medium term period. The major drawback is their cost, compared with an FRA or a swap, which can also be used to fix an interest rate (but in an 'unconditional' binding agreement).

5 Interest rate hedging strategies

FAST FORWARD

When deciding which techniques to use to hedge against interest rate risk, issues such as cost, flexibility, expectations and ability to take advantage of favourable interest rate movements should be considered.

Financial instruments should not be chosen in isolation – their impact on the overall financial strategy of the company should also be taken into consideration.

While it is essential to know about the different financial instruments that are available to reduce interest rate risk, it is also very important to be able to determine which instrument(s) should be used in particular circumstances or when devising strategies.

If you have to discuss which instrument should be used to hedge interest rate risk, consider **cost**, **flexibility**, **expectations** and **ability to benefit** from favourable interest rate movements.

Different hedging instruments often offer alternative ways of managing risk in a specific situation. In the following example, we consider the different ways in which a company can hedge interest rate risk.

5.1 Example – interest rate hedging strategies

It is 31 December. Octavo needs to borrow £6 million in three months' time for a period of six months. For the type of loan finance which Octavo would use, the rate of interest is currently 13% per year and the corporate treasurer is unwilling to pay a higher rate.

The treasurer is concerned about possible future fluctuations in interest rates, and is considering the following possibilities:

- Forward rate agreements (FRAs)
- Interest rate futures
- Interest rate guarantees or short-term interest rate caps

Required

Explain briefly how each of these three alternatives might be useful to Octavo.

Solution

Forward rate agreements (FRAs)

Entering into an FRA with a bank will allow the treasurer of Octavo to **effectively lock in an interest rate** for the six months of the loan. This agreement is independent of the loan itself, upon which the prevailing rate will be paid. If the FRA were negotiated to be at a rate of 13%, and the actual interest rate paid on the loan were higher than this, the bank will pay the difference between the rate paid and 13% to Octavo. Conversely, if the interest paid by Octavo turned out to be lower than 13%, they would have to pay the difference to the bank. Thus the cost to Octavo will be 13% regardless of movements in actual interest rates.

Interest rate futures

Interest rate futures have the same effect as FRAs, in effectively **locking in an interest rate**, but they are standardised in terms of size, duration (see chapter 21, section 3.5) and terms. They can be **traded on an exchange** (such as LIFFE in London), and they will generally be **closed out before the maturity date**, yielding a profit or loss that is offset against the loss or profit on the money transaction that is being hedged. So, for example, as Octavo is concerned about rises in interest rates, the treasurer can sell future contracts now; if that rate does rise, their value will fall, and they can then be bought at a lower price, yielding a profit which will compensate for the increase in Octavo's loan interest cost. If interest rates fall, the lower interest cost of the loan will be offset by a loss on their futures contracts.

There may not be an **exact match** between the **loan and the future contract** (100% hedge), due to the standardised nature of the contracts, and margin payments may be required while the futures are still held.

Interest rate guarantees

Interest rate guarantees (or short-term interest rate options) give Octavo the opportunity to **benefit from favourable interest rate movements** as well as protecting them from the effects of adverse movements. They give the holder the **right** but not the **obligation** to deal at an agreed interest rate at a future maturity date. This means that if interest rates rise, the treasurer would exercise the option, and 'lock in' to the predetermined borrowing rate. If, however, interest rates fall, then the option would simply lapse, and Octavo would feel the benefit of lower interest rates.

The main disadvantage of options is that a premium will be payable to the seller of the option, whether or not it is exercised. This will therefore add to the interest cost. The treasurer of Octavo will need to consider whether this cost, which can be quite expensive, is justified by the potential benefits to be gained from favourable interest rate movements.

> When considering interest rate or currency risk hedging, don't discuss every possible technique that you can recall. Marks will only be awarded for techniques that are *appropriate* to the circumstances described in the question.

Chapter Roundup

- The range of **derivative instruments** available for the **elimination of interest rate risk** includes **forward rate agreements, interest rate futures contracts**, **interest rate swaps** and **options**.
- Futures can be used to hedge an exposure to a rise or fall in short term interest rates over a period of up to approximately two years.
- Swaps can be used for the management of interest rate risk.

  There are two broad types of interest rate swap: a coupon swap and a basis swap.
- An option can be used to hedge an interest rate exposure by locking in a worst-case interest rate for borrowing or lending/investing.

  The option provides interest rate protection, and at the same time allows the option holder to benefit from a favourable change in the market rate.
- Under a cap agreement, the seller (writer) agrees to compensate the buyer (holder) if interest rates rise above the strike price at each reset date (rollover date) for the loan.

  The cap buyer pays the seller a premium, normally in advance of the transaction being made.
- An interest rate floor is comparable to a cap in the same way that a lender's option can be compared to a borrower's option.
- Collars are a lower cost alternative to caps and floors.
- When deciding which techniques to use to hedge against interest rate risk, issues such as cost, flexibility, expectations and ability to take advantage of favourable movements in interest rates should be considered.
- Financial instruments should not be chosen in isolation – their impact on the overall financial strategy of the company should be taken into consideration.

Quick Quiz

1 What kind of interest rate movement is not hedged by an forward rate agreement?

2 What are the main disadvantages of interest rate futures as hedging tools?

3 If a company wants to fix the interest rate on anticipated borrowing should the company buy or sell futures contracts?

4 In a basis swap the parties agree to exchange a stream of .... rate payments for a stream of .... rate payments.

(a) fixed, floating
(b) fixed, fixed
(c) floating, floating
(d) floating, fixed

5 A borrower's option can be used to secure a .... effective interest rate for future short-term borrowing while allowing the option holder to benefit from .... market rates of interest.

(a) minimum, lower
(b) maximum, higher
(c) minimum, higher
(d) maximum, lower

6 What is the main advantage of a collar compared to a cap or floor?

Answers to Quick Quiz

1 The changes in interest rates due to changes in credit quality are not hedged by a FRA.

2 The main disadvantages of interest futures as hedging tools is the fact that initial and variation margins tie up cash in deposits until the position is closed.

3 The company should sell futures contracts

4 (c) floating, floating

5 (d) maximum, lower

6 The main advantage of a collar compared to a cap or floor is its lower cost.

Now try the question below from the Exam Question Bank

Number	Level	Marks	Time
31	Introductory	15	27 mins
32	Introductory	15	27 mins
33	Examination	20	36 mins

Other forms of risk

Topic list	Syllabus reference
1 Political, economic, regulatory and fiscal risks	E (4) (a)
2 Credit risk	E (4) (b)
3 Credit spreads and the cost of debt capital	E (4) (b)
4 Hedging against credit risk	E (4) (b)
5 Assessing default risk using option pricing models	E (4) (c)

Introduction

The previous chapter dealt with what is known as **market risk**, that is, a change in the value of a position due to a change in the price of financial assets. The present chapter discusses all **other risks** that **multinational companies** are exposed to, such as **political, economic, regulatory** and **fiscal risks**, how these risks arise and how companies may mitigate their impact. The chapter then examines **credit risk** in detail and how this is assessed using **credit rating systems** and **option pricing models**. The impact of **credit risk** on the **cost** of **debt capital** is also examined.

Study guide

		Intellectual level
E4	**Other forms of risk**	
(a)	Assess the firm's exposure to political, economic, regulatory and fiscal risk and the strategies available for the mitigation of such risk.	3
(b)	Assess the firm's exposure to credit risk, including: (i) Explain the role of, and the risk assessment models used by, the principal rating agencies. (ii) Estimate the likely credit spread over risk free. (iii) Estimate the firm's current cost of debt capital using the appropriate term structure of interest rates and the credit spread.	2
(c)	Explain the role of option pricing models in the assessment of default risk, the value of debt and its potential recoverability	1

1 Political, economic, regulatory and fiscal risks

1.1 Political risk

Key term

> **Political risk** is the risk that political action will affect the position and value of a company.

When a multinational company invests in another country, either by setting up a subsidiary or by entering into a joint venture, it may face a political risk of action by that country's government which may affect the operation of the company. The ultimate political risk is the expropriation of the company's investment by the government of the host country. Although expropriation or nationalisation is not very common today, a multinational company is still exposed to political risk in the form of various restrictions.

(a) Import quotas could be used to limit the quantities of goods that a subsidiary can buy from its parent company and import for resale in its domestic markets.

(b) Exchange control regulations could be applied that may affect the ability of the subsidiary to remit profits to the parent company.

(c) Government actions that could restrict the ability of foreign companies to buy domestic companies, especially those that operate in politically sensitive industries such as defence contracting, communications, energy supply and so on.

(d) Government legislation that may specify minimum shareholding in companies by residents. This would force a multinational to offer some of the equity in a subsidiary to investors in the country where the subsidiary operates.

There are a large number of factors that can be considered to assess political risk, for example government stability, remittance restrictions and product boycotting as a result of deterioration in the relationships between the host country and the country where the parent company is based. Measurement is often by subjective weighting of these factors. Industry specific factors are also important.

1.2 Economic risk

Key term

> **Economic risk** arises from changes in economic policy in the host country that affect the macroeconomic environment in which the multinational company operates.

Examples of political risk include:

- A highly restricted monetary policy may lead to high interest rates and a recession affecting aggregate demand and the demand for the products of the multinational in the host country. On the

other hand a inflation in the host country may lead to a devaluation of the currency and it may decrease the value of remittances to the parent company.

- Currency inconvertibility for a limited period of time.
- The host country may also be subjected to economic shocks, e.g. falling commodity prices which may also affect its exchange rate of fiscal and monetary policy which may affect again the state of the economy and the exchange rate.

1.3 Fiscal risk

Key term

Fiscal risk is the risk that a multinational company is exposed to that the tax arrangements in the host country may change after the investment in the host country is undertaken.

Fiscal risks include:

- The imposition of indirect taxes such as VAT on the products of the company, raising the price of its products and potentially reducing demand.
- The imposition of excise duties on imported goods and services that are used by the subsidiary.
- An increase in the corporate tax rate
- The abolition of the accelerated tax depreciation allowances for new investments
- Changes in the tax law regarding admissibility of expenses for tax deductibility

1.4 Regulatory risk

Key term

Regulatory risk is the risk that arises from the change in the legal and regulatory environment which determines the operation of a company.

For example a change in employment legislation making the firing of workers more difficult may increase costs of production and may affect the profitability of a company. Anti-monopoly laws may also restrict the capacity of a company to expand and it may restrict its profitability. Disclosure requirements or stricter corporate governance may also affect the freedom of a company to operate in the host country. Also legal standards of safety or quality (non-tariff barriers) could be imposed on imported goods to prevent multinationals from selling goods through a subsidiary which have been banned as dangerous in other countries.

1.5 Strategies to deal with risks

There are various strategies that multinational companies can adopt to limit the effects of political and other risks.

Negotiations with host government

The aim of these negotiations is generally to obtain a **concession agreement**. This would cover matters such as the transfer of capital, remittances and products, access to local finance, government intervention and taxation, and transfer pricing. The main problem with concession agreements can be that the initial terms of the agreement may not prove to be satisfactory subsequently. Companies may have different reasons for choosing to set up initially and choosing to stay, whilst the local government may be concerned if profits are too high.

Insurance

In the UK the Export Credits Guarantee Department (ECGD) provides protection against various threats including nationalisation, currency conversion problems, war and revolution.

Production strategies

It may be necessary to strike a balance between contracting out to local sources (thus losing control) and producing directly (which increases the investment and hence increases the potential loss.) Alternatively it may be better to locate key parts of the production process or the distribution channels abroad. Control of patents is another possibility, since these can be enforced internationally.

Contacts with markets

Multinationals may have contacts with customers which interventionist governments cannot obtain.

Financial management

If a multinational obtains funds in local investment markets, these may be on terms that are less favourable than on markets abroad, but would mean that local institutions suffered if the local government intervened. However governments often do limit the ability of multinationals to obtain funds locally.

Alternatively guarantees can be obtained from the government for the investment that can be enforced by the multinational if the government takes action.

Management structure

Possible methods include joint ventures or ceding control to local investors and obtaining profits by a management contract.

If governments do intervene, multinationals may have to make use of the advantages they hold or threaten withdrawal. The threat of expropriation may be reduced by negotiation or legal threats.

2 Credit risk

Key term

Credit risk, also referred to as **default risk**, is the risk undertaken by the lender that the borrower will default either on **interest payments** or on the **repayment of principal** on the due date, or on both.

2.1 Credit risk aspects

Credit risk arises from the inability of a party to fulfil its obligation under the terms of a contract. We have already discussed credit risk in relation to the OTC derivatives and how exchanges deal with it through the introduction of margins. Creditors to companies such as corporate bondholders and banks are also exposed to credit risk. The credit risk of an individual loan or bond is determined by the following two factors:

The probability of default

This is the probability that the borrower or counterparty will default on its contractual obligations to repay its debt

The recovery rate

This is the fraction of the face value of an obligation that can be recovered once the borrower has defaulted. When an company defaults, bond holders do not necessarily lose their entire investment. Part of the investment may be recovered depending on the **recovery rate**.

Key term

The **loss given default** (LGD) is the difference between the **amount of money owed** by the borrower less the **amount of money recovered**.

For example, a bond has a face value of $100 and the recovery rate is 80 percent. The **loss given default** in this case is:

Loss given default = $100 – $80 = $20

Key term

The **expected loss** (EL) from credit risk shows the amount of money the lender should expect to lose from the investment in a bond or loan with credit risk.

The **expected loss** (EL) is the product of the **loss given default** (LGD) and the **probability of default** (PD).

$$EL = PD \times LGD$$

If the probability of default is, say, 10 percent, the expected loss form investing in the above bond is:

EL = 0.10 × 20 = $2

2.2 Credit risk measurement

We have already discussed how to measure **market risk**, using measures such as the **standard deviation** or the **beta**. The measurement of **credit risk** is slightly more complex. All the approaches concentrate on the estimation of the **default probability** and the **recovery rate**.

The oldest and most common approach is to assess the probability of default using financial and other information on the borrowers and assign a rating that reflects the expected loss from investing in the particular bond. This assignment of **credit risk ratings** is done by **credit rating companies** such Standard & Poor, Moody's Investor Services or Fitch. These ratings are widely accepted as indicators of the credit risk of a bond. Table 1 shows the credit rating used by the two largest credit rating agencies.

Table 1: Credit Risk Rating

Standard & Poor	Moodys	Description of Category
AAA	Aaa	Highest quality, lowest default risk
AA	Aa	High quality
A	A	Upper medium grade quality
BBB	Baa	Medium grade quality
BB	Ba	Lower medium grade quality
B	B	Speculative
CCC	Caa	Poor quality (high default risk)
CC	Ca	Highly speculative
C	C	Lowest grade quality

Both credit rating agencies estimate default probabilities from the **empirical performance** of issued **corporate bonds** of each category. In Table 2 the probability of default for certain credit categories is shown over different investment horizons. The probability of default within a year for AAA, AA,or A bonds is practically zero whereas for a CCC bond is 19.70%. However, although the probability of default for a AAA company is **practically zero** over a single year, it becomes 1.40% over a fifteen year period. Similar increases are apparent for the other categories. For example for a B rated company, the default probability increases from 5.20% over a single year to 19.40 over a period of four years and to 30.65% over a period of fifteen years.

Table 2: Standard and Poor cumulative default probabilities

Initial Rating Term	Years							
	1	2	3	4	5	7	10	15
AAA	0.00%	0.00	0.07	0.15	0.24	0.66	1.40	1.40
AA	0.00%	0.02	0.12	0.25	0.43	0.89	1.29	1.48
A	0.06%	0.16	0.27	0.44	0.67	1.12	2.17	3.00
BBB	0.18%	0.44	0.72	1.27	1.78	2.99	4.34	4.70
BB	1.06%	3.48	6.12	8.68	10.97	14.46	17.73	19.91
B	5.20%	11.00	15.95	19.40	21.88	25.14	29.02	30.65
CCC	19.79%	26.92	31.63	35.97	40.15	42.64	45.10	45.10

2.2.1 Criteria for establishing credit ratings

The criteria for rating international organisations encompasses the following.

Country risk	No issuer's debt will be rated higher than the country of origin of the issuer (the 'Sovereign Ceiling' concept)
Universal/Country Importance	The company's standing relative to other companies in the country of domicile and globally (measured in terms of sales, profits, relationship with government, importance of the industry to the country, etc)
Industry risk	The strength of the industry within the country, measured by the impact of economic forces, cyclical nature of the industry, demand factors, etc.
Industry position	Issuer's position in the relevant industry compared with competitors in terms of operating efficiency.
Management evaluation	The company's planning, controls, financing policies and strategies, overall quality of management and succession, merger and acquisition performance and record of achievement in financial results.
Accounting quality	Auditor's qualifications (if any) of the accounts, and accounting policies for inventory, goodwill, depreciation policies and so on.
Earnings protection	Earnings power including return on capital, pre-tax and net profit margins, sources of future earnings growth.
Financial gearing	Long-term debt and total debt in relation to capital, gearing, nature of assets, off-balance sheet commitments, working capital, management, etc.
Cash flow adequacy	Relationship of cash flow to gearing and ability to finance all business cash needs.
Financial flexibility	Evaluation of financing needs, plans and alternatives under stress (ability to attract capital), banking relationships, debt covenants.

2.3 Credit migration

FAST FORWARD

The credit rating of a borrower may change after a bond is issued. This is referred to as credit migration.

There is another aspect of **credit risk** which should be taken into account when investors are investing in **corporate bonds**, beyond the **probability of default** .

A borrower may not default, but due to changing economic conditions or management actions the borrower may be become more or less risky than at the time the bond was issued and as a result, the bond issuer will be assigned by the credit agency a different credit rating. This is called **credit migration**. The significance of credit migration lies in the fact that the assignment of **lower credit rating** will **decrease the market value** of the corporate bond. This is discussed in the next section in the context of credit spreads.

3 Credit spreads and the cost of debt capital

FAST FORWARD

The cost of debt capital and the market price of corporate bonds depend on the credit risk of the bond.

3.1 Credit spreads

Key term

The **credit spread** is the premium required by an investor in a corporate bond to compensate for the **credit risk** of the bond.

The yield to a government bond holder is the compensation to the investor for foregoing consumption today and saving. However, corporate bond holders should require compensation not only for foregoing consumption, but also for the credit risk that they are exposed to. As we discussed in the previous section, this is a function of the probability of default, the recovery rate and the probability of migration. Assuming that a government bond such as the one issued by the US or an EU government is **free** of **credit risk**, the yield on a corporate bond will be

Formula to Learn

Yield on corporate bond = risk free rate + credit spread

Or in symbols $y = r + s$

Where y is the yield on the corporate bond
r is the risk-free rate, ie the rate on a government bond with no default risk
s is the credit spread

Since **credit spreads** reflect the **credit risk** of a bond, they will be inversely related to the credit quality of the bond. Low credit quality bonds will be characterised by large spreads and high credit quality bonds will be characterised by low spreads. An example of credit spreads by type of bond and maturity is given below.

Table 4: Credit Spreads (in basis points)

Rating	1–3 years Spread	3–5 years Spread	5–7 years spread	7–10 years spread
AAA	49.50	63.86	70.47	73.95
AA	58.97	71.22	82.36	88.57
A	88.82	102.91	110.71	117.52
BBB	168.99	170.89	185.34	179.63
BB	421.20	364.55	345.37	322.32
B	760.84	691.81	571.94	512.43

Source: J.D. Amato and E.M. Remolona, BIS Quarterly Review, December 2003

The table above shows that investors in bonds of low credit quality require a large premium over a corresponding government bond of similar maturity to compensate them for the risk they are bearing.

For example, the holder of a B bond with a maturity of 7 – 10 years would require 5.12% over the risk free rate to compensate for the risk of the bond.

3.2 The cost of debt capital

The cost of debt capital for a company will therefore be determined by the following:

(a) its credit rating
(b) the maturity of the debt.
(c) the risk-free rate at the appropriate maturity
(d) the corporate tax rate

Formula to learn

Cost of debt capital = (1 – tax rate)(risk free rate + credit spread)

Question

Cost of Capital

Consider a corporate bond with a maturity of 4 years and a credit rating of BBB. The 4-year risk-free rate is 5% and the credit spread is 200 basis points. The corporate tax rate is 30 percent. Find the cost of debt capital

Answer

Cost of debt capital = $(1-0.3)(5\%+2\%) = 0.7 \times 7 = 4.9\%$

3.3 Impact of credit spreads on bond values

FAST FORWARD

The deterioration in the credit quality of a bond, referred to as credit migration, will affect the market value of the bond.

We have already mentioned that credit risk is affected by the probability of migration of a certain debt or loan to another credit category. In markets where loans or corporate bonds are traded this migration is reflected in increased spreads. Using only the probability of default and ignoring the probability of migration from one category to another may give a misleading estimate of the risk exposure. Thus a company that has a very low or even zero probability of default but a high probability of being downgraded will have its credit risk significantly underestimated.

To explain how credit migration may impact on bond values consider a bond which is currently rated as BBB. In a year's time the bond may still be rated BBB, or it may have a higher or lower credit rating. The probability of being at the same or a different rating in a year's time is given in the corresponding row of Table 3 and is reproduced in Table 5.

Table 5: Value of BBB bond for different credit ratings

Year-end rating	Probability of migration
AAA	0.02%
AA	0.33%
A	5.95%
BBB	86.93%
BB	5.30%
B	1.17%
CCC	0.12%
Default	0.18%

As we have discussed, each credit category implies a different credit spread which in turn implies a different cost of debt capital. Table 6 is an example of the cost of debt capital for bonds of different credit ratings and different maturities. The cost of debt capital for a AAA bond with a maturity of one year is 3.6% , whereas the cost of capital for a CCC bond with a maturity of 4 years is 13.52%.

Table 6: Forward rates by credit category (%)

Category	Year 1	Year 2	Year 3	Year 4
AAA	3.60	4.17	4.73	5.12
AA	3.65	4.22	4.78	5.17
A	3.72	4.32	4.93	5.32
BBB	4.10	4.67	5.25	5.63
BB	5.55	6.02	6.78	7.27
B	6.05	7.02	8.03	8.52
CCC	15.05	15.02	14.03	13.52

Source: CreditMetrics Manual

The value of a bond is the **present value** of the coupons and the redemption value, **discounted** using the appropriate cost of debt capital.

For the BBB bond of our example we need to assume a coupon rate and a face value. Suppose the bond has a face value of \$100 and pays an annual coupon of 6%. Using the discount factors from Table 6 we calculate the value of the bond at the end of a year if it remained rated BBB using:

$$P_{BBB} = \frac{6}{1.041} + \frac{6}{(1.0467)^2} + \frac{6}{(1.0525)^3} + \frac{106}{(1.0563)^4} = 101.53$$

If it is upgraded to A, it will be worth \$102.64.

$$P_A = \frac{6}{1.0372} + \frac{6}{(1.0432)^2} + \frac{6}{(1.0493)^3} + \frac{106}{(1.0532)^4} = 102.64$$

If it is downgraded to CCC, it will be worth .\$77.63

$$P_{CCC} = \frac{6}{1.1505} + \frac{6}{(1.1502)^2} + \frac{6}{(1.1403)^3} + \frac{106}{(1.1352)^4} = 77.63$$

Calculating the values of the BBB bond for all possible ratings results in the values that are shown in Table 7.

Table 7: Value of BBB bond for different credit ratings

Year-end rating	bond value
AAA	\$103.35
AA	\$103.17
A	\$102.64
BBB	\$101.53
BB	\$96.01
B	\$92.09
CCC	\$77.63

The value of the bond when it defaults will not be zero, as the issuing firm will have some assets. The available empirical evidence from credit rating agencies shows that about 51 percent of the value of a BBB bond is recovered when the issuing firm defaults.

If bondholders expect to recover in case of bankruptcy,the non-recoverable amount is \$49 per \$100 of face value. The Loss Given Default for a BBB bond will therefore be:

LGD = 0.49 × 100 = \$49

The expected loss for the BBB bond in the example is:

EL = 0.0018 × \$49 = \$0.0882

The low probability of default reduces the credit risk of a BBB bond despite the fact that it loses nearly 50 percent of its value in the case of a default.

3.4 Predicting credit ratings

Exam focus point

> If a question on the Kaplan-Urwitz model comes up in an exam, the formulae will be given.

As we have already discussed in Chapter 15, credit rating companies use financial ratios and other information in order to arrive at the credit score of a company. Many researchers have tried to 'guess' the models that are employed by credit rating agencies and have estimated models which link the observed credit rating to financial characteristics of a company. The first and best known attempt is due to Kaplan and Urwitz in 1979, and the equations they estimated have become known as the Kaplan Urwitz models. The models produce a numerical value which is used to classify a company into a credit rating category.

Their first model which they estimated for quoted companies is

Y = 5.67 + 0.0011 SIZE + 5.13 PROFITABILITY – 2.36 DEBT – 2.85 LEVERAGE + 0.007 INTEREST – 0.87 BETA – 2.90 $\sigma_{UNSYSTEMATIC}$

Y is the score that the model produces.

SIZE is the size of a firm measured in total assets.

PROFITABILITY is net income/total assets.

DEBT is a variable that takes the value of zero if debt is unsubordinated or the value of 1 if the debt is subordinated.

LEVERAGE is long-term debt to total assets.

INTEREST is the useful cover derived as income before taxes and interested dividend by interest payment.

BETA is the beta of the stock estimated using the capital asset pricing model.

$\sigma_{UNSYSTEMATIC}$ is the unsystematic risk estimated as the variance of the residuals from the CAPM regression equation.

The second of Kaplan-Urwitz model was estimated using data on unquoted companies:

Y = 4.41 + 0.001 SIZE = 6.40 PROFITABILITY – 2.56 DEBT – 2.72 LEVERAGE + 0.006 INTEREST – 0.53 COV

where COV is the coefficient of variations of the last five year's of the company's earnings.

The classification of companies into credit rating categories is done in the following way

Score (Y)	*Rating category*
Y > 6.76	AAA
Y > 5.19	AA
Y > 3.28	A
Y > 1.57	BBB
Y > 0	BB

Use the Kaplan-Urwitz model to classify this company.

Key term

> **Unsubordinated debt** is the debt that has priority claim.

In contrast, subordinated debt has no priority claim as it is subordinated to other debt.

Question — Kaplan-Urwitz Model

The following data are available for Epsilon Inc, a software company.

TOTAL ASSETS = $650m

NET INCOME = $250m

TYPE OF DEBT = unsubordinated

LONG-TERM DEBT = $200m

Income before interest and taxes = $500m

Interest payments = $40m

In addition, the following CAPM model was estimated:

$r_{EPSILON}$ = 0.045 + 0.800 ERP

with the stock and market volatility equal to:

$\sigma_{EPSILON} = 22\%$
$\sigma_{MARKET} = 20\%$

Answer

The inputs for the Kaplan-Urwitz model are

SIZE = $650m

PROFITABILITY = Net income/Total assets = 250/650 = 38.5%

DEBT = 0

LEVERAGE = long-term debt/total assets = 200/650 = 30.77

INTEREST = Income before tax and interest/interest payable = 500/40 = 12.50

BETA = 0.800

$\sigma_{UNSYSTEMATIC} = \sqrt{\sigma_{EPSILON}{}^2 - \beta^2\ \sigma_{MARKET}{}^2} = 0.18$ or 18%

Using the data for Epsilon, the Kaplan-Urwitz model yields

$Y = 5.67 + 0.0011 \times 650 + 5.13 \times 0.385 - 2.36 \times 0 - 2.85 \times 0.308 + 0.007 \times 12.5 - 0.87 \times 0.8 - 2.9 \times 0.18 = 6.35$

The model predicts that the company is AA.

3.5 Duration

FAST FORWARD

Duration (also known as Macaulay duration) is the weighted average length of time to the receipt of a bond's benefits (coupon and redemption value), the weights being the present value of the benefits involved.

3.5.1 What is duration?

This calculation gives each bond an overall **risk weighting** that allows two bonds to be compared. In simple terms, it is a **composite** measure of the risk expressed in years.

Duration is the **weighted average** length of time to the receipt of a bond's **benefits** (coupon and redemption value), the weights being the **present value** of the benefits involved.

3.5.2 Calculating duration

Step 1 Multiply the present value of cash flows for each time period by the time period and add together.

Step 2 Add the present value of the cash flows in each time period together.

Step 3 Divide the result of step 1 by the result of step 2

3.5.3 Example of calculating duration

Using an example of a 10%, five-year annual coupon bond trading at £97.25 with a gross redemption yield (GRY) of 10.743%, the duration would be as follows.

	Time period				
	1	2	3	4	5
Flow	10	10	10	10	110
Present value @ GRY	9.03	8.15	7.36	6.66	66.05

Using the above steps, the duration is:

$$\frac{(9.03\times1)+(8.15\times2)+(7.36\times3)+6.66\times4)+(66.05)\times5)}{9.03+8.15+7.36+6.66+66.05}$$

$$\frac{404.3}{97.25} = 4.157 \text{ years}$$

Note that the total present value of the bond's flows of 97.25 is equal to the price, as would be expected.

3.5.4 Properties of duration

The basic features of sensitivity to interest rate risk will all be mirrored in the duration calculation.

- **Longer-dated bonds** will have longer durations.
- **Lower-coupon bonds** will have longer durations. The ultimate low-coupon bond is a zero-coupon bond where the duration will be the maturity.
- **Lower yields** will give longer durations. In this case, the present value of flows in the future will rise if the yield falls, extending the point of balance, therefore lengthening the duration.

The duration of a bond will shorten as the life span of the bond decays. However, the rate of decay will not be at the same rate. In our example above, a five-year bond has a duration of 4.157 years. In a year's time the bond will have a remaining life of four years and a duration based on the same GRY of 3.480 years. The life span has decayed by a full year, but the duration by only 0.677 of a year.

3.6 Modified duration

3.6.1 The use of modified duration

At the same time as the Macaulay duration was being promoted as a means of expressing the sensitivity of a bond to movements in the interest rate, Hicks was developing a formula to explain the impact of yield change on price. Not surprisingly, the two measures are linked.

Hicks' basic proposition was that the change in yield (ΔY), multiplied by this sensitivity measure, would give the proportionate change in price (ΔP).

$$\frac{\Delta P}{P} = -\text{Modified duration} \times \Delta Y$$

which can also be expressed as:

$$\Delta P = -\text{Modified duration} \times \Delta Y \times P$$

3.6.2 The calculation of modified duration

The modified duration used in this formula is Hicks' measure of sensitivity and is simply:

$$\frac{\text{Macaulay duration}}{1 + \text{GRY}} = \text{Modified duration}$$

Using the example from above

$$\text{Modified duration} = \frac{4.157}{1+0.10743} = 3.753$$

As the modified duration is derived from the Macaulay duration, it shares the same properties.

- **Longer dated bonds** will have higher modified durations.
- **Lower coupon bonds** will have higher modified durations.
- **Lower yields** will give higher modified durations.

The higher the modified duration, then the greater the sensitivity of that bond to a change in the yield.

4 Hedging against credit risk

FAST FORWARD

Credit derivatives are financial contracts that isolate specific aspects of credit risk and transfer that risk between two parties.

Credit derivatives separate the ownership and management of credit risk.

Exam focus point

You will be expected to know how derivatives can be used for risk management purposes and how derivatives have developed in the credit markets.

4.1 What are credit derivatives?

Credit derivatives are financial contracts that isolate specific aspects of credit risk from an underlying instrument and transfer that risk between two parties. In doing so, credit derivatives separate the ownership and management of credit risk from other qualitative and quantitative aspects of ownership of financial assets.

The efficiency gains from disaggregating risk can be likened to an auction process. An auctioneer may sell a number of risks individually, each to the highest bidder, rather than selling these risks as an entire 'package'. In most cases the sale of the individual risks will yield a higher aggregate sales price than the 'package' of risks. In other words, by separating specific aspects of credit risk from other risks, credit derivatives allow even the most illiquid credit exposures to be transferred from one portfolio to another, even when the underlying asset cannot be transferred in the same way.

By mid-2007, the volume of credit derivatives was approximately $45.46 trillion – an increase of 32% on the end of 2006. However the credit crunch of late 2007 and early 2008 has had a major effect on the volume of credit derivatives' trading.

4.2 Types of credit derivatives

4.2.1 Credit swaps

A credit swap is a financial contract in which one counterparty (the 'Protection Buyer') pays a periodic fee in return for a contingent payment by the 'Protection Seller' following a 'credit event' with respect to the party whose credit risk is being transferred.

In a credit swap, the buyer is basically buying protection insurance, for a fee, against a credit event on a reference asset they (usually) own.

Credit events are normally defined as the occurrence of one or more of the following.

(a) Failure to meet payment obligations when due.
(b) Bankruptcy
(c) Material adverse restructuring of debt

4.2.2 Credit options

Credit options are put or call options on the price of either

(a) A floating rate note, bond or loan

(b) an 'asset swap' package, which consists of a credit-risky instrument with any payment characteristics and a corresponding derivative contract that exchanges the cash flows of that instrument for a floating rate cash flow stream.

In the case of (a), the credit option grants the option buyer the right, but not the obligation, to sell (put option) or buy (call option) a specified floating rate asset at a pre-specified price (the strike price). Settlement may be on a cash or physical basis.

In the case of (b), the put option buyer would pay a premium for the right to sell an asset to the put option seller and simultaneously enter into a swap in which the put option seller would pay the coupon on the asset and receive three or six month LIBOR plus a predetermined spread (the' strike spread'). The put option seller would make an up-front payment for this combined package when it is exercised.

4.2.3 Uses of credit options

Credit options may be used by borrowers wishing to lock in future borrowing costs without inflating their balance sheet. A borrower with a known future funding requirement could hedge exposure to outright interest rates using interest rate derivatives (see Chapter 20).

Prior to the advent of credit derivatives, exposure to changes in the level of the issuer's borrowing spreads could not be hedged without issuing debt immediately and investing funds in other assets. This had the adverse effect of inflating the current balance sheet unnecessarily and exposing the issuer to reinvestment risk.

4.2.4 Catastrophic risk-transfer (CAT) bonds

The ultimate payoff on derivative transactions is associated with a distinct event, making interest rate risk and credit risk particularly suited to this financial instrument.

CAT bonds embody the closest thing to emerge as a generic structure for unique risks. Such bonds usually take the fom of insurance contracts rather than derivative agreements but still function in a similar way. They protect investors against specific risks such as weather, natural disasters and even record sales for musical artists.

Case Study

(a) Oriental Land Co, the owner and operator of Tokyo Disneyland, hedged the risk of costly property damage due to the park being located on a site in a prime earthquake zone. The company entered into a $200 million privately arranged risk transfer bond, which, in the event of significant earthquake damage within five years of the bond being issued, would pay out for repairs.

(b) Hurricane bonds to the value of $200 million were created for the United Services Automobile Association (USAA) – much of whose clients live in Texas and Florida – to hedge against the possibility of huge property claims in the event of a major hurricane.

5 Assessing default risk using option pricing models

FAST FORWARD

Option pricing models can be used to calculate the expected loss associated with a corporate bond.

Exam focus point

You will not be examined on the numerical derivation of default probability and risk from option pricing models.

5.1 Options and default probability

FAST FORWARD

The role of **option pricing models** in the assessment of **default risk** is based on the **limited liability property** of **equity investments**.

The **equity** of a company can be seen as **a call option** on the **assets** of the company with an **exercise price** equal to the **outstanding debt**.

The role of **option pricing models** in the assessment of **default risk** is based on the **limited liability property** of **equity investments**. Whereas shareholders can participate in a increase in the profits of a company, their losses are limited to the values of their holding. To see how this property is exploited, consider a firm with assets whose market value is denoted by V. Furthermore the firm is assumed to have a very simple capital structure where the acquisition of assets is funded by equity whose market value is denoted by E and by debt with market value D. The balance sheet of this firm is given by

Assets	Liabilities
V	Equity E
	Debt D

The **debt** issued by the firm is a **one year zero coupon bond** with **one year maturity** and **face value F**. The **market value** of **debt** is:

$$D = \frac{F}{1+y}$$

Note that y is not the risk-free return but includes a risk premium over the risk-free rate to reflect the fact that bondholders are exposed to credit risk and they may not receive the promised payment F. This can happen when on the date the debt matures, the value of the assets V_1 are not sufficient to pay the bondholders. The company will default on its debt if $V_1 < F$ in which case bond holders will receive not F but V_1, suffering a loss of $F - V_1$. The lower the value of the assets on maturity the higher the loss suffered by the bond holders.

Equity is a residual claim on the assets of the company and the value of equity on maturity date will be the difference between the value of the assets and the face value of debt. It will be positive if the value of the assets is higher than the outstanding debt, and zero if the value of the assets is lower than the outstanding debt. In summary the value of the equity E_1 will be:

$E_1 = V_1 - F$ if $V_1 > F$

$E_1 = 0$ if $V_1 \leq F$

The value of equity on maturity date is shown in Figure 1 below. The value of equity is positive when $V_1 > F$ and zero when $V_1 \leq F$. Because of the limited liability feature of equity, the lowest value it can reach is zero.

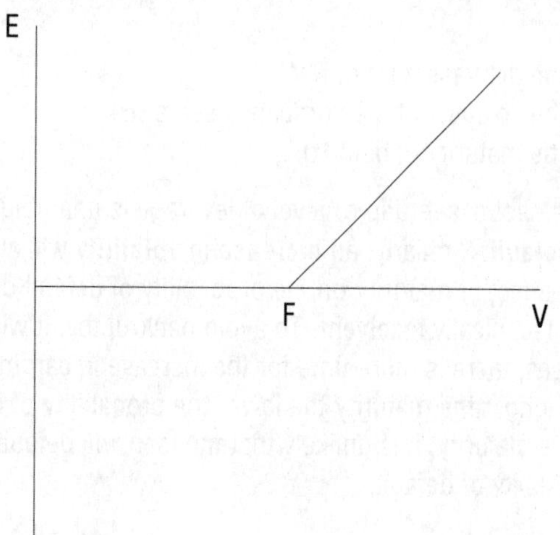

Figure 1

As we have already discussed in Chapter 8, this is the payoff of a call option on the assets of a company with an exercise price equal to the face value of debt F.

The value of the firm's equity can therefore be estimated using a variation of the **Black-Scholes model** for the valuation of a European call option.

$$E = N(d_1)V - N(d_2)Fe^{-rt}$$

$$\text{Where } d_1 = \frac{\ln(V/F) + (r + 0.5\sigma^2)t}{\sigma\sqrt{t}}$$

$$d_2 = d_1 - \sigma\sqrt{t}$$

Where σ = the volatility of V
r = the risk-free rate
t = the time to expiration

The value of $N(d_1)$ shows how the value of equity changes when the value of the assets change. This is the delta of the call option. The value of $N(d_2)$ is the probability that a call option will be in the money at expiration. In this case it is the probability that the value of the asset will exceed the outstanding debt, i.e. $V_1 > F$. The probability of default is therefore given by $1 - N(d_2)$. This is shown as the shaded part in Figure 2 below.

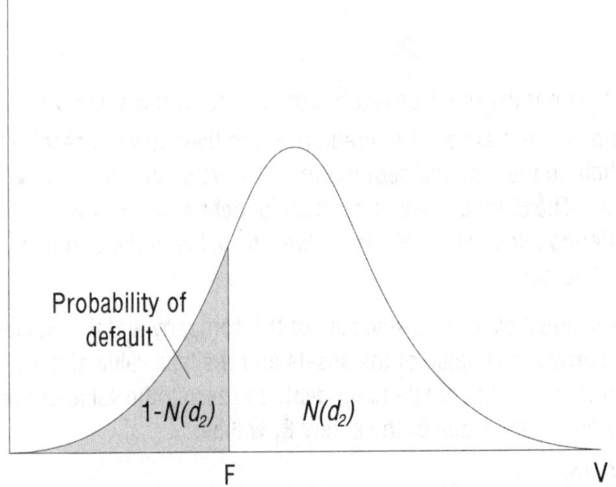

Figure 2

The option pricing model provides useful insights on what determines the probability of default of a bond and it can therefore be used to asses the impact of its determinants on credit risk and the cost of debt capital. From the Black –Scholes formula, it can be seen that the probability of default depends on three factors.

- The debt/asset ratio, F/V
- The volatility of the company assets (σ).
- The maturity of debt (t).

The effect of the debt/asset ratio or level of leverage is unambiguous. A **higher F/V ratio increases** the **probability of default**. Similarly, an **increase** in **volatility** will also **increase** the **probability of default**. Remember that effect of maturity on the probability of default depends on whether F>V or whether F<V. If F>V, the firm is technically insolvent. To avoid bankruptcy, it will need to have increasing earnings. As maturity increases, there is more time for the increase in earnings to occur and for the risk to be reduced. In this case the longer the maturity the lower the probability of default. If F<V and the loan has only a short time to go before maturity, it is unlikely that the loan will default. In this case the longer the maturity the higher the probability of default.

Question

Default Probability

The market value of the assets is $100, and the face value of the 1-year debt is 70. The risk free rate is 5% and the volatility of asset value is 40%. Find the value of the default probability using the Black-Scholes model.

Answer

For this problem we have

V = 100
F = 70
r = ln (1 + 0.05) = 0.0488
σ = 0.40

The Black –Scholes model parameters are:

$$d_1 = \frac{\ln(V/F)+(r+0.5\sigma^2)t}{\sigma\sqrt{t}} = \frac{\ln(100/70)+(0.0488+0.5\times0.4^2)}{0.4} = 1.213$$

d_2 = 1.213 – 0.4 = 0.813

The delta of the option is:

$N(d_1)$ = Probability ($z \le 1.213$) = 0.888 $N(d_2)$ = Probability ($z \le 0.813$) = 0.792

From which we have:

$1 - N(d_2) = 1 - 0.792 = 0.208$

Thus the probability of default is 20.8 percent.

5.2 Options and expected losses

FAST FORWARD

Expected losses are a put option on the assets of the firm with an exercise price equal to the value of the outstanding debt.

Apart from the probability of default the option pricing model can be used to measure the expected loss associated with a corporate bond. We have already stated that bond holders are exposed to credit risk and to losses. The expected loss for the bondholder is

Loss = 0 if V_1>F
Loss = F – V_1 if V_1<F

The expected losses can be seen in Figure 3 below

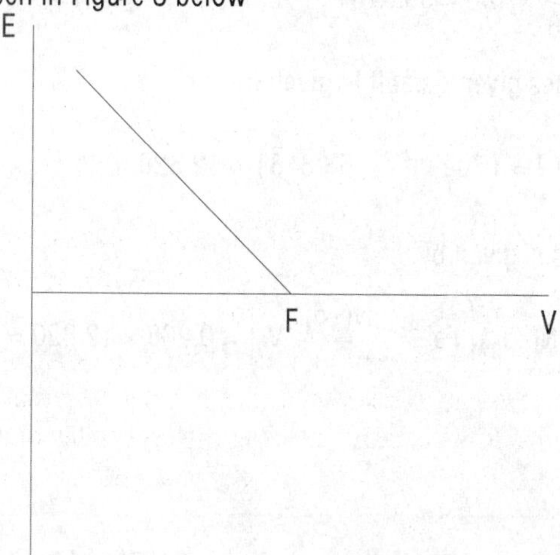

Figure 3

This is the **payoff** of a **put option** written on the **assets** of the **company** V, with **exercise price** F. The expected losses at expiration can be estimated from the **value** of the **put option**. Using the **Black Scholes** model the value of the put option and consequently the expected losses is given by the formula for a European put option with exercise price F and underlying value V:

Put Option = Losses = $(1-N(d_2))Fe^{-rt} - (1-N(-d_1))V$

Using the fact that:

$N(-d_1) = 1 - N(d_1)$ and $N(-d_2) = 1 - N(d_2)$, the formula for a European put option can be written as:

$$\text{Put Option} = \text{Losses} = N(-d_2)Fe^{-rt} - N(-d_1)V$$

The expected losses are represented by the difference between the face value of the bond and the value of the assets which is unknown prior to maturity date. This can be seen by rewriting the formula for the put option as:

$$\text{Put Option} = \text{Expected Loss} = N(-d_2)\left(Fe^{-rt} - \frac{N(-d_1)}{N(-d_2)}V\right)$$

The term $\frac{N(-d_1)}{N(-d_2)}V$ shows the recovery value of the asset.

Question — Recovery value

The market value of the assets is $100, and the face value of the 1-year debt is 70. The risk free rate is 5% and the volatility of asset value is 40%. What is the recovery value and the expected loss?

Answer

We have already found from the previous question that for $V=100$, $F=70$, $r=\ln(1+0.05)=0.0488$, and $s = 0.40$ the Black-Scholes formula yields $d_1=1.213$

$d_2 = 0.813$

$N(d_1) = 0.888$

$N(d_2) = 0.792$

$N(-d_1) = 0.112$

$N(-d_2) = 0.208$

The discounted recovery amount is:

$$\frac{N(-d_1)}{N(-d_2)}V = \frac{0.112}{0.208} \times 100 = 53.846$$

The discounted loss given default is given by

$$\left(Fe^{-rt} - \frac{N(-d_1)}{N(-d_2)}V\right) = \left(70e^{-0.0488} - 53.846\right) = 12.820$$

The expected loss is given by:

$$\text{Expected Loss} = N(-d_2)\left(Fe^{-rt} - \frac{N(-d_1)}{N(-d_2)}V\right) = 0.208 \times 12.820 = \$2.667$$

Question — Equity Value

The market value of the assets of a company is $100, and the face value of the 1-year debt is 70. The risk free rate is 5% and the volatility of asset value is 40%. What is the market value of equity?

Answer

We have already found from the previous questions that for $V=100$, $F=70$, $r=\ln(1+0.05)=0.0488$, and $s = 0.40$ the Black-Scholes formula yields $d_1=1.213$

$d_2 = 0.813$

$N(d_1) = 0.888$

$N(d_2) = 0.792$

$N(-d_1) = 0.112$

$N(-d_2) = 0.208$

Using the Black-Scholes formula for the value of a European call option yields

$$E = N(d_1)V - N(d_2)Fe^{-rt} = 0.888 \times 100 - 0.792 \times 70 \times e^{-0.0488} = \$36.021$$

Question

Credit Spread

The market value of the assets of a company is \$100, and the face value of the 1-year debt is 70. The risk free rate is 5% and the volatility of asset value is 40%. What is the credit spread of the bond?

Answer

We have already found from the previous questions that for V = 100, F = 70, $r = \ln(1 + 0.05) = 0.0488$, and s = 0.40 the Black-Scholes formula yields E = \$36.021

The market value of debt is the discounted present value of the face value, discounted at the interest rate that includes a credit spread:

$$D = \frac{F}{1 + r + s}$$

The credit spread can be calculated by rearranging the above formula:

$$s = \frac{F}{D} - 1 - r$$

The market value of debt is calculated as the difference between the market value of assets and the market value of equity, where the latter is calculated using the Black Scholes model.

The market value of debt is therefore given by:

$D = V - E = 100 - 36.021 = \$63.979$

The credit spread is given by:

$$s = \frac{70}{63.979} - 1 - 0.05 = 0.044 = 4.4\%$$

Chapter Roundup

- The credit rating of a borrower may change after a bond is issued. This is referred to as credit migration.
- The cost of debt capital and the market price of corporate bonds depend on the credit risk of the bond.
- The deterioration in the credit quality of a bond, referred to as credit migration, will affect the market value of the bond.
- Duration (also known as Macaulay duration) is the weighted average length of time to the receipt of a bond's benefits (coupon and redemption value), the weights being the present value of the benefits involved.
- Credit derivatives are financial contracts that isolate specific aspects of credit risk and transfer that risk between two parties.
- Credit derivatives separate the ownership and management of credit risk.
- Option pricing models can be used to calculate the expected loss associated with a corporate bond.
- The role of **option pricing models** in the assessment of **default risk** is based on the **limited liability property** of **equity investments**.

  The **equity** of a company can be seen as **a call option** on the **assets** of the company with an **exercise price** equal to the **outstanding debt.**
- Expected losses are a put option on the assets of the firm with an exercise price equal to the value of the outstanding debt.

Quick Quiz

1. You have invested in a bond with a default probability of 10 percent. In the event of default you hold collateral that amount to about 70 percent of the value of the bond. What is your expected loss?
2. What is the relationship between credit rating and the cost of debt capital?
3. What is the most likely rating next year of a BBB bond?
4. What will happen to the value of a corporate bond if its credit rating is downgraded?
5. Explain why the equity liability of a company can be considered as a call option.
6. If the equity of a company is considered as a call option on the underlying assets what is the exercise price of the call option?
7. What are the factors that determine the probability of default according to the option pricing approach?

Answers to Quick Quiz

1 The expected loss is equal to 0.10 x (1-0.70) = 0.03 or 3 percent.

2 The lower the credit rating the higher the credit spread and consequently the higher the cost of capital.

3 From the historical migration tables the most likely rating for a BBB bond will be a BBB rating.

4 The value of the bond will fall.

5 Because of the limited liability provision, the loss arising from holding equity is limited to zero, whereas there is unlimited profit.

6 If the equity of a company is considered as a call option on the underlying assets, the exercise price of the call option is the value of the outstanding debt.

7 The debt to equity ratio
The volatility of the company assets
The maturity of the debt

Now try the question below from the Exam Question Bank

Number	Level	Marks	Time
34	Examination	10	18 mins

Dividend policy in multinationals and transfer pricing

Topic list	Syllabus reference
1 Dividend capacity	E (5) (a)
2 Dividend repatriation policies	E (5) (a)
3 Transfer pricing	E (5) (b)
4 Regulation of transfer pricing	E (5) (b)

Introduction

Multinational companies have operations in the form of **subsidiaries**, **affiliates** or **joint ventures** in more than one country and produce and sell products around the world. The revenues of international operations are repatriated to the parent company in the form of dividends, royalties or licences. Overseas operations can therefore have a significant impact on the parent company's ability to pay dividends to its external shareholders or to finance its investment plans.

Multinational companies are either **horizontally integrated** (different affiliates produce the same product in different markets) or **vertically integrated** (upstream affiliates produce intermediate products that are further processed by downstream affiliates prior to final sale) or both. Irrespective of their organisation structure multinational companies are integrated enterprises, their affiliates engage in substantial amounts of intrafirm transactions.

This chapter examines the **dividend capacity** of a **multinational company** and how it is affected by dividend repatriation, investment plans and share repurchases. It also discusses factors, such as tax, managerial incentives and timing that may affect dividend repatriation. The chapter then examines the various economic, tax and legal factors which may influence the choice of transfer pricing used in multinational corporations. Motives for the setting of transfer prices are analysed, along with guidelines that multinational companies need to observe in order to prevent them from exploiting the host country.

Study guide

		Intellectual level
E5	**Dividend policy in multinationals and transfer pricing**	
(a)	Determine a firm's dividend capacity and its policy given: (i) The firm's short- and long-term reinvestment strategy (ii) The impact of any other capital reconstruction programmes on free cash flow to equity such as share repurchase agreements and new capital issues (iii) The availability and timing of central remittances (iv) The corporate tax regime within the host jurisdiction	3
(b)	Develop company policy on the transfer pricing of goods and services across international borders and be able to determine the most appropriate transfer pricing strategy in a given situation reflecting local regulations and tax regimes.	3

1 Dividend capacity

FAST FORWARD

The dividend capacity of a company depends on its after tax profits, investment plans and foreign dividends.

Exam focus point

There was a six mark section in a compulsory 30 mark question in the December 2007 exam that asked students to calculate a multinational company's maximum dividend capacity.

We have already discussed how to estimate the dividend capacity of a firm in Chapter 6. Here we extend the treatment to the case of a multinational company and highlight the role of special factors such as remittances from subsidiaries, and the timing of payments.

The starting point again is the cash budget identity which may be expressed as follows:

Sources = Uses

$$R_t + FD_t + \Delta S_t + \Delta B_t = OE_t + Int_t + Div_t + Taxes_t + \Delta I_t + \Delta WC_t$$

where subscript (t) is used to index these components of cash flow according to date, and

- R = operating revenue from domestic operations
- FD = Dividends from foreign affiliates and subsidiaries
- ΔS = net equity issuance (i.e., new issues net of repurchases)
- ΔB = net debt issuance (i.e., new borrowing net of repayment)
- OE = operating costs
- Int = interest payments on debt, less any interest income
- Div = dividends on common stock
- Taxes = total taxes paid
- Dep = Depreciation
- ΔI = net investment in non-current assets (ie net of asset sales)
- ΔWC = net investment in working capital, inclusive of cash and marketable securities.

The potential dividend that can be paid, ie the dividend capacity of the firm can be estimated by rearranging the terms in the above equation.

$$Div_t = [R_t - OE_t - Int_t - Taxes_t] + FD_t - [\Delta I_t + \Delta WC_t] + \Delta B_t + \Delta S_t$$

Adding and subtracting depreciation the above equation can be restated as the **Free Cash Flow to Equity** (FCFE).

$$FCFE_t = [R_t - OE_t - Dep_t - Int_t - Taxes_t] + Dep_t + FD_t - [\Delta I_t + \Delta WC_t] + \Delta B_t + \Delta S_t$$

= Net profit after tax + Depreciation + Foreign Dividends – Total Net Investment + Net debt Issuance + Net Share Issuance

The FCFE represents dividends that could be paid to shareholders. This is usually not the same as actual dividends in a given year because normally the management of a company deliberately smoothes dividend payments across time. In the rest of this section we look in greater detail at three of the factors, total net investment, share repurchases and foreign dividends.

Exam focus point

You should know how the various parts of the FCFE equation affect dividend capacity.

1.1 Effect of investment plans

Total net investment is the single most important factor in determining dividend payouts to the shareholders. According to pecking order hypothesis funding investments with internal funds is the first choice of management, followed by borrowing or share issues. Consequently, fast growing companies would be associated with low dividend distributions.

1.2 Effect of share repurchases

A company that opts to repurchase its shares transfers funds from the company to the shareholders. The repurchase is financed from the firm's distributable reserves. The effect of a share repurchase is to increase the earnings per share, as the number of issued shares is reduced. The evidence suggests that markets react favourably to announcements of share repurchases. The rationale for the positive reaction is that when there are no investment opportunities then it is preferable for the excess cash to be returned to shareholders rather than to be retained within the company.

Share repurchases as a method of distribution represented a larger amount than dividends in the US. The reason for this is the more favourable tax treatment of share repurchases, which is subject to capital gains tax, whereas dividend payments are subject to income tax which is higher.

1.3 Dividends from overseas operations

Corporations paying dividends to common shareholders could, for example, fund these payments by triggering repatriations. Repatriations help parent companies meet their financing needs as larger dividends to external shareholders are associated with larger dividend repatriations inside the firm, and highly levered parent companies with profitable domestic investment opportunities draw more heavily on the resources of their foreign affiliates. In fact dividend repatriations represent sizeable financial flows for the US companies. For example in 1999 U.S. corporations listed in Compustat paid $198 billion in dividends to common shareholders and foreign affiliates of U.S. multinational firms repatriated $97 billion to the United States as dividends.

The importance of repatriated dividends is not limited to quoted companies, which it may be argued face pressure from the markets to distribute dividends to shareholders. Even private companies rely heavily on their overseas subsidiaries to finance dividend distributions. The evidence suggests that this is happening even when dividend repatriation is not tax efficient.

2 Dividend repatriation policies

FAST FORWARD

The amount of dividends subsidiaries pay to the parent company depend on the parent company's dividend policies, financing needs, taxation and managerial control.

The choice of whether to repatriate earnings from a foreign subsidiary is one of the most important decisions in multinational financial management. As mentioned in the previous section dividend repatriations represent significant financial flows for parent companies and contribute to dividend payments. The factors that affect dividend repatriation policies can be grouped as follows:

(a) Financing Factors
(b) Tax Factors
(c) Managerial Factors
(d) Timing Factors

2.1 Financing factors

Note that the equation for repatriated dividends can be written in terms of its use as:

$$FD_t = Div_t + \Delta I_t + \Delta WC_t - [R_t - OE_t - Taxes_t - Int_t] - [\Delta S_t + \Delta B_t]$$

The equation shows that the factors that shape **repatriation dividend policy** within the multinational firm are the **payment of dividends to external shareholders**, the level **of investment planned by the parent company, after tax profits** and **financing policies**.

Repatriation policies may reflect financing concerns of parents who draw on subsidiary cash flows to finance domestic expenses. Two examples of such domestic expenses are **dividend payments** to **external shareholders** and **capital expenditures in the home countries**.

2.2 Investment financing

Dividend repatriations from foreign affiliates may offer an attractive source of finance for domestic investment expenditures, despite possible associated tax costs especially, when alternative forms of finance are costly. This is true for parent companies with profitable domestic investment opportunities that already maintain large amounts of external debt and do not wish to increase the level of borrowing even further. Another case is when companies need to expand fast into areas and profitability is not sufficient to finance the expansion.

One of the strong implications of the U.S. tax treatment of foreign income is that American multinational corporations should not simultaneously remit dividends from low-tax foreign locations and transfer equity funds into the same foreign locations. Doing so generates a home-country tax liability that could be easily avoided simply by reducing both dividends and equity transfers.

2.3 Dividend policy

Dividend repatriations from foreign affiliates may also offer an attractive source of finance for payments of dividends to common shareholders especially when the parent company may prefer a smooth dividend payment pattern and domestic profitability is in decline. The dividend payments of a subsidiary may also be affected by the dividend policy of the parent company. For example if the parent company operates a constant payout ratio policy, then the subsidiary will have to adopt a constant payout ratio policy too.

The empirical evidence shows (Desai, Foley and Hines (2001)) that dividend payments to parent companies tend to be regular and multinational firms behave as though they select target payouts for their foreign affiliates, gradually adjusting payouts over time in response to changes in earnings.

2.4 Tax regime and dividend payments

Tax considerations are thought to be the primary reason for the dividend policies inside the multinational firm. For example the parent company may reduce its overall tax liability by, for example, receiving larger amounts of dividends from subsidiaries in countries where undistributed earnings are taxed.

For subsidiaries of UK companies, all foreign profits, whether repatriated or not, are liable to UK corporation tax, with a credit for the tax that has already been paid to the host country. Similarly, the US government does not distinguish between income earned abroad and income earned at home and gives credit to MNCs headquartered in the US for the amount of tax paid to foreign governments.

Example

Assume that the corporate tax rate in the home country is 40% and in the overseas country where a subsidiary is located is 30 percent. Assume that both the parent company and the subsidiary have pretax profits of $1000.

Taxes to foreign government = 1000 × 30% = 300
MNC's profit after foreign tax = 1,000 – 300 = 700

US taxes = 1000 × 40% = 400
Foreign tax credit = 300
Net tax to IRS = 400 – 300 = 100.
Total taxes = 300 + 100 = 400.

2.5 Managerial control

Another reason that may determine repatriation policies is the inability to fully monitor foreign managers. Regularized dividend payments restrict the financial discretion of foreign managers, thereby reducing associated agency problems. Conflicts of interest are most apt to arise when ownership is divided, as local owners may influence managers to undertake transactions at other than market prices. Control considerations inside the firm may explain the tax-penalized behaviour especially when affiliates are partially owned.

Finally, the desire to control corporate managers around the world carries implications for dividend policies. A multinational firm's central management can use financial flows within the firm to evaluate the financial prospects and needs of far-flung foreign affiliates and to limit the discretion of foreign managers. As this observation suggests, it may be sensible to mandate dividend payments to police and monitor foreign managers, limit their ability to misallocate funds, and to extract returns on investments – much as public shareholders use dividends to monitor and control their firms.

2.6 Timing of dividend payments

So far we have concentrated on the size of repatriated dividends. The timing of payments may also be equally important. For example, a subsidiary may adjust its dividend payments to a parent company in order to benefit from expected movements in exchange rates. A company would like to collect early (lead) payments from currencies vulnerable to depreciation and to collect late (lag) from currencies which are expected to appreciate.

Also given that tax liabilities are triggered by repatriation, these tax liabilities can be deferred by reinvesting earnings abroad rather than remitting dividends to parent companies. The incentive to defer repatriation is much stronger for affiliates in low-tax countries, whose dividends trigger significant parent tax obligations, than they are for affiliates in high-tax countries – particularly since taxpayers receive net credits for repatriations from affiliates in countries with tax rates that exceed the parent country tax rate.

3 Transfer pricing

FAST FORWARD

Transfer prices are set by the multinational corporation not only to recover the cost of services and goods provided but also to achieve objectives such as tax liability minimisation and to offset host country policies.

Multinational corporations supply their affiliates with capital, technology, and managerial skills, for which the parent firm receives a stream of dividend and interest payments, royalties, and license fees. At the same time significant intrafirm transfers of goods and services also occur. For example the subsidiary may provide the parent company with raw materials, whereas the parent company may provide the subsidiary with final goods for distribution to consumers in the host country. For intrafirm trade both the parent company and the subsidiary need to charge prices. These prices for goods, technology, or services between wholly or partly owned affiliates of the multinational are called **transfer prices**.

Key term

A **transfer price** may be defined as the price at which goods or services are transferred from one process or department to another or from one member of a group to another.

The extent to which costs and profit are covered by the transfer price is a matter of company policy. A transfer price may be based upon any of the following.

- Standard cost
- Marginal cost: at marginal cost or with a gross profit margin added

- Opportunity cost
- Full cost: at full cost, or at a full cost plus price
- Market price
- Market price less a discount
- Negotiated price, which could be based on any of the other bases

A transfer price based on cost might be at **marginal cost** or **full cost**, with no profit or contribution margin but in a profit centre system it is more likely to be a price based on **marginal cost** or **full cost** plus a margin for contribution or profit. This is to allow profit centres to make a profit on work they do for other profit centres, and so earn a reward for their effort and use of resources on the work.

Transfers based on **market price** might be any of the following.

(a) The **actual market price** at which the transferred goods or services could be sold on an external market

(b) The **actual external market price**, minus an amount that reflects the savings in costs (for example selling costs and bad debts) when goods are transferred internally

(c) The **market price** of **similar goods** which are sold on an external market, although the transferred goods are not exactly the same and do not themselves have an external market

(d) A **price** sufficient to give an appropriate share of profit to each party

3.1 The level of transfer prices

The size of the transfer price will affect the costs of one profit centre and the revenues of another. Since profit centre managers are held accountable for their costs, revenues, and profits, they are likely to **dispute** the size of transfer prices with each other, or disagree about whether one profit centre should do work for another or not. Transfer prices affect behaviour and decisions by profit centre managers.

If managers of individual profit centres are tempted to take decisions that are harmful to other divisions and are not congruent with the goals of the organisation as a whole, the problem is likely to emerge in disputes about the transfer price.

Disagreements about output levels tend to focus on the transfer price. There is presumably a profit-maximising level of output and sales for the organisation as a whole. However, unless each profit centre also **maximises** its **own profit** at the corresponding level of output, there will be **inter-divisional disagreements** about output levels and the profit-maximising output will not be achieved.

3.2 The advantages of market value transfer prices

Giving profit centre managers the freedom to negotiate prices with other profit centres as though they were independent companies will tend to result in **market-based transfer prices**.

(a) In most cases where the transfer price is at market price, internal transfers should be expected, because the buying division is likely to benefit from a **better quality of service**, **greater flexibility**, and **dependability of supply**.

(b) Both divisions may benefit from **lower costs** of **administration**, **selling** and **transport**.

A market price as the transfer price would therefore result in decisions which would be in the best interests of the company or group as a whole.

3.3 The disadvantages of market value transfer prices

Market value as a transfer price does have certain disadvantages.

(a) The **market price** may be **temporary**, induced by adverse economic conditions, or dumping, or the market price might depend on the volume of output supplied to the external market by the profit centre.

(b) A **transfer price** at market value might, under some circumstances, act as a **disincentive** to use up any spare capacity in the divisions. A price based on incremental cost, in contrast, might provide an incentive to use up the spare resources in order to provide a marginal contribution to profit.

(c) Many products do **not have** an **equivalent market price**, so that the price of a similar product might be chosen. In such circumstances, the option to sell or buy on the open market does not exist.

(d) There might be an **imperfect external market** for the transferred item, so that if the transferring division tried to sell more externally, it would have to reduce its selling price.

(e) **Internal transfers** are often **cheaper** than **external sales**, with savings in selling costs, bad debt risks and possibly transport costs. It would therefore seem reasonable for the buying division to expect a discount on the external market price, and to negotiate for such a discount.

Question — Transfer pricing

A company has two profit centres, X and Y. Each will work at full capacity. X's total annual costs are £3,570,000 and Y's total annual costs excluding purchases from X are $1,500,000. 40% of X's output is transferred to Y, and the remaining 60% is sold externally for $4,800,000. All of Y's output is sold externally for $7,000,000.

Compute the profits of X, Y and the company as a whole:

(a) Using a transfer price equal to market value
(b) Using a transfer price equal to full cost

Answer

(a) *Transfer price equal to market value*

	X		*Y*		*Total*
	$'000	$'000	$'000	$'000	$'000
External sales		4,800		7,000	11,800
Transfer sales		3,200		0	
		8,000		7,000	
Transfer costs	0		3,200		
Own costs	3,570		1,500		5,070
		3,570		4,700	
Profit		4,430		2,300	6,730

(b) *Transfer price equal to full cost*

	X		*Y*		*Total*
	$'000	$'000	$'000	$'000	$'000
External sales		4,800		7,000	11,800
Transfer sales*		1,428		0	
		6,228		7,000	
Transfer costs	0		1,428		
Own costs	3,570		1,500		5,070
		3,570		2,928	
		2,658		4,072	6,730

* (3,570 × 0.4)

3.4 Example: Transfer prices

A multinational company based in Beeland has subsidiary companies in Ceeland and in the UK. The UK subsidiary manufactures machinery parts which are sold to the Ceeland subsidiary for a unit price of B$420 (420 Beeland dollars), where the parts are assembled. The UK subsidiary shows a profit of B$80 per unit; 200,000 units are sold annually.

The Ceeland subsidiary incurs further costs of B$400 per unit and sells the finished goods on for an equivalent of B$1,050.

All of the profits from the foreign subsidiaries are remitted to the parent company as dividends. Double taxation treaties between Beeland, Ceeland and the UK allow companies to set foreign tax liabilities against their domestic tax liability.

The following rates of taxation apply.

	UK	*Beeland*	*Ceeland*
Tax on company profits	25%	35%	40%
Withholding tax on dividends	–	12%	10%

Required

Show the tax effect of increasing the transfer price between the UK and Ceeland subsidiaries by 25%.

Solution

The current position is as follows.

	UK company B$'000	*Ceeland company* B$'000	*Total* B$'000
Revenues and taxes in the local country			
Sales	84,000	210,000	294,000
Production expenses	(68,000)	(164,000)	(232,000)
Taxable profit	16,000	46,000	62,000
Tax (1)	(4,000)	(18,400)	(22,400)
Dividends to Beeland	12,000	27,600	39,600
Withholding tax (2)	0	2,760	2,760
Revenues and taxes in Beeland			
Dividend	12,000	27,600	39,600
Add back foreign tax paid	4,000	18,400	22,400
Taxable income	16,000	46,000	62,000
Beeland tax due	5,600	16,100	21,700
Foreign tax credit	(4,000)	(16,100)	(20,100)
Tax paid in Beeland (3)	1,600	–	1,600
Total tax (1) + (2) + (3)	5,600	21,160	26,760

An increase of 25% in the transfer price would have the following effect.

	UK company B$'000	*Ceeland company* B$'000	*Total* B$'000
Revenues and taxes in the local country			
Sales	105,000	210,000	315,000
Production expenses	(68,000)	(185,000)	(253,000)
Taxable profit	37,000	25,000	62,000
Tax (1)	(9,250)	(10,000)	(19,250)
Dividends to Beeland	27,750	15,000	42,750
Withholding tax (2)	0	1,500	1,500
Revenues and taxes in Beeland			
Dividend	27,750	15,000	42,750
Add back foreign tax paid	9,250	10,000	19,250
Taxable income	37,000	25,000	62,000
Beeland tax due	12,950	8,750	21,700
Foreign tax credit	(9,250)	(8,750)	(18,000)
Tax paid in Beeland (3)	3,700	–	3,700
Total tax (1) + (2) + (3)	12,950	11,500	24,450

The total tax payable by the company is therefore reduced by B$2,310,000 to B$24,450,000.

3.5 Motivations for transfer pricing

In deciding on their transfer pricing policies, multinational companies take into account many internal and external factors or motivations for transfer pricing. In terms of internal motivations these include

Performance evaluation

When different affiliates within a multinational are treated as stand-alone profit centres, transfer prices are needed internally by the multinational to determine profitability of the individual divisions. Transfer prices which deviate too much from the actual prices will make it difficult to properly monitor the performance of an affiliated unit.

Management incentives

If transfer prices are used for internal measures of performance by individual affiliates deviate from the true economic prices, and managers are evaluated and rewarded on the basis of the distorted profitability, then it may result in corporate managers behaving in an irresponsible way.

Cost Allocation

When units within the multinational are run as cost centres, subsidiaries are charged a share of the costs of providing the group service function so that the service provider covers its costs plus a small mark-up. Lower or higher transfer prices may result in a subsidiary bearing less or more of the overheads.

Financing Considerations

Transfer pricing may be used in order to boost the profitability of a subsidiary, with the parent company undercharging the subsidiary. Such a boost in the profitability and its credit rating may be needed by the subsidiary in order to succeed in obtaining funds from the host country.

Transfer pricing can also be used to disguise the profitability of the subsidiary in order to justify high prices for its products in the host country and to be able to resist demands for higher wages.

Several external motivations can affect the multinational's choice of transfer prices. Because multinationals operate in two or more jurisdictions, transfer prices must be assigned for intrafirm trade that crosses national borders.

Taxes

Multinational corporations use transfer pricing to channel profits out of high tax rate countries into lower ones. A parent company may sell goods at lower than normal prices to its subsidiaries in lower tax rate countries and buy from them at higher than normal prices. The resultant loss in the parent's high tax country adds significantly to the profits of the subsidiaries . An MNC reports most of its profits in a low-tax country, even though the actual profits are earned in a high tax country.

Tariffs

Border taxes such as tariffs and export taxes, are often levied on crossborder trade. Where the tax is levied on an ad valorem basis, the higher the transfer price, the larger the tax paid per unit. Whether a MNC will follow high transfer price strategy or not may depend on its impact on the tax burden. When border taxes are levied on a per-unit basis (i.e. specific taxes), the transfer price is irrelevant for tax purposes.

Rule of Origin Rule

Another external factor is the need to meet the rule of origin that applies to crossborder flows within a free trade area. Since border taxes are eliminated within the area, rules of origin must be used to determine eligibility for duty-free status. Over-or under-invoicing inputs is one way to avoid customs duties levied on products that do not meet the rule of origin test.

Exchange Control and Quotas

Transfer pricing can be used to avoid currency controls in the host country. For example a constraint in profit repatriation could be avoided by the parent company charging higher prices for raw materials, or higher fees for services provided to the subsidiary. The parent company will have higher profits and a higher tax liability and the subsidiary will have lower profitability and a lower tax liability.

When the host country restricts the amount of foreign exchange that can be used to import goods, then a lower transfer price allows a greater quantity of goods to be imported.

4 Regulation of transfer pricing

FAST FORWARD

Multinational companies have to adhere to pricing guidelines to prevent exploitation of the host country.

4.1 The problem of transfer price manipulation

As we have discussed in the previous section, transfer pricing is a normal, legitimate, and, in fact, required activity. Firms set prices on intrafirm transactions for a variety of perfectly legal and rational internal reasons, and, even where pricing is not required for internal reasons, governments may require it in order to determine how much tax revenues and customs duties are owed by the multinational corporation. **Transfer price manipulation** on the other hand exists, when multinational companies use transfer prices to evade or avoid payment of taxes and tariffs, or other controls that the government of the host country has put in place.

Governments worry about transfer price manipulation because they are concerned with the loss of revenues through tax avoidance or evasion and they dislike the loss of control. Overall MNC profits after taxes may be raised by either under-or over-invoicing the transfer price; such manipulation for tax purposes, however, comes at the expense of distorting other goals of the firm, in particular, evaluating management performance.

4.2 The arm's length standard

Key term

The **arm's length standard** states that intra-firm trade of multinationals should be priced as if they took place between unrelated parties acting at arm's length in competitive markets.

The most common solution that tax authorities have adopted to reduce the probability of the transfer price manipulation is to develop particular transfer pricing regulations as part of the corporate income tax code. These regulations are generally based on the concept of the arm's length standard, which says that all MNC intra-firm activities should be priced as if they took place between unrelated parties acting at arm's length in competitive markets. The 1979 OECD Report defines the arm's length standard as "prices which would have been agreed upon between unrelated parties engaged in the same or similar transactions under the same or similar conditions in the open market" (OECD 1979).

The arm's length standard has two methods.

Method 1: use the price negotiated between two unrelated parties C and D to proxy for the transfer between A and B.

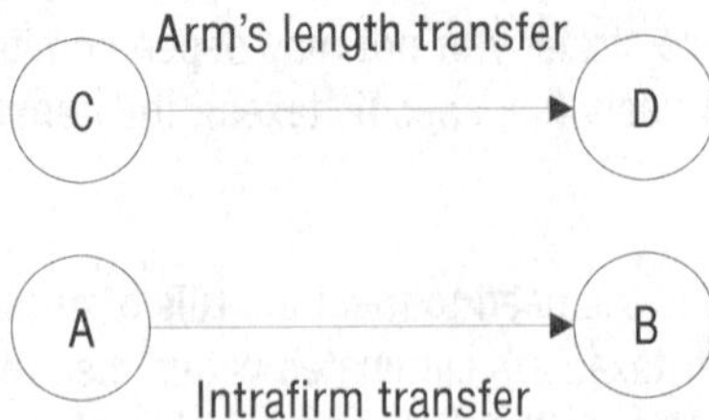

Method 2: use the price at which A sells to unrelated party C to proxy for the transfer price between A and B.

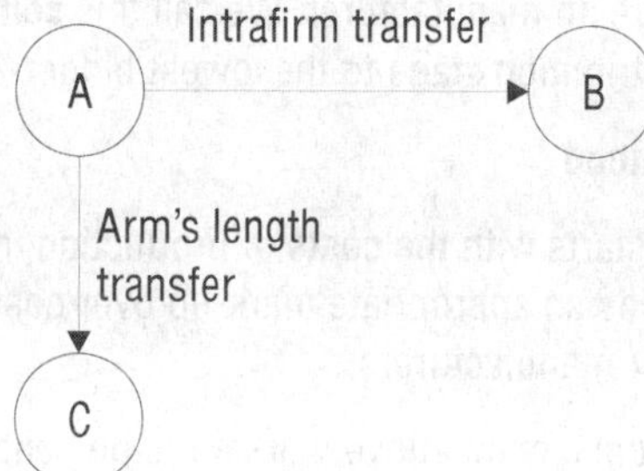

In practice, the method used will depend on the available data. That is the existence of unrelated parties that engage in the same, or nearly the same, transactions under the same or nearly the same, circumstances. Does one of the related parties also engage in the same, or nearly the same, transactions with an unrelated party under the same, or nearly the same circumstances? Where there are differences, are they quantifiable? Do the results seem reasonable in the circumstances?

If the answers to these questions are yes, then the arm's length standard will yield a reasonable result. If the answers are no, then alternative methods must be used.

The main methods of establishing "arm's length" transfer prices of tangible goods include:

- comparable uncontrolled price (CUP)
- resale price (RP)
- cost plus (C+)
- comparable profit method(CPM)
- profit split (PS)

The first three are transactions-based approach, while the latter two are profit-based.

The comparable uncontrolled price (CUP) method

The CUP method looks for a comparable product to the transaction in question, either in terms of the same product being bought or sold by the MNC in a comparable transaction with an unrelated party, or the same or similar product being traded between two unrelated parties under the same or similar circumstances. The product so identified is called a **product comparable**. All the facts and circumstances that could materially affect the price must be considered.

Tax authorities prefer the CUP method over all other pricing methods for at least two reasons. First, it incorporates more information about the specific transaction than does any other method; ie it is transaction and product specific. Second, CUP takes both the interests of the buyer and seller into account since it looks at the price as determined by the intersection of demand and supply.

The resale price method (RPM)

Where a product comparable is not available, and the *CUP* method cannot be used, an alternative method is to focus on one side of the transaction, either the manufacturer or the distributor, and to estimate the transfer price using a functional approach.

Under the resale price method, the tax auditor looks for firms at similar trade levels that perform similar distribution function (ie. a **functional comparable***)*. The **RPM** method is best used when the distributor adds relatively little value to the product so that the value of its functions is easier to estimate. The assumption behind the **RP** method is that competition among distributors means that similar margins (returns) on sales are earned for similar functions.

The resale price method backs into the transfer price by subtracting a profit margin, derived from margins earned by comparable distributors engaged in comparable functions, from the known retail price to determine the transfer price. As a result, the **RPM** method evaluates the transaction only in terms of **the buyer**. The method ensures that the buyer receives an arm's length return consistent with returns earned by similar firms engaged in similar transactions. Since the resale margin is determined in an arm's length manner, but nothing is done to ensure that the manufacturer's profit margin is consistent with margins earned by other manufacturers, the adjustment is one-sided. Under the RPM method, having determined

the buyer's arm's length margin, all excess profit on the transaction is assigned to the seller. Thus the resale price method tends to **overestimate** the transfer price since it gives all unallocated profits on the transaction to the upstream manufacturer. We call this **contract distributor** case, since the manufacturer is contracting out the distribution stage to the lowest bidder.

The cost plus (C+) method

The cost plus method starts with the costs of production, measured using recognized accounting principles, and then adds an appropriate mark-up over costs. The appropriate mark-up is estimated from those earned by similar manufacturers.

The assumption is that in a competitive market the percentage mark-ups over cost that could be earned by other arms length manufacturers would be roughly the same. The cost plus method works best when the producer is a simple manufacturer without complicated activities so that its costs and returns can be move easily estimated.

In order to use the cost plus method, the tax authority or the multinational company must know the accounting approach adopted by the unrelated parties. Such as what costs are included in the cost base before the mark-up over costs is calculated? Is it actual cost or standard cost?

Are only manufacturing costs included or is the cost base the sum of manufacturing costs plus some portion of operating costs? The larger the cost base, the smaller should be the profit mark-up, or gross margin, over costs.

The comparable profit (CPM) method

The comparable profits method is based on the premise that companies in similar industries will tend to have similar financial performance and to have similar financial characteristics. This similarity in performance will be indicated by the similarity in financial ratios. For instance if the return on assets (ROA) is the profit level indicator, then knowledge of the rate of ROAs for comparable companies or for the industry coupled with knowledge of the assets of the company would determine the taxable profits of the company.

The comparable profits method (CPM) has the following shortcomings: (1) it is not a transactions-based method, (2) it does not take the contractual obligations of the parties into account, (3) it does not reflect the facts and circumstances of the case, and (4) it could lead to substantial double taxation of income if other governments did not accept the method.

The Profit Split Method (PSM)

When there are no suitable product comparables (the *CUP* method) or functional comparables (the RPM and C+ methods), the most common alternative method is the profit split (PSM) method, whereby the profits on a transaction earned by two related parties are split between the parties.

The profit split method allocates the consolidated profit from a transaction, or group of transactions, between the related parties. Where there are no comparables that can be used to estimate the transfer price, this method provides an alternative way to calculate or 'back into' the transfer price. The most commonly recommended ratios to split the profits on the transaction between the related parties is return on operating assets (the ratio of operating profits to operating assets).

The profit split method ensures that both related parties earn the same return on assets; the CPM, on the other hand, ensures that one of the two parties earns the average or median of returns earned by comparable uncontrolled parties. CPM is somewhat like the cost plus and resale price methods in that it focuses on only one side of total profits whereas the PS method looks to both sides.

Chapter Roundup

- The dividend capacity of a company depends on its after tax profits, investment plans and foreign dividends.
- The amount of dividends subsidiaries pay to the parent company depend on the parent company's dividend policies, financing needs, taxation and managerial control.
- Transfer prices are set by the multinational corporation not only to recover the cost of services and goods provided but also to achieve objectives such as tax liability minimisation and to offset host country policies.
- Multinational companies have to adhere to pricing guidelines to prevent exploitation of the host country.

Quick Quiz

1 What are the main motivations for transfer pricing?

2 What is meant by transfer price manipulation?

3 What are the main methods of establishing "arm's length" transfer prices?

4 What are the main factors that affect dividend repatriation policies?

Answers to Quick Quiz

The main motivations for transfer pricing are:

1 (a) Performance evaluation
  (b) Management incentives
  (c) Cost Allocation
  (d) Financing Considerations
  (e) Taxes
  (f) Tariffs
  (g) Rule of Origin Rule
  (h) Exchange Control and Quotas

2 *Transfer price manipulation* is the use of transfer prices to avoid the payment of taxes or tarrifs.

3 The main methods of establishing an "arm's length transfer price" are:

- Comparable uncontrolled price (CUP)
- Resale price (RP)
- Cost plus (C+)
- Comparable profit method(CPM)
- Profit split (PS)

4 The main factors that affect dividend repatriation policies are:

  (a) Financing Factors
  (b) Tax Factors
  (c) Managerial Factors
  (d) Timing Factors

Now try the question below from the Exam Question Bank

Number	Level	Marks	Time
35	Introductory	10	18

PART F

Economic environment for multinationals

Management of international trade and finance

Topic list	Syllabus reference
1 Theory and practice of international trade	F 1(a)
2 Trade agreements	F 1(b)
3 The World Trade Organisation (WTO)	F 1(c)
4 International monetary institutions	F 1(d)
5 International financial markets and global financial stability	F 1(e)

Introduction

In this chapter we look at the international environment within which companies need to make financial decisions. We discuss the growth of international trade and its benefits and risks for the corporation, the development of common markets and free trade areas, the establishment of the World Trade Organisation and the role of international financial institutions such as the World Bank and the International Monetary Fund. Finally we discuss how the globalisation of international markets facilitates the flow of funds to emerging markets but may create instability.

Study guide

		Intellectual level
F1	**Management of international trade and finance**	
(a)	Advise on the theory and practice of free trade and the management of barriers to trade	3
(b)	Demonstrate an up to date understanding of the major trade agreements and common markets and, on the basis of contemporary circumstances, advise on their policy and strategic implications for a given business.	3
(c)	Discuss the objectives of the World Trade Organisation.	2
(d)	Discuss the role of international financial institutions within the context of a globalised economy, with particular attention to the International Monetary Fund, the Bank of International Settlements, The World Bank and the principal Central Banks (the Fed, Bank of England, European Central Bank and the Bank of Japan).	2
(e)	Assess the role of the international financial markets with respect to the management of global debt, the financial development of the emerging economies and the maintenance of global financial stability.	2

1 Theory and practice of international trade

FAST FORWARD

World output of **goods** and **services** will increase if countries specialise in the production of goods/services in which they have a **comparative advantage** and **trade** to obtain other goods and services.

Business enterprises are now also becoming increasingly **'internationalised'** by the development of **multinational activities** beyond pure import and export trade.

1.1 Theory of international trade

In the modern economy, production is based on a high degree of **specialisation**. Within a country individuals specialise, factories specialise and whole regions specialise. Specialisation increases productivity and raises the standard of living. International trade extends the principle of the division of labour and specialisation to countries. International trade originated on the basis of nations exchanging their products for others which they could not produce for themselves.

International trade arises for a number of reasons.

- Different goods require **different proportions** of **factor inputs** in their production.
- Economic resources are **unevenly distributed** throughout the world.
- The **international mobility** of **resources** is extremely **limited.**

Since it is difficult to move resources between nations, the goods which 'embody' the resources must move. The main reason for trade therefore is that there are differences in the relative efficiency with which different countries can produce different goods and services.

1.2 The law of comparative advantage

The significance of the law of comparative advantage is that it provides a justification for the following beliefs.

(a) Countries should **specialise** in what they produce, even when they are less efficient (in absolute terms) in producing every type of good. They should specialise in the goods where they have a **comparative advantage** (they are **relatively** more efficient in producing).

(b) **International trade** should be allowed to take place **without restrictions** on imports or exports – ie there should be **free trade**.

1.2.1 Does the law apply in practice?

The law of **comparative advantage** does apply in practice, and countries do specialise in the production of certain goods. However, there are certain limitations or restrictions on how it operates.

(a) **Free trade does not always exist**. Some countries take action to protect domestic industries and discourage imports. This means that a country might produce goods in which it does not have a comparative advantage.

(b) **Transport costs** (assumed to be nil in the examples above) can be **very high** in international trade so that it is cheaper to produce goods in the home country rather than to import them.

1.3 The advantages of international trade

The law of comparative advantage is perhaps the major advantage of encouraging international trade. However, there are other advantages to the countries of the world from encouraging international trade. These are as follows.

(a) Some countries have a **surplus** of **raw materials** to their needs, and others have a deficit. A country with a surplus (eg of oil) can take advantage of its resources to export them. A country with a deficit of a raw material must either import it, or accept restrictions on its economic prosperity and standard of living.

(b) International trade **increases competition** amongst suppliers in the world's markets. Greater competition reduces the likelihood of a market for a good in a country being dominated by a monopolist. The greater competition will force firms to be competitive and so will increase the pressures on them to be **efficient**, and also perhaps to produce goods of a high quality.

(c) International trade creates larger markets for a firm's output, and so some firms can benefit from **economies of scale** by engaging in export activities.

(d) There may be **political advantages** to international trade, because the development of **trading links** provides a foundation for **closer political links**. An example is the development of political links based on trade is the **European Union**.

1.4 Barriers to entry

Key term

Barriers to entry are factors which make it difficult for suppliers to enter a market.

Multinationals may face various entry barriers. All of these barriers may be more difficult to overcome if a multinational is investing abroad because of factors such as unfamiliarity with local consumers or government favouring local firms.

Strategies of expansion and diversification imply some logic in carrying on operations. It might be a better decision, although a much harder one, to cease operations or to pull out of a market completely. There are likely to be **exit barriers** making it difficult to pull out of a market.

1.4.1 Product differentiation barriers

An **existing major supplier** would be able to exploit its position as supplier of an established product that the consumer/ customer can be persuaded to believe is better. A new entrant to the market would have to design a better product, or convince customers of the product's qualities, and this might involve spending substantial sums of money on research and development, advertising and sales promotion.

1.4.2 Absolute cost barriers

These exist where an existing supplier has access to **cheaper raw material sources** or to know-how that the new entrant would not have. This gives the existing supplier an advantage because its input costs would be cheaper in absolute terms than those of a new entrant.

1.4.3 Economy of scale barriers

These exist where the **minimum level of production** needed to achieve the greatest economies of scale is at a high level. New entrants to the market would have to be able to achieve a substantial market share before they could gain full advantage of potential scale economies, and so the existing firms would be able to produce their output more cheaply.

1.4.4 Fixed costs

The amount of **fixed costs** that a firm would have to sustain, regardless of its market share, could be a significant entry barrier.

1.4.5 Legal barriers

These are barriers where a supplier is fully or partially protected by law. For example, there are some **legal monopolies** (nationalised industries perhaps) and a company's products might be protected by **patent** (for example computer hardware or software).

2 Trade agreements

FAST FORWARD

Justifications for **protection** include prevention of the import of cheap goods and dumping, and protection of infant or declining industries.

Free trade can lead to greater competition and efficiency, and achieve better economic growth worldwide.

2.1 Free trade

Free trade exists where there is no restriction on imports from other countries or exports to other countries. The **European Union** (EU) is a free trade area for trade between its member countries. In practice, however, there exist many barriers to free trade because governments wish to protect home industries against foreign competition. **Protectionism** would in effect be intended to hinder the operation of the law of comparative advantage.

2.2 Protectionist measures

Protectionist measures may be implemented by a government, but **popular demand** for protection commonly exceeds what governments are prepared to allow. In the UK, for example, some protectionist measures have been taken against Japanese imports (eg a voluntary restriction on car imports by Japanese manufacturers) although more severe measures are called for from time to time by popular demand or lobbying interests.

Protection can be applied in several ways, including the following.

- Tariffs or customs duties
- Import quotas
- Embargoes
- Hidden subsidies for exporters and domestic producers
- Import restrictions
- Deliberately restrictive bureaucratic procedures ('red tape') or product standards
- Government action to devalue the domestic currency

2.2.1 Tariffs or customs duties

Tariffs or customs duties are taxes on imported goods. The effect of a tariff is to raise the price paid for the imported goods by domestic consumers, while leaving the price paid to foreign producers the same, or even lower. The difference is transferred to the government sector.

For example, if goods imported to the UK are bought for £100 per unit, which is paid to the foreign supplier, and a tariff of £20 is imposed, the full cost to the UK buyer will be £120, with £20 going to the government.

An **ad valorem** tariff is one which is applied as a percentage of the value of goods imported. A **specific** tariff is a fixed tax per unit of goods.

2.2.2 Import quotas

Import quotas are restrictions on the **quantity** of a product that is allowed to be imported into the country. The quota has a similar effect on consumer welfare to that of import tariffs, but the overall effects are more complicated.

- Both domestic and foreign suppliers enjoy a higher price, while consumers buy less.
- Domestic producers supply more.
- There are fewer imports (in volume).
- The government collects no revenue.

An **embargo** on imports from one particular country is a total ban, ie effectively a zero quota.

2.2.3 Hidden export subsidies and import restrictions

An enormous range of government subsidies and assistance for exports and deterrents against imports have been practised, such as:

(a) **For exports** – export credit guarantees (government-backed insurance against bad debts for overseas sales), financial help (such as government grants to the aircraft or shipbuilding industry) and state assistance via the Foreign Office

(b) **For imports** – complex import regulations and documentation, or special safety standards demanded from imported goods and so on

2.2.4 Government action to devalue the currency

If a government allows its currency to fall in value, imports will become more expensive to buy. This will reduce imports by means of the price mechanism, especially if the demand and supply curves for the products are elastic.

2.3 Arguments against protection

Arguments against protection are as follows:

Reduced international trade

Because protectionist measures taken by one country will almost inevitably provoke retaliation by others, protection will reduce the volume of international trade. This means that the following benefits of international trade will be reduced.

(a) **Specialisation**
(b) **Greater competition**, and so greater efficiency amongst producers
(c) The advantages of **economies of scale** amongst producers who need world markets to achieve their economies and so produce at lower costs

Retaliation

Obviously it is to a nation's advantage if it can apply protectionist measures while other nations do not. But because of **retaliation by other countries**, protectionist measures to reverse a balance of trade deficit are unlikely to succeed. Imports might be reduced, but so too would exports.

Effect on economic growth

It is generally argued that widespread protection will damage the **prospects for economic growth** amongst the countries of the world, and protectionist measures ought to be restricted to 'special cases' which might be discussed and negotiated with other countries.

Political consequences

Although from a nation's own point of view, protection may improve its position, protectionism leads to a **worse outcome for all**. Protection also creates political ill-will amongst countries of the world and so there are **political disadvantages** in a policy of protection.

2.4 Arguments in favour of protection

Arguments for protection are as follows:

Imports of cheap goods

Measures can be taken against imports of cheap goods that compete with higher priced domestically produced goods, and so **preserve output and employment** in domestic industries. In the UK, advocates of protection have argued that UK industries are declining because of competition from overseas, especially the Far East, and the advantages of more employment at a reasonably high wage for UK labour are greater than the disadvantages that protectionist measures would bring.

Dumping

Measures might be necessary to counter **'dumping'** of surplus production by other countries at an uneconomically low price. Although dumping has short-term benefits for the countries receiving the cheap goods, the longer term consequences would be a **reduction** in **domestic output** and **employment**, even when domestic industries in the longer term might be more efficient.

Retaliation

This is why protection tends to spiral once it has begun. Any country that does not take protectionist measures when other countries are doing so is likely to find that it suffers all of the disadvantages and none of the advantages of protection.

Infant industries

Protectionism can protect a country's **'infant industries'** that have not yet developed to the size where they can compete in international markets. **Less developed countries** in particular might need to protect industries against competition from advanced or developing countries.

Declining industries

Without protection, the industries might collapse and there would be severe problems of sudden mass unemployment amongst workers in the industry.

Reduction in balance of trade deficit

However, because of retaliation by other countries, the success of such measures by one country would depend on the demand by other countries for its exports being inelastic with regard to price and its demand for imports being fairly elastic.

2.5 The 'optimal tariff' argument

In each of the above cases, tariffs and other protectionist measures are being advocated instead of alternative policies specifically targeted on the objectives sought.

Another argument in favour of tariffs targets directly the problem of a divergence between social and private marginal costs arising from trade itself. This **optimal tariff argument** provides a clearer demonstration of the possibility of gains in welfare from a tariff.

If a country's imports make up a significant share of the world market for a particular good, an increase in imports is likely to result in the world price of the good rising. The economic agents in the country collectively 'bid up' the price of imports. In a free market, each individual will buy imports up to the point at which the benefit to the individual equals the world price. Because of the price-raising effect referred to above, the cost to the economy as a whole of the last import exceeds the world price, and therefore exceeds its benefit.

In such a case, society can gain by restricting imports up to the point at which the **benefit of the last import equals its cost to society as a whole**. A tariff set to achieve this result is called an 'optimal tariff'.

Tariffs would decrease the welfare of a country in circumstances in which the optimal tariff is zero and there is no longer a need to discourage imports. This is when a country does not 'bid up' the world price of imports, as with a relatively small country in a large world market for a good.

2.6 Other measures

As an alternative to protection, a country can try to stimulate its export competitiveness by making efforts to improve the productivity and lower the costs of domestic industries, thus making them more competitive against foreign producers. **Hidden subsidies** and **exchange rate devaluation** are examples of indirect protectionist measures, but other measures, such as **funding industrial training schemes and educational policies**, might in the longer term result in improvements in domestic productivity.

2.7 The European Union

The **EU** is one of several international economic associations. It dates back to 1957 (the Treaty of Rome) and now consists of twenty-seven countries including formerly communist Eastern European countries.

The EU incorporates a **common market** combining different aspects.

(a) A **free trade area exists** when there is no restriction on the movement of goods and services between countries. This has been extended into a **customs union** (see below).

(b) A **common market** encompasses the idea of a customs union but has a number of additional features. In addition to free trade among member countries there is also **complete mobility** of the **factors of production**. A British citizen has the freedom to work in any other country of the European Union, for example. A common market will also aim to achieve stronger links between member countries, for example by harmonising government economic policies and by establishing a closer political confederation.

(c) The **single European currency**, the **euro**, was adopted by eleven countries of the EU from the inception of the currency at the beginning of 1999.

2.8 The customs union

The customs union of the EU **establishes a free trade area between member states**, and also erects **common external tariffs** to charge on imports from non-member countries. The EU thus promotes free trade among member states, while acting as a **protectionist bloc** against the rest of the world. It is accordingly consistent that the EU negotiates in GATT talks as a single body.

2.9 The single European market

The EU set the end of 1992 as the target date for the removal of all existing physical, technical and fiscal barriers among member states, thus creating a large multinational **European Single Market**. In practice, these changes have not occurred 'overnight', and many of them are still in progress.

2.9.1 Elimination of trade restrictions

(a) **Physical barriers** (eg customs inspection) on good and services have been removed for most products. Companies have had to adjust to a new VAT regime as a consequence.

(b) **Technical standards** (eg for quality and safety) should be harmonised.

(c) Governments should not **discriminate** between EU companies in awarding public works contracts.

(d) **Telecommunications** should be subject to greater competition.

(e) It should be possible to provide **financial services** in any country.

(f) There should be **free movement of capital** within the community.

(g) **Professional qualifications** awarded in one member state should be recognised in the others.

(h) The EU is taking a **co-ordinated stand** on matters related to consumer protection.

2.9.2 Remaining barriers

There are many areas where harmonisation is a long way from being achieved. Here are some examples.

(a) **Company tax rates**, which can affect the viability of investment plans, vary from country to country within the EU.

(b) Whilst there have been moves to harmonisation, there are still differences between **indirect tax** rates imposed by member states.

(c) There are considerable **differences in prosperity** between the wealthiest EU economies (eg Germany), and the poorest (eg Greece). This has meant that grants are sometimes available to depressed regions, which might affect investment decisions; and that different marketing strategies are appropriate for different markets.

(d) **Differences in workforce skills** can have a significant effect on investment decisions. The workforce in Germany is perhaps the most highly trained, but also the most highly paid, and so might be suitable for products of a high added value.

(e) Some countries are better provided with road and rail infrastructure than others. Where accessibility to a market is an important issue, **infrastructure** can mean significant variations in distribution costs.

2.10 The European Free Trade Area (EFTA)

The European Free Trade Area (EFTA) was established in 1959, with seven member countries, one of which was the UK. The UK, Denmark and Portugal have since transferred to the EU, while Finland and Iceland joined the other original member states, Sweden, Norway, Austria and Switzerland. More recently, Finland, Sweden and Austria have also joined the EU. There is free trade between EFTA member countries but there is no harmonisation of tariffs with non-EFTA countries.

2.11 North American Free Trade Agreement (NAFTA)

Canada, the USA and Mexico formed the North American Free Trade Agreement (NAFTA) which came into force in 1994. This free trade area covering a population of 360 million and accounting for economic output of US$6,000 billion annually is almost as large as the European Economic Area, and is thus the second largest free trade area after the EEA.

Under NAFTA, virtually all tariff and other (non-tariff) barriers to trade and investment between the NAFTA members are to be eliminated over a 15-year period. In the case of trade with non-NAFTA members, each NAFTA member will continue to set its own external tariffs, subject to obligations under GATT. The NAFTA agreement covers most business sectors, with special rules applying to especially sensitive sectors, including agriculture, the automotive industry, financial services and textiles and clothing.

3 The World Trade Organisation (WTO)

FAST FORWARD

The **World Trade Organisation** (WTO) is the a global international organization dealing with the rules of trade between nations.

3.1 The World Trade Organisation (WTO)

The **World Trade Organisation (WTO)** was formed in 1995 to continue to implement the General Agreement on Tariffs and Trade (GATT). The WTO has well over 100 members including the entire European Union. Its aims include:

(a) To **reduce existing barriers** to free trade

(b) To **eliminate discrimination** in international trade such as tariffs and subsidies

(c) To **prevent the growth of protection** by getting member countries to consult with others before taking any protectionist measures

(d) To act as a **forum** for assisting free trade, by for example administering agreements, helping countries negotiate and **offering a disputes settlement process**

(e) Establishing **rules and guidelines** to make **world trade more predictable**

3.1.1 The most favoured nation principle

Key term

Most favoured nation: a principle in the GATT international trade agreement binding the parties to grant to each other treatment which is as favourable as that offered to any other GATT member in respect of tariffs and other trading conditions.

The WTO encourages free trade by applying the **'most favoured nation'** principle where one country (which is a member of GATT) that offers a reduction in tariffs to another country must offer the same reduction to all other member countries of GATT.

3.1.2 Impact on protectionist measures

Although the WTO has helped reduce the level of protection, some problems still remain:

(a) Special circumstances (for example economic crises, the protection of an infant industry, the rules of the EU) have to be **admitted** when protection or special low tariffs between a group of countries are allowed.

(b) A country in the WTO may **prefer not to offer a tariff reduction** to another country because it would have to offer the same reduction to all other GATT members.

(c) In spite of much success in reducing tariffs, the WTO has had **less effect** in dealing with **many non-tariff barriers** to trade that countries may set up. Some such barriers, for example those in the guise of health and safety requirements, can be very difficult to identify.

(d) New agreements are **not always accepted initially** by all members.

Nevertheless the WTO exists to help business, and ultimately businesses should be able to benefit from the **expanded opportunities** a freer global market brings, even if in certain countries some businesses may suffer through losing the benefits of protection.

4 International monetary institutions

> The IMF was set up partly with the role of providing finance for any countries with temporary balance of payments deficits.
>
> The World Bank and the IDA have tried to provide long-term finance for **developing countries**, to help them to continue developing.

4.1 The International Monetary Fund

Most countries of the world have membership of the IMF. The three broad aims of the IMF are:

- To **promote international monetary** co-operation, and to establish a code of conduct for making international payments
- To **provide financial support** to countries with **temporary balance of payments deficits**
- To provide for the **orderly growth** of international liquidity, through its Special Drawing Rights (SDR) scheme (launched in 1970).

4.2 The IMF and financial support for countries with balance of payment difficulties

If a country has a balance of payments deficit on current account, it must **either borrow capital** or use up official reserves to offset this deficit. Since a country's official reserves will be insufficient to support a balance of payments deficit on current account for very long, it must borrow to offset the deficit.

The IMF can provide financial support to member countries. Most IMF loans are repayable in 3 to 5 years.

Of course, to lend money, the IMF must also have funds. Funds are made available from subscriptions or 'quotas' of member countries. The IMF uses these subscriptions to lend foreign currencies to countries which apply to the IMF for help.

4.3 IMF loan conditions

The pre-conditions that the IMF places on its loans to debtor countries vary according to the individual situation of each country, but the general position is as follows.

(a) The IMF wants countries which borrow from the IMF to get into a position to start **repaying the loans fairly quickly**. To do this, the countries must take effective action to improve their balance of payments position.

(b) To make this improvement, the IMF generally believes that a country should take action to **reduce the demand for goods and services** in the economy (eg by increasing taxes and cutting government spending). This will reduce imports and help to put a brake on any price rises. The country's industries should then also be able to divert more resources into export markets and hence exports should improve in the longer-term.

(c) With 'deflationary' measures along these lines, **standards of living will fall** (at least in the short term) and unemployment may rise. The IMF regards these short-term hardships to be necessary if a country is to succeed in sorting out its balance of payments and international debt problems.

4.4 Borrowing to supplement liquidity

Countries which have balance of payments deficits can borrow their way out of trouble, at least temporarily. There are various sources of borrowing:

(a) The IMF (IMF lending has already been described)

(b) Other institutions, such as the World Bank, the International Development Association (IDA), and the Bank for International Settlements (BIS)

(c) Borrowing from private banks (in the eurocurrency markets)

4.5 The World Bank (IBRD)

The **World Bank** (more properly called the **International Bank for Reconstruction and Development** or **IBRD**) began operations in 1946. Its chief aim now is to **supplement private finance** and lend money on a commercial basis for capital projects. Loans are usually direct to governments or government agencies, for a long-term period of over 10 years (typically 20 years). Lending is usually tied to specific projects, although the Bank's lending policy has been more flexible in recent years.

Case Study

In June 2003, the World Bank approved a $59.6 million credit to help meet the needs of Afghanistan's rural population, whose health is amongst the worst in the world.

The World Bank's funds are obtained from **capital subscriptions** by member countries of the IMF, its profits, and borrowing. The major source of funds is borrowing, and the World Bank makes bond issues on the world's capital markets (eg New York).

4.6 The IDA

World Bank lending is for projects concerned with the development of agriculture, electricity, transport and so on. The cost of World Bank loans was (and still is) high to developing countries, and in 1960, the **International Development Association (IDA)** was set up to provide 'soft' loans – ie loans at a low cost with easy repayment terms – to less developed countries, for similar types of projects financed by the World Bank. The IDA is a subsidiary of the World Bank and member countries of the IDA are also members of the World Bank.

4.7 The BIS

The **Bank for International Settlements (BIS)** is the banker for the central banks of other countries. It is situated in Basle, where it was founded in 1930. Most of its deposits are from the central banks of various countries and some are shareholders and represented on its board. It is a profit making institution, and lends money at commercial rates. The Bank of England, for example, has a 10% stake in the BIS.

The main functions of the BIS are to

- Promote co-operation between central banks
- Provide facilities for international co-operation

5 International financial markets and global financial stability

FAST FORWARD

The globalisation of the financial markets has facilitated the transfer of funds to emerging markets but it has contributed to financial instability.

5.1 The rise of global financial markets.

One of the main developments of the last decades has been the globalisation of the financial markets. This globalisation has been buoyed by the creation of the Euro and the expansion of the European Union, the rise of China and India as important trading players in the world economy and the creation of the World Trade Organisations. The globalisation in financial markets is manifested in developments in international equity markets, in international bond markets and in international money markets.

5.2 International capital markets and emerging economies development

Private capital flows are important for emerging economies, and the transfer of flows has increased significantly as a result of the development in international capital markets. The capital flows to emerging markets take three forms:

(a) **Foreign direct investment** by multinational companies .

(b) **Borrowing from international banks.** Borrowing from international banks is becoming more important. There are several advantages in borrowing from international banks. It is possible to obtain better terms and in currencies which may be more appropriate in term of the overall risk exposure of the company.

(c) **Portfolio investment** in emerging markets capital markets. Emerging markets equity hs become a distinct .

5.3 The European Monetary System (EMS)

FAST FORWARD

European Monetary System (EMS) reduces exchange dealing costs and enhances economic policies, but limits the ability of governments to pursue independent economic policies.

The purposes of the EMS are:

(a) To **stabilise exchange rates** between the currencies of the member countries

(b) To promote **economic convergence** in Europe, pushing inflation rates down by forcing economic policies on partner governments similar to the policies of the more successful members

(c) To develop **European Economic and Monetary Union (EMU)**

5.4 European Economic and Monetary Union

EMU was a long-standing objective of the EU, reaffirmed in the Single European Act of 1985 and in the Maastricht agreement of 1992. It culminated in the introduction of the single currency, the Euro, in 1999.

(a) **Monetary union** can be defined as a single currency area, which has required a monetary policy for the area as a whole, implemented by the **European Central Bank**.

(b) **Economic union** can be described as an unrestricted common market for trade, with some economic policy co-ordination between different regions in the union.

Gordon Brown, the UK's Chancellor of the Exchequer, has explained in the House of Commons that the UK Treasury has 'made a detailed assessment of five economic tests' believed to define whether a clear and unambiguous case could be made to support Britain joining a single currency. These were:

- **Convergence** between the **UK and the economies** of a single currency
- Whether there is **sufficient flexibility** to cope with economic change
- The **effect on investment**
- The **impact on the financial services industry**
- Whether it is **good for employment**

5.5 For and against EMU

The arguments for and against EMU can be summarised as shown below, with particular reference to the UK's position.

<table>
<tr><th>For</th><th>Against</th></tr>
<tr><td>

Economic policy stability

- EMU members are expected to keep to strict economic criteria.
- Politicians in member countries will be less able to pursue short-term economic policies, for example just before an election, to gain political advantage

Facilitation of trade

- Eliminates risk of currency fluctuations affecting trade and investment between EMU member countries
- Eliminates need to 'hedge' against such risks
- Savings in foreign exchange transaction costs for companies, as well as tourists
- Enhances ease of trade with non EU countries

Lower interest rates

- Reduces risk of inflation and depreciating currencies, reducing interest rates
- Stabilises interest rates at a level closer to that of Germany, reducing interest costs for businesses and government

Preservation of the City's position.

- If the UK stays out of EMU, the City's position as one of the major European financial capitals will be threatened
- In turn, the City's role as a leading global financial market would also be jeopardised
- Inward investment from the rest of the EU would also be likely to diminish

</td><td>

Loss of national control over economic policy

- Under EMU, monetary policy is largely in the hands of the new European central bank
- Individual countries' fiscal policies also need to stay in line with European policy criteria
- The European economic policy framework puts greater emphasis on price stability than some individual governments may want
- Restrictive monetary policies could result in disproportionate unemployment and output effects

The need to compensate for weaker economies

- For the UK, the possible benefits of being economically linked to stronger European economies are reduced and possibly even outweighed by the need to compensate for weaker economies
- Stronger economies could be under pressure to 'bail out' member countries which borrow too much in order to hold the system together

Confusion in the transition to EMU

- Introduction of a new currency and coinage may cause confusion to businesses and consumers

Lower confidence arising from loss of national pride

- Sterling is a symbol of national cohesion
- EMU puts its members on the road to a federal Europe, it is suggested, making the UK parliament into little more than a regional town hall within Europe, with no more power than local government. Such a move might dent national pride and adversely affect economic confidence

</td></tr>
</table>

5.6 International capital markets and financial stability

The globalisation of the financial markets has created more liquid, efficient and transparent market, but it has also created volatility in the capital flows especially in emerging markets. One important feature of the second half of the 1990s has been the phenomenon of financial contagion which creates global instability. Financial contagion occurs when crisis in one country spills to other countries. The phenomenon started when the collapse of Thailand's currency triggered the crises in other Asian emerging markets.

The experience of the Asian crisis shows that globalisation also needs a series of measures to improve financial stability in emerging-market economies and thus to reduce the frequency and intensity of future crises. These measures include both an improved framework for macroeconomic policy and improved corporate governance.

5.7 The global debt crisis

A **global debt crisis** arose as governments in **less developed countries (LDCs)** took on levels of debt to fund their development programmes which are beyond their ability to finance. As a result, the level of debt rose and their ability to repay decreased, as increasing amounts of GDP were absorbed in servicing the debt rather in financing development. A further factor was that, in some countries with substantial oil reserves, banks were keen to lend against the fact of these reserves combined with high world oil prices. Examples of such countries include Nigeria and Venezuela. As the oil price fell, the fall in oil revenues to the LDCs precipitated a debt crisis.

Case Study

'Most of the 41 countries classified as heavily indebted are in sub-Saharan Africa (SSA), including 25 of the 32 countries rated as severely indebted. In 1962, SSA owed $3bn (£1.8bn). Twenty years later it had reached $142bn. Today it's about $235bn – or 76 per cent of GNP. The most heavily indebted countries are: Nigeria ($35bn), followed by Côte D'Ivoire ($19bn) and Sudan ($18bn).

Latin America's debt is much bigger – about $650bn – but the nature of its problem has been very different. Most of its 1980s debt was owed to commercial banks, and a series of relief agreements and stronger economic growth combined to make it more manageable for all but a few countries, including Nicaragua, Bolivia and Guyana.

'Unlike Latin America, Africa owes more than two-thirds of its debt to foreign government and multilateral lenders. Multilateral lenders – including the IMF, the World Bank, and the African Development Bank – account for 32 per cent of the debt; governments are owed 42 per cent, and private lenders, mainly commercial banks, account for the balance – 26 per cent.'

(Financial Times, 15 September 1997)

5.8 Resolving the global debt crisis

Various approaches have been taken in attempts to overcome these problems. Where the situation has arisen due to a sudden (and hopefully temporary) fall in commodity prices, one solution may be for the country to take on **additional short-term debt** to cover the temporary shortfall.

Where the problem is of a longer term nature, approaches include the following.

(a) The **debt** may be **restructured** and/or rescheduled in order to allow the government a longer time to repay the loan.

(b) Restructuring is often linked to a **package of economic reforms** which are aimed at improving the balance of trade and stimulating growth. Some countries may initiate such reforms themselves as a way out of their problem – in other cases, reforms are linked to the rescheduling package and are approved and monitored by the IMF.

(c) Some of the debt may be **written off** by the lending governments and banks thereby reducing the interest burden and enhancing the prospects of eventual payment.

(d) Some of the debt may be **converted to equity**, giving foreign companies a stake in local industries and reducing the level of interest payments.

5.9 Negative impacts on multinational firms

The debt crisis has a number of adverse consequences for multinational firms which undertake FDI in less developed countries. Many of these adverse consequences result from the policies of 'economic adjustment' which are imposed on debtor countries by the IMF.

5.9.1 Effects of deflationary policies

Deflationary policies imposed on LDCs by the IMF are likely to **damage** the **profitability of multinationals' subsidiaries** by reducing their sales in the local market. These deflationary policies are designed to improve the balance of payments position of the debtor countries by reducing their imports and boosting exports. Higher interest rates are likely to be introduced to suppress domestic consumer's demand for imports. However, higher interest rates will tend to dampen domestic investment and could result in increased unemployment and loss of business confidence.

5.9.2 Effects of devaluation

Devaluation of the domestic currency is a policy which the debtor country may **adopt** to try to **boost exports**. The country will be able to sell its exports more cheaply in foreign currency terms – while imports to the country will become more expensive. This will adversely affect the level of operating costs for multinational firms which make use of imported inputs to their production process.

5.9.3 Sourcing of imports

Debtor countries' **lack of foreign currency** (arising from the need to service their debt) means that **less can be imported**. Host countries may require that multinationals increase their use of local inputs which may be of higher cost or lower quality than the same goods obtained from elsewhere.

5.9.4 Lack of capital inflows

Measures such as the Baker Plan were intended to increase the level of lending available to debtor countries. Nevertheless, as already indicated, the international banks have **not been willing** to provide these **increased capital inflows** to the less developed countries. As a result, multinational firms operating in these countries have been forced to rely more heavily on **host country funding** for their activities in those countries, which they may have preferred not to do.

Chapter Roundup

- World output of goods and services will increase if countries specialise in the production of goods/services in which they have a comparative advantage and trade to obtain other goods and services.

  Business enterprises are now also becoming increasingly 'internationalised' by the development of multinational activities beyond pure import and export trade.
- Justifications for protection include prevention of the import of cheap goods and dumping, and protection of infant or declining industries.

  Free trade can lead to greater competition and efficiency, and achieve better economic growth worldwide.
- The World Trade Organisation (WTO) is the a global international organization dealing with the rules of trade between nations.
- The IMF was set up partly with the role of providing finance for any countries with temporary balance of payments deficits.
- The World Bank and the IDA have tried to provide long-term finance for developing countries, to help them to continue developing.
- The globalisation of the financial markets has facilitated the transfer of funds to emerging markets but it has contributed to financial instability.
- European Monetary System (EMS) reduces exchange dealing costs and enhances economic policies, but limits the ability of governments to pursue independent economic policies.

Quick Quiz

1 Define a multinational enterprise.

2 What is meant by the law of comparative advantage?

3 What is meant by:

(a) a free trade area
(b) a customs union
(c) a common market

4 Assume that two small countries, X and Y, produce two commodities P and Q, and that there are no transport costs. One unit of resource in Country X produces 4 units of P or 8 units of Q. One unit of resource is Country Y produces 1 unit of P or 3 units of Q. Which of the following statements is true?

A Country X has an absolute advantage over Country Y in producing P and Q, and so will not trade.
B Country X does not have an absolute advantage over Country Y in producing P and Q.
C Country Y has a comparative advantage over Country X in producing Q.
D Country X has a comparative advantage over Country Y in producing both P and Q.

5 How do deflationary measures help to eliminate a balance of payments deficit?

6 **Fill in the blank.** ______________________ are countries with lenient tax rules or low tax rates, often designed to attract foreign investment.

7 What according to Eiteman, Stonehill and Moffett are the five main strategic reasons for undertaking foreign direct investment?

8 Give three examples of barriers to entry that multinationals might face.

Answers to Quick Quiz

1 A multinational enterprise is one which has a physical presence or property interests in more than one country.

2 The law of comparative advantage or comparative costs states that two countries can gain from trade when each specialises in the industries in which it has the lowest opportunity costs.

3 A free trade area exists when there is no restriction on trade between countries. This is extended into a customs union when common external tariffs are levied on imports from non-member countries. A common market adds free movement of the factors of production, including labour and may harmonise economic policy.

4 C. Country Y has a comparative advantage over country X in producing Q.

5 Domestic deflation cuts demand including demand for imports. Industry is therefore encouraged to switch to export markets.

6 Tax havens

7 Market; Raw material; Production efficiency; Knowledge; Political safety

8 Any three of: Product differentiation barriers; Absolute cost barriers; Economy of scale barriers; Fixed costs; Legal barriers

Now try the question below from the Exam Question Bank

Number	Level	Marks	Time
36	Introductory	12	20 mins

24 Strategic business and financial planning for multinationals

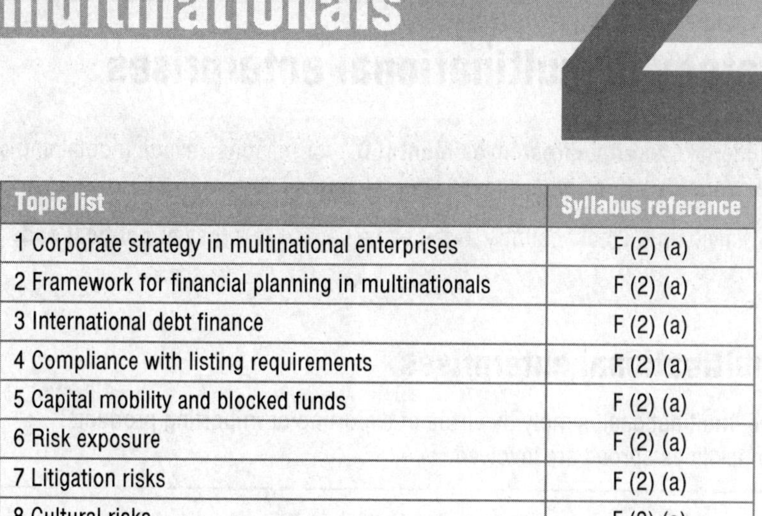

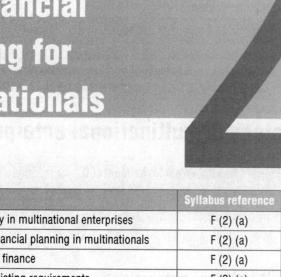

Topic list	Syllabus reference
1 Corporate strategy in multinational enterprises	F (2) (a)
2 Framework for financial planning in multinationals	F (2) (a)
3 International debt finance	F (2) (a)
4 Compliance with listing requirements	F (2) (a)
5 Capital mobility and blocked funds	F (2) (a)
6 Risk exposure	F (2) (a)
7 Litigation risks	F (2) (a)
8 Cultural risks	F (2) (a)
9 Agency issues	F (2) (a)

Introduction

In this chapter, we discuss the various aspects of strategic decision making in a multinational corporation, such as the decision to invest abroad, how it deals with barriers to entry and blocked funds, the capital structure decision and the various risks it is exposed to and finally the agency problem that exists between the subsidiary and the parent organisation.

Study guide

		Intellectual level
F2	**Strategic business and financial planning for multinationals**	
(a)	Advise on the development of a financial planning framework for a multinational taking into account:	3
	(i) Compliance with national governance requirements (for example the LSE requirements for admission for trading)	
	(ii) The mobility of capital across borders and national limitations on remittances and transfer pricing	
	(iii) The pattern of economic and other risk exposures in the different national markets	
	(iv) Agency issues in the central coordination of overseas operations and the balancing of local financial autonomy with effective central control	

1 Corporate strategy in multinational enterprises

FAST FORWARD

Multinational enterprises undertake **foreign direct investment (FDI)** for reasons including obtaining **cost and revenue advantages, tax considerations** and **process specialisation**.

FDI can stimulate economic activity in the host country, but it can also lead to a **loss of political and economic sovereignty**.

1.1 The nature of multinational enterprises

A company does not become 'multinational' simply by virtue of exporting or importing products: ownership and the control of facilities abroad are involved.

Key term

A **multinational enterprise** is one which owns or controls production facilities or subsidiaries or service facilities outside the country in which it is based.

Multinational enterprises range from medium-sized companies having only a few facilities (or 'affiliates') abroad to giant companies having an annual turnover larger than the gross national product (GNP) of some smaller countries of the world. Indeed, the largest – such as the US multinationals Ford, General Motors and Exxon – each have a turnover similar to the GNP a medium-sized national economy.

The **size and significance of multinationals** is increasing. Many companies in 'middle-income' countries such as Singapore are now becoming multinationals, and the annual growth in output of existing multinationals is in the range 10-15%.

The extensive activities of multinational enterprises, particularly the larger ones, raises questions about the problems of controlling them. Individual governments may be largely powerless if multinationals are able to exploit the tax regimes of **'tax haven'** countries through **transfer pricing** policies or if the multinationals' production is switched from one country to another.

Key term

Tax havens are countries with lenient tax rules or relatively low tax rates, which are often designed to attract foreign investment.

The empirical evidence on the growth of multinational companies shows that companies become multinational in a gradual way. First companies expand their operations into overseas markets by exporting. Then they create overseas sale subsidiaries and enter into licensing agreements. And finally they invest and create production facilities in overseas locations. The key element of the process of expansion is the creation of competitive advantages

1.2 Competitive advantages of multinationals

FAST FORWARD

There are many strategic reasons for engaging in foreign investment which include seeking **new markets** for goods, **new sources** of **raw materials**, **production efficiency**, expertise and **political safety**.

The main strategic reasons for engaging in foreign direct investment (FDI) include:

1.2.1 Market seeking

'Market seeking' firms engage in FDI either to meet **local demand** or as a way of exporting to markets other than the home market. Examples of this are the manufacturing operations of US and Japanese car producers in Europe. Some FDI is undertaken to provide a sales and market organisation in the overseas economy for the exporter's goods.

1.2.2 Raw material seeking

Firms in industries such as oil, mining, plantation and forestry will extract raw materials in the **places where they can be found**, whether for export or for further processing and sale in the host country.

1.2.3 Production efficiency seeking

The labour-intensive manufacture of electronic components in Taiwan, Malaysia and Mexico is an example of locating production where one or more **factors of production** are **cheap** relative to their productivity.

1.2.4 Knowledge seeking

Knowledge seeking firms choose to set up operations in countries in which they can **gain access to technology or management expertise**. For example, German, Japanese and Dutch companies have acquired technology by buying US-based electronics companies.

1.2.5 Political safety seekers

Firms which are seeking 'political safety' will acquire or set up new operations in those countries which are thought to be **unlikely to expropriate or interfere** with **private enterprise or impose import controls**. More positively these companies may offer grants and tax concessions.

1.2.6 Economies of scale

There are advantages to be gained in production, marketing, finance, research and development, transport and purchasing by virtue of firms being large. **Production economies** can arise from use of large-scale plant or from the possibility of rationalising production by adopting worldwide specialisation. Multinational car manufacturers produce engines in one country, transmissions in another, bodies in another, and assemble cars in yet another country.

1.2.7 Managerial and marketing expertise

Managerial expertise may be fostered in the environment of the larger multinational enterprise, and can be developed from previous knowledge of foreign markets. Empirical studies show that multinationals tend to **export to markets** before **establishing production operations** there, thus partly overcoming the possibly superior local knowledge of firms based in the host country.

1.2.8 Technology

Empirical studies suggest a link between **research and development (R & D)** work, which enhances technological, scientific and engineering skills and the larger multinationals engaged in FDI. Vernon's **product cycle theory** is based on the idea that multinational firms originate much new technology as a result of R&D activities on new products initially launched in their home markets. Host nations are often interested in FDI for the reason that technology transfer may result from it.

1.2.9 Financial economies

Multinationals enjoy considerable cost advantages in relation to finance. They have the advantage of access to the **full range of financial instruments** such as Eurocurrency and Eurobonds, which reduces their borrowing costs. Multinationals' financial strength is also achieved through their ability to **reduce risk** by **diversifying their operations** and their sources of borrowing.

1.2.10 Differentiated products

Firms create their own firm-specific advantages by **producing** and **marketing differentiated products**, which are similar products differentiated mainly by branding. Once the firm has developed differentiated products for the home market, it can maximise return on the heavy marketing costs by marketing them worldwide. Competitors will find it expensive and possibly difficult to imitate such products.

1.3 Issues in overseas production decisions

FAST FORWARD

Commonly used means to establish an **interest abroad** include:

- Joint ventures
- Licensing agreements
- Management contracts
- Subsidiary
- Branches

Most of the two-way traffic in investment by multinational companies (**foreign direct investment** or **FDI**) is between the developed countries of the world. While the present pattern of FDI can be traced back to the initial wave of investment in Europe by the USA following the Second World War, more recently Europe and Japan have become substantial overseas investors.

Developments in international capital markets have provided an environment conducive to FDI.

Key term

Globalisation describes the process by which the capital markets of each country have become internationally integrated.

The process of integration is facilitated by improved telecommunications and the deregulation of markets in many countries.

There have been significant changes affecting the pattern of multinationals' activities over the last twenty years or so.

1.3.1 Destination countries

The focus has shifted from Canada and Latin America in the days when the USA was the major source of FDI to other areas, including the countries of South East Asia which receive significant direct investment from Japanese companies in particular.

1.3.2 Centralised control

Centralised control of production activities within multinationals has increased, prompted partly by the need for **strategic management of production planning** and worldwide resource allocation. This process of centralisation has been facilitated by the development of sophisticated worldwide computer and telecommunications links.

1.3.3 Type of integration

A firm might develop **horizontally** in different countries, replicating its existing operations on a global basis. **Vertical integration** might have an international dimension through FDI to acquire raw material or component sources overseas (**backwards integration**) or to establish final production and distribution in

other countries (**forward integration**). **Diversification** might alternatively provide the impetus to developing international interests.

Different forms of expansion overseas are available to meet various strategic objectives.

(a) Firms may expand by means of **new 'start-up' investments**, for example in manufacturing plants. This does allow flexibility, although it may be slow to achieve, expensive to maintain and slow to yield satisfactory results.

(b) A firm might **take over or merge** with established firms abroad. This provides a means of **purchasing market information**, **market share** and **distribution channels**. If speed of entry into the overseas market is a high priority, then acquisition may be preferred to start-up. However, the better acquisitions may only be available at a **premium**.

(c) **A joint venture with a local overseas partner** might be entered into. A joint venture may be defined as 'the commitment, for more than a very short duration, of funds, facilities and services by two or more legally separate interests to an enterprise for their mutual benefit.' Different forms of joint venture are distinguished below.

1.3.4 Joint ventures

The two distinct types of joint venture are **industrial co-operation (contractual)** and **joint-equity**. A **contractual joint venture** is for a fixed period and the duties and responsibility of the parties are contractually defined. A **joint-equity venture** involves investment, is of no fixed duration and continually evolves. Depending on government regulations, joint ventures may be the **only** means of access to a particular market.

The main advantages of joint ventures are:

(a) Relatively **low cost access** to new markets

(b) **Easier access** to **local capital markets**, possibly with accompanying tax incentives or grants

(c) **Use of joint venture partner's existing management expertise**, local knowledge, distribution network, technology, brands, patents and marketing or other skills

(d) **Sharing of risks**

(e) **Sharing of costs**, providing economies of scale

The main disadvantages of joint ventures are:

(a) **Managerial freedom** may be **restricted** by the need to take account of the views of all the joint venture partners.

(b) There may be **problems** in **agreeing on partners' percentage ownership**, transfer prices, reinvestment decisions, nationality of key personnel, remuneration and sourcing of raw materials and components.

(c) Finding a **reliable joint venture partner** may take a long time.

(d) Joint ventures are **difficult to value**, particularly where one or more partners have made intangible contributions.

1.3.5 Exploiting and licensing

Exporting and **licensing** stand as alternatives to FDI. **Exporting** may be direct selling by the firm's own export division into the overseas markets, or it may be indirect through agents, distributors, trading companies and various other such channels. **Licensing** involves conferring rights to make use of the licensor company's production process on producers located in the overseas market.

Key terms

Licensing is an alternative to foreign direct investment by which overseas producers are given rights to use the licensor's production process in return for royalty payments.

Exporting may be unattractive because of tariffs, quotas or other import restrictions in overseas markets, and local production may be the only feasible option in the case of bulky products such as cement and flat glass.

The main advantages of licensing are:

(a) It can allow fairly **rapid penetration of** overseas markets.

(b) It does **not require substantial financial resources**.

(c) **Political risks** are **reduced** since the licensee is likely to be a local company.

(d) **Licensing** may be a **possibility** where direct investment is restricted or prevented by a country.

(e) For a multinational company, licensing agreements provide a way for **funds** to be **remitted** to the parent company in the form of licence fees.

The main disadvantages of licensing are:

(a) The arrangement may give to the licensee **know-how** and **technology** which it can use in competing with the licensor after the license agreement has expired.

(b) It may be more **difficult to maintain quality standards**, and lower quality might affect the standing of a brand name in international markets.

(c) It might be possible for the licensee to **compete** with the licensor by exporting the produce to markets outside the licensee's area.

(d) Although relatively insubstantial financial resources are required, on the other hand **relatively small cash inflows** will be **generated**.

1.3.6 Management contracts

Management contracts whereby a firm agrees to sell management skills are sometimes used in combination with licensing. Such contracts can serve as a means of obtaining funds from subsidiaries, and may be a useful way of maintaining cash flows where other remittance restrictions apply. Many multinationals use a **combination** of various methods of servicing international markets, depending on the particular circumstances.

1.3.7 Overseas subsidiaries

The basic structure of many multinationals consists of a parent company (a holding company) with subsidiaries in several countries. The subsidiaries may be wholly owned or just partly owned, and some may be owned through other subsidiaries. Whatever the reason for setting up subsidiaries abroad, the aim is to increase the profits of the multinational's parent company. However there are different approaches to increasing profits that the multinational might take. At one extreme, the parent company might choose **to get as much money as it can** from the subsidiary, and **as quickly as it can**. This would involve the transfer of all or most of the subsidiary's profits to the parent company.

At the other extreme, the parent company might encourage a foreign subsidiary to **develop its business gradually**, to achieve long-term growth in sales and profits. To encourage growth, the subsidiary would be allowed to retain a large proportion of its profits, instead of remitting the profits to the parent company.

1.3.8 Branches

Firms who want to establish a definite presence in an overseas country may choose to establish a **branch** rather than a subsidiary. Key elements in this choice are as follows.

Taxation

In many countries the remitted profits of a subsidiary will be taxed at a higher rate than those of a branch, as profits paid in the form of dividends are likely to be subject to a withholding tax. How much impact the withholding tax has however, is questionable, particularly as a double tax treaty can reduce its import. In many instances a multinational will establish a branch and utilise its initial losses against other profits, and then turn the branch into a subsidiary when it starts making profits.

Formalities

As a separate entity, a subsidiary may be subject to more legal and accounting formalities than a branch. However, as a separate legal entity, a subsidiary may be able to claim more reliefs and grants than a branch.

Marketing

A local subsidiary may have a greater profile for sales and marketing purposes than a branch.

2 Framework for financial planning in multinationals

FAST FORWARD

Multinational companies need to develop a **financial planning framework** in order to make sure that the strategic objectives and competitive advantages are realised. Such a financial **planning framework** will include ways of raising **capital** and **risks** related to overseas operations and the **repatriation of profits**.

2.1 Financing an overseas subsidiary

Once the decision is taken by a multinational company to start overseas operations in any of the forms that have been discussed in the previous section, there is a need to decide on the source of funds for the proposed expansion. There are some differences in methods of financing the **parent company** itself, and the **foreign subsidiaries**. The parent company itself is more likely than companies which have no foreign interests to raise finance in a foreign currency, or in its home currency from foreign sources.

The **need to finance a foreign subsidiary** raises the following questions.

(a) How much **equity capital** should the parent company put into the subsidiary?

(b) Should the subsidiary be allowed to **retain a large proportion** of its profits, to build up its equity reserves, or not?

(c) Should the parent company hold **100% of the equity** of the subsidiary, or should it try to create a minority shareholding, perhaps by floating the subsidiary on the country's domestic stock exchange?

(d) Should the subsidiary be encouraged to **borrow** as much **long-term debt** as it can, for example by raising large bank loans? If so, should the loans be in the domestic currency of the subsidiary's country, or should it try to raise a foreign currency loan?

(e) Should the subsidiary be listed on the local stock exchange, raising funds from the local equity markets?

(f) Should the subsidiary be encouraged to minimise its working capital investment by relying heavily on trade credit?

The **method of financing** a subsidiary will give some indication of the **nature and length of time** of the investment that the parent company is prepared to make. A sizeable equity investment (or long-term loans from the parent company to the subsidiary) would indicate a long-term investment by the parent company.

2.2 Choice of finance for an overseas investment

The choice of the source of funds will depend on:

(a) The **local finance costs**, and any subsidies which may be available

(b) **Taxation systems** of the countries in which the subsidiary is operating. Different tax rates can favour borrowing in high tax regimes, and no borrowing elsewhere.

(c) Any **restrictions on dividend remittances**

(d) The possibility of **flexibility in repayments** which may arise from the parent/subsidiary relationship

Tax-saving opportunities may be maximised by **structuring the group** and its subsidiaries in such a way as to **take the best advantage** of the different local tax systems.

Because subsidiaries may be operating with a guarantee from the parent company, different gearing structures may be possible. Thus, a subsidiary may be able to operate with a higher level of debt that would be acceptable for the group as a whole.

Parent companies should also consider the following factors.

(a) **Reduced systematic risk.** There may be a small incremental reduction in systematic risk from investing abroad due to the segmentation of capital markets.

(b) **Access to capital.** Obtaining capital from foreign markets may increase liquidity, lower costs and make it easier to maintain optimum gearing.

(c) **Agency costs.** These may be higher due to political risk, market imperfections and complexity, leading to a higher cost of capital.

2.3 Dealing with currency risk

To reduce or to eliminate the currency risk of an overseas investment, a company might **finance** it with **funds** in the **same currency** as the investment. The advantages of borrowing in the same currency as an investment are as follows.

(a) Assets and liabilities in the same currency can be **matched**, thus avoiding exchange losses on conversion in the group's annual accounts.

(b) **Revenues** in the foreign currency can be used to **repay borrowings** in the same currency, thus eliminating losses due to fluctuating exchange rates.

Exam focus point

You must be prepared to answer questions about various methods of financing an overseas subsidiary.

3 International debt finance

FAST FORWARD

Multinational companies will have access to international debt, such as **Eurobonds**.

3.1 International borrowing

Borrowing markets are becoming increasingly internationalised, particularly for larger companies. Companies are able to borrow long-term funds on the **eurocurrency (money) markets** and on the markets for **eurobonds**. These markets are collectively called '**euromarkets**'. Large companies can also borrow on the **syndicated loan market** where a syndicate of banks provides medium to long-term currency loans.

If a company is receiving income in a foreign currency or has a long-term investment overseas, it can try to **limit the risk** of adverse exchange rate movements by **matching**. It can take out a long-term loan and use the foreign currency receipts to repay the loan.

3.2 Eurocurrency markets

Key terms

Eurocurrency is currency which is held by individuals and institutions outside the country of issue of that currency.

Eurodollars are US dollars deposited with, or borrowed from, a bank outside the USA. *(OT 2005)*

A UK company might borrow money from a bank or from the investing public, in sterling. However it might also borrow in a foreign currency, especially if it trades abroad, or if it already has assets or liabilities abroad denominated in a foreign currency. When a company borrows in a foreign currency, the loan is known as a **eurocurrency loan**. (As with euro-equity, it is not only the euro that is involved, and so the 'euro-' prefix is a misnomer.) Banks involved in the euro currency market are **not subject to central bank reserve requirements** or regulations in respect of their involvement.

The eurocurrency markets involve the **depositing of funds** with a **bank outside the country** of the currency in which the funds are denominated and **re-lending these funds for a fairly short term**, typically three months, normally at a floating rate of interest. **Eurocredits** are medium to long-term international bank

loans which may be arranged by individual banks or by **syndicates of banks**. Syndication of loans increases the amounts available to hundreds of millions, while reducing the exposure of individual banks.

3.3 Eurobonds

Key term

A **eurobond** is a bond sold outside the jurisdiction of the country in whose currency the bond is denominated. *(OT 2005)*

In recent years, a strong market has built up which allows very large companies to borrow in this way, long-term or short-term. Again, the market is not subject to national regulations.

Eurobonds are **long-term loans raised by international companies** or other institutions and **sold to investors in several countries** at the same time. Eurobonds are normally repaid after 5-15 years, and are for major amounts of capital ie $10m or more.

Exam focus point

Don't make the common mistake of thinking that eurobonds are issued in Europe or only denominated in euros.

3.3.1 How are Eurobonds issued?

Step 1 A lead manager is appointed from a major merchant bank; the lead manager liaises with the credit rating agencies and organises a **credit rating** of the Eurobond.

Step 2 The lead manager organises an **underwriting syndicate** (of other merchant banks) who agree the terms of the bond (eg interest rate, maturity date) and buy the bond.

Step 3 The underwriting syndicate then organise the sale of the bond; this normally involves **placing** the bond with **institutional investors**.

3.3.2 Advantages of Eurobonds

(a) Eurobonds are '**bearer instruments**', which means that the owner does not have to declare his identity.

(b) Interest is paid gross and this has meant that Eurobonds have been used by investors to avoid tax.

(c) Eurobonds create a liability in a foreign currency to **match** against a foreign currency asset.

(d) They are often **cheaper** than a foreign currency bank loan because they can be sold on by the investor, who will therefore accept a lower yield in return for this greater liquidity.

(e) They are also extremely **flexible**. Most eurobonds are fixed rate but they can be floating rate or linked to the financial success of the company.

(f) They are typically issued by companies with excellent credit ratings and are normally **unsecured**, which makes it easier for companies to raise debt finance in the future.

(g) Eurobond issues are not normally advertised because they are **placed** with institutional investors and this reduces issue costs.

3.3.3 Disadvantages of Eurobonds

Like any form of debt finance there will be **issue costs** to consider (approximately 2% of funds raised in the case of Eurobonds) and there may also be problems if gearing levels are too high.

A borrower contemplating a eurobond issue must consider the **foreign exchange risk** of a long-term foreign currency loan. If the money is to be used to purchase assets which will earn revenue in a currency different to that of the bond issue, the borrower will run the risk of exchange losses if the currency of the loan strengthens against the currency of the revenues out of which the bond (and interest) must be repaid.

4 Compliance with listing requirements

When a company decides to raise funds form the local equity markets, the company must comply with the requirements of the local exchanges for listing.

4.1 Listing requirements for the London Stock Exchange

The listing requirements for the London Stock Exchange are:

4.1.1 Track record requirements

The track record requirements are:

(a) At least 75 percent of the entity's business must be supported by a revenue earnings record for the three years period. The UK listing authority has the discretion to allow a shorter period in certain circumstances.

(b) Must report significant acquisitions in the three year running up to the flotation.

4.1.2 Market capitalisation

Market capitalisation and share in public hands:

(a) At least £700,000 for shares at the time of listing.

(b) At least 25% of shares should be in public hands.

4.1.3 Future prospects

The company must show that it has enough working capital for its current needs and for at least the next 12 months.

The company must be able to carry on its business independently and at arm's length from any shareholders with economic interest.

A general description of the future plans and prospects must be given.

If the company gives n optional profit forecast in the document or has already given one publicly, a report will be required from the sponsor and the Reporting Accountant.

4.1.4 Audited historical financial information

Cover latest three full years and any published later interim period.

If latest audited financial data is more than 6 months old, interim audited financial information is required.

4.1.5 Corporate governance

Although the UK corporate governance rules do not apply to the non-UK companies, investors would expect similar standard, and an explanation for any differences. UK companies are expected to:

(a) Splitting the roles of Chairman and CEO.

(b) Except for smaller companies (below FTSE 350), at least half of the board, excluding the chairman, should comprise independent non-executive directors. Smaller companies should have at least two independent non-executive directors.

(c) Have an independent audit committee, a remuneration committee and a nomination committee.

(d) Provide evidence of a high standard of financial controls and accounting systems.

4.1.6 Acceptable jurisdiction and accounting standards

The company must be properly incorporated

IFRS and equivalent accounting standards are acceptable.

4.1.7 Other considerations

Sponsors/Underwriters usually recommend that existing shareholders should be barred form selling their shares for a period after initial listing offering of their shares.

The sponsor will need to make sure through due and careful enquiry, that the applicant has established procedures that enable it to comply with the listing rules and disclosure rules, as well having established procedures which provide a reasonable basis for the applicant to make proper judgements on an ongoing basis as to its financial position and prospects.

5 Capital mobility and blocked funds

FAST FORWARD

Multinationals can take various measures to combat the risks of political **interference** or **turbulence** including agreements with governments, insurance, and location elsewhere of key parts of the production process.

Multinationals can **counter exchange controls** by management charges or royalties.

5.1 Blocked funds

Exchange controls block the flow of foreign exchange into and out of a country, usually to defend the local currency or to protect reserves of foreign currencies. Exchange controls are generally more restrictive in developing and less developed countries although some still exist in developed countries. Typically, a government might enforce regulations:

(a) **Rationing the supply of foreign exchange**. Anyone wishing to make payments abroad in a foreign currency will be restricted by the limited supply, which stops them from buying as much as they want from abroad.

(b) **Restricting the types of transaction** for which payments abroad are allowed, for example by suspending or banning the payment of dividends to foreign shareholders, such as parent companies in multinationals, who will then have the problem of **blocked funds**.

5.2 Dealing with blocked funds

Ways of overcoming blocked funds include the following.

(a) The parent company could **sell goods or services** to the subsidiary and obtain payment. The amount of this payment will depend on the volume of sales and also on the transfer price for the sales.

(b) A parent company which grants a subsidiary the right to make goods protected by patents can charge a **royalty** on any goods that the subsidiary sells. The size of any royalty can be adjusted to suit the wishes of the parent company's management.

(c) If the parent company makes a **loan** to a subsidiary, it can set the interest rate high or low, thereby affecting the profits of both companies. A high rate of interest on a loan, for example, would improve the parent company's profits to the detriment of the subsidiary's profits.

(d) **Management charges** may be levied by the parent company for costs incurred in the management of international operations.

6 Risk exposure

FAST FORWARD

The methods of financing overseas subsidiaries will depend on the **length of investment period** envisaged, also the **local finance costs, taxation systems** and **restrictions on dividend remittances**.

6.1 Political risks for multinationals

Key term

Political risk is the risk that political action will affect the position and value of a company.

When a multinational company invests in another country, by setting up a subsidiary, it may face a **political risk** of action by that country's government which restricts the multinational's freedom.

If a government tries to prevent the exploitation of its country by multinationals, it may take various measures.

(a) Import **quotas** could be used to limit the quantities of goods that a subsidiary can buy from its parent company and import for resale in its domestic markets.

(b) Import **tariffs** could make imports (such as from parent companies) more expensive and domestically produced goods therefore more competitive.

(c) Legal standards of safety or quality (**non-tariff barriers**) could be imposed on imported goods to prevent multinationals from selling goods through a subsidiary which have been banned as dangerous in other countries.

(d) **Exchange control regulations** could be applied (see below).

(e) A government could **restrict** the ability of foreign companies to buy domestic companies, especially those that operate in politically sensitive industries such as defence contracting, communications, energy supply and so on.

(f) A government could **nationalise** foreign-owned companies and their assets (with or without compensation to the parent company).

(g) A government could insist on a **minimum shareholding** in companies by residents. This would force a multinational to offer some of the equity in a subsidiary to investors in the country where the subsidiary operates.

6.2 Assessment of political risk

There are a large number of factors that can be taken into account when assessing political risk, for example:

- Government stability
- Political and business ethics
- Economic stability/inflation
- Degree of international indebtedness
- Financial infrastructure
- Level of import restrictions
- Remittance restrictions
- Assets seized
- Existence of special taxes and regulations on overseas investors, or investment incentives

In addition **micro factors**, factors only affecting the company or the industry in which it invests, may be more significant than macro factors, particularly in companies such as hi-tech organisations.

Measurement is often by **subjective weighting** of these factors. Macro analysis may involve use of measures such as those developed by Euromoney or the Economist Intelligence Unit. Micro analysis may be more problematic; specially tailored consultancy reports may be needed, also visits to the country or drawing on the experience of those who know the country

6.3 Dealing with political risks

There are various strategies that multinational companies can adopt to limit the effects of political risk.

6.3.1 Negotiations with host government

The aim of these negotiations is generally to obtain a **concession agreement**. This would cover matters such as the transfer of capital, remittances and products, access to local finance, government intervention and taxation, and transfer pricing.

6.3.2 Insurance

In the UK the Export Credits Guarantee Department (ECGD) provides **protection against various threats** including nationalisation, currency conversion problems, war and revolution.

6.3.3 Production strategies

It may be necessary to strike a balance between **contracting out to local sources** (thus losing control) and **producing directly** (which increases the investment and hence increases the potential loss). Alternatively it may be better to locate key parts of the production process or the distribution channels abroad. Control of patents is another possibility, since these can be enforced internationally.

6.3.4 Contacts with markets

Multinationals may have **contacts with customers** which interventionist governments cannot obtain.

6.3.5 Financial management

If a multinational obtains funds in local investment markets, these may be on terms that are **less favourable** than on markets abroad, but would mean that local institutions suffered if the local government intervened. However governments often do limit the ability of multinationals to obtain funds locally.

Alternatively guarantees can be obtained from the government for the investment that can be enforced by the multinational if the government takes action.

6.3.6 Management structure

Possible methods include **joint ventures** or **ceding control** to local investors and obtaining profits by a management contract.

If governments do intervene, multinationals may have to make use of the advantages they hold or threaten withdrawal. The threat of expropriation may be reduced by negotiation or legal threats.

Exam focus point

The political risks of investing overseas may be examined in a number of ways. Discussion of the risks may be part of a longer question involving a numerical analysis of an overseas investment. Alternatively political risks may be examined as a shorter optional question or part of one.

7 Litigation risks

FAST FORWARD

Litigation risks can be reduced by keeping abreast of changes, acting as a good corporate citizen and lobbying.

7.1 Legal impacts

Companies may face government legislation or action in any jurisdiction that extend over its whole range of activities. Important areas may include:

(a) **Export and import controls** for political, environmental, or health and safety reasons. Such controls may not be overt but instead take the form of bureaucratic procedures designed to discourage international trade or protect home producers.

(b) **Favourable trade status** for particular countries, eg EU membership, former Commonwealth countries.

(c) **Monopolies and mergers legislation**, which may be interpreted not only within a country but also across nations. Thus the acquisition of a company in country A, by company B, which both sell in country C may be seen as a monopolistic restraint of trade.

(d) **Law of ownership**. Especially in developing countries, there may be legislation requiring local majority ownership of a firm or its subsidiary in that country, for example.

(e) **Acceptance of international trademark, copyright and patent conventions**. Not all countries recognise such international conventions.

(f) Determination of minimum **technical standards** that the goods must meet eg noise levels, contents and so on.

(g) **Standardisation measures** such as packaging sizes.

(h) **Pricing regulations**, including credit (eg, some countries require importers to deposit payment in advance and may require the price to be no lower than those of domestic competitors).

(i) **Restrictions on promotional messages**, methods and media.

(j) **Product liability**. Different countries have different rules regarding product liability (ie the manufacturer's/retailer's responsibility for defects in the product sold and/or injury caused). US juries are notoriously generous in this respect.

Bear in mind that organisations may also face legal risks from lack of legislation (or lack of enforcement of legislation) designed to protect them.

Case Study

The lax enforcement of intellectual property legislation can cause problems for companies trading in certain markets. Britain's Imperial Tobacco group has had difficulties with its operations in Indonesia. A provincial trader, Sumatra stole the trademark of its premier cigarette brand, Davidoff, and Imperial Tobacco had major problems enforcing its rights.

The problem lay not in the law, which was strengthened about 10 years ago, but in the reluctance of the courts to enforce the law. Eventually Imperial needed a decision by the Indonesian Supreme Court to enforce its rights. The lower courts had refused to consider evidence that the sale of the trademark to Sumatra was fraudulent, and ignored claims that Sumatra was not actively using the trademark as it was required to do by Indonesian law.

Imperial Tobacco's problems could have had serious consequences for the Indonesian economy as a whole. Not only had Imperial Tobacco planned to invest in a hi-tech factory generating hundreds of jobs, but Imperial's problems might have deterred other companies from investing even though 2003 was designated by the Indonesian government as the year of investment.

Far Eastern Economic Review 22 May 2003

7.2 Dealing with legal risks

7.2.1 Consequences of non-compliance

Businesses that fail to comply with the law run the risk of **legal penalties** and accompanying **bad publicity**. Companies may also be forced into legal action to counter claims of allegedly bad practice that is not actually illegal; as the McDonalds case demonstrates, even a victory in such an action cannot prevent much bad publicity.

The issues of legal standards and costs have very significant implications for companies that trade internationally. Companies that meet a strict set of standards in one country may face accusations of **hypocrisy** if their practices are laxer elsewhere. Ultimately higher costs of compliance, as well as costs of labour may mean that companies **relocate** to countries where costs and regulatory burdens are lower.

7.2.2 The legislative process

Policy in many areas only changes slowly over time. Industries and organisations must however be alert for **likely changes in policy.**

Businesses also need to consider the impact of changes in how powers are **devolved** outside central government. In America state legislatures have been described as 'the forum for the ideas of the nation'. Directly elected mayors also wield considerable power in major cities.

7.2.3 Good citizenship

One aspect of minimising problems from governmental intervention is social and commercial good citizenship, **complying with best practice** and being responsive to **ethical concerns**. Often what is considered good practice at present is likely to acquire some regulatory force in the future. In addition, compliance with voluntary codes, particularly those relating to best practice or relations with consumers, can be **marketed positively**.

7.2.4 Other steps

Companies may wish to take all possible steps to avoid the bad publicity resulting from a court action. This includes implementing systems to make sure that the company **keeps abreast** of **changes in the law**, and staff are kept fully informed. Internal procedures may be designed to minimise the risks from legal action, for example **human resource policies** that minimise the chances of the company suffering an adverse judgement in a case brought by a disgruntled ex-employee. Contracts may be drawn up requiring **binding arbitration** in the case of disputes.

Of course compliance with legislation may involve **extra costs**, including the extra procedures and investment necessary to conform to safety standards, staff training costs and legal costs. However these costs may also act as a **significant barrier to entry**, benefiting companies that are already in the industry.

8 Cultural risks

FAST FORWARD

Cultural risks affect the products and services produced and the way organisations are managed and staffed. Businesses should take cultural issues into account when deciding where to sell abroad, and how much to **centralise** activities.

8.1 Challenges of different cultures

Where a business trades with, or invests in, a foreign country additional uncertainty is introduced by the existence of different customs, laws and language. Communication between parties can be hindered, and potential deals put into jeopardy by ignorance of the expected manner in which such transactions should be conducted.

The following areas may be particularly important.

(a) The **cultures and practices of customers** and consumers in individual markets

(b) The **media and distribution systems** in overseas markets

(c) The **different ways of doing business** (eg it is reputed that Japanese companies are concerned to avoid excessive legalism) in overseas markets

(d) The degree to which **national cultural differences matter** for the product concerned (a great deal for some consumer products, eg washing machines where some countries prefer front-loading machines and others prefer top-loading machines, but less so for products such as gas turbines)

(e) The degree to which a firm can use its own **'national culture'** as a selling point

8.2 Dealing with cultural risk

8.2.1 Deciding which markets to enter

Making the right choices about which markets to enter is a key element in dealing with cultural risk. When deciding what types of country it should enter (in terms of environmental factors, economic development, language used, cultural similarities and so on), the major criteria for this decision should be as follows.

(a) **Market attractiveness**. This concerns such indicators as GNP/head and forecast demand.

(b) **Competitive advantage**. This is principally dependent on prior experience in similar markets, language and cultural understanding.

(c) **Risk**. This involves an analysis of political stability, the possibility of government intervention and similar external influences.

Some products are extremely sensitive to the **environmental differences**, which bring about the need for adaptation; others are not at all sensitive to these differences, in which case standardisation is possible.

Environmentally sensitive	Environmentally insensitive
Adaptation necessary • Fashion clothes • Convenience foods	Standardisation possible • Industrial and agricultural products • World market products, eg jeans

8.2.2 Use of control systems

Local conditions and the scale of operations will influence the organisation structure of companies trading internationally. Conglomerates with widely differing product groups may organise globally by product, with each operating division having its own geographic structure suited to its own needs.

Companies with more integrated operations may prefer their top-level structure to be broken down **geographically** with product management conducted locally.

Very large and complex companies may be organised as a **heterarchy,** an organic structure with significant local control.

(a) **Some headquarters functions are diffused geographically**. For example, R&D might be in the UK, marketing in the US. Some central functions might be split up: many firms are experimenting with having several centres for R&D.

(b) **Subsidiary managers have a strategic role for the corporation as a whole** (eg through bargaining and coalition forming).

(c) **Co-ordination is achieved through corporate culture and shared values** rather than a formal hierarchy. Employees with long experience might have worked in a number of different product divisions.

(d) **Alliances** can be formed with other company parts and other firms, perhaps in joint ventures or consortia.

8.2.3 Management of human resources

The balance between local and expatriate staff must be managed. There are a number of influences.

- The availability of technical skills such as financial management
- The need for control
- The importance of product and company experience
- The need to provide promotion opportunities
- Costs associated with expatriates such as travel and higher salaries
- Cultural factors

For an international company, which has to think globally as well as act locally, there are a number of problems.

- Do you employ mainly **expatriate staff** to control local operations?
- Do you employ **local managers**, with the possible loss of central control?
- Is there such a thing as the **global manager**, equally at home in different cultures?

Expatriate staff are sometimes favoured over local staff.

(a) Poor **educational opportunities** in the market may require the import of skilled technicians and managers. For example, expatriates have been needed in many western firms' operations in Russia and Eastern Europe, simply because they understand the importance of profit.

(b) Some senior managers believe that a business run by expatriates is easier to **control** than one run by local staff.

(c) Expatriates might be better able than locals to **communicate** with the corporate centre.

(d) The expatriate may **know more about the firm** overall, which is especially important if he or she is fronting a sales office.

The use of expatriates in overseas markets has certain disadvantages.

(a) They **cost** more (eg subsidised housing, school fees).

(b) **Culture shock**. The expatriate may fail to adjust to the culture (eg by associating only with other expatriates). This is likely to lead to poor management effectiveness, especially if the business requires personal contact.

(c) A substantial training programme might be needed.

(i) **Basic facts** about the country will be given with basic language training, and some briefings about cultural differences.

(ii) **Immersion training** involves detailed language and cultural training and simulation of field social and business experiences. This is necessary to obtain an intellectual understanding and practical awareness of the culture.

Employing local managers raises the following issues.

(a) A **glass ceiling** might exist in some companies. Talented local managers may not make it to board level if, most members of the board are drawn from one country.

(b) In some cases, it may be hard for locals to **assimilate** into the **corporate culture**, and this might led to communication problems.

(c) Locals will **have greater knowledge of the country**, but may find it difficult to understand the wider corporate picture.

The following issues may also be important.

(a) **Recruitment and training**. In countries with low levels of literacy, more effort might need to be spent on basic training.

(b) **Career management**. Can overseas staff realistically expect promotion to the firm's highest levels if they do well?

(c) **Appraisal schemes**. These can be a minefield at the best of times, and the possibilities for communications failure are endless. For example, in some cultures, an appraisal is a two way discussion whereas in others arguing back might be considered a sign of insubordination.

(d) Problems associated with the **status of women**.

(e) **Communications**. Human resources management tries to mobilise employees' commitment to the goals of the organisation. In far-flung global firms, the normal panoply of staff newsletters and team briefings may be hard to institute but are vital. Time differences also make communication difficult.

9 Agency issues

FAST FORWARD

Agency issues can be observed in all types and at all levels of organisations for example between managers at headquarters and managers of subsidiaries. These issues can be addressed by a bundle of corporate governance mechanisms.

9.1 Agency problems in multinational companies

We have already studied in Chapter 1 of this text the **agency problem** between **shareholders** and **managers**. However, these are not the only kinds of dyadic agency relationships. In fact, agency relationships are fairly general and can be observed in all types and levels of organisations. For example, **agency relationships** exist between the CEOs of conglomerates (the principals) and the strategic business unit (SBU) managers that report to these CEOs (agents). The interests of the individual SBU managers may be **incongruent** not only with the interests of the CEOs, but also with those of the other SBU managers. Each SBU manager may try to make sure his or her unit gets access to **critical resources** and achieves the **best performance** at the expense of the performance of other SBUs and the whole organization.

Similarly, **agency relationships** exist between the **managers** at the **headquarters** of **multinational corporations (principals)** and the managers that run the **subsidiaries** of **multinational corporations (agents)**. The **agency relationships** are created between the headquarters and subsidiaries of multinational corporations because, the interests of the managers at the headquarters who are responsible for the performance of the whole organization can be considerably different from the interests of the managers that run the subsidiaries.

The incongruence of interests between the multinationals' headquarters and subsidiaries can arise, not only due to concerns that can be seen in any parent-subsidiary relationship, but also due to the fact that the multinationals' headquarters and subsidiaries operate in different cultures and have divergent backgrounds.

Finally, similar to what we observe in shareholder-manager relationships, the subsidiary managers in the headquarters-subsidiary relationships are monitored and bonded via bundles of **subsidiary specific corporate governance mechanisms**, so that the **agency costs** are **minimised**. These **subsidiary specific bundles** of **monitoring** and **bonding contracts** represent the **headquarters-subsidiary corporate governance relationships**.

It is also possible that the **corporate governance** mechanisms that make-up the bundles that represent corporate governance relationships are institutions that are **internal** to the firm, such as

- The board of directors
- Large outside shareholders
- Mutual monitoring among managers
- Managerial share ownership
- Managerial compensation packages
- Financial leverage

Other mechanisms involve institutions that are external to the firm, such as

- Capital market
- Market for corporate control
- External managerial labour market
- Product market

In the following paragraphs, we review two of the major **internal corporate governance mechanisms** extensively to demonstrate how they work to align the interests of the **shareholders** and **managers**, and the **headquarters** and **subsidiaries**.

9.2 Solutions to the agency problems in multinational companies

9.2.1 Board of directors

One way of reducing **agency costs** is to separate the **ratification** and **monitoring** of managerial decisions from their **initiation** and **implementation**. Boards of directors, which consist of top level executives of firms and non-executive outside members, are institutions that carry out the role of **ratifying** and **monitoring** the managerial decisions with the help of their **non-executive** outside members.

As is the case with all **corporate governance** mechanisms, monitoring by boards of directors is not without costs. Outsiders on the board may lack the expertise about the firm that the managers of the firm have, therefore, the outsiders may accept unsound managerial proposals and reject sound ones. The outsiders may also lack the incentives to challenge managerial decisions. **Subsidiary boards** of directors have similar characteristics to the **corporate boards** of directors. However, it must be noted that in subsidiary boards the role of outsiders may be played not only by directors that are not affiliated with the parent company or the subsidiary in any way, but also by **directors** that are **employees** of the **parent** but not of the **subsidiary**.

9.2.2 Managerial compensation packages

FAST FORWARD

Managerial compensation packages can be used to reduce **agency costs** in aligning the interests of top executives with shareholders and the interests of subsidiary managers to those of head office.

Top executive incentive systems can reduce **agency costs** and align the interests of the managers to those of the shareholders by making top **executives' pay contingent** upon the **value** they **create** for the **shareholders**. **Value** created for the **shareholders** can be measured by various criteria such as the **growth** in the **firm's market value**, **accounting returns**, **cash flows**, and even **subjective measures**.

Tying managerial compensation to firm value is not without costs. As managers' exposure to firm specific risk increases, the risk averse managers may ask to be compensated at higher levels to make up for the risk they are undertaking.

Managerial compensation packages can be used to align the interests of the **subsidiary managers** to those of the headquarters, too. An additional friction that makes using contingent compensation more costly in subsidiaries is that most subsidiaries of multinational corporations are not publicly traded companies. As a result, market value based standards and rewards can not be used in subsidiary contingent compensation schemes.

9.2.3 Bundles of corporate governance mechanisms as the nexus of contracts

As we have emphasized in our review of each **corporate governance mechanism**, none of the mechanisms operates without costs or frictions. As a result, any single mechanism cannot mitigate the agency problem completely. In order to address the agency problem a firm faces, a **multiple of** these **mechanisms** need to work in **unison**. Another important characteristic of corporate governance mechanisms is that they substitute for and complement each other. The frictions related to each mechanism and substitution effects between mechanisms suggest that the mechanisms do not operate independently (i.e., their effects are not additive), rather the mechanisms work as **bundles** of **mechanisms** in reducing the **agency costs**.

Finally, we can say that the bundles of corporate governance mechanisms are the **nexus of contracts**, which align the interests of the shareholders and the managers in the public corporation and the interests of the headquarters and the subsidiaries in the multinational corporation. Therefore, the bundles of corporate governance mechanisms represent **shareholder-manager** and **parent-subsidiary corporate governance relationships**.

Chapter Roundup

- **Multinational enterprises** undertake **foreign direct investment (FDI)** for reasons including obtaining **cost and revenue advantages, tax considerations** and **process specialisation**.

  FDI can stimulate economic activity in the host country, but it can also lead to a **loss of political and economic sovereignty**.
- There are many strategic reasons for engaging in foreign investment which include seeking new markets for goods, new sources of raw materials, production efficiency, expertise and political safety.
- Commonly used means to establish an **interest abroad** include:
  - Joint ventures
  - Licensing agreements
  - Management contracts
  - Subsidiaries
  - Branches
- **Multinational companies** need to develop a **financial planning framework** in order to make sure that the strategic objectives and competitive advantages are realised. Such a financial **planning framework** will include ways of raising **capital** and **risks** related to overseas operations and the **repatriation of profits**.
- Multinational companies will have access to international debt, such as **Eurobonds**.
- When a company decides to raise funds form the local equity markets, the company must comply with the requirements of the local exchanges for listing.
- Multinationals can take various measures to combat the risks of political **interference** or **turbulence** including agreements with governments, insurance, and location elsewhere of key parts of the production process.
- Multinationals can **counter exchange controls** by management charges or royalties.
- The methods of financing overseas subsidiaries will depend on the **length of investment period** envisaged, also the **local finance costs**, **taxation systems** and **restrictions on dividend remittances**.
- **Litigation risks** can be reduced by keeping abreast of changes, acting as a good corporate citizen and lobbying.
- **Cultural risks** affect the products and services produced and the way organisations are managed and staffed. Businesses should take cultural issues into account when deciding where to sell abroad, and how much to **centralise** activities.
- **Agency issues** can be observed in all types and at all levels of organisations for example between managers at headquarters and managers of subsidiaries. These issues can be addressed by a bundle of corporate governance mechanisms.
- **Managerial compensation packages** can be used to reduce **agency costs** in aligning the interests of top executives with shareholders and the interests of subsidiary managers to those of head office.

Quick Quiz

1 Give three reasons why a multinational might establish an overseas subsidiary.

2 Give three factors that might influence the choice of finance for an overseas subsidiary.

3 By what methods do governments impose exchange controls?

4 Give four examples of ways companies can overcome exchange controls.

5 Forward integration would involve acquiring final production and distribution facilities in other countries.

True ☐

False ☐

6 What principal characteristics is a tax haven most likely to have?

7 Why might a firm looking to establish an overseas presence choose to set up a branch rather than a subsidiary?

8 What are the main differences between a contractual joint venture and a joint-equity venture?

Answers to Quick Quiz

1 Any three of:

(a) Location of markets
(b) Need for a sales organisation
(c) Opportunity to produce goods more cheaply
(d) Need to avoid import controls
(e) Need to obtain access for raw materials
(f) Availability of grants and tax concessions

2 Any three of:

(a) Local finance costs
(b) Taxation systems
(c) Restrictions on dividend remittances
(d) Flexibility in repayments

3 (a) Rationing the supply of foreign exchange
(b) Restricting the types of transaction for which payments abroad are allowed

4 (a) Selling goods or services to subsidiary
(b) Charging a royalty on goods sold by subsidiary
(c) Interest rate manipulation
(d) Management charges

5 True

6 (a) Tax on foreign investment or sales income earned by resident companies, and withholding tax on dividends paid to parent should be low

(b) Stable government and stable currency

(c) Adequate financial service support facilities

7 (a) More favourable tax (not subject to withholding tax)
(b) Fewer legal formalities

8 A contractual joint venture is for a fixed period, duties and responsibilities are defined in a contract
A joint-equity venture involves investment, is of no fixed duration and continually evolves.

Now try the questions below from the Exam Question Bank

Number	Level	Marks	Time
37	Examination	19	34 mins

PART G

Emerging issues

25 Recent developments and trends in world financial markets and international trade

Topic list	Syllabus reference
1 Overview	G(1)
2 Developments in world financial markets	G (3)
3 Developments in international trade and finance	G (3)

Introduction

In this chapter we discuss developments in global financial markets as well as developments in international trade and finance and how they impact on the operations of a multinational company.

Study guide

		Intellectual level
G1	**Developments in world financial markets**	
	Demonstrate awareness, and discuss the significance to the firm, of latest developments in the world financial markets with particular reference to the removal of barriers to the free movement of capital and the international regulations on money laundering.	2
G3	**Developments in international trade and finance**	
	Demonstrate an awareness of new developments in the macroeconomic environment, establishing their impact upon the firm, and advising on the appropriate response to those developments both internally and externally.	2

1 Overview

The previous chapters have examined a number of issues regarding the financial decision making in a corporation, together with the impact of the economic and financial environment on multinational companies. In this chapter we first review the most important developments in financial markets, such as the growth in derivatives, globalization and the creation of the euro. We then discuss some recent developments in international trade and finance and how they impact on the operations of multinational companies.

2 Developments in world financial markets

FAST FORWARD

Developments in international financial markets have facilitated the growth in trade and the funding of overseas expansion strategies and have opened up more opportunities for investors. The main developments are:

- Globalisation
- Growth in derivatives
- Securitisation
- The single European currency
- The adoption of common accounting standards

2.1 Integration and globalisation

Perhaps foremost among recent changes in world financial markets has been their accelerating **integration** and **globalisation**. This development, has been fostered by the **liberalisation of markets**, the rapid **technological progress** especially in computer power, and major advances in **telecommunications**. **Globalisation** has created **new investment** and **financing opportunities** for businesses and people around the world. It has made easier the access to **global financial markets** for **individuals** and **corporations** and this leads to a more **efficient allocation** of capital, which, in turn, will promote **economic growth** and **prosperity**.

2.2 The growth of derivatives markets

A second interesting development in world financial markets include the continued **broadening** and **expansion** of **derivatives** markets. The broadening of these markets has largely come about because rapid advances in technology, **financial engineering**, and **risk management** have helped to enhance both the **supply** of and the **demand** for more **complex** and **sophisticated derivatives** products. The increased use of derivatives to adjust exposure to risk in financial markets has also contributed to the rise in the notional amounts of outstanding derivatives contracts seen in recent years, in particular in over-the-counter (OTC) derivatives markets. While the leveraged nature of derivative instruments poses risks to individual

investors, derivatives also provide scope for a more efficient allocation of risks in the economy, which is beneficial for the functioning of financial markets, and hence enhances the conditions for **economic growth**.

The size of the market for both the Over the Counter (OTC) and the exchange-traded instruments has increased significantly over the last few years. The size of the OTC market is estimated using the notional amounts of outstanding derivatives produced by the Bank for International Settlements (BIS) in tits triennial survey. Other estimates are produced by the International Swap and Derivatives Association (ISDA).

The following table shows the size of the market by instrument for 2001 and 2004. Both measures show that the size of the derivatives market more than doubled between 2001 and 2004 to $220 trillion.

Global Positions in OTC markets by type of instrument ($billion)

	Notional amounts at end-June 2001	*Notional amounts at end-June 2004*
Foreign exchange contracts	20,435	31,500
Interest rate contracts	75,813	177,457
Equity-linked contracts	2,039	5,094
Commodity contracts	674	1,354
Credit-linked and other contracts	698	4,664
Total contracts	99,659	220,069

Source: BIS Triennial Report

The market for exchange-traded derivatives is not as large as the OTC market. The BIS survey of organized derivatives markets across the world, reports that the notional amount of derivatives was $52.8 trillion in 2004, and $19.5 trillion in 2001.

Global Position in exchange-traded derivative instruments ($billion)

	Position at end-June 2001	*Position at end-June 2004*
Exchange-traded currency contracts	66	98
Exchange-traded interest rate contracts	17,515	49,385
Exchange-traded equity index contracts	1,912	3,318
	19,493	52,801

Source: BIS, Triennial Report

2.3 Securitisation

Apart from this ongoing **integration** and **globalisation**, world financial markets have also recently experienced increased **securitisation**. Securitisation (covered in Chapter 18) refers to the process of **creating assets from cash flows** and selling those assets to investors. Examples of securitization include the sale of loans by banks. In part, this development has been spurred by the surge in mergers and acquisitions and leveraged buy-outs. Securitisation has become a very common form of financing and it has led to an increase in corporate bond issuance, which has also coincided with a diminishing supply of government bonds in many countries, particularly in the United States.

2.4 Convergence of financial institutions

Traditionally, financial institutions were operating within clearly delineated boundaries. Banks were engaged in **deposit taking** and **loan provision**, **insurance companies** in the **transfer of risks, securities firms** and **investment banks** in the provision of **services** related to **capital markets**. The separation of activities was reflected in separate regulatory authorities. In the UK, for example, banks were regulated by the Bank of England, whereas insurance companies were regulated by the Department of Trade and Industry.

Similarly, in the US, the Glass-Steagall Act of 1933 barred banks, brokerages and insurance companies from entering each others' industries, and investment banking and commercial banking were separated.

In the UK, the Financial Services Act 1986 abolished the barriers between the various financial firms, allowing banks to enter the insurance and securities markets and creating a **single regulatory authority**. Similarly, in the US the Financial Services Modernization Act of 1999 also did away with restrictions on the integration of banking, insurance and stock trading.

The result of abolishing the barriers to entry in the various segments of the financial services industries has led to the creation of **financial conglomerates** with operations in **banking**, **securities** and **insurance**. The effect of this convergence is:

(a) The creation of **economies of scale** as operations that were previously performed by different companies are now performed by one company

(b) The creation of **economies of scope** since one factor of production can be employed in the production of more that one products

(c) The **reduction of volatility of earnings** since some of the earnings are fee-based and not influenced by the economic cycle.

(d) The **saving** of consumers **significant search costs** since they can buy all financial product from one source.

2.5 The creation of the euro

The launch of the euro on 1 January 1999 by converting initially 11 and later with the addition of Greece, 12 national currencies into one single currency overnight had tremendous implications for the world financial markets, beyond its political importance in the creation of a stable, prosperous and peaceful Europe.

The creation of the euro has been an important element in the process of integration in European financial markets and has been influenced and has in turn influenced the trend towards globalisation. The euro created a **single monetary policy**, a **uniform policy implementation framework** for all euro area countries, and introduced a **unified payment system** providing for **real-time gross settlement** transfers throughout the Euro area.

2.5.1 The banking sector

The creation of the euro and the transparency brought about by a single currency and a single monetary policy makes it easier for customers to compare **bank products** and **costs**. This, in turn, fostered competition among banks. Although this increased competition may lead to lower bank margins, it has promoted restructuring and consolidation among banks in the euro area, which has helped them to compete globally. Banks all over Europe are merging or forming alliances on an unprecedented scale, thereby drastically changing the national banking environment and creating **international networks**. Hence, the introduction of the euro has not only provided banks with a market large enough to support their efforts in global competition, but also pressured them to undertake the **restructuring** and **consolidation** they need in order to be successful in an **increasingly global market**.

2.5.2 Securities markets

In addition to these changes in the banking sector, the advent of the euro also provided the basis for a **Europe-wide securities market**. The euro area money market underwent a wide-ranging process of integration and standardisation following the introduction of the single monetary policy framework. The unsecured deposit markets and the derivatives markets became fully integrated in early 1999. Moreover, the need to redistribute liquidity among euro area countries, including liquidity provided by the eurosystem as part of its refinancing operations, fostered the development of area-wide transactions in the money markets.

2.5.3 Bond markets

Another sector in which impressive changes have taken place following the introduction of the euro is the **euro-denominated bond market**. There was a marked rise in private bond issuance in the euro area after 1999 which has continued broadly unabated since then. Following the introduction of the euro, the euro-

denominated component of international bond markets played a far larger role than the predecessor currencies of the euro had hitherto. In other words, the whole has turned out to be much greater than the sum of the parts. Apart from this, it also became clear that various characteristics of newly issued debt securities were changing. In particular, the average size of new bond issues rose considerably in 1999, as the number of very large issues, of 1 billion euro or more, grew significantly. These changes show that the newly created **euro-denominated bond market**, by virtue of its size and high degree of openness, is more able to absorb very large issues than the individual bond markets of the predecessor currencies of the euro. Hence, the introduction of the single currency has resulted in more efficient and well-functioning markets, which benefit not only euro area residents, but also market participants outside the euro area. Furthermore, this market still has great potential since the use of securities finance by the corporate sector, relative to bank finance, is still only about half that of its counterpart in the United States.

2.5.4 Asset management

Similar efficiency gains can be reaped in the **asset management industry**. The European investment funds currently manage over 5 trillion euro of assets. It is a vital link between financial markets and the real economy and household investors. The single currency will lead to simplifying notification procedures; delivering a real simplified prospectus; opening up distribution systems; facilitating fund mergers and pooling; allowing management company passports; and tackling regulatory arbitrage from substitute products.

2.6 Financial reporting

From 1 January 2006 all EU listed companies must use IFRS for their consolidated financial statements. Common accounting standards increase **transparency** and **comparability** for investors. This should lead to a more **efficient capital market**, much more transparency and greater cross-border investment, thereby promoting growth and employment in Europe. Making IFRS work in the EU will also allow greater access of EU companies to global capital markets since it will include removal of the reconciliation requirement to US GAAP for companies which list in the US.

2.7 Effect on the corporate sector

Globalisation and the single European currency have led to the restructuring of the global and European corporate sector, and the emergence of new companies. The raising of capital through **global equity** and **bond markets** has become commonplace and has made easier **cross-border mergers** as well as **foreign direct investment**. These developments can only favour those companies which may have found it difficult in the past to finance themselves, but which will now be able to raise equity more easily.

The ongoing integration process of the national stock exchanges has also been conducive to this development. Primary issues of European equities has been steadily increasing with whole new markets, such as the Neuer Markt in Frankfurt, becoming prominent internationally. In addition, a number of **Europe-wide equity indices** have been established, thereby contributing to extending the trading possibilities and the position-taking opportunities for institutional investors from many European countries. The elimination of exchange rate risks has also allowed many European institutional investors which were previously constrained to investing in the domestic market to invest in any European market, increasing the supply of capital.

Finally, alliances between stock exchanges also foster the integration of stock market infrastructures and trading platforms creating more competition and making the European markets more resilient and fit for the global economy.

2.8 Money laundering legislation

FAST FORWARD

The growth of globalisation has created however more opportunities for money laundering which governments and international bodies are trying to combat with legislation.

One of the side effects of globalisation and the free movement of capital has been the growth in **money laundering**.

Key term

Money laundering constitutes any financial transactions whose purpose is to conceal the identity of the parties to the transaction or to make the tracing of the money difficult.

Money laundering is used by organised crime and terrorist organisations but it is also used in order to avoid the payment of taxes or to distort accounting information. Money laundering involves therefore a number of agents and entities from criminals and terrorists to companies and corrupt officials or states as well as tax havens.

The increasing complexity of financial crime and its increase has prompted national governments and the European Union to legislate and regulate the contact of transactions. The Third Money Laundering Directive of the EU was formally adopted on 26th October 2005 and it will be implemented by the 15th December 2007.

At the same time the Financial Services Authority requires that professionals who engage in the provision of financial services should warn the authorities when they discover that illegal transactions have taken place.

3 Developments in international trade and finance

FAST FORWARD

The globalisation and integration of financial markets has contributed to expansion of international trade, but it has also created potentially more uncertainty for multinational companies.

The macroeconomic environment has a catalytic effect on business activities. A **stable macroeconomic environment** with **minimal exchange rate** and **interest rate fluctuations** allows business to plan their activities and to predict the key drivers of their value. An economic environment in which there is **uncertainty** about the cost of capital or currency rates, is not conducive to long-term planning. In this section we review some developments that have taken place recently and which have an impact on multinational companies.

3.1 Trade and world deflation

Trade among nations is a common occurrence and normally benefits both the exporter and the importer. In many countries international trade accounts for more than 20 percent of their national incomes. **Foreign trade** can usually be justified on the principle of **comparative advantage**. According to this economic principle, it is economically profitable for a country to specialize in the production of that commodity in which the producer country has the greater comparative advantage and to allow the other country to produce that commodity in which it has the lesser comparative disadvantage. We have already concluded in previous chapters that the risks of foreign trade increase as a company moves from exporting to direct foreign investment and when its activities are directed to less developed countries rather than to developed countries.

The most important application of the principle of **comparative advantage** has been the Chinese economy. China has exploited its comparative advantage stemming from low wages to dominate the production of labour-intensive products which being produced at a fraction of the production cost in developed countries has contributed to the world-wide low inflation regime of the last few years. The reduction of the cost has kept prices down and has increased consumer purchasing power world wide.

3.2 Contact of monetary policy

One of the most important developments in the macroeconomic environment has been the way monetary policy has been conducted in the advanced economies. Monetary policy has been assigned the task of controlling inflation and is largely outside the control of the national governments.

The **Bank of England** became independent of the government in 1997 and sets interest rates so as to meet the inflationary target set out by the government. Similarly, the **European Central Bank** sets the interest rates in the euro zone. The **independence of central banks** from government interference has given credibility to their policies and has stabilised the financial markets. This in turn has affected the expectations about inflation of market participants and has lowered inflation. A **low inflation environment** is conducive to **long-term planning** by business and **stimulates investment**.

3.3 Trade zones and international trade

We have already discussed in previous chapters that the main obstacles to international trade are capital restrictions and tariffs imposed upon imports as well as restrictions on capital mobility. Tariffs are usually imposed to provide revenue or to protect a home industry. The basic arguments for tariffs are:

(a) To protect infant or key industries
(b) To equalize costs of production between domestic and foreign producers
(c) To protect domestic jobs
(d) To prevent capital flight

Other measures that have been used selectively to control imports are **import quotas** which set the maximum absolute amount of a particular commodity that can be imported. **Export subsidies** are also used to encourage exports of certain goods or to prevent discrimination against overseas exporters who sell in a foreign market at a world price lower than the domestic price. **Exchange controls** are also used to control the flow of international trade. Some controls are used to ration a country's scarce foreign exchange. Some countries use different exchange rates for different commodities to encourage or discourage imports.

However, in the last few years there has been an increasing realisation that **tariffs** deny individuals and nations the benefits of **greater productivity** and a higher standard of living and tariffs eliminate or reduce the advantages of specialization and exchange among nations and prevent the best use of scare world resources. The presence of tariffs also hinders the expansion of multinational companies and international trade and inhibits their growth and the benefits of consumers.

As a result of the growing movement towards freer trade which culminated with the creation of the World Trade Organisation many countries have come together to create free trade areas. The European Community was a free trade area, before it became the European Union. The **North American Free Trade Area** is also a free trade area created by the United States, Mexico and Canada in 1994. The members of the trade zone have established preferential tariff treatment for certain products traded between these countries, in the form of reduced or zero rate tariffs. By eliminating **trade barriers**, the **trade zone** facilitates **cross-border movement** of **goods and services**, increases **investment opportunities**, promotes fair competition, and enforces **intellectual property rights** in the three countries.

3.4 Trade financing

A significant development which has boosted international trade is that **trade financing** has become easier to be obtained by companies. Financing sources for international trade transactions include **commercial bank loans** within the host country and loans from **international lending agencies**. Foreign banks can also be used to **discount trade bills** to finance short term financing. Eurodollar financing is another method for providing foreign financing. A **Eurodollar** is a **dollar deposit** held in a bank outside the United States. An active market exists for these deposits. Banks use Eurodollars to make dollar loans to borrowers; the interest rate is usually in excess of the deposit rate. Such loans are usually in very large amounts, are short-term working-capital loans, and are unsecured. U.S. firms frequently arrange for lines of credit and revolving credits from Eurodollar banks. No compensating balances are usually required.

The Eurobond market is widely used for long-term funds for multinational U.S. companies. A Eurobond is a long-term security issued by an internationally recognized borrower in several countries simultaneously. The bonds are denominated in a single currency. Such bonds are usually fixed-income bonds or floating-rate bonds; some bonds are convertible into common stock.

Many countries have organized **development banks** that provide intermediate and long-term loans to private enterprises. Such loans are made to provide **economic development** within a country.

3.5 Developments in the non market environment

We have discussed so far the impact of developments in financial market and how they may facilitate the funding of investment strategies and the management of risks, These are all the benign effect of globalisation on multinational companies. However, globalisation may also create more uncertainty. This is created in turn by changes in the non-market environments in which multinational companies operate.

The **non-market environments** consist of the **social**, **political**, and **legal arrangements** that determine the firms' interactions outside of, and in conjunction with, markets. These **non-market environments** are shaped by both **global** and **country-specific factors** and the successful implementation of a multi-domestic strategy involves issue-specific action plans that are tailored to the configuration of institutions and interests in individual countries.

3.5.1 Regulation

Many governments have responded to **globalisation** and the loss of control through **tariffs** and other methods of control by introducing regulation. For example the wave of **cross-border mergers** and acquisitions of 1990s, an integral component of globalisation, have created oligopolies in many industries. Major industries (such as automobiles, petroleum exploration, semiconductors, consumer electronics, insurance, banking) now have eight to ten key players that account for 70-80 percent of the global output. Not surprisingly then, there is an increased level of **antitrust scrutiny**, especially in the US and the EU, the scrutiny of the Boeing-McDonnell Douglas merger, British Airways–American Airlines alliance, being notable examples of regulators restraining the emergence of (potential or actual) **cross-border oligopolies**.

Thus antitrust actions become non-tariff barriers or cartel-sponsored private barriers become obstacles to trade and investment flows, key issues are whether, when, and how to establish an international regime (or modify an extant one) on competition policy. Needless to say, this has an immense bearing on multinational corporations' (MNCs) non-market environments.

Globalisation also creates incentives for governments to intervene in favour of domestic MNCs in terms of 'macroeconomic' and 'macro-structural' policies. It was argued in the 1980s that in industries marked by **imperfect competition, high positive externalities** and **supernormal profits** (characteristics of the new oligopolies as well), firms are often locked in a zero-sum game, and governments have incentives to intervene in favour of domestic firms. Boundaries between domestic and international are blurred because domestic interventions can tilt the scale in favour of domestic firms in global markets. Arguably, given the fast pace of product obsolescence, a winner-takes-all situation is developing in many industries. Consequently, MNCs have incentives to emerge as winners, if not through market processes then through non-market strategies. Thus, globalisation processes create incentives for MNCs to enlist support from their home governments and create an obligation for governments to support them.

3.5.2 Pressure groups

Although domestic governments may be willing to support MNCs, a major threat has emerged from **transnationally networked pressure groups**, which influence the public and put pressure on governments to take measures against multinational companies.

Case Study

A telling example is the controversy over the dumping of the Brent Spar oil platform in the North Sea in 1995. The main actors were Greenpeace and Royal Dutch/Shell (3rd largest MNC in terms of assets; with 1997 sales of $128 billion). Shell used the Brent Spar buoy as storage and tanker loading facility for its Brent oil field in the North Sea. In 1991 the buoy was decommissioned, and after extensive internal scientific evaluation, discussions with British governmental agencies, and consultation with British stakeholders regrading the environmental and safety aspects of various disposal options, Shell decided to dump it in the North Sea rather than to bring it onshore for dismantling. Greenpeace opposed dumping of the buoy in the sea, a position that had considerable support in continental Europe, though not in the UK. Through dramatic actions (such as boarding and occupying the buoy) that were captured on television, excellent media management and grassroots mobilization across countries (including consumer boycotts and the firebombing of Shell stations in Germany), Greenpeace forced Shell to bring the buoy back onshore for disassembly. Subsequently, Greenpeace admitted that its favoured option had worse environmental consequences than Shell's. Nevertheless, in the heat of the controversy, the media gave prominence to Greenpeace over Shell.

3.5.3 Political risks

Because globalisation leads to a high degree of cross -border economic linkages, MNCs become vulnerable to political developments in their home and host countries. Citizen groups in home/host countries can impact MNCs' strategies in yet another country.

Case Study

US citizen groups, notably the Natural Resources Defense Council, in alliance with Mexican groups, forced Mitsubishi to shelve a $100 million investment in a salt plant on the shores of Laguna San Ignacio where gray whales breed: 'And as Mexico received $11.6 billion last year in long-term investments from abroad, it also discovered that it cannot ignore the other forces, like the environmental movement, that are criss-crossing borders and making politics into a global game'.

The message is clear: if MNCs invest in multiple markets, they need to deal with citizen groups in multiple countries. And this would require MNCs to integrate their supranational and multi-domestic non-market strategies.

Chapter Roundup

- Developments in international financial markets have facilitated the growth in trade and the funding of overseas expansion strategies and have opened up more opportunities for investors. The main developments are:
  - Globalisation
  - Growth in derivatives
  - Securitisation
  - The single European currency
  - The adoption of common accounting standards
- The growth of globalisation has created however more opportunities for **money laundering** which governments and international bodies are trying to combat with legislation.
- The globalisation and integration of financial markets has contributed to expansion of international trade, but it has also created potentially more uncertainty for multinational companies.

Quick Quiz

1. Give three effects of the convergence of financial institutions.
2. Give three reasons for the use of tariffs countries.
3. By what methods do governments try to combat money laundering?
4. Give four reasons why a government may want to impose tariffs.
5. Regulation has replaced tariffs.

   True ☐

   False ☐
6. Who is responsible for monetary policy in the UK?

Answers to Quick Quiz

1 Any three of:

(a) Create economies of scale
(b) Create economies of scope
(c) It diversifies revenue sources and reduces risk
(d) It reduces search costs for consumers

2 Any three of:

(a) Protect infant and key industries
(b) Equalise costs of production between domestic and foreign producers
(c) Protect domestic jobs
(d) Prevent capital flight

3 (a) Legislation that makes it more difficult to happen
(b) Asking professionals to report suspect transactions

4 (a) Protect infant and key industries
(b) Equalise costs of production between domestic and foreign producers
(c) Protect domestic jobs
(d) Prevent capital flight

5 True

6 The Bank of England

Now try the questions below from the Exam Question Bank

Number	Level	Marks	Time
38	Introductory	17	31 mins

Financial engineering and emerging derivative products

26

Topic list	Syllabus reference
1 Overview and latest derivative products	G (2) (a)
2 Derivatives markets for the firm	G (2) (a)
3 Risks from the use of derivatives	G (2) (a)
4 Measuring derivatives risk using value at risk	G (2) (a)
5 Risks of options	G (2) (a)
6 Risk of forward and futures instruments	G (2) (a)
7 Risk of swaps	G (2) (a)
8 Scenario analysis	G (2) (a)
9 Stress testing	G (2) (a)

Introduction

In this chapter we discuss the risks associated with derivatives. First we present some data on the growth of derivatives and examine reasons for their growth. Then we explain how to measure derivatives risk using value at risk, scenario analysis and stress testing.

Study guide

		Intellectual level
G2	**Financial Engineering and emerging derivative products**	
(a)	Demonstrate awareness, and discuss the significance to the firm, of latest derivative products with particular emphasis on the risks in derivative trading and the application of the following in their management:	2
(i)	Value at risk	
(ii)	Scenario Analysis	
(iii)	Stress testing	

1 Overview and latest derivative products

FAST FORWARD

Financial engineering deals with the design and valuation of new derivative products.

We have already discussed in previous chapters the **basic derivative products**, such as **options, forward** and **futures contracts** and **swaps.** These basic derivative products, combined with the underlying or cash instruments can be used as the basis for a variety of new instruments to create new products. In fact, there is no limit to the products that can be designed, hence a new finance discipline called **financial engineering** has been developed, which deals with the **design** and **valuation** of **new derivative products**. Some of these new products are: **convertible** and **callable bonds, equity swaps, delayed start swaps, collapsible swaps, indexed principal swaps, and credit derivatives**. A great variety of options contracts has also been designed such as **barrier options, compound options, look back options and Asian options**. Chapters 18, 19 and 20 discussed in greater detail the use of **derivative instruments** in **risk management**. In this chapter we look at the **risks** that are associated with derivatives and how to **measure** those **risks**.

1.1 Exotic options

FAST FORWARD

A great variety of options has been designed that vary in terms of the exercise price or the underlying. There are options where the underlying is a non-financial asset such as the amount of rainfall or snow.

There are several variations of options that vary in terms of the **underlying**, the **exercise price** or one of the other distinguishing characteristics of the option. Two examples of exotic options are given below:

A **barrier option** is an option that comes into existence or ceases to exist if the price of the underlying exceeds or falls short of a certain specified value. Options that come into existence are called **knock-in options**, whereas options that cease to exist are called **knock-out options**. If the trigger price is touched at any time before maturity, it causes an option with pre-determined characteristics to come into existence (in the case of a knock-in option) or it will cause an existing option to cease to exist (in the case of a knock-out option).

A **compound option** is an **option-on-an-option**. It could be a **call-on-a-call** giving the owner for instance the right to buy in 1 month's time a 6 month 1.52 US dollar call/Canadian dollar put expiring 7 months from today (or 6 months from the expiry of the compound). The **strike price** on the compound is the premium that we would pay in 1 month's time if we exercised the compound for the option expiring 6 months from that point in time. It could be a **put-on-a-call** giving the owner the right to sell in 1 month's time a 6 month 1.52 US dollar call/Canadian dollar put expiring 7 months from today.

These types of products are often used by corporations to **hedge** the **foreign exchange risk** involved with **overseas acquisitions** when the success of the acquisition itself is uncertain. Why buy a vanilla hedge or enter into a forward contract before you are sure that you will be buying the foreign company? Sophisticated speculators use **compound options** to speculate on **the volatility of volatility**.

1.2 Insurance derivatives

While the underlying assets for most derivatives include financial instruments ranging from **common stocks** to **foreign exchange rates**, there are also derivatives based on **non-financial 'assets'** such as the amount of snow at a particular location. **Insurance derivatives**, are designed to help insurance companies hedge their exposure to insurance losses. In most cases, they are used as a protection against catastrophic losses such as those caused by a hurricane or an earthquake. As other derivatives, in addition to hedging, insurance derivatives could be used by investors for speculative purposes or to improve portfolio diversification.

A simple example of an **insurance derivative** is an option that gives its buyer the right to a cash payment if a specific index of insured earthquake losses reaches a specified level ('strike price'). Alternatively, the index might be based not on the level of losses, but on the severity of the catastrophic event.

1.3 Weather derivatives

Weather derivatives like insurance derivatives are derivatives whose underlying is an indicator of **weather conditions**. Such derivatives are used by farmers for example to hedge against a **poor harvest** due to **drought or frost**. The underlying 'asset' in this case is the level of **frost or drought**.

1.4 Real estate derivatives

Real estate derivatives are derivatives whose underlying is an index of **real estate values**. Investors can invest in the index instead of the real estate assets.

2 Derivatives markets for the firm

2.1 Rationale for the use of derivatives

The previous chapter presented the tremendous increase in both the traded and the over the counter derivatives products. In this section we discuss the reasons for this tremendous growth and the ways in which derivatives are used by firms.

FAST FORWARD

Two general arguments have been put forward for the growth in derivatives.

- The first is that derivatives complete the market
- The second argument is that they make markets more efficient.

2.1.1 Market completeness

Derivatives allow investors to achieve payoffs that would be impossible without using them. Although in theory continuous trading can create the payoffs of derivatives, rendering derivatives redundant, in practice this is not possible because investors face **trading costs** that make replicating closely the payoff of even as simple a derivative as a call option **prohibitively expensive**. In the case of call options the payoff of the call option on shares, for instance, can be replicated by holding treasury bills and shares. When the price of the shares rises, the portfolio is adjusted in favour of shares so that it behaves more or less like the underlying. When the price of shares falls the portfolio is adjusted in favour of treasury bills, creating a minimum value in the portfolio which is the value of the treasury bill position. Replication also requires the investor to trade every time the price changes. In the absence of continuous trading, the replication is only approximate. Finally, the correct replicating strategy is often difficult to work out because there is uncertainty as to which is the true statistical process that drives asset prices. For example, if price changes are characterised by trends, then a policy of replication will be successful since a rebalancing of the portfolio in favour of equities following a change in share prices will be followed by further rises in share prices. If on the other hand prices change in a random way, then rebalancing the portfolio in favour of equities, as a result of an increase in share prices, will not be effective if the prices subsequently fall.

2.1.2 Market efficiency

Derivatives make markets more efficient by providing investors with **information** that **cash markets** alone **cannot generate**. For example, swaps can generate **yield curves** even in the absence of corresponding cash markets. The option markets can produce valuable estimates of the implied volatilities in the various markets.

2.2 The role of hedging for the firm

Derivative instruments are used either for **speculation** or for **hedging**. Derivatives are used for speculation when they are used on their own and not in conjunction with the underlying instrument. For example a long position in a futures contract, is a bet that the price of the underlying will move in a certain direction by a certain date. Similarly the writer of a call option bets that the price will not move above a certain range over a period of time. In both cases the derivatives position can result in losses if the price does not move in the anticipated direction. When derivatives are used for **hedging** they are always used in combination with the **underlying**. The principle of **hedging** as has already been explained in Chapters 19 and 20 is that any profits or losses in the **cash position** will be offset by losses or profits in the **derivatives position**.

The empirical evidence on the use of derivatives by corporations shows that firms primarily use derivatives for **hedging** rather than **speculation**. Examples of the use of derivatives in the hedging of interest and exchange rate risk have been discussed in previous chapters.

One unresolved issue is why companies need to hedge their risks since investors can themselves diversify away all risks by including the shares of the company in a portfolio. Here we review the arguments that have been put forward to explain the use of hedging. The main arguments are:

(a) Hedging reduces the risk imposed on the firm's managers, employees, suppliers and customers

(b) Hedging can control the conflict of interest between bondholders and shareholders, thus reducing the agency costs of debt;

(c) The use of derivatives increases the value of a firm. As we have already discussed in Chapter 7, Modigliani and Miller showed that firm value and financial policy decisions are unrelated in the absence of market imperfections. Models have been developed that show that hedging can increase the value of a firm if capital market imperfections exist. Thus the following additional justifications have been provided:

   (i) Hedging **lowers the probability** of the firm encountering **financial distress** which in turn lowers the expected costs of financial distress and the cost of capital.

   (ii) Hedging encourages investment by the firm. According to the **agency theory** between shareholders and bondholders developed by Myers, the issuance of bonds which have higher priority than equity creates incentives for the firm's equity holders to underinvest. Hedging reduces the incentive to underinvest since hedging reduces uncertainty and the risk of loss. Because firms with more valuable growth opportunities and higher leverage are more likely to be affected by the underinvestment problem, these firms are also more likely to hedge.

3 Risks from the use of derivatives

FAST FORWARD

The main risks from the use of derivatives are the role of mispricing (**valuation** or **model risk**), **liquidity risk** and **reporting risk**.

Firms that use derivatives are exposed to the following risks:

Valuation (model) risk

The most common risk for OTC derivative users is the **risk of mispricing** the derivatives position. Since OTC derivatives do not trade in **liquid markets** where they can always be bought or sold at the market price, valuation models need to be used. These models however are based on assumptions which may not be valid.

For example the Black-Scholes option valuation model assumes that markets have no frictions, that the stock price is lognormally distributed, that interest rates are fixed, that the volatility of return is constant and that trading is possible all the time.

However, it is well known that these assumptions are at variance with reality. Interest rates are not constant and neither is the volatility. Demand and supply may have an impact on prices and there are certainly frictions in the market.

There are many examples of firms losing money due to valuation errors. Chase Manhattan lost $60 million in 1999 when one of its foreign exchange traders misvalued forward contracts. In January 2004, the National Australian Bank reported currency option losses in excess of $360 million Australian dollars (approximately $280 million in U.S. dollars) that were attributed to rogue traders and risk management failures and involved incorrect valuations and misreporting. It is much harder to value more complicated derivatives.

The use of value-at-risk and stress tests to monitor derivative risks means that firms that use derivatives regularly know their risks reasonably well. But these measurement tools do not always work well; for example, during the Russian crisis, banks exceeded their value-at-risk more than they theoretically should have.

Liquidity risk

Exchange-traded derivative products are highly liquid and a transaction can take place at the market price. The market value of a derivatives contract is thus realized when it is sold. In the case of OTC derivatives and especially where complex contracts are involved it is not always possible for these contracts to be sold, and their model-calculated value to be realised. The reasons for this are:

(a) Uncertainty about the **valuation model** and the **risks** of the **position**.

(b) In the case of complex contracts, there may be only a small number of counterparties who both want that particular set of risk characteristics and are confident that they understand what they are receiving

A good example of the problems of closing derivatives position is Warren Buffett's inability to sell a derivatives subsidiary when he acquired General Re in 1992.

Reporting risk

OTC complex derivative positions especially with long maturities can be manipulated so that the true value and the true risks of the positions are not revealed. For example, Enron had a huge portfolio of derivatives, including many contracts with extremely long maturities, whose risks were not revealed before it collapsed.

4 Measuring derivatives risk using value at risk

Key term

> **Value at risk (VAR)** is the maximum amount by which the value of a position will fall over a given period of time at a given level of confidence.

For example, if VAR is $1m at a confidence level of 95% for one week, this indicates that there is a 5% probability that the losses will exceed $1m over the next week. The interpretation of this number is that one would expect the $1m loss to be exceeded once every 20 weeks.

Although the VAR gives us the frequency with which the specific loss will be exceeded, it does not provide us with an estimate of the expected loss once the $1m mark has been exceeded.

Thus another way to look at the VAR is to say that the portfolio will lose at least $1m every 20 weeks or that there is a probability of 5% that the portfolio will lose at least $1m.

Key term

> **Value at risk** is the minimum amount by which the value of a position will fall over a given period of time at a given level of probability.

The **value at risk** at 5 percent level, if assuming that the distribution of returns of the underlying asset is normal, is defined as

$$VAR = 1.645 \times \sigma$$

Where σ is the **standard deviation** of the **asset price** or **return**.

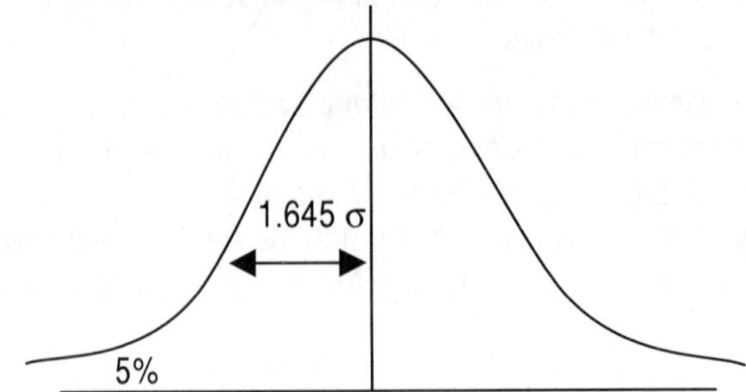

In calculating the value at risk for derivative products we shall need to find the standard deviation of the return of each derivative instrument.

5 Risks of options

FAST FORWARD

Changes in the value of an option can be measured in terms of its **Greeks**, that is in terms of its **risk factors**.

5.1 Risk factors in options positions

We have already seen that the factors that affect the value of a call or put option are:

- The value of the underlying
- The exercise price
- The risk-free interest rate
- The volatility
- The time to expiration

Since these factors are the ones that may adversely affect the value of an option they are also known as **risk factors**.

The Black Scholes model we used in Chapter 8 gives a mathematical expression of the relationship between the **value of an option** and the **factors** that **affect** its **value**. This is reproduced below.

The Black-Scholes model states that the value (P_c) of a call option is given by the following formula.

Exam formula

$$c = P_aN(d_1) - P_eN(d_2)e^{-rt}$$

Where

$$d_1 = \frac{\ln(P_a/P_e) + (r + 0.5s^2)t}{s\sqrt{T}}$$

$$d_2 = d_1 - s\sqrt{T}$$

The model has three main elements to it.

(a) The share price, P_a

(b) The delta value, $N(d_1)$, which measures how option prices vary with share prices (discussed below)

(c) ($Pe\ N(d_2)e^{-rt}$), which represents the borrowing element that must be combined with the share investment to produce an option equivalent.

Exam focus point

Remember that the volatility is represented by the standard deviation, **not** the variance. The variance is the standard deviation squared.

Within the model

(a) The difference between the share price and the option exercise price ($P_a - P_e$) is the intrinsic value of the option.

(b) e^{-rt} is a discount factor, reflecting the fact that the option will be exercised in the future.

(c) The model is very dependent upon σ, the factor representing the share price volatility. This is likely to be calculated on the basis of historical movements, and different conditions may apply in the future.

5.2 Measuring the impact of risk factors: the Greeks

FAST FORWARD

The 'Greeks' are an important element in option theory.

- **Delta** – change in call option price/change in value of share
- **Gamma** – change in delta value/change in value of share
- **Theta** – change in option price over time
- **Rho** – change in option price as interest rates change
- **Vega** – change in option price as volatility changes

Various elements of the Black-Scholes model can be analysed separately. Collectively they are known as the Greeks.

5.3 Delta

If we accept the Black-Scholes model, the value of N(d1) can be used to indicate the amount of the underlying shares (or other instrument) which the writer of an option should hold in order to hedge (eliminate the risk of) the option position.

The appropriate 'hedge ratio' N(d1) is referred to as the delta value: hence the term delta hedge. The delta value is valid if the price changes are small.

Key term

Delta = change in call option price ÷ change in the price of the shares ($\frac{\Delta C}{\Delta S}$ = delta *)*

Delta is used to measure the slope of the option value line at any particular time/price point.

For example, if we know that a change in share price of 3 cents results in a change in the option price of 1 cent, then:

Delta = 1c ÷ 3c = 1/3

5.4 Delta hedging

The significance of the delta value is illustrated by the process of delta hedging. Delta hedging allows us to determine the number of shares that we must buy to create the equivalent portfolio to an option, and cent hedge it.

We have seen that:

Buying call options = Buying share portfolio + Borrowing at risk free rate

As the opposite of borrowing is investing, therefore:

Buying call options + Investing at risk free rate = Buying share portfolio

As the opposite of buying call options is selling call options therefore:

Investing at risk free rate = Buying share portfolio + Selling call options

Therefore we can eliminate investment risk by buying shares and selling call options, as an adverse movement in the share price will be offset by a favourable movement in the option price. Delta hedging tells us in what proportion shares should be purchased and call options sold.

Delta hedges are only valid for small movements in the share price. The delta value is likely to change during the period of the option, and so the option writer may need to change her holdings to maintain a delta hedge position.

5.4.1 Example: Delta hedge

What is the number of call options that you would have to sell in order to hedge a holding of 200,000 shares, if the delta value ($N(d_1)$) of options is 0.8?

Assume that option contracts are for the purchase or sale of units of 1,000 shares.

Solution

The delta hedge can be calculated by the following formula.

$$\text{Number of contracts} = \frac{\text{Number of shares}}{\text{Delta of option} \times \text{size of contract}}$$

$$= \frac{200{,}000}{0.8 \times 1{,}000}$$

$$= 250$$

If in this example the price of shares increased by $1, the value of the call options would increase by $800 per contract (80c per share). Since however we were selling these contracts the increase in the value of our holding of shares, 200,000 × $1, would be matched by the decrease in our holding of option contracts 250 × $800.

The portfolio would need to be adjusted as the delta value moved. If the delta value moved from 0.8 to 0.9, the number of extra contracts that would be required to maintain the hedge would be:

250 × (0.9 – 0.8)= 25.

5.5 Other points about delta values

Note also the following points about delta values.

(a) If an **option is 'at the money'** (ie if the share price equals the exercise price), then the **delta value is approximately 0.5**.

(b) As an option moves **'out of the money'** (ie the share price moves below the exercise price), the **delta value falls towards zero**.

(c) As an option moves further **'into the money'**, the delta hedge ratio increases towards a value of 1.

(d) At expiry the value of the delta will either be 1, if the options is **in the money**, or 0, if the option is **out of the money.**

(e) A **small change** in the **share price** can result in a **large change** in the **delta value**.

The factors influencing delta when the option is either in the money or out of the money can be appreciated by looking at the variables in the $N(d_1)$ formula given earlier. These factors are:

- The exercise price of the option relative to the share price (ie its intrinsic value)
- The time to expiration
- The risk-free rate of return
- The volatility of returns on the share

5.6 Uses of delta factors

Delta factors are often used when deciding which options to **sell** or **buy**, with investors considering

- The delta value
- The trend – are delta values of options currently held getting stronger or weaker?

5.7 Gamma

The **gamma value** measures the amount by which the delta value changes as the share price changes.

Key term

> **Gamma** = Change in delta value ÷ Change in the price of the underlying share

The **higher** the **gamma value**, the more difficult it is for the option writer to **maintain** a **delta hedge** because the delta value increases more for a given change in share price. Gamma is effectively, a measure of how easy risk management will be.

Gamma is the same for both call and puts and is always positive.

Gamma values will be highest for a share which is **close to expiry** and is **'at the money'**. For example, suppose that an option has an exercise price of 340 pence and is due to expire in a few minutes' time.

(a) If the share price is 338 pence, there is a very low chance of the option being exercised. The delta hedge ratio will be approximately zero; in other words, no hedge is necessary.

(b) If the share price rises suddenly to 342 pence, it becomes highly probable that the option will be exercised and the delta hedge ratio will approximate to 1, suggesting the need to hedge through holding the underlying shares.

On the delta value graph, gamma is the rate of change of the slope of the option value line. Gamma is expressed as a number between zero and one for both puts and calls. If a call option's delta is 0.4 and its gamma is 0.05, a one point increase in the underlying assets should result in a delta increase of 0.05 to 0.45.

5.8 Theta

Key term

> **Theta** is the change in an option's price (specifically its time premium) over time.

Remember that an option's price has two components, its **intrinsic value** and its **time premium**. When it expires, an option has no time premium.

Thus the time premium of an option diminishes over time towards zero and theta measures **how much value is lost over time,** how much therefore the option holder will lose through retaining her options. Theta is usually expressed as an amount lost per day. If a dollar option has a theta of –0.05, it will theoretically lose 5 cents a day, assuming there are no other changes in conditions.

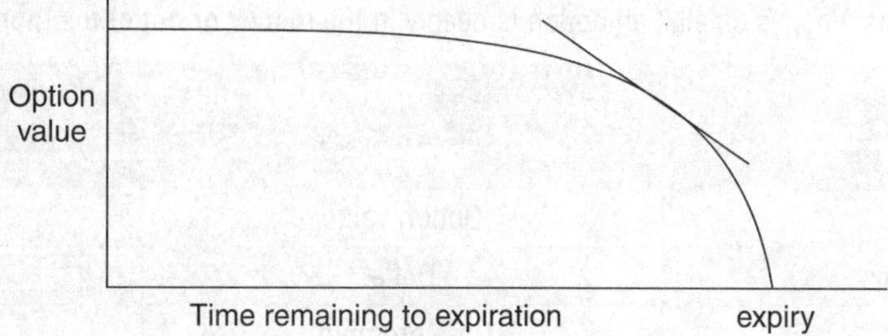

At **the money options** have the **greatest time premium** and thus the **greatest theta**. Their time decay is not linear; their theta increases as the date of expiration approaches. By contrast, the more in the money or out of the money the option is, the more its theta decays in a straight line.

Generally, options that have a **negative theta** have a **positive gamma** (and vice versa). A **positive gamma** means a **position benefits from movement**. **Negative theta** means that the **position loses money** if the **underlying asset** does **not move**.

5.9 Rho

Key term

> **Rho** measures the sensitivity of options prices to interest rate changes.

An option's rho is the amount of change in value for a 1% change in the risk-free interest rate. Rho is positive for calls and negative for puts, ie

Prices	*Interest rate rises*	*Interest rate falls*
Calls	Increase	Decrease
Puts	Decrease	Increase

If a dollar call option that has one year until expiration has a rho of 0.2, a 1% increase in interest rates will result in a 20 cent increase in the price of the option. However, the impact on the price of an option that has six months left until expiry would only be a 10 cent increase.

Generally, the **interest rate** is the **least significant influence** on change in price, and in addition interest rates tend to change slowly and in small amounts.

Long-term options have larger rhos than short-term options. The more time there is until expiration, the greater the effect of a change in interest rates.

5.10 Vega

Key term

> **Vega** measures the sensitivity of an option's price to a change in its implied volatility. ($\frac{\Delta C}{\Delta \sigma} = \text{Vega}$)

Vega is the **change in value of an option that results from a 1% point change in its volatility**. If a dollar option has a vega of 0.2, its price will increase by 20 cents for a one percentage point increase in its volatility. Vega is the same for both calls and puts

We have seen earlier that the Black-Scholes model is very dependent upon accurately estimating the volatility of the option price. Vega is a measure of the consequences of an incorrect estimation.

Long-term options have **larger vegas** than **short-term options**. The longer the time period until the option expires, the more uncertainty there is about the expiry price. Therefore a given change in volatility will have more impact on an option with longer until expiration than one with less time until expiration.

Volatility means the market's current assessment of volatility. It is influenced by the balance between option **demand** and **supply** (the greater the balance the less the volatility), also matters such as takeover rumours. Once announcements of definite plans have been made volatility will generally decrease.

With company options with the same month of expiry, **vega** is generally greatest **for at the money options**. Vega is small if an option is deeply in the money or out of the money.

SUMMARY OF GREEKS		
	Change in	**With**
Delta	Option value	Underlying asset value
Gamma	Delta	Underlying asset value
Theta	Time premium	Time
Rho	Option value	Interest rates

Exam focus point

> Both optional and compulsory questions covering the components of the Black-Scholes model are likely to be tested.

5.11 Greeks and risk measurement

The values of the Greek parameters can give an approximate estimate of the value of a position if one or more of the factors that determine the value of an option change. The change in the value of the option can be approximated using the formula

Change in option value = delta × (change in underlying) + ½ × gamma × (change in underlying)^2 + vega × (change in volatility) + theta × (change in time) + rho × (change in interest rate)

$$\Delta C = \text{Delta} \times \Delta S + \tfrac{1}{2}\,\text{Gamma} \times (\Delta S)^2 + \text{Vega} \times \Delta\sigma + \text{Theta} \times \Delta t + \text{Rho} \times \Delta r$$

The gamma term is added to explain the fact that delta itself changes when the price of the underlying changes.

Question — **Using the Greeks**

Suppose that the Greeks of a call option are as follows:

Delta = 0.5
Gamma = 0.03

What will the value of the call option be if the value of the underlying increase by 5 units?

Answer

The value of the option will change by

$\Delta C = 0.5 \times 5 + ½\ 0.03 \times (5)^2 = 2.5 + 0.375 = 2.875$

Note that the changes in the option price could have been calculated directly using the Black-Scholes option pricing model. However, using the Greeks is convenient for two reasons:

- First, this method provides a quick way to calculate the Greeks of a portfolio of options
- The second reason is that the methods allow a simple estimation of the value at risk of an option position to be calculated

5.12 Portfolio Greeks

The Greeks of a portfolio of options is simply the sum of the Greeks of the individual contracts. For example if the portfolio is made up of two call options, a long and a short position with deltas of 1 and -0.3, the portfolio delta is 0.7.

5.13 The VAR of options

Under the assumption of normality the calculation of the value at risk requires the estimation of the standard deviation of the price or the return of the underlying asset. If we assume that the changes in the price of the underlying asset follows the normal distribution with a standard deviation $\sigma_{UNDERLYING}$, the standard deviation of the option contract or the portfolio of options can be approximated by:

$$\sigma_{OPTION} = \text{delta} \times \sigma_{UNDERLYING}$$

The value at risk of the option position is given by:

$$VAR_{OPTION} = 1.645 \times \sigma_{OPTION} = 1.645 \times \text{delta} \times \sigma_{UNDERLYING}$$

This approach shows that for a portfolio with a delta of zero, the value at risk is zero. That is a zero delta position does not bear any risk. However a delta-neutral position still has a positive gamma, so the delta neutral position may not be entirely free of risk.

6 Risk of forward and futures instruments

FAST FORWARD

Changes in the value of a futures position reflect the changes in the value of the underlying asset.

6.1 Valuation models

In Chapter 18 we showed that the value of a forward contract when agreed between two counter-parties is given by:

$$F(t,T) = S_t(1+r)^{T-t}$$

Where F(t, T) is the price of the futures contract agreed in period t, with maturity period T.
S_t is the price of the underlying at time t
r is the interest rate

In order to see how the value of the futures contract changes when the underlying changes, suppose that its value 5 days later is: $F(t+5,T) = S_{t+5}(1+r)^{T-(t+5)}$

If the interest rate is assumed to be constant then the value of the futures contract will change in **exactly the same way** as the **value** of the **underlying asset** and the risk of the futures or forward position will be the same as the **risk** of the **underlying asset**.

6.2 Finding the VAR of forwards and futures

Since the **risk** of the **futures position** is the same as the **risk** of the **underlying asset**, the **standard deviation** of a **forward** or **futures contract** is the same as the standard deviation of the underlying. ie:

$$\sigma_{FORWARD} = \sigma_{UNDERLYING}$$

The value at risk of a futures or forward contract is:

$$VAR_{FUTURES} = 1.645 \times \sigma_{FUTURES}$$

7 Risk of swaps

7.1 Swaps as portfolios of bonds

FAST FORWARD

Changes in the value of swaps positions reflect the changes in the value of interest rates.

In order to measure the risk of swap position, we need to view a swap as a portfolio which is made up of a floating rate bond and a fixed rate bond. The value of the swap is the difference between the values of the two bonds.

$$V_{SWAP} = V_{FIXED} - V_{FLOATING}$$

The value of the fixed-coupon bond with a maturity say of 4 years is given by:

$$V_{FIXED} = \frac{C}{(1+r)} + \frac{C}{(1+r)^2} + \frac{C}{(1+r)^3} + \frac{F+C}{(1+r)^4}$$

A floating rate bond carries little interest rate risk. If market rates rise, a fixed rate bond declines in value. However, the expected coupons of the floating rate bond increase in line with the increase in forward rates. This means the price remains constant. As floating rate bonds are almost immune to interest rate risk, they are considered conservative investments for investors who believe market rates will increase. The risk that remains is:

$$V_{FLOATING} = \frac{100r}{(1+r)} + \frac{100r}{(1+r)^2} + \frac{100r}{(1+r)^3} + \frac{100+100r}{(1+r)^4} = 100$$

When the two parties first agree to the swap, its value equals zero because the market-determined coupon rate, *c*, is set so that the fixed-rate component of the swap sells for its par value, that is, the coupon equals the fixed-rate bond's initial yield to maturity so that $V_{FIXED} = 100$. The subsequent value of the swap position will be given by:

$$V_{SWAP} = V_{FIXED} - 100$$

When interest rates go down the value of the fixed coupon bond will be above 100, and the value of the swap will be positive. When on the other hand interest rates go up, the value of the fixed coupon bond will be less than 100, and the value of the swap will be negative.

Question

Swap valuation

A 4-year $100 million swap was agreed to 2 years ago with a C = 6.00% coupon rate. Currently, the swap has exactly 2 years to maturity and the semi-annually compounded yields on ½, 1, 1½, and 2 year zero coupon bonds are 3.1%, 3.2%, 3.3%, and 3.5%, respectively. What is the current value of the swap?

Answer

$$V_{FIXED} = \frac{3}{\left(1+\frac{0.031}{2}\right)} + \frac{3}{\left(1+\frac{0.032}{2}\right)^2} + \frac{3}{\left(1+\frac{0.033}{2}\right)^3} + \frac{100+3}{\left(1+\frac{0.035}{2}\right)^4}$$

$$= 2.95 + 2.91 + 2.86 + 96.09 = 104.8$$

Therefore

$$V_{SWAP} = V_{FIXED} - V_{FLOATING} = 104.8 - 100 = \$4.8$$

Changes in the value of a swaps position depend on the sensitivity of the value of the fixed coupon rate to changes in interest rates. This sensitivity is measured by the duration of the bond. The idea behind duration is simple. Suppose a bond has a duration of 3 years. Then that bond's value will decline about 3% for each 1% increase in interest rates – or rise about 3% for each 1% decrease in interest rates. Such a bond is less risky than one which has a 10-year duration. That bond is going to decline in value about 10% for each 1% rise in interest rates. Using the duration of a bond as a measure of the sensitivity of the bond we can approximate the change in the value of the bond by:

$$\Delta V_{FIXED} = -\text{Duration} \times \Delta r$$

Since the value of the swap changes only due to changes in the value of the fixed coupon bond the change in the value of the swap will be:

$$\Delta V_{SWAP} = -\text{Duration} \times \Delta r$$

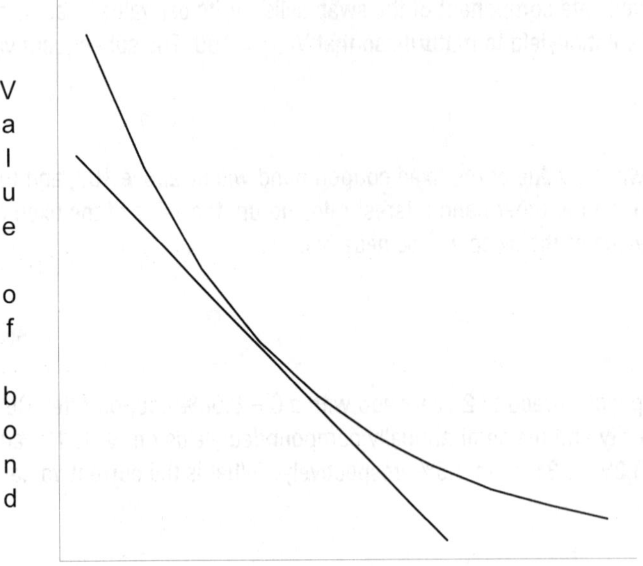

7.2 Finding the VAR of swaps

The standard deviation of a swap is given by:

$\sigma_{SWAP} = \text{Duration} \times \sigma_{INTEREST\ RATE}$

The value at risk of a swap is given by:

$VAR_{SWAP} = 1.645 \times \sigma_{SWAP} = 1.645 \times \text{Duration} \times \sigma_{INTEREST\ RATE}$

7.3 Multi-period VAR

Exam focus point

> You may be asked in the examination to convert daily volatility into annual volatility and vice versa.

The value at risk calculated so far was for a single period. The calculations of VAR for many periods has already been mentioned in Chapter 6 in the context of the calculation of project VAR.

If the daily volatility is denoted by σ_{DAILY} then the volatility of N days is given by:

$\sigma_{N\text{-}DAY} = \sqrt{N} \times \sigma_{DAILY}$

For example, if N = 5, then:

$\sigma_{5\text{-}DAY} = \sqrt{5} \times \sigma_{DAILY}$

The annual volatility is calculated assuming that there are 250 trading days in a year and is given therefore by:

$\sigma_{ANNUAL} = \sqrt{250} \times \sigma_{DAILY}$

Thus the daily VAR can be transformed into an N-day VAR by simply multiplying the Daily VAR by $\sqrt{N}$, the square root of N

$VAR_{N\text{-}DAY} = \sqrt{N}\ V_{DAILY} = 1.645\ \sqrt{N}\ \sigma_{DAILY}$

Example

The daily volatility is 0.72%. What is the weekly volatility? What is the annual volatility?

Weekly volatility = $\sqrt{5} \times 0.72 = 1.61\%$

Annual volatility = $\sqrt{250} \times 0.72 = 11.38\%$

Similarly we can convert annual volatility into daily volatility using

$\sigma_{ANNUAL} / \sqrt{250} = \sigma_{DAILY}$

8 Scenario analysis

FAST FORWARD

Scenario analysis analyses the losses likely to be incurred in a range of different scenarios without identifying the likelihood of any particular scenario.

A second group of approaches to the measurement of risk are known as **stress testing** and **scenario analysis**. Whereas **value at risk** measures the maximum losses that a portfolio may experience under normal circumstances, **stress testing** measures risk under unusual or low probability circumstances that cannot be captured by VAR. The two approaches are therefore complementary.

Scenario analysis is when we analyze the losses incurred in a limited range of scenarios. It does not identify how likely it is that a particular scenario will occur. This is one of the limitations of scenario analysis. Other problems of scenario analysis are highlighted below.

This is in contrast to VAR, which specifies a probability of a loss beyond a certain level arising, but does not indicate the actual amount of loss.

8.1 Types of scenario analysis

Scenarios may be selected in the following ways.

(a) **Stylized scenarios.** Simulating movement in a particular variable, such as interest rates, stock prices, commodity prices or exchange rates. The movement can be small or large. The Derivatives Policy Group recommends the following seven scenarios

- (i) Parallel yield curve shift by +/–100 basis points (1 percentage point)
- (ii) Yield curve twisting by +/–25 basis points
- (iii) Each of the four combinations of the above shifts and twists
- (iv) Implied volatilities changing by +/–20 percent from the current levels
- (v) Equity index levels changing by +/–10 percent
- (vi) Major currencies moving +/–6 percent and other currencies by +/–20 percent.
- (vii) Swap spread changing by +/–20 basis points

(b) Actual **extreme events** that have occurred, for example, the impact of another stock market crash.

(c) **Hypothetical** extreme events that may occur. This requires thinking about possible events and following through the likely impact of these events. For example, nuclear war in Asia, terrorist attack in London.

8.2 Evaluating scenarios

When evaluating scenarios, it is necessary to evaluate the impact of the relevant risk factors on the firm's positions such as the impact of a change in the exchange rate on a yen currency position or changes in option values.

The overall impact on the portfolio is the sum of the impact on all the individual positions. In times of stress, markets may not act in a normal way. Estimates of sensitivities should not be based on normal market conditions. Examples of particular problems include:

- There may be no market liquidity. Assumptions about the effectiveness of hedges may therefore be wrong.
- Volatility and correlations may change dramatically.

8.3 Benefits of scenario analysis

Scenario analysis has the flexibility to deal with changes that VAR finds harder to accommodate, as follows.

- Establish our exposure to hidden risks. For example, a firm that uses delta hedging may look adequately hedged when looking at normal market movements. However, it may be exposed to large market movements.
- Look at the impact of changes in volatility. For example, a currency may be pegged to the dollar. If it is subsequently allowed to free float, its volatility will increase.
- Look at the impact of changes in correlations. Highlight vulnerabilities in risk management.
- By forcing managers to consider adverse circumstances, it can highlight risks that they have ignored and improve ability to respond to risks.

8.4 Problems with scenario analysis

The following are major problems with scenario analysis:

(a) Analysis is highly dependent on the scenarios selected.

(b) The analysis is also dependent on the expertise of the people conducting the analysis.

(c) Failure to anticipate feasible adverse events makes the results of the analysis less reliable.

(d) It is difficult to allow for all relevant risk factors.

(e) The analysis is highly subjective and judgmental.

(f) Difficult to complete the analysis of scenarios without suffering information overload.

(g) Having identified scenarios, we need to work through all their implications. This could be extremely complicated (e.g. interactions between interest rates, equities, bonds, and exchange rates).

(h) When looking at risks, we need to consider how the risks may interact. It may be unrealistic to assume that two losses will occur together. This increases the complexity of the analysis.

(i) There is a need to eliminate price movements that would breach arbitrage conditions. Allowing for this increases complexity.

The fact that scenario analysis does not indicate the likelihood of a scenario arising is a potential limitation of scenario analysis. However, it should not be viewed as a criticism, since scenario analysis was not intended to give this information in the first place.

9 Stress testing

FAST FORWARD

Stress testing analyses a large number of possible events in order to identify the combination of events that produce the highest losses. Different forms are:

- Factor push analysis
- Maximum loss optimisation
- Worst case scenario analysis

9.1 Types of stress testing

Scenario analysis selects a limited number of plausible adverse scenarios. Model stressing approaches are concerned with the analysis of a large number of possible events.

Key term

Model stressing analyses a very large number of possible events in order to identify the combination of events that produce the **highest losses**.

Model stressing approaches are more extensive than **scenario analysis** but they give more computational complexity. Different forms of model stressing approaches are the following:

(a) Factor push analysis.
(b) Maximum loss optimization.
(c) Worst case scenario analysis.

9.2 Factor push analysis

Key term

Factor push analysis is when the prices of securities (or the risk factors that drive those prices) are pushed in an adverse direction. The impact of these pushes on the value of the portfolio is then calculated.

For example, we can decide on a confidence limit and then push each price by the number of standard deviations implied by the confidence limit. This will then give the worst price movements for the given confidence limit (this is similar to the VAR approach).

The **benefits** of factor push analysis are as follows.

(a) It is easy to program.
(b) Identifies the worst case, indicating areas of danger.
(c) Less reliance on underlying assumptions than VAR (e.g. no need to assume linear portfolios).
(d) Can vary correlations used in the analysis to see the impact of changing correlations.
(e) If limiting assumptions are used (e.g. about the shape of a distribution), can get an estimate of the probability of the loss arising (i.e. effectively do a VAR calculation).

Problems with factor push analysis are as follows.

(a) Investments having different sensitivities to the same risk factor. This can be resolved by analyzing risk factors rather than the prices themselves but this involves further estimates.
(b) The analysis assumes that maximum loss occurs when a risk reaches an extreme value. This is not always true (for example, a long straddle actually makes more profit at extreme values).

9.3 Maximum loss optimisation

Key term

Maximum loss optimisation identifies the movement in the risk factor that gives the maximum loss, rather than concentrating on the maximum movement for the risk factor.

Maximum loss optimisation is more complex and computationally intensive than factor push analysis due to the need to consider a wider range of possibilities.

Where a portfolio is simple, **factor push analysis** should be sufficient. When a portfolio has more complex exposures, maximum loss optimization is appropriate.

9.4 Worst case scenario

This deals with the worst case situation that **is expected** to occur, in contrast to **factor push** analysis, which considers the worst case that **could** occur. It is less conservative.

Chapter Roundup

- Financial engineering deals with the design and valuation of new derivative products.
- A great variety of options has been designed that vary in terms of the exercise price or the underlying. There are options where the underlying is a non-financial asset such as the amount of rainfall or snow.
- Two general arguments have been put forward for the growth in derivatives.
  - The first is that derivatives complete the market
  - The second argument is that they make markets more efficient
- The main risks from the use of derivatives are the role of mispricing (**valuation** or **model risk**), **liquidity risk** and **reporting risk**.
- Changes in the value of an option can be measured in terms of its **Greeks**, that is in terms of its **risk factors**.
- The 'Greeks' are an important element in option theory.
  - **Delta** – change in call option price/change in value of share
  - **Gamma** – change in delta value/change in value of share
  - **Theta** – change in option price over time
  - **Rho** – change in option price as interest rates change
  - **Vega** – change in option price as volatility changes
- Changes in the value of a futures position reflects the changes in the value of the underlying asset.
- Changes in the value of swaps positions reflect the changes in the value of interest rates.
- Scenario analysis analyses the losses likely to be incurred in a range of different scenarios without identifying the likelihood of any particular scenario.
- Stress testing analyses a large number of possible events in order to identify the combination of events that produce the highest losses. Different forms are:
  - Factor push analysis
  - Maximum loss optimisation
  - Worst case scenario analysis

Quick Quiz

1 If the delta of an option is 0.7 and the volatility of the underlying is 20%

(a) what is the volatility of the option?
(b) what is the 5% value at risk?

2 Why is the VAR of a futures contract the same as the VAR of an equivalent position on the underlying?

3 What is the duration of a floating rate bond?

4 If the duration of a bond is 5 years and the interest rate volatility is 0.02% is

(a) what is the volatility of the bond?
(b) what is the volatility of the swap?
(c) what is the VAR of the swap?

5 What types of scenarios are normally used in scenario analysis?

6 What are the main types of stress testing employed?

Answers to Quick Quiz

1 (a) The volatility of the option is given by

$$\sigma_{OPTION} = \text{delta} \times \sigma_{UNDERLYING}$$
$$= 0.7 \times 0.20 = 0.14 \text{ or } 14\%$$

(b) The 5% value at risk is

$$VAR_{OPTION} = 1.645 \times 0.14 = 0.2303$$

2 Because the volatility of the two positions is the same.

3 The duration of a floating rate bond is practically zero, meaning that exchange rate changes do not affect the value of the bond.

4 (a) The volatility of the bond is

$$\sigma_{BOND} = \text{Duration} \times \sigma_{INTEREST\ RATE}$$
$$= 5 \times 0.02\% = 0.1\%$$

(b) The volatility of the swap is simply the volatility of the bond $\sigma_{SWAP} = 0.1\%$

(c) $$VAR_{SWAP} = 1.645\ \sigma_{SWAP}$$
$$= 1.645 \times 0.1 = 0.1645$$

5 Stylised scenarios, extreme events that have happened, hypothetical extreme events.

6 Factor push analysis, maximum loss optimisation, worst case scenario.

Now try the questions below from the Exam Question Bank

Number	Level	Marks	Time
39	Introductory	15	27 mins

Appendix – Mathematical tables and exam formulae

Present Value Table

Present value of 1 i.e. $(1 + r)^{-n}$

Where r = discount rate
n = number of periods until payment

Discount rate (r)

Periods (n)	1%	2%	3%	4%	5%	6%	7%	8%	9%	10%	
1	0·990	0·980	0·971	0·962	0·952	0·943	0·935	0·926	0·917	0·909	1
2	0·980	0·961	0·943	0·925	0·907	0·890	0·873	0·857	0·842	0·826	2
3	0·971	0·942	0·915	0·889	0·864	0·840	0·816	0·794	0·772	0·751	3
4	0·961	0·924	0·888	0·855	0·823	0·792	0·763	0·735	0·708	0·683	4
5	0·951	0·906	0·863	0·822	0·784	0·747	0·713	0·681	0·650	0·621	5
6	0·942	0·888	0·837	0·790	0·746	0·705	0·666	0·630	0·596	0·564	6
7	0·933	0·871	0·813	0·760	0·711	0·665	0·623	0·583	0·547	0·513	7
8	0·923	0·853	0·789	0·731	0·677	0·627	0·582	0·540	0·502	0·467	8
9	0·914	0·837	0·766	0·703	0·645	0·592	0·544	0·500	0·460	0·424	9
10	0·905	0·820	0·744	0·676	0·614	0·558	0·508	0·463	0·422	0·386	10
11	0·896	0·804	0·722	0·650	0·585	0·527	0·475	0·429	0·388	0·350	11
12	0·887	0·788	0·701	0·625	0·557	0·497	0·444	0·397	0·356	0·319	12
13	0·879	0·773	0·681	0·601	0·530	0·469	0·415	0·368	0·326	0·290	13
14	0·870	0·758	0·661	0·577	0·505	0·442	0·388	0·340	0·299	0·263	14
15	0·861	0·743	0·642	0·555	0·481	0·417	0·362	0·315	0·275	0·239	15

(n)	11%	12%	13%	14%	15%	16%	17%	18%	19%	20%	
1	0·901	0·893	0·885	0·877	0·870	0·862	0·855	0·847	0·840	0·833	1
2	0·812	0·797	0·783	0·769	0·756	0·743	0·731	0·718	0·706	0·694	2
3	0·731	0·712	0·693	0·675	0·658	0·641	0·624	0·609	0·593	0·579	3
4	0·659	0·636	0·613	0·592	0·572	0·552	0·534	0·516	0·499	0·482	4
5	0·593	0·567	0·543	0·519	0·497	0·476	0·456	0·437	0·419	0·402	5
6	0·535	0·507	0·480	0·456	0·432	0·410	0·390	0·370	0·352	0·335	6
7	0·482	0·452	0·425	0·400	0·376	0·354	0·333	0·314	0·296	0·279	7
8	0·434	0·404	0·376	0·351	0·327	0·305	0·285	0·266	0·249	0·233	8
9	0·391	0·361	0·333	0·308	0·284	0·263	0·243	0·225	0·209	0·194	9
10	0·352	0·322	0·295	0·270	0·247	0·227	0·208	0·191	0·176	0·162	10
11	0·317	0·287	0·261	0·237	0·215	0·195	0·178	0·162	0·148	0·135	11
12	0·286	0·257	0·231	0·208	0·187	0·168	0·152	0·137	0·124	0·112	12
13	0·258	0·229	0·204	0·182	0·163	0·145	0·130	0·116	0·104	0·093	13
14	0·232	0·205	0·181	0·160	0·141	0·125	0·111	0·099	0·088	0·078	14
15	0·209	0·183	0·160	0·140	0·123	0·108	0·095	0·084	0·074	0·065	15

Annuity Table

Present value of an annuity of 1 i.e. $\frac{1-(1+r)^{-n}}{r}$

Where r = discount rate
n = number of periods

Discount rate (r)

Periods (n)	1%	2%	3%	4%	5%	6%	7%	8%	9%	10%	
1	0·990	0·980	0·971	0·962	0·952	0·943	0·935	0·926	0·917	0·909	1
2	1·970	1·942	1·913	1·886	1·859	1·833	1·808	1·783	1·759	1·736	2
3	2·941	2·884	2·829	2·775	2·723	2·673	2·624	2·577	2·531	2·487	3
4	3·902	3·808	3·717	3·630	3·546	3·465	3·387	3·312	3·240	3·170	4
5	4·853	4·713	4·580	4·452	4·329	4·212	4·100	3·993	3·890	3·791	5
6	5·795	5·601	5·417	5·242	5·076	4·917	4·767	4·623	4·486	4·355	6
7	6·728	6·472	6·230	6·002	5·786	5·582	5·389	5·206	5·033	4·868	7
8	7·652	7·325	7·020	6·733	6·463	6·210	5·971	5·747	5·535	5·335	8
9	8·566	8·162	7·786	7·435	7·108	6·802	6·515	6·247	5·995	5·759	9
10	9·471	8·983	8·530	8·111	7·722	7·360	7·024	6·710	6·418	6·145	10
11	10·37	9·787	9·253	8·760	8·306	7·887	7·499	7·139	6·805	6·495	11
12	11·26	10·58	9·954	9·385	8·863	8·384	7·943	7·536	7·161	6·814	12
13	12·13	11·35	10·63	9·986	9·394	8·853	8·358	7·904	7·487	7·103	13
14	13·00	12·11	11·30	10·56	9·899	9·295	8·745	8·244	7·786	7·367	14
15	13·87	12·85	11·94	11·12	10·38	9·712	9·108	8·559	8·061	7·606	15

(n)	11%	12%	13%	14%	15%	16%	17%	18%	19%	20%	
1	0·901	0·893	0·885	0·877	0·870	0·862	0·855	0·847	0·840	0·833	1
2	1·713	1·690	1·668	1·647	1·626	1·605	1·585	1·566	1·547	1·528	2
3	2·444	2·402	2·361	2·322	2·283	2·246	2·210	2·174	2·140	2·106	3
4	3·102	3·037	2·974	2·914	2·855	2·798	2·743	2·690	2·639	2·589	4
5	3·696	3·605	3·517	3·433	3·352	3·274	3·199	3·127	3·058	2·991	5
6	4·231	4·111	3·998	3·889	3·784	3·685	3·589	3·498	3·410	3·326	6
7	4·712	4·564	4·423	4·288	4·160	4·039	3·922	3·812	3·706	3·605	7
8	5·146	4·968	4·799	4·639	4·487	4·344	4·207	4·078	3·954	3·837	8
9	5·537	5·328	5·132	4·946	4·772	4·607	4·451	4·303	4·163	4·031	9
10	5·889	5·650	5·426	5·216	5·019	4·833	4·659	4·494	4·339	4·192	10
11	6·207	5·938	5·687	5·453	5·234	5·029	4·836	4·656	4·486	4·327	11
12	6·492	6·194	5·918	5·660	5·421	5·197	4·988	4·793	4·611	4·439	12
13	6·750	6·424	6·122	5·842	5·583	5·342	5·118	4·910	4·715	4·533	13
14	6·982	6·628	6·302	6·002	5·724	5·468	5·229	5·008	4·802	4·611	14
15	7·191	6·811	6·462	6·142	5·847	5·575	5·324	5·092	4·876	4·675	15

Standard normal distribution table

	0·00	0·01	0·02	0·03	0·04	0·05	0·06	0·07	0·08	0·09
0·0	0·0000	0·0040	0·0080	0·0120	0·0160	0·0199	0·0239	0·0279	0·0319	0·0359
0·1	0·0398	0·0438	0·0478	0·0517	0·0557	0·0596	0·0636	0·0675	0·0714	0·0753
0·2	0·0793	0·0832	0·0871	0·0910	0·0948	0·0987	0·1026	0·1064	0·1103	0·1141
0·3	0·1179	0·1217	0·1255	0·1293	0·1331	0·1368	0·1406	0·1443	0·1480	0·1517
0·4	0·1554	0·1591	0·1628	0·1664	0·1700	0·1736	0·1772	0·1808	0·1844	0·1879
0·5	0·1915	0·1950	0·1985	0·2019	0·2054	0·2088	0·2123	0·2157	0·2190	0·2224
0·6	0·2257	0·2291	0·2324	0·2357	0·2389	0·2422	0·2454	0·2486	0·2517	0·2549
0·7	0·2580	0·2611	0·2642	0·2673	0·2703	0·2734	0·2764	0·2794	0·2823	0·2852
0·8	0·2881	0·2910	0·2939	0·2967	0·2995	0·3023	0·3051	0·3078	0·3106	0·3133
0·9	0·3159	0·3186	0·3212	0·3238	0·3264	0·3289	0·3315	0·3340	0·3365	0·3389
1·0	0·3413	0·3438	0·3461	0·3485	0·3508	0·3531	0·3554	0·3577	0·3599	0·3621
1·1	0·3643	0·3665	0·3686	0·3708	0·3729	0·3749	0·3770	0·3790	0·3810	0·3830
1·2	0·3849	0·3869	0·3888	0·3907	0·3925	0·3944	0·3962	0·3980	0·3997	0·4015
1·3	0·4032	0·4049	0·4066	0·4082	0·4099	0·4115	0·4131	0·4147	0·4162	0·4177
1·4	0·4192	0·4207	0·4222	0·4236	0·4251	0·4265	0·4279	0·4292	0·4306	0·4319
1·5	0·4332	0·4345	0·4357	0·4370	0·4382	0·4394	0·4406	0·4418	0·4429	0·4441
1·6	0·4452	0·4463	0·4474	0·4484	0·4495	0·4505	0·4515	0·4525	0·4535	0·4545
1·7	0·4554	0·4564	0·4573	0·4582	0·4591	0·4599	0·4608	0·4616	0·4625	0·4633
1·8	0·4641	0·4649	0·4656	0·4664	0·4671	0·4678	0·4686	0·4693	0·4699	0·4706
1·9	0·4713	0·4719	0·4726	0·4732	0·4738	0·4744	0·4750	0·4756	0·4761	0·4767
2·0	0·4772	0·4778	0·4783	0·4788	0·4793	0·4798	0·4803	0·4808	0·4812	0·4817
2·1	0·4821	0·4826	0·4830	0·4834	0·4838	0·4842	0·4846	0·4850	0·4854	0·4857
2·2	0·4861	0·4864	0·4868	0·4871	0·4875	0·4878	0·4881	0·4884	0·4887	0·4890
2·3	0·4893	0·4896	0·4898	0·4901	0·4904	0·4906	0·4909	0·4911	0·4913	0·4916
2·4	0·4918	0·4920	0·4922	0·4925	0·4927	0·4929	0·4931	0·4932	0·4934	0·4936
2·5	0·4938	0·4940	0·4941	0·4943	0·4945	0·4946	0·4948	0·4949	0·4951	0·4952
2·6	0·4953	0·4955	0·4956	0·4957	0·4959	0·4960	0·4961	0·4962	0·4963	0·4964
2·7	0·4965	0·4966	0·4967	0·4968	0·4969	0·4970	0·4971	0·4972	0·4973	0·4974
2·8	0·4974	0·4975	0·4976	0·4977	0·4977	0·4978	0·4979	0·4979	0·4980	0·4981
2·9	0·4981	0·4982	0·4982	0·4983	0·4984	0·4984	0·4985	0·4985	0·4986	0·4986
3·0	0·4987	0·4987	0·4987	0·4988	0·4988	0·4989	0·4989	0·4989	0·4990	0·4990

This table can be used to calculate $N(d_i)$, the cumulative normal distribution functions needed for the Black-Scholes model of option pricing. If $d_i > 0$, add 0·5 to the relevant number above. If $d_i < 0$, subtract the relevant number above from 0·5.

End of Question Paper

Formula Sheet

Modigliani and Miller Proposition 2 (with tax)

$$k_e = k_e^i + (1-T)(k_e^i - k_d)\frac{V_d}{V_e}$$

Two asset portfolio

$$s_p = \sqrt{w_a^2 s_a^2 + w_b^2 s_b^2 + 2w_a w_b r_{ab} s_a s_b}$$

The Capital Asset Pricing Model

$$E(r_i) = R_f + \beta_i(E(r_m) - R_f)$$

The asset beta formula

$$\beta_a = \left[\frac{V_e}{(V_e + V_d(1-T))}\beta_e\right] + \left[\frac{V_d(1-T)}{(V_e + V_d(1-T))}\beta_d\right]$$

The Growth Model

$$P_o = \frac{D_0(1+g)}{(r_e - g)}$$

Gordon's growth approximation

$$g = br_e$$

The weighted average cost of capital

$$WACC = \left[\frac{V_e}{V_e + V_d}\right]k_e + \left[\frac{V_d}{V_e + V_d}\right]k_d(1-T)$$

The Fisher formula

$$(1+i) = (1+r)(1+h)$$

Purchasing power parity and interest rate parity

$$s_1 = S_0 x \frac{(1+h_c)}{(1+h_b)} \qquad f_0 = s_0 x \frac{(1+i_c)}{(1+i_b)}$$

The Black Scholes Option Pricing Model	The FOREX modified Black and Scholes option pricing model
$c=P_aN(d_1)-P_eN(d_2)e^{-rt}$ Where: $d_1=\frac{\ln(P_a/P_e)+(r+0.5s^2)t}{s\sqrt{t}}$ $d_2=d_1-s\sqrt{t}$	$c=e^{-rt}\left[F_0N(d_1)-XN(d_2)\right]$ Or $p=e^{-rt}\ XN(-d_2)-F_0N(-d_1)$ Where: $d_1=\frac{1n(F_0/X)+s^2T/2}{s\sqrt{T}}$ and $d_2=d_1-s\sqrt{T}$

The Put Call Parity relationship

$$p=c-P_a+P_ee^{-rt}$$

Exam question and answer bank

1 Remuneration **22 mins**

A company is considering improving the methods of remuneration for its senior employees. As a member of the executive board, you are asked to give your opinions on the following suggestions:

(a) A high basic salary with usual 'perks' such as company car, pension scheme etc but no performance-related bonuses

(b) A lower basic salary with usual 'perks' plus a bonus related to their division's profit before tax

(c) A lower basic salary with usual 'perks' plus a share option scheme which allows senior employees to buy a given number of shares in the company at a fixed price at the end of each financial year

Required

Discuss the arguments for and against each of the three options from the point of view of both the company and its employees. Detailed comments on the taxation implications are not required.

(12 marks)

2 Goals **36 mins**

Assume you are Finance Director of a large multinational company, listed on a number of international stock markets. The company is reviewing its corporate plan. At present, the company focuses on maximising shareholder wealth as its major goal. The Managing Director thinks this single goal is inappropriate and asks his co-directors for their views on giving greater emphasis to the following:

(a) Cash flow generation

(b) Profitability as measured by profits after tax and return on investment

(c) Risk-adjusted returns to shareholders

(d) Performance improvement in a number of areas such as concern for the environment, employees' remuneration and quality of working conditions and customer satisfaction

Required

Provide the Managing Director with a report for presentation at the next board meeting which:

(a) Evaluates the argument that maximisation of shareholder wealth should be the only true objective of a company, and

(b) Discusses the advantages and disadvantages of the MD's suggestions about alternative goals

(20 marks)

3 Stakeholders **27 mins**

(a) Many decisions in financial management are taken in a framework of conflicting stakeholder viewpoints. Identify the stakeholders and some of the financial management issues involved in the situation of a company seeking a stock market listing. **(5 marks)**

(b) XYZ plc is a medium-sized company operating in the chemical industry. It is a profitable business, currently producing at below maximum capacity. It has one large factory located on the outskirts of a small industrial town. It is the region's main employer. The company is evaluating a project which has substantial environmental implications.

Required

Discuss the inclusion of environmental costs and benefits into the investment appraisal procedure and explain how this might be done. **(10 marks)**

(Total = 15 marks)

4 XYZ **27 mins**

The table below shows earnings and dividends for XYZ plc over the past five years.

Year	*Net earnings per share* £	*Net dividend per share* £
20W9	1.40	0.84
20X0	1.35	0.88
20X1	1.35	0.90
20X2	1.30	0.95
20X3	1.25	1.00

There are 10,000,000 shares issued and the majority of these shares are owned by private investors. There is no debt in the capital structure.

It is clear from the table that the company has experienced difficult trading conditions over the past few years. In the current year, net earnings are likely to be £10 million, which will be just sufficient to pay a maintained dividend of £1 per share.

Members of the board are considering a number of strategies for the company, some of which will have an impact on the company's future dividend policy.

The company's shareholders require a return of 15% on their investment.

Four options are being considered, as follows.

(1) Pay out all earnings as dividends.
(2) Pay a reduced dividend of 50% of earnings and retain the remaining 50% for future investment.
(3) Pay a reduced dividend of 25% of earnings and retain the remaining 75% for future investment.
(4) Retain all earnings for an aggressive expansion programme and pay no dividend at all.

The directors cannot agree on any of the four options discussed so far. Some of them prefer option (1) because they believe to do anything else would have an adverse impact on the share price. Others favour either option (2) or option (3) because the company has identified some good investment opportunities and they believe one of these options would be in the best long-term interests of shareholders. An adventurous minority favours option (4) and thinks this will allow the company to take over a small competitor.

Required

(a) Discuss the company's dividend policy between 20W9 and 20X3 and its possible consequences for earnings. **(4 marks)**

(b) Advise the directors of the share price for XYZ plc which might be expected immediately following the announcement of their decision if they pursued each of the four options, using an appropriate valuation model. You should also show what percentage of total return is provided by dividend and capital gain in each case. You should ignore taxation for this part of the question. Make (and indicate) any realistic assumptions you think necessary to answer this question. **(6 marks)**

(c) Discuss the reliability you can place on the figures you have just produced and on the usefulness of this information to the company's directors. **(5 marks)**

(Total = 15 marks)

5 Ethical dimension 36 mins

(a) According to Carroll, what are the four main responsibilities faced by companies when developing an ethical framework, and in what ways can these responsibilities be addressed? **(10 marks)**

(b) Discuss how ethical considerations impact on each of the main functional areas of a firm. **(10 marks)**

(Total = 20 marks)

6 Solden 36 mins

Solden plc is a UK company which is considering setting up a manufacturing operation to make ski-boot warmers in a country called Ober. The currency of Ober is the Gurgle and these are currently G16 to the pound sterling. If the operation were to be set up the plant would be purchased in Ober costing G600,000 now and some equipment would be sent from the UK immediately. This equipment is fully written off in the UK but has a market value of £12,500 or G200,000. All plant and equipment is written off on a straight line basis by Solden plc over 5 years.

The ski-boot warmers will sell for an initial price of G160 but this price will increase in line with inflation in Ober which is expected to continue at its current rate of 10% pa. It is also expected that 4,000 ski-boot warmers will be sold in the first year increasing at a rate of 5% each year. The costs of making ski-boot warmers consist of local variable costs of G80 per unit and selling and administration costs of G40,000 pa, both of which will increase in line with inflation in Ober. The warmers also require some specialist parts sent over from the UK each year. These will be transferred at the beginning of the first year of production at a cost of G40,000 (£2,500) which includes a 25% mark up on cost. The transfer price and cost of these items are expected to increase by 5% pa, and they will be billed to the Ober operation at the beginning of the year and paid for at the end of the year. The working capital for this project will be required at the beginning of each year and will be equal to10% of the expected sales value for the year.

Solden plc estimates that it will lose some of its own exports worth £5,000 now and increasing by 5% pa due to the setting up of the operation in Ober. However, Solden plc will be receiving a licence fee from the Ober operation equal to 10% of sales each year.

Corporation tax in Ober is only 20% and operating costs, licence fees and depreciation at 25% on a straight line basis are all tax allowable expenses. Corporation tax in the UK is at 33%. There is a one year tax delay in both countries.

Solden plc wishes to assess this project from the point of view of both investors in Ober (required return 15%) and investors in the UK (required return 10%). The assessment will take place using Solden's usual 5 year time 'horizon' and valuing and Ober operation at three times its net cash inflow during the fifth year. If the operation were to be sold at this value, tax would be payable at 30% on the proceeds.

It is expected that the Gurgle will depreciate against the pound by 4% pa from year 2, the first depreciation affecting year 2 cash flows. Assume that all prices have just altered, and that all cash flows occur at the end of the year unless specified otherwise.

Required

(a) Calculate (to the nearest 100 Gurgles) whether the operation would be worthwhile for investors based in Ober. **(12 marks)**

(b) If all cash surpluses can be remitted to the UK calculate whether Solden plc should set up the operation. Assume no further UK tax is payable on income taxed on Ober. **(8 marks)**

(Total = 20 marks)

7 Mover **36 mins**

(a) You have been asked to provide preliminary advice on whether or not your company's pension fund should make an investment in the shares of Mover plc, a large construction company which is leading a consortium that is proposing to build a rail tunnel between Gibraltar and Morocco. The tunnel is scheduled to open in 20X4. The only information available to you at this time is the cash flow projections published by the tunnel consortium.

Projected cash flows of the tunnel project

	£m
20X0	–450
20X1	–500
20X2	–550
20X3	–650
20X4	–200
20X5	200
20X6	300
20X7	320
20X8	340
20X9	360
20Y0	400
Each year after 20Y0	400

All projections exclude inflation, which is expected to remain at approximately 4% per year.

Required

Undertake an analysis of the proposed tunnel project and advise on whether or not the pension fund should invest in shares of Mover plc. Relevant calculations must be shown.

State clearly all assumptions that you make. In this question *only* reasoned assumptions regarding a discount rate are encouraged. **(15 marks)**

(b) Explain how inflation affects the rate of return required on an investment project, and the distinction between a real and a nominal (or 'money terms') approach to the evaluation of an investment project under inflation. **(5 marks)**

(Total = 20 marks)

8 Nile plc **27 mins**

Nile plc is considering an investment of capital to be raised from the issue of new ordinary shares and debentures in a mix which will hold its gearing ratio approximately constant. It wishes to estimate its weighted average cost of capital.

The company has an issued share capital of 1 million ordinary shares of £1 each; it has also issued £800,000 of 8% debentures. The market price of ordinary shares is £4.76 per share and debentures are priced at £77 per cent. Dividends and interest are payable annually. An ordinary dividend has just been paid; the next instalment of interest is payable in the near future. Debentures are redeemable at par in twenty years time.

A summary of the most recent balance sheet runs as follows:

	£'000		£'000	£'000
Ordinary share capital	1,000	Fixed assets		1,276
Reserves	1,553	Current assets	4,166	
Deferred taxation	164	Less: current		
Debentures	800	liabilities	1,925	
				2,241
	3,517			3,517

Dividends and earnings have been as follows:

	Dividends (excluding tax credit)	*Earnings before tax*	*Earnings after tax*
	£'000	£'000	£'000
20X4	200	575	350
20X5	230	723	452
20X6	230	682	410
20X7	260	853	536
20X8	300	906	606

Assume that there have been no changes in the system or rates of taxation during the last five years, that the rate of corporation tax is 35% and that the standard rate of income tax is 30%. Assume that 'now' is 20X8.

Required

(a) Calculate Nile plc's weighted average cost of capital; and **(10 marks)**

(b) discuss briefly any difficulties and uncertainties in your estimation. **(5 marks)**

(Total = 15 marks)

9 Crystal plc

27 mins

The following figures have been extracted from the most recent accounts of Crystal plc.

BALANCE SHEET AS ON 30 JUNE 20X9

	£'000	£'000
Fixed assets		10,115
Investments		821
Current assets	3,658	
Less current liabilities	1,735	
		1,923
		12,859
Ordinary share capital		
Authorised: 4,000,000shares of £1		
Issued: 3,000,000 shares of £1		3,000
Reserves		6,542
Shareholders' funds		9,542
7% Debentures		1,300
Deferred taxation		583
Corporation tax		1,434
		12,859

Summary of profits and dividends

Year ended 30 June:	*20X5*	*20X6*	*20X7*	*20X8*	*20X9*
	£'000	£'000	£'000	£'000	£'000
Profit after interest and before tax	1,737	2,090	1,940	1,866	2,179
Less tax	573	690	640	616	719
Profit after interest and tax	1,164	1,400	1,300	1,250	1,460
Less dividends	620	680	740	740	810
Added to reserves	544	720	560	510	650

The current (1 July 20X9) market value of Crystal plc's ordinary shares is £3.27 per share cum div. An annual dividend of £810,000 is due for payment shortly. The debentures are redeemable at par in ten years time. Their current market value is £77.10 per cent. Annual interest has just been paid on the debentures. There have been no issues or redemptions of ordinary shares or debentures during the past five years.

The current rate of corporation tax is 30%, and the current basic rate of income tax is 25%. Assume that there have been no changes in the system or rates of taxation during the last five years.

Required

(a) Estimate the cost of capital which Crystal plc should use as a discount rate when appraising new investment opportunities. **(10 marks)**

(b) Discuss any difficulties and uncertainties in your estimates. **(5 marks)**

(Total = 15 marks)

10 PS Ltd **54 mins**

(a) A European call option on shares has 3 months to expiry. The exercise price of the option is £2.50, and the current price of the share is £3. The standard deviation of the share is 20% and the risk free rate is 5%.

Required

Calculate the value of the call option per share using the Black-Scholes formula. **(10 marks)**

(b) Explain

(i) The five input variables involved in the Black-Scholes pricing model

(ii) How the five input variables can be adapted to value real options as opposed to traded share options **(10 marks)**

(c) Discuss the advantages to a company of using swap arrangements as part of its treasury management strategies. Explain, briefly, the risks involved in using swap techniques. **(10 marks)**

(Total = 30 marks)

11 Canada **27 mins**

PG plc is considering investing in a new project in Canada which will have a life of four years. The initial investment is C$150,000, including working capital. The net after-tax cash flows which the project will generate are C$60,000 per annum for years 1, 2 and 3 and C$45,000 in year 4. The terminal value of the project is estimated at C$50,000, net of tax.

The current spot rate of C$ against the pound sterling is 1.7000. Economic forecasters expect the pound to strengthen against the Canadian dollar by 5% per annum over the next 4 years.

The company evaluates UK projects of similar risk at 14%.

Required

(a) Calculate the NPV of the Canadian project using the following two methods:

(i) Convert the currency cash flows into sterling and discount the sterling cash flows at a sterling discount rate

(ii) Discount the cash flows in C$ using an adjusted discount rate which incorporates the 12-month forecast spot rate and explain briefly the theories and/or assumptions which underlie the use of the adjusted discount rate approach in (ii). **(10 marks)**

(b) The company had originally planned to finance the project with internal funds generated in the UK. However, the finance director has suggested that there would be advantages in raising debt finance in Canada.

Discuss the advantages and disadvantages of matching investment and borrowing overseas as compared with UK-sourced debt or equity.

Wherever possible, relate your answer to the details in this question for PG plc. **(5 marks)**

(Total = 15 marks)

12 Drive plc **36 mins**

(a) Drive plc is a car hire company with operations based solely in the UK. It is currently considering setting up a new outlet with the following predicted earnings:

	Year				
	1	*2*	*3*	*4*	*5*
Earnings before tax (£m)	2.5	2.6	3.5	4.2	4.5

Initial investment in the new premises will be £8m, for which first year tax allowances of 40% are available, with the remainder being written down over a four year period. Tax is charged at 30%.

Required

(i) Calculate the tax liability and the after tax earnings for each year of the project. **(6 marks)**

(ii) How would earnings be affected if the first year allowance was 50%? **(4 marks)**

(b) Drive plc is also considering setting up in Goldland, whose currency – the Gold dollar (G$), has been quite volatile in the past.

Required

Write a memo to the financial director of Drive plc, which covers the following areas:

(i) The potential effects on the financial statements of operating in a country with a volatile economy;

(ii) The problems in alleviating these effects. **(10 marks)**

(Total = 20 marks)

13 Organic growth **15 mins**

Discuss the advantages to a company of establishing an overseas operating subsidiary by:

either (i) Organic growth
or (ii) Acquisition **(8 marks)**

14 Canon Burger **36 mins**

Canon Burger has been expanding its operation rapidly by acquiring a number of restaurants. Canon has been funding its acquisitions by bank borrowing and it has a high level of leverage. Canon Burger has been specialising in fast food outlets and although the market is supported by a booming young population, the older generation prefer more traditional outlets. Canon is considering the acquisition of Templar Restaurant, a continental type of establishment with a steady clientele and good reputation. The owners of Templar have been rather conservative and have not exploited the brand value of the restaurant to expand, as they approach retirement. The owners of Templar are prepared to accept a cash offer of £200,000. Canon Burger has a cost of capital of 16 percent due to its high leverage. Templar Restaurant on the other hand is free of debt. As a result of the acquisition, Canon Burger expects the debt equity ratio of the combined equity to decrease and the cost of capital to fall to 12 percent. The acquisition of Templar Restaurant is expected to increase Canon's cash flow by £25,000 per year forever.

(a) What kind of synergies will the acquisition of Templar Restaurants create? **(6 marks)**

(b) Should Canon Burger proceed with the acquisition? **(7 marks)**

(c) If the acquisition was funded by borrowing so that there is no impact on the level of leverage of the combined entity and the cost of capital was not reduced, should Canon still proceed with the acquisition? **(7 marks)**

(Total = 20 marks)

15 Univo plc **27 mins**

Summarised financial data for Univo plc is shown below.

PROFIT AND LOSS ACCOUNTS

	20W9	*20X0*	*20X1*[1]
	£'000	£'000	£'000
Turnover	76,270	89,410	102,300
Taxable income	10,140	12,260	14,190
Taxation	3,346	4,046	4,683
	6,794	8,214	9,507
Dividend	2,335	2,557	2,800
Retained earnings	4,459	5,657	6,707

BALANCE SHEET

	20X1[1]
	£'000
Fixed assets	54,200
Current assets	39,500
Current liabilities	(26,200)
	67,500
Ordinary shares (50 pence par value)	20,000
Reserves	32,500
10% debentures 20X6 (£100 par value)	15,000
	67,500

[1] 20X1 figures are unaudited estimates.

As a result of recent capital investment, stock market analysts expect post tax earnings and dividends to increase by 25% for two years and then to revert to the company's existing growth rates.

Univo's asset (overall) beta is 0.763, beta of debt is 0.20 and beta of equity is 0.82. The risk free rate is 12% and the market return 17%.

The current market price of Univo's shares is 217 pence cum 20X1 dividend.

Required

(a) Using the dividend growth model estimate what a fundamental analyst might consider to be the intrinsic (or realistic) value of the company's shares. Comment upon the significance of your estimate for the fundamental analyst.

Assume, for this part of the question only, that the cost of equity is not expected to change. The cost of equity may be estimated by using the CAPM. **(10 marks)**

(b) If interest rates were to increase by 2% and expected dividend growth to remain unchanged, estimate what effect this would be likely to have on the intrinsic value of the company's shares. **(5 marks)**

(Total = 15 marks)

16 Black Raven Ltd **54 mins**

Black Raven Ltd is a prosperous private company, whose owners are also the directors. The directors have decided to sell their business, and have begun a search for organisations interested in its purchase. They have asked for your assessment of the price per ordinary share a purchaser might be expected to offer. Relevant information is as follows.

MOST RECENT BALANCE SHEET

	£'000	£'000	£'000
Fixed assets (net book value)			
Land and buildings			800
Plant and equipment			450
Motor vehicles			55
Patents			2
			1,307
Current assets			
Stock		250	
Debtors		125	
Cash		8	
		383	
Current liabilities			
Creditors	180		
Taxation	50		
		230	
			153
			1,460
Long-term liability			
Loan secured on property			400
			1,060
Share capital (300,000 ordinary shares of £1)			300
Reserves			760
			1,060

The profits after tax and interest but before dividends over the last five years have been as follows.

Year	£
1	90,000
2	80,000
3	105,000
4	90,000
5 (most recent)	100,000

The company's five year plan forecasts an after-tax profit of £100,000 for the next 12 months, with an increase of 4% a year over each of the next four years. The annual dividend has been £45,000 (gross) for the last six years.

As part of their preparations to sell the company, the directors of Black Raven Ltd have had the fixed assets revalued by an independent expert, with the following results.

	£
Land and buildings	1,075,000
Plant and equipment	480,000
Motor vehicles	45,000

The gross dividend yields and P/E ratios of three quoted companies in the same industry as Black Raven Ltd over the last three years have been as follows.

	Albatross plc		*Bullfinch plc*		*Crow plc*	
	Div. yield	*P/E ratio*	*Div. yield*	*P/E ratio*	*Div. yield*	*P/E ratio*
	%		%		%	
Recent year	12	8.5	11.0	9.0	13.0	10.0
Previous year	12	8.0	10.6	8.5	12.6	9.5
Three years ago	12	8.5	9.3	8.0	12.4	9.0
Average	12	8.33	10.3	8.5	12.7	9.5

Large companies in the industry apply an after-tax cost of capital of about 18% to acquisition proposals when the investment is not backed by tangible assets, as opposed to a rate of only 14% on the net tangible assets.

Your assessment of the net cash flows which would accrue to a purchasing company, allowing for taxation and the capital expenditure required after the acquisition to achieve the company's target five year plan, is as follows.

	£
Year 1	120,000
Year 2	120,000
Year 3	140,000
Year 4	70,000
Year 5	120,000

Required

Use the information provided to suggest alternative valuations which prospective purchasers might make.

(Total = 30 marks)

17 Margate **72 mins**

Margate Group plc is a large, long-established company whose primary interests are in transport and distribution within the United Kingdom. It is considering a bid to acquire Hastings plc, a company also in the transport and distribution industry. Hastings plc, however, has a strong operations base in Europe as well as in the UK. Both companies are listed on a recognised stock exchange. They both have a wide share ownership including many institutional investors.

Hastings plc has recently fought off a bid from a company based in the United States of America and has made a public statement that it will defend itself against any future bids. The company has recently won a fiercely contested five-year contract to undertake transport and distribution services for a major supermarket group. Margate Group plc also tendered for this contract. Press comment suggests this contract will allow Hastings plc's earnings to grow at 10% a year for at least the next five years. However, some industry experts believe Hastings plc tendered a price that was so low that the contract could result in very little profit, or even losses.

If the acquisition were to succeed, it would create the largest company of its kind in the UK. A concern is that this would attract the interest of the competition authorities. However, as both companies have recently restructured their operations, redundancies are likely to be few and concentrated mainly in central administration.

Financial Statements

Key financial information for the two companies for the latest financial year is given below. All figures are in £ million unless otherwise stated.

PROFIT AND LOSS ACCOUNTS
FOR THE YEAR TO 31 AUGUST 20X1

	Margate Group plc	*Hastings plc*
	£m	£m
Turnover	2,763	1,850
Operating costs	1,950	1,380
Operating profit	813	470
Net interest	125	85
Profit before tax	688	385
Tax	185	85
Earnings	503	300
Dividends declared	201	135
Retained profit for the year	302	165
Earnings per shares (pence)	47.90	35.29
EPS for year to 31 August 20X0 (pence)	34.85	29.50

BALANCE SHEETS AT 31 AUGUST 20X1

	Margate Group plc	*Hastings plc*
	£m	£m
Fixed assets (net book value)	3,250	2,580
Current assets		
	125	175
	550	425
	450	45
Creditors: due within 1 year		
	0	420
	755	365
Creditors: due after 1 year		
	1,450	950
	150	40
Net assets	2,020	1,450
Capital and reserves		
	1,050	850
	220	150
	750	450
Total shareholder's funds	2,020	1,450

Note. Margate Group plc's debenture is 8%, repayable 20X5. Hastings plc's is 9%, repayable 20X4.

Share price information (prices in pence)

		Margate Group plc	*Hastings plc*
Share price movements:	High for last financial year	705	590
	Low for last financial year	470	440
Share price today (20 November 20X1)		671	565
P/E ratios today		14	16
Equity betas		1.1	1.2

Other information

- The average P/E for the industry is currently estimated as 13.
- The return on the market is currently estimated as 12%, the risk-free rate as 6%. These rates are expected to remain constant for the next 12 months and are post-tax.
- The average debt ratio for the industry (long-term debt as proportion of total long-term funding) is 30% based on book values.
- Economic forecasts provided by Margate Group plc's financial advisors expect inflation and interest rates to remain at their current levels for the foreseeable future. Inflation is currently 2% a year.

Terms of the proposed bid

Margate Group plc's directors are planning to offer a share exchange to Hastings plc's shareholders.

Required

(a) Calculate and discuss briefly three key ratios for both companies that are relevant to the evaluation of the proposed acquisition. **(7 marks)**

(b) Calculate a range of possible values that Margate Group plc could place on Hastings plc, using both P/E basis and the dividend growth model.

Accompany your calculations by brief comments or explanations. Where necessary, explain any assumptions you have made **(7 marks)**

(c) Assume you are the Financial Manager with Margate Group plc. Write a report to the directors of the group that evaluates the proposed acquisition.

You should use the figures you have calculated in answer to parts (a) and (b) to support your recommendations/advice where relevant. If you have not been able to do the calculations for parts (a) and (b), you should make, and state, appropriate assumptions.

Your report should include the following topics.

(i) Recommendation to the directors of a bid price and offer terms, assuming a share-for-share exchange.

(ii) Advice on a strategy for making the offer to Hastings plc to minimise the likelihood of outright rejection by the Hastings plc board, and a discussion of the other risks involved in making the bid.

(iii) Discussion of the strategic and financial advantages that might arise from the acquisition by Margate Group plc of Hastings plc.

Support your discussion with calculations of the post-acquisition value of the combined group and how the estimated gains are likely to be split between the shareholders of Margate Group plc and Hastings plc. **(26 marks)**

(Total = 40 marks)

18 Canadian plc — 72 mins

Canadian plc is a regional electricity generating company with several coal, oil and gas powered generating stations. The opportunity to bid for the coal mine supplying one of its local stations has arisen, and you have been asked to assess the project. If Canadian does not bid for the pit, then it is likely to close, in which case coal for the station would have to be obtained from overseas.

Canadian's bid is likely to be successful if priced at £6 million. Regional development fund finance is available at a subsidised interest rate of 4% for the full cost of the purchase, as against Canadian's marginal cost of debt if financed commercially. If Canadian invests a further £6 million in updated machinery, the pit is likely to generate £10 million of coal per annum for the next five years at current UK coal prices. Operating costs will total £3 million per annum, plus depreciation. Thereafter it will have to close, at a net cost after asset sales of £17 million, which includes redundancy, cleanup and associated costs, at present prices.

You have ascertained the following information about the coal industry.

	Coal industry (average)
Gearing (debt/equity):	
Book values	1 to 0.5
Market values	1:1
Equity beta	0.7
Debt beta	0.2

Capital allowances would be available at 25% on a reducing balance basis for all new machinery. The purchase price of the mine can be depreciated for tax at 25% per annum straight line. All other costs are tax allowable in full.

Other than the regional development fund loan (repayable after 5 years), the project would be financed by retained earnings. The project is likely to add another £3 million of borrowing capacity to Canadian, in addition to the £6 million regional development fund loan. Corporation tax is expected to remain to 30% during the life of the project. The company as a whole expects to be in a tax payable position for all years except the third year of the project.

Assume that all prices rise with the RPI, currently by 3% pa, except coal prices, which in view of reduced demand are set to remain static. You may assume that original investment cash flows arise at the start of the first year, and that all other cash flows arise at the end of the year in which the costs are incurred, except for tax, which lags one year. Treasury bills currently yield 8%, and the return required of the market portfolio is currently 16%.

You have discovered the following information concerning Canadian.

	Canadian plc
Gearing (debt/equity):	
	1 to 1
	1:2
Equity beta	1.0
Debt beta	0.25
P/E ratio	14
Dividend yield	6%
Share price	220 pence
Number of ordinary shares	8 million

Required

Write a memorandum for the finance director advising on whether the mine should be acquired. you should divide your memorandum into the following sections:

(a)	Overall summary and conclusion	**(6 marks)**
(b)	Detailed numerical workings	**(23 marks)**
(c)	Assumptions behind the report	**(8 marks)**
(d)	Areas for further research	**(3 marks)**
		(Total = 40 marks)

Approaching the answer

You should read through the requirement before working through and annotating the question as we have so you are aware of what things you are looking for.

19 Peden and Tulen — 27 mins

The total values (equity plus debt) of two companies, Peden and Tulen are expected to fluctuate according to the state of the economy.

	Economic state		
	Recession	*Slow growth*	*Rapid growth*
Probability	0.15	0.65	0.20
Total values			
Peden (£m)	42	55	75
Tulen (£m)	63	80	120

Peden currently has £45 million of debt, and Tulen £10 million of debt.

Required

(a) If the two companies were to merge, and assuming that no operational synergy occurs as a result of the merger, calculate the expected value of debt and equity of the merged company. Explain the reasons for any difference that exists from the expected values of debt and equity if they do not merge. **(11 marks)**

(b) Discuss the importance of financial post-audits following a merger or takeover. **(4 marks)**

(Total = 15 marks)

20 Takeover regulation — 36 mins

(a) Discuss the key aspects of takeover regulation in the UK and continental Europe in the context of European harmonisation.

(b) As hostile takeovers increase discuss some of the defensive measures that could be taken by a target in Europe and compare these briefly with what would be permissible in the US regulatory environment. **(20 marks)**

21 Atlas International — 27 mins

Atlas International plc is considering a bid for Olympic Global plc. The following information is given for both companies:

	Atlas	*Olympics*
	£	£
Earnings per share	4	0.90
Share price	70	22
Number of shares	1,000,000	500,000

The consensus view is that Olympic will grow at a rate of 5 percent. The management of Atlas believe that without additional investment they can raise the growth rate to 7%.

(a) What is the gain from the acquisition? **(5 marks)**

(b) What is the cost of acquisition if Atlas pays £30 per share in cash for each share of Global? Should the acquisition go ahead? **(5 marks)**

(c) What is the cost of acquisition if Atlas offers one of its own shares for every two shares of Global? Should the acquisition go ahead? **(5 marks)**

(Total = 15 marks)

22 Dolly Ltd

36 mins

Dolly Ltd, a toy manufacturer, has received a letter from a company that specialises in the prediction of corporate failure. The letter suggests that Dolly Ltd has a high probability of failure and has offered to supply a full report at a cost of £150,000.

Dolly Ltd's managing director is seriously considering the purchase of the report, as publication of its contents could have an adverse effect on the company's value.

The most recent summarised financial statements for Dolly Ltd are as follows:

Income statement	*31 Dec 20X6*	*31 Dec 20X5*
	£m	£m
Turnover	403	377
Earnings before interest and tax	28	34
Interest	13	12
Profit before tax	15	22
Taxation	5	4
Profit available to shareholders	10	18
Dividend	11	11
Retained earnings	(1)	7

Balance sheet		*31 Dec 20X6*		*31 Dec 20X5*
		£m		£m
Fixed assets (NBV)				
Land and buildings		137		127
Plant and machinery		128		122
Other		32		31
		297		280
Current assets				
Stock	101		83	
Debtors	21		22	
Cash	3		2	
		125		107
Creditors: amounts falling due within one year				
Creditors	127		108	
Taxation	5		7	
Proposed dividends	8		8	
		(140)		(123)
Creditors: amounts falling due after more than one year				
10% debentures	98		98	
Bank loan	61		42	
		(159)		(140)
		123		124
Shareholders' Funds				
Ordinary shares (25p)	49		49	
Reserves	74		75	
		123		124

Other information:

(i) Corporate tax rate is 30%.
(ii) Dolly Ltd's share price is currently 151 pence.
(iii) Dolly Ltd's cost of capital is 10%.
(iv) Current interest rate on the bank loan is 5%.
(v) Depreciation allowable for tax purposes is £25m.
(vi) For production to remain at current levels, annual investment of approximately £23m is required.

The managing director is aware of the Z-score method of predicting corporate failure, which is calculated using the following formula:

$Z = 1.2X_1 + 1.4X_2 + 3.3X_3 + 0.6X_4 + 1.0X_5$

Where X_1 = Working Capital/Total Assets
X_2 = Retained Earnings/Total Assets
X_3 = EBIT/Total Assets
X_4 = Market Value of Equity/Book Value of Debt
X_5 = Turnover/Total Assets

A Z-score that is greater than or equal to 2.7 indicates a very low probability of failure; a score of 1.8 or less suggests a high probability of failure. Any score between 1.8 and 2.7 is inconclusive.

Required

(a) Calculate Dolly Ltd's Z-score for the year ended 31 December 20X6 **(5 marks)**

(b) Discuss the significance of the Z-score for Dolly Ltd's future **(6 marks)**

(c) The Z-score is one method of predicting corporate failure. Briefly discuss alternative means of predicting such failure **(5 marks)**

(d) Should Dolly Ltd purchase the full report for the asking price of £150,000? Give reasons for your answer. **(4 marks)**

(Total = 20 marks)

23 Brive plc

54 mins

The latest balance sheet for Brive plc is summarised below.

	£'000	£'000	£'000
Fixed assets at net book value			5,700
Current assets			
Stock and work in progress		3,500	
Debtors		1,800	
		5,300	
Less current liabilities			
Unsecured creditors	4,000		
Bank overdraft (unsecured)	1,600		
		5,600	
Working capital			(300)
Total assets less current liabilities			5,400
Liabilities falling due after more than one year			
10% secured debentures			3,000
Net assets			2,400
			£'000
Capital and reserves			
Called up share capital			4,000
Profit and loss account			(1,600)
			2,400

Brive plc's called up capital consists of 4,000,000 £1 ordinary shares issued and fully paid. The fixed assets comprise freehold property with a book value of £3,000,000 and plant and machinery with a book value of £2,700,000. The debentures are secured on the freehold property.

In recent years the company has suffered a series of trading losses which have brought it to the brink of liquidation. The directors estimate that in a forced sale the assets will realise the following amounts.

	£
Freehold premises	2,000,000
Plant and machinery	1,000,000
Stock	1,700,000
Debtors	1,700,000

The costs of liquidation are estimated at £770,000. However, trading conditions are now improving and the directors estimate that if new investment in plant and machinery costing £2,500,000 were undertaken the company should be able to generate annual profits before interest of £1,750,000. In order to take advantage of this they have put forward the following proposed reconstruction scheme.

(a) Freehold premises should be written down by £1,000,000, plant and machinery by £1,100,000, stocks and work in progress by £800,000 and debtors by £100,000.

(b) The ordinary shares should be written down by £3,000,000 and the debit balance on the profit and loss account written off.

(c) The secured debenture holders would exchange their debentures for £1,500,000 ordinary shares and £1,300,000 14% unsecured loan stock repayable in five years' time.

(d) The bank overdraft should be written off and the bank should receive £1,200,000 of 14% unsecured loan stock repayable in five years time in compensation.

(e) The unsecured creditors should be written down by 25%.

(f) A rights issue of 1 for 1 at par is to be made on the share capital after the above adjustments have been made.

(g) £2,500,000 will be invested in new plant and machinery.

Required

(a) Prepare the balance sheet of the company after the completion of the reconstruction. **(8 marks)**

(b) Prepare a report, including appropriate calculations, discussing the advantages and disadvantages of the proposed reconstruction from the point of view of:

(i) The ordinary shareholders
(ii) The secured debenture holders
(iii) The bank
(iv) The unsecured creditors

Ignore taxation. **(22 marks)**

(Total = 30 marks)

24 Reorganisation 22 mins

(a) Discuss the potential problems with management buyouts. **(5 marks)**

(b) Company X's hotel division is experiencing considerable financial difficulties. The management is prepared to undertake a buyout, and Company X is willing to sell for £15 million. After an analysis of the division's performance, the management concluded that the division required a capital injection of £10 million.

Possible funding sources for the buyout and the additional capital injection are as follows:

From management:

Equity shares of 25p each	£12 million
From venture capitalist:	
Equity shares of 25p each	£5.5 million
Debt: 9.5% fixed rate loan	£7.5 million

The fixed rate loan principal is repayable in 10 years' time.

Forecasts of earnings before interest and tax for the next 5 years following the buyout are as follows:

	Year 1	*Year 2*	*Year 3*	*Year 4*	*Year 5*
	£'000	£'000	£'000	£'000	£'000
EBIT	2,200	3,100	3,900	4,200	4,500

Corporation tax is charged at 30%. Dividends are expected to be no more than 12 % of profits for the first five years.

Management has forecast that the value of equity capital is likely to increase by approximately 15 % per annum for the next 5 years.

Required

On the basis of the above forecasts, determine whether management's estimate that the value of equity will increase by 15% per annum is a viable one. **(7 marks)**

(Total = 12 marks)

25 Kilber plc **27 mins**

Kilber plc is a mining company with exclusive rights to the mining of Kilbe in Wales. Kilbe is a new metal that used in the construction industry. The demand for Kilbe is highly dependant on the state of the housing and market and the price is highly volatile. Kilber would like to hedge its exposure but there are no traded derivatives for Kilbe. The treasurer of Kilbe has approached a number of banks but have found the OTC market is expensive, as Kilbe is considered to be too risky, and are therefore reluctant to use forward contracts for hedging. One of the bankers they have sought advice from, suggested that they should use futures contracts on copper. She explained that the price of Kilbe is highly correlated with the price of copper and therefore copper futures contracts are good substitutes.

Required

(a) Explain why the company should care about hedging its risks and comment on the risks that Kilber plc may face if it adopts the recommendation and use copper futures contracts as a hedging instrument. **(6 marks)**

(b) Discuss some of the advantages and disadvantages of OTC derivatives. **(3 marks)**

(c) The management of Kilber is currently reviewing its funding strategies. All its borrowing is at variable rate and as there are strong indications that interest rates will increase they seek your advise on how to reduce the impact of higher rates on its interest payments. **(6 marks)**

(Total = 15 marks)

26 Expo plc **27 mins**

Expo plc is an importer/exporter of textiles and textile machinery. It is based in the UK but trades extensively with countries throughout Europe. It has a small subsidiary based in Switzerland. The company is about to invoice a customer in Switzerland 750,000 Swiss francs, payable in three months' time. Expo plc's treasurer is considering two methods of hedging the exchange risk. These are:

Method 1: Borrow Fr 750,000 for three months, convert the loan into sterling and repay the loan out of eventual receipts.

Method 2: Enter into a 3-month forward exchange contract with the company's bank to sell Fr 750,000.

The spot rate of exchange is Fr 2.3834 to £1. The 3-month forward rate of exchange is Fr 2.3688 to £1. Annual interest rates for 3 months' borrowing are: Switzerland 3%, UK 6%.

Required

(a) Advise the treasurer on:

(i) Which of the two methods is the most financially advantageous for Expo plc, and

(ii) The factors to consider before deciding whether to hedge the risk using the foreign currency markets

Include relevant calculations in your advice. **(10 marks)**

(b) Assume that Expo plc is trading in and with developing countries rather than Europe and has a subsidiary in a country with no developed capital or currency markets. Expo plc is now about to invoice a customer in that country in the local currency. Advise Expo plc's treasurer about ways in which the risk can be managed in these circumstances. No calculations are required for this part of the question. **(5 marks)**

(Total = 15 marks)

27 Fidden plc

(a) Discuss briefly four techniques a company might use to hedge against the foreign exchange risk involved in foreign trade. **(8 marks)**

(b) Fidden plc is a medium sized UK company with export and import trade with the USA. The following transactions are due within the next six months. Transactions are in the currency specified.

Purchases of components, cash payment due in three months: £116,000.
Sale of finished goods, cash receipt due in three months: $197,000.
Purchase of finished goods for resale, cash payment due in six months: $447,000.
Sale of finished goods, cash receipt due in six months: $154,000.

Exchange rates (London market)	$/£
Spot	1.7106–1.7140
Three months forward	0.82–0.77 cents premium
Six months forward	1.39–1.34 cents premium

Interest rates		
Three months or six months	*Borrowing*	*Lending*
Sterling	12.5%	9.5%
Dollars	9%	6%

Foreign currency option prices (New York market)
Prices are cents per £, contract size £12,500

		Calls			*Puts*	
Exercise price ($)	*March*	*June*	*Sept*	*March*	*June*	*Sept*
1.60	–	15.20	–	–	–	2.75
1.70	5.65	7.75	–	–	3.45	6.40
1.80	1.70	3.60	7.90	–	9.32	15.35

Assume that it is now December with three months to the expiry of March contracts and that the option price is not payable until the end of the option period, or when the option is exercised.

Required

(i) Calculate the net sterling receipts and payments that Fidden might expect for both its three and six month transactions if the company hedges foreign exchange risk on

1 the forward foreign exchange market
2 the money market **(7 marks)**

(ii) If the actual spot rate in six months time turned out to be exactly the present six months forward rate, calculate whether Fidden would have done better to have hedged through foreign currency options rather than the forward market or the money market. **(7 marks)**

(iii) Explain briefly what you consider to be the main advantage of foreign currency options. **(3 marks)**

(Total = 25 marks)

28 Exchange rate forecasts **27 mins**

(a) Your managing director has received forecasts of Euro exchange rates in two years' time from three leading banks.

Euro/£ two year forecasts

Lottobank	1.452
Kadbank	1.514
Gross bank	1.782

The current spot mid-rate Euro 1.667/£

A non-executive director of your company has suggested that in order to forecast future exchange rates, the interest rate differential between countries should be used. She states that 'as short term interest rates are currently 6% in the UK, and 2.5% in the Euro bloc, the exchange rate in two years' time will be Euro 1.747/£'.

Required

(i) Prepare a brief report discussing the likely validity of the non-executive director's estimate. **(4 marks)**

(ii) Explain briefly whether or not forecasts of future exchange rates using current interest rate differentials are likely to be accurate. **(3 marks)**

(b) You have also been asked to give advice to your managing director about a tender by the company's Italian subsidiary for an order in Kuwait. The tender conditions state that payment will be made in Kuwait dinars 18 months from now. The subsidiary is unsure as to what price to tender. The marginal cost of producing the goods at that time is estimated to be Euro 340,000 and a 25% mark-up is normal for the company.

Exchange rates
Euro/Dinar
Spot 0.256 – 0.260

No forward rate exists for 18 months' time.

		Italy	*Kuwait*
		%	%
Annual inflation rates		3	9
Annual interest rates available to the Italian subsidiary:	Borrowing	6	11
	Lending	2.5	8

Required

Discuss how the Italian subsidiary might protect itself against foreign exchange rate changes, and recommend what tender price should be used. **(8 marks)**

All relevant calculations must be shown. **(Total = 15 marks)**

29 USA Options

27 mins

(a) Your UK based company has won an export order worth \$1.8 million from the USA. Payment is due to be made to you in dollars in six months time. It is now 15 November. You wish to protect the exchange rate risk with currency options, but do not wish to pay an option premium of more than £10,000.

Your bank has suggested using a particular currency option which has no premium. The option would allow a worst case exchange rate at which the option could be exercised of \$1.65/£. If the contract moved in your favour then the bank would share (participate in) the profits, and would take 50% of any gains relative to the current spot exchange rate.

You also have access to currency options on the Philadelphia Stock Exchange.

Current option prices are:

Sterling contacts, £31,250 contract size. Premium is US cents per £.

		Calls			*Puts*	
Exercise price	*Dec*	*March*	*June*	*Dec*	*March*	*June*
1.55	6.8	7.9	10.1	0.2	0.5	0.9
1.60	2.1	3.8	5.3	1.9	3.1	4.0
1.65	0.6	0.9	1.1	5.1	7.2	9.6
1.70	0.1	0.2	0.4	10.1	12.3	14.1

The current spot rate is \$1.6055 – 1.6100/£. Any option premium would be payable immediately.

Required

Evaluate whether a participating option or traded option is likely to offer a better foreign exchange hedge. **(10 marks)**

(b) Your company is trading in and with developing countries and has a subsidiary in a country with no developed capital or currency markets. Your company is now about to invoice a customer in that country in the local currency. Advise your treasurer about ways in which the risk can be managed in these circumstances. **(5 marks)**

(Total = 15 marks)

30 Curropt plc **54 mins**

It is now 1 March and the treasury department of Curropt plc, a quoted UK company, faces a problem. At the end of June the treasury department may need to advance to Curropt's US subsidiary the amount of $15,000,000. This depends on whether the subsidiary is successful in winning a franchise. The department's view is that the US dollar will strengthen over the next few months, and it believes that a currency hedge would be sensible. The following data is relevant.

Exchange rates US$/£
1 March spot 1.4461 – 1.4492; 4 months forward 1.4310 – 1.4351.
Futures market contract prices
Sterling £62,500 contracts:
March contract 1.4440; June contract 1.4302.
Currency options: Sterling £31,250 contracts (cents per £)

	Calls	*Puts*
Exercise price	June	June
$1.400/£	3.40	0.38
$1.425/£	1.20	0.68
$1.450/£	0.40	2.38

Required

(a) Explain whether the treasury department is justified in its belief that the US dollar is likely to strengthen against the pound. **(3 marks)**

(b) Explain the relative merits of forward currency contracts, currency futures contracts and currency options as instruments for hedging in the given situation. **(7 marks)**

(c) Assuming the franchise is won, illustrate the results of using forward, future and option currency hedges if the US$/£ spot exchange rate at the end of June is:

(i) 1.3500
(ii) 1.4500
(iii) 1.5500 **(20 marks)**

Note: Assume that the difference between future and spot price is the same at the end of June as now

(Total = 30 marks)

Approaching the answer

You should read through the requirement before working through and annotating the question as we have done so that you are aware of what things you are looking for.

30 Curropt plc

54 mins

Futures date

Uncertainty

Which rate to use?

It is now 1 March and the treasury department of Curropt plc, a quoted UK company, faces a problem. At the end of June the treasury department may need to advance to Curropt's US subsidiary the amount of $15,000,000. This depends on whether the subsidiary is successful in winning a franchise. The department's view is that the US dollar will strengthen over the next few months, and it believes that a currency hedge would be sensible. The following data is relevant.

Exchange rates US$/£

1 March spot 1.4461 – 1.4492; 4 months forward 1.4310 – 1.4351.

Futures market contract prices

Which contract to use?

Sterling £62,500 contracts:

March contract 1.4440; June contract 1.4302.

Currency options: Sterling £31,250 contracts (cents per £)

Premiums

Exercise price	*Calls* June	*Puts* June
$1.400/£	3.40	0.38
$1.425/£	1.20	0.68
$1.450/£	0.40	2.38

Which exercise price?

What demonstrates market views?

Narrative

(a) Explain whether the treasury department is justified in its belief that the US dollar is likely to strengthen against the pound. **(3 marks)**

(b) Explain the relative merits of forward currency contracts, currency futures contracts and currency options as instruments for hedging in the given situation. **(7 marks)**

(c) Assuming the franchise is won, illustrate the results of using forward, future and option currency hedges if the US$/£ spot exchange rate at the end of June is:

(i) 1.3500
(ii) 1.4500
(iii) 1.5500 **(20 marks)**

Note: Assume that the difference between the future and spot price is the same at the end of June as now.

(Total = 30 marks)

Answer plan

Then organise the things have noticed and your points arising into a coherent answer plan. Not all the points you have noticed will have to go into your answer – you should spend a few minutes thinking them through and prioritising them.

(a) (i) Market indicators (forward/futures)
(ii) Other factors

(b) Forward contract

(i) Fix exchange contract
(ii) Option forward contract
(iii) Committed to buying dollars, maybe unfavourable rate

Future contract

(i) Mechanism
(ii) Hedge inefficiencies
(iii) Committed to buying

Option contract

(i) Don't have to use
(ii) Windfall gain

(c) (i) Use proforma for futures and options
(ii) Futures at same basis
(iii) Use spot price when assessing options
(iv) Need to take into account unhedged amounts if any

31 Carrick plc — 27 mins

(a) Explain the term risk management in respect of interest rates and discuss how interest risk might be managed. **(7 marks)**

(b) It is currently 1 January 20X7. Carrick plc receives interest of 6% per annum on short-term deposits on the London money markets amounting to £6 million. The company wishes to explore the use of a collar to protect, for a period of seven months, the interest yield it currently earns. The following prices are available, with the premium cost being quoted in annual percentage terms.

LIFFE interest rate options on three month money market futures (Contract size: £500,000).

	Calls		*Puts*	
Strike price	*Jun*	*Sept*	*Jun*	*Sept*
92.50	0.71	1.40	0.02	0.06
93.00	0.36	1.08	0.10	0.14
93.50	0.12	0.74	0.20	0.35
94.00	0.01	0.40	0.57	0.80
94.50	–	0.06	0.97	1.12

Required

Evaluate the use of a collar by Carrick plc for the purpose proposed above. Include calculations of the cost involved and indicate appropriate exercise price(s) for the collar. Ignore taxation, commission and margin requirements. **(8 marks)**

(Total = 15 marks)

32 Burger-Queen — 27 mins

The three-month sterling interest rate futures are quoted as follows on 30 July:

September	92.50
December	92.70
March	92.90

Each futures contract has a notional of $500,000. Burger Queen will need to borrow $10 million floating at the end of December, for three months and is concerned that interest rates may rise.

(a) Suggest a hedging strategy that Burger Queen could use to reduce interest rate risk **(5 marks)**

(b) What is the effective rate of interest that Burger Queen will have to pay if it hedged its exposure and interest rates have risen to 9 percent in December? **(5 marks)**

(c) What is the effective rate of interest after taking into account the derivative transaction if three month spot rates are 6 percent in December? **(5 marks)**

(Total = 15 marks)

33 Theta plc

36 mins

(a) Theta plc wants to borrow £10 million for five years with interest payable at six-monthly intervals. It can borrow from a bank at a floating rate of LIBOR plus 1% but wants to obtain a fixed rate for the full five-year period. A swap bank has indicated that it will be willing to receive a fixed rate of 8.5% in exchange for payments of six-month LIBOR.

Required

Calculate the fixed interest six-monthly payment with the swap in place. **(4 marks)**

(b) Calculate

(i) The interest payments if LIBOR is 10 percent **(4 marks)**

(ii) The interest payment if LIBOR is 7.5 percent **(4 marks)**

(c) Discuss the advantages to a company of using swap arrangements as part of its treasury management strategies. Explain, briefly, the risks involved in using swap techniques. **(8 marks)**

(Total = 20 marks)

34 Espondera Inc

18 mins

Espondera Inc is a small unquoted company that needs to raise funds in order to invest in a new project. The company wants to issue 10-year bonds and its finance director is trying to work out the cost of debt in order to assess the profitability of the company.

The following information is available for the company

Total assets	$120 million
Net income	$6 million
Type of proposed debt	Subordinated
Long-term debt	$5 million
Income before interest and taxes	$8 million
Interest payments	$1.0 million

The earnings of the company for the last 5 years are as follows

Year	Earnings
2006	$5m
2005	$4.2m
2004	$3.2m
2003	$3.8m
2002	$2.2m

The finance director has decided to use the Kaplan Urwitz model for unquoted companies to asses the cost of debt.

The Kaplan-Urwitz model for unquoted companies is given by

Y=4.41+0.001SIZE+6.40PROFITABILITY -2.56DEBT-2.72LEVERAGE + 0.006INTEREST-0.53COV

The following table gives the yield to maturity for 10-year corporate bonds by credit category

Rating	Cost of debt (Yield to maturity)
AAA	6.8%
AA	7.3%
A	7.8%
BBB	8.4%
BB	9.4%
B	10.5%

Calculate the cost of debt for Espondera Inc. **(10 marks)**

35 Transfer prices **18 mins**

A multinational company based in Beeland has subsidiary companies in Ceeland and in the UK.

The UK subsidiary manufactures machinery parts which are sold to the Ceeland subsidiary for a unit price of B$420 (420 Beeland dollars), where the parts are assembled. The UK subsidiary shows a profit of B$80 per unit; 200,000 units are sold annually.

The Ceeland subsidiary incurs further costs of B$400 per unit and sells the finished goods on for an equivalent of B$1,050.

All of the profits from the foreign subsidiaries are remitted to the parent company as dividends.

Double taxation treaties between Beeland, Ceeland and the UK allow companies to set foreign tax liabilities against their domestic tax liability.

The following rates of taxation apply.

	UK	*Beeland*	*Ceeland*
Tax on company profits	25%	35%	40%
Withholding tax on dividends	–	12%	10%

Required

(a) Show the tax effect of increasing the transfer price between the UK and Ceeland subsidiaries by 25%. **(6 marks)**

(b) Outline the various problems which might be encountered by a company which adjusts a transfer price substantially. **(4 marks)**

(Total = 10 marks)

36 Common market **20 mins**

(a) State the differences between free trade areas and common markets.
(b) What economic benefits might countries gain from forming a common market? **(12 marks)**

37 Multinationals **34 mins**

By operating in a large number of countries, multinational organisations are exposed to political, cultural and legal risks.

Required

(a) Define each of the three risks mentioned above and the effects they may have on a multinational company's business **(10 marks)**

(b) What steps could a multinational company take to deal with these risks? **(9 marks)**

(Total = 19 marks)

38 Developments **31 mins**

(a) The launch of the Euro on 1 January 1999 had major implications for the world financial markets.

Required

Discuss the impact that the launch of a single European currency had on financial institutions such as the securities and bond markets **(9 marks)**

(b) International trade has expanded substantially in the last few decades; however this has led to greater uncertainty for multinational companies.

Required

Discuss ways in which increased globalisation may adversely affect multinational organisations. **(8 marks)**

(Total = 17 marks)

39 Engineering Ltd **27 mins**

The directors of Engineering Ltd, a manufacturing organisation with factories in several countries, are considering the use of derivatives to hedge against risk. However they are concerned about the potential risks involved in using financial instruments and how these risks may be measured.

Required

Prepare a memo to the directors which:

(a) Outlines the role that hedging can play in reducing a company's risk

(b) Describes the main risks that are associated with the use of derivatives in general

(c) Describes the benefits and problems of using scenario analysis as a specific means of measuring risk **(15 marks)**

ANSWERS

1 Remuneration

> **Top tips**. You may need to discuss these issues in the written part of a longer question. You have to think beyond the pure financial issues (what costs most) and consider also what will motivate staff to give their best, and how to ensure that the staff's best efforts are properly directed (goal congruence). Although you will only have had time to have written a few lines on each option, it is important that your treatment of each is balanced, with sufficient time spent on advantages and disadvantages.

The choice of an appropriate remuneration policy by a company will depend, among other things, on:

(a) **Cost**: the extent to which the package provides value for money.

(b) **Motivation**: the extent to which the package motivates employees both to stay with the company and to work to their full potential.

(c) **Fiscal effects**: government tax incentives may promote different types of pay. At present there are tax benefits in offering share options and profit-related pay schemes (although PRP schemes are due to be phased out starting from 1998). At times of wage control and high taxation this can act as an incentive to make the 'perks' a more significant part of the package.

(d) **Goal congruence**: the extent to which the package encourages employees to work in such a way as to achieve the objectives of the firm – perhaps to maximise rather than to satisfice.

High basic salary

In this context, Option (i) is likely to be **relatively expensive** with no payback to the firm in times of low profitability. It is unlikely to encourage staff to maximise their efforts, although the extent to which it acts as a motivator will depend on the individual psychological make-up of the employees concerned. Many staff prefer this type of package however, since they know where they are financially. In the same way the company is also able to budget accurately for its staff costs.

Profit bonus

The firm will be able to gain benefits from operating a **profit-related pay scheme** (Option (ii)), as **costs** will be **lower**, though not proportionately so, during a time of low profits. The effect on motivation will vary with the individual concerned, and will also depend on whether it is an individual or a group performance calculation. There is a further risk that figures and performance may be **manipulated** by managers in such a way as to maximise their bonus to the detriment of the overall longer term company benefit.

Share option scheme

A share option scheme (Option (iii)) carries **fiscal benefits**. It also minimises the cost to the firm since this is effectively borne by the existing shareholders through the dilution of their holdings. Depending on how pricing is determined, it may assist in **achieving goal congruence**. However, since the share price depends on many factors which are external to the firm, it is possible for the scheme to operate in a way which is unrelated to the individual's performance. Thus such a scheme is unlikely to motivate directly through links with performance. Staff will continue to obtain the vast majority of their income from salary and perks and are thus likely to be more concerned with maximising these elements of their income than with working to raise the share price.

2 Goals

Top tips. You would probably not get a full question on this area but the question does test a number of concepts that might need to be brought into your answers. You need to remember that maximisation of shareholder wealth involves maximisation of the net present value of the organisation, not maximisation of short-term dividend flows.

The answer first concentrates on maximisation of shareholder wealth and puts up against it the main modification, the stakeholder view.

The second part of the answer deals with the other suggestions made. Note the clear distinction drawn between the first three measures and performance improvement. The first three objectives are discussed in terms of how good a measure they are of maximisation of shareholder value. The performance improvement discussion develops further the points made about stakeholders in (a).

The conclusion sums up how the possible objectives can be fitted into the overall strategy of the organisation.

(a) and (b) REPORT

To: Managing Director
From: Finance Director
Date: 17 November 20X5
Subject: Definition of corporate objectives

Introduction

1 This report has been drafted for use as a discussion document at the forthcoming board meeting. It deals with the validity of continuing to operate with the single major goal of **shareholder wealth maximisation**. The remaining sections of the report contain an analysis of the advantages and disadvantages of some of the alternative objectives that have been put forward in recent discussions.

Maximisation of shareholder wealth

2 The concept that the **primary financial objective** of the firm is to **maximise** the **wealth** of shareholders underpins much of modern financial theory. However, there has been some recent debate as to whether this should or can be the only true objective, particularly in the context of the multinational company.

3 The **stakeholder view** of corporate objectives is that **many groups** of people have a stake in what the company does. Each of these groups, which include suppliers, workers, manager, customers and governments as well as shareholders, has its own objectives, and this means that a compromise is required. For example, in the case of the multinational firm with a facility in a politically unstable third world economy, the directors may at times need to place the **interests of local government and economy** ahead of those of its shareholder, in part at least to ensure its own continued stability there.

4 While the relevance of the wealth maximisation goal is under discussion, it might also be useful to consider the way in which this type of objective is defined, since this will impact upon both parallel and subsidiary objectives. A widely adopted approach is to seek to **maximise the present value of the projected cash flows**. In this way, the objective is both made measurable and can be translated into a yardstick for financial decision making. It cannot be defined as a single attainable target but rather as a criterion for the continuing allocation of the company's resources.

Cash flow generation

5 The validity of **cash flow generation** as a major corporate objective depends on the timescale over which performance is measured. If the business maximises the net present value of the cash flows generated in the medium to long term, then this objective is effectively the same as that discussed above. However, if the aim is to **maximise all cash flows**, then decisions are likely to be

disproportionately focused on **short-term performance**, and this can work against the long-term health of the business. Defining objectives in terms of long-term cash flow generation makes the shareholder wealth maximisation goal more clearly definable and measurable.

Profitability

6 Many companies use **return on investment (ROI)** targets to **assess performance** and **control the business**. This is useful for the comparison of widely differing divisions within a diverse multinational company, and can provide something approaching a 'level playing field' when setting targets for the different parts of the business. It is important that the **measurement techniques** to be used in respect of both profits and the asset base are **very clearly defined**, and that there is a clear and consistent approach to accounting for inflation. As with the cash flow generation targets discussed above, the selection of the time frame is also important in ensuring that the selected objectives do work for the long-term health of the business.

Risk adjusted returns

7 It is assumed that the use of **risk adjusted returns** relates to the criteria used for investment appraisal, rather than to the performance of the group as a whole. As such, risk adjusted returns cannot be used in defining the top level major corporate goals; however they can be one way in which **corporate goals** are made **congruent** with operating decisions. At the same time, they do provide a **useful input** to the goal setting process in that they focus attention on the company's policy with regard to making risky investments. Once the overall corporate approach to risk has been decided, this can be made effective in operating decisions, for example by **specifying the amount** by which the **cost of capital** is to be **augmented** to allow for risk in various types of investment decisions.

Performance improvement in non-financial areas

8 As discussed in the first section of this report, recent work on corporate objectives suggests that firms should take specific account of those areas which impact only indirectly, if at all, on **financial performance**. The firm has responsibilities towards many groups in addition to the shareholders, including:

(i) **Employees:** to provide good working conditions and remuneration, the opportunity for personal development, outplacement help in the event of redundancy and so on

(ii) **Customers:** to provide a product of good and consistent quality, good service and communication, and open and fair commercial practice

(iii) **The public:** to ensure responsible disposal of waste products.

9 There are many **other interest groups** that should also be included in the discussion process. Non-financial objectives may often work indirectly to the financial benefit of the firm in the long term, but in the short term they do often appear to compromise the primary financial objectives.

Conclusions

10 It is very difficult to find a comprehensive and appropriate alternative primary financial objective to that of **shareholder wealth maximisation**. However, achievement of this goal can be pursued, at least in part, through the setting of specific **subsidiary targets** in terms of items such as return on investment and risk adjusted returns. The definition of non-financial objectives should also be addressed in the context of the overall review of the corporate plan.

Signed: Finance Director

3 Stakeholders

Top tips. (a) is an introduction to issues that will often be relevant in questions on mergers as well as questions about change of company status. The answer concentrates on financial benefits, and even just concentrating on these indicates potential conflicts. These may be significant in a merger situation, as co-operation of senior managers and employees will often be essential for the merger to succeed.

The discussion in (b) talks about longer-term technological charges as well as short-term direct costs. Real options may be involved (if action only has to be taken when demand exceeds a certain level). (ii) is important as reputation as a good corporate citizen may be thought to be worth the extra costs incurred in maximising environmental benefits.

(a) **A company seeking a stock market listing**

When an unlisted company converts into a listed company, some of the existing shareholder/managers will sell their shares to outside investors. In addition, new shares will probably be issued. The dilution of ownership might cause loss of control by the existing management.

The stakeholders involved in potential conflicts are as follows.

(i) **Existing shareholder/managers**

They will want to sell some of their shareholding at as high a price as possible. This may motivate them to overstate their company's prospects. Those shareholder/managers who wish to retire from the business may be in conflict with those who wish to stay in control – the latter may oppose the conversion into a listed company.

(ii) **New outside shareholders**

Most of these will hold minority stakes in the company and will receive their rewards as dividends only. This may put them in conflict with the existing shareholder/managers who receive rewards as salaries as well as dividends. On conversion to a listed company there should be clear policies on dividends and directors' remuneration.

(iii) **Employees, including managers who are not shareholders**

Part of the reason for the success of the company will be the efforts made by employees. They may feel that they should benefit when the company seeks a listing. One way of organising this is to create employee share options or other bonus schemes.

(b) **Directly attributable costs**

The way in which **environmental costs and benefits** are included in the appraisal process will depend on the nature of the environmental implications, and the way in which the company intends to approach them. One method is to include in the appraisal only those elements of environmental cost that are **directly attributable** to undertaking the project, and to evaluate any further actions that the company may wish to undertake as a separate issue. In some cases, this may be relatively simple, particularly if legislation exists that defines the environmental standards to be applied.

Technological options

The company will then be faced with a variety of **technological options** that it could use to reduce the contamination to the required levels; for example, if volumes are large enough, it may be appropriate to build a treatment plant to decontaminate the effluent – alternatively it could enter into an agreement with a waste treatment company to tanker away the waste and dispose of it off site. Each of these options will have a **definable cost** which can be evaluated and incorporated into the overall project appraisal. In this situation, there are **no quantifiable benefits** as such, since the environmental issues take the form of a constraint on the project. The costs arise as a direct result of undertaking the project, and as such must be incorporated into the appraisal.

Further expenditure

The problems arise where the company sees the opportunity to go beyond its statutory duties and to act in such a way as to **maximise** the **environmental benefits**. In the example cited above, it may be that the most cost effective method from the point of view of the company is to **tanker the waste** to a remote treatment plant. However, it may view this as unacceptable on the grounds that it wishes to **minimise** the **disturbance** to the area around the site, and thus not to generate high volumes of tanker traffic in the local area. In this situation, the **higher cost option** of **on-site treatment** may become more attractive, although this is not a direct requirement of the project being undertaken. The benefits that arise are difficult to quantify and will not accrue directly to the company undertaking the investment.

In this situation, two approaches are possible.

(i) The company could decide that its own environmental standards form a financial constraint upon the project, and thus that the project should be **evaluated at its full environmental cost**.

(ii) Alternatively, it could decide that the additional costs of on-site treatment over and above the cost of meeting the statutory requirements represent a **separate environmental investment**. If the company sets aside a budget for environmental and social issues, these excess costs could then be taken away from the project and allocated against this environmental budget.

Both approaches are valid and will depend on the objectives and policies of the company with regard to environmental issues.

4 XYZ

Top tips. (a) provides an excellent example of how various ratios link together.

(b) involves the use of the dividend valuation model. You need to explain what assumptions you have had to make in arriving at your answer since the information provided in the question is limited. Option 4 illustrates the limitations of the dividend growth model in a situation where no dividends are paid out.

In (c) it is helpful to consider some of the other factors that influence share price, as well as addressing the investment decisions that surround the choice of dividend policy.

You may come across scrip dividends in the exam as they have proved to be popular with some companies. Don't forget the point about possible dilution of shareholding.

(a) **Ratios**

During this period, **earnings per share** have declined by 10.7% while at the same time **dividend per share** has increased by 19.0%. The **payout ratio** has increased from 60% in 20W9 to 80% in 20X3, and thus the proportion of earnings retained has fallen to 20%. If it is assumed that the capital structure has not changed over the period, then it can be seen that both **actual earnings** and the **return on capital employed** have declined over the period.

Retention policy

One possible implication of this policy is that **insufficient earnings** have been **retained** to finance the investment required to at least maintain the rate of return on capital employed. If this means that the company is falling behind its competitors, then this could have a serious **impact** on the **long-term profitability** of the business.

(b) **Rate of return**

For the purposes of calculation it is assumed that any new investment will earn a rate of return equivalent to that **required by the shareholders** (ie 15%), and that this will also be the level of return that is earned on existing investments for the foreseeable future. It is further assumed that investors are indifferent as to whether they receive their returns in the form of dividend or as capital appreciation.

Option 1

The amount of dividend per share is £1 with no growth forecast. The rate of return required by shareholders is 15%. The theoretical share price can be estimated using the dividend valuation model.

$Ke = d_1/p_0$

Where Ke = Cost of equity

d_1 = Dividend per share
= Market price per share

$15\% = 1.00/p_0$

p_0 = £6.67, or £7.67 cum div

100% of the total return is provided in the form of dividend.

Option 2

Under the assumptions relating to earnings stated above, the share price will be the same as that calculated for option 1, ie £6.67 per share. However in this case 50% of the expected return is in the form of dividend and 50% as capital appreciation.

A numerical example will clarify the position.

The rate of growth of dividends g may be expressed as:

$g = rb$

Where r = required rate of return
b = proportion of profits retained

In this case therefore, with dividends at 50 pence per share:

$g = 0.15 \times 0.5 = 0.075$

$$p_0 = \frac{d_1}{r-g} = \frac{0.5 \times 1.075}{0.15 - 0.075} = £7.17$$

£7.17 plus 50p dividend at t_0 = £7.67 cum div.

Option 3

This is the same as for option 2, but 25% of the expected return is in the form of dividend and 75% as capital growth.

$g = 0.15 \times 0.75 = 0.1125$

$$p_0 = \frac{0.25 \times 1.1125}{0.15 - 0.1125} = 7.42$$

£7.42 plus 25p dividend at t_0 = £7.67 cum div

Option 4

In this case, for a share price of £6.67, investors would need to believe that retained profits will be invested in projects yielding annual growth of 15% and that the share price will grow at this rate. 100% of the expected return is provided in the form of capital appreciation under this option.

(c) **Factors influencing share price**

The figures calculated above assume that the **share price** is wholly dependent on the **rate of return required by shareholders** and that the shareholders are indifferent as to the form which the return takes. In practice, this is but one element in the range of factors which influence share prices. Other significant influences include the following.

(i) The **level of funds available for investment**
(ii) **Investor confidence**
(iii) The **tax situation and income requirements of investors**
(iv) The **availability of alternative investments**

The figures calculated are helpful to the directors only in so far as they direct attention away from the share price: they demonstrate that it is the **level of returns** and the **rate of return required** by investors which drive the share price.

Investment policy

It would be more helpful for the directors to look in detail at the options available to them in terms of **investment** and to assess these against the **cost of capital**, taking account of the differing **degrees of risk** entailed. For the share price to be maximised in the long term, it is the effect of **investment policy** on the net worth of the business which is important, ie the **net present value** of operating cash flows. This may mean that in the short term the share price declines, but the directors may decide that this is a worthwhile sacrifice to make for the long-term profitability of the business. They may also need to consider whether the company needs a further injection of capital in addition to an increase in retentions in order to fund its development.

5 Ethical dimension

(a) The main responsibilities faced by companies when developing an ethical framework are:

(i) Economic
(ii) Legal
(iii) Ethical
(iv) Philanthropic

The ways in which these responsibilities can be addressed are:

Economic

(i) Management should always be acting in the best interests of the company's shareholders, and should therefore always be actively making decisions that will increase shareholders' wealth.

(ii) Projects that have positive NPVs should be pursued as far as funds will allow, as such projects will increase the value of the company and thus shareholders' wealth.

(iii) Whilst management may have a different attitude towards risk than do the shareholders, they should always manage risk according to shareholders' requirements.

(iv) Financing – the optimal financing mix between debt and equity should be chosen as far as possible.

(v) Dividends – there is no legal obligation to pay dividends to ordinary shareholders, but the reasons for withholding dividends must be in the interests of the company as a whole (for example, maintaining funds within the company in order to finance future investment projects).

Legal

(i) Companies must ensure that they are abiding by the rules and regulations that govern how they operate. Company law, health and safety, accounting standards and environmental standards are examples of these boundaries.

(ii) Failure to abide by the rules can cost companies dearly. One only has go look at the fate of WorldCom and Enron bosses, as well as Nick Leeson of Barings Bank, for examples of how failure to operate within the legal framework can cause companies to collapse, taking with them the jobs (and often pension funds) of thousands of employees.

Ethical

(i) Ethical responsibilities arise from a moral requirement for companies to act in an ethical manner.

(ii) Pursuit of ethical behaviour can be governed by such elements as:

- Mission statements
- Ethics managers
- Reporting channels to allow employees to expose unethical behaviour.
- Ethics training and education (including ethics manuals)

Philanthropic

(i) Anything that improves the welfare of employees, the local community or the wider environment.

(ii) Examples include Tesco's "Computers for Schools" campaign (UK); provision of an employees' gym; sponsorship of sporting events; charitable donations.

(b) Main functional areas of a firm include:

(i) Human resources
(ii) Marketing
(iii) Market behaviour
(iv) Product development

Human Resources

(i) Provision of minimum wage. In recent years, much has been made of 'cheap labour' and 'sweat shops'. The introduction of the minimum wage is designed to show that companies have an ethical approach to how they treat their employees and are prepared to pay them an acceptable amount for the work they do.

(ii) Discrimination – whether by age, gender, race or religion. It is no longer acceptable for employers to discriminate against employees for any reason – all employees are deemed to be equal and should not be prevented from progressing within the company for any discriminatory reason.

Marketing

(i) Marketing campaigns should be truthful and should not claim that products or services do something that they in fact cannot. This is why such campaigns have to be very carefully worded to avoid repercussions under Trades Descriptions Acts etc.

(ii) Campaigns should avoid creating artificial wants. This is particularly true with children's toys, as children are very receptive to aggressive advertising.

(iii) Do not target vulnerable groups (linked with above) or create a feeling of inferiority. Again, particularly true with children and teenagers, who are very easily led by what their peer groups have. The elderly are also vulnerable, particularly when it comes to such things as electricity and gas charges – making false promises regarding cheaper heating for example may cause the elderly to change companies when such action is not necessary and may in fact be detrimental.

Market Behaviour

(i) Companies should not exploit their dominant market position by charging vastly inflated prices (this was particularly true when utilities were first privatised in the UK; also transport companies such as railway operators which have monopolies on certain routes).

(ii) Large companies should also avoid exploiting suppliers if these suppliers rely on large company business for survival. Unethical behaviour could include refusing to pay a fair price for the goods and forcing suppliers to provide goods and services at uneconomical

prices. In the past this has been a particular problem for suppliers in developing countries providing goods and services to large companies in developed countries.

Product Development

(i) Companies should strive to use ethical means to develop new products – for example, more and more cosmetics companies are not testing on animals, an idea pioneered by such companies as the Body Shop.

(ii) Companies should be sympathetic to the potential beliefs of shareholders – for example, there may be large blocks of shareholders who are strongly opposed to animal testing. Managers could of course argue that if potential investors were aware that the company tested their products on animals then they should not have purchased shares.

(iii) When developing products, be sympathetic to the public mood on certain issues – the use of real fur is now frowned upon in many countries; dolphin friendly tuna is now commonplace.

(iv) Use of Fairtrade products and services – for example, Green and Blacks Fairtrade chocolate; Marks and Spencer using Fairtrade cotton in clothing and selling Fairtrade coffee.

6 Solden

Top tips. Exam questions would not be purely numerical as this one is, but this question does provide an excellent demonstration of the level of detail you will have to cope with in a foreign investment appraisal. Planning is very important, working out what format you will need and what workings will be required.

You can assume that the rates of return are money rates of return, which means that the sales and costs have to be adjusted for price increases.

Possible pitfalls in this question are getting the timing of the exchange rates movements wrong, forgetting that the working capital figure in the cash flow analysis is the **change** in working capital (not the total amount) and including the full cost of materials in (b) rather than just the contribution (remember the UK company is going to have to pay cost price to obtain new materials).

(a) **Investors in Ober**

Year		*0*	*1*	*2*	*3*	*4*	*5*	*6*
		G'000	G'000	G'000	G'000	G'000	G'000	G'000
Contribution	1		320.0	369.6	426.9	493.0	569.5	
Materials – UK	2		(40.0)	(43.7)	(47.7)	(52.1)	(56.9)	
Selling costs			(40.0)	(44.0)	(48.4)	(53.2)	(58.6)	
Licence fee (10% sales)			(64.0)	(73.9)	(85.6)	(98.6)	(113.8)	
Tax allowable depreciation (800 × 25%)			(200.0)	(200.0)	(200.0)	(200.0)		
Taxable profit/(loss)			(24.0)	8.0	45.2	89.1	340.2	
Tax at 20%				4.8	(1.6)	(9.0)	(17.8)	(68.0)
Plant		(600.0)						
Equipment		(200.0)						
Tax allowable depreciation			200.0	200.0	200.0	200.0		
Working capital		(64.0)	(9.9)	(11.7)	(13.0)	(15.3)	113.9	
Terminal value (3 × 436.3*)							1,308.9	
Tax on terminal value at 30%								(392.6)
Net cash flow in year		(864.0)	166.1	201.1	230.6	264.8	1,745.2	(460.6)
Discount factor at 15%		1,000	0.870	0.756	0.658	0.572	0.497	0.432
PV		(864.0)	144.5	152.0	151.7	151.4	867.4	(199.0)
NPV		404.0						

*436.3 = Year 5 cash flows to this point.

The project is acceptable to investors in Ober.

Workings

	Year	*0*	*1*	*2*	*3*	*4*	*5*	*6*
	Exchange rate	16.00	16.00	16.64	17.31	18.00	18.72	19.47
(1)	Sales – units		4,000	4,200	4,410	4,630	4,862	
	Ober contribution per unit (160 – 80, increasing by 10%)		80.0	88.0	96.8	106.5	117.1	
	Ober contribution (G'000s)		320.0	369.6	426.9	493.0	569.5	
(2)	*Materials (UK) – assuming fixed cost increasing with inflation*							
	Cost in pounds		2,500	2,625	2,756	2,894	3,039	
	Cost in gurgles (G'000s)		40.0	43.7	47.7	52.1	56.9	
(3)	*Working capital*							
	Balance – 10% sales	64.0	73.9	85.6	98.8	113.9		
	Increase/(decrease)	64.0	9.9	11.7	13.0	15.3	(113.9)	

(b) **Investors in UK**

Year		*0*	*1*	*2*	*3*	*4*	*5*	*6*
		£	£	£	£	£	£	£
From Ober subsidiary	(W1)	(54,000)	10,381	12,085	13,325	14,711	93,221	(23,662)
Adjustments in UK								
Licence fee	(W2)		4,000	4,441	4,946	5,478	6,080	
Contribution on materials			500	525	551	579	608	
Lost exports			(5,000)	(5,250)	(5,513)	(5,788)	(6,078)	
Total adjustments			(500)	(284)	(16)	269	610	
Tax thereon, lagged one year				165	94	5	(89)	(201)
Net		(54,000)	9,881	11,966	13,403	14,985	93,742	(23,863)
DF at 10%		1.000	0.909	0.826	0.751	0.683	0.621	0.564
PV		(54,000)	8,982	9,884	10,066	10,235	58,214	(13,459)

The NPV is positive, at £29,922.

Workings

		0	*1*	*2*	*3*	*4*	*5*	*6*
1	From Ober subsidiary:							
	Cashflow in G'000s	(864.0)	166.1	201.1	230.6	264.8	1,744.9	(460.6)
	Pound equivalent	(54,000)	10,381	12,085	13,325	14,711	93,221	(23,662)
2	Licence fee, in G'000s		64	73.9	85.6	98.6	113.8	
	Licence fee, in pounds		4,000	4,441	4,946	5,478	6,080	

7 Mover

Top tips. Unusually in (a) you are not given a discount rate. In this case you need to fall back on the assumption that the market risk premium for shares above the risk free rate is in the range 7% to 8%. The inflation figure is not needed, as the cash flows are given in real terms, and hence a real discount rate is needed. Do not assume that because a tunnel is a very high risk project its discount rate must be extremely high. For a diversified investor, the relevant risk in the discount rate is systematic risk. However, construction as an industry does have fairly high systematic risk.

Examiner's comment. In (a) candidates needed to use a realistic (not too low) discount rate, justify the discount rate used, and treat estimates beyond year 10 in a sensible fashion. However many discount rates used were too low, and in some cases the inflation rate was used. Some candidates also failed to appreciate the difference between real and nominal rates. Most candidates also failed to discuss wider issues such as the reliability of the cash flows, or the risks, or Mover's activities other than the tunnel project.

(a) **Use of real rate**

The expected cash flows of the tunnel should be discounted at a suitable cost of capital, taking into account the **risk** of the project. Since the cash flow projections exclude inflation, the cost of capital should also be a **real rate.**

Estimate of the real rate

(i) In the UK the current **risk free rate** is approximately 6% whilst inflation is approximately 2%, giving an approximate real risk free rate of 4%.

(ii) The **market premium** is assumed to be in the range 7 – 8%, although several market commentators are using much lower rates today (closer to 4.5%).

(iii) The tunnel project is assumed to have a **high level** of **systematic risk**, say a beta of 1.3.

(iv) The pension fund is well diversified and therefore only subject to **systematic risk.**

This implies a real discount rate of approximately 4% + (7% × 1.3) = approx. 13%

Assuming the tunnel has an indefinite life, post 20Y0 cashflows are discounted in perpetuity:

Year		*13% df*	*PV*
	£m		£m
20X0	(450)	0.885	(398)
20X1	(500)	0.783	(392)
20X2	(550)	0.693	(381)
20X3	(650)	0.613	(398)
20X4	(200)	0.543	(109)
20X5	200	0.480	96
20X6	300	0.425	128
20X7	320	0.376	120
20X8	340	0.333	113
20X9	360	0.295	106
20Y0	400	0.261	104
20Y1 onwards*	400	0.261/0.13	803
			(208)

*These are PVs of perpetuity cash flows.

At this estimated discount rate the NPV is **negative**, and therefore the project should be rejected. For a more comprehensive assessment **sensitivity analysis** should be used.

Other considerations

(i) The use of NPV ignores the value of any **embedded or real options**. Such options might include the option to develop land either side of the tunnel.

(ii) **Economic factors** may be critical to the accuracy of the forecast cashflows.

(iii) **Assumptions** concerning costs and competitive issues (the costs of alternative transport links) should be reviewed. In particular there may be a high probability that costs will be greater than forecast, and also that the project will be delayed, leading to further costs and delays in revenues. In addition the costs of **upkeep** of the tunnel have not been included in the calculations.

(iv) The **contractual role** of the construction company should be reviewed – is the project Government supported?

(v) Whilst the tunnel project is presumably the most important project that Mover will be undertaking over the next few years, the company's continued existence may not depend upon it. The trustees should therefore consider the likely results of the **other contracts** that Mover will be undertaking over the next few years.

On a project of this size, and dependent on the level of the pension fund investment, such factors should be modelled in more detail, perhaps using **sensitivity analysis** or **simulation**.

(b) **Effect of inflation**

Inflation erodes the **purchasing power** of money. It therefore has an **effect** on the **returns** an investor will require, and consequently on the appraisal of capital investment decisions by companies. As the **inflation rate increases so will the minimum return required** by an investor.

Example

A return of 5% on a sum invested of £100 will provide £105 back in one year's time. If inflation is running at 15% then at the end of one year £105 will only buy 105/1.15 = £91.30 worth of goods at today's prices. In order to be able to purchase £105 worth of goods at today's prices the investor will need a nominal return of 1.05 × 1.15 = 1.2075, ie 20.75%. Thus with inflation at 15%, a nominal rate of interest of 20.75% is required to give the investor a real return of 5%. This effect can be expressed as:

(1 + money (or nominal) rate) = (1 + real rate) × (1 + inflation rate)

Choice of approaches

Companies therefore have a **choice** of approaches when accounting for inflation in the appraisal of capital projects. They can either **inflate all the elements** of the cash flow at the appropriate rates and then **discount at the nominal (or money) rate of return**. Alternatively they can **exclude inflation** from the cash flows and **discount at the real rate**.

8 Nile plc

(a) The net dividend has increased 1.5 times from the end of 20X4 to the end of 20X8, a period of 4 years. This represents an approximate annualised growth rate of 10.67% (being $4\sqrt{1.5}$).

Cost of ordinary share capital in after tax terms = $\frac{30(1.1067)}{476} + 0.1067 = 0.176$ or 17.6%

Cost of debentures: = £77 (with interest) is the current market price per cent. The cost of debentures (%) is the internal rate of return of the following cash flows:

Year	*MV*	*Interest*	*Tax Saving*	*Cash Flow*
	£	£	£	£
0	(77)	8		(69.0)
1-20		8	(2.8)	5.2
20		100		100.0

At a discount rate of 7% the NPV is + £11.9, and at a discount rate of 9% the NPV is – £3.69. The IRR is (by interpolation)

$$7\% + \left(\frac{11.9}{11.9 + 3.69} \times 2\%\right) = 8.5\%$$

It is assumed that the new issue of shares and debentures will be weighted in accordance with the existing gearing ratio as measured by market values.

The weighted average cost of capital is:

	Cost (%)	*Market Value*		*Hash Total*
Ordinary share capital	17.6% ×	4,760,00	=	837,760
Debentures	8.5% ×	552,00	=	46,920
		5,312,000		844,680

$$\text{Weighted average cost of capital} = \frac{£884,680}{5,312,000} \times 100\% = 16.6\%$$

(b) *Difficulties and uncertainties that should be mentioned are:*

(i) will the growth rate in dividend remain the same as in previous years?

(ii) should a premium for risk be added to the weighted average cost of capital; e.g. should the test discount rate for projects be, say, 20% or more rather than 16.6% (or 17%)?

9 Crystal plc

Top tips. (a) demonstrates the complications that may occur in weighted average cost of capital calculations. When you calculate the cost of equity, you will need to do more than just plug the figures into the formula. Don't forget to check whether shares are quoted cum or ex div. Here also you need to use Gordon's growth model to calculate g.

With debentures, the most serious mistake you can make is to treat redeemable debentures as irredeemable. Because the debentures are redeemable, you need to carry out an IRR analysis. Remember this calculation is done from the viewpoint of the **investor**. The investor pays the market price for the debentures at time 0, and then receives the interest and the conversion value in subsequent years. You must bring tax into your calculation, although you could have assumed that tax was paid with a one year time delay.

Lastly don't forget that the weightings in the WACC calculation are based on **market** values, **not book** values.

(b) demonstrates that the calculation of the weighted average cost of capital is not a purely mechanical process. It makes assumptions about the shareholders, the proposed investment and the company's capital structure and future dividend prospects. Given all the assumptions involved, the result of the calculations may need to be taken with a large pinch of salt!

Questions focusing on WACC calculations have been set by the examiner, but having even more complications than those described above.

(a) The post-tax weighted average cost of capital should first be calculated.

(i) **Ordinary shares**

	£
Market value of shares cum div.	3.27
Less dividend per share (810 ÷ 3,000)	0.27
Market value of shares ex div.	3.00

The formula for calculating the cost of equity when there is dividend growth is:

$$r = \frac{D_0(1+g)}{P_0} + g$$

where r = cost of equity
D_0 = current dividend
g = rate of growth
P_0 = current ex div market value.

In this case we shall estimate the future rate of growth (g) from the average growth in dividends over the past four years.

$810 = 620\,(1 + g)^4$

$$(1 + g)^4 = \frac{810}{620} = 1.3065$$

$(1 + g) = 1.069$

$g = 0.069 = 6.9\%$

$$r = \frac{0.27 \times 1.069}{3} + 0.069 = 16.5\%$$

(ii) **7% Debentures**

In order to find the post-tax cost of the debentures, which are redeemable in ten years time, it is necessary to find the discount rate (IRR) which will give the future post-tax cash flows a present value of £77.10.

The relevant cash flows are:

(1) Annual interest payments, net of tax, which are £1,300 × 7% × 70% = £63.70 (for ten years)

(2) A capital repayment of £1,300 (in ten years time)

It is assumed that tax relief on the debenture interest arises at the same time as the interest payment. In practice the cash flow effect is unlikely to be felt for about a year, but this will have no significant effect on the calculations.

	Present value
Try 8%	£'000
Current market value of debentures (1,300 at £77.10 per cent)	(1,002.3)
Annual interest payments net of tax £63.70 × 6.710 (8% for ten years)	427.4
Capital repayment £1,300 × 0.463 (8% in ten years time)	601.9
NPV	27.0

Try 9%	£ '000
Current market value of debentures	(1,002.3)
Annual interest payments net of tax 63.70 × 6.418	408.8
Capital repayment 1,300 × 0.422	548.6
NPV	(44.9)

$$\text{IRR} = 8\% + \left[\frac{27.0}{27.0 - -44.9} \times (9-8)\right]\%$$

$= 8.38\%$

(iii) **The weighted average cost of capital**

	Market value	*Cost*	*Product*
	£'000	%	
Equity	9,000	16.50	1,485
7% Debentures	1,002	8.38	84
	10,002		1,569

$$\frac{1,569}{10,002} \times 100 = 15.7\%$$

The above calculations suggest that a discount rate in the region of 16% might be appropriate for the appraisal of new investment opportunities.

(b) Difficulties and uncertainties in the above estimates arise in a number of areas.

(i) **The cost of equity**. The above calculation assumes that all shareholders have the **same** marginal cost of capital and the same **dividend expectations**, which is unrealistic. In addition, it is assumed that dividend growth has been and will be at a **constant rate** of 6.9%. In fact, actual growth in the years 20X5/6 and 20X8/9 was in excess of 9%, while in the year 20X7/8 there was no dividend growth. 6.9% is merely the average rate of growth for the past four years. The rate of future growth will depend more on the return from future projects undertaken than on the past dividend record.

(ii) **The use of the weighted average cost of capital**. Use of the weighted average cost of capital as a discount rate is only justified where the company in question has achieved what it believes to be the optimal capital structure (the mix of debt and equity) and where it intends to maintain this structure in the long term.

(iii) **The projects themselves**. The weighted average cost of capital makes no allowance for the business risk of individual projects. In practice some companies, having calculated the WACC, then add a premium for risk. In this case, for example, if one used a risk premium of 5% the final discount rate would be 21%. Ideally the risk premium should vary from project to project, since not all projects are equally risky. In general, the riskier the project the higher the discount rate which should be used.

10 PS Ltd

> **Top tips.** Part (a) gives you practice in using the Black-Scholes formula. Go back to Chapter 15 and work again through the example if you got stuck. We have used interpolation to find N (d_1) and N (d_2). However, the examiner has indicated that understanding the principles behind the Black-Scholes formula are more important than being able to plug numbers into the formula. Expect therefore to see discussion parts similar to parts (b)(i) and (ii) featuring in questions on Black-Scholes. Although you will not be asked to use Black-Scholes in an investment appraisal question, you are expected to know that it can be used to evaluate real options that arise in investment appraisal questions.
>
> Part (c) is a good test of your understanding of swaps. Don't forget swaptions.

(a) Using the Black-Scholes Formula

$$d_1 = \frac{\ln\left(\frac{P_s}{X}\right) + rT}{\sigma\sqrt{T}} + 0.5\sigma\sqrt{T} \quad d_1 = \frac{\ln(P_a \div P_e) + \left(r + 0.5s^2\right)t}{s\sqrt{t}}$$

$$= \frac{\ln\left(\frac{3}{2.50}\right) + (0.05 \times 0.25)}{0.2 \times \sqrt{0.25}} + \left(0.5 \times 0.2 \times \sqrt{0.25}\right)$$

$$= \frac{0.1823 + 0.0125}{0.1} + 0.05$$

$$= 1.9982$$

$$d_2 = d_1 - s\sqrt{T}$$
$$= 1.9982 - 0.2\sqrt{0.25}$$
$$= 1.9982 - 0.1$$
$$= 1.8982$$

$$N(d_1) = 0.5 + 0.4767 + \frac{82}{100}(0.4772 - 0.4767)$$
$$= 0.9771$$

$$N(d_2) = 0.5 + 0.4706 + \frac{82}{100}(0.4713 - 0.4706)$$
$$= 0.9712$$

$$P_c = P_s N(d_1) - Xe^{-rT} N(d_2)$$
$$= (3 \times 0.9771) - (2.50e^{-0.05 \times 0.25} \times 0.9712)$$
$$= 2.9313 - (2.50 \times 0.9876 \times 0.9712)$$
$$= 53.35p$$

(b) (i) The **Black-Scholes pricing model** was developed to value traded call options on quoted shares and can be adapted to value any options. The input variables are:

(1) **The market price of the underlying share**

If the **share price rises**, the **value** of the **call option** will **increase**.

(2) **The exercise price (or strike price)**

A **call option** gives the holder the **right to buy** the share at a fixed price, known as the **exercise price**. The **higher the price** of the **underlying share** compared with the exercise price (above), the **more valuable** is the **option**.

(3) **The time to expiry**

The longer an option has to run before it expires, the more chance there is that the **value of the underlying share will increase**. Time to expiry therefore **adds value** to an option.

(4) **The volatility of the underlying share (standard deviation of share price variations)**

Options provide **unlimited opportunities for gains** but **losses** are **limited to the purchase price**. This asymmetrical probability distribution of gains/losses means that volatility of the underlying share **adds value** to the option.

(5) **The interest rate**

This is the **risk free rate of interest**, which gives the **time value of money** and is relevant because the option is valued today but is exercisable on a future date.

The difference between 1 and 2 is known as the '**intrinsic value'** of the option, but it has a minimum value of zero. The combination of 3, 4 and 5 gives its '**time value'**. The total value of the option is the sum of intrinsic and time values.

(ii) **Real options**

Real options are **choices** which **arise** in **real capital investments**, for example the opportunity to renew a lease at a fixed price or to renew a license agreement after an introductory period. The party able to make the choice effectively holds an option, the value of which should be considered when appraising the investment.

Example

Suppose a capital project involves paying a franchise fee to a company which has patented a key process. Our agreement gives us the **right** (but not the obligation) to **renew this franchise** after 3 years for a further 5 year period at a fixed cost of $5 million. The value of this option can be estimated by adapting the 5 input variables:

(1) The **current market cost** of a 5-year franchise (say $4m). This would need to take into account potential competitors who may wish to take over our business.

(2) The **$5m cost of the 5 year renewal license** agreed in our contract (i.e. the **exercise price**). This option currently has an intrinsic value of zero.

(3) The **3-year period** until we have to choose.

(4) The **volatility of the franchise price**, which depends on its susceptibility to general market factors and specific factors including our success at using it.

(5) The **risk-free interest rate**, as in the original model.

(c) **Nature of interest rate swap**

A swap is an **exchange** of a stream of **future cash obligations** with another party. For example interest on loans can be swapped in the same currency or different currencies. A swap is particularly useful if **high transactions costs prevent** the **early redemption** of a loan in order to take out one with different characteristics.

Uses of swap

If markets are efficient, the main use of a swap is to **alter the risk and/or repayment characteristics** of cash flows to a **more desirable pattern**. For example, floating rate interest may be exchanged for fixed in order to **improve predictability**, or, as in this example, the **currency swap** is used effectively as a money market **hedge**, so that currency fluctuations in foreign earnings are offset by interest costs in the same currency. Swap products have been developed to meet **specific requirements**, for example '**swaptions**' which give the holder the option to swap payment patterns.

Market imperfections

Sometimes **gains** can also be made from **market imperfections**. The interest charged may not be high enough to compensate for the expected currency depreciation. This is a market imperfection which results in a gain in the net present value of the project.

Other advantages of swaps

(i) **Credit rating**

Swaps offer the ability to **take advantage** of a **relatively better credit rating** in the company's own country than in a foreign country. If two organisations borrow in their home currencies and swap, they may achieve lower interest rates than if they attempt to borrow directly in foreign currencies.

(ii) **Comparative advantage**

Comparative advantage of **fixed or floating rate borrowing** can be **exploited**. For example if a company can obtain **relatively cheaper rates** if it borrows at floating rate, but it requires a fixed rate loan, it may achieve a lower fixed interest rate by borrowing at floating rate and swapping into fixed rate.

Disadvantages of swaps

(i) **Risk of default by the other party to the swap (counter-party risk)**

If one company became **unable** to meet its **swap payment obligations**, this could mean that the other risked having to make them itself.

(ii) **Apparent gains in expected value**

These might be made at the expense of accepting much riskier cash flow characteristics. A company whose main business lies outside the field of finance should **not increase financial risk** in order to make **speculative gains**.

(iii) **Arrangement fees**

Swaps have arrangement fees payable to third parties. Although these may appear to be cheap, this is because the intermediary accepts **no liability** for the swap.

11 Canada

Top tips. Method (i) involves a year-by-year conversion of the receipts, making sure that you adjust the exchange rate by the correct amount each year. In method (ii) the adjusted discount rate is computed in the same way as a nominal discount rate is computed from a real discount rate and an inflation rate.

Your answer to (b) needs to bring out the costs that will be incurred, and how the risks of loss (and chance of gain) will be limited or enhanced by borrowing abroad.

(a) **Method (i)**

Years	*0*	*1*	*2*	*3*	*4*
Investment C$'000	(150)				50
After tax cash flows C$'000		60	60	60	45
Net cash C$'000	(150)	60	60	60	95
Exchange rate	1.7000	1.7850	1.8743	1.9680	2.0664
Net cash £'000	(88.24)	33.61	32.01	30.49	45.97
14% discount factors	1.000	0.877	0.769	0.675	0.592
PV in £'000	(88.24)	29.48	24.62	20.58	27.21
NPV in £'000	**13.65**				

Method (ii)

Adjusted discount rate: equivalent discount rate in C$, allowing for 5% appreciation of the pound, is given by $1 + r = 1.14 \times 1.05 = 1.197$. Discount rate = 19.7%.

Years	*0*	*1*	*2*	*3*	*4*
Net cash C$'000	(150)	60	60	60	95
19.7% discount factors	1.000	0.835	0.698	0.583	0.487
PV C$'000	(150)	50.10	41.88	34.98	46.27
NPV C$'000	23.23				
Exchange rate	1.7000				
NPV £'000	**13.66**				

To provide a 14% rate on return in UK and to cope with a 5% annual strengthening of the pound, a dollar invested in Canada would have to grow by 14% to \$1.14 and by a further 5% to \$1.14 × 1.05 = \$1.197. In other words it would have to show a rate of return of 19.7%. The company's cost of capital, translated into Canadian dollars is therefore 19.7%.

In a system of **free floating exchange rates**, if the C$ depreciates by 5% per year against sterling, the cost of borrowing in C$ is likely to be about 5% more expensive than borrowing in sterling.

(b) **Finance by borrowing**

The decision to **finance** a **foreign investment** by **borrowing** in the foreign country's currency is influenced by a number of factors.

Loan in the same currency

For any income-generating foreign investment there is a risk that the foreign currency **depreciates**, resulting in a reduced value of income when converted to the home currency. If, however, borrowings are taken out in the **same currency** as that in which the **income** is generated, then the **reduced income** is at least partially offset by reduced **loan interest costs**. It should be noted, however, that this hedging effect also **reduces** the chances of **currency gains**: if the foreign currency appreciates, then the increased value of income is offset by an increased loan interest cost when converted to the home currency.

Unexpected losses

In the example, the Canadian dollar steadily devalues against the pound. Borrowing in Canadian dollars would therefore enable currency risk to be managed better than if borrowing is arranged in

sterling. However, in a system of free floating exchange rates, if the C$ depreciates by 5% per year against sterling, the cost of borrowing in C$ is likely to be about 5% **more expensive than borrowing** in sterling. This **increased interest cost** will take away the advantage of the devaluation of the C$ loan. If currencies always moved in predictable ways, there would be little advantage in financing the Canadian investment with a Canadian loan. However, currency **devaluations** can sometimes be **unexpected** and much larger than predicted. It is to prevent these **unexpected losses** that hedging using a foreign loan is recommended.

Cost of foreign loans

The **cost of foreign loans** may be higher than the theoretical equivalent cost of a domestic loan because the company does not have such a **good credit standing** in the foreign country. Better rates may be obtained from the **euromarkets** or by arranging a **currency loan swap**. Care should be taken to match the duration of the loan with the **expected duration** of the project (4 years in this question), unless further foreign investments are anticipated. A further consideration is the availability of **tax savings** on the loan interest. The effect on the company's **overall tax charge needs** to be included in the decision process.

Impact of political risk

For countries with high political risk, which may impose exchange controls, or even expropriate assets, **borrowing** in the **local currency** is recommended to **offset** investment losses which might result from political action.

12 Drive plc

(a) (i) Calculation of tax liability and after tax earnings when first year allowances (FYA)are 40%:

	1	*2*	*3*	*4*	*5*
	£m	£m	£m	£m	£m
EBIT	2.5	2.6	3.5	4.2	4.50
Allowances					
FYA	3.2	–	–	–	–
Allowance b/f	–	0.7	–	–	–
Depreciation for tax purposes	–	1.2	1.2	1.2	1.20
	3.2	1.9	1.2	1.2	1.20
Taxable earnings	–	0.7	2.3	3.0	3.30
Tax at 30%	–	0.21	0.69	0.9	0.99
Earnings after tax	2.5	0.49	1.61	2.1	2.31

(ii) Calculation of tax liability and after tax earnings when first year allowances are 50%:

	1	*2*	*3*	*4*	*5*
	£m	£m	£m	£m	£m
EBIT	2.5	2.6	3.5	4.2	4.50
Allowances					
FYA	4.0	–	–	–	–
Allowance b/f	–	1.5	0.1	–	–
Depreciation for tax purposes	–	1.2	1.2	1.2	1.20
	4.0	2.7	1.3	1.2	1.20
Taxable earnings	–	–	2.20	3.0	3.30
Tax at 30%	–	–	0.66	0.9	0.99
Earnings after tax	2.5	2.6	1.54	2.1	2.31

(b) **MEMORANDUM**

To: Financial Director
From: An adviser
Re: Effects on financial statements of operating in a country with a volatile currency

Please find below a summary of how financial statements may be affected by operating in a country with a volatile currency and how these problems may be alleviated.

Translation Risk

(i) Changes the value of remittances from the subsidiary to the parent, therefore consolidated sales figures may be distorted if exchange rates change quickly and significantly.

(ii) Any investments made in Goldland will be shown as different sterling values in the Balance Sheet depending on exchange rate movements.

(iii) Large 'exchange differences' may be offputting when analysing the financial statements.

It could be argued that translation does not really represent a genuine risk as it does not involve the flow of cash into or out of the business. However volatile exchange rates can significantly affect values of assets, liabilities, income and expenditure in the financial statements – such volatility may not be popular with investors.

Alleviating Translation Risk

Match foreign investment as much as possible with loans in the same currency which means that a fall in the sterling value of the asset will be matched with an equivalent fall in value of the liability.

Transaction Risk

(i) If a new facility is set up in Goldland, this means that cash flows generated from this facility will be in Gold dollars (G$). If the exchange rate is volatile, the value of these cash flows may vary significantly.

(ii) This risk may also occur due to the solution to translation risk above – that is, borrowing money denominated in G$. On such loans, Drive plc will have to make interest and capital repayments in the foreign currency – if the exchange rate is volatile, the sterling value of these payments will fluctuate, not only in the financial statements, but in real value.

Alleviating Transaction Risk

(i) Forward market hedging – where a contract is entered into to secure a fixed exchange rate at some point in the future. In this way, Drive plc will know the sterling value of G$ transactions in advance.

(ii) Futures contracts – this would normally be an option for alleviating transaction risk, but such contracts are only available in a limited number of currencies. Given that the G$ is not a major currency, it is unlikely that futures contracts will be available for this currency.

Interest Rates

Volatile currency exchange rates generally means volatile interest rates, given the interest rate parity theorem. This can create problems if the company has taken out loans in the foreign country (see above) as interest expenses will fluctuate, not just in the home currency but also in the overseas currency.

Alleviating volatile interest rate problems

Only borrow in the home markets and the home currency. This is unfortunately at odds with the solution to translation risk above.

When a country has volatile exchange rates, this suggests that interest rates and inflation rates are volatile. It is difficult to conduct business in such an unstable environment therefore careful consideration of the financial consequences of operating in Goldland will be necessary prior to making a final decision.

13 Organic growth

(a) **Advantages of organic growth**

(1) The company will be developing a new vehicle that has the group's existing culture rather than acquiring a **subsidiary** with a **different culture**.

(2) Growing organically may be cheaper in the long-run as it is more likely to **be financed** by **retained earnings** rather than new sources with issue costs, and it will not involve paying a premium for a desirable subsidiary.

(3) Planned development of a subsidiary should mean that there is **no duplication of resources** with existing operations.

(4) Organic growth offers **more opportunities** for **current employees**.

(5) Organic growth is more likely to be in areas where a company **currently has expertise**, limiting the risk of failure.

(b) **Advantages of acquisition**

(1) Acquisition can offer **speedier entry** into an overseas market than organic growth.

(2) Merging with **established firms abroad** can be a means of **purchasing market information**, **market share**, **distribution channels** and **reputation**.

(3) **Other synergies** include **acquisition of management skills** and **knowledge**, **intangibles** such as brands and trademarks, or **additional cash** and **debt capacity**.

(4) Acquiring a subsidiary may be a means of **removing trade barriers**.

(5) Acquisition can be a means of **removing a competitor**.

(6) **Start-up costs** will not be incurred.

Ultimately the risk of acquiring an established operation may well be less than starting up a subsidiary in an area where the company has **not previously operated**.

14 Canon Burger

(a) There are a number of synergies that the acquisition of Templar can create.

Financial synergies arising from the diversification into other areas reducing the volatility of earnings. The acquisition will also increase the debt capacity of Canon as Templar has no debt.

Revenue synergies are also expected to arise as Templar will be able to use the marketing and advertising services of Canon

The management of Canon may also improve the performance of Templar and may exploit its brand value and clientele.

(b) Present value of additional cash flow in perpetuity = $\frac{£25,000}{0.12}$ = £208,333

The net present value of the acquisition is given by value from the acquisition minus the cost of the acquisition

NPV = £208,333 – £200,000 = £8,333

The acquisition should proceed

(c) Unchanged level of leverage of the combined entity means that the cost of capital remains the same at 16%

$$NPV = \frac{£25,000}{0.16} - £200,000 = £156,950 - £200,000$$

$$= - £43,750$$

The acquisition should not proceed if there is no reduction in the cost of capital.

15 Univo plc

> **Top tips.** Hopefully you remembered that the fundamental theory of share values is based on linking share values with **future** dividend patterns, whatever these patterns are assumed to be. (Chartism assumes that past dividend patterns will be repeated in the future).
>
> This question gives you the beta of equity, so you can just insert it into the formula. In the exam you are more likely to have to calculate it using the principles of gearing and ungearing betas (which we shall be covering in Chapter 11). The main complication in (a) is knowing how to cope with the different dividend growth rates. The calculation of the intrinsic value of share has two elements:
>
> (a) The present value of dividends in 20X2 and 20X3
> (b) The market value of the shares in 20X3, using the formula but remembering to discount its result.
>
> In (b) you have to carry out the same calculation making the assumption that as the return on fixed interest securities has increased, the return required from shares must also have increased. Don't get confused into making adjustments to the actual dividends received (the question tells you that they are unaffected by the change in interest rates); it is the discount factor that needs to change.

(a) The **dividend growth model** may be formulated as follows.

$$P_0 = \frac{D_0(1+g)}{(r-g)}$$

where: P_0 = market price of the share (ex div)
D_0 = current net dividend
r = cost of equity capital
g = expected annual rate of dividend growth

In this example, the first step is to calculate the cost of equity capital. This may be done using the CAPM, assuming that debt and equity betas are weighted using market values. The CAPM takes the form:

$$E(r_j) = r_f + [E(r_m) - r_f]\beta_j$$

where: $E(r_j)$ = cost of capital
β_j = beta factor relating to the type of capital in question
$E(r_m)$ = expected market rate of return
F_r = risk free rate of return
$E(r_j) = 12\% + (17\% - 12\%) \times 0.82 = 16.1\%$

Dividend growth between 20W9 and 20X1 has been 9.5% per year. It is estimated that growth in 20X2 and 20X3 will be 25%, thereafter reverting to 9.5%. Dividends for the next three years can be estimated as follows.

	Total dividend	*Dividend per share*
	£	pence
20X1	2,800,000	7.00
20X2	3,500,000	8.75
20X3	4,375,000	10.94
20X4	4,790,625	11.98

Then we can estimate the intrinsic share value as follows.

	p	Discount factor @ 16%	PV Pence
20X1 Dividend	7.00	–	–
20X2 Dividend	8.75	0.862	7.54
20X3 Dividend	10.94	0.743	8.13
20X3 Value of shares in 20X3 per dividend model	181.50*	0.743	134.85
			150.52

$$* \frac{d_{20X3}(1+g)}{K_e - g} = \frac{10.94(1+0.095)}{0.161-0.095} = 181.50 \text{ pence}$$

Estimated intrinsic value = 150.52p

The actual market price of the shares (ex div) is 210 pence per share. A fundamental analyst would therefore regard the shares as being overpriced and would recommend their sale.

(b) If the interest rate increased by 2%, the return required on equity is likely to increase by a similar amount to approximately 18%. The PV of dividends to be used in calculations will therefore fall.

	Total dividend £	*Dividend per share* Pence	*Discount factor @ 18%*	*PV* Pence
20X1	2,800,000	7.00p		
20X2	3,500,000	8.75p	0.847	7.41
20X3	4,375,000	10.94p	0.718	7.85
20X4	4,790,625	11.98p		
				15.26

The PV of the expected dividend from 20X4 onwards will fall to 8.6p (11.98p × 0.718).

$$P_0 = \frac{D_1}{(r-g)}$$

where: P_0 = market price of the share (ex div)

D_1 = net dividend (8.6p)

r = cost of equity capital (18%)

g = expected annual rate of dividend growth (9.5%)

$$P_0 = \frac{8.6}{(18\% - 9.5\%)} = 101.18\text{p}$$

To this must be added the PV of the dividend for 20X2 and 20X3:

Estimated intrinsic value = 101.18 + 15.26 = 116.44p

16 Black Raven Ltd

Top tips. This question provides comprehensive practice of valuation techniques. In the exam you would most likely be expected to use three or four of these techniques to carry out calculations that would form the basis of discussions. Even in this question, you do need to make clear the basis of your calculations and the assumptions you are making (in (a) the assumption is that the purchaser will accept the valuation, in (b) that the last five years are an appropriate indicator and so on).

Other important issues which this question raises include:

- Valuation (if any) of intangible assets
- Lack of likelihood that asset valuation basis would be used
- Adjustment to P/E ratios used in calculations because company is unquoted

Don't take all of the figures used in this answer as the only possibilities. You could for example have made adjustments to estimated earnings in (c) to allow for uncertainty, or used a different figure to 17% in (d).

(a) **Earnings basis valuations**

If the purchaser believes that earnings over the last five years are an appropriate measure for valuation, we could take average earnings in these years, which were:

$$\frac{£465,000}{5} = £93,000$$

An appropriate P/E ratio for an earnings basis valuation might be the average of the three publicly quoted companies for the recent year. (A trend towards an increase in the P/E ratio over three years is assumed, and even though average earnings have been taken, the most recent year's P/E ratios are considered to be the only figures which are appropriate.)

	P/E ratio	
Albatross plc	8.5	
Bullfinch plc	9.0	
Crow plc	10.0	
Average	9.167	(i)
Reduce by about 40% to allow for unquoted status	5.5	(ii)

Share valuations on a past earnings basis are as follows.

	P/E ratio	*Earnings*	*Valuation*	*Number of shares*	*Value per share*
		£'000	£'000		
(i)	9.167	93	852.5	300,000	£2.84
(ii)	5.5	93	511.5	300,000	£1.71

Because of the unquoted status of Black Raven Ltd, purchasers would probably apply a lower P/E ratio, and an offer of about £1.71 per share would be more likely than one of £2.84.z

Future earnings might be used. Forecast earnings based on the company's five year plan will be used.

		£	
Expected earnings:	Year 1	100,000	
	Year 2	104,000	
	Year 3	108,160	
	Year 4	112,486	
	Year 5	116,986	
	Average	108,326.4	(say £108,000)

A share valuation on an expected earnings basis would be as follows.

P/E ratio	*Average future earnings*	*Valuation*	*Value per share*
5.5	£108,000	£594,000	£1.98

It is not clear whether the purchasing company would accept Black Raven's own estimates of earnings.

(b) **A dividend yield basis of valuation with no growth**

There seems to have been a general pattern of increase in dividend yields to shareholders in quoted companies, and it is reasonable to suppose that investors in Black Raven would require at least the same yield.

An average yield for the recent year for the three quoted companies will be used. This is 12%. The only reliable dividend figure for Black Raven Ltd is £45,000 a year gross, in spite of the expected increase in future earnings. A yield basis valuation would therefore be:

$$\frac{£45{,}000}{12\%} = £375{,}000 \text{ or } £1.25 \text{ per share.}$$

A purchasing company would, however, be more concerned with earnings than with dividends if it intended to buy the entire company, and an offer price of £1.25 should be considered too low. On the other hand, since Black Raven Ltd is an unquoted company, a higher yield than 12% might be expected.

(c) **A dividend yield basis of valuation, with growth**

Since earnings are expected to increase by 4% a year, it could be argued that a similar growth rate in dividends would be expected. We shall assume that the required yield is 17%, rather more than the 12% for quoted companies because Black Raven Ltd is unquoted. However, in the absence of information about the expected growth of dividends in the quoted companies, the choice of 12%, 17% or whatever, is not much better than a guess.

$$P_0 = \frac{D_0(1+g)}{(r-g)} = \frac{45{,}000(1.04)}{(0.17-0.04)} = £360{,}000 \text{ or } £1.20 \text{ per share}$$

(d) **The discounted value of future cash flows**

The present value of cash inflows from an investment by a purchaser of Black Raven Ltd's shares would be discounted at either 18% or 14%, depending on the view taken of Black Raven Ltd's assets. Although the loan of £400,000 is secured on some of the company's property, there are enough assets against which there is no charge to assume that a purchaser would consider the investment to be backed by tangible assets.

The present value of the benefits from the investment would be as follows.

Year	*Cash flow*	*Discount factor*	*PV of cash flow*
	£'000	14%	£'000
1	120	0.877	105.24
2	120	0.769	92.28
3	140	0.675	94.50
4	70	0.592	41.44
5	120	0.519	62.28
			395.74

A valuation per share of £1.32 might therefore be made. This basis of valuation is one which a purchasing company ought to consider. It might be argued that cash flows beyond year 5 should be considered and a higher valuation could be appropriate, but a figure of less than £2 per share would be offered on a DCF valuation basis.

(e) **Summary**

Any of the preceding valuations might be made, but since share valuation is largely a subjective matter, many other prices might be offered. In view of the high asset values of the company an asset stripping purchaser might come forward.

17 Margate

Top tips. In this case study there are *many* alternative answers for all parts of the question, but the main requirement throughout the question is to demonstrate your knowledge of the principles involved by writing explanatory notes and comments.

In part (a), try to choose three ratios with different purposes (e.g. profitability, liquidity, gearing) – but the P/E ratios are already given – so presumably no marks for calculating them, even though it is a relevant ratio!

In part (b), there is a huge range of justifiable values for the company, even without estimating possible merger gains, on which no information is given. Again, the key is to justify the assumptions you make, Giving a range of possible answers means the expectations of different commentators are taken into account, and an indication of the risk involved is given.

For the report in part (c), the most sensible figure to choose for a bid price would be something with a premium over current market value. The 'offer terms' means suggesting how many shares of Margate would be exchanged for a given number of Hastings' shares (eg 7 for 8). The bulk of the discussion marks can be earned by considering principles of takeover defences and reasons for merger synergy and needs to range quite widely. Your calculation for the value of the combined company should show how much would be owned by the original shareholders of Margate and how much by former Hastings shareholders.

(a) **Three key ratios**

Profitability: Return on shareholders' funds

	Margate Group plc £m	*Hastings plc* £m
Earnings £m	503	300
Shareholders' funds £m	2,020	1,450
Return on shareholders' funds	25%	21%

This ratio shows the **rate of return of equity earnings** compared with the book value of shareholders' funds. Margate Group plc has a **higher return** at present, a fact that is consistent with its lower P/E ratio, but inconsistent with its lower equity beta. The measure is **limited** by the fact that **book values** are used.

Gearing: Debt ratio

	Margate Group plc £m	*Hastings plc* £m
Long term debt	1,450	950
Shareholders' funds	2,020	1,450
Total long term funds	3,470	2,400
Debt ratio	42%	40%

Both companies have **higher debt ratios** than the industry average (30%), indicating that use of **debt finance** for the merger would probably be **inadvisable**. The figure for Hastings could be understated if its substantial overdraft is effectively used as long-term debt. Including the overdraft of £420 million, the debt ratio becomes 1,370/2,820 = 49%.

Liquidity: Current ratio

	Margate Group plc £m	*Hastings plc* £m
Current assets £m	1,125	645
Current liabilities £m	755	785
Current ratio	1.490	0.822

At less than 1, the current ratio of Hastings looks low. This is despite the fact that it carries **higher stock levels** than Margate. The high overdraft probably needs restructuring into long term funds, otherwise a period of rapid growth may cause severe liquidity difficulties.

(b) **Range of possible values for Hastings plc**

P/E ratios

Hastings' **current P/E ratio** is 16, giving its equity shares a current market value of 16 × equity earnings £300 million = £4,800 million. It is highly unlikely that any offer below this figure would be attractive to shareholders, who would have no incentive to sell. Measured by the industry average P/E of 13, Hastings would be worth 13 × £300 million = £3,900 million. The higher value that Hastings enjoys at present is because of its **above-average growth expectations** and, probably, expectations of gains from a merger with another company.

The dividend valuation model

Top tips. Many different calculation assumptions may be offered here. Two or three valuations would be sufficient.

The current dividend is £135 million. The cost of equity for Hastings can be estimated from the **Capital Asset Pricing Model**, k_e = 6% + (12% – 6%) 1.2 =13.2%.

Possible valuation method

Using this cost of equity in the dividend valuation model, we obtain the following possible valuation figures:

(i) If, as some experts believe, the **supermarket contract results in zero growth**, the company's equity value would be 135/0.132 = £1,023 million, well below current market value.

(ii) On the optimistic side, if there was **dividend growth of 10% per year to perpetuity**, the equity value would be 135 × 1.1 / (0.132 – 0.10) = £4,640 million. This is more in line with current market value.

(iii) Dividend growth of 10% per annum for 5 years followed by a period of lower growth would result in a **valuation figure between these two values**.

Adjusted present value method

Hastings is relatively highly geared, which has the effect of increasing its equity beta. Since the acquisition would be financed by equity shares, the Adjusted Present Value method would use a discount rate based on the **cost of ungeared equity** to value Hastings, and there would be no gearing side effect. The cost of ungeared equity for Hastings would be lower than 1.2, let us say 1.0, giving a cost of equity of 12%. The computations above would then lead to higher figures:

(i) **No dividend growth**: 135/0.12 = £1,125 million
(ii) **Growth of 10% p.a. to perpetuity**: 135 × 1.1 / (0.12 – 0.10) = £7,425 million
(iii) **Growth of 10% for 5 years**, followed by slower growth: a figure between these two values

Summary

Based on existing information, the value of Hastings' equity can be calculated as somewhere between £1,023 and £7,425 million, with its **current market value** at £4,800 million.

(c) To: Board of Directors, Margate Group plc
From: Financial Manager
Date: 13 December 20X1
Subject: Report on the proposed acquisition of Hastings plc

Introduction

This report provides a financial evaluation of the proposed acquisition, recommends offer terms and discusses strategic issues.

(i) **Recommended bid price and offer terms**

Our calculations show that the intrinsic value of Hastings as a stand-alone company is somewhere in the **range** £1,000 million to £7,400 million. On the basis of the efficient market hypothesis, the **current market value** of £4,800 million is probably as good a guide to the company's value as any, but it should be remembered that the market will undoubtedly have factored some expected merger gains (see below) into the share price as a result of the recent bid by the US company.

Premium

However, if we are to make a bid, we will not be successful unless we offer a **premium over current market value**, giving the Hastings shareholders an incentive to sell. An offer price of approximately £5,000 million is suggested.

Synergy

It should be noted that if the possibility of merger gains is already factored into Hastings' share price, this offer price can only be justified if we have clear **plans** for **creating synergy** from the combination. Before going ahead, I suggest that we thoroughly investigate the possibilities, as indicated below.

Consideration

A share-for-share exchange should be offered as the terms for this merger, because:

(1) We have **insufficient cash**.

(2) As the **debt ratios** of both companies are above the industry average, I do **not recommend** any further **increase in borrowings** to finance this deal.

(3) Our company's shares have an **above average P/E ratio that**, though not as high as Hastings', indicates that they are a relatively good 'currency' at the moment.

I recommend that we offer **7 of our own shares for every 8 in Hastings**. At our current share price this would value Hastings shares at $7 \times 671\text{p} / 8$ =587.125 pence, giving a total market value for Hastings equity of £4,991 million, a premium of 3.9% over the current market value.

Workings

Our share price is currently 671 pence.

Hastings' total number of shares in issue are £300m/35.29p EPS = 850.1 million. At a total value of £5,000 million, Hastings' share price would be 588 pence.

The terms of the offer should be 588 of our shares for 671 of Hastings, which are approximately 7 of ours for 8 of theirs.

Revised bid

When we make our initial bid, the market will assess it. The effect on the share price will depend on whether the market anticipated the sort of bid that we shall be making, but it is possible that we may have to make a revised offer.

(ii) **Strategy for making the offer**

To minimise the **risk of outright rejection** by the Hastings plc board, our strategy needs to take the following factors into account.

(1) We must follow the **City Code** on Takeovers and Mergers, Stock Exchange regulations and the law, especially that on **insider dealing**. We are allowed to approach the board of directors of Hastings for informal talks, but must maintain **absolute secrecy** until we make a formal offer.

(2) We will need to ensure that Hastings' directors are given **key roles** on the board of the combined company. This bid is most likely to succeed if management arrangements are those of a genuine merger rather than a takeover by ourselves.

(3) We need to **emphasise the similarities** between the management styles of our companies, and the advantages of joining forces to compete effectively in Europe against world competition.

Risks in making the bid

(1) The American company may decide to make a **counter offer**, resulting in an auction for Hastings' business, bidding up the price to an unrealistic level.

(2) Hastings may appeal for an **investigation** by the Competition Commission, on the grounds that our bid is against the public interest.

(3) Hastings' board may decide to **counter our offer** by making an offer to acquire us.

(4) Hastings staff may decide to **mobilise public opinion** against us. Some key members may leave (see below).

(5) Hastings' directors may have strengthened their **contract termination terms**: this needs to be investigated.

Risks of post-merger failure

(1) There may be a **conflict of cultures** between the management of the two companies. Disagreements at board level may lead to widespread loss of morale. Key staff of Hastings may leave and set up on their own or join another competing company. For example the American company may decide to poach staff rather than making an increased offer for Hastings' business.

(2) Our objective of achieving synergy may not be realised because of **poor planning**, lack of resolve to tackle the key issues, or shortage of funds for necessary capital investment.

(3) **Incompatibility of information systems** between the companies is a common merger problem.

(iii) **Strategic and financial issues**

The rationale for the bid depends on the advantages that a combination of our companies would have over the existing 'stand-alone' businesses. Such combinations can create synergetic merger gains (the whole is worth more than the sum of the parts) by a number of mechanisms.

Increased market power

Elimination of Hastings as a major competitor might allow us to charge **more realistic prices** to customers on some of our less profitable operations. We are also likely to be able to negotiate **more favourable deals** with suppliers in terms of costs and payment terms. However, in this respect we must be careful to avoid the accusation that we have become a monopoly. Our combination will have more than a 25% share of the UK market and the Competition Commission may decide to mount an investigation.

Access to new market

The merger would enable us to **grow more rapidly** in Europe, where Hastings already has a strong base.

Combining complementary resources

Hastings' **superior knowledge of markets in Europe** fits well with our dominant position in the UK.

Achieving critical mass to enable effective competition

As trade barriers fall, our competition is worldwide rather than just the UK. Our defence to the potential monopoly accusation is that our **market share** in the **European Union** is still relatively small and we need this merger in order to be able to compete effectively in international markets.

Elimination of duplicated resources

Our research shows that recent restructuring of both our companies does **not** leave **much scope** for **staff reductions** except at the head offices, but there will be possibilities for rationalising our warehouse and depot locations, for example.

Elimination of management inefficiencies

For example, Hastings' **financial management** could be **improved** with savings in financing costs.

Post-acquisition value of combined group

Our company has 1,050 million shares in issue and Hastings has 850 million.

At offer terms of 7 for 8, we will issue 7/8 × 850m new shares in Margate = 743.8m.

Total Margate shares in issue would then be 1,050 +743.8 = 1,793.8m shares.

To maintain our existing share price, the value of the combined company would need to be 1,793.8 × 671p = £12,036m, shared as follows:

	No of shares	*Share price* (p)	*Value* £m
Original Margate shareholders	1,050.0	671	7,045
New shareholders from Hastings	743.8	671	4,991
	1,793.8		12,036

The existing market capitalisation of the two companies is as follows:

		£m
Margate	as above	7,045
Hastings	£300m × P/E16	4,800
		11,845

Size of synergistic gains

To maintain our existing share price, we would need to generate synergetic gains of £191 million (above those gains which have already been factored into the current share prices), which would accrue to the new shareholders from Hastings (£4,991m – £4,800m).

(1) On the down side, if we assume that a more realistic value for Hastings as a stand-alone company is in the region of £4,000 million, the synergy needed is closer to £1,000 million. Clearly we need to start work immediately on evaluating whether this is a **realistic proposition** and, if so, developing plans for implementing our ideas as swiftly as possible.

(2) On the optimistic side, if the market value of Hastings is realistic and our offer is accepted and we can generate an **additional synergy** of **£500 million**, say, the value of the company would be £12,345 million, split as follows:

	No of shares	*Share price* (p)	*Value* £m	*Original value* £m	*Gain* £m	*% gain*
Original						
Margate shareholders	1,050.0	688.22	7,226	7,045	181	2.6%
New shareholders						
from Hastings	743.8	688.22	5,119	4,800	319	6.6%
	1,793.8		12,345		500	

The gains made by Hastings shareholders would be higher in percentage terms.

Financial advantages

Given that the preferred bid strategy is a share-for-share exchange, if the bid goes through the combined group's debt: equity ratio will be lower than either of the current companies. We can either accept that this reduction in financial risk would be beneficial (as the gearing of both companies currently is high for the industry), or we can take the opportunity to issue further debt. Perceived business risk is unlikely to fall because the merger does not involve diversification, and because of the uncertainties surrounding the supermarket project.

Conclusion

Whilst a merger would have some significant benefits, we would need to convince our shareholders that Hastings is not overvalued, before they approve the issue of the consideration shares. Other issues, in particular the reaction of Hastings and the Competition Commission, also need to be considered carefully.

18 Canadian plc

MEMORANDUM

To: The Finance Director
From: Accountant
Date: 12 December 20X5
Subject: Proposed investment in local coal mine

(a) **Overall summary and conclusion**

I have performed an analysis of the available figures using the adjusted present value technique (APV). This method is appropriate because the project:

Justify APV

(i) Represents an activity **fundamentally different** from that of the company
(ii) Has a **different risk profile**, as evidenced by the differing betas, from Canadian
(iii) Is to be financed using a **gearing ratio different** from the company
(iv) Is a **significant investment** for the company (ie is not a marginal investment)

An alternative to this method might be the **adjusted discount rate method**, in which an estimate is made of the appropriate discount rate to use and the project cash flows discounted at this rate. However, insufficient data is available to perform this sort of analysis.

Summarise main effects of using APV

APV demonstrates that while the project appears to be marginally attractive under the stated assumptions (a positive NPV of £86,000), the total project allowing for the financing effects has a positive net present value of £2,010,000. These positive financing effects result from the interest savings on the Regional Development Board loan, plus the tax effects of the additional debt capacity of the firm.

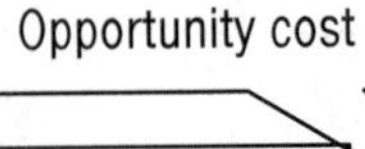

However, I should stress that these figures assume a great deal about the future, both as regards the values of the factors that have been taken into account, and the factors that have been ignored. I would refer you to the later sections of this memo, but broadly:

Risk management

(i) There would be **substantial implications** for power station X if this pit were to close. These costs should also be considered in coming to our conclusion.
(ii) Even if the power station is judged viable in the absence of the pit, **buying coal from overseas** will expose us to **currency fluctuations** which would need to be managed.
(iii) **No sensitivity analysis** has been carried out. It would appear likely that the project is highly sensitive to the price of coal, and to the level of redundancy and environmental cleanup costs. This implies a high degree of political risk, which will be outstanding for five years

(b) **Workings**

The adjusted present value represents the NPV of the project based on an all equity financed situation, adjusted for any finance costs/benefits.

The appropriate discount rate is found from the formula:

$$\beta \text{ asset} = \beta_e \frac{E}{E+D(1-t)} + \beta_d \frac{D(1-t)}{E+D(1-t)}$$

This should be based on the betas for the coal mining industry, which obviously has a different risk profile from that of the power generation industry.

$$\beta \text{ asset} = 0.7 \times \frac{1}{1+1(1-0.3)} + 0.2 \times \frac{(1-0.3)}{1+1(1-0.3)} = 0.494$$

Therefore the appropriate discount rate is:

$$\begin{aligned} Ke &= 8\% + (16\% - 8\%) \times 0.494 \\ &= 12\% \end{aligned}$$

The cashflows generated by the project are therefore discounted at 12% to find the base NPV.

Cashflow forecast, £'000s

Don't Inflate

Take inflation into account

Year	*0*	*1*	*2*	*3*	*4*	*5*	*6*
Inflows							
Value of coal production		10,000	10,000	10,000	10,000	10,000	
Outflows							
Operating costs (3,000 × 3% inflation factor)		(3,090)	(3,183)	(3,278)	(3,377)	(3,478)	
Initial investment	(12,000)						
Final payment (17,000 × 1.03^5)						(19,708)	
Tax			(1,173)		(1,313)	(1,347)	4,525
Tax from year 3					(1,258)		
Net cashflow	(12,000)	6,910	5,644	6,722	4,052	(14,533)	4,525
NPV factor (12%)	1.000	0.893	0.797	0.712	0.636	0.567	0.507
NPV	(12,000)	6,171	4,498	4,786	2,577	(8,240)	2,294
Total NPV	86						

Working

Year	*1*	*2*	*3*	*4*	*5*
Tax calculations					
Operating cashflows					
Inflows	10,000	10,000	10,000	10,000	10,000
Outflows	(3,090)	(3,183)	(3,278)	(3,377)	(3,478)
Capital allowances					
On equipment	(1,500)	(1,125)	(844)	(633)	(1,898)
On mine	(1,500)	(1,500)	(1,500)	(1,500)	
Termination costs					(19,708)
Net taxable flow	3,910	4,192	4,378	4,490	(15,084)
Tax on taxable flow	1,173	1,258	1,313	1,347	(4,525)

Financing effects are as follows.

Borrowing effect

The company can borrow a total of £6 million (the regional development loan) plus the £3 million increase in the borrowing capacity as a result of this project. This means that debt benefits flow on a total of £9 million of additional debt. This is worth:

Debt benefit = Total debt × Canadian's borrowing rate × tax rate

Canadian's borrowing rate can be found using CAPM as:

Use Canadian beta

$K_d = 8\% + (16\% - 8\%) \times 0.25 = 10\%$

Therefore the increase in debt capacity is worth:

£9 million × 10% × 30% = £270,000 pa

Discounting adjustments

This tax benefit will be received between the years 2 and 6, and should be discounted at the cost of debt (10%).

$£270{,}000 \times 3.791 \times \frac{1}{1.10} = £931{,}000$

Regional development loan

The value of the subsidy can be related directly to the cost of debt that Canadian plc would otherwise have paid (10%).

Therefore the saving in interest charges is:

£6 million × (10% – 4%) = £360,000 pa

Again, this is discounted at the cost of debt. However, there are two things to notice:

(i) The benefit of the interest rate reduction is received in years 1-5.

(ii) There is an associated reduction in the tax benefit, detrimental in years 2-6, of the interest cost × tax charge.

Don't forget to discount

Present value of interest saved in years 1-5:

£360,000 × 3.791 = £1,365,000

Present value of tax benefit foregone in years 2-6:

$£6m \times 6\% \times 30\% \times 3.791 \times \frac{1}{1.10} = £372,000$

The expected APV of the project, including financing effects, will therefore be:

	£'000
NPV of project	86
NPV of tax shelter on interest	931
NPV of interest saved	1,365
NPV of tax benefit forgone on interest saved	(372)
	2,010

(c) **Assumptions behind this report**

As regards the data used in the report, it assumes the following.

(i) The various output and costing **figures** are reasonably **accurate**.

(ii) The **cleanup** and **redundancy costs** are **correctly estimated** – this assumes a stable political environment over the next five years.

(iii) The **price of coal** will **stay at the current level** for the foreseeable future.

(iv) The **RPI** can be **accurately used** as a measure of the cost inflation factors that will affect the pit.

Available funds very important

(v) The Regional Development Board **loan is obtained**.

(vi) **Retained earnings** are **available** to finance the equity component of the project. If additional equity finance were required then issue costs could make this project unviable.

(vii) That the **debt capacity** added to the firm is **accurate**. It is not known how this figure is arrived at, but the project might well affect the total perceived risk of the firm for both equity and debt, and therefore change borrowing capacities for the rest of the firm.

Change in risk

(viii) The **tax regime** is at least as **favourable** as regards capital allowances as at present over the next five years

As regards the APV model, it assumes the following.

(i) The value of the **tax shield** is the **full corporate tax rate**. This is questionable when shareholders obtain the benefit of a dividend imputation system and annual capital gains tax allowances.

Must include APV assumptions

(ii) The **project** will **contribute** a **full £9 million** to the borrowing capacity of the group for the whole of its useful life. In reality it is likely that the asset base, and hence the borrowing capacity, will diminish over time.

(iii) The **CAPM** can be used to arrive at an **ungeared cost of capital**, which can then be used to discount the cash flows over five years. The CAPM is an annual model, so the assumption must be questioned.

(d) **Areas for further research**

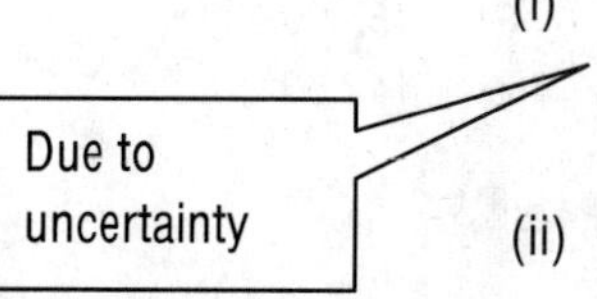

(i) This memo is incomplete without a **detailed sensitivity analysis** being carried out. Such an analysis would seek to determine which of the above assumptions was likely to change, and by how much.

(ii) It is also not possible to assess whether this project is advisable in isolation from other **capital opportunities** and needs of the firm. It is unclear whether capital is in short supply.

(iii) The scenario presumes that there is **no alternative bidder for** the mine. However, it is possible that supplies to Station X might be secured by offering a fixed price contract to an alternative bidder for the supply of coal. In this case we ourselves can avoid the risks inherent in this industry, about which we know so little, and concentrate on our strengths.

19 Peden and Tulen

Top tips. (a) illustrates how shareholders gain from creditors in a bankruptcy scenario because of their limited liability. The key is that when Peden is a stand-alone company, the minimum value of its equity is zero, causing a drop in the value of debt, but when combined with a low-geared company the debt recovers its value at the expense of equity.

Examiner's comment. Many candidates aggregated equity and debt without considering their individual values, and produced implausible solutions. Candidates also ignored the narrative in the question that stated that operational synergy did not occur.

(a) **Value of Peden's shares**

To find the **value of Peden's equity shares**, subtract debt of £45m from the total value:

Peden	*Recession*	*Slow growth*	*Rapid growth*
	£m	£m	£m
Equity	(3)	10	30
Debt	45	45	45
Total	42	55	75

This gives a **negative value to equity** in the recession scenario, which cannot happen because the shares have limited liability. Assume the shares are zero value and the debt has declined to £42m because of bankruptcy risk. The expected value of equity of debt can then be computed:

Peden	*Recession*	*Slow growth*	*Rapid growth*	*Expected value*
Equity	0	10	30	12.50
Debt	42	45	45	44.55
Total	42	55	75	57.05

Value of Tulen's shares

To find the value of Tulen's equity shares, subtract debt of £10m from the total value:

Tulen	*Recession*	*Slow growth*	*Rapid growth*	*Expected value*
Equity	53	70	110	75.45
Debt	10	10	10	10.00
Total	63	80	120	85.45

Effect of merger

When the companies merge, **add** the **economic values** of **equity** and **debt** together. This means using the negative £3 million value for Peden's equity in the recession scenario. Its debt will be restored to £45 million because the bankruptcy risk will have disappeared by combination with a low geared company. This is known as the coinsurance effect.

Combined	*Recession*	*Slow growth*	*Rapid growth*	*Expected value*
Equity	50	80	140	87.50
Debt	55	55	55	55.00
Total	105	135	195	142.50

Summary

Expected equity values

	£m
Peden	12.50
Tulen	75.45
Total	87.95
Combined company	87.50
Loss in equity value after combination	0.45

Expected debt values

	£m
Peden	44.55
Tulen	10.00
Total	54.55
Combined company	55.00
Gain in debt value after combination	0.45

After the combination, in the absence of synergy, the total economic value of the businesses remains at £142.5 million, but the total expected value of debt has increased by £0.45m at the expense of equity. This is because, under the recession scenario, there is **no longer** a **bankruptcy risk** for the debt holders of Peden. The previous advantage conferred on Peden equity by limited liability has now disappeared.

Furthermore, the cash flows of the combined company may **reduce in volatility** because of the portfolio effect and this may further reduce the cost of debt, increasing its value.

(b) **Significance of financial post-audits**

(i) **Incentive for strategic planning**

The knowledge that a post-audit will take place will **discourage growth** by acquisition **without** proper strategic **analysis** and **planning**.

(ii) **Problem identification**

They **identify problems** which have occurred since the merger or acquisition, identify whether these were unexpected or whether contingency plans had been made, and ensure that management confront the problems.

(iii) **Forecasting methods assessment**

By **analysing results** against **forecasts** made before the merger or takeover, they provide valuable feedback on the **reliability** of the **forecasting** and **planning** methods used.

(iv) **Future plans**

They identify **factors** which may have been **overlooked** and which need to be incorporated into future merger and takeover proposals.

20 Takeover regulation

(a) Takeover regulation in the UK, centred around the City Code, is based upon what is often referred to as a **'market-based model'** designed to protect a wide and **dispersed shareholder base**. This system which also prevails in the Commonwealth countries and the US is based on **case law** and the legal rules resulting from it. These seek to a great extent the protection of shareholder rights.

The second system, prevalent in continental Europe, is referred to as the **'block-holder'** or **stakeholder system** and relies on codified or civil law seeking to protect a broader group of stakeholders such as creditors, employees and the wider national interest.

The two systems differ not only in terms of their **regulatory framework** (**civil** versus **common law**) but also in terms of the underlying structure of ownership and control that they seek to address.

In the UK and the US the system is characterised by **wider share ownership** than in continental Europe where companies tend to be owned by **majority** or **near-majority stakes** held by a small number of investors.

In the Anglo-American model, the emphasis is on the **agency problem** and the protection of the **widely distributed shareholder base**.

The civil law countries rely via **legislation** on the monitoring by large shareholders, **creditors** and **employees**.

The **Takeovers Directive** lays down for the first time minimum EU rules concerning the regulation of takeovers of companies whose shares are traded on regulated markets. It is one of the measures adopted under the EU Financial Services Action Plan and aims to strengthen the single market in financial services.

The **Takeover Directive** requires that certain of the activities of the **Takeover Panel** are placed within a legal framework brining an end to the non-statutory approach to regulation in the UK. In terms of approach, the new regulatory model leads to the **convergence** of the **European system** to the **UK-US** one by adopting many of the elements of the **City Code**.

The City Code is divided into general principles and detailed rules which must be observed by persons involved in a merger or takeover transaction. The ten principles of the City Code are the following:

1 All the shareholders of the target company must be treated similarly

2 All information disclosed to one or more shareholders of the target company must be disclosed to all

3 An offer should only be made if it can be implemented in full

4 Sufficient information, advice and time to be given for a properly informed decision

5 All documentation should be of the highest standards of accuracy

6 All parties must do everything to ensure that a false market is not created in the shares of the target company

7 Shareholder approval

8 'Rights of control must be exercised in good faith and the oppression of a minority is wholly unacceptable'

9 The directors of both target and bidder must act in the interest of their respective companies

10 'Where control of a company is acquired ... a general offer to all other shareholders is normally required'

(b) Some mergers, referred to as friendly, take place when the management of the respective firms negotiate an agreement that is beneficial to both sides.

However, not all takeovers are negotiated in this way and those that are perceived as hostile are likely to be resisted by the directors.

The defensive measures that can be taken to resist a hostile bid have developed over the years, mainly in the US during the wave of takeover bids of the 1980s.

The more aggressive tactics are designed to make the target less attractive to the bidder, often risk shareholders interests in favour of those management.

Examples of such aggressive tactics include the following:

Golden parachute

This is where large compensation payments are agreed with top management in the case of a takeover.

Poison pill

Poison pills have many variants but the basic objective behind them is to give rights to existing shareholders to buy shares at a very low price or special preferential terms.

Crown jewels

This tactics is where the directors decide to sell the firm's most valuable assets making the firm less attractive as a result.

Restricted voting rights

Multiple voting rights can often be used as a means of allocation to certain shareholders disproportionate voting rights, enabling them to frustrate a bid.

In the US these takeover defences are allowed to a greater extent as they are subject to a very sophisticated and ever-developing set of rulings based on case law established during a period of over 25 years of court judgements.

In the UK, one of the principles of the Takeover Code is the requirement that the directors of the target company are not permitted to take any steps to frustrate a bid without the prior approval of the shareholders. This principle seeks to minimise the danger of the directors adopting measures that would risk the shareholders' interests in favour of their own.

In Europe an attempt was made by the Takeover Directive to introduce the break-through rule whereby a bidder with a specified proportion of shares would be able to break-through the company's multiple voting rights and exercise control as if one share one vote existed. However, this was considered unpopular and was introduced as an optional measure in continental Europe.

21 Atlas International

(a) We need to find the value of Global under the assumption that it will grow at 7%. We do not know the cost of equity for Global so we find it implicitly for the share price.

$$P = \frac{EPS}{k - g}$$

$$\text{Or } £22 = \frac{£0.90}{k - 0.05} \text{ or } k = \frac{£0.90}{£22} + 0.05 = 0.09$$

The value of the target company is:

$$\frac{£0.90}{0.09 - 0.07} = £43.04 \text{ per share}$$

The value of Global's equity will therefore be:

43.04 × 500,000 = £21,521,739

The value will increase by:

21,521,739 – 11,000,000 = 10,521,739

(b) The acquisition premium is:

£30 – £22 = £8 per share

or £4000,000

The NPV of acquisition is:

NPV = Additional Revenues – Costs of Acquisition
= 10,521,739 – 4,000,000
= 6,521,739

The acquisition should proceed

(c) Atlas needs to issue another 250,000 shares. The value of the combined company will be 70,000,000 + 21,521,739 = 91,521,739

The value of each share will be:

$$\frac{91{,}521{,}739}{1{,}250{,}000} = £73.22$$

Cost of acquisition = 250,000 × 73.22 – 11,000,000 = 7,304,348

NPV of acquisition = 10,521,739 – 7,304,348 = 3,217,391

The acquisition should proceed

22 Dolly Ltd

(a) Calculation of Dolly Ltd's Z-score for year ended 31 December 20X6:

Working Capital = 125 – 140 = (15)
Total Assets = 422
EBIT = 28
MV of Equity = 151p x (49/0.25) = 295.96
BV of Total Debt = 159
Turnover = 403

$$\text{Z-score} = 1.2 \times \frac{(15)}{422} + 1.4 \times \frac{(1)}{422} + 3.3 \times \frac{28}{422} + 0.6 \times \frac{295.96}{159} + 1.0 \times \frac{403}{422}$$

$$= \underline{\underline{2.24}}$$

(b) The Z-score calculated in (a) above lies almost exactly in the middle of the "inconclusive" range so it is not certain how vulnerable Dolly Ltd is to failure. If the Z-score had been in the "danger zone" – that is, 1.8 or under, remedial action could have been taken to prevent bankruptcy. In this case, management should take actions that will push Dolly Ltd's Z-score towards the 2.7 hurdle.

Z-scores have been successful in predicting up to 94% of bankruptcy cases, and can predict bankruptcy up to 2 years before it actually happens (with 72% accuracy). It is therefore worthwhile to monitor the Z-score over time to determine whether Dolly Ltd's position has worsened or improved. The Z-score for y/e 31 December 20X5 was 2.47, which shows that Dolly Ltd's financial health is deteriorating. Management should keep a close watch on performance and take steps to prevent the position deteriorating further.

Whilst Z-scores have had considerable success in predicting corporate failure, Dolly Ltd should be aware that this model can hide vital statistics. Dolly Ltd has negative working capital and negative retained earnings in 20X6 which cannot be sustained in the long term. The Z-score does not reveal such statistics, therefore its significance may be limited.

Dolly Ltd should also be aware that Z-scores are often developed specifically for a particular industry, therefore its construction is not necessarily applicable to Dolly Ltd's line of business. The result may be significant for the wrong reasons – that is, it may be completely misleading.

As with many models, Z-scores can be manipulated – Dolly Ltd should therefore carry out more in-depth investigations regarding its financial health before placing too much significance on the Z-score results. It is possible for Z-scores to predict that firms with high probabilities of failure are actually financially sound and vice versa.

(c) Other means of predicting corporate failure include:

(i) Financial ratios (but not in isolation – they must be compared either from year to year for the same company or with similar sized companies in the same industry).

(ii) Accurate audit reports.

(iii) Credit rating ratios such as Standard and Poor.

(iv) Other predictive models such as the Zeta model.

(v) Information in the press.

(vi) Information in published accounts, such as post balance sheet events; large contingent liabilities.

(vii) Competitors' behaviour – are they expanding whilst your own company is either remaining static or contracting?

(d) Dolly Ltd may consider purchasing the report if it cannot easily reproduce the analysis and if the company (which is deemed to be reputable) has a good history of making accurate predictions. However, Dolly Ltd's share price may already reflect the information contained in the analysis and report if it operates in an efficient market. If this is the case, there is no point in purchasing the report.

If the market is inefficient and the Z-score predictions are considered to be more accurate, purchasing the report may be worthwhile. If the report contains significant information that the market is unaware of, the company selling the report may do so only on the condition that the information is not released to third parties. However, such behaviour may be deemed to be unethical.

23 Brive plc

Top tips. In this question you are given details of the proposed reconstruction whereas in the exam you may have some input into its design.

There are no real traps in answer to (a), and if you adopted a methodical layout you should have scored full marks. The principal advantage of the layout we've used is that it highlights the adjustments.

In (b) with each of the parties you first assess what the position would be if liquidation did occur, and then the consequences (certain and uncertain) of reconstruction. Knowledge of the order of priority in a liquidation is vital. You need to show that the shareholders' and debentureholders' position is not clear-cut. If liquidation proceeds, they will certainly lose money; however if the reconstruction proceeds, they will have to pay out more money in return for uncertain future returns **and** other possibly undesirable consequences (change in control, lack of security).

Don't forget when considering the debentureholders' and bank's position in the event of reconstruction to include the opportunity cost of the cash foregone from liquidation.

The conclusion sums up the benefits to everyone but also emphasises the uncertainties.

(a) and (b)

REPORT

To:	Board of Directors
From:	M Accountant
Date:	17 September 20X1
Subject:	Proposed capital reconstruction

Introduction

The purpose of this report is to evaluate the implications of the proposed capital reconstruction of Brive plc for the various affected parties, including the shareholders, debenture holders, unsecured creditors and the bank. Calculations showing the effect of the reconstruction on the balance sheet are included as an appendix to this report.

Ordinary shareholders

In the event of Brive going into liquidation, the ordinary shareholders would be most unlikely to receive anything for their shares, since the net proceeds of the liquidation would be as follows.

	£
Property	2,000,000
Plant	1,000,000
Stock	1,700,000
Debtors	1,700,000
Liquidation costs	(770,000)
	5,630,000

The total amount due to the creditors, bank and debenture holders is £8,600,000, leaving nothing available for the shareholders.

If the reconstruction is undertaken, the existing shareholders will have to provide an additional £1m of capital in subscribing to the rights issue. However, if the projections are correct the effect of this should be to bring Brive back into profit, with earnings after interest amounting to £1.4m (£1.75m – £0.35m) per annum. This amounts to earnings per share of 28p which should permit Brive to start paying a dividend and providing some return to the shareholders again. The fact that the company is returning to profit should also make it possible to sell the shares if required which is presumably difficult at the present time. However there would be a substantial shift in the balance of control with the existing shareholders being left with only 40% of the equity, the balance being in the hands of the present debenture holders.

Secured debenture holders

Under the existing arrangements, the amount owing to the debenture holders is £3m. Although the debentures are secured on the property which has a book value of £3m, in the event of a forced sale this would only be likely to realise £2m giving a shortfall of £1m. The debenture holders would rank alongside the bank and the other creditors for repayment of this balance. As has been calculated above, the amount that would be realised on liquidation and available to the unsecured creditors would be £3.63m (net of property proceeds). The total amount owed is:

	£m
Debenture holders	1.0
Bank (overdraft)	1.6
Creditors	4.0
	6.6

The debenture holders would therefore only receive 55 pence in the pound on the balance owing, giving a total payout of 85 pence in the pound ((£2m + £0.55m)/£3.0m).

Under the proposed scheme, the debenture holders would receive £2.8m of new capital in return for the old debentures ie 93.33 pence in the pound in the form of capital rather than cash. Of this, £1.3m would be in the form of 14% unsecured loan stock, and the remainder in the form of equity. They would also have to subscribe an additional £1.5m to take up the rights issue. Their total investment in the reconstruction would therefore be:

	£m
Cash foregone from liquidation	2.55
Additional cash investment	1.50
	4.05

Returns would be:

	£
Interest (£1.3m × 14%)	182,000
Return on equity (£3m × 0.28)	840,000
	1,022,000

This represents a return of 25.23% which is likely to be above that which could be earned elsewhere thus making the scheme attractive to the debenture holders. However, in addition they would have to forgo their security on the property and rank partly with the unsecured creditors and partly with the equity. They should therefore be confident of the ability of the management to deliver the projected returns before consenting to the scheme.

The bank

Since the overdraft is unsecured, the bank would rank for repayment alongside the unsecured creditors. As calculated above, the amount to be repaid would be 55 pence in the pound, and the bank would thus recover £880,000 in the event of a liquidation. In the reconstruction, the bank would have to write off £400,000 (£1,600,000 debt – £1,200,000 loan stock), but would receive interest of 14% per annum leading to repayment of the balance in five years time.

The investment that the bank would be making would therefore be the cash forgone from the liquidation of £880,000. The annual returns would be £168,000 (14% × £1.2m) which represents a return on the incremental investment of 19.1%. Provided that the bank is confident of the financial projections of the management, it stands to receive £1.2m in five years' time. The effective return of 19.1% in the meantime is in **excess of current overdraft rates**, and the level of security is improved since there would no longer be secured debenture holders ranking ahead of the bank for repayment. The scheme is therefore likely to be attractive to the bank.

Unsecured creditors

If Brive goes into liquidation the unsecured creditors will receive 55 pence in the pound ie £2.2m. Under the proposed scheme they would stand to receive 75 pence (25% written down) in the pound with apparently no significant delay in payment. If Brive continues to operate they will be able to continue to trade with the company and generate further profits from the business. The proposed scheme therefore seems **attractive** from their point of view.

Conclusions

The proposed scheme appears to hold benefits for all the parties involved. It is also in the interests of Brive's customers and workforce for the company to continue to trade. However these benefits will only be realised if the directors are correct in their forecast of trading conditions and if the new investment can achieve the projected returns. All parties should satisfy themselves as to these points before considering proceeding further with the reconstruction.

	Before			*Adjustment*			*After*
	£'000	*a*	*b*	*c*	*d*	*e–g*	£'000
Fixed assets	5,700	(2,100)				2,500	6,100
Current assets							
Stock	3,500	(800)					2,700
Debtors	1,800	(100)					1,700
	5,300						4,400
Creditors	(4,000)					1,000	(3,000)
Overdraft	(1,600)				1,600		0
Working capital	(300)						1,400
Total assets	5,400						7,500
10% Debentures	(3,000)			3,000			0
14% Stock				(1,300)	(1,200)		(2,500)
Net assets	2,400						5,000
Capital and reserves							
Share capital	4,000		(3,000)	1,500		2,500	5,000
P&L account	(1,600)		1,600				0
	2,400						5,000

24 Reorganisation

(a) Potential problems with management buy outs:

(i) Deciding on a fair price – management will obviously want to pay the lowest price possible, whilst the vendor will want to secure the highest possible price.

(ii) Any geographical relocation may result in the loss of key workers.

(iii) Maintaining a good relationship with suppliers and customers, particularly if key contacts that suppliers and customers were used to dealing with decide to leave as a result of the buy out.

(iv) Availability of sufficient cash flow to maintain and replace fixed assets. This is one of the main problems with buy outs – cash is often very tight at the beginning of the venture.

(v) Changes in work practices may not suit all employees.

(vi) Maintaining financial arrangements with previous employees may be difficult – for example, pension rights.

(vii) Many suppliers of funds will insist on representation at board level in order to maintain some control over how the funds are being used.

(b) In order to estimate the change in the value of equity, we can use forecast retained earnings figures, assuming dividends to be at the maximum 12 % level:

(All figures are in £000)

	0	*1*	*2*	*3*	*4*	*5*
EBIT	–	2,200	3,100	3,900	4,200	4,500
9.5% interest	–	713	713	713	713	713
Earnings before tax	–	1,487	2,387	3,187	3,487	3,787
Tax	–	446	716	956	1,046	1,136
Earnings after tax	–	1,041	1,671	2,231	2,441	2,651
Dividend (12%)	–	125	201	268	293	318
Retained earnings	–	916	1,470	1,963	2,148	2,333
Equity	17,500	18,416	19,886	21,849	23,997	26,330

$$\text{Compound growth interest rate} = \left[\sqrt[5]{\frac{26{,}330}{17{,}500}}\right] - 1 = 8.5\%$$

The 8.5% growth rate is considerably less than the 15% rise predicted by management, therefore it can be concluded that the management's estimate does not appear to be viable.

25 Kilber plc

(a) The management of risk is one of the most important aspects of the treasury function. Excessive volatility in the cash flows of the company, caused by changing business conditions, changes in exchange rates or interest rates will affect adversely the value of the firm. Hedging is in general considered to enhance the value of the company.

The most serious risk that Kilber faces is the falling kilbe prices. Since kilbe prices are highly correlated with copper prices, it is reasonable to use copper futures contract to lock into certain future value. Suppose that Kilber has sold a sufficient number of copper futures contract maturing in three months. Suppose further that during this period, the price of both kilbe and copper have fallen. On expiration of the contract, the company will have a loss due to the fall in the price of the kilbe but a gain on the copper futures contract.

Whether the gain in the futures contract will offset the loss due to the fall in the price of the kilbe it will depend on whether the price of copper has fallen by the same percentage as the price of kilbe. If it has fallen by the same percentage then the price of copper will be behaving exactly like the price of kilbe, the copper futures contract will be the exact equivalent of a kilbe futures contract.

However when the price of kilbe and copper is not perfectly correlated, then the copper futures contract is an imperfect hedge.

The remaining risk is called basis risk and arises from the imperfect correlation between the hedging instrument and the hedged asset.

(b) The main benefit of OTC derivatives is that they can be tailored to the needs of the two parties; their major drawback is that they pose a higher risk of default than do exchange-traded derivatives. Some very specialized agreements may also be illiquid.

(c) Kilber could use a variety of instruments to hedge interest rate risk depending on its time horizon. For short-term protection the company could use forward rate agreements, short-term interest rate futures and interest rate options. For long-term protection, it could use interest rate swaps to convert the variable interest rate debt to fixed rate.

Note that forward rate agreements, futures and swaps lock into a particular borrowing rate and the company does not benefit from a fall in interest rate. Interest rate options on the other hand set a ceiling on the interest rate to be paid but allow the company to benefit from a fall in interest rates.

26 Expo plc

> **Top tips.** The numerical part of this question is a good example of how you might be tested on forward and money market alternatives to hedging. However the rest of the question demonstrates that you need to be able to discuss why and how risk can be dealt with. Remember that hedging everything will be expensive, but only hedging certain transactions may be more expensive still. (b) shows the importance of matching; remember that the company may be able to use a hard currency if the local currency cannot be used. There are however other possibilities and your answer should briefly mention these.

(a) To: The Treasurer
From: Assistant
Date: 12 November 20X7

(i) Comparison of two methods of hedging exchange risk

Method 1

Expo borrows SFr750,000.

Three months interest is SFr750,000 × 3% × 3/12 = SFr5,625.

The customer pays SFr750,000, which repays the loan principal but not the interest. The interest must be paid by converting pounds. Since the interest is known in advance, this can be covered on the forward market at a cost of 5625/2.3688 = £2,375.

Meanwhile, the SFr750,000 is converted to sterling at the original spot rate 2.3834 to give £314,677. Assume that this is used to repay the company's short-term borrowings. Interest saved will be £314,677 × 6% × 3/12 = £4,720.

So, at the end of three months, the net sterling cash from the transaction is:

£314,677 + £4,720 – £2,375 = £317,022.

Method 2

The exchange rate is agreed in advance. Cash received in three months is converted to produce 750,000/2.3688 = £316,616.

Conclusion

On the basis of the above calculations, Method 1 gives a slightly better receipt. Banker's commission has been omitted from the figures.

(ii) **Factors to consider before deciding whether to hedge foreign exchange risk using the foreign currency markets**

Risk-averse strategy

The company should have a clear strategy concerning how much foreign exchange risk it is prepared to bear. A highly risk-averse or 'defensive' strategy of hedging all transactions is expensive in terms of commission costs but recognises that floating exchange rates are very unpredictable and can cause losses high enough to bankrupt the company.

Predictive strategy

An alternative 'predictive' strategy recognises that if all transactions are hedged, then the chance of currency gains is lost. The company could therefore attempt to forecast foreign exchange movements and only hedge those transactions where currency losses are predicted. The fact is that some currencies are relatively predictable (for example, if inflation is high the currency will devalue and there is little to be gained by hedging payments in that currency).

This is, of course, a much more risky strategy but in the long run, if predictions are made sensibly, the strategy should lead to a higher expected value than that of hedging everything and will incur lower commission costs as well. The risk remains, though, that a single large uncovered transaction could cause severe problems if the currency moves in the opposite direction to that predicted.

Best strategy

A sensible strategy for our company could be to set a cash size for a foreign currency exposure above which all amounts must be hedged, but below this limit a predictive approach is taken or even, possibly, all amounts are left unhedged.

Matching

Before using any technique to hedge foreign currency transactions, receipts and payments in the same currency at the same date should be offset. This technique is known as 'matching'. For example, if the company is expecting to receive SFr750,000 on 31 March and to pay SFr600,000 on the same day, only the net amount of SFr150,000 needs to be considered.

Matching can be extended to receipts and payments which do not take place on exactly the same day by simply hedging the period and amount of the difference between the receipt and payment. A company like ours which has many receipts and payments in European currencies should consider matching assets with liabilities in the same currency. For example if we have total Swiss debtors of SFr2million, we should borrow SFr2million on overdraft to match the debtor.

(b) **Matching**

If the foreign subsidiary is selling predominantly **matching** in its own country, the principle of matching assets and liabilities says that the subsidiary should be **financed as far as possible** in the **currency of that country**. Ideally the subsidiary will be highly geared with loans and overdrafts in the developing country's currency. If local finance has not been used and the sales invoice which is about to be sent is large, then an overdraft in the same currency should be taken out and the receipt converted to sterling immediately.

Positively correlated currency

If it is impossible to borrow in the local currency, Expo plc should attempt to find a **hard currency** which is **highly positively correlated** with the local currency. For example, some countries have a policy of pegging their currency to the US dollar. The receipt can then be hedged by selling the US dollar forward.

This technique is, however, open to the risk that the local currency suddenly devalues against the dollar, as happened in 1997 with a number of Asian currencies. The likelihood of this happening is high if there is high inflation in the country and it has low reserves.

If Expo plc is fairly certain that the local currency is going to devalue and that it cannot borrow in that currency, the remaining alternatives are:

(i) To **increase the sales price** by the amount of the expected devaluation and bear the risk

(ii) To **invoice in a hard currency**, for example US dollars, which can then be sold forward

(iii) To **arrange a 'counter-trade' agreement** (ie barter) in which the sale of Expo's textiles is paid for by the purchase of local raw materials or other products

27 Fidden plc

(a) Techniques for protecting against the risk of adverse foreign exchange movements include the following.

(i) A company could trade only in its own currency, thus transferring all risks to suppliers and customers.

(ii) A company could ensure that its assets and liabilities in any one currency are as nearly equal as possible, so that losses on assets (or liabilities) are matched by gains on liabilities (or assets).

(iii) A company could enter into forward contracts, under which an agreed amount of a currency will be bought or sold at an agreed rate at some fixed future date or, under a forward option contract, at some date in a fixed future period.

(iv) A company could buy foreign currency options, under which the buyer acquires the right to buy (call options) or sell (put options) a certain amount of a currency at a fixed rate at some future date. If rates move in such a way that the option rate is unfavourable, the option is simply allowed to lapse.

(v) A company could buy foreign currency futures on a financial futures exchange. Futures are effectively forward contracts, in standard sizes and with fixed maturity dates. Their prices move in response to exchange rate movements, and they are usually sold before maturity, the profit or loss on sale corresponding approximately to the exchange loss or profit on the currency transaction they were intended to hedge.

(vi) A company could enter into a money market hedge. One currency is borrowed and converted into another, which is then invested until the funds are required or funds are received to repay the original loan. The early conversion protects against adverse exchange rate movements, but at a cost equal to the difference between the cost of borrowing in one currency and the return available on investment in the other currency.

(b) (i) 1 Forward exchange market

The rates are:

	\$/£
Spot	1.7106 – 1.7140
3 months forward	1.7024 – 1.7063
6 months forward	1.6967 – 1.7006

The net payment three months hence is $\frac{£116{,}000 - \$197{,}000}{1.7063} = £546$.

The net payment six months hence is $\frac{\$(447{,}000 - 154{,}000}{1.6967} = £172{,}688$.

Note that the dollar receipts can be used in part settlement of the dollar payments, so only the net payment is hedged.

2 Money market

\$197,000 will be received three months hence, so:

$$\frac{\$197{,}000}{(1+0.09\times 3/12)}$$

may be borrowed now and converted into sterling, the dollar loan to be repaid from the receipts.

The net sterling payment three months hence is:

$$£116{,}000 - \frac{\$197{,}000}{1+(0.09\times 3/12)}\times\frac{1}{1.7140}\times(1+(.0.095\times 3/12)) = £924$$

The equation for the \$197,000 receipt in three months is to calculate the amount of dollars to borrow now (divide by the dollar borrowing rate) and then to find out how much that will give now in sterling (divide by the exchange rate). The final amount of sterling after three months is given by multiplying by the sterling lending rate.

\$293,000 (net) must be paid six months hence. We can borrow sterling now and convert it into dollars, such that the fund in six months will equal \$293,000. The sterling payment in six months time will be the principal and the interest thereon. A similar logic applies as for the equation above except that the situation is one of making a final payment rather than a receipt.

The sterling payment six months hence is therefore

$$\frac{293{,}000}{1+0.06\times 6/12}\times\frac{1}{1.7106}\times(1+0.125\times 6/12)=£176{,}690$$

(ii) Available put options (put, because sterling is to be sold) are at \$1.70 (cost 3.45 cents per £) and at \$1.80 (cost 9.32 cents per £).

Using options at \$1.70 gives the following results.

$$\frac{\$293{,}000}{1.70\$/£}=£172{,}353$$

$$\text{Contracts required}=\frac{£172{,}353}{£12{,}500}=14\text{(to the next whole number)}$$

Cost of options = 14 × 12,500 × 3.45 cents = \$6,038.

14 contracts will provide, for £12,500 × 14 = £175,000, \$(175,000 × 1.70) = \$297,500.

$$\text{The overall cost is £175,000 + }\frac{\$293{,}000+\$6{,}038-\$297{,}500}{1.6967}=£175{,}906$$

As this figure exceeds the cost of hedging through the forward exchange market (£172,688), use of \$1.70 options would have been disadvantageous.

Note. The rate of 1.6967 is used instead of 1.7006 because buying 14 contracts leaves the company slightly short of dollars (by \$293,000 + \$6,038 – \$297,500 = \$1,538).

Using options at \$1.80:

$$\frac{\$293{,}000}{1.80\$/£}=£162{,}778$$

$$\text{Contracts required}=\frac{£162{,}778}{£12{,}500}=14\text{(to next whole number)}$$

Cost of options = 14 × 12,500 × 9.32 cents = \$16,310

14 contracts will provide, for £12,500 × 14 = £175,000, 175,000 × 1.80 = \$315,000.

$$\text{The overall cost is £175,000 + }\frac{\$293{,}000+\$16{,}310-\$315{,}000}{1.7006}=£171{,}654$$

This figure is less than the cost of hedging through the forward exchange market, so use of \$1.80 options would have been preferable.

(iii) Foreign currency options have the advantage that while offering protection against adverse currency movements, they need not be exercised if movements are favourable. Thus the maximum cost is the option price, while there is no comparable limit on the potential gains.

28 Exchange rate forecasts

> **Top tips**. In (a) (i) and (b) there are two alternative versions of the International Fisher Effect and Purchasing Power Parity formulae. Either one will give the correct result. In (a)(ii) you must distinguish between the terms 'unbiased' and 'accurate', and state some of the assumptions behind the IFE formula. In (b) the best type of hedge where it is uncertain whether cash is needed is a currency option.
>
> In (a) marks were split 50% IFE calculations, 50% comment. 5 out of 8 marks were available in (b) for calculations of the tender price and conclusion, with 3 marks being available for the alternative hedges.

(a) (i) To: Managing Director

From: Financial analyst

Predictions of Euro/£ exchange rate

If exchange rates are freely floating and interest rates are also freely determined by market forces, then, according to the International Fisher Effect, interest rate differentials between two countries can be applied to the current exchange rate to give an unbiased predictor of the future exchange rate.

Predicted future exchange rate = spot rate $\times$ $(1 + i_f)/(1 + i_{uk})$

This gives year 1 exchange rate as $1.667 \times 1.035/1.06 = 1.6277$, and year 2 as $1.6277 \times 1.035/1.06 = 1.589$ Euro/£.

The non-executive director is wrong, having applied the formula wrongly as $1.667 \times (1 + 0.02358)^2 = 1.747$ Euro/£.

> **Top tips**. An alternative version of the formula gives the predicted figure as follows:
>
> Using the formula $(i_f - i_{uk})/(1 + i_{uk})$, the predicted future exchange rate would change by:
>
> $(0.035 - 0.6)/1.06 = -2.358\%$. This implies that the Euro is predicted to strengthen against the pound by 2.36%.
>
> If this happens for two years, the predicted exchange rate will be $1.667 \times (1 - 0.02358)^2 = 1.667 \times 0.97642^2 = 1.589$ Euro/£.

(ii) **Errors in prediction**

The fact that a predicted exchange rate is **unbiased** does not make it accurate. Unbiased simply means that the rate is as likely to be above the prediction as below it. The margin of error on the prediction over two years will be very large, even if other factors remain the same, which is unlikely. Over the next two years interest rates are almost certain to change with changing economic conditions.

Assumptions

The **assumptions** behind the IFE model are also **unlikely to hold**. The model assumes that the currencies are freely traded on the market with, for example, no government intervention, and that the current exchange rate represents an equilibrium position. The forecast exchange rate is therefore very unlikely to be accurate.

(b) **Currency options**

The best form of protection against foreign exchange risk, in a situation where it is uncertain whether there will be a need for the currency to be exchanged, is a **currency option**. A forward contract cannot be avoided if the contract is lost and could create a currency loss, whereas a currency option can be allowed to lapse if it is not advantageous. The disadvantage of a currency option is the 'up-front' premium, which is non-refundable and can be expensive.

Period of option

The option is needed **from the date** the **tender is made** to **the date the results are announced**. Beyond that point, if the contract is won, currency protection could be achieved by a money market hedge (borrowing Dinars on the strength of the future sales proceeds), or by another option, but forward contracts do not appear to be available.

Since the date of award of the contract is unknown, an alternative hedge would be to take out an **option** for the **whole 18 month period**. The company would purchase an option to sell (put) Dinars for Euros in 18 months time.

Prediction of exchange rate

If no hedge is used, a prediction of the exchange rate in 18 months is needed to estimate the tender price.

The spot rate is 0.256 – 0.260 Euros per Dinar. The rate for selling Dinars is 0.256 (when you sell Dinars you will get the lower number of Dinars).

Using purchasing power parity:

The formula is: $\dfrac{\left(\dfrac{1+i_E}{1+i_D}-1\right)}{(1+i_D)}$

Alternative solution

The formula is: $\dfrac{(i_E - i_D)}{(1+i_D)}$

The Euro is predicted to strengthen against the Dinar: $\dfrac{(3\% - 9\%)}{1.09} = -5.505\%$ per year.

In 18 months (1.5 years) the exchange rate is predicted to be:

$0.256 \times (1 - 0.0505)^{1.5} = 0.235$ Euros per Dinar.

Purchasing power parity has been used instead of the International Fisher effect as it is regarded as more reliable.

The Euro cost in 18 months time is predicted to be 340,000. A 25% margin gives a price of €425,000.

If no hedge is used, the recommended tender price is: $\dfrac{425{,}000}{0.235} = 1{,}808{,}511$ Dinars.

If an option hedge using today's exchange rate is used, the price should be 425,000/0.256 = 1,660,156 Dinars *plus* the cost of the option.

29 USA Options

Top tips. To compare the participating option with the traded option, it is best to look at the same exercise price for both (£1 = $1.65). Since you need to look at the outcomes for a range of possible exchange rate movements, it is convenient to use the range from $1.55 to $1.70 given in the traded option table. The company is selling its dollar (term currency) receipt, therefore the bank is buying the dollars high. Collars are often worth mentioning in questions on options.

(b) provides useful revision of other hedging methods. Matching can be an important technique. Watch out also for references to currencies being pegged to another currency (generally the $).

Examiner's comment. Poorer candidates confused futures and options, showed a lack of understanding of option premia or the possibility of options lapsing.

(a) **Current spot rate**

At the current exchange rate of £1 = $1.6100, the receipt of $1,800,000 will produce £1,118,012.

Participating option

Using the **participating option**, there is no premium. An examination of possible receipts under 4 possible exchange rates in 6 months time shows the following.

	$1.55	*$1.60*	*$1.65*	*$1.70*
	£	£	£	£
Spot market				
At opening spot rate				
$1.8 million/$1.61	1,118,012	1,118,012	1,118,012	1,118,012
At closing spot rate $1.8 million/closing rate	1,161,290	1,125,000	1,090,909	1,058,824
Gain/(loss)	43,278	6,988	(27,103)	(59,188)
Options market				
Buy at	1.65	1.65	1.65	1.65
Sell at	1.55	1.60	1.65	1.70
Exercise?	No	No	Yes/No	Yes

Outcome of option position

			As for $1.65 on spot market	*As for $1.65 on spot market*
Net outcome	£	£	£	£
Gain/(loss)	43,278	6,988	(27,103)	(27,103)
Half gain to bank	(21,639)	(3,494)		
Net gain/(loss)	21,639	3,494		

Traded option

Set up option

(i) Contract date June

(ii) Option type call

(iii) Strike price $1.65 and $1.70 have premium costs less than £10,000. Choose $1.65 for comparison

(iv) Number of contracts

$$\frac{1{,}800{,}000 \div 1.65}{31{,}250} \approx 34.9 \text{ contracts, say 35}$$

(v) Tick size = 31,250 × 0.0001
= $3.125

(vi) Premium = $\frac{1.1}{100} \times 31{,}250 \times 35$
= \$12,031 @ 1.605
= £7,494

Closing prices

As for participating option.

Outcome

		\$1.55	*\$1.60*	*\$1.65*		*\$1.70*
(i)	Options market					
	Strike price call	\$1.65	\$1.65	\$1.65		\$1.65
	Closing price	\$1.55	\$1.60	\$1.65		\$1.65
	Exercise ?	No	No	Yes/no		Yes
	Tick movement				500	
	Options outcome				500 × 35 × 3.125 = \$54,688	

(ii)	Net outcome	£	£	£	£
	Spot market gain/(loss) as for participating option	43,278	6,988	(27,103)	(59,188)
	Options market gain ÷ spot rate				32,169
	Options premium	(7,494)	(7,494)	(7,494)	(7,494)
		35,784	(506)	(34,597)	(34,513)

Comparison of the two pay-off schedules shows that using the participating option is probably preferable, as the resulting cash receipt is less sensitive to exchange rate fluctuations and, in particular, shows a lower maximum loss.

Creation of straddle option

As a more advanced use of traded options, the company could consider creating a straddle option. In order to hedge the purchase of pounds with dollars, the company should buy call options and sell put options at the same exercise price.

For example, the cost of purchasing \$1.60 options (5.3 cents) can be offset by selling \$1.60 put options (4.0 cents). The net premium cost per £ is 1.3 cents.

Receipt = 1,800,000/1.60
= £1,125,000

Premium = \$1.3/100 × 1,125,000
= \$14,625, which at today's spot rate of \$1.6055 would be £9,109, which is within the £10,000 limit.

Effect of straddle

The combination of two options on the same exercise price *fixes* the exchange rate to £1 = \$1.60. When the net premium cost is added, the effective exchange rate for buying pounds with dollars is £1 = \$1.613. This is an alternative to using forward or futures contracts.

Collars

Use of collars with calls and puts on different exercise prices gives a **pay off schedule** with a **risk profile intermediate** between a fixed return and the call option pay off shown above.

(b) **Matching assets and liabilities**

If the foreign subsidiary is selling predominantly in its own country, the principle of **matching assets and liabilities** says that the subsidiary should be financed as far as possible in the currency of that country. Ideally the subsidiary will be highly geared with loans and overdrafts in the developing country's currency. If local finance has not been used and the sales invoice which is about to be sent is large, then an overdraft in the same currency should be taken out and the receipt converted to sterling immediately.

Use of hard currency

If it is impossible to borrow in the local currency, the company should attempt to find a hard currency which is highly positively correlated with the local currency. For example, some countries have a policy of pegging their currency to the US dollar. The receipt can then be hedged by selling the US dollar forward.

This technique is, however, open to the risk that the local currency suddenly devalues against the dollar, as happened in 1997 with a number of Asian currencies. The likelihood of this happening is high if there is high inflation in the country and it has low reserves.

Other options

If the company is fairly certain that the local currency is going to devalue and that it cannot borrow in that currency, the **remaining alternatives** are:

(i) **Increase the sales price** by the amount of the expected devaluation and bear the risk

(ii) **Invoice in a hard currency**, for example US dollars, which can then be sold forward

(iii) **Arrange a 'countertrade' agreement** (ie barter) in which the sale of the company's textiles is paid for by the purchase of local raw materials or other products

30 Curropt plc

(a) The department's view that the US dollar will strengthen is in **agreement** with the **indications** of the forward market and the futures market. Forward and futures rates show a **stronger dollar** than the spot rate. The forward rate is often taken as an **unbiased** predictor of what the spot rate will be in future. However, future events could cause large currency movements in **either direction**.

(b) The **company needs to buy dollars in June.**

Forward contract

Lack of flexibility

A forward currency contract will fix the exchange rate for the date required near the end of June. If the exact date is not known, a range of dates can be specified, using an **option forward contract**. This will remove currency risk **provided that the franchise is won**. If the **franchise is not won** and the group has no use for US dollars, it will still have to buy the dollars at the forward rate. It will than have to sell them back for pounds at the spot rate which might result in an exchange loss.

Futures contract

Use sterling futures

A currency hedge using futures contracts will attempt to create a **compensating gain** on the futures market which will **offset** the **increase** in the **sterling cost** if the dollar strengthens. The hedge works by **selling sterling futures** contracts now and closing out by **buying sterling futures** in **June** at a lower dollar price if the dollar has strengthened. Like a forward contract, the exchange rate in June is effectively fixed because, if the dollar weakens, the futures hedge will produce a loss which counter-balances the cheaper sterling cost. However, because of inefficiencies in future market hedges, the exchange rate is not fixed to the same level of accuracy as a forward hedge.

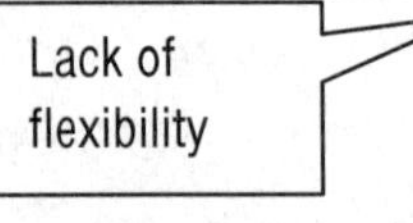

A futures market hedge has the same weakness as a forward currency contract in the franchise situation. If the franchise is not won, an **exchange loss** may result.

Currency option

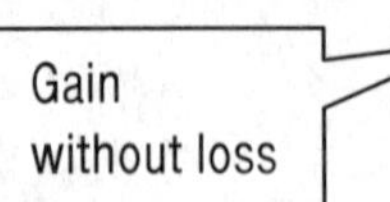

A currency option is an ideal hedge in the franchise situation. It gives the company the **right but not the obligation** to sell pounds for dollars in June. It is only exercised if it is to the company's advantage, that is if the dollar has strengthened. If the **dollar strengthens** and the franchise is won, the exchange rate has been **protected**. If the dollar strengthens and the **franchise is not won**, a **windfall gain** will result by **selling pounds** at the exercise price and buying them more cheaply at spot with a stronger dollar.

(c) **Results of using currency hedges if the franchise is won**

Forward market

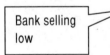

Bank selling low

Using the forward market, the rate for **buying dollars** at the end of June is 1.4310 US$/£. The cost in sterling is 15 million/1.4310 = £10,482,180.

Futures

Date of contract

June future

Type of contract

Sell sterling futures

Number of contracts

$$\frac{15{,}000{,}000}{1.4302 \times 62{,}500} = 167.8 \approx 168 \text{ contracts}$$

Tick size

$0.001 \times 62{,}500 = \$6.25$

Closing futures price

Three possible spot price scenarios

1.3500
1.4500
1.5500

As told futures price is in the same relationship to spot price, futures price at end of June

(i) 1.3500 + (1.4302 – 1.4461) = 1.3341
(ii) 1.4500 + (1.4302 – 1.4461) = 1.4341
(iii) 1.5500 + (1.4302 – 1.4461) = 1.5341

Basis

Hedge outcome

	1.3500	1.4500	1.5500
	$	$	$
Opening futures price	1.4302	1.4302	1.4302
Closing futures price	1.3341	1.4341	1.5341
Movement in ticks	961	(39)	(1039)
Futures profits /(losses)	1,009,050	(40,950)	(1,090,950)
168 × tick movement × 6.25	1,009,050	(40,950)	(1,090,950)

Net outcome

	$	$	$
Spot market payment	(15,000,000)	(15,000,000)	(15,000,000)
Futures market (profits)/losses	1,009,050	(40,950)	(1,090,950)
	(13,990,950)	(15,040,950)	(16,090,950)
Translated at closing rate	£10,363,667	£10,373,069	£10,381,258

Options

Date of contract

June

Option type

Buy put

Exercise price

Exercise price	*Premium*	*Net*
1.4000	0.0038	1.3962
1.4250	0.0068	1.4182
1.4500	0.0238	1.4262

Choose 1.4500

Number of contracts

$$\frac{15{,}000{,}000 \div 1.4500}{31{,}250} = 331.03 \approx 331 \text{ contracts}$$

Tick size

31,250 × 0.0001 = $3.125

Unhedged amount

Premium

0.0238 × 31,250 × 331 = $246,181 at 1.4461
= £170,238

Outcome

	1.3500	1.4500	1.5500
	$	$	$
Option market			
Strike price	1.4500	1.4500	1.4500
Closing price	1.3500	1.4500	1.5500
Exercise?	Yes	No	No
Tick movement	1,000	–	–
Outcome of options position	1,000 × 331 × 3.125 = 1,034,375		

Net outcome

	1.3500	1.4500	1.5500
	$	$	$
Spot market payment	(15,000,000)	(15,000,000)	(15,000,000)
Options	1,034,375		
	(13,965,625)	(15,000,000)	(15,000,000)
	£	£	£
Translated at closing spot rate	(10,344,907)	(10,344,828)	(9,677,419)
Premium	(170,238)	(170,238)	(170,238)
	10,515,145	10,515,066	9,847,657

Complications in choice

Summary

The company will either choose to purchase a **future** or an **option.** Although futures are more advantageous at lower exchange rates, the net benefits of using an option if the rate is $1.5500 are much greater than the difference between futures and options at 1.3500 and 1.4500.

31 Carrick plc

> **Top tips.** The first part of this question should be fairly straightforward. It is easy however to write more than is strictly necessary on these areas, and leave yourself insufficient time for the rest of the question. The key things to bring out is how each instrument limits interest rate risk by limiting or eliminating the effects of interest rate changes on the company.
>
> In (b) remember that Carrick is **receiving** interest so it must buy a call option to limit its exposure to falls in interest rates. As a collar is being constructed, Carrick must sell a put option to counterbalance buying the call option.
>
> The answer works through the key stages:
>
> - Choice of options
> - No of contracts
> - Premium payable
> - Effects of collar
> - Results of collar
>
> You need to show in the answer:
>
> - Technical expertise (choosing 9400 for the initial option, evaluating the other possible prices but ignoring 9450 as it's not relevant)
> - Numerical abilities (getting the premium, number of contracts and gain calculation right)
> - Depth of discussion (the question asks you to evaluate and that implies detailed analysis, explaining what will happen at the various rates, and also explaining that the choice is not clear-cut – 9250 has the largest potential benefits but also the largest definite costs)

(a) **Interest rate exposure**

Interest rate exposure arises when a company's borrowing is such that a change in interest rates might expose it to interest charges that are unacceptably high. For example, if a company has a large tranche of debt at a fixed rate of interest that is due for repayment in the near future, and the loan is to be replaced or renegotiated, the company would be vulnerable to a sudden increase in market interest rates.

Risk management

Risk management in this context involves using **hedging techniques** to reduce or 'cover' an exposure. However, hedging has a cost, which will either take the form of a **fee** to a financial institution or a **reduction in profit**, and this must be weighed against the reduction in financial risks that the hedge achieves. The extent to which the exposure is covered is known as the **'hedge efficiency'**. A perfect hedge has an efficiency of 100%.

Methods of managing interest rate risk include the following.

Forward interest rate agreements (FRAs)

A FRA is an agreement, usually between a company and a bank, about the **interest rate** on a future loan or deposit. The agreement will **fix the rate of interest** for borrowing for a certain time in the future. If the actual rate of interest at that time is above that agreed, the bank pays the company the difference, and vice versa. Thus the company benefits from effectively fixing the rate of interest on a loan for a given period, but it may miss the opportunity to benefit from any favourable movements in rates during that time. A FRA is simply an agreement about rates – it does not involve the movement of the principal sum – the actual borrowing must be arranged separately.

Futures

A financial future is an agreement on the **future price** of a **financial variable**. Interest rate futures are similar in all respects to FRAs, except that the terms, sums involved, and periods are **standardised**. They are traded on the London International Futures and Options Exchange (LIFFE).

Their standardised nature makes them less attractive to corporate borrowers because it is not always possible to match them exactly to specific rate exposures. Each contract will require the payment of a small initial deposit.

Interest rate options

An interest rate guarantee (or option) provides the **right to borrow** a **specified amount** at a guaranteed rate of interest. The option guarantees that the **interest rate will not rise** above a specified level during a specified period. On the date of expiry of the option the buyer must decide whether or not to exercise his right to borrow. He will only exercise the option if actual **interest rates** have **risen above the option rate**. The advantage of options is that the buyer cannot lose on the interest rate and can take advantage of any favourable rate movements. However, a **premium** must be paid regardless of whether or not the option is exercised. Options can be negotiated directly with the bank or traded in a standardised form on the LIFFE.

Caps and collars

These can be used to set a **floor** and a **ceiling** to the range of interest rates that might be incurred. A **premium** must be paid for this service. These agreements do not provide a perfect hedge, but they do limit the range of possibilities and thus reduce the level of exposure.

(b) Collars make use of **interest rate options** to limit exposure to the risk of movement in rates. The company would arrange both a ceiling (an upper limit) and a floor (a lower limit) on its interest yield. The use of the ceiling means that the cost is lower than for a floor alone.

Choice of options

Since Carrick requires protection for the next seven months, it can use **September options** in order to cover the full period. It is assumed that the floor will be fixed at the current yield of 6%. This implies that it will buy call options at 9400. At the same time, Carrick will limit its ability to benefit from rises in rates by selling a put option at a higher rate, for example 7% (or 9300).

The level of **premiums payable** will **depend** on the different **sizes of collar**. The number of three-month contracts required for seven months' cover will be:

$$\frac{£6m}{£0.5m} \times \frac{7}{3} = 28 \text{ contracts } (£14m)$$

The premiums payable at different sizes of collar (in annual percentage terms) will be:

Call	*Premium*	*Put*	*Premium*	*Net premium*	*£ cost**
9400	0.40	9350	0.35	0.05	1,750
9400	0.40	9300	0.14	0.26	9,100
9400	0.40	9250	0.06	0.34	11,900

(* eg £14m × 0.05% × ¼ = £1,750)

If Carrick does take out the options as described above, the effect will be as follows.

(i) If interest rates fall below 6%, Carrick will **exercise the call option** and effectively fix its interest rate at 6%. The loss on the interest rate will be borne by the seller of the call option.

(ii) If interest rates remain between the 6% floor and the 7% ceiling, Carrick will **do nothing** but will benefit from the effect of any increase in rates above 6% within this band.

(iii) If interest rates rise above 7% the buyer of the put option will **exercise** their **option**, provided that the futures price falls below 9300. Carrick will effectively achieve an interest rate of 7%, but the benefit of any premium on rates above 7% will accrue to the buyer of the put option.

In practice, costs will be higher due to the transaction costs that will be incurred.

The potential gross interest rate gain, and the net gain taking premiums into account if rates do rise to the various exercise prices, are as follows. The interest rate gain is calculated on £6m for seven months.

	Interest rate % rise	*Interest gain £*	*Premium £ cost (above)*	*Net gain £*
9350	0.50	17,500	1,750	15,750
9300	1.00	35,000	9,100	25,900
9250	1.50	52,500	11,900	40,600

This suggests that Carrick could make the greatest potential gain by **selling put options** at 9250. However, this gain will only be realised if actual rates rise to 7.5%. If they stay at around 6% then Carrick will still incur costs without realising benefits. The actual put price chosen will depend on the view of the directors on the likely movements in rates over the period in question, but if it seems likely that rates will increase by up to 1%, then a put price of 9300 would be the most appropriate.

32 Burger-Queen

(a) Burger-Queen could sell the December futures contract for 92.70. Since each contract has a notional value of £500,000 it should sell

$$\frac{£10,000,000}{£500,000} = 20 \text{ contracts.}$$

(b) Since interest rates have risen to 9 percent the price of the futures contract will fall to 91 (=100-9).

The gain on the futures contract is as follows:

92.70 – 91 = 170 ticks

Each tick is worth £12.5 and the profit on the futures contract is

170 × £12.5 × 20 = £42,500

Although there is gain in the futures position, the company has to pay a higher rate for the loan. The extra amount of interest paid on the loan is: 9 – 7.3 = 1.70 percent or

£10 million × 0.017 × $^3/_{12}$ = £42,500

This extra cost is offset by the profit on the futures position so the effective rate is 7.3% even though interest rates have risen

(c) The effective rate is still 7.3%

This time there will be loss on the futures contract since the price of the futures contract has risen. The price of the futures contract is now 94 (= 100-6). The loss is 94- 92.70 = 130 ticks or

130 × £12.50 × 20 = £32,500

The lower interest rate on the loan means that there is a saving on interest payments equal to

£10 million × (0.073 – 0.06) × $^3/_{12}$ = £32,500

The gain on the interest is again offset by the loss on the futures position, so that the cost of borrowing remains the same at 7.3 percent

33 Theta plc

Theta borrows £10 million with interest at six-month LIBOR plus 1%. In the swap, it receives six-month LIBOR and pays fixed interest at 8.5%. The net effect is to acquire a fixed rate obligation at 9.5% for the full term of the swap.

	%
Borrow at LIBOR plus 1%	– (LIBOR + 1%)
Swap: receive (floating rate)	+LIBOR
pay (fixed rate)	–8.5%
Net payment (fixed rate)	–9.5%

Theta will therefore fix its payments at £475,000 (10 million × 9.5% × 6/12) every six months for the five-year term of the swap.

At each six-monthly fixing date for the swap, the payment due from Theta to the swaps bank or from the bank to Theta will depend on the market rate for six-month LIBOR at that date.

LIBOR 10%

Suppose that on the first fixing date for the swap, at the end of month six in the first year, six-month LIBOR is 10%. The payments due by each party to the swap will be as follows:

	£
Theta pays fixed rate of 8.5%	
(£10 million × 8.7% × 6/12)	425,000
Swaps bank pays LIBOR rate of 10%	
(10million × 10% × 6/12)	500,000
Net payment from bank to Theta	75,000

This payment will be made six months later at the end of the notional interest rate period. Theta will pay interest on its loan at LIBOR + 1% which for this six-month period is 11% (10% + 1%). Taken with the payment received under the swap agreement, the net cost to Gamma is equivalent to interest payable at 9.5%.

	£
Loan payment at 11%	
(£10 million x 11% x 6/12)	550,000
Payment received from the swaps bank	(75,000)
Net payment (equivalent to 10.7% interest)	475,000

LIBOR 7.5%

Suppose that at the next six-monthly fixing date, six-month LIBOR is 7.5%. The swap payments will be as follows:

	£
Theta to swaps bank (fixed at 8.5%)	425,000
Swaps bank to Theta (at 7.5%)	375,000
Net payment by Theta to swaps bank	50,000

Under its loan arrangement, Theta will pay 8.5% (LIBOR + 1%) for the six-month period. Adding the net swap payment gives a total cost for the six-month period of £475,000, equivalent to an interest rate of 8.5% for the period.

	£
Loan payment at 8.5%	
(£10 million × 8.5% × 6/12)	425,000
Swap payment	50,000
Total payment (equivalent to 10.7% interest)	475,000

34 Espondera Inc

In order to calculate the cost of debt we need first to assign a credit rating to the company. The values of the equation variables are as follows

SIZE = Total Assets =$120 million

$$\text{PROFITABILITY} = \frac{\text{Net income}}{\text{Total assets}} = \frac{\$6\text{ million}}{\$120\text{ million}} = 0.05$$

DEBT = Subordinated = 1

$$\text{LEVERAGE} = \frac{\text{Long term debt}}{\text{Total assets}} = \frac{\$14\text{ million}}{£120\text{ million}} = 0.117$$

$$\text{INTEREST} = \frac{\text{Income before interest and taxes}}{\text{Inataearest payments}} = \frac{\$8\text{ million}}{\$1\text{ million}} = 8$$

$$\text{COV} = \frac{\text{Standard deviation of earnings}}{\text{Average value of earnings}} = \frac{1.055}{3.68} = 0.287$$

Workings

The average value of earnings is: (5 + 4.2 + 3.2 + 3.8 + 2.2) = \$3.68m

The variance of earnings is:

$$\frac{(5-3.68)^2 + (4.2-3.68)^2 + (3.2-3.68)^2 + (3.8-3.68)^2 + (2.2-3.68)^2}{4} = 1.12$$

The standard deviation of earnings is the square root of the variance and is: $\sqrt{1.112} = 1.055$

Inserting the values of the variables in The Kaplan – Urwitz model we have:

$$Y = 4.41 + 0.001 \times 120 + 6.40 \times 0.05 - 2.56 \times 1 - 2.72 \times 0.1178 + 0.006 \times 8 - 0.53 \times 0.287 = 1.87$$

The value of the model assigns a credit rating of BBB and on the basis of observed market rates for bonds of this rating the cost of debt is 8.4%.

35 Transfer prices

Top tips. You would probably not see an exam question covering both transfer pricing and treasury management, but this question gives you a good insight into the most important issues in these areas.

You can go wrong quite easily in part (a) if you don't think carefully about the layout of your computation. For each of the options you need to split the calculation between what happens in the countries where the subsidiaries are located, and what happens in the country where the holding company is located. Remember also to assess the effect of the withholding tax separately from the other local taxes.

(b) demonstrates how strategic issues can be brought into the discussion part of an answer. It is not sufficient just to discuss government action. Local issues are important, also trying to ensure goal congruence throughout the group.

The answer to (c) starts off by explaining the cost centre approach as that is mentioned in the question, but then goes on to consider the implications of the profit centre approach. Again strategic issues are significant including risk management, resources (staff), internal pricing and performance evaluation.

(a) The current position is as follows.

	UK company B$'000	Ceeland company B$'000	Total B$'000
Revenue and taxes in the local country			
Sales	84,000	210,000	294,000
Production expenses	(68,000)	(164,000)	(232,000)
Taxable profit	16,000	46,000	62,000
Tax (1)	(4,000)	(18,400)	(22,400)
Dividends to Beeland	12,000	27,600	39,600
Withholding tax (2)	0	2,760	2,760
Revenue and taxes in Beeland			
Dividend	12,000	27,600	39,600
Add back foreign tax paid	4,000	18,400	22,400
Taxable income	16,000	46,000	62,000
Beeland tax due	5,600	16,100	21,700
Foreign tax credit	(4,000)	(16,100)	(20,100)
Tax paid in Beeland (3)	1,600	–	1,600
Total tax (1) + (2) + (3)	5,600	21,160	26,760

An increase of 25% in the transfer price would have the following effect.

	UK company B$'000	Ceeland company B$'000	Total B$'000
Revenues and taxes in the local country			
Sales	105,000	210,000	315,000
Production expenses	(68,000)	(185,000)	(253,000)
Taxable profit	37,000	25,000	62,000
Tax (1)	(9,250)	(10,000)	(19,250)
Dividends to Beeland	27,750	15,000	42,750
Withholding tax (2)	0	1,500	1,500
Revenues and taxes in Beeland			
Dividend	27,750	15,000	42,750
Add back foreign tax paid	= 9,250	10,000	19,250
Taxable income	37,000	25,000	62,000
Beeland tax due	12,950	8,750	21,700
Foreign tax credit	(9,250)	(8,750)	(18,000)
Tax paid in Beeland (3)	3,700	–	3,700
Total tax (1) + (2) + (3)	12,950	11,500	24,450

The total tax payable by the company is therefore reduced by B$2,310,000 to B$24,450,000.

(b) **Government action**

In practice, governments usually seek to prevent multinationals reducing their tax liability through the manipulation of transfer prices. For tax purposes governments will normally demand that an **'arms length' price** is used in the computation of the taxable profit and not an artificial transfer price. If no such 'arms length' price is available then there may be some scope for tax minimisation through the choice of transfer price.

Other factors

If it is possible to manipulate the transfer price in this way, there are further factors that the company must take into consideration before making a final decision.

(i) The level of transfer prices will affect the **movement of funds** within the group. If inter company sales involve the use of different currencies the level of the transfer price will also affect the group's **foreign exchange exposure**. These factors must be taken into account as well as the tax situation.

(ii) The level of profit reported by the subsidiary could affect its **local credit rating** and this could be important if the company wishes to raise funds locally. It could also affect the ease with which credit can be obtained from suppliers.

(iii) The reported profit is likely to have an **effect** on the **motivation** of managers and staff in the subsidiary. If reported profits are high then they may become complacent and cost control may become weak. If on the other hand profits are continually low they may become demotivated.

(iv) Transfer prices that **do not reflect market levels** may lead to subsidiaries making 'make or buy' decisions that do not optimise the performance of the group as a whole.

36 Common market

Top tips. This question is a good test of your understanding of the features of a common market. It is probably more straightforward than you would get in the exam; the examiner might be tempted to focus more on implications of recent developments in Europe such as the introduction of the common currency and the expansion of the European Union.

If you are tempted to choose a question on this subject, note that the case for the common market is underpinned by economic arguments – comparative advantage, different factor endowments, economies of scale and financial contagion. If you are not confident on the economics, it's best to avoid the question.

(a) **Free trade area**

A free trade area exists when there is **no restriction** on the **movement of goods** and services between countries. This may be extended into a customs union when there is a free trade area between all member countries of the union, and in addition there are common external tariffs applying to imports from non-member countries into any part of the union. In other words, the union promotes free trade among its members but acts as a protectionist bloc against the rest of the world.

Common market

A common market encompasses the idea of a customs union but has a number of **additional features**. In addition to free trade among member countries there is also **complete mobility** of the factors of production. A British citizen has the freedom to work in any other country of the European community, for example. A common market will also aim to achieve stronger links between member countries, for example by harmonising government economic policies and by establishing a closer political confederation.

(b) **Comparative advantage**

The most obvious benefits which countries might gain from forming a common market are associated with **free trade** between them. The benefits of free trade are illustrated by the law of comparative advantage which states that countries should specialise in producing those goods where they have a comparative advantage. Specialisation, together with free trade, will result in an increase in total output and all countries will be able, to a great or lesser extent, to share in the benefits.

Larger range

In particular, different countries have **different factor endowments** and, as the international mobility of these factors tends to be severely limited, **trade increases the range of goods** and services available in a particular country. By becoming part of a common market, imports from other member countries are available more cheaply and easily. Imports of certain raw materials or types of capital equipment not otherwise available in a particular country will improve its

productive potential, enabling a faster rate of economic growth to be achieved. Similarly, improvements in the range and quality of consumer goods available will tend to enhance a country's standard of living.

Larger markets

In addition, there is a **larger market for domestic output** and firms may be able to benefit from economies of scale by engaging in export activities. **Economies of scale** improve efficiency in the use of resources and enable output to be produced at lower cost. This also raises the possibility of benefits to consumers if these cost savings are passed on in the form of lower prices. In addition, the extension of the market in which firms operate increases the amount of competition they face and hence should improve efficiency.

Exchange rate agreement

Establishment of a common market is often accompanied by some form of **exchange rate agreement** between members and this in turn is likely to encourage further trade as it reduces uncertainty for both exporters and importers. Stability of exchange rates is also beneficial to a government in formulating its domestic economic policies.

Smaller economics

Membership of a common market may be particularly beneficial to smaller or weaker economies as, in addition to increasing the availability of essential factors of production and the range of goods and services available to domestic consumers, it also enables them to **benefit** from any **economic growth** experienced by their fellow members. Spin-offs may be in the form of larger markets for their exports, lower import prices, improved employment opportunities and so on.

Political links

In addition to fostering economic ties between countries, common markets provide the basis for **stronger political links**. Again, this may be particularly important for smaller countries enabling them to benefit from an enhanced position in the world economy. It may also encourage further international economic co-operation, in turn providing an additional stimulus to growth.

37 Multinationals

(a) **Political Risk**

(i) The risk that political action will affect the position and value of a company.

(ii) This risk can adversely affect multinationals in the following ways:

- Import quotas and tariffs may limit the quantity of goods that a subsidiary can buy from the parent.
- Potential nationalisation of subsidiaries and their assets can lead to financial loss as there may be no compensation from the foreign government for doing so.
- The foreign government may place restrictions on the ability of the parent to purchase domestic companies, particularly in strategic industries.
- Different countries have different legal standards of safety or quality. The subsidiary's country may have stricter standards that the parent is unwilling to adhere to, given that it could lead to inconsistent standards of goods in different countries.

Cultural Risk

(i) The risk that different cultural beliefs and styles will affect the products and services provided and the ways in which the organisation is managed and staffed.

(ii) Effect on multinationals:

- The host country's beliefs and cultural approach may affect the means by which the product/service is advertised or distributed. Some countries' media is much more rigorously regulated and at times censored therefore it is important to avoid any controversial messages. Poorer countries' residents may have little or no access to television or internet, therefore alternative means of getting the message across may be necessary.
- Customers and consumers may differ depending on the country in which multinationals operate. It would be of no benefit in a strictly Muslim country for health clubs to direct marketing campaigns showing men and women exercising in the same complex for example.
- The extent to which cultural differences matter will play a large part in the exposure to cultural risk. Although China is a Communist country, its inhabitants respond to many Western marketing campaigns, although there is a much greater emphasis on family. However it would be worthless to advertise pork products in Muslim countries because of religious and cultural beliefs.

Legal Risk

(i) The risk that legislation may affect the efficient and effective operations of an organisation.

(ii) Effect on multinationals:

- Minimum technical standards may differ in certain countries which may result in a particular product having different specifications depending on which country it is manufactured in.
- Some countries do not accept the legality of international trademarks or patents. As such intellectual property is often the core of business, multinationals may find it difficult to accept that local companies can copy their trademarks or have very similar ones. One example is in China where the food chain Pizza Hut operates alongside the Chinese equivalent Pizza Hill, whose company colours and logos are very similar to those of the Western chain.

(b) Steps to deal with political, cultural and legal risks:

Political Risk

(i) Negotiate with host government on matters such as transfer of capital and access to local finance.

(ii) Production strategies – create a balance between contracting out to local sources and producing directly.

(iii) Take out insurance against various threats – for example, war, revolution, currency conversion problems.

Cultural Risk

(i) Do your homework – identify the best markets to enter based on forecast demand, comparative advantage, risk.

(ii) Management of human resources – have a balance between local works and ex-pats. Have to look at such matters as:

- Recruitment and training – ex-pats take away the need to recruit locally and train new people in the ways of the organisation in general and the job in particular.
- Status of women – certain countries do not allow women to work, or men do not respect women's authority.
- Locals may have a greater knowledge of the local culture but less appreciation of the wider corporate picture. The reverse is true for ex-pats.

- Employing locals is generally much cheaper, as ex-pat packages include paying for housing, schools, international health care, air travel and so on.

(iii) Make use of such systems as joint ventures, to take advantage of local knowledge but at the same time using the company's own expertise.

Legal Risk

(i) Good citizenship – comply with best practice, be responsive to ethical concerns, respect the host country's legal requirements.

(ii) Keep abreast of changes in the law in the broader sense and human resource policies internally.

(iii) Be aware of the consequences of non-compliance, such as bad publicity and potential court cases and take actions to avoid such exposure.

38 Developments

(a) Impact of launch of a single European currency on financial institutions:

Banks

(i) As it is now easier for customers to compare bank products (as they are based in the same currency) bank margins may have to have been reduced to maintain competitiveness.

(ii) The single currency has promoted restructuring and consolidation among banks in the Euro area, resulting in mergers and alliances.

(iii) Banks have been forced to restructure and consolidate on a global scale as well as within the Euro area.

Securities Markets

(i) Rather than individual markets, the securities markets have undergone integration and standardisation to form the Europe-wide securities market.

(ii) There is now a fully integrated unsecured deposit market and derivatives market.

Bond Markets

(i) There was a rise in private bond issuance in the Euro area post-1999.

(ii) Average size of new bond issues rose considerably, showing that the Euro-dominated bond market is more able to absorb very large issues more easily than individual bond markets of predecessor currencies.

(iii) The introduction of a single currency has resulted in more efficient, well-functioning markets.

(b) Adverse effects of increased globalisation on multinational companies:

Government regulation

(i) Increased regulation due to greater number of industries being characterised by oligopoly.

(ii) Anti-trust scrutiny – for example, British Airways and American Airlines alliance to prevent cross-border oligopolies.

(iii) Such regulation creates obstacles to trade, as companies must comply with regulations that may prevent efficient and effective operations.

Pressure groups

Pressure is being put on governments to take measures against multinational companies – in the UK for example there is increasing resistance to supermarket chains setting up in opposition to small shops in city suburbs. The pressure groups are becoming more and more successful at curbing multinationals' activities.

Political risks

(i) Multinational companies are becoming more vulnerable to political developments in home and host countries. Global conflicts have led to trade embargoes, restrictions on operating in certain countries and sanctions. Airlines have been badly hit as their routes have been restricted – the Asian crisis in the late 1990s severely curtailed the number of flights to such areas as Japan, Singapore and Hong Kong.

(ii) Tariffs and capital restrictions; import quotas; export subsidies; exchange controls are all barriers that can affect multinational activity, as host countries try to protect domestic industries.

39 Engineering Ltd

MEMORANDUM

To: Directors of Engineering Ltd
From: Adviser
Re: Financial instruments

This memo outlines the role that hedging can play in reducing Engineering Ltd's risk; the main risk associated with the use of derivatives in general; and the benefits and problems of using scenario analysis as a specific means of measuring risk.

Hedging and the reduction of risk

Hedging reduces risk by allowing the company to be in greater control of what happens in the future with regard to such issues as interest rates and currency rates. It allows interest rates and currency rates to be fixed at a particular time in the future, which removes the uncertainty of, for example, the sterling value of foreign currency receipts and payments.

As interest rates can also be fixed at a particular rate, hedging can control the conflict of interest between bondholders and shareholders, thus reducing the agency cost of debt.

If capital market imperfections exist, hedging can lower the probability of firms suffering financial distress as there is less uncertainty about such things as interest payments and foreign currency values. By lowering the probability of financial distress, hedging can also reduce the cost of capital and debt, as investors will see the firm as being a less risky investment. Greater certainty encourages investment due to increased confidence in the firm's abilities to make money.

Main risks associated with derivatives in general

There is a risk of mispricing derivatives due to the use of predictive valuation models. The Black-Scholes model for example assumes no market friction, the existence of fixed interest rates and a constant volatility of return, none of which exist in reality. Derivatives are therefore priced on the basis of unrealistic assumptions and as predictions are only as good as the model used, the results may be misleading.

Liquidity risk can also be a problem as it is not always possible for Over the Counter (OTC) derivatives to be sold due to uncertainty about valuation and the risks of the position taken. As OTC derivatives are constructed specifically to a particular organisation's requirements, there may be very few counterparties who want the set of risk characteristics offered by that derivative and are confident about what they are receiving.

Also there is the risk of manipulation. As with any financial information, it is possible to manipulate OTC derivatives' positions so that the true values and true risks are not revealed. Although in the UK firms are now required to report on the fair value of their derivatives' positions, the complexity of these instruments are such that users of financial information find it virtually impossible to check the validity of these values.

Scenario analysis

This method of measuring risk tests plans against various possible scenarios to determine the outcome should things not go to plan. It is an important technique in risk management, helping firms and financial institutions ensure that they don't take on too much risk. Its usefulness however depends on risk managers coming up with the right scenarios.

One of the benefits of scenario analysis is that it establishes any exposure to hidden risk such as large market movements. A firm may have a delta hedge in place to protect against normal market movements but not against larger movements. Scenario analysis can highlight this exposure and allow firms to take protective action.

Scenario analysis also allows managers to examine the impact of increased volatility of, for example, exchange rates. Whilst a currency may currently be pegged to a stronger currency such as the US dollar if it is allowed to float freely it will become more volatile. As scenario analysis allows focus on such possibilities, firms are more prepared for the potential effects of such volatility.

Managers are forced to confront adverse circumstances when using scenario analysis that might otherwise have been ignored. This will improve their ability to respond to risks which will make the firm less vulnerable to financial distress.

However scenario analysis is not without its problems. The method is very subjective and judgemental and greatly depends on the scenarios selected (their feasibility for example). There is no point analysing scenarios that are not going to happen.

Scenario analysis can become very complex and unwieldy as managers have to work through all the implications of scenarios, often resulting in too much information than is necessary or possible to work with. There is a danger that managers will become so caught up in the complexities of the process that they forget what they are trying to achieve.

Any attempt to analyse a real life scenario can often lead to difficulties in allowing for all relevant risk factors. It is very easy to miss a possible outcome or the effect of a particular factor on the final outcome, which can render the entire process useless as it may lead to a result that will never occur in reality.

In summary, hedging can be an effective tool in reducing a company's risk, although managers should be aware of the risks associated with these financial instruments themselves. Whilst scenario analysis is useful as a specific means of measuring risk, the benefits of this technique should be weighed up against the problems before a final decision is taken on whether to use it. As with all risk measurement and risk reduction techniques, care should be taken when analysing the results of scenario analysis and hedging and also before any reliance is placed on these results.

Index

Note. **Key Terms** and their page references are given in **bold**.

Review Form & Free Prize Draw – Paper P4 Advanced Financial Management (6/08)

All original review forms from the entire BPP range, completed with genuine comments, will be entered into one of two draws on 31 January 2009 and 31 July 2009. The names on the first four forms picked out on each occasion will be sent a cheque for £50.

Name: ______________________ **Address:** ______________________

____

____

How have you used this Text?
(Tick one box only)

☐ Home study (book only)
☐ On a course: college ______________
☐ With 'correspondence' package
☐ Other ______________

Why did you decide to purchase this Text? *(Tick one box only)*

☐ Have used BPP Texts in the past
☐ Recommendation by friend/colleague
☐ Recommendation by a lecturer at college
☐ Saw advertising
☐ Saw information on BPP website
☐ Other ______________

During the past six months do you recall seeing/receiving any of the following?
(Tick as many boxes as are relevant)

☐ Our advertisement in *ACCA Student Accountant*
☐ Our advertisement in *Pass*
☐ Our advertisement in *PQ*
☐ Our brochure with a letter through the post
☐ Our website www.bpp.com

Which (if any) aspects of our advertising do you find useful?
(Tick as many boxes as are relevant)

☐ Prices and publication dates of new editions
☐ Information on Text content
☐ Facility to order books off-the-page
☐ None of the above

Which BPP products have you used?

Text	☑	*Success CD*	☐	*Learn Online*	☐
Kit	☐	*i-Learn*	☐	*Home Study Package*	☐
Passcard	☐	*i-Pass*	☐	*Home Study PLUS*	☐

Your ratings, comments and suggestions would be appreciated on the following areas.

	Very useful	*Useful*	*Not useful*
Introductory section (Key study steps, personal study)	☐	☐	☐
Chapter introductions	☐	☐	☐
Key terms	☐	☐	☐
Quality of explanations	☐	☐	☐
Case studies and other examples	☐	☐	☐
Exam focus points	☐	☐	☐
Questions and answers in each chapter	☐	☐	☐
Fast forwards and chapter roundups	☐	☐	☐
Quick quizzes	☐	☐	☐
Question Bank	☐	☐	☐
Answer Bank	☐	☐	☐
Index	☐	☐	☐

Overall opinion of this Study Text *Excellent* ☐ *Good* ☐ *Adequate* ☐ *Poor* ☐

Do you intend to continue using BPP products? *Yes* ☐ *No* ☐

On the reverse of this page are noted particular areas of the text about which we would welcome your feedback.

The BPP author of this edition can be e-mailed at: lesleybulck@bpp.com

Please return this form to: Lesley Buick, ACCA Publishing Manager, BPP Learning Media Ltd, FREEPOST, London, W12 8BR

Review Form & Free Prize Draw (continued)

TELL US WHAT YOU THINK

Please note any further comments and suggestions/errors below

Free Prize Draw Rules

1 Closing date for 31 January 2009 draw is 31 December 2008. Closing date for 31 July 2009 draw is 30 June 2009.

2 Restricted to entries with UK and Eire addresses only. BPP employees, their families and business associates are excluded.

3 No purchase necessary. Entry forms are available upon request from BPP Learning Media Ltd. No more than one entry per title, per person. Draw restricted to persons aged 16 and over.

4 Winners will be notified by post and receive their cheques not later than 6 weeks after the relevant draw date.

5 The decision of the promoter in all matters is final and binding. No correspondence will be entered into.